Records and Processes of Dispute Settlement in Early Medieval Societies

Medieval Law and Its Practice

VOLUME 41

The titles published in this series are listed at *brill.com/mlip*

Records and Processes of Dispute Settlement in Early Medieval Societies

Iberia and Beyond

Edited by

Isabel Alfonso
José M. Andrade
André Evangelista Marques

BRILL

LEIDEN | BOSTON

Cover illustration: Psychostasia scene in the north crypt of the former cathedral of Roda de Isábena (Huesca), attributted to the Master of Navasa, c. 1200. © Photo: A. García Omedes.

Library of Congress Cataloging-in-Publication Data

Names: Alfonso Antón, Isabel, editor. | Andrade, José M., editor. | Marques, André Evangelista, 1982- editor.
Title: Records and processes of dispute settlement in early medieval societies : Iberia and beyond / edited by Isabel Alfonso, José M. Andrade, André Evangelista Marques.
Description: Leiden ; Boston : Brill, 2023. | Series: Medieval law and its practice, 1873-8176 ; 41 | Includes bibliographical references and index.
Identifiers: LCCN 2023031798 (print) | LCCN 2023031799 (ebook) | ISBN 9789004682955 (hardback) | ISBN 9789004683006 (ebook)
Subjects: LCSH: Dispute resolution (Law)–History. | Law, Medieval–History.
Classification: LCC K445 .R43 2023 (print) | LCC K445 (ebook) | DDC 347/.46090903–dc23/eng/20230926
LC record available at https://lccn.loc.gov/2023031798
LC ebook record available at https://lccn.loc.gov/2023031799

Typeface for the Latin, Greek, and Cyrillic scripts: "Brill". See and download: brill.com/brill-typeface.

ISSN 1873-8176
ISBN 978-90-04-68295-5 (hardback)
ISBN 978-90-04-68300-6 (e-book)
DOI 10.1163/9789004683006

Contents

PART 2
Recording Disputes: The Textual Construction of Judicial Process

PART 3
Framing Disputes: Judicial Authorities and Social Order

Acknowledgments

This volume is the outcome of a research project that has thoroughly catalogued and published online the corpus of northern Iberian dispute records dated until 1100 (nearly 2000 documents).[1] Led by Isabel Alfonso, the PRJ project brought together medievalists from several Spanish and Portuguese universities and a group of international scholars from British, French, Italian, and American universities, with the aim of contrasting the Iberian material against similar corpora of dispute records extant for other areas in western Europe. If only a restricted group of Spanish and Portuguese researchers worked on the project's database and online edition of the Iberian records, the whole team gathered for a couple of working meetings and took part in a final conference held at the University of Santiago de Compostela (12–13 November 2015) that was aimed at a comparative reflection about dispute processing in early medieval societies. This volume has grown out of the papers presented there.

The book has been far too long in the making.[2] We should like to thank all contributors for their support and kind forbearance throughout the process, as well as Marcella Mulder and the staff at Brill for patiently helping us bring this project to completion. We are also extremely grateful to a number of other people who helped us with different technical tasks: Deirdre Casey translated into English several chapters originally written in Spanish (1–5, 10, 12), Patricia Stirnemann translated the chapter by François Bougard (9), and Antonio Uriarte (CSIC) drew all the maps in the introduction. The editors are also indebted to Wendy Davies and Adam Kosto for precious advice on English terminology, and to Julio Escalona for his unstinting support throughout the whole editorial process. Finally, we wish to express our thanks to the Centro

1 *Procesos Judiciales en las sociedades medievales del norte peninsular (siglos IX–XI) = Judicial Processes in Early Medieval Societies in Northern Iberia (9th–11th centuries)*, funded by the Spanish National R&D Plan (Ref. HUM2007–61233—HAR2011–26685) and carried out at the Centro de Ciencias Humanas y Sociales, CSIC (Madrid) between 2008–2015; PRJ hereafter. The PRJ database offers access to the text of every single dispute record and full-text search capacities on the whole corpus. Complex queries are also available, allowing for cross comparison between different time frames, regions, the institutions where the records were originally produced/transmitted, forms of transmission (originals/copies), and ratios of dispute records to the overall number of extant records. The database is available at http://prj.csic.es/ (accessed 15 April 2022).

2 This means that some data collected in earlier versions of the PRJ database may now be slightly outdated, and that more recent editions of primary sources may have been overlooked. An effort was made to minor these shortcomings, but the editors are aware that this may not have always succeeded.

de Ciencias Humanas y Sociales—CSIC (Madrid) and to the Facultad de Geografía e Historia—Universidad de Santiago de Compostela for institutional and logistical support to, respectively, the PRJ project's several working meetings and its final conference.

Illustrations

Figures

Tables

Graphs

Maps

Notes on Contributors

Isabel Alfonso

received her doctorate from the U. Complutense, where she was *Profesora Titular* of Institutional History, and went on to join the Instituto de Historia—CSIC as *Investigadora Científica* until she retired in 2016. Her research interests include different aspects of rural society (peasant communities, social differentiation), as well as the use of political and legal anthropology in the study of conflicts, political discourse and legitimation, topics on which she has directed several research projects. She is the editor of *The Rural History of Medieval European Societies: Trends and Perspectives* (Brepols, 2007) and co-editor of (with Hugh Kennedy and Julio Escalona) *Building Legitimacy: Political Discourses and Forms of Legitimation in Medieval Societies* (Brill, 2004), (with Julio Escalona and Georges Martin) *Lucha política: Condena y legitimación en la España medieval* (ENS, 2004), and (with José Antonio Jara Fuente and Georges Martin) *Construir la identidad en la Edad Media* (Universidad de Castilla-La Mancha, 2010).

José M. Andrade

is Professor of Medieval History at the University of Santiago de Compostela. He has published on several aspects of medieval Galician history, with a special focus on monasteries and their social impact. He is the author of *El monacato benedictino y la sociedad de la Galicia medieval (siglos X al XIII)* (Ediciós do Castro, 1997) and the editor of *O Tombo de Celanova*, 2 vols (Consello da Cultura Galega, 1995). More recently, he has been working on judicial documentation and the settlement of disputes in north-western Iberia during the early and high Middle Ages.

François Bougard

is Director of the Institut de recherche et d'histoire des textes (CNRS, Paris). He is the author of *La justice dans le royaume d'Italie de la fin du VIII*e *siècle au début du XI*e *siècle* (EFR, 1995). Other publications include several essays on history of justice and practices of documentation during the early middle ages. His most recent book is *Le royaume d'Italie de Louis II à Otton I*er *(840–968). Histoire politique* (Eudora Verlag, 2022).

Warren C. Brown

is Professor for Medieval History at the California Institute of Technology. He studies the social and political history of medieval Europe, especially power, law, and written culture. His publications include *Unjust Seizure: Conflict, Interest, and Authority in an Early Medieval Society* (Cornell, 2001), *Violence in Medieval Europe* (Longman, 2011), (as co-author and editor) *Documentary Culture and the Laity in the early Middle Ages* (Cambridge UP, 2013), and *Beyond the Monastery Walls: Lay Men and Women in Early Medieval Legal Formularies* (Cambridge UP, 2023).

Wendy Davies
is Professor of History Emerita UCL and an associate member of the History Faculty, University of Oxford. Until her retirement from UCL in 2007, she taught medieval European history and was also successively Head of the History Department, Deans of Arts and of Social and Historical Sciences, and Pro-Provost (Europe). In research she has run interdisciplinary projects which explore the interaction between text and field evidence (hence, with James Graham-Campbell and others, *The Inscriptions of Early Medieval Brittany* (2000) and the long series of archaeological publications with Grenville Astill). She remains active in research: in the last twenty years northern Iberia has been her focus and her most recent monograph is *Windows on Justice in Northern Iberia 800–1000* (Routledge, 2016).

Julio Escalona
(Madrid, 1963) received his doctorate in 1996 from the U. Complutense and he is currently *Investigador Científico* at the Instituto de Historia—CSIC. His main research field is early medieval society and territory. He is co-editor of (with Andrew Reynolds) *Scale and Scale Change in the Early Middle Ages: Exploring Landscape, Local Society and the World Beyond* (Brepols, 2011) and of (with Orri Vésteinsson and Stuart Brookes) *Polity and Neighbourhood in Early Medieval Europe* (Brepols, 2019).

Kim Esmark
is Associate Professor in Medieval History at Roskilde University. His scholarly interests center on the historical anthropology of medieval society and methodological issues of applying Bourdieusian sociology to historical analysis. He has published articles and co-edited books on gift-giving, ritual, kinship, memory, and dispute processing in Denmark and France, ca. 1000–1300. He is currently involved in an interdisciplinary collective research project about civil war in medieval Scandinavia.

Adam Kosto
is Professor of History at Columbia University (New York). He specializes in the institutional and legal history of medieval Europe, with a focus on Cata-

lonia and the Mediterranean. He received his B.A. from Yale University (1989), an M.Phil. from the University of Cambridge (1990), and his Ph.D. from Harvard University (1996). His most recent books are *Hostages in the Middle Ages* (Oxford UP, 2012) and (as co-editor) *Documentary Practices and the Laity in the Early Middle Ages* (Cambridge UP, 2012). He is a member of the Commission Internationale de Diplomatique.

Juan José Larrea
is Professor of Medieval History at the University of the Basque Country (Vitoria). He received his Ph.D at the University of Toulouse-Le Mirail. His main research interests lie in the rural societies of the early and high Middle Ages, a topic on which he has coordinated several research projects. He has also co-directed with Francesca Tinti the *Digital Edition of the Becerro Galicano de San Millán de la Cogolla*. Amongst his main publications is *La Navarre du IVe au XIIe siècle. Peuplement et société* (De Boeck, 1998).

André Evangelista Marques
is an independent scholar, member of the Institute for Medieval Studies at NOVA University Lisbon. He specialises in the social and material history of early-to-high medieval Portugal. His books include: *O casal: uma unidade de organização social do espaço no Entre-Douro-e-Lima (906–1200)* (Toxosoutos, 2008), *Da representação documental à materialidade do espaço. Território da diocese de Braga (séculos IX–XI)* (Afrontamento, 2014), and (as co-editor) *Livro de Mumadona, Cartulário do Mosteiro de Guimarães: Edição crítica* (Academia das Ciências de Lisboa, 2016).

Josep M. Salrach
is Professor Emeritus of Medieval History at the Pompeu Fabra University (Barcelona). He has published widely on early medieval Catalonia. His books include *El procés de feudalització, segles III–XII* (Edicions 62, 1987), *Catalunya a la fi del primer mil·lenni* (Eumo, 2004) and *Justícia i poder a Catalunya abans de l'any mil* (Eumo, 2013). He has also directed and co-directed the edition of large collections of medieval Catalan sources: *Els pergamins de l'Arxiu Comtal de Barcelona, de Ramon Borrell a Ramon Berenguer I* (1999), *Els pergamins de l'Arxiu Comtal de Barcelona, de Ramon Berenguer I a Ramon Berenguer IV* (2010), and *Justícia i resolució de conflictes a la Catalunya medieval* (2018).

Igor Santos Salazar
teaches Medieval History at the University of Trento (Italy), and is particularly interested in the evolution of the structures of territorial organisation and

the articulation of the different societies in various European areas between the sixth and twelfth centuries, through the study of both written sources and material records.

Francesca Tinti
held research and teaching positions at the Universities of Cambridge and Bologna, before joining the Universidad del País Vasco (UPV/EHU) as Ikerbasque Research Professor in 2009. While in Cambridge she worked for five years as post-doctoral research associate for the *Prosopography of Anglo-Saxon England*. She has directed several research projects, including the *Digital Edition of the Becerro Galicano de San Millán de la Cogolla* (with Juan José Larrea) and *The Languages of Early Medieval Charters: Anglo-Saxon England and Eastern Francia: c. 700–c. 1100*. She has published extensively on the documentary, social and religious history of early medieval Europe, with a special focus on cartularies and the role of language in the production of early medieval records.

Introduction

Isabel Alfonso, José Andrade and André Evangelista Marques

How can early medieval dispute records—a broad category comprising different types of texts directly or indirectly related to conflicts—shed light on dispute settlement processes and their social and political underpinnings? The contributions gathered here attempt to answer this question by looking into the interplay between record-making, disputing process, and the overall social and political context of conflicts. In exploring the interaction between these three elements, and especially the ways in which dispute records condition the study of dispute settlement processes and of their underlying power politics, the authors aim at contributing to the design of an agenda for a comparative survey of medieval European dispute records and their corpora, without forgetting that the extant documentary sources tend to focus on judicial court process and formal justice, thus concealing other (non-judicial, or at least less formal) modes of conflict resolution which often combined with the former.

The PRJ project's comparative aim and the collaborative work in which the team engaged led to the discussion of a common framework to examine early medieval dispute records; which does not necessarily entail a common vocabulary.[1] Such a framework is illustrated in Part 1 of this volume, which is made up of a series of regional surveys presenting the corpus of Iberian dispute records catalogued in the PRJ database,[2] while also aiming to address general issues that can be of interest in the study of similar corpora elsewhere in Europe.[3] Part 2 addresses several issues with a bearing on the recording of dispute settlement in Iberia and Italy. Finally, Part 3 deals with the agency behind the settlement of disputes in court in Iberia and Denmark (encompassing both judicial

1 The problem with harmonizing the words (and their correlative concepts) used by both early medieval scribes and modern commentators to classify the multiple documentary forms associated with dispute records is that any such attempt will necessarily overshadow the intrinsic variety of the vocabulary used in different documentary corpora and in different historiographical traditions. Our efforts at terminology harmonization throughout this volume proved unproductive even within Iberia, where significant variation is to be found in this respect, especially between east and west. Albeit handy, traditional diplomatic classifications and their broad categories are of little use when it comes to transregional enquiries.

2 http://prj.csic.es/ (accessed 15 April 2022).

3 John Hudson, "Legal history and the history of disputes," in *Disputing Strategies in Medieval Scandinavia*, ed. Kim Esmark et al. (Leiden: Brill, 2013), 333–341, at 333, sees charters as the "most obvious" type of source on which a comparative approach to the study of disputes across different European regions can be based.

 | DOI:10.1163/9789004683006_002

procedures and extra-judicial mechanisms) and investigates the role of dispute settlement in the enactment of social order. The two elements that form part of the volume's title—records and processes—are closely intertwined and must necessarily be studied together. Thus, the chapters in Parts 1 and 2 pay close attention to how the making of dispute records interacted with the processes of dispute settlement, whereas the chapters in Part 3 approach such processes based on a thorough assessment of the evidentiary value of dispute texts, which calls for consideration of how documents themselves were used in, and affected, court practice.

Despite its focus on the ninth to eleventh centuries, this volume includes papers that stretch back to late antiquity (Brown) and forward until the late twelfth century (Esmark, who nonetheless deals with some of the oldest charters extant in Scandinavia). Spanning such a long period allows one to understand continuity and change in judicial practice and its recording throughout a period of significant legal innovation. 'Peripheral' areas, such as Iberia and Scandinavia, are especially relevant to assess how 'new' and 'effective' the changes wrought by the revival of Roman and canon law actually were when it comes to issues such as: the uses of law and custom, the workings of procedure, the status and functions of officers, the nature of judicial authority, the role of assemblies, etc. This is also why, despite its focus on northern Iberia, this volume is very much concerned with confronting the manifold Iberian reality against other regions in western Europe that can be seen either as central (Italy) or peripheral (Scandinavia).[4]

1 Outline of the Volume

Drawing on the catalogue put together by the PRJ project, the chapters in Part 1 outline the overall documentary landscape of northern Iberia before 1100 and examine the corpora of dispute records extant for the main 'historical' regions across the northern half of the peninsula.[5] Each author engages in a thorough analysis of one or more regional corpora, paying attention not only to the texts themselves and their formal characteristics but also to the procedural models and the judicial forums they stem from, as well as to the sociopolitical contexts in which they were written. These chapters investigate the

4 Four chapters engage in direct comparison: Brown (Iberian and Frankish formulas), Santos (Castile/Álava and Tuscany), Bougard (inside and outside Italy) and Larrea (western Pyrenees, Italy and Germany).

5 The chapter on Portugal by André Evangelista Marques unfortunately did not make it into this volume.

idiosyncrasies involved in the production and transmission of dispute records in each region while confronting them with the more general patterns that characterize the Iberian corpus.

The common questionnaire underpinning Chapters 1–5 addresses the key topics of the volume. Texts themselves are dealt with by examining time and place distributions within each regional corpus, the format and structure of dispute records, their materiality, and the transmission processes that account for the exact corpora extant for each region. The connection between texts and judicial court procedure is approached by looking at the types of disputes and their object, the statuses and agency of litigants, judges, and court officials, as well as the role played by the authorities before which cases were brought. Finally, the interplay between record-making, disputing process and sociopolitical contexts is tackled by taking into account the rhetorical dimension of dispute records. From simple charters recording property transfers determined by (or contested before) a court, to more elaborate narrative texts giving a detailed account of dispute settlement processes, these records were normally designed to legitimize some sort of social, economic, or political action, and to achieve precise goals in given contexts.

Chapters 1–5 aim to lay the foundations for further enquiries on court practice, on legal culture and its uses, and on the wider social and political circumstances in which disputes arose and were settled in early medieval Iberia. At the same time, the authors try to make a larger argument about the importance of corpora analysis, once it is set against the social, political, and cultural backdrop of documentary production. This sort of analysis is key to assess the evidentiary value of extant records, which means engaging not only in the sort of enquiry carried out in these chapters, but also in a meta-analysis of how a given corpus was assembled, constructed and made available, either through printing or online.[6] Thus, a final paper in Part 1 by Francesca Tinti assesses the PRJ database by exploiting its possibilities and pointing out some of the directions in which it could be enhanced in the light of recent work on medieval textual corpora and thematic databases. This means examining not only the selection criteria but also the norms used to structure information within the database and the strategies chosen to present both the texts and their meta-information, which includes the design of search options.[7]

6 See also François Bougard's remarks about Italy in his chapter below.

7 Whereas the chapters in Part 1 explicitly attempt to showcase the possibilities presented by the PRJ database for the study of justice and dispute settlement across northern Iberia, chapters such as those by Adam Kosto and Juan José Larrea in Part 3 are also good examples of how the investigation of specific topics can benefit from the establishment of regional corpora of dispute records and from the analytical possibilities opened up by the PRJ database.

The four chapters in Part 2 take a closer look at the modes in which dispute settlement was recorded, with an eye on the complex relationship between the texts themselves, the contexts in which they were written and the actual (and often broader) conflicts they depict. Drawing on charter material from Iberia and Italy, the two areas in western Europe where early medieval evidence about judicial disputes is arguably richer, these chapters make a strong argument for a broad typology of dispute records. This should encompass not only texts that are directly related to court activity, either recording specific procedures or giving an overall account of a case, but also records of transactions or other legal arrangements that indirectly refer to (or stem from) judicial process. Furthermore, as Wendy Davies shows with her "deconstruction" of some remarkable Iberian texts, and François Bougard notes about the different elements of Italian "judicial dossiers", no classification system can dispense with giving serious thought to the relationship between the different types of records and the different moments in which they were written vis-à-vis the original court proceedings or the original transactions they record.

Key topics addressed by the papers in this section include the ways in which legal texts and concepts, procedural models, formularies, and the notariate all have influenced the writing of dispute records, which were themselves part and parcel of judicial practice. Two papers choose to zoom in some of these topics, namely Warren Brown's analysis of conflict and judicial processes in the *Formulae Visigothicae*, which he examines in tandem with the Frankish formulas; and Igor Santos's consideration of the levels of literacy associated with the judicial sphere, as well as of the ratio of dispute records actually preserved to those originally produced, which he tries to assess through the references to lay *deperdita* in dispute texts from Castile-Álava and Tuscany.

Finally, the five papers assembled in Part 3 address the contexts surrounding—and the dense interactions underpinning—the uses of justice and the settlement of disputes. Competition and collaboration between different levels and scales of power make dichotomies such as 'public' vs. 'private' and 'formal' vs. 'informal' insufficient to describe dispute processes that were often more fluid and diversified, and to capture the dynamic interplay between different (but not necessarily opposing) modes of conflict resolution. Having this in mind, these chapters take a closer look at the agency of individuals and groups acting as judicial authorities, judges, officials, scribes, litigants, or even appearing in court as patrons and representatives of the parties, with some occasionally taking on two or more of these roles, like the "versatile participants" identified by Adam Kosto in Catalonian records.

This kind of approach shows litigation as a means of political action, designed to (re)shape social order. The disputes known to us are mostly concerned with property and territorial control, but the conflicting political, jurisdictional, and economic interests that underpin legal action are legion; and they would vary according to the status of the litigants, whom recent scholarship—increasingly interested in non-elite agency—has been showing to span the social spectrum. Besides, such conflicting interests, and the uses of litigation made by the different actors, were often intertwined in ways that escape the eye of the modern historian. It is not infrequent that an apparently restricted, localized case developed in fact against a wider background, casting its net wider to include players other than the litigants and to impact on matters other than those under discussion.

Chapters in this part look into different types of cases opposing either members of the lay and ecclesiastical elite, as in Kim Esmark's analysis of a dispute between Archbishop Eskil and Canon Florentius of Lund; or local communities and ecclesiastical lords, as in Julio Escalona's examination of a 'hidden' dispute between the monastery of Sahagún and its dependent communities in a small territory, and in Juan José Larrea's exploration of the role of delimitations and conflicts in the construction of monastic territories in the Western Pyrenees; or even opposing peasant communities against one another, a sort of conflict also explored by Larrea. Despite such different sociopolitical frameworks, some common elements can be seen to play a part in most, if not all, dispute settlement processes studied in these chapters. This is the case with the centrality of micropolitical power games, the resort to mediation through patrons, friends, kinsmen, and neighbours as a means to reach and enforce settlement, and the procedural use of compromise, ritual ceremonies, and the written (and sometimes performed) word in judicial court process. By presenting case studies based on detailed reconstructions of events, places, individuals, and local contexts, these three papers show how micro-analysis is particularly instructive to understand the workings of court procedure and the dynamics of dispute settlement in all its complexity; provided that it engages in the sort of "thick description" (Clifford Geertz) that accounts for the stance of the litigants and of other participants in the disputing process, which is ultimately a good proxy for social order in any given society.

2 Northern Iberia: A Case Study

2.1 *A Fragmented Political Landscape with a Common Legal and Procedural Framework*

Research on political power in early medieval northern Iberia has made a huge progress over the last decades, and basically transitioned from a classical approach centred on the state, and dominated by nationalistic views which tended to back-project the map and the institutional architecture of high medieval Christian kingdoms and their state apparatuses, to a new paradigm based on the notion of 'territorial fragmentation'—seen as stretching back as far as the Visigothic period—and mostly concerned with the local articulation of different spheres of power.[8] The resulting image is that of a very fragmented political and institutional landscape, in which local and supra-local elites were able to get the upper hand over kings, despite the rhetoric of delegation deployed by royal propagandists in narrative texts and charters alike.[9] A key attribute of power, the exercise of justice—with its associated authority to channel the law and other types of social norms into the resolution of disputes and the punishment of crimes—was equally fragmented. On the one hand, royal justice proved unable to sustain any overarching, permanent judicial system, rather acting as a regulatory mechanism for social and political relations between the different players amongst the realm's political community;[10] on the other hand, local and regional courts seem to have become the standard judicial fora, at least as far as the extant evidence will let us know.[11]

Early medieval justice, in Iberia as elsewhere, was predominantly the work not of a centralized political body committed to enforce the law and court decrees deriving from it, but rather an emanation of politics at a much more localized scale. Beyond a very few cases brought before the royal court, what we

8 For general context, see Roger Collins, *Caliphs and Kings: Spain, 796–1031* (Chichester: Wiley-Blackwell, 2014); Amancio Isla Frez, *La Alta Edad Media: siglos VIII–XI* (Madrid: Síntesis, 2002).

9 Santiago Castellanos and Iñaki Martín Viso, "The local articulation of central power in the north of the Iberian Peninsula (500–1000)," *Early Medieval Europe* 13, no. 1 (2005), 1–42; Juan Antonio Quirós Castillo, "Early medieval landscapes in north-west Spain: local powers and communities, fifth–tenth centuries," *Early Medieval Europe* 19, no. 3 (2011), 285–311; Álvaro Carvajal Castro, *Bajo la máscara del "regnum": la monarquía asturleonesa en León (854–1037)* (Madrid: Consejo Superior de Investigaciones Científicas, 2017).

10 Carvajal Castro, *Bajo la máscara*, esp. ch 8; Iñaki Martín Viso, "Authority and justice in the formation of the Kingdom of Asturias–León," *Al-Masāq* 29, no. 2 (2017), 114–132.

11 Wendy Davies, *Windows on Justice in Northern Iberia, 800–1000* (Abingdon: Routledge, 2016).

find is, first, lordly courts (both lay and ecclesiastical[12]), which were often called upon to settle matters involving a lord that may act both as plaintiff (sometimes by proxy) and member/president of the tribunal, but also to deal with disputes and criminal cases involving peasants; and second, courts that were seemingly more 'public' in nature, in which notable men—from magnates to well off-peasants—sat alongside professional judges to hear all sorts of cases.[13] Although these latter courts often acted at a supra-local level, the great majority of cases brought before both types of court dealt with matters of local significance, either property disputes confined to small territories, or crimes affecting a limited number of individuals/families within the same village community, or at best impacting on the relationship between neighbouring communities or between communities and lords. No wonder, thus, that the justice delivered by this kind of court is conciliatory in its nature, or at least in its rhetoric, as notions of peace and reconciliation were key to keep the balance and good functioning of local communities, as well as the authority of the court itself. This does not mean that there were not hierarchies and power struggles at stake when a court was asked to mediate a dispute between groups or individuals—in which case the judges often acted as guardians of the judicial process rather than adjudicators—or to pass judgment on felony cases.[14] In fact, justice constituted a primary political arena in early medieval societies;[15] which means that judicial court process cannot avoid mirroring the tensions and hierarchies that cut across local and supra-local communities.

12 The intervention of churchmen as judges became commonplace already in Visigothic times: Carlos Petit, *Ivstitia gothica: Historia social y teología del proceso en la Lex Visigothorum* (Huelva: Universidad de Huelva, 2001), 339–361; Céline Martin, *La géographie du pouvoir dans l'espace visigothique* (Villeneuve d'Ascq: Presses universitaires du Septentrion, 2003), 199–200.

13 On the legitimation derived from the presence of *boni homines* in court, and the different functions these men might perform (judging, oath taking, intercession, price-fixing and enforcement of transactions), see Wendy Davies, "Boni homines in northern Iberia: A particularity that raises some general questions," in *Italy and Early Medieval Europe*, ed. Ross Balzaretti et al. (Oxford: Oxford University Press, 2018), 60–72.

14 Judges and *saiones* had the ability to enforce court decisions in northern Iberia, as opposed to what happened in other Europeans areas; Davies, *Windows on Justice*, 155–168. On *saiones* see also below, Chapter 11, pp. 317–325.

15 Wendy Davies and Paul Fouracre, eds., *The Settlement of Disputes in Early Medieval Europe* (Cambridge: Cambridge University Press, 1986); Warren Brown and Piotr Górecki, eds., *Conflict in Medieval Europe: Changing Perspectives on Society and Culture* (Aldershot: Ashgate, 2003); Kim Esmark et al., *Disputing Strategies.*

Such a fragmented, and yet highly condensed, political landscape did not translate, however, into an equally fragmented legal and procedural framework for the settlement of disputes. Against the traditional view that describes the early Middle Ages as a period of 'weak' legal and institutional frameworks, because of a near absence of royal/public power, and in which custom (as opposed to law) and mediation (as opposed to adjudication) prevailed, recent scholarship has been drawing a more complex picture.[16] In her latest book about justice in northern Iberia before 1000, Wendy Davies has clearly shown that a "long-established judicial system" defined by some standard procedures and a common legal framework was in place across northern Iberia (from Portugal and Galicia to Navarre and Aragon) already in the ninth and tenth centuries;[17] and the same is true of Catalonia, despite some procedural and documentary nuances and an even stronger influence of Visigothic law.[18] Some of the features of such 'system' look distinctive, namely the frequent references to written law in charters, the high number of criminal cases, and the office of *saio*, but most elements of Iberian judicial process can also be traced

16 For the first view, see e.g. José María Mínguez Fernández, "Justicia y poder en el marco de la feudalización de la sociedad leonesa," in *La giustizia nell'alto medioevo (secoli IX–XI)* (Spoleto: Centro Italiano di Studi sull'Alto Medioevo, 1997), 1:491–548; for the latter, Isabel Alfonso, "Resolución de disputas y prácticas judiciales en el Burgos medieval," in *Burgos en la Plena Edad Media. III Jornadas burgalesas de historia* (Burgos: Asociación Provincial de Libreros de Burgos, 1994), 211–241; Isabel Alfonso, "Litigios por la tierra y "malfetrías" entre la nobleza medieval castellano-leonesa," *Hispania* 197 (Desarrollo legal, prácticas judiciales y acción política en la Europa medieval, ed. Isabel Alfonso) (1997), 917–955; Isabel Alfonso, "Judicial rhetoric and political legitimation in medieval León-Castile," in *Building Legitimacy: Political Discourses and Forms of Legitimacy in Medieval Societies*, ed. I. Alfonso, H. Kennedy, and J. Escalona (Leiden: Brill, 2004), 51–87; Isabel Alfonso, "The language and practice of negotiation in medieval conflict resolution (Castille-Leon, 11th–13th centuries)," in *Feud, Violence and Practice: Essays in Medieval Studies in Honor of Stephen D. White*, ed. Belle S. Tuten and Tracey L. Billado (Farnham: Ashgate, 2010), 157–174; Pascual Martínez Sopena, "La justicia en la época asturleonesa: entre el *liber* y los mediadores sociales," in *El lugar del campesino. En torno a la obra de Reyna Pastor*, ed. Ana Rodríguez (València: Universitat de València, CSIC, 2007), 239–260; Jeffrey Bowman, "From Galicia to the Rhône. Legal practice in northern Spain around the Year 1000," in *Culture and Society in Medieval Galicia. A Cultural Crossroads at the Edge of Europe*, ed. James D'Emilio (Leiden: Brill, 2015), 343–360; and the articles collected in *Al-Masāq* 29 (2), 99–185 (special issue on "Justice in Early Medieval Northern Iberia").

17 Davies, *Windows on Justice*, 155, 202–203, 245–246 (quoted phrase on p. 256).

18 Adam J. Kosto, *Making Agreements in Medieval Catalonia: Power, Order, and the Written Word, 1000–1200* (Cambridge: Cambridge University Press, 2001); Jeffrey A. Bowman, *Shifting Landmarks: Property, Proof, and Dispute in Catalonia around the Year 1000* (Ithaca: Cornell University Press, 2004); Josep M. Salrach, *Justícia i poder a Catalunya abans de l'any mil* (Vic: Eumo, 2013).

in other areas of western Europe.[19] This 'system' extended beyond the royal, comital and episcopal courts to encompass lordly courts (whether lay or monastic), which followed the same procedure.[20] No major changes seem to occur in the eleventh century, according to the few micro-regional analyses available;[21] and legal historians have suggested that the Visigothic legal tradition, transmitted by the *Forum Iudicum* as well as by "custom, memory or even formulas", dominated judicial procedure in northern Iberia through the ninth to twelfth century.[22] This very long persistence can perhaps be seen as another argument that confirms the vision of Visigothic law as deriving to a significant extent from late Roman vulgar law, that is, a legal framework firmly implemented in large stretches of the Peninsula since before the fifth century.[23] And it helps to explain the "remarkable penetration of judicial experience and procedure into Catalan society", deduced by Adam Kosto from the "relative lack of overlap in officials' roles."[24]

In any case, this was not an institutional system—as posited by traditional legal history and critiqued by the anthropologically inspired school of dispute studies—but rather a practical system defined by a common legal framework

---

19 Davies, *Windows on Justice*, 232–254 (elements found elsewhere summarized on p. 233); Wendy Davies, "Settling disputes in early medieval Spain and Portugal: A contrast with Wales and Brittany?," in *Wales and the Welsh in the Middle Ages: Essays Presented to J. Beverley Smith*, ed. Ralph A. Griffiths and Phillipp R. Schofield (Cardiff: University of Wales Press, 2011), 89–107.

20 Wendy Davies, "Summary justice and seigneurial justice in northern Iberia on the eve of the Millennium," *Haskins Society Journal* 22 (2010 [2012]), 43–58, at 54–55.

21 E.g. Martínez Sopena, "La justicia," 241.

22 Agustín Prieto Morera, "El proceso en el reino de León a la luz de los diplomas," in *El reino de León en la Alta Edad Media, II: Ordenamiento jurídico del reino*, 381–518 (León: Centro de Estudios e Investigación 'San Isidoro', 1992), citation on p. 517. On the influence of the *Liber iudiciorum* in Visigothic court documents, see Nicholas Everett, "Lay documents and archives in early medieval Spain and Italy, c. 400–700," in *Documentary Culture and the Laity in the Early Middle Ages*, ed. Warren Brown et al. (Cambridge: Cambridge University Press, 2012), 63–94, at 88–89. For its uses in the ninth to eleventh century, see Roger Collins, "'Sicut lex Gothorum continet': law and charters in ninth- and tenth-century León and Catalonia," *The English Historical Review* 100, no. 396 (1985), 489–512; Michel Zimmermann, *Écrire et lire en Catalogne (IXe-XIIe siècle)*, 2 vols (Madrid: Casa de Velázquez, 2003), 922–949; Pascual Martínez Sopena, "El uso de la Ley Gótica en el reino de León," in *Remploi, citation, plagiat. Conduites et pratiques médiévales (Xe-XIIe siècle)*, ed. Pierre Toubert and Pierre Moret (Madrid: Casa de Velázquez, 2009), 97–114; Amancio Isla Frez, "La pervivencia de la tradición legal visigótica en el reino asturleonés," *Mélanges de la Casa de Velázquez* 41, no. 2 (2011), 75–86; Davies, *Windows on Justice*, 26–27, 235–237; Graham Barrett, "The text of Visigothic law in practice," *Visigothic Symposium* 4 (2020–2021), 18–63, at https://visigothicsymposia.org/graham-barrett/ (accessed 15 April 2022).

23 For a brief summary of the discussion, see Roger Collins, *Early Medieval Spain: Unity in Diversity, 400–1000*, 2nd ed. (New York: St. Martin's Press, 1995), 27–29.

24 See below, Chapter 11, p. 329.

which encompassed not only common laws but above all a common way of recording judicial court process. It comes as no surprise that such a judicial system was defined by some sort of recording system, as much as by legal and procedural norms. One might ask whether this recording system is partly responsible for conveying the image of a judicial system as such, which raises the question of whether the idiosyncrasies of other types of courts (less formal and undocumented) are not downplayed by the 'correct' way of recording judicial proceedings that is used in the extant charter material. But what should be stressed here is that already in the ninth and tenth centuries, dispute records reveal some standard features in terms of structure, materiality, formulas, and language, which led Davies to speak of a "common recording tradition".[25] The consistent use of some formulas in dispute texts (mainly those reflecting specific procedures and the utterance of ritual words in court) denotes less variation than is to be found in some gift and sale formulas and reflects a long-established judicial practice.[26] Furthermore, and despite the absence of a comprehensive study of the eleventh-century material, dispute records dated after 1000 seem to have kept that same tradition, whether they were written in monastic scriptoria or in the royal circles.[27]

2.2 *The Corpus of Northern Iberian Charters up to 1100*

More broadly, a diplomatic tradition was indeed in place in Visigothic Iberia and it remained as the general framework of documentary practice until the twelfth century; not least in the northern regions from the Atlantic shores of Portugal and Galicia to the Pyrenees, a vast stretch of land which escaped the grip of Muslim power from an early stage and where several Christian polities came to take root after the late eighth century.[28] In fact, a steadily growing

25 Davies, *Windows on Justice*, 234. An impressive analysis of the Asturian-Leonese material considering all four aspects is offered throughout chs. 2–5.

26 Davies, *Windows on Justice*, 148. Davies suggests, however, that the lesser variation of dispute texts reveals a more recent and restricted writing practice that owes less to Visigothic models and more to post-Visigothic developments and the new diplomatic practices of large monasteries from the tenth century onwards, Davies, *Windows on Justice*, 144, 258–259; cf. José Antonio Fernández Flórez, *La elaboración de los documentos en los reinos hispánicos occidentales* (ss. VI–XIII) (Burgos: Institución Fernán González, Academia Burguense de Historia y Bellas Artes, 2002), 77.

27 Isabel Alfonso, "El formato de la información judicial en la Alta Edad Media peninsular," in *Chartes et cartulaires comme instruments de pouvoir: Espagne et Occident chrétien* (VIIIe–XIIe *siècles*), ed. Julio Escalona and Hélène Sirantoine (Toulouse: Université de Toulouse-Le Mirail, 2013), 191–218, at 209.

28 Roger Collins, "Literacy and the laity in early mediaeval Spain," in *The Uses of Literacy in Early Mediaeval Europe*, ed. Rosamond McKitterick (Cambridge: Cambridge University Press, 1990), 109–133; Everett, "Lay documents."; Zimmermann, *Écrire et lire*; Fernández

number of monasteries and cathedrals assured the continuity of late antique scribal practices in this area. Most importantly, they were responsible for keeping and transmitting a significant amount of early medieval records written by both clerical and lay scribes who shared a 'common culture of documentary practice'.[29] The use of standard formulas and language cannot be equated, though, with the formal lay notarial tradition found in Italy, or its offshoots in some other parts of the Carolingian Empire. Public notaries (*notarii publici*) are mentioned in the *Liber iudiciorum*, but the fact that a document was drawn up by one of these professionals "had no effect on the document's legal validity" already in the seventh-century.[30] Professional notariate seems to have disappeared in post-Visigothic Iberia, largely replaced by beneficiary production, sometimes committed to local scribes by peasants and even lords.[31] And although comital scribes could be found in Catalonia since Carolingian times and royal notaries were at work in the kingdom of Asturias-León (encompassing northwest Iberia stretching as far east as Castille) from the end of the tenth century and in the kingdoms of Pamplona (Navarre) and Aragon from, respectively, the first third and the middle of the eleventh century, royal chanceries do not seem to have been in place in Iberia before the twelfth century.[32]

Flórez, *La Elaboración*, 62–92; Miguel Calleja Puerta, "Ecos de las *Fórmulas* visigóticas en la documentación altomedieval astur-leonesa," in *Les formulaires. Compilation et circulation des modèles d'actes dans l'Europe médiévale et moderne: XIIIe congrès de la Commission internationale de diplomatique (Paris, 3–4 septembre 2012)*, ed. O. Guyotjeannin, L. Morelle, and S.P. Scalfati (Paris: Éditions en ligne de l'École des chartes, 2016), at http://elec.enc.sorbonne.fr/cid2012/part4 (accessed 15 April 2022); Graham Barrett, *Text and Textuality in Early Medieval Iberia: The Written and the World, 711–1031* (Oxford: Oxford University Press, 2023).

29 Adam J. Kosto, "*Sicut mos esse solet*: documentary practices in Christian Iberia, c. 700–1000," in *Documentary Culture and the Laity in the Early Middle Ages*, ed. Warren Brown et al. (Cambridge: Cambridge University Press, 2012), 259–282, citation on p. 260.

30 Everett, "Lay documents," 70, 85; "Lex Visigothorum," in Karl Zeumer, ed., *Leges Visigothorum*, MGH LL nat. Germ. 1 (Hanover: Hahn, 1902), VII.5.9, pp. 308–309.

31 Wendy Davies, "Local priests and the writing of charters in northern Iberia in the tenth century," in *Chartes et cartulaires comme instruments de pouvoir: Espagne et Occident chrétien (VIIIe–XIIe siècles)*, ed. Julio Escalona and Hélène Sirantoine (Toulouse: Université de Toulouse-Le Mirail, 2013), 29–43; Zimmermann, *Écrire et lire*, 113–135.

32 Collins, "Literacy and the laity," 125. Manuel Lucas Álvarez, *El Reino de León en la alta Edad Media. VIII: La documentación real astur-leonesa (718–1072)* (León: Centro de Estudios e Investigación 'San Isidoro', 1995), 219–233; cf. Andrés Gambra, *Alfonso VI: cancillería, curia e imperio*, 2 vols (León: Centro de Estudios e Investigación 'San Isidoro', 1997), 1:103–174. Guadalupe Lopetegui Semprena, "Escribas y notarios en la Cancillería real de Navarra durante el siglo XII," in *Los cimientos del Estado en la Edad Media: Cancillerías, notariado y privilegios reales en la construcción del Estado en la Edad Media*, ed. Juan Antonio Barrio Barrio (Alicante: Marfil, 2004), 65–92. Ángel Canellas López, "La cancillería real

For more than a century after the Arab conquest (711), which marked the end of the Visigothic kingdom, there survive little more than 200 documents in northern Iberia.[33] This figure is not very different from that for the whole Iberian Peninsula in the sixth and seventh centuries, although the Visigothic material tends to be more fragmentary and less elaborate. Less than ten original charters and about two dozen texts transmitted in parchment copies (mostly fragmentary and not all charters) are extant;[34] to which one can add the ever growing corpus of 163 texts written in slate (also fragmentary and mostly found in the north-western area of the *Meseta*, around Salamanca and Ávila)[35] and an apparently loose collection of 46 formulas, known as *Formulae Visigothicae*.[36]

From the mid-ninth century onwards, and especially in the tenth century, the charter evidence becomes more consistent in the Asturian-Leonese king-

del reino de Aragón (1035–1134)," in *Folia Budapestina* (Zaragoza: Institución Fernando el Católico, 1983), 23–46; María de los Desamparados Cabanes Pecourt, "Diplomas y cancillería," in *Sancho Ramírez, rey de Aragón, y su tiempo (1064–1094)*, ed. Esteban Sarasa Sánchez (Huesca: Instituto de Estudios Altoaragoneses, 1994), 25–45. Thanks are due to Josep M. Salrach and Juan José Larrea for their help with this point.

33 The PRJ database lists 222 documents from 850 and before across northern Iberia (50 of which with some bearing on disputes), but only 23 are dated eighth century. There remain very few originals, Calleja Puerta, "Ecos," 8; and many were forged or interpolated, Antonio C. Floriano, *Diplomática española del período astur (718–910)*, 2 vols (Oviedo: Instituto de Estudios Asturianos, 1949–1951), and the several volumes in the *Catalunya carolíngia* series, a full list of which is available at https://www.iec.cat/recerca/projecte1.asp?codi=PIN2012-S01-FELIU01 (accessed 15 April 2022).

34 Originals: *Chartae Latinae antiquiores: Facsimile-edition of the Latin charters. 2nd series, Ninth century*, ed. Guglielmo Cavallo and Giovanna Nicolaj, vol. 114: Spain 3-Portugal, ed. Miguel Calleja Puerta et al. (Dietikon-Zurich: Urs-Graf Verlag, 2018); cf. *Chartae Latinae antiquiores: Facsimile-edition of the Latin charters prior to the ninth century*, ed. A. Bruckner, R. Marichal, and T. Dorandi, vol. 46: Belgium, Greece, Ireland, Israel, Norway, Holland, Republic of Georgia, Spain, ed. Tiziano Dorandi (Dietikon-Zurich: Urs-Graf Verlag, 1995); copies: Ángel Canellas López, *Diplomática hispano-visigoda* (Zaragoza: Institución "Fernando el Católico", 1979), 15–17. Four complete sixth-century charters from the Aragonese monastery of San Martin de Asán were recently found preserved in later copies: Guillermo Tomás Faci and José Carlos Martín Iglesias, "Cuatro documentos inéditos del monasterio visigodo de San Martín de Asán (522–586)," *Mittellateinisches Jahrbuch* 52 (2017), 261–286; Céline Martin and Juan José Larrea, eds., *Nouvelles chartes visigothiques du monastère pyrénéen d'Asán* (Bordeaux: Ausonius Éditions, 2021).

35 Isabel Velázquez Soriano, *Las Pizarras Visigodas (Entre el latín y su disgregación. La lengua hablada en Hispania, siglos VI–VIII)* (Madrid; Salamanca: Real Academia Española, Fundación Instituto Castellano y Leonés de la Lengua, 2004).

36 "Formulae Visigothicae," in Karl Zeumer, ed., *Formulae Merowingici et Karolini Aevi*, MGH LL 5 (Hanover: Hahn, 1886), 572–595; "Formulae Wisigothicae," in Juan Gil, ed. *Miscellanea Wisigothica* (Seville: Publicaciones de la Universidad de Sevilla, 1972), 69–112 (where formula 46 is missing). This collection, preserved in a sixteenth-century copy of a twelfth-century Oviedo codex, raises several diplomatic issues, which fuelled the discussion on

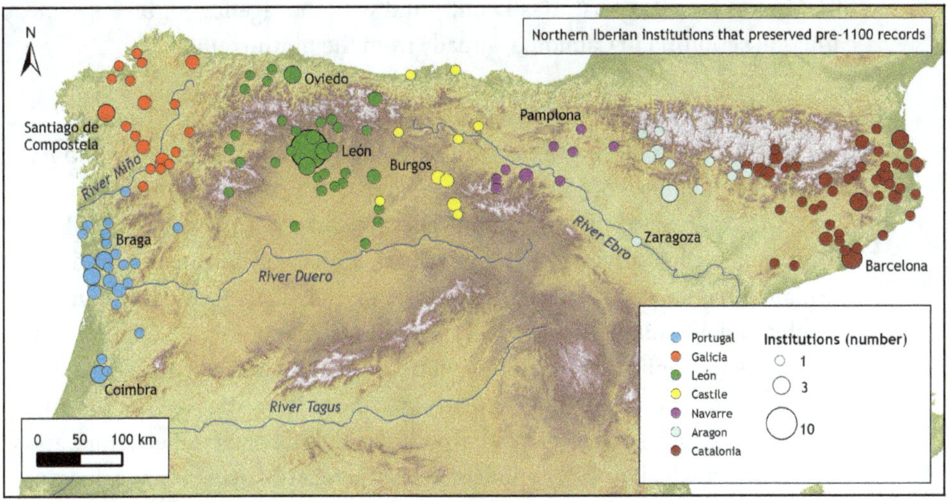

MAP 0.1 Northern Iberian institutions that preserved pre-1100 records
MAP DRAWN BY ANTONIO URIARTE (LABORATORIO DE ARQUEOLOGÍA DEL PAISAJE Y TELEDETECCIÓN. CSIC-INSTITUTO DE HISTORIA. MADRID)

dom,[37] and even more so in the Catalan counties, where the early medieval charter material is plentiful by any standard of comparison in Europe (let alone its northern neighbours of Aragon and Navarre).[38] By 1000, we can see that a standard documentary practice, deeply rooted in the Visigothic tradition, was still in place, despite pockets of local variation that show more recent developments, particularly associated with "the establishment of large monastic scrip-

whether it was compiled in or after the Visigothic period, on which see Edorta Corcoles Olaitz, "About the origin of the *Formulae Wisigothicae*," *Anuario da Facultade de Dereito da Universidade da Coruña* 12 (2008), 199–222; Calleja Puerta, "Ecos;" and below, Chapter 7.

37 Leonor Sierra Macarrón, "Producción y conservación de la documentación altomedieval: del Cantábrico al Duero (siglos IX–XI)," *Signo* 13 (2004), 99–120; on tenth-century charters, see Wendy Davies, *Acts of Giving: Individual, Community, and Church in Tenth-Century Christian Spain* (Oxford: Oxford University Press, 2007), 22–26. For the Asturian-Leonese kingdom, the PRJ database lists 180 documents dated before 900 (23 dispute records), 2.490 dated 901–1000 (265 dispute records), and 4.875 dated 1001–1100 (694 dispute records) (see below, Appendix).

38 Jonathan Jarrett, "Comparing the earliest documentary culture in Carolingian Catalonia," in *Problems and Possibilities of Early Medieval Charters*, ed. Jonathan Jarrett and Allan Scott McKinley (Turnhout: Brepols, 2013), 89–126, at 89–91. For Catalonia alone, the PRJ database lists 486 documents dated before 900 (53 dispute records), 4.270 dated 901–1000 (122 dispute records), and 7.349 dated 1001–1100 (611 dispute records). For Navarre and Aragon, it lists 111 dated before 900 (only 4 dispute records); 401 dated 901–1000 (17 dispute records), and 2.253 dated 1001–1100 (142 dispute records) (see below, Appendix).

toria" in tenth-century Asturias-León;[39] and with the "agency" of bishops and cathedral scriptoria in Catalonia, already from the ninth-century.[40]

2.3 *The PRJ Database of North-Iberian Dispute Records up to 1100*

Over the past generation, different scholarly traditions have shown the importance of documentary corpora analysis as a requisite for research into the social uses and implications of the written record. 'Literacy', '*memoria*' and '*cartularisation*' are three keywords, among others, which can help us to pin down the main directions which research has taken in the Anglo-Saxon, German and French scholarly milieus, respectively.[41] By showing that no phenomenon can be conveniently approached without thinking about its representations in the written record, these different scholarly traditions have stressed the significance of assessing the documentary corpora available for each subject, time, and place, without which no full appreciation of the records' evidentiary value can be gained. Conflict and justice are no exception, which is why the PRJ project devoted a great effort to establish and describe the corpus of dispute records extant for northern Iberia (from Portugal to Catalonia) prior to the twelfth century.

The PRJ database is a relational database designed to provide digital access to these texts and to structured information on the corpus. It includes (1) a census of all published documents dated until 1100, which were counted year by year and ascribed to the exact institution in whose archive each document was kept, and therefore to a specific region;[42] and (2) a catalogue of documents containing any kind of information on judicial proceedings and dispute resolution mechanisms in general—a corpus of documents here termed 'dispute records' for the sake of brevity.[43] The database currently stands at approximately 22,000 documents, nearly 10% of which contain some kind of dispute

39 Davies, *Windows on Justice*, ch. 2–5 (citation on p. 120); Ernesto Pastor Díaz de Garayo, "Los testimonios escritos del sector meridional de Castilla (siglos X–XI). Ensayo de crítica documental," *Historia. Instituciones. Documentos* 24 (1997), 355–379, at 359, 379; Calleja Puerta, "Ecos."

40 Jarrett, "Comparing," who draws a "comparison of target formulae" between ninth-century gifts and sales from Catalonia and Asturias-León, to conclude that the documents are "similar" but the formulas used by the scribes of the two areas show considerable variation in their wording (p. 114).

41 Pierre Chastang, "L'archéologie du texte médiéval," *Bulletin du centre d'études médiévales d'Auxerre* (*BUCEMA*) Hors-série no. 2 (2009), at http://journals.openedition.org/cem/8702 (accessed 15 April 2022).

42 This is the most thorough attempt, to date, at measuring this corpus and its distributions over time and space.

43 The catalogue details for each record the date, textual transmission (original/copy), authenticity (authentic, suspect, false), and a summary (regesta) of its content.

information (see Table 0.1 below).[44] On account of the conceptual rationale for the twofold composition of the database being that the material with some kind of dispute content can only be assessed in relation to the rest of the existing documentation, the project has managed to produce a key resource for historians working on any topic related to early medieval Iberia, and not only on conflict and justice.

The PRJ database also allows the user to access and download the text of every single dispute record in its most recent edition and to perform full-text searches on the whole corpus. A few multiple search queries to the database are also available, both on the corpus of dispute records and on the census of the overall number of records extant. These queries allow for cross comparison between different time frames, regions, the institutions where the records were originally produced/transmitted, forms of transmission (originals/copies), and ratios of dispute records to the overall number of extant records.[45] The database is organized according to two criteria: regions and institutions. Searches can be performed using both, and also allowing for the distinction between the overall number of records and that of dispute records for most of the variables considered. This enables researchers to conduct comparative enquiries at regional level across north Iberia, but also between the archives of different institutions, which in many cases, and save for the major monasteries and episcopal sees, are associated with much smaller territories and tend to reflect rather more localized realities.[46]

For operational purposes seven regions were identified which correspond broadly to the north of Portugal and six of the current autonomous communit-

44 The documents from Catalonia are still being processed and will be made available soon. At present, the public version of the PRJ database allows searches on the records from the remaining regions only, the overall number of which is 10.312, of which 1.145 are dispute records.

45 The PRJ database was originally aimed at supporting more complex research on the writing and preservation of dispute records and on dispute settlement processes. A module dealing with the information about litigation in these texts has been designed to perform structured analysis of specific variables such as the venues and fora in which litigation took place, the status of the litigants, the types of disputes, procedures, evidence, resolutions, and results, etc. This module is still under development and will be included in future versions of the database. Until such a comprehensive analytical tool is available, we must rely on occasional studies of one or more such variables, which often focus on specific regions and timeframes. This helps to explain the imbalance in the treatment of judicial court process and other methods of dispute settlement in the chapters in Part 1 of this volume.

46 When comparing the size of regional corpora one must bear in mind that they correlate with very different territorial extensions; and the same is true of institutional corpora.

ies in Spain: Galicia, León, Castile, Navarre, Aragon, and Catalonia. (Asturias were included in the León region, Cantabria in Castile and León, and La Rioja in Navarre).[47] No early medieval political and institutional framework should be read into this sevenfold regional division, let alone any absolute territorial coincidence between early medieval and modern administrative units. Despite all its shortcomings, such a regional grid makes it easier to correlate the data in the database with an historiography that has remained for the past decades—especially in Spain—markedly regional in its scope.[48]

Institutional affiliation was another consideration used to organize the PRJ database. The reason is that the documentation included in the database was largely preserved in ecclesiastic institutions, and that this material has been predominantly published by institution.[49] The publication of early medieval charters has experienced a substantial increase in Spain since the 1970s and 1980s, and greater numbers of critical editions of ever-increasing quality have been published in recent decades.[50] Editorial criteria have also evolved and, while it is true that some compilations of documents related to a specific territory, a political entity or a reign do still appear occasionally, the 'institution/edition' rationale has largely become the standard model.[51]

47 See above, Map 0.1. Given the fluctuations of political geography during the medieval period, regional boundaries have not been marked on the map.

48 On the need to overcome this fragmented historiographical framework, see Álvaro Carvajal Castro et al., "Towards a trans-regional approach to early medieval Iberia," *History Compass* 20, no. 6 (2022), e12743, at https://compass.onlinelibrary.wiley.com/doi/abs/10.1111/hic3.12743 (accessed 15 August 2022).

49 This institutional classification of documents allows for an easy way to map the location of archives, which proves much more difficult with large editions of regional corpora such as, for example, the *Portugaliae Monumenta Historica* and the *Catalunya Carolingia*.

50 J.Á. García de Cortázar, J.A. Munita Loinaz and L.J. Fortún Pérez de Ciriza, eds., *CODIPHIS: catálogo de colecciones diplomáticas hispano-lusas de época medieval*, 2 vols (Santander: Fundación Marcelino Botín, 1999); updated by Luis Javier Fortún Pérez de Ciriza, "La edición de fuentes documentales para el estudio de la Edad Media hispana," in *XXV años de historiografía hispana (1980–2004): Historia medieval, moderna y de América*, ed. José Antonio Munita Loinaz and José Ramón Díaz de Durana Ortíz de Urbina (Bilbao: Universidad del País Vasco, 2007), 15–53; André Evangelista Marques, "Para um inventário da documentação diplomática anterior a 1101 conservada em arquivos portugueses," in *Mundos medievales: espacios, sociedades y poder: homenaje al profesor José Ángel García de Cortázar y Ruiz de Aguirre*, ed. Beatriz Arízaga Bolumburo et al. (Santander: Universidad de Cantabria, 2012), 2:705–718. For a recent overview, Carvajal Castro et al., "Trans-regional approach." The PRJ database source list is available at http://prj.csic.es/bibliografia_en.php?c=4 (accessed 15 April, 2022).

51 The criteria adopted in different editions often lack consistency in key aspects such as distinguishing between documents preserved in single-sheet parchments or copied in cartularies, dating techniques, whether or not to include those records which are known to

In any case, the connection between documents and institutions is seldom straightforward, since records were often the object of complex transmission processes which saw them transition from the place where they were originally produced and stored to one or more archives in which they ended up being kept. The documentary collections of large ecclesiastic institutions (both monasteries and diocesan sees) were mainly assembled by the incorporation of archives from other minor monastic entities when the latter were merged into the former—something that occurred in parallel with their institutional development; and it is now widely accepted that ecclesiastical collections also included documentation from lay archives.[52] Such accumulative dynamics raise some issues in terms of quantifying the charters preserved for any of these institutions. It is not easy to provide a general, standard solution for all cases, since very often no data exists as to the origin of the documents from minor entities that have been incorporated into a larger one, sometimes at the end of a rather long archival route. Some experimental strategies have been proposed in the PRJ database regarding certain documentary collections that may be classified by their 'institution of origin'. Special attention has been paid to the structure of cartularies where the documents from incorporated monasteries were copied with some indication of their provenance, as is the case, for example, with the cartularies from three cathedrals, namely the *Tumbo Legionense* from León, the *Liber Fidei* from Braga and the *Livro Preto* from Coimbra.[53]

Appendix: Illustrations

Technical Note

- All tables and graphs included in this Appendix and in the chapters in Part 1 were retrieved through the PRJ database search tools available online, which allow structured data searches by 'region', 'institution' and multi-layered comparison.[54]

---

have been lost, the consideration of false and interpolated documents, and even the very concept of document unit. Although an attempt was made to overcome some of these shortcomings in the PRJ database, they must be borne in mind when managing its data.

52 Kosto, "*Sicut mos*." These "lay dossiers" are not singled out in the PRJ database, though.

53 See below, Chapter 2, p. 70.

54 See the database user guide at http://prj.csic.es/guia_en.php?m=1&c=8 (accessed 15 April 2022).

- The PRJ database allows detailed analyses of time distributions of both the overall number of records ('All') and of 'Dispute' records. For the sake of illustration, distributions across two different time spans (100 and 25 years) were represented using bar and line graphs (both types available on the database online interface), which work best with longer and shorter time spans, respectively. It should be noted that the start date of the tables and graphs compiled here may vary according to the data series for each region.
- Counts of charters dated to an interval in the PRJ database are based on end dates, which in the case of many undated documents means the last year of a given century. This leads to an inflation in years such as 900, 1000 and 1100, which must be borne in mind when looking at time distributions.
- Through a careful identification of the institution where each record was originally kept (but not necessarily written), the PRJ database also provides us with relevant information about spatial distributions within each region and across the whole northern Iberia. The maps in this volume try to convey basic distributions, although such information lends itself to further analysis and mapping.

Tables

TABLE 0.1 Iberian records before 1100, by region

Region	Institutions (n)	All records (n)	Dispute records (n)	Dispute records (%)	Years
Aragon	19	1357	81	5.97	(814–1100)
Castile	13	999	61	6.11	(804–1100)
Catalonia	67	12105	786	6.49	(780–1100)
Galicia	25	1303	266	20.41	(569–1100)
León	61	3963	443	11.18	(767–1100)
Navarre	11	1408	82	5.82	(759–1100)
Portugal	33	1282	212	16.54	(832–1100)
Total	229	22417	1931	8.61	

TABLE 0.2 Iberian records before 1100, by region/century

Region	Century	All records (n)	Dispute records (n)	Dispute records (%)
Aragon	9th	91	3	3.3
	10th	251	12	4.78
	11th	1015	66	6.5
Castile	9th	16	1	6.25
	10th	342	23	6.73
	11th	641	37	5.77
Catalonia	8th	3	0	0
	9th	483	53	10.97
	10th	4270	122	2.86
	11th	7349	611	8.31
Galicia	8th	11	0	0
	9th	77	15	19.48
	10th	567	96	16.93
	11th	646	155	23.99
León	8th	5	0	0
	9th	63	5	7.94
	10th	1378	117	8.48
	11th	2517	321	12.75
Navarre	8th	2	0	0
	9th	18	1	5.56
	10th	150	5	3.33
	11th	1238	76	6.14
Portugal	9th	8	2	25
	10th	203	29	14.29
	11th	1071	81	16.9

TABLE 0.3 Iberian dispute records before 1100 (originals/copies), by region

Region	Dispute records (n)	Originals (n)	Originals (%)	Copies (n)	Copies (%)	Years
Aragon	81	9	11.25	72	88.89	(958–1098)
Castile	61	8	13.11	53	86.89	(911–1093)
Catalonia	786	478	60.81	308	39.19	(780–1100)
Galicia	266	30	11.28	236	88.72	(861–1098)
León	443	208	46.95	235	53.05	(804–1100)
Navarre	82	3	3.66	79	96.34	(1050–1086)
Portugal	212	90	42.45	122	57.55	(915–1100)

Graphs

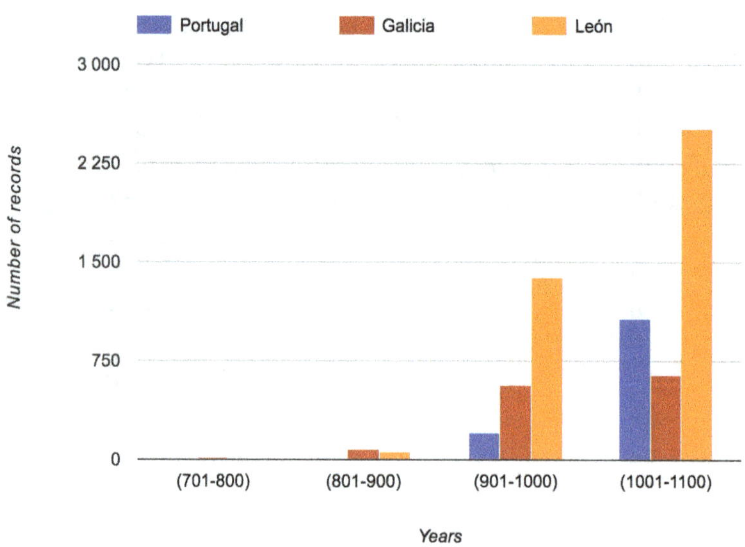

GRAPH 0.1 Western Iberian records before 1100, by region/century

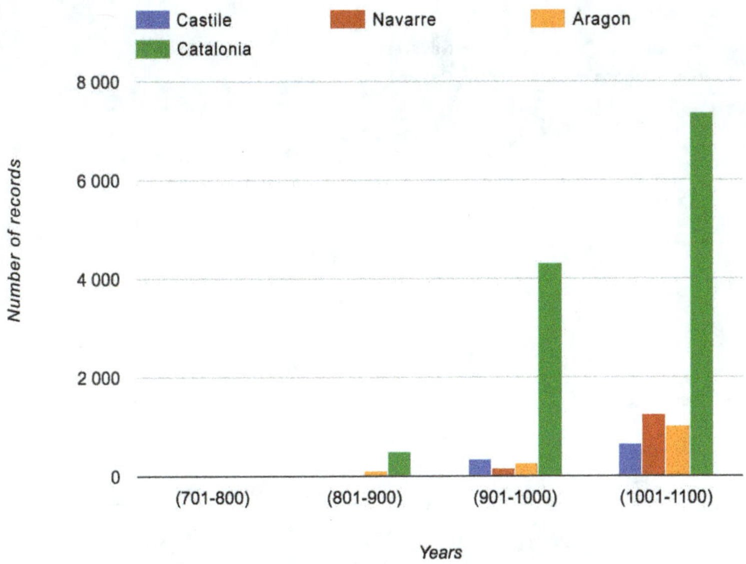

GRAPH 0.2 Eastern Iberian records before 1100, by region/century

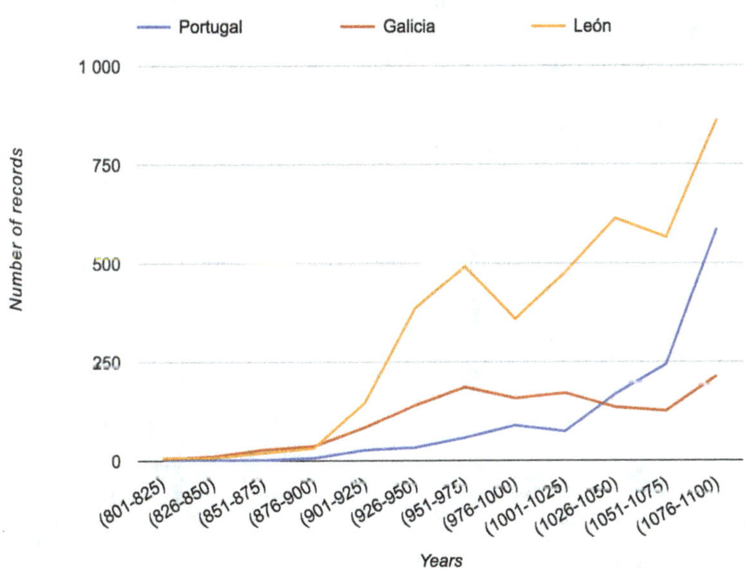

GRAPH 0.3 Western Iberian records before 1100, by region/quarter-century

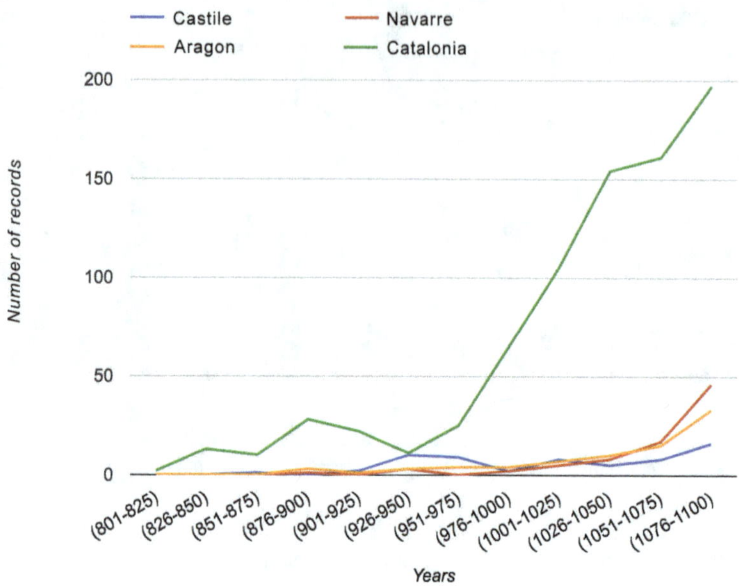

GRAPH 0.4 Eastern Iberian records before 1100, by region/quarter-century

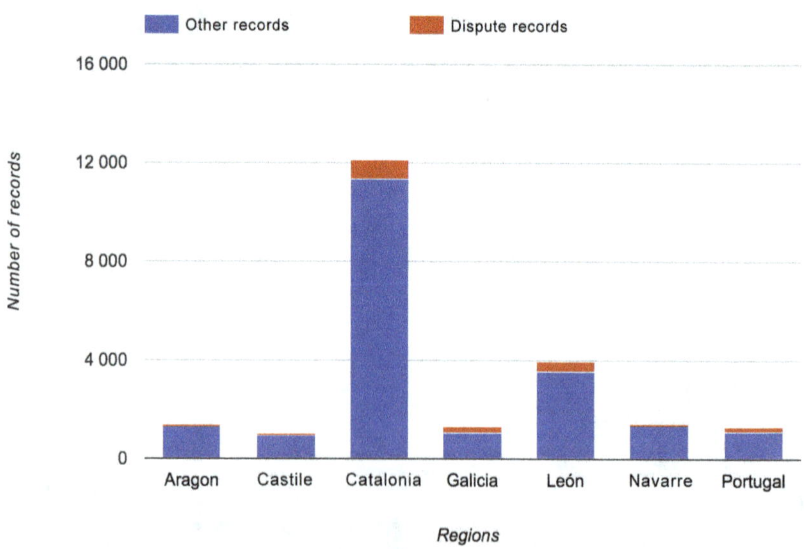

GRAPH 0.5 Proportion of Iberian dispute records before 1100, by region

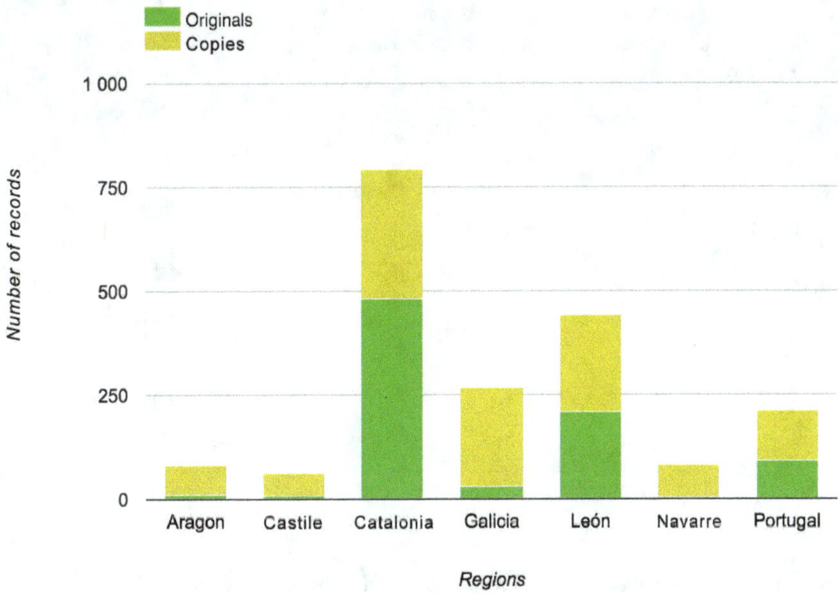

GRAPH 0.6 Iberian dispute records before 1100 (originals/copies), by region

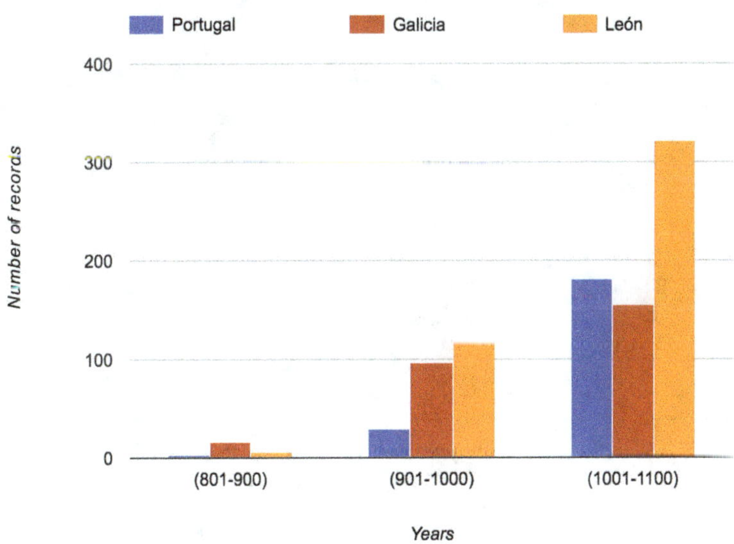

GRAPH 0.7 Western Iberian dispute records before 1100, by region/century

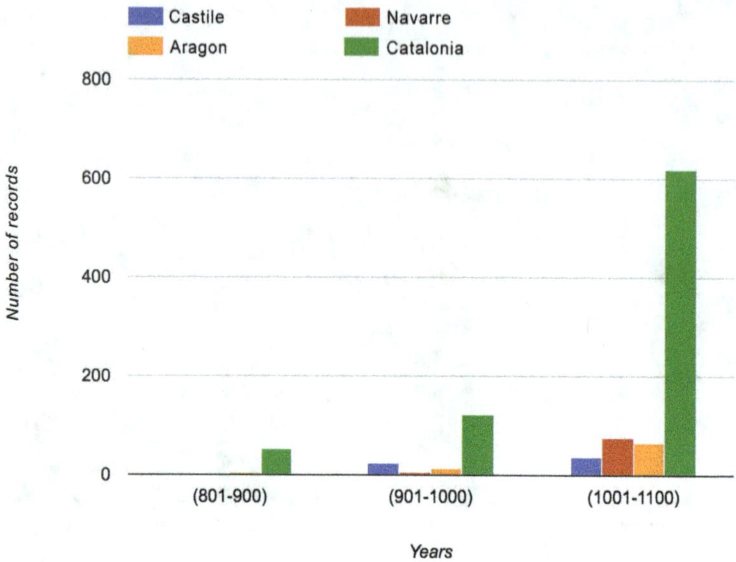

GRAPH 0.8 Eastern Iberian dispute records before 1100, by region/century

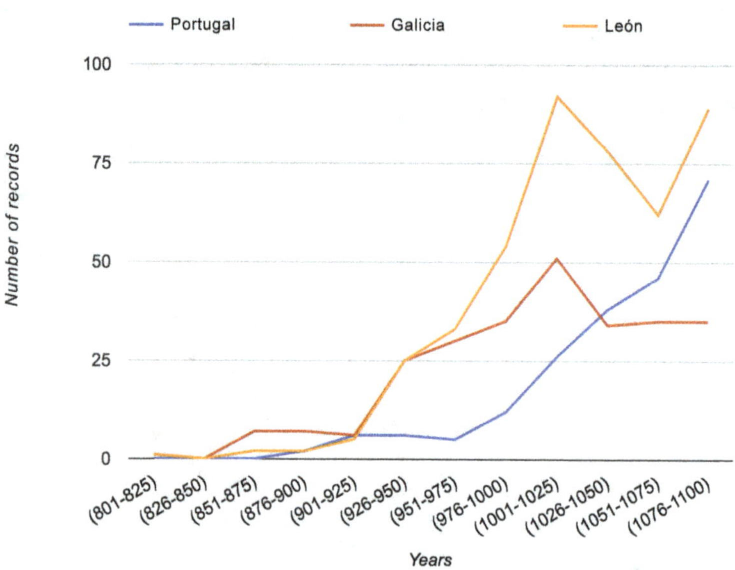

GRAPH 0.9 Western Iberian dispute records before 1100, by region/quarter-century

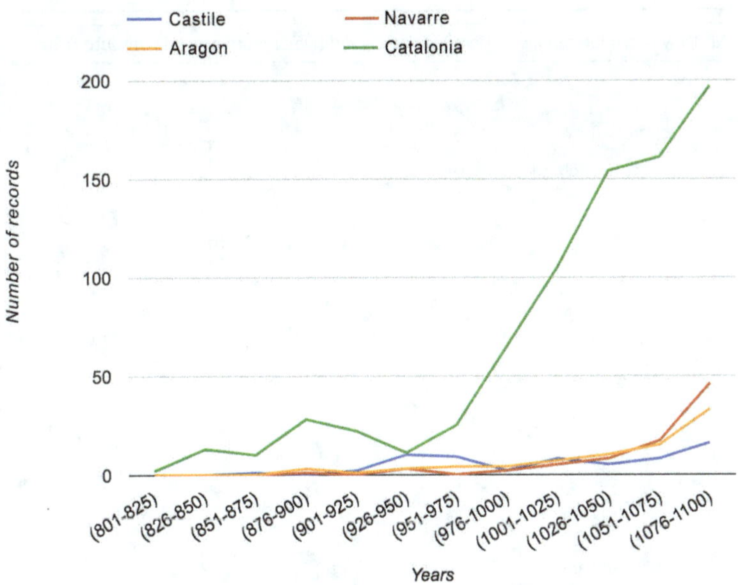

GRAPH 0.10 Eastern Iberian dispute records before 1100, by region/quarter-century

Maps

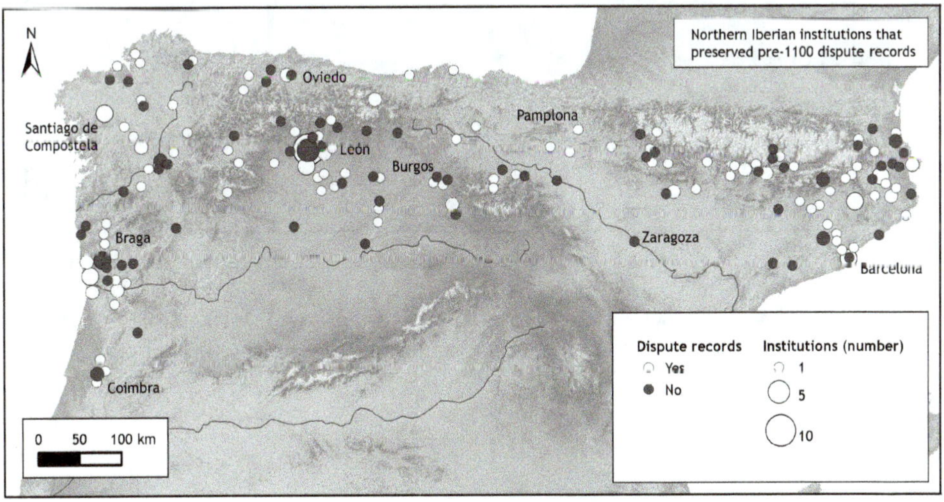

MAP 0.2 Northern Iberian institutions that preserved pre-1100 dispute records
MAP DRAWN BY ANTONIO URIARTE (LABORATORIO DE ARQUEOLOGÍA DEL PAISAJE Y TELEDETECCIÓN. CSIC-INSTITUTO DE HISTORIA. MADRID)

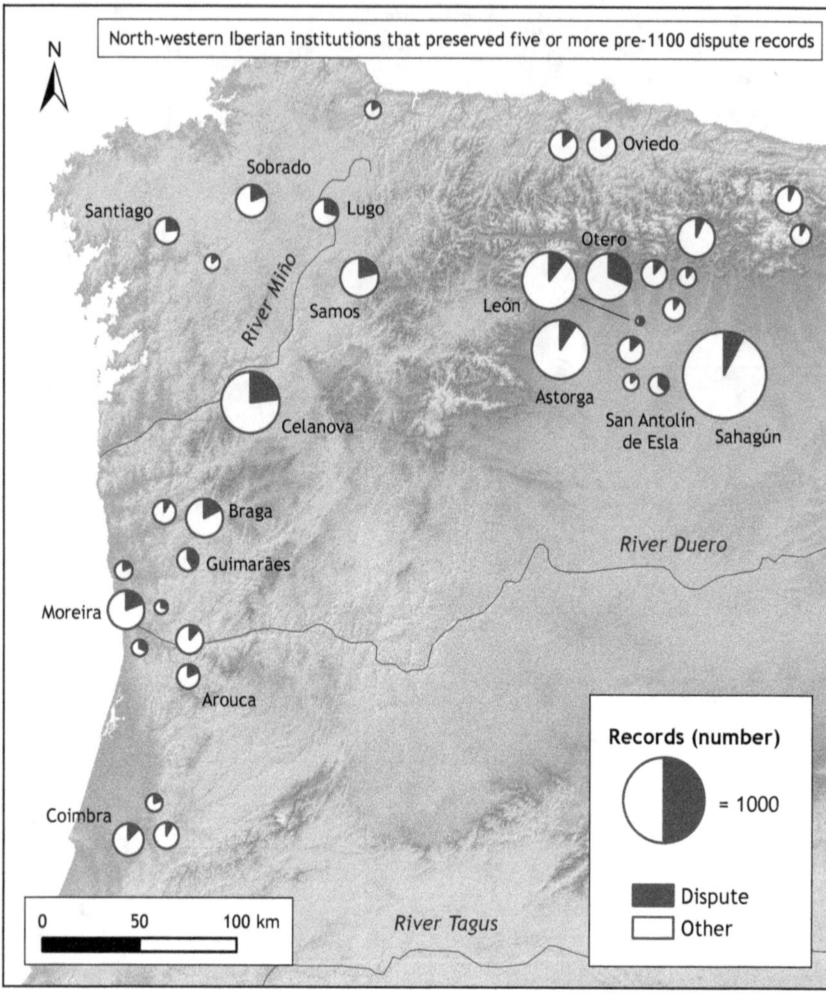

MAP 0.3 North-western Iberian institutions that preserved five or more pre-1100 dispute records
MAP DRAWN BY ANTONIO URIARTE (LABORATORIO DE ARQUEOLOGÍA DEL PAISAJE Y TELEDETECCIÓN. CSIC-INSTITUTO DE HISTORIA. MADRID)

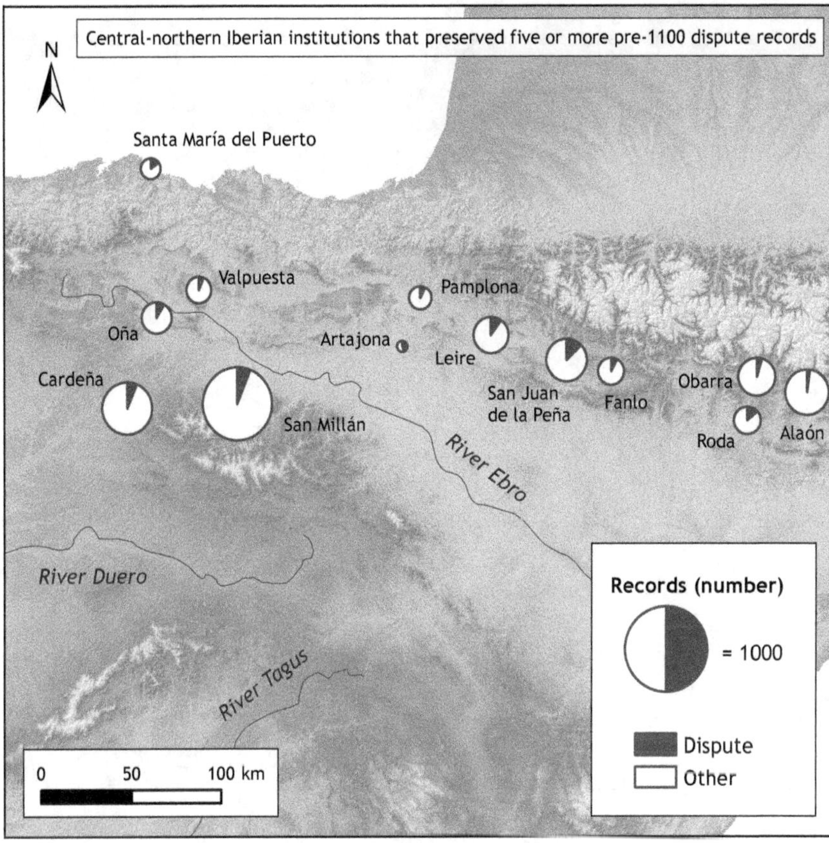

MAP 0.4 Central-northern Iberian institutions that preserved five or more pre-1100 dispute records

MAP DRAWN BY ANTONIO URIARTE (LABORATORIO DE ARQUEOLOGÍA DEL PAISAJE Y TELEDETECCIÓN, CSIC-INSTITUTO DE HISTORIA. MADRID)

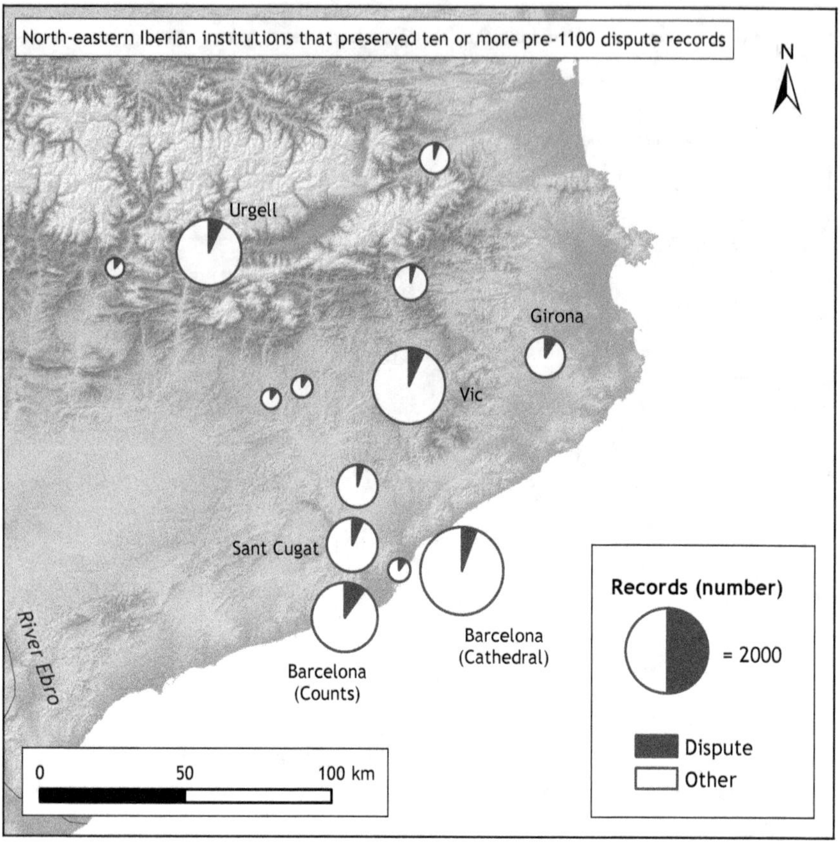

MAP 0.5 North-eastern Iberian institutions that preserved ten or more pre-1100 dispute records

MAP DRAWN BY ANTONIO URIARTE (LABORATORIO DE ARQUEOLOGÍA DEL PAISAJE Y TELEDETECCIÓN. CSIC-INSTITUTO DE HISTORIA. MADRID)

Bibliography

Primary Sources

Chartae Latinae antiquiores: Facsimile-edition of the Latin charters prior to the ninth century, edited by Albert Bruckner, Robert Marichal, and Tiziano Dorandi. Vol. 46: Belgium, Greece, Ireland, Israel, Norway, Holland, Republic of Georgia, Spain, edited by Tiziano Dorandi. Dietikon-Zurich: Urs-Graf Verlag, 1995.

Chartae Latinae antiquiores: Facsimile-edition of the Latin charters. 2nd series, Ninth century, edited by Guglielmo Cavallo and Giovanna Nicolaj. Vol. 114: Spain 3-Portugal, edited by Miguel Calleja Puerta, Pilar Ostos-Salcedo, M.L. Pardo Rodríguez, and M.J. Sanz Fuentes. Dietikon-Zurich: Urs-Graf Verlag, 2018.

Floriano, Antonio C. *Diplomática española del período astur (718–910)*. 2 vols. Oviedo: Instituto de Estudios Asturianos, 1949–1951.

Gil, Juan, ed. *Miscellanea Wisigothica*. Seville: Publicaciones de la Universidad de Sevilla, 1972.

PRJ: *PRocesos Judiciales en las sociedades medievales del norte peninsular*. Accessed 15 April 2022. http://prj.csic.es/.

Tomás Faci, Guillermo, and José Carlos Martín Iglesias. "Cuatro documentos inéditos del monasterio visigodo de San Martín de Asán (522–586)." *Mittellateinisches Jahrbuch* 52 (2017), 261–286.

Velázquez Soriano, Isabel. *Las Pizarras Visigodas (Entre el latín y su disgregación. La lengua hablada en Hispania, siglos VI–VIII)*. Madrid; Salamanca: Real Academia Española, Fundación Instituto Castellano y Leonés de la Lengua, 2004.

Zeumer, Karl, ed. *Formulae Merowingici et Karolini Aevi*. Monumenta Germaniae Historica, Legum Sectio v. Hanover: Hahn, 1886.

Zeumer, Karl, ed. *Leges Visigothorum*. Monumenta Germaniae Historica, Leges nationum Germanicarum 1. Hanover: Hahn, 1902.

Secondary Works

Alfonso, Isabel. "Resolución de disputas y prácticas judiciales en el Burgos medieval." In *Burgos en la Plena Edad Media. III Jornadas burgalesas de historia*, 211–241. Burgos: Asociación Provincial de Libreros de Burgos, 1994.

Alfonso, Isabel. "Litigios por la tierra y "malfetrías" entre la nobleza medieval castellano-leonesa." *Hispania* 197 (Desarrollo legal, prácticas judiciales y acción política en la Europa medieval, ed. Isabel Alfonso) (1997), 917–955.

Alfonso, Isabel. "Judicial rhetoric and political legitimation in medieval León-Castile." In *Building Legitimacy: Political Discourses and Forms of Legitimacy in Medieval Societies*, edited by Isabel Alfonso, Hugh Kennedy, and Julio Escalona, 51–87. Leiden: Brill, 2004.

Alfonso, Isabel. "The language and practice of negotiation in medieval conflict resolution (Castille-Leon, 11th–13th centuries)." In *Feud, Violence and Practice: Essays in Medieval Studies in Honor of Stephen D. White*, edited by Belle S. Tuten and Tracey L. Billado, 157–174. Farnham: Ashgate, 2010.

Alfonso, Isabel. "El formato de la información judicial en la Alta Edad Media peninsular." In *Chartes et cartulaires comme instruments de pouvoir: Espagne et Occident chrétien (VIIIe–XIIe siècles)*, edited by Julio Escalona and Hélène Sirantoine, 191–218. Toulouse: Université de Toulouse-Le Mirail, 2013.

Barrett, Graham. "The text of Visigothic law in practice." *Visigothic Symposium* 4 (2020–2021), 18–63. Accessed 15 April 2022. https://visigothicsymposia.org/graham-barrett/.

Barrett, Graham. *Text and Textuality in Early Medieval Iberia: The Written and the World, 711–1031*. Oxford: Oxford University Press, 2023.

Bowman, Jeffrey A. *Shifting Landmarks: Property, Proof, and Dispute in Catalonia around the Year 1000*. Ithaca: Cornell University Press, 2004.

Bowman, Jeffrey. "From Galicia to the Rhône. Legal practice in northern Spain around the Year 1000." In *Culture and Society in Medieval Galicia. A Cultural Crossroads at the Edge of Europe*, edited by James D'Emilio (Leiden: Brill, 2015), 343–360.

Brown, Warren, and Piotr Górecki, editors. *Conflict in Medieval Europe: Changing Perspectives on Society and Culture*. Aldershot: Ashgate, 2003.

Cabanes Pecourt, María de los Desamparados. "Diplomas y cancillería." In *Sancho Ramírez, rey de Aragón, y su tiempo (1064–1094)*, edited by Esteban Sarasa Sánchez, 25–45. Huesca: Instituto de Estudios Altoaragoneses, 1994.

Calleja Puerta, Miguel. "Ecos de las *Fórmulas* visigóticas en la documentación altomedieval astur-leonesa." In *Les formulaires. Compilation et circulation des modèles d'actes dans l'Europe médiévale et moderne: XIIIe congrès de la Commission internationale de diplomatique (Paris, 3–4 septembre 2012)*, edited by Olivier Guyotjeannin, Laurent Morelle, and Silio P. Scalfati. Paris: Éditions en ligne de l'École des chartes, 2016. Accessed 15 April 2022. http://elec.enc.sorbonne.fr/cid2012/part4.

Canellas López, Ángel. "La cancillería real del reino de Aragón (1035–1134)." In *Folia Budapestina*, 23–46. Zaragoza: Institución Fernando el Católico, 1983.

Carvajal Castro, Álvaro. *Bajo la máscara del "regnum": la monarquía asturleonesa en León (854–1037)*. Madrid: Consejo Superior de Investigaciones Científicas, 2017.

Carvajal Castro, Álvaro, et al. "Towards a trans-regional approach to early medieval Iberia." *History Compass* 20, no. 6 (2022), e12743. Accessed 15 August 2022. https://compass.onlinelibrary.wiley.com/doi/abs/10.1111/hic3.12743.

Castellanos, Santiago, and Iñaki Martín Viso. "The local articulation of central power in the north of the Iberian Peninsula (500–1000)." *Early Medieval Europe* 13, no. 1 (2005), 1–42.

Chastang, Pierre. "L'archéologie du texte médiéval." *Bulletin du centre d'études médiévales d'Auxerre (BUCEMA)* Hors-série no. 2 (2009). Accessed 15 April 2022. http://journals.openedition.org/cem/8702.

Collins, Roger. "'Sicut lex Gothorum continet': law and charters in ninth- and tenth-century León and Catalonia." *The English Historical Review* 100, no. 396 (July 1, 1985 1985), 489–512.

Collins, Roger. "Literacy and the laity in early mediaeval Spain." In *The Uses of Literacy in Early Mediaeval Europe*, edited by Rosamond McKitterick, 109–133. Cambridge: Cambridge University Press, 1990.

Collins, Roger. *Early Medieval Spain: Unity in Diversity, 400–1000*. 2nd ed. New York: St. Martin's Press, 1995.

Collins, Roger. *Caliphs and Kings: Spain, 796–1031*. Chichester: Wiley-Blackwell, 2014.

Corcoles Olaitz, Edorta. "About the origin of the *Formulae Wisigothicae*." *Anuario da Facultade de Dereito da Universidade da Coruña* 12 (2008), 199–222.

Davies, Wendy. *Acts of Giving: Individual, Community, and Church in Tenth-Century Christian Spain*. Oxford: Oxford University Press, 2007.

Davies, Wendy. "Summary justice and seigneurial justice in northern Iberia on the eve of the Millennium." *Haskins Society Journal* 22 (2010 [2012]), 43–58.

Davies, Wendy. "Settling disputes in early medieval Spain and Portugal: A contrast with Wales and Brittany?". In *Wales and the Welsh in the Middle Ages: Essays Presented to J. Beverley Smith*, edited by Ralph A. Griffiths and Phillipp R. Schofield, 89–107. Cardiff: University of Wales Press, 2011.

Davies, Wendy. "Local priests and the writing of charters in northern Iberia in the tenth century." In *Chartes et cartulaires comme instruments de pouvoir: Espagne et Occident chrétien (VIIIe–XIIe siècles)*, edited by Julio Escalona and Hélène Sirantoine, 29–43. Toulouse: Méridiennes-Université de Toulouse-Le Mirail, CSIC, 2013.

Davies, Wendy. *Windows on Justice in Northern Iberia, 800–1000*. Abingdon: Routledge, 2016.

Davies, Wendy. "Boni homines in northern Iberia: A particularity that raises some general questions." In *Italy and Early Medieval Europe*, edited by Ross Balzaretti, Julia Barrow, and Patricia Skinner, 60–72. Oxford: Oxford University Press, 2018.

Davies, Wendy, and Paul Fouracre, editors. *The Settlement of Disputes in Early Medieval Europe*. Cambridge: Cambridge University Press, 1986.

Esmark, Kim, Lars Hermanson, Hans Jacob Orning, and Helle Vogt, editors. *Disputing Strategies in Medieval Scandinavia*. Leiden: Brill, 2013.

Everett, Nicholas. "Lay documents and archives in early medieval Spain and Italy, c. 400–700." In *Documentary Culture and the Laity in the Early Middle Ages*, edited by Warren Brown, Marios Costambeys, Matthew Innes, and Adam J. Kosto, 63–94. Cambridge: Cambridge University Press, 2012.

Fernández Flórez, José Antonio. *La elaboración de los documentos en los reinos hispánicos occidentales (ss. VI–XIII)*. Burgos: Institución Fernán González, Academia Burguense de Historia y Bellas Artes, 2002.

Fortún Pérez de Ciriza, Luis Javier. "La edición de fuentes documentales para el estudio de la Edad Media hispana." In *XXV años de historiografía hispana (1980–2004): Historia medieval, moderna y de América*, edited by José Antonio Munita Loinaz and José Ramón Díaz de Durana Ortíz de Urbina, 15–53. Bilbao: Universidad del País Vasco, 2007.

Gambra, Andrés. *Alfonso VI: cancillería, curia e imperio*. 2 vols. León: Centro de Estudios e Investigación 'San Isidoro', 1997.

García de Cortázar, José Ángel, José Antonio Munita Loinaz, and Luis Javier Fortún Pérez de Ciriza, editors. *CODIPHIS: catálogo de colecciones diplomáticas hispano-lusas de época medieval*. 2 vols. Santander: Fundación Marcelino Botín, 1999.

Hudson, John. "Legal history and the history of disputes." In *Disputing Strategies in Medieval Scandinavia*, edited by Kim Esmark, Lars Hermanson, Hans Jacob Orning, and Helle Vogt, 333–341. Leiden: Brill, 2013.

Isla Frez, Amancio. *La Alta Edad Media: siglos VIII–XI*. Madrid: Síntesis, 2002.

Isla Frez, Amancio. "La pervivencia de la tradición legal visigótica en el reino astur-leonés." *Mélanges de la Casa de Velázquez* 41, no. 2 (2011), 75–86.

Jarrett, Jonathan. "Comparing the earliest documentary culture in Carolingian Catalonia." In *Problems and Possibilities of Early Medieval Charters*, edited by Jonathan Jarrett and Allan Scott McKinley, 89–126. Turnhout: Brepols, 2013.

Kosto, Adam J. *Making Agreements in Medieval Catalonia: Power, Order, and the Written Word, 1000–1200*. Cambridge: Cambridge University Press, 2001.

Kosto, Adam J. "*Sicut mos esse solet*: documentary practices in Christian Iberia, c. 700–1000." In *Documentary Culture and the Laity in the Early Middle Ages*, edited by Warren Brown, Marios Costambeys, Matthew Innes, and Adam J. Kosto, 259–282. Cambridge: Cambridge University Press, 2012.

Lopetegui Semprena, Guadalupe. "Escribas y notarios en la Cancillería real de Navarra durante el siglo XII." In *Los cimientos del Estado en la Edad Media: Cancillerías, notariado y privilegios reales en la construcción del Estado en la Edad Media*, edited by Juan Antonio Barrio Barrio, 65–92. Alicante: Marfil, 2004.

Lucas Álvarez, Manuel. *El Reino de León en la alta Edad Media. VIII: La documentación real astur-leonesa (718–1072)*. León: Centro de Estudios e Investigación 'San Isidoro', 1995.

Marques, André Evangelista. "Para um inventário da documentação diplomática anterior a 1101 conservada em arquivos portugueses." In *Mundos medievales: espacios, sociedades y poder: homenaje al profesor José Ángel García de Cortázar y Ruiz de Aguirre*, edited by Beatriz Arízaga Bolumburo, et al. Vol. 2, 705–718. Santander: Universidad de Cantabria, 2012.

Martin, Céline. *La géographie du pouvoir dans l'espace visigothique*. Villeneuve d'Ascq: Presses universitaires du Septentrion, 2003.

Martin, Céline, and Juan José Larrea, editors. *Nouvelles chartes visigothiques du monastère pyrénéen d'Asán*. Bordeaux: Ausonius Éditions, 2021.

Martín Viso, Iñaki. "Authority and justice in the formation of the Kingdom of Asturias–León." *Al-Masāq* 29, no. 2 (2017/05/04 2017), 114–132.

Martínez Sopena, Pascual. "La justicia en la época asturleonesa: entre el *liber* y los mediadores sociales." In *El lugar del campesino. En torno a la obra de Reyna Pastor*, edited by Ana Rodríguez, 239–260. València: Universitat de València, CSIC, 2007.

Martínez Sopena, Pascual. "El uso de la Ley Gótica en el reino de León." In *Remploi, citation, plagiat. Conduites et pratiques médiévales (X^e^-XIIe siècle)*, edited by Pierre Toubert and Pierre Moret, 97–114. Madrid: Casa de Velázquez, 2009.

Mínguez Fernández, José María. "Justicia y poder en el marco de la feudalización de la sociedad leonesa." In *La giustizia nell'alto medioevo (secoli IX–XI)*. Vol. 1, 491–548. Spoleto: Centro Italiano di Studi sull'Alto Medioevo, 1997.

Pastor Díaz de Garayo, Ernesto. "Los testimonios escritos del sector meridional de Castilla (siglos X–XI). Ensayo de crítica documental." *Historia. Instituciones. Documentos* 24 (1997), 355–379.

Petit, Carlos. *Ivstitia gothica: Historia social y teología del proceso en la Lex Visigothorum*. Huelva: Universidad de Huelva, 2001.

Prieto Morera, Agustín. "El proceso en el reino de León a la luz de los diplomas." In *El reino de León en la Alta Edad Media, II: Ordenamiento jurídico del reino*, 381–518. León: Centro de Estudios e Investigación 'San Isidoro', 1992.

Quirós Castillo, Juan Antonio. "Early medieval landscapes in north-west Spain: local powers and communities, fifth–tenth centuries." *Early Medieval Europe* 19, no. 3 (2011), 285–311.

Salrach, Josep M. *Justícia i poder a Catalunya abans de l'any mil*. Vic: Eumo, 2013.

Sierra Macarrón, Leonor. "Producción y conservación de la documentación altomedieval: del Cantábrico al Duero (siglos IX–XI)." *Signo* 13 (2004), 99–120.

Zimmermann, Michel. *Écrire et lire en Catalogne (IXe-XIIe siècle)*. 2 vols. Madrid: Casa de Velázquez, 2003.

PART 1

Surveying the Corpus of Iberian Dispute Records, 800–1100

CHAPTER 1

Documentary Production and Dispute Records in Galicia before the Year 1100

José M. Andrade

1 Galician Documents from the Eighth to the Eleventh Century

The overall number of extant documents from Galicia from before the twelfth century is 1303.[1] This puts Galicia in fifth place among the seven regions into which the PRJ project has divided northern Iberia, far behind Catalonia and León and also, though very much less so, behind Navarre and Aragon. However, if we take into account the close historical and political relationship between Galicia and northern Portugal during much of the period under analysis here and include the documentation from both territories, the old Roman province of *Gallaecia* would rank third among northern Iberian regions in terms of the overall number of documents preserved (see above, Table 0.1).

As is the case for all the regions, documentation from the ninth century is scarce, with only 77 extant documents. However, this figure puts Galicia in third place behind Catalonia and Aragon only. In addition, there is the important fact that some of the Galician documents are from very early in that century. For the tenth and eleventh centuries, it should be noted that the number of Galician documents is not that different from that of the rest of the regions. There are 567 extant documents from the tenth century and 646 from the eleventh. The similar number of documents from these two centuries is, in fact, one of most singular characteristics of early medieval Galician documentation.[2] It should be noted that the documents from the tenth century represent 43 per cent of the total documentation before the year 1100 and that this is the highest percentage for any of the regions considered in the PRJ project. Moreover, in absolute terms, the number of Galician documents

1 This figure is taken from the PRJ database at http://prj.csic.es/ (accessed 20 April 2020), which also provides the full texts of all dispute records cited here. The abbreviations used in this paper for editions of charters are listed in the bibliography.

2 The eleventh- to tenth-century documents in the other regions varies from two-to-one up to eight-to-one in the most extreme case, Navarre.

 | DOI:10.1163/9789004683006_003

from the tenth century is the third highest among the entire corpus of Iberian documents from this century (see above, Graphs 0.1 and 0.2). The copiousness of Galician documentation from the tenth century is related, as we will see, to an important group of monasteries founded during that century, which generated new documents and preserved older ones.

Even so, it is important not to forget that the eleventh century, especially its first half, is the period with the largest number of documents, as well as of dispute records in particular.

1.1 *The Predominance of Monasteries and the Reign of the Cartulary*

Let us begin by looking at the geographic distribution of the centres that produced and/or preserved this documentation. We can see immediately that, except for Xubia, none of the institutions were located on or near the coast. Although the notion that the Galician coast was inhospitable and scarcely habitable during these centuries is no longer accepted by historians, the fact is that the main cities and monasteries were located inland (see above, Map 0.1).

We can identify five areas where the production/preservation of documents was concentrated during these centuries:

1) The north of today's provinces of Lugo and A Coruña, whose main centre was the episcopal see of Mondoñedo. In addition to this cathedral, there were three monasteries of roughly equal importance: Xubia, Caaveiro, and Lourenzá.
2) The highlands in the interior of what is today A Coruña: it is here where the important family monastery of Sobrado is located, along with the relatively small monasteries of Toques, Soandres, and Cis.
3) The city of Santiago and its environs: here, in addition to the cathedral of Santiago itself, we need to include the urban monasteries of Pinario and Antealtares, as well as Carboeiro, which is outside of Compostela but at a short distance.
4) The area around the city and episcopal see of Ourense and the banks of the Miño and Sil rivers. This is the area that will come to be called *Ribeira Sacra* (Sacred Riverbank), where a relatively large number of monasteries were concentrated.
5) Lastly, two monasteries that were geographically isolated from the other zones but were extremely important both socially and with respect to documents: Samos, located in what is now the Lugo province near one of the busiest roads in the medieval period, and Celanova, in the Ourense province, more specifically in the region of Limia, close to the border with Portugal.

Samos and Celanova bring me to my next subject: the main institutions responsible for preserving documents in Galicia and the way that these documents were transmitted. Galician documents dated before 1100 come mostly from monasteries. In fact, almost 84 per cent of these documents were written or preserved in monastic scriptoria. That said, it is important to keep in mind that a substantial number of Galician monasteries, particularly those founded in the tenth century, were endowed by aristocrats, and thus it is not uncommon to find among their document collections relatively large groups of texts that come from the archives of the founding families or other lay collections. This is true, for example, of the cartularies of Celanova[3] and Sobrado, compiled in the thirteenth century, with the latter containing transcriptions of documents not only from the period when Sobrado was a family monastery but also, possibly, from the original archive of the founding family.[4]

In contrast, the number of documents preserved in episcopal sees is one of the lowest from any part of Iberia before the twelfth century. Only Navarre and Castile have a much lower percentage, while Aragon's is only slightly lower. Conversely, in Catalonia this type of document represents 45 per cent of the whole, and in both León and Portugal, areas much more closely related to Galicia, it represents c. 27 per cent.[5] One possible explanation for the meagreness of extant episcopal documents from Galicia is that the archives from which they proceed might have suffered disproportionate losses. Although document loss is a general phenomenon, it might have had a larger effect on

3 The history of Rosendo Gutiérrez's family, the founders of Celanova, has been reconstructed mainly from the monastery's documents by Emilio Sáez, "Los ascendientes de San Rosendo. Notas para el estudio de la monarquía astur-leonesa durante los siglos IX y X," *Hispania* 8 (1948), 3–76 and 179–233; and more recently by Ermelindo Portela and María Carmen Pallares, "Elementos para el análisis de la aristocracia altomedieval de Galicia: parentesco y patrimonio," *Studia Historica. Historia Medieval* 5 (1987), 17–32.

4 Adam J. Kosto, "*Sicut mos esse solet.* Documentary practices in Christian Iberia, c. 700–1000," in *Documentary Culture and the Laity in the Early Middle Ages*, ed. Warren Brown et al. (Cambridge: Cambridge University Press, 2012), 259–282, at 269–273. On how the Sobrado cartularies were put together and how the documents they contain were organized, see Ana I. Suárez González, "Los *Libri cartarum Superaddi*: notas para otra lectura (AHN, codices 976 and 977)," in *Galicia Monástica. Estudos en lembranza da profesora María José Portela Silva*, ed. Raquel Casal et al. (Santiago: Universidade de Santiago de Compostela, 2009), 39–59.

5 This figure does not include the documents originating in monasteries that came to be absorbed, with their properties and archives, by the sees of León, Braga and Coimbra, as these monasteries were considered independently in the PRJ database; see below, Chapter 2, as well as the introduction to this volume.

TABLE 1.1 Galician institutions that preserved more than 30 pre-1100 records

S. Salvador de Celanova	513
S. Julián de Samos	212
Sta María de Sobrado	144
Santiago Cathedral	96
Lugo Cathedral	101
S. Salvador de Lourenzá	40
S. Lorenzo de Carboeiro	36

episcopal centres, especially the see of Iria-Santiago, whose importance during the ninth to eleventh centuries is not at all reflected in the small number of documents that have survived from this diocese.[6]

The main collections of documents are, therefore, from monasteries. Table 1.1 shows the number of documents from each institution. Clearly, there is one institution that stands out among the rest: the monastery of Celanova. Moreover, its importance in terms of preserved documents transcends Galicia; if we leave out Catalonia, Celanova has the third largest number of documents among all Iberian institutions, behind only Sahagún (1043) and San Millán de la Cogolla (742).

If we look at the tenth century alone—which is especially important for Galician documentation, as mentioned above—Celanova occupies the second place in number of documents (233). It is ahead of San Millán (101) and is surpassed only by Sahagún (370), and by a much smaller margin than that of the overall numbers.

Celanova can also be seen as an example of another feature of Galician documentation from these centuries: the great reliance on cartulary copies.

6 It has been suggested that there were approximately one thousand documents from prior to the year 1000 in the Santiago cathedral archive, of which only about 10 per cent have survived; Fernando López Alsina, *La ciudad de Santiago de Compostela en la Alta Edad Media* (Santiago de Compostela: Ayuntamiento de Santiago de Compostela, 1985), 28–43. This topic has been studied recently, with a focus on the monastery of Antealtares in Santiago by José M. Andrade, "La Concordia de Antealtares en su contexto histórico," in *Los reyes de Asturias y los orígenes del culto a la tumba del apóstol Santiago*, ed. Francisco J. Fernández Conde and Raquel Alonso (Gijón: Trea, 2017), 109–126.

More than 500 Celanova documents have come down to us almost exclusively through the copies in its *tumbo*, which began to be compiled in the late twelfth century.[7] In fact, for the period that concerns us here, there is only one extant single-sheet document from Celanova, and it is not even an original but rather a copy from the eleventh century.

The reliance on cartulary copies is obviously not unique to early medieval Galicia, but here the cartularies were also compiled relatively late. They were all made, either partially or totally, in the thirteenth century and make up part of what Miguel Calleja calls the second generation of Iberian cartularies.[8] Another indication of the importance of copied documents is the fact that, among the Galician institutions with the largest document collections prior to the twelfth century, there is only one, the monastery of Carboeiro, that does not have a single cartulary. When studying the rest of them, we rely essentially on documents transcribed into these diplomatic codices. In fact, most single-sheet copies and originals come from Lugo, Santiago, and Samos, and even there the numbers are minimal.[9]

1.2 *The Documents as Historical Sources*

As to the potential and the limits of this corpus, one should stress two spheres which the documents illuminate particularly well. First and not surprisingly, they allow us to glimpse the important social role played by monasteries and the aristocracy that founded most of them in early medieval Galicia. At the same time, they do not present a dichotomous image of a society split between the powerful and a uniform mass of peasants; instead, they open a window onto a world that is much more diversified both socially and economically, with dif-

7 'Tumbo' is the word used in Galicia and occasionally in Portugal for cartulary. In the absence of a thorough codicological study on Celanova's cartulary, see the brief introductory remarks in TC, 1:x–xviii; and Carlos Sáez and Almudena Gutiérrez, "Hacia una interpretación del tumbo de Celanova," in *Iglesia y religiosidad en España. Historia y archivos*, 3 vols (Guadalajara: Junta de Comunidades de Castilla la Mancha, 2002), 2:997–1008.

8 Miguel Calleja, "Cartularios y construcción de la memoria monástica en los reinos de León y Castilla durante el siglo XII," in *Les cartulaires médiévaux: écrire et conserver la mémoire du pouvoir, le pouvoir de le mémoire. Los cartularios medievales: escribir y conservar la memoria del poder, el poder de la memoria*, ed. Véronique Lamazou-Duplan and Eloísa Ramírez Vaquero (Pau: Presses universitaires de Pau et des Pays de l'Adour, 2013), 187–200.

9 For a study of documents written in Visigothic script that provides some information about the survival of originals and single-sheet copies, see Ainoa Castro, *Colección diplomática altomedieval de Galicia I (662–1234)* (Noia: Toxosoutos, 2011).

ferent ranks of aristocrats, a range of peasants going from well-to-do farmers to destitute peasants, and everything in between, as well as slaves (slavery was still common before the year 1100).[10]

The land, the territory, and its organization and demarcation are other aspects that the documentation addresses in some detail. It speaks of a densely settled and highly organized space, at least in many of the areas that are most documented, in which the *villa*, now understood preferably as a village,[11] is a key element.

These two facets of early medieval Galicia are the fundamental avenues for historical research that this corpus opens up to us. Moreover, the documents that we have called 'dispute records' constitute some of the richest sources of information on these questions.

2 The Corpus of Galician Dispute Records

In about 1120, a French cleric, the author of the famous *Liber Sancti Iacobi*, a guide for pilgrims, characterized the people of Galicia as quarrelsome and litigious. This image would eventually become a hackneyed stereotype in the early modern period and has persisted right up to contemporary times. The fact is, however, that the French pilgrim's impression is corroborated by the contents of our corpus. Dispute records make up a much larger percentage of the overall number of documents in Galicia than in the other regions: a little more than 20 per cent of documents contain some kind of information about disputes. Although there are differences between the three centuries considered, the percentage of dispute records is very high in each of them, especially in the eleventh, where they make up almost 24 per cent of the whole (see above, Tables 0.1 and 0.2, Graph 0.5, and Map 0.2).[12]

---

10 Robert Portass, "Rethinking the "small worlds" of tenth-century Galicia," *Studia Historica. Historia Medieval* 31 (2013), 83–103. On the judicial role of intermediary groups, though not exclusively in Galicia, see also Robert Portass, "The middling sort at court in early medieval Christian Iberia," *Al-Masáq* 29, no. 2 (2017), 99–113. On slavery, see José M. Andrade, *El monacato benedictino y la sociedad de la Galicia medieval (siglos X–XIII)* (Sada-A Coruña: Ediciós do Castro, 1997), 139–149; Marcos Fernández Ferreiro, *Servos e escravos altomedievais no noroeste da Península Ibérica* (Noia: Toxosoutos, 2010).

11 Ermelindo Portela and María Carmen Pallares, "La *villa*, por dentro," *Studia Historica. Historia Medieval* 16 (1998), 13–43.

12 Only in the ninth century is there another region, Portugal, with a higher proportion of dispute records than Galicia's. In the tenth and eleventh centuries, Galicia has the highest proportion of such records. It is interesting to note that Portugal and León come right

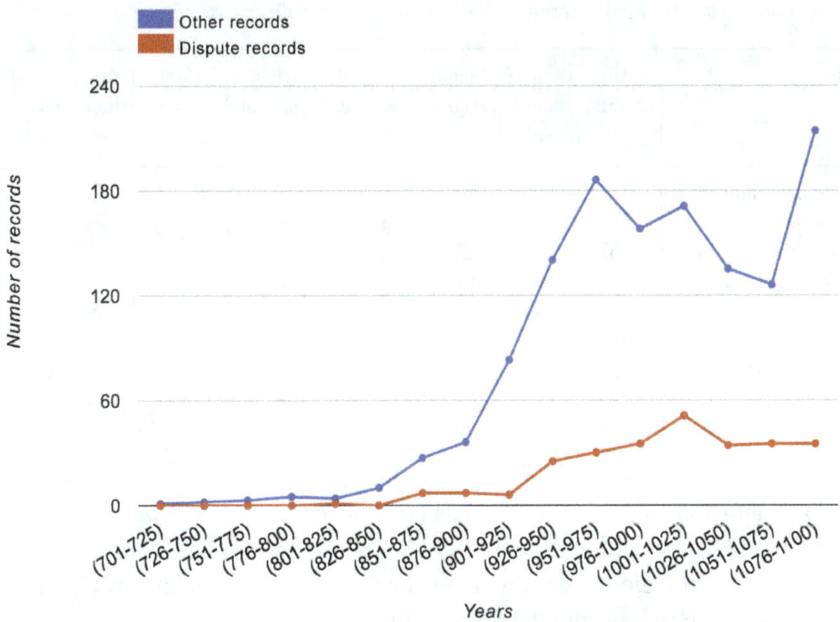

GRAPH 1.1 Proportion of Galician dispute records before 1100, by quarter-century

When we analyse this documentation by institution, we see that Celanova clearly outranks all the others in terms of raw numbers. With 118 dispute records, it has more than twice the number preserved by Samos (44), with all other institutions coming far behind. Moreover, there is a rather close correlation between the number of total documents and that of dispute records preserved by Galician institutions. This correlation might seem self-evident, but actually it is not. A review of the data from other regions shows that, for example, in León, Navarre, and Portugal, the institutions with larger numbers of documents are not the same ones with large collections of dispute records (see above, Maps 0.3, 0.4 and 0.5).

Still, it is interesting to note how the size of Celanova's corpus of dispute texts puts it well beyond almost any other institution in northern Iberia. In fact, this monastery is second only to the Barcelona cathedral, whose collection of dispute records exceeds that of Celanova only slightly.[13] For this type of

behind. Was there possibly a distinctive documentary practice in the western part of the Iberia Peninsula that would explain the greater preponderance of judicial documents in these regions?

13 120 dispute records from Barcelona as opposed to 118 from Celanova, though it should be added that the Catalan materials in the PRJ database are still under review.

TABLE 1.2 Galician institutions that preserved five or more pre-1100 dispute records

Institution	All records (n)	Dispute records (n)	Dispute records (%)	9th c.	10th c.	11th c.	Originals	Copies	Authentic	Suspect	False
S. Salvador de Celanova	513	118	23	1	39	78	0	118	118	0	0
S. Julián de Samos	212	44	20.75	2	13	29	5	39	43	1	0
Lugo Cathedral	101	29	28.71	3	12	14	8	21	26	3	0
Sta. María de Sobrado	144	27	18.75	2	16	9	0	27	27	0	0
Santiago Cathedral	96	22	22.92	6	7	9	1	21	21	1	0
S. Salvador de Lourenzá	40	6	15	0	0	6	2	4	6	0	0
S. Lorenzo de Carboeiro	36	5	13.89	0	2	3	5	0	5	0	0
TOTAL	1142	251		14	89	148	21	230	246	5	0

document, Celanova outpaces monasteries and cathedrals with larger archives, such as Sahagún or the cathedrals of Vic and Astorga, to name two examples from different regions.[14] Further along I will attempt to explain why Celanova preserved such a large number of dispute records.

Looking at the proportion of dispute records to the overall number of extant documents, the Lugo cathedral comes clearly ahead, followed by Celanova and, in third place, the Iria-Santiago cathedral.[15] This information qualifies somewhat the observation above that documentation preserved in monasteries predominated in early medieval Galicia (Table 1.2 and below, Graph 1.2).

As for the material aspects, let us just recall that Galician documents in general are characterized by a reliance on cartulary copies.[16] In fact, only 30 dispute records (11 per cent of the whole) have come down to us as single-sheet parchments. Although this is not a feature that is unique to the Galician corpus,[17] it does clearly contrast with the situation in Portugal and León, whose document collections otherwise share some common features with those of Galicia, as has been mentioned (see above, Table 0.3 and Graph 0.6).[18]

---

14 80 extant judicial documents from Sahagún out of a total of more than 1000; 112 out of a total of 1604 from the Vic cathedral; and lastly, 46 out of a total of 491 from Astorga.

15 The percentages are 28.7, 23, and 22.9 per cent, respectively.

16 Wendy Davies devoted an extensive chapter to this in her monograph on the justice system in early medieval Hispania, *Windows on Justice in Northern Iberia. 800–1000* (Abingdon: Routledge, 2016), ch. 3.

17 The proportion of single sheets is even lower in the case of Navarre, while the percentages in Aragon and Castile are almost identical to Galicia's.

18 In both Portugal and León the percentage of judicial documents transmitted on single sheets is more than 40 per cent.

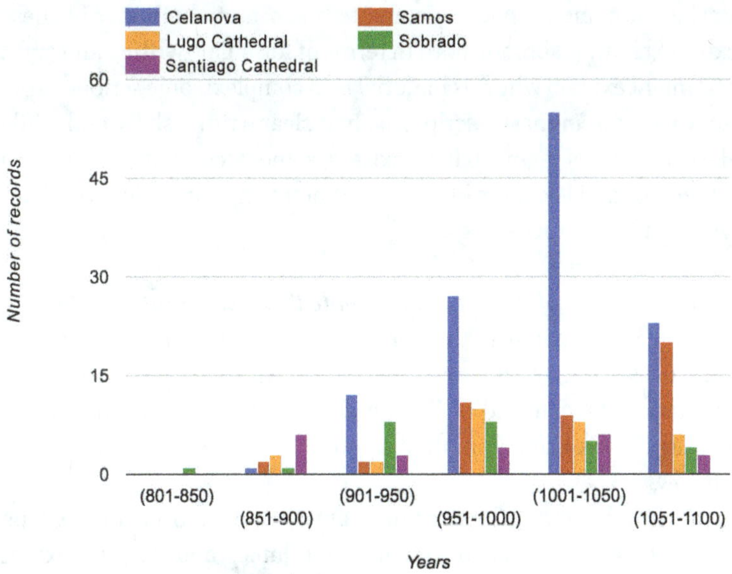

GRAPH 1.2 Largest Galician collections of pre-1100 dispute records, by half-century

When it comes to the thorny issue authenticity, as with the other regions and collections considered in the PRJ database, we rely mainly on the opinion that has been offered by the different editors.[19] That said, it should be noted that only a small number of dispute texts have been identified as suspect.[20] Prominent among them are three royal documents transmitted in Lugo's *Tumbo Viejo*, a cartulary that includes other documents known for their debatable authenticity.[21]

---

19 One needs to assess, in addition to the editors' opinions, a series of partial studies that help us to better understand the originals, pseudo-originals, single copies, etc. See, for example, Julio Escalona, "Antes de los cartularios: gestión de archivos y transmisión de los documentos de la Castilla Condal (siglo IX-1038)," in *Chartes et cartulaires comme instruments de pouvoir. Espagne et Occident chrétien (VIIIe–XIIe siècles)*, ed. Julio Escalona and Hélène Sirantoine (Toulouse: Université de Toulouse-Le Mirail, 2013), 131–151.

20 Only seven documents (2.6 per cent). None have been identified as false.

21 TVL 10, 19 and 81. On the famous and much debated documents related to the eighth-century Bishop Odoario, see, among others, Luis Vázquez de Parga, "Los documentos sobre las presuras del Obispo Odoario, de Lugo," *Hispania* 41 (1950), 635–680; James D'Emilio, "The legend of Bishop Odoario and the early medieval church in Galicia," in *Church, State, Vellum, and Stone: Essays on Medieval Spain in Honor of John Williams*, ed. Therese Martin and Julie Harris (Leiden: Brill, 2005), 47–83; and the recent edition and commentary on all Odoarian documents by Ernesto Pastor Díaz de Garayo and Ainoa Castro Correa, *Las presuras de Odoario "el africano" en Lugo y Braga: textos, objetos y contextos para la*

Setting aside false and suspect documents, a substantial number of these dispute texts are highly elaborate, both in terms of formulaic writing and style. Certain facts might explain why this material is so complex: some scribes, especially those working in monastic scriptoria, had clear writing skills; and while nothing like trial records seems to have existed, some documents contained a montage of records and accounts of several different legal procedures and different stages in judicial proceedings.

2.1 *A Brief Overview of the Types of Dispute Records Extant in Galicia*

One of the first features to note in this corpus is that the majority of references are to criminal cases rather than civil ones. Although the importance of the criminal corpus can be detected in Iberian documentation from prior to the eleventh century,[22] this is much more pronounced in Galicia for the reasons explained below.

In effect, the fact that judicial transactions are by far the most common type of document among Galician dispute records determines, and to a great extent explains, the preponderance of criminal references over civil ones.[23] There are 78 examples of judicial transactions, as compared to 42 accounts of dispute cases, the second most common type. Judicial transactions predominate in Celanova's dispute material, whose quantitative importance is accounted for in part by the number of documents with this format. This is also the most-common type of document among dispute records from Sobrado's, and the second most common among those from Samos, Lugo and Santiago.

One of the things that is most often recorded in these transactions is compensation for unpaid loans called *renovos*.[24] These make up half of the judicial transactions in Sobrado, and one third of Celanova's documents. They also make up an important part of the documentation from Samos. In contrast, they rarely appear among episcopal documents. Although we cannot be sure that

---

construcción de la memoria y la legitimación de la dominación personal y política (Bilbao: Universidad del País Vasco, 2020).

22 Davies, *Windows on Justice*, 235. On Galicia in particular, see Jeffrey Bowman, "From Galicia to the Rhône. Legal practice in northern Spain around the Year 1000," in *Culture and Society in Medieval Galicia. A Cultural Crossroads at the Edge of Europe*, ed. James D'Emilio (Leiden: Brill, 2015), 343–360, at 348.

23 I follow here the definitions of the different formats of dispute records given in Isabel Alfonso, "El formato de la información judicial en la Alta Edad Media peninsular," in *Chartes et cartulaires*, ed. Escalona and Sirantoine, 191–218.

24 Luis García de Valdeavellano, "El *renovo*. Notas y documentos sobre los préstamos usurarios en el reino astur-leonés (siglos x–xi)," *Cuadernos de Historia de España* 57–58 (1973), 408–448.

the practice of lending existed only in monasteries,[25] it does appear that the preservation of documents recording this practice was unique to them, due among other things to the peculiar bias of Galician episcopal cartularies.

Another kind of judicial transaction that accounts for a higher proportion of criminal cases than civil ones are records of fines. They reflect the influence wielded by the powerful, especially monasteries, and at the same time the public manner in which justice was administered during this period.[26] Again, Celanova accounts for a good part of these cases, many of them hidden in long inventories enumerating the properties acquired by abbots and provosts.[27]

The judicial transactions to be found among episcopal documents are mostly mentions of confiscations made by kings in response to rebellions, which ended up benefitting the bishoprics. These also appear in some monastic collections, such as those of Celanova and Samos, but they are especially prominent in the *Tumbo A* from Santiago, particularly in ninth-century documents related to the reign of Alfonso III (r. 866–910), and in the *Tumbo Viejo* from Lugo.[28]

The documents that provide the most accurate reflection of legal disputes and the workings of judicial process are without a doubt the accounts of judicial proceedings and to a lesser extent the agreements and confessions (*placita*, *agnitiones*, etc.). As in the other regions, in Galicia these kinds of documents reflect a wide range of conflicts. However, there is a theme that comes up more frequently than in other regions: disputes over the status of dependent men or over who should control them.[29] In fact, this is the main kind of conflict that we see in the dispute records from Celanova, and it is prevalent as well in the documentation from other leading institutions such as the Santiago cathedral and the Samos monastery. The importance of conflicts around the issue of personal servitude is certainly a reflection of early medieval Galician society, as is the persistence of slavery and servitude in general in Galicia.[30]

---

25 As explained below, some of Sobrado's *renovos* come from documents pertaining to the monastery's founding family and not from the monastery's own lending activities. On loans made to and by private individuals, see also Portass, "The middling," 110–111.

26 Davies, *Windows on Justice*, 43.

27 On the role of the provost, one of whose functions was "judicial," see José M. Andrade, "Aproximación a la figura del prepósito monástico en el monacato gallego medieval: siglo X al XII," *Estudios Mindonienses* 11 (1995), 279–292.

28 See also, with respect to royal confiscations in León, Álvaro Carvajal, *Bajo la máscara del* Regnum. *La monarquía asturleonesa en León (854–1037)* (Madrid: CSIC, 2017), 132–137.

29 Bowman, "From Galicia," 348.

30 Fernández, *Servos*.

3 Best-Documented Judicial Processes in Galicia

3.1 *Loans and Debts: The* Renovos

As mentioned above, unpaid debts are one of the judicial matters most often mentioned in Galician documents.[31] Credit was a universal practice throughout the West during the early Middle Ages and was addressed in most of the legal codes produced at the time. The Iberian Peninsula was no exception, although certain nuances made it distinct. Thus, the terminology used in most of Europe is scarcely to be found in documentary sources from Iberia, while the interest rate to be applied to loans is specified in the *Liber iudiciorum* only.[32]

At least some of those who took out loans—which were almost always in kind[33]—seem to have been humble peasant families. This can be deduced from the fact that the loan often amounted to a small quantity of bread, wine, or grains and the tract of land with which they settled their default was, in general, of small size. Sometimes the document even specifies that the loan was disbursed in circumstances of real necessity, during years of famine. This is the case in a document mentioning a woman named Columba, who in the year 1001 handed over one of her properties to the Celanova monastery, from which she had received diverse goods *in tempore et dies de sterelitate fame*.[34]

Though there is scarce information that we can glean from these documents that is strictly judicial, we can surmise certain things.[35] This is the case in sev-

31 Some of these loans, which were not always defined as *renovos*, may have been resolved through non-judicial agreements; Portass, "The middling," 104 and 111. It is worth comparing the Galician material with the copious Catalan documents recording pledges as well as foreclosures and enforcement proceedings against collateral, on which see below, Chapter 5.

32 See below, n. 35. On both these points, see François Bougard, "Le crédit dans l'Occident du Haut Moyen Âge: documentation et pratique," in *Les élites et la richesse au Haut Moyen Âge*, ed. Jean P. Devroey, Laurent Feller, and Regine Le Jan (Turnhout: Brepols, 2010), 439–478, at 450–451.

33 Loans of money are rare. On this, see García de Valdeavellano, "El *renovo*," 415 and 417–418. Loans of foodstuffs are well documented in Iberia, including Catalonia, but they are extremely rare in the rest of Western Christendom. See Bougard, "Le crédit," 465–467.

34 TC 192. We should note that this case does not mention a *renovo*. But we are given to understand that the recouping of unpaid debts would have intensified during times of great need. These references to hunger as a driving force behind credit can be highly ambiguous; see Bougard, "Le credit," 470.

35 The *Liber iudiciorum* makes a distinction between loans of money and loans in kind: Karl Zeumer, ed., *Leges Visigothorum*, MGH LL nat. Germ. 1 (Hanover: Hahn, 1902), V.5.4 and

eral documents from Sobrado that belong to what we might call the lay archive of its founding family. Let us take a look at two of these documents. Both have the same date (December 22, 952) and involve two couples living in the same village; and they must have been preserved together, given the fact that the compilers of the Sobrado *tumbos* copied them next to each other.[36] In these documents, the two couples hand over small parcels in an orchard (consisting of twenty apple trees in one case and ten in the other) as compensation for having failed to pay back a debt of grain that they had received from Hermenegildo and Paterna at their *domus* in Sobrado,[37] an estate where we can assume that the family monastery would be built years later. Moreover, the fact that both 'repayments' are dated the same day and were made for the same reason might be evidence that an assembly was held, or at least a public ceremony, certainly in the same *domus* where the loans had been made, also as part of a public event. We might even suppose that the proximity of Christmas is an indication that these hearings or judicial meetings were held seasonally in courts presided over by Hermenegildo and Paterna. These examples also serve to demonstrate that the practice of lending and the legal consequences of default were not the exclusive domain of monasteries.[38]

Even so, it is clear that the information that has come down to us about the practice of lending with interest has done so mainly through monastic documents. This is especially true of Celanova, as was pointed a while ago by García de Valdeavellano.[39] In effect, among the 118 judicial documents from Celanova that we have identified, there are 29 in which a *renovo* is mentioned. This figure is by far the largest among all the institutions in the PRJ database. If to this we add the fact that the institution with the second largest number of *renovos* is the monastery of Samos, and that the first documented *renovo* seems to come from the Portuguese monastery of Guimarães, in the year 973,[40] we cannot help but

---

v.5.8 (pp. 228 and 230) on the former; and 5.5.9 (p. 230) on the latter. In neither case does the law lay out the legal procedure to be followed, other than stipulating the interest rate.

36 TSob 98 and 99.

37 *Inprestada de vestra casa de Superado*, TSob 98.

38 For other *renovos* granted by another Galician count, Vermudo Vegilaz, see García de Valdeavellano, "El *renovo*," 426 and 438. The author includes references to documents that show that other lay families besides those of counts engaged in lending, and therefore were parties to demands for repayment. The examples given by Valdeavellano, however, come not from Galicia but from León; ibid., 427. On the lending activities of laypeople in other European regions, see Bougard, "Le credit," 468–469.

39 García de Valdeavellano, "El *renovo*," 409.

40 García de Valdeavellano, "El *renovo*," 417. I am grateful to André Marques for verifying the latter fact for me. See LM 63.

conclude that this is a practice that was transmitted mainly by monastic documents from the northwest, at least so far as the practice is known by this very name.[41]

The *renovo* documents from Celanova come mostly from the period 989–1045. In fact, there is only one case that does not fall within this range of years and is dated to the last quarter of the eleventh century.[42] Lending seems to have been a solidly established custom of this monastery, at least during that period. The people who were involved in this activity were mainly the provosts of the monastery. They are the ones who seem to have received the properties that were handed over in lieu of repayment of loans. In addition to the well-documented case of Cresconio, there are at least four other provosts who are known to have acted in this capacity, either alone or together with their respective abbots.[43] It should come as no surprise that the provosts played such a large role in this regard, since they were the ones to shoulder much of the monastery's intense judicial activity. But, besides them, there were other members of the community who played this role.[44] Here we should mention Abbot Aloito (1011–1045), who is documented on seven different occasions as being the sole receiver of properties in compensation for unpaid loans.

From what we can deduce from some of the documents, the loans that would eventually result in *renovos* were granted in the monastery and their repayment was supposed to happen there as well. We also know that they could be granted in several of Celanova's dependencies. Both the disbursement of the loan and the payment of compensation for default seem to have been made in public and coincided, at least sometimes, with what we might call sessions of the judicial court that operated in the monastery, as was the case with the above-mentioned loans made by Hermenegildo and Paterna. The public and judicial nature, both of the disbursement and of compensation for debt, can

41 The involvement of judicial courts in sanctioning and regulating loan defaults is very well documented in Catalonia. Here, even though it was based on the same law, judicial practice in this matter seems to have been very different from what we observe in Galicia; see Josep M. Salrach, *Justícia i poder a Catalunya abans de l'any mil* (Vic: Eumo, 2013), 144–150; and below, Chapter 5.

42 TC 443, on which see more below.

43 On Cresconio, see María Inés Carzoglio, "Cresconio, prepósito de Celanova. Un personaje gallego al filo del siglo XI," *Cuadernos de Historia de España* 57–58 (1973), 225–279. The other provosts who are mentioned as being involved in recouping *renovos* are Munio, Sandino, Gutier and Vimara Cagitiz.

44 For example, Deacon Vermudo or *Frater* Raupario.

be clearly seen in one document from Celanova, a sale of properties by a certain Bezto and his wife to the monastery in the year 1002.[45] The couple ceded to Celanova a group of properties located near the city of Ourense. One of them was a small country retreat and its surrounding fields, which was located next to one of the monastery's dependent houses.[46] This is where Bezto and his wife acknowledged the receipt, *in meas manus*, of a sizeable loan,[47] whose default occasioned the compensatory 'sale' of these properties. The document recording the public act of the debt's cancelation was signed not in the outlying house but *in capitulo Cellenove*, in the presence of the entire community and of those who *adpreciaverunt ipsas villas*, that is, those who were charged with assessing the value of the properties handed over to the monastery.[48]

The borrowers mentioned in these documents came from a wide geographical area, but they were especially numerous in places closest to Celanova or where the monastery's assets were concentrated. The clearest example of this may be the eight *renovos* involving residents of Bobadela, which was one of the enclaves where the monastery was most active in acquiring property and attempting to take control of the village.[49]

The amount of the loan was sometimes as high as hundreds of *modii* (a measure of capacity and a system of valuation), and the penalty for non-repayment might be even higher.[50] A good example is the aforementioned case of Bezto and his family.[51] The reason for the transfer of properties to Celanova was the default on a loan of 60 *modii* of wheat, 48 of rye and 2000 of wine. Another example is the case of Guntino and his wife, who had borrowed from Celanova 440 *modii* of unspecified goods.[52] The variety of situations is proof that borrowing was practiced by a wider swath of society than we usually ima-

45 TC 556.

46 *Adicimus aliam pausatellam qui est in Mellanes prope vestra deganea sic de Mellanes*, ibid. On the meaning of *pausatellam*, see Xaime Varela Sieiro, *Léxico cotián na Alta Idade Media de Galicia: a arquitectura civil* (Santiago de Compostela: Universidade de Santiago de Compostela, 2008), 186–187. The dependent house might very well have been located in what is today the parish of Santa María de Melias.

47 *Pro que tenui pro vestro renovo in meas manus in vestra deganea de Mellanes*, TC 556.

48 Ibid.

49 Andrade, *El monacato*, 149–152; and Portela y Pallares, "La villa," 13–43.

50 According to the *Liber iudiciorum*, the interest rate for in-kind loans was 50 per cent. On this and on the repayment of these loans in the tenth and eleventh centuries, see García de Valdeavellano, "El *renovo*," 411 and 429–430.

51 TC 556.

52 TC 333.

gine.[53] They also might indicate that not everyone who took out a loan did it because they were pressed by necessity; there could have been other reasons, such as the desire to take part in the land market.[54]

There is another *renovo* document in which the parties involved are people of considerable social standing and the amount of the debt is substantial, and this one is especially interesting because it includes more procedural information than is usually found in this kind of record. It is another document from Celanova's collection and it dates from 1096, later than most *renovo* documents. From it we know that a pair of brothers, Gontrode and Iermias Gudesteiz, were sued before the count of Lemos, Froila Díaz, by two monks from Celanova acting on behalf of their abbot.[55] A complaint was lodged because of a debt the Gudesteiz brothers had incurred with one of Celanova's subsidiary monasteries in the amount of 160 *modii* of wine, 11 of wheat and 30 of rye and millet, *sicut in suis scripturas resonat*. Once both sides had been heard, it was decided that the monastery's representatives should swear an oath that the loan was in fact disbursed, as was stipulated in the *Lex gotorum*.[56] At this point Gontrode agrees to an *agnitionem placiti* with Celanova's representatives before the *concilio*; below, the document provides details concerning the origin of the property that was going to be handed over as compensation for the unpaid debt.[57]

It is difficult to know if this document is indicative of all unrepaid loans. It is possible that there were differences between the practices at the beginning of the tenth century that we see in the lay documentation from Sobrado and the practices at the end of the eleventh, during the reign of Alfonso VI (r. 1065–1109), a time of rapid change. It is also highly likely that the steps taken in the example above, which involved a dispute between a great monastery and another somewhat important party, would not have been identical to the steps taken in the case of default by a family of humble peasants. Surely the way such a family preserved its written records would not have

53 Recall that Bezto was the owner of a *pausatellam*, a type of property that only people of means would have owned. Examples from elsewhere in Western Christendom corroborate the diversity of social classes to which borrowers might belong; Bougard, "Le crédit," 454–458.

54 On both topics, see Portass, "Rethinking," 96–98.

55 TC 443.

56 *Et iurassent ipse renovo sicut lex gotorum de rebus ecclesie promulgata denimticit relatio*; ibid.

57 *Pario vobis illa pro vestro renovo integra*; ibid.

involved the same degree of detail that we find in the Celanova document from 1098. But this text does prove that legal complaints resulting from unpaid loans also might invoke the *lex*, as happens in so many other legal spheres in early medieval Iberia.[58] It also shows that some loans were recorded in writing and that the corresponding judicial procedure might include recourse to a sworn oath, a practice that is amply attested in judicial documents from Galicia.

3.2 *A World of* Servi, *Oaths and Ordeals*

As is true for all northern Iberian regions, the disputes about which we have extant records reflect a wide range of conflicts. However, there is one issue that appears more frequently in Galicia than in other regions: disputes regarding the status of groups of dependents or control over these groups. This is the main kind of conflict recorded in the accounts of dispute cases from Celanova, and it is prominent as well among the documentation from other important institutions such as the sees of Santiago and Lugo and the monasteries of Samos and Sobrado.

Chronologically speaking, the documents recording this kind of conflict are quite evenly distributed over the tenth and eleventh centuries, although there is somewhat of a concentration during the last stretch of the eleventh century, coinciding with the reign of Alfonso VI.[59] As to the documents' form, there is also some variety, with examples of several of the types of records mentioned above.[60] However, the accounts of dispute cases predominate, as well as other types such as inventories[61] and rulings[62] that seem to be directly connected to the former even if they scarcely mention them.

In these documents, ecclesiastical institutions are seen suing in court over their lordly rights against all different kinds of opponents, such as another

58 Claudio Rodiño, "A Lex Gótica e o Liber Iudicum no reino de León," *Cuadernos de Estudios Gallegos* 44 (1997), 9–52, and Amancio Isla, "La pervivencia de la tradición legal visigótica en el reino asturleonés," *Mélanges de la Casa de Velázquez, Nouvelle sèrie* 41 (2011), 75–86.

59 The case of Santiago is striking for chronological reasons, since three out of the four documents that address conflicts over dependency status date from the tenth century.

60 Alfonso, "Formato," 199–209.

61 The very lengthy inventory of the men of Loúzara, from 1057, can be understood as the result of a lawsuit about which this document provides only a few details, TS 123.

62 In the year 999, Vermudo II (r. 985–999) handed down a sentence that resolved a suit between the see of Iria/Santiago and a layman regarding the offspring of a marriage between a man from Iria and a woman who belonged to the layman. The text centres on the ruling in the suit and not on the details leading up to it, TA 58.

ecclesiastical institution,[63] a count,[64] or an aristocrat.[65] However, kings were without a doubt the main rivals of cathedrals and monasteries in disputes over lordly and seigneurial rights.[66] And not only kings but also members of the royal family,[67] monasteries belonging to the *infantado* (created for daughters of the royal family)[68] or linked in some way to the royal patrimony, people who forced dependents of a church into royal service,[69] royal representatives without an official position,[70] and as of the middle of the eleventh century, a group of royal officials such as *tenentes*,[71] *merinos*[72] and *vicarii*.[73]

Paradoxically, perhaps, the preferred forum for resolving many of these disputes was a hearing before the king or his representative.[74] From the earliest documents to the latest we see kings presiding over trials,[75] while in other cases monarchs appear together with royal judges,[76] kings entrust one of their delegates to oversee a suit,[77] or disputes are ruled on by royal judges or *merinos*.[78] No other matter seems to have involved royal courts to the extent that we see here.

63 This is the case in the dispute dated 999 between Bishop Pelayo of Lugo and Pedro, bishop of Iria, in his capacity as former abbot of Sobrado, TSob 109. On this document, its structure and authorship, see Davies, *Windows on Justice*, 39. It has also been carefully studied and even translated into Spanish by Agustín Prieto, "El proceso en el reino de León a la luz de los diplomas," in *El reino de León en la alta edad media, II. Ordenamiento jurídico del reino* (León: Centro de Estudios e Investigación 'San Isidoro', 1992), 381–518, at 476–478. On the recourse to testimony from the elderly, see José M. Andrade, "La voz de los ancianos. La intervención de los viejos en los pleitos y disputas de la Galicia medieval," *Hispania* 240 (2012), 11–34, especially 14–16.

64 In 1062, Celanova brings a suit against Count Ordoño over a group of *villae* and the men living in them, TC 526.

65 An example would be the legal battle that took place in 1078 between Celanova and Velasco Fernandi regarding lordly rights, TC 293.

66 On conflicts between ecclesiastical institutions and royal delegates, see Amancio Isla, *Realezas hispánicas del año Mil* (Sada-A Coruña: Ediciós do Castro, 1999), 110.

67 The *infante* Fruela was engaged in a legal dispute with Samos in the year 975, TS 44.

68 TS, 112.

69 The *homines* of Souto de Vide were dependents of the see of Santiago. Due to the intervention of an individual named Gimundo, these men had come under royal jurisdiction and had been freed. In the year 958, Ordoño IV (r. 958–960) *coram concilio* signs an *agnitio* according to which the men are returned to Santiago, TA 46.

70 For example, TC 552 and 369.

71 TC 260.

72 TS 113.

73 TC 147 and 526.

74 This is perfectly understandable if we keep in mind that the litigants are people and institutions belonging to the elite; Carvajal, *Bajo la máscara*, 273–274.

75 TS 44.

76 TC 552.

77 TC 260.

78 TS 113.

In records of disputes over the status of dependents there are occasional references to documentary evidence. Thus, for example, in the suit brought in the year 999 by Vegila against the church of Santiago regarding the descendants of a married man and women who were in the service of two different *domini*, one of the arguments put forward by Bishop Pedro of Iria/Santiago involved *testamenta que in tesauro Sancti Iacobi roborata et afirmata sunt.*[79] However, the majority of extant documents make clear that the burden of proof fell mainly on the testimony of the persons affected or of others who could be considered to know the facts of the case. This testimony was almost invariably accompanied by a sworn oath.[80]

This oath was sometimes taken by the very individuals who were the object of the dispute. This is the case in a lawsuit between Velasco Núñez, a representative of Celanova, and Nausti Diaz, who held the *mandamentum* of Ludro, regarding the men of the *villa* of Froiás, recorded in a document dated 1007.[81] The suit was argued before the royal judge at Limia and the men whose service was being disputed were the very ones obliged to take an oath:

> que dedissent ipsos homines iuramento de sua parte sicut et dederunt, quomodo fuerunt suos avolos de Cellanova sicut et illos sunt quomodo desursum resonat. Et iurarunt illos per si.[82]

But, as though this was not enough, a monk from Celanova who had authority over the men also took an oath, as did two people from the neighbourhood who, by virtue of their age or social status, must have been considered well acquainted with the case.[83]

In fact, sworn witnesses tended to be third parties. Who were these witnesses? Most documents meticulously record the names of oath takers—both

---

79 TA 58. In TSob 109 there is a similar mention, when Lugo's bishop argued that the *notitias per nomina* of the parents of the disputed *homines* were kept in the archives of the Lugo see: *in scriniis uel thesaurum*. I am grateful to Marcos Fernández for having made me aware of this reference.

80 Sometimes, the sworn oath also served to confirm documentary evidence. See, for example, TS S-8 and TC 513.

81 On the Galician *mandamenta* from the end of the tenth century onward, see Amancio Isla, *La sociedad gallega en la Alta Edad Media* (Madrid: CSIC, 1992), 244–246; this lawsuit is mentioned on p. 244.

82 TC 552.

83 *Et cum eis iuravit frater Andrias qui ipso mandamento tenebat, et alios duos Ramiro et Vistremiro, qui de ipso territorio sunt et sapiebant veritate*, ibid.

their Christian name and their patronymic, which was uncommon. The number of sworn witnesses is variable. Sometimes three[84] or ten[85] are mentioned, sometimes twelve,[86] but the most common number is five.[87] They had to be people close to the party for whom they were giving witness, but at the same time they had to have a certain social and economic standing, which made their testimony doubly valuable.[88]

The sworn oath—which had a sacred and symbolic value and a judicial validity about which there is much to be said—could put an end to a suit. In fact, some accounts of judicial proceedings end with the sworn oath, which can be understood to mean that this oath was considered sufficient proof for resolving the dispute. In effect, in most cases, after the oath is pronounced, the opposing side acknowledges their culpability or, at least, that they are not entitled to pursue the litigation, and resorts to the formula of confession or *agnitio*.[89]

But in some other cases—amounting to a fifth of our sample—the oath is a prelude to another kind of evidence that constitutes definitive proof: the ordeal. In the documentation from Galicia, this is referred to by the simple name of *pena* and is accompanied by the verb *eicio*.[90] All of the references in our corpus involve use of the hand, though we do not know whether this entailed placing a hot stone or other burning object on it or introducing the hand into a boiling liquid.[91] The cases in which this procedure is resorted to are characterized by involving litigants with equal power and a similar social status.

84 TC 260.

85 TC 252.

86 TC 369.

87 TS 113.

88 Bowman, "From Galicia," 351, compares various aspects of judicial documentation in Catalonia and Galicia and concludes that in Galicia the number of oath takers seems to carry more weight than their social standing and their familiarity with the circumstances of the dispute. These people would be, rather, "oath-helpers" for bolstering the cases of the different parties. Davies, *Windows on Justice*, 28–29, 195, 243–244, points out the difficulty in distinguishing between "oath-helpers" and "sworn witnesses".

89 TC 369.

90 According to Bowman, "From Galicia," 352, the ordeal is not well documented in Galicia. However, and despite the absence of a definitive comparative study, I suspect that it is precisely in Galicia where this practice is most well documented.

91 One document with highly detailed information about ordeals—though it describes a case that deals only tangentially with *homines*—is TS S-12. Galician documentation does not mention other forms of ordeal such as immersion in cold water, which we do find in Catalonia; Salrach, *Justícia*, 231.

An example would be the aforementioned dispute between Bishop Pelayo of Lugo and Bishop Pedro of Iria, regarding the lordly rights over some men from the valley of Présaras.[92]

To conclude this section, I would like to comment on a document that exhibits many of the features mentioned above. This document dates from 1038 and was preserved in the Lugo cathedral archive. It records a lawsuit between Oveco Rodosendiz (a representative of the *infanta* Sancha) and the priest Leoncio (on behalf of the church of Lugo) regarding two women, whose names are omitted but who are referred to as the wives of Sisnando and Bello. Curiously—and exceptionally for Galician judicial documents—there are two extant copies of this suit, the document that must be the original and its cartulary copy in Lugo's *Tumbo Viejo*.[93]

The document begins by mentioning that Sancha's representative and the *merinos* of the church of Lugo appeared before none other than Lugo's Bishop Pedro and the *infanta*, in addition to the judicial court made up of three members. Both sides made their arguments: one side argued that the women belonged to Sancha's *criatione*; the other, that these women were the daughters of *homines de ingenuitate*. Once these declarations were made, the two sides and the judges made arrangements for the *placitum*, which was set for the third day following the feast of Saint Michael, when they were to present six witnesses. Only four witnesses are mentioned for Sancha, and five for Lugo. Both sides stuck to their testimony, although the document only gives an account of the declaration made by the church of Lugo.

Next *dederunt lege in ipso concilio* for the witnesses for Lugo to take an oath. The oath was taken *per conditiones* at the cathedral's altar in the presence of Sancha and the *merinos*. As a colophon to the oath, an ordeal is agreed to that is to be undergone *per manu ipsius sagione*, most probably the *saio* Paulino, who was mentioned during the first round of testimony. The church of San Vicente de Pedreda—located in the modern municipality of Lugo, though in a rural area well beyond the city walls—was the scene of the ordeal.

Three days later, the ordeal was held in the presence of Bishop Aloito of Mondoñedo, along with three other judges identified by name. The hand of the *nocente*—that is, the individual who underwent the ordeal—was declared to be "clean." It is only at this point that Sancha gives her *agnitio*, acknowledging that the women do not belong to her.

---

92 TSob 109.

93 Ainoa Castro and Manuel Rodríguez Sánchez, eds., *Colección diplomática altomedieval de Galicia II: documentación en escritura visigótica de la sede lucense*, 2 vols (Lugo: Publicaciones Diócesis de Lugo, 2019), 1: no. 64, pp. 353–358; TVL 132.

3.3 *Justice in the Cloisters: Intramural Rulings and Original Jurisdiction*

The judicial role performed by and in some monasteries is of special interest in the case of Galicia. The monastery of Celanova stands out from other institutions in this respect as well.[94] There is documentation of a court operating there, beginning in the tenth century, that has all the features that are commonly and characteristically found in other courts presided over by more powerful lords than a monastery, even one as important as Celanova. This monastic court ruled primarily on matters affecting Celanova's own patrimony,[95] as was illustrated by the cases involving *renovos*. Here, the monastery acted both as judge and as party to the suit, following procedures that were, nonetheless, eminently public.[96] Let us take a look at some examples of how this justice of original jurisdiction—which was simultaneously public and private—functioned.

The first example dates from 1007 and has come down to us in a document that we can classify as a judicial transaction.[97] In it we learn of a case involving the "robbery" of some properties that the defendants, a family of peasants, had previously sold to the provost Cresconio, as stated in a record of sale written at the time. As a result, the peasants were taken by the *saio* Sigila to the monastery, where they were judged *in presentia iudicum prepositum domno Munio et maurino domno Sandino et aliorum iudicum*. These judges, the document says, should *pro lex cotica inquirere* the abovementioned robbery. The judges, who were mentioned by name, were members of the monastic community at Celanova (as was the *saio*, most likely), but the document makes clear that they are going to proceed in accordance with the law.[98]

The second example is from a year later and is also recorded in a judicial transaction.[99] A man named Trastino and his family, who appear to have been relatively well off compared to their fellow peasants, had been accused of vandalizing a property belonging to the monastery. They therefore were required to appear in Celanova before a judge who was none other than Cresconio,[100] who heard the case together with *aliorum judicum*. The *saio* is again mentioned, here one Sisgundo Fafilaz, as an agent who forces the accused to be present,

94 Davies, *Windows on Justice*, 157–158.

95 It has been established that this is also the case in some large monasteries in León; Carvajal, *Bajo la máscara*, 274.

96 I agree with Wendy Davis's recent assessment that the administration of justice in the tenth century was a "public" affair. Davies, *Windows on Justice*, 246.

97 TC 193.

98 On non-royal judges and *saiones* in León, see Carvajal, *Bajo la máscara*, 271.

99 TC 495.

100 See Carzolio, "Cresconio."

and now we hear of a *mandator*, Sandino Sendamiriz, who acts on behalf of Celanova as plaintiff against Trastino and his family.[101] Trastino refuses to put forward a defence or possibly even to enter into litigation.[102] It should be noted that the term and the concept of *agnitio* is avoided, despite the basic similarity between this case and the 1038 dispute between Lugo and the *infanta* Sancha discussed above, perhaps because the *agnitio* was formally reserved for persons of higher status. Is the social position of the litigant what determines the document format used to record the case? The text explains that the properties were ceded to Celanova as a *iudicato* due to a different member of Celanova, the provost Aloito. He had not been mentioned previously as one of the judges in the case, but he clearly must have participated in it.

However, there were other disputes that were first heard in Celanova but ended up being ruled upon by another court. This happens when the matter to be resolved transcends the monastery's domanial and seigneurial claims and needs to be settled by what we might call a higher authority. One especially detailed example of this kind of situation is the dispute between the monastery and the married couple Tetone and Egilo. This couple was accused of killing a man from Celanova named Baldemaro in the year 1056. This case—which is much richer and more complex than any we have looked at thus far—provides insight into a different period, the reign of Fernando I (r. 1037–1065), which was characterized by broad changes and innovation.[103]

The compilers of the *Tumbo* copied two documents that describe the proceedings in detail, each focusing on a different phase and a different site/location, and each using a completely different format. The two documents are copied consecutively, although as separate pieces and in reverse chronological order. On 2 March 1056, Egilo signed a *placitum pregarium* with the *vicarius* of Celanova's abbot, Arias.[104] She did so *in concilio Cellenove*, at and before the monastery's court, since her husband, Tetone, was imprisoned there. He had been taken to the monastery for the murder of Baldemaro, who was a dependent belonging to Celanova. The compromise reached consisted of freeing the prisoner, who was to appear before the court three days later. Although the place in which the trial is to be held is not specified, it seems clear that it was to be at Celanova. At this trial, the document says, *faciat quantum lex*

101 *Dedistis nostro mandator nomine Sandino Sendamiriz qui vestra voce obtinebit contra me Trastino*, TC 495.

102 The text of the document admits of this interpretation when it says *et ego Trastino nolui questionem*, ibid.

103 Isla, *Realezas*, 149–175.

104 TC 475.

et veritas docet pro illo omicidio. That is, the document invokes the *lex* as well as the truth, as proof of the public and regular nature of the proceedings. In the event of Tetone's failure to appear in court, his wife pledged to forfeit a plot in the village of Morteira. The document is signed by three witnesses, one of whom is Ero, the *carzereiro* (jailor), who was in charge of the monastery's prison, whom we can imagine releasing the accused at the very moment of the signing.

A little more than a month later, on 7 April, an *agnitio* is signed as part of a lengthy and elaborate document that fills out the details of what had happened up to the moment in which a formal commitment to appear in court was signed and, at the same time, follows up on everything that happened afterward.[105] To begin, it clarifies the social status of the murderer, who is identified as a *mallato* of a count, Sancho, and it describes the circumstances surrounding the murder in a flourish that is noteworthy as an example of narrative discourse:

> essent omnes adunati una domnica die ad eclesiam nunccupatam vocabulo Sancto Iacobo in villa Mortaria, prope fluvio Arnogie. Accidit ibi occasio sicut mos est in orbem terrarum. Postquam se inhebriarunt commiscuerunt baralia et ibi percusserunt uno homine de lancea nomine Baldemaro, homine proprio de monasterio Cellenove, unde cicius venit ad mortem.[106]

The witnesses to the murder are the same people who seem to have arrested Tetone and taken him to Celanova, where *iactaverunt eum in carcere et in vinculia ferreis quomodo dignus erat supplicio pati*, as we already knew from the earlier *placitum*. In fact, one of the signers of this document is also the jailor Ero. The abbot of the monastery comes and interrogates Tetone without any intermediary, the document recounts, hoping to find out the truth about what had happened.[107] In answering the abbot's questions, the murderer acknowledges his guilt, though he attempts to exculpate himself using the argument that *vino fui ebriatus*. After hearing this admission of guilt, the abbot returns the murderer to the monastery's jail. He then received a visit from the murderer's wife, who begs him to release her husband and to jail her instead or to set the prisoner free in exchange for a guarantee (bail) and a promise that he

105 TC 474.

106 Ibid.

107 On the importance of the term *ueritas*, which is repeatedly invoked in this text, and its implications in tenth-century judicial documents, especially in Galicia, see Davies, *Windows on Justice*, 123 and 144.

will appear at the trial, as was recorded in the document discussed above: *saccabo eum in fiato, et pono vobis hereditatem meam in placito et, ut inquirat alios fideiussores, et veniat ad diem placito*.[108]

The abbot takes pity on the wife and decides to free the murderer. Up to this point, the matter seems to fall exclusively within the jurisdiction of the monastery, exactly as we have seen in the cases discussed previously. This might be explained by the fact that what is at stake concerns the monastery's seigneurial lordship[109] and by the social status of the persons directly involved in the case (the murderer and his victim), who were both dependents. But what happens after Tetone is released turns the matter into something that goes beyond the monastery's jurisdiction. In effect, after leaving the monastery's jail, Tetone goes directly to see his lord, Count Sancho. He throws himself at his feet and tells him a completely different version of events (*multa fallacia narrante*, the document says) and complains of his mistreatment by Celanova.

The angry count decides to intervene. He authorizes a *homine bono* to go to the abbot and find out what happened. This attempt at mediation is fruitless, and once the count has heard from his emissary, he decides to resort to interrogation *ipsa com\l\latione qui ibidem fuerant ubi ipso omicidio fuit*. That is, he moves the trial to the scene of the murder, where it can be attended by the community who witnessed it.[110] This represents a new phase in the trial in which it is no longer Celanova taking the lead but rather the count, who will now act as judge.

The process for settling the matter is agreed upon: one monk and four of the *homines meliores* are to swear an oath *super ipso Tetone et super sua mulier qui illo homine tenuerat ad capillos quando eum plagaverunt lancea*, with the additional obligation to submit to an ordeal. The count orders his *vicarius* (there is no reference here to a *saio*) to oversee this stage of the proceedings.

On the day stipulated, the witnesses finally testify under oath, as the count-judge had ordered, in the same church where the murder had taken place. And three days later the ordeal is agreed upon that the *nocente*, a man named Sarracino, will undergo as a representative of Celanova. As is customary, the scene of the trial by fire is a church other than the one where the sworn testimony was given. Three days after that, and at a different location,[111] the *ino-*

108 TC 474.

109 Recall that the victim was a serf belonging to Celanova. The document never identifies him by name; he is simply referred to as *ille homine*.

110 On the term *collatio* and its synonyms, see Carvajal, *Bajo la máscara*, 214.

111 In contrast to the fact that, in its early stages, this case was dealt with 'domestically' (i.e.,

cente is presented to the count, along with a crowd of *benenatorum*. The latter confirm that his hand was *lenpeda* ("clean"). The count, in his capacity as judge, then orders the married couple to pay for the murder, *sicut sua ueritas erat*.

The trial does not end here. Tetone and Egilo did not have enough to pay the amount of the fine for the murder and, moreover, they do not appear at the *concilium* arranged for that purpose. At this point the judge-count orders his *saio* to award to the abbot and the community of Celanova the plot of land that Tetone and Egilo had given as guarantee. And the document adds: *Et teneant ea usque reddat ipse Tetone et sua mulier ipso omicidio sicut veritas docet*. The count signs this *agnicio*, for which he also acted as judge, the document reminds us, and a group of people certify and sign together with him. All these signatures are put down in the presence of the entire community of Celanova, from the least to the most important.[112] In other words, the case—which originated in Celanova and went through all the procedural vicissitudes described here—comes to a close in the most symbolic way possible with the signing of the ruling in the monastery itself.

Lastly, this case is illuminating in that it provides a series of temporal signposts, which allows us to measure the speed with which some trials were carried out. The original *placitum* was dated March 1056, and the final ruling, following all of the phases described, was signed in April. Although this is not the most frequent scenario, it is not the only documented case reflecting a system of judicial courts that provided, at least occasionally, a speedy trial.[113]

within the monastery or the count's court), the later stages were characterized by the clearly itinerant nature of the proceedings and demonstrate the public aspects and the publicity of delivering justice.

112 *Et omnis congregatio monasterii Cellenove a minimo usque ad magnum hac vere confirmans*, TC 474. On the significance of the fact that children were part of the communities that were present for the ruling on some suits, see José M. Andrade, "Las edades del hombre en los monasterios benedictinos y cistercienses: de la infancia a la vejez," in *El ritmo de la vida cotidiana en el monasterio*, ed. José A. García de Cortazar and Ramón Teja (Aguilar de Campoo: Fundación Santa María la Real, 2015), 111–141.

113 Another example, dated to 1038, that permits us to observe the details of a conflict's development over time and its speedy resolution is TVL 132.

Bibliography

Abbreviations

LM: Amaral, Luís, André Evangelista Marques, José Meirinhos, Maria Cristina Almeida e Cunha, and Maria João Oliveira e Silva, eds. *Livro de Mumadona: Cartulário do Mosteiro de Guimarães: Edição crítica.* Lisbon: Academia das Ciências de Lisboa, 2016 [2018].

PRJ: *PRocesos Judiciales en las sociedades medievales del norte peninsular.* Accessed 20 April 2020. http://prj.csic.es/.

TA: Lucas, Manuel, ed. *Tumbo A de la Catedral de Santiago.* Santiago de Compostela: Cabildo de la S.A.M.I. Catedral—Seminario de Estudos Galegos, 1998.

TC: Andrade Cernadas, José Miguel, with Marta Díaz Tie and Francisco J. Pérez Rodríguez, eds. *O Tombo de Celanova: estudio introductorio, edición e índices (ss. IX–XII).* 2 vols. Santiago de Compostela: Consello da Cultura Galega, 1995.

TS: Lucas, Manuel, ed. *El Tumbo de San Julián de Samos: (siglos VIII–XII).* Santiago de Compostela: Caixa Galicia, 1985.

TSob: Loscertales de García de Valdeavellano, Pilar, ed. *Tumbos del monasterio de Sobrado de los Monjes.* 2 vols. Madrid: Dirección General del Patrimonio Artístico y Cultural, Archivo Histórico Nacional, 1976.

TVL: López Sangil, José Luis, and Manuel Vidán, eds. "Tumbo Viejo de Lugo (transcripción completa)." *Estudios Mindonienses* 27 (2011), 11–373.

Other Primary Sources

Castro, Ainoa, and M. Rodríguez Sánchez, eds. *Colección diplomática altomedieval de Galicia II: documentación en escritura visigótica de la sede lucense.* 2 vols. Lugo: Publicaciones Diócesis de Lugo, 2019.

Zeumer, Karl, ed. *Leges Visigothorum.* Monumenta Germaniae Historica, Leges nationum Germanicarum 1. Hanover: Hahn, 1902.

Secondary Works

Alfonso, Isabel. "El formato de la información judicial en la Alta Edad Media peninsular." In *Chartes et cartulaires comme instruments de pouvoir. Espagne et Occident chrétien (VIIIe-XIIe siècles)*, edited by Julio Escalona and Hélène Sirantoine, 191–218. Toulouse: Université de Toulouse-Le Mirail, 2013.

Andrade, José M. "Aproximación a la figura del prepósito monástico en el monacato gallego medieval: siglo X al XII." *Estudios Mindonienses* 11 (1995), 279–292.

Andrade, José M. *El monacato benedictino y la sociedad de la Galicia medieval (siglos X–XIII).* Sada-A Coruña: Ediciós do Castro, 1997.

Andrade, José M. "La voz de los ancianos. La intervención de los viejos en los pleitos y disputas de la Galicia medieval." *Hispania* 240 (2012), 11–34.

Andrade, José M. "Las edades del hombre en los monasterios benedictinos y cistercienses: de la infancia a la vejez." In *El ritmo de la vida cotidiana en el monasterio*, edited by José A. García de Cortazar and Ramón Teja, 111–141. Aguilar de Campoo: Fundación Santa María la Real, 2015.

Andrade, José M. "La Concordia de Antealtares en su contexto histórico." In *Los reyes de Asturias y los orígenes del culto a la tumba del apóstol Santiago*, edited by Francisco J. Fernández Conde and Raquel Alonso, 109–126. Gijón: Trea, 2017.

Bougard, François. "Le crédit dans l'Occident du Haut Moyen Âge: documentation et pratique." In *Les élites et la richesse au Haut Moyen Âge*, edited by Jean P. Devroey, Laurent Feller, and Regine Le Jan, 439–478. Turnhout: Brepols, 2010.

Bowman, Jeffrey. "From Galicia to the Rhône. Legal practice in northern Spain around the Year 1000." In *Culture and Society in Medieval Galicia. A Cultural Crossroads at the Edge of Europe*, edited by James D'Emilio (Leiden: Brill, 2015), 343–360.

Calleja, Miguel. "Cartularios y construcción de la memoria monástica en los reinos de León y Castilla durante el siglo XII." In *Les cartulaires médiévaux: écrire et conserver la mémoire du pouvoir, le pouvoir de le mémoire. Los cartularios medievales: escribir y conservar la memoria del poder, el poder de la memoria*, edited by Véronique Lamazou-Duplan and Eloísa Ramírez Vaquero, 187–200. Pau: Presses universitaires de Pau et des Pays de l'Adour, 2013.

Carvajal, Álvaro. *Bajo la máscara del* Regnum. *La monarquía asturleonesa en León (854–1037)*. Madrid: CSIC, 2017.

Carzoglio, María Inés. "Cresconio, prepósito de Celanova. Un personaje gallego al filo del siglo XI." *Cuadernos de Historia de España* 57–58 (1973), 225–279.

Castro, Ainoa. *Colección diplomática altomedieval de Galicia I (662–1234)*. Noia: Toxosoutos, 2011.

Davies, Wendy. *Windows on Justice in Northern Iberia. 800–1000*. Abingdon: Routledge, 2016.

D'Emilio, James. "The legend of Bishop Odoario and the early medieval church in Galicia." In *Church, State, Vellum, and Stone: Essays on Medieval Spain in Honor of John Williams*, edited by Therese Martin and Julie Harris, 47–83. Leiden: Brill, 2005.

Escalona, Julio. "Antes de los cartularios: gestión de archivos y transmisión de los documentos de la Castilla Condal (siglo IX-1038)." In *Chartes et cartulaires comme instruments de pouvoir. Espagne et Occident chrétien (VIIIe–XIIe siècles)*, edited by Julio Escalona and Hélène Sirantoine, 131–151. Toulouse: Université de Toulouse-Le Mirail, 2013.

Fernández Ferreiro, Marcos. *Servos e escravos altomedievais no noroeste da Península* Ibérica. Noia: Toxosoutos, 2010.

García de Valdeavellano, Luis. "El *renovo*. Notas y documentos sobre los préstamos usurarios en el reino astur-leonés (siglos X–XI)." *Cuadernos de Historia de España* 57–58 (1973), 408–448.

Isla, Amancio. *La sociedad gallega en la Alta Edad Media*. Madrid: CSIC, 1992.

Isla, Amancio. *Realezas hispánicas del año Mil*. Sada-A Coruña: Ediciós do Castro, 1999.

Isla, Amancio. "La pervivencia de la tradición legal visigótica en el reino asturleonés." *Mélanges de la Casa de Velázquez, Nouvelle sèrie* 41 (2011), 75–86.

Kosto, Adam J. "*Sicut mos esse solet*. Documentary practices in Christian Iberia, c. 700–1000." In *Documentary Culture and the Laity in the Early Middle Ages*, eds. Warren Brown, Marios Costambeys, Matthew Innes, and Adam J. Kosto, 259–282. Cambridge: Cambridge University Press, 2012.

López Alsina, Fernando. *La ciudad de Santiago de Compostela en la Alta Edad Media*. Santiago de Compostela: Ayuntamiento de Santiago de Compostela, 1985.

Pastor Díaz de Garayo, Ernesto, and Ainoa Castro Correa. *Las presuras de Odoario "el africano" en Lugo y Braga: textos, objetos y contextos para la construcción de la memoria y la legitimación de la dominación personal y política*. Bilbao: Universidad del País Vasco, 2020.

Portass, Robert. "Rethinking the "small worlds" of tenth-century Galicia." *Studia Historica. Historia Medieval* 31 (2013), 83–103.

Portass, Robert. "The middling sort at court in early medieval Christian Iberia." *Al-Masáq* 29, no. 2 (2017), 99–113.

Portela, Ermelindo, and María Carmen Pallares. "Elementos para el análisis de la aristocracia altomedieval de Galicia: parentesco y patrimonio." *Studia Historica. Historia Medieval* 5 (1987), 17–32.

Portela, Ermelindo, and María Carmen Pallares. "La villa, por dentro." *Studia Historica. Historia Medieval* 16 (1998), 13–43.

Prieto, Agustín. "El proceso en el reino de León a la luz de los diplomas." In *El reino de León en la alta edad media, II. Ordenamiento jurídico del reino*, 381–518. León: Centro de Estudios e Investigación 'San Isidoro', 1992.

Rodiño, Claudio. "A Lex Gótica e o Liber Iudicum no reino de León." *Cuadernos de Estudios Gallegos* 44 (1997), 9–52.

Sáez, Carlos, and Almudena Gutiérrez. "Hacia una interpretación del tumbo de Celanova." In *Iglesia y religiosidad en España. Historia y archivos*, 3 vols, vol. 2, 997–1008. Guadalajara: Junta de Comunidades de Castilla la Mancha, 2002.

Sáez, Emilio. "Los ascendientes de San Rosendo. Notas para el estudio de la monarquía astur-leonesa durante los siglos IX y X." *Hispania* 8 (1948), 3–76 and 179–233.

Salrach, Josep M. *Justícia i poder a Catalunya abans de l'any mil*. Vic: Eumo, 2013.

Suárez González, Ana I. "Los *Libri cartarum Superaddi*: notas para otra lectura (AHN, codices 976 and 977)." In *Galicia Monástica. Estudos en lembranza da profesora María José Portela Silva*, edited by Raquel Casal García, José M. Andrade, and Roberto J. López, 39–59. Santiago: Universidade de Santiago de Compostela, 2009.

Varela Sieiro, Xaime. *Léxico cotián na Alta Idade Media de Galicia: a arquitectura civil.* Santiago de Compostela: Universidade de Santiago de Compostela, 2008.

Vázquez de Parga, Luis. "Los documentos sobre las presuras del Obispo Odoario, de Lugo." *Hispania* 41 (1950), 635–680.

CHAPTER 2

Documentary Production and Dispute Records in León before the Year 1100

Isabel Alfonso

1 Leonese Documents from the Ninth to the Eleventh Century

Like the rest of the northern Iberian regions, León has ill-defined borders that shifted throughout the period considered here, which is something that needs to be taken into account as we evaluate the extant documentation preserved by the institutions ascribed to the Leonese area in the PRJ database. Furthermore, this documentation sometimes refers to areas that are clearly outside of León's borders. In any case, the Leonese corpus for the entire period before 1100 has close to 4000 documents, which makes León the region with the second highest number of documents in northern Iberia, only behind Catalonia. Although it trails the latter by a significant amount, it has practically twice the number of documents as the other regions (see above, Table 0.1).

There is nothing particularly striking about the chronological distribution of this documentation by century, except that it is rather irregular and has some significant peaks. This makes sense when we consider the institutions, both monasteries and cathedrals, that preserved it. The number of documents begins to increase at the end of the ninth century and continues upward until reaching a high point in the middle of the tenth. There is a marked decrease at the end of the 960s which continues almost to the end of that century, when the numbers again start to increase, slowly but surely, with this trend continuing throughout the eleventh century (see above, Table 0.2 and Graphs 0.1 and 0.3).

The spatial distribution of the Leonese records is noteworthy, with 61 different ecclesiastical institutions having been identified as centres where records were originally produced and/or preserved. However, during the Middle Ages this documentation was brought into a much smaller number of archives. This concentration process was the product of a growing hierarchization of ecclesiastical institutions that took place, like in the other regions, mainly during the eleventh century.[1] As a result, and despite the appearance of 'decentraliza-

1 E.g., Julio Escalona, "Antes de los cartularios: gestión de archivos y transmisión de los docu-

 | DOI:10.1163/9789004683006_004

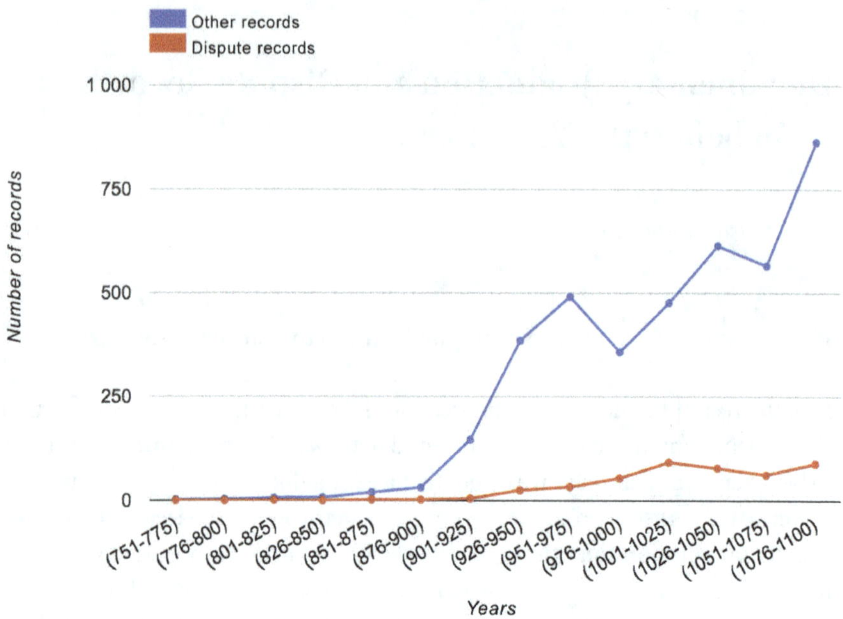

GRAPH 2.1 Proportion of Leonese dispute records before 1100, by quarter-century

tion' arising from the fact that the documents' original provenance has been identified in the PRJ project with as much detail as possible, there are many differences in the information that we have about some geographical areas compared to others (see above, Map 0.1).[2] The volume of documents from each institution is very unequal; ten institutions have more than 100 documents, but the majority have fewer than twenty.

As is the case in other regions, in León as well there are numerous ecclesiastical centres that compiled at least one cartulary. Prominent among them are the cartularies from Sahagún and the León, Oviedo and Astorga cathedrals, but there are also extant examples from smaller institutions (San Pedro de

mentos de la Castilla condal (siglo IX-1038)," in *Chartes et cartulaires comme instruments de pouvoir. Espagne et Occident chrétien (VIIIe-XIIe siècles)*, ed. Julio Escalona and Hélène Sirantoine (Toulouse: Université de Toulouse-Le Mirail, 2013), 147–167, at 134–135. The abbreviations used in this paper for editions of charters are listed in the bibliography.

2 In a recent work based on León's documentation up to the year 1037, Álvaro Carvajal Castro, *Bajo la máscara del* Regnum. *La monarquía asturleonesa en León (854–1037)* (Madrid: Consejo Superior de Investigaciones Científicas, 2017), 51, emphasizes this point as well as the irregular distribution of the documentation over time, suggesting the need for research on whether this distribution was the result primarily of general tendencies, regional factors, or the particular history of each monastic centre.

Montes, Castañeda, Carracedo, Santo Toribio de Liébana, etc.) However, notwithstanding the abundance of cartularies, an important distinctive feature of the Leonese documentation is that almost half of the texts have come down to us in the form of single-sheet parchments (many of them originals). Moreover, one of the most notable Iberian collections of single sheets is made up of the two largest groups of lay documents from this area and period, those belonging to counts Fruela Muñoz and Pedro Flaínez, which were to be preserved in the archive of Otero de las Dueñas, a Cistercian convent founded in the thirteenth century.

Although a detailed evaluation of the entire corpus of documents from León is not possible here, it is necessary, in order to contextualize the information on disputes that can be drawn from that corpus, to provide a rundown of the main archives and what we know about their creation and preservation.

The León cathedral archive kept the largest number of records from the period in question: more than 1300, only a third of which originated in the cathedral itself, with the rest coming from monasteries elsewhere in the Leonese area. This copious body of texts for the period before 1100 has been published in four volumes with introductory studies that describe the documents' main diplomatic and palaeographical characteristics and provide an outline of the complex process of their transmission.[3] We thus know that the documents from the León cathedral are unique among the Leonese episcopal collections for being earlier, more numerous, and more diverse and for the larger number of originals and the smaller number of falsifications. By contrast, the archive of the Astorga cathedral went up in flames,[4] that of the Oviedo cathedral, in addition to having lost many pieces, contains many false documents,[5] and those

3 See the introductory material to CL1, CL2, CL3, and CL4.

4 A much later cartulary, compiled in the eighteenth century, only includes regesta of a great many Astorga documents. Gregoria Cavero Domínguez and Encarnación Martín López, eds., *Colección documental de la Catedral de Astorga, I (646–1126)* (León: Centro de Estudios e Investigación 'San Isidoro', 1999). See also Mercedes Durany Castrillo and María Carmen Rodríguez González, "Puntualizaciones sobre la datación de algunos documentos de la Catedral de Astorga del primer tercio del siglo XI. De Jimeno a Sampiro," *Estudios Humanísticos. Historia* 3 (2004), 275–302; and María Josefa Sanz Fuentes, *El Tumbo Negro de la Catedral de Astorga: una aproximación a su historia* (Astorga: Centro de Estudios Astorganos Marcelo Macías, 2010).

5 María Josefa Sanz Fuentes et al., eds., *El "Liber Testamentorum" de la catedral de Oviedo* (Barcelona: Moleiro Editor, 1995); also of interest is Miguel Calleja Puerta, "La Catedral de Oviedo como centro de conservación de documentos en la alta Edad Media," in *Estudos em homenagem ao Professor Doutor José Marques* (Porto: Faculdade de Letras da Universidade do Porto, 2006), IV:179–191.

of the Zamora, Palencia, and Valladolid cathedrals only go back to the eleventh century.[6] Another distinctive feature of the León cathedral archive is that its organization is reflected in the structure of its cartulary, the *Tumbo Legionense* (1124).[7] The documents originating in each of the monasteries that ended up being incorporated into the patrimony of the León cathedral are grouped together in the cartulary, thus forming independent sections. This makes it possible to determine with relative confidence where each document came from, since the documents were incorporated into the cathedral's archive when each of the monasteries—which were spread out all over the diocese—was annexed to the cathedral, despite the fact that 'the archives of these monastic centres remained separate entities for a long time after having been integrated administratively into the see.'[8] Because of this underlying archival organization, a decision was made in the PRJ database of isolating the documents belonging to the cathedral itself from those proceeding from the monastic collections that are differentiated from one another in the cartulary, following the indications of the editors of the published collection.[9] Thus, out of the more than 1300 documents recorded in the cathedral archive before the itemization, only 441 were assigned to the León Cathedral itself.[10] This itemization makes it possible, among other things, to deal separately with each of the document collections that were added to the cathedral's own. In fact, some of them had already been the subject of previous editions and/or monographic studies.[11]

---

6 For all of the above, see Ruiz Asencio's introduction to CL3, pp. ix–xi.

7 León, Archivo de la Catedral de León, Códice 11. See CL3, pp. xxviii–xxix; José María Fernández Catón, "El Tumbo Legionense. Notas sobre su origen, reacción, estructura, contenido y utilización," in *Actas do IV Congreso Internacional de Latim Medieval Hispânico* (Lisbon: Centro de Estudos Clássicos, 2007), 415–435; Marta Herrero de la Fuente, "Cartularios leoneses: Del *Becerro Gótico de Sahagún* al *Tumbo Legionense* y al *Libro de las Estampas*," in *La escritura de la memoria: los cartularios*, ed. Elena E. Rodríguez Díaz and Antonio Claret García Martínez (Huelva: Universidad de Huelva, 2011), 111–152.

8 CL3, p. ix. On the almost absolute preponderance of monastic collections compared to those of the cathedral up to the second half of the eleventh century and the difficulties involved in reconstructing the process by which these collections were incorporated, see CL3, p. xiii.

9 For these documents' provenance, see, in CL1, appendix 4, pp. 374–380; in CL2, appendix 4, pp. 340–348; in CL3, pp. xiii–xv; and in CL4, pp. xxi–xiii. A similar breakdown was done on the documentation collected in the Braga cathedral's *Liber Fidei* and in the Coimbra Cathedral's *Livro Preto*.

10 It should be kept in mind that the 'private documents' whose provenance could not be assigned by the editors have not been itemized and remain included among the cathedral's documents. More research is needed to be able to offer more detail about both the provenance and the transmission of all these documents.

11 Justiniano Rodríguez Fernández, *El monasterio de Ardón. Estudio histórico sobre los centros*

The more than 1000 documents that were held at the monastery of Sahagún make its archive particularly important among those of the Leonese region. These documents, like those of the León cathedral, have come down to us both as single-sheet parchments and in the monastery's well-known cartulary, the *Becerro Gótico de Sahagún*.[12] But unlike the "institutional and geographical" variety of the documentation from the cathedral archive, Sahagún "comes across as a powerful institution with a well-organized scriptorium where virtually all the legal transactions affecting the monastery were written down, including issues having to do with the Crown, although such transactions were made to fit into a rigid formulary" and were repetitive in their subject matter.[13] However, despite the relatively concise and homogeneous nature of this group of documents, it is possible to discern that it was also augmented by the incorporation of other monastic and lay collections, though the structure of the cartulary in this case does not permit such a straightforward itemization of the contents as in the case of the León cathedral.[14]

In contrast to the previous cases, the more than 300 diplomas from before the year 1100 regarding the counts Fruela Muñoz and Pedro Flaínez have come down to us exclusively as single-sheet parchments. And it is noteworthy as well that the Otero de las Dueñas convent, where these documents were preserved, was not founded until the thirteenth century by a descendant of the counts. These documents are, therefore, much earlier than the institution that held them, and it is important to point out that we do not know which archives preserved them up until the time that Otero was founded.[15] In my opinion, it is misleading to speak of a 'comital' archive, since it implies that the two counts kept an archive that was then passed down to the heir who founded Otero in

monásticos medievales de Cillanueva y Rozuela (León, Centro de Estudios e Investigación 'San Isidoro', 1964); María del Pilar Yañez Cifuentes, *El monasterio de Santiago de León* (León: Centro de Estudios e Investigación 'San Isidoro', 1972); María José Carbajo Serrano, "El monasterio de los santos Cosme y Damián de Abellar. Monacato y sociedad en la época astur-leonesa," *Archivos Leoneses* 81–82 (1987), 7–300.

12 S1, S2, and S3. For a study of the *Becerro*, see Leticia Agúndez San Miguel, *La memoria escrita en el monasterio de Sahagún (años 904–1300)* (Madrid: Consejo Superior de Investigaciones Científicas, 2019), 77–144.

13 Ruiz Asencio, introduction to CL4, pp. x–xi.

14 Adam J. Kosto, "*Sicut mos esse solet*: documentary practices in Christian Iberia, c. 700–1000," in *Documentary Culture and the Laity in the Early Middle Ages*, ed. Warren Brown et al. (Cambridge: Cambridge University Press, 2013), 259–282, at 276–280, identifies seven lay dossiers of documents.

15 OD. On this particular archive, see Alfonso García Leal, *El archivo de los condes Fruela Muñoz y Pedro Flaínez: la formación de un patrimonio nobiliario en la montaña asturleonesa (854–1048)* (León: Universidad de León, 2010).

1230. Although we have almost no information about their institutional histories, we cannot rule out the possibility that one of the monasteries linked to the families of the two counts served as the initial archive for their documents. For example, it may have been San Pedro de Valdoré, which is located at the very centre of Count Pedro Flaínez's—and afterward his daughter-in-law María Froilaz's—domains in the region, and which was ceded to the León cathedral in 1052.[16] Also to be taken into account are the documents connected to these comital families that were held in the archives of other monasteries (Sahagún, Eslonza, San Antolín del Esla, San Juan de León, Carrizo) and in those of the León and Oviedo cathedrals.[17]

2 The Corpus of Leonese Dispute Records

A comparison of the ratios of dispute records to the overall number of documents across all northern Iberian regions shows that León, with 11.2 per cent, is in third place among the westernmost regions, behind Galicia (20.4 per cent) and Portugal (16.5 per cent). However, in absolute terms, the 443 documents that contain some kind of information about disputes and judicial process make León first among the same group since that number is twice the corresponding figure both in Galicia (266) and in Portugal (212) (see above, Table 0.1 and Graph 0.5). The distribution of dispute records from one century to the next is very uneven, with the eleventh century producing more than twice the number of records (321) that the tenth century produced (117) (see above, Table 0.2 and Graphs 0.7, 0.9 and 2.1). And the distribution over time for the specific institutions is likewise uneven, each showing its own pattern which reflects its particular development (Table 2.1 and Graph 2.2 below).[18]

16 CL4 1083. A document dated 1073 (CL4 1091) tells of the monastery's vicissitudes during this twenty-year interim.

17 Mariel Pérez, "El control de lo sagrado como instrumento de poder: los monasterios particulares de la aristocracia altomedieval leonesa," *Anuario de Estudios Medievales* 42, no. 2 (2012), 799–822, compiles information about and a bibliography on the aristocratic proprietary monasteries.

18 Otero de las Dueñas, for example, with only 16 dispute records in the tenth century, especially in its last decade, preserves 78 from the eleventh, with a relative majority coming from the 1020s, after which the numbers fall off precipitously. This is very different from Sahagún, where the largest number of dispute records were produced in the 970s and in the 1090s.

TABLE 2.1 Leonese institutions that preserved five or more pre-1100 dispute records

Institution	All records (n)	Dispute records (n)	Dispute records (%)	9th c.	10th c.	11th c.	Originals	Copies	Authentic	Suspect	False
Sta. María de Otero de Dueñas	305	95	31.15	1	16	78	77	1	78	0	0
Sahagún	1043	80	7.67	0	25	55	25	55	76	3	1
León Cathedral (CL)	441	49	11.04	1	16	32	33	16	49	0	0
Astorga Cathedral	491	46	9.37	1	5	40	1	45	44	0	2
S. Antolín del Esla-CL	59	22	37.29	0	5	17	2	20	21	0	1
S. Vicente de Oviedo	125	17	13.6	0	0	17	17	0	16	1	0
Oviedo Cathedral	119	15	12.61	1	3	11	3	12	12	2	1
S. Cosme y S. Damián de Abellar-CL	213	15	7.04	0	11	4	2	13	14	1	0
Stos. Justo y Pastor de Ardón-CL	101	13	12.87	0	10	3	1	12	13	0	0
Santiago de León-CL	100	11	11	0	2	9	6	5	11	0	0
S. Pedro de Eslonza	71	7	9.86	0	0	7	5	2	7	0	
Sto. Toribio de Liébana	104	7	6.73	1	4	2	0	7	7	0	0
S. Miguel de la Vega-CL	53	6	11.32	0	1	5	2	4	6	0	0
S. Pedro de la Puerta del Obispo-CL	10	5	50	0	0	5	0	5	5	0	0
Sta María de Valdevimbre-CL	37	5	13.51	0	4	1	0	5	4	1	0
Sta. María de Piasca	64	5	7.81	0	2	3	1	4	4	0	1
TOTAL	3337	398		5	104	289	175	206	367	8	6

It is also noteworthy that, despite the large number of institutions from which this documentation originates, it is in the Leonese region that we find four of the largest collections of dispute records in the whole northern Iberia: Otero (95), Sahagún (80), and the cathedrals of León (49)[19] and Astorga (46) (see above, Maps 0.2 and 0.3).[20]

19 As was mentioned above, this figure is the result of separating out the documents from the monasteries incorporated into the cathedral and assigning to the cathedral only those of unknown provenance having to do with private individuals. Without this itemization, the entire group of dispute records preserved at the cathedral would be 152 (11.7 per cent of the cathedral's total documentation).

20 The list of institutions having preserved more than 40 dispute records is headed by the Counts of Barcelona (135), the Barcelona and Vic cathedrals (120 and 112), and the monastery of Celanova (118), but it also includes the Urgell and Girona cathedrals (86 and 41) and

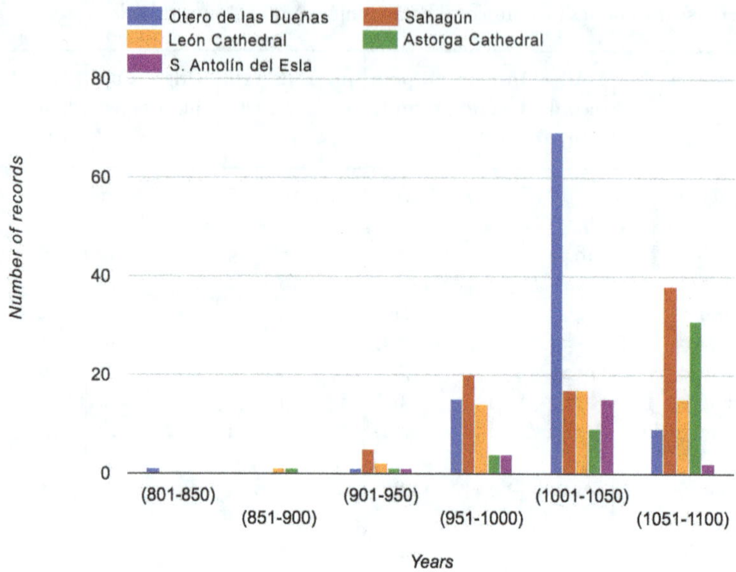

GRAPH 2.2 Largest Leonese collections of pre-1100 dispute records, by half-century

As we have seen with the total documentation for the region, there are two main differences to be observed also between these collections. First, that of Otero has exclusively lay documents, as compared to the mainly ecclesiastical holdings of the other three institutions. Second, the records at Otero have been preserved as single-sheet parchments, while those from the cathedrals and the monastery of Sahagún have come down to us mainly in cartularies, though some single-sheet parchments are also extant. However, these differences need to be qualified, among other things because the archives of the latter three ecclesiastical centres also incorporated lay documents.[21]

That said, in the analysis that follows, only in the case of the León cathedral will a distinction be made between documentation from the cathedral itself and documentation from incorporated monasteries, and this is because the structure of the cartulary allows such a distinction. Among these monasteries, I have decided to focus on San Antolín del Esla, because it raises some

the monasteries of Sant Cugat del Vallès (55), San Millán de la Cogolla (46), and S. Julián de Samos (44); see above, Table 1.2, and below, Tables 4.2 and 5.2.

21 The documentation from the Astorga cathedral is not included in this analysis. Because of the significant losses that this archive has suffered, a large part of its documentation is preserved only in very late copies. See above, n. 4.

important issues relating to the transmission of its documentation and makes it possible to draw very interesting comparisons between the mainly lay content of this documentation and the group of documents from Otero. San Antolín del Esla's collection includes only 59 documents, which were presumably also transmitted in single-sheet parchments, as were those from Otero, until they were copied into the *Tumbo Legionense*. Thus, my study of the Leonese corpus of dispute records will be based on two collections of mostly ecclesiastical documents—from Sahagún and the León Cathedral—and two collections of mostly lay documents—from Otero de las Dueñas and San Antolín del Esla.

2.1 *Sahagún and the León Cathedral: Two Ecclesiastical Centres*

The two most important institutions in the Leonese region in terms both of their patrimony and their ecclesiastical role were the monastery of Sahagún and the León cathedral, both of which enjoyed royal favour from the time of their founding.[22] They produced two important cartularies at the beginning of the twelfth century in which much of their documentation has been transmitted: the *Becerro Gótico de Sahagún* (1110) and the *Tumbo Legionense* (1124), though they also preserved a significant number of single-sheet parchments. This has made it possible to carry out comparative studies between the two kinds of records, thus gaining insight into the multi-faceted process of compiling the cartularies and the sophistication of both scriptoria.[23] Precisely because of the large number of extant parchments, the collections of these two institutions have been published, both originals and copies, in chronological order; unfortunately, however, the publication of the cartularies themselves, though it has been announced, has yet to appear.[24]

22 According to Andrés Gambra, *Alfonso VI, cancillería, curia e imperio*, vol. 1 *Estudio* (León: Centro de Estudios e Investigación 'San Isidoro', 1997), 106, they were both "institutions with close links to the monarchy and scriptoria with qualified scribes capable of giving these diplomas an appearance consistent with the dignity of their author and the style of the royal chancery, an institution whose development they influenced", despite it being still at an early stage before 1100.

23 José Antonio Fernández Flórez and Marta Herrero de la Fuente, "Libertades de los copistas en la confección de cartularios: el caso del Becerro Gótico de Sahagún," in *Scribi e colofoni: le sottoscrizioni di copisti dalle origini all'avvento della stampa* (*Atti del Seminario di Erice: X Colloquio del Comité international de paléographie latine, 23–28 ottobre 1993*), ed. Emma Condello and Giuseppe De Gregorio (Spoleto: Centro Italiano di Studi sull'alto Medioevo, 1995), 301–324.

24 Herrero de la Fuente, "Cartularios leoneses," 116.

These two institutions—unlike Otero and San Antolín—also do not differ greatly in the ratio of dispute records to the total number of extant documents. The figure is somewhat higher for the León cathedral than for Sahagún (11 per cent compared to 7.7 per cent), though in absolute terms the latter has almost twice as many extant dispute records as the cathedral (80 compared to 49; see above, Table 2.1).

Among the many possible perspectives that might be used to evaluate each collection of dispute records, I have opted here to look at the document formats used in the two scriptoria to record information about disputes and judicial process, and to explore the similarities and differences between them and with the dispute records from the other two lay archives. The goal is not only to understand the relationship between form and content in their varied aspects but also to substantiate the impact that the patronage network of each of these institutions—and therefore their sphere of action—had both on the volume and the nature of the documents that were preserved, as well as on the format in which these were recorded.

In Sahagún's collection, the 'account' format is most prevalent, with nearly thirty records that can be identified as such. The most striking features of these texts, based on a detailed study of the documents, are as follows.[25] This format is the predominant one for recording judicial information throughout the entire period, but it becomes increasingly so in the eleventh century, especially in the final decade. Most records of civil suits (disputes over land, chiefly) in which Sahagún is one of the parties to the dispute, while the other litigant is a layperson of very high social status, are framed as accounts of the dispute settlement process.[26] This is one of the main features that, as we will see below, differentiates both this collection and that of the León cathedral from those at Otero and San Antolín. In this type of record we can see a close connection between the social status of the litigants, the number and the size of the properties in dispute and the forum in which the dispute is settled: the larger the size of the property (*villae*), the higher the status of those litigating with the monastery (counts, aristocrats) and the more exalted the forum

25 I provide a summary here of my conclusions in Isabel Alfonso, "El formato de la información judicial en la Alta Edad Media peninsular," in *Chartes et cartulaires comme instruments de pouvoir. Espagne et Occident chrétien (VIIIe–XIIe siècles)*, ed. Julio Escalona and Helène Sirantoine (Toulouse: Université de Toulouse-Le Mirail, 2013), 191–218.

26 Dated to the eleventh century, only three of them have been identified as criminal cases, one of which was brought before a count, S2 451 (1037); while no mention of the forum is made in the other two, S2 670 (1068) and 725 (1073). All are disputes between private individuals, with no mention of Sahagún. They are very short documents for which we only have copies in the *Becerro Gótico de Sahagún*.

(royal); the smaller properties (plots of land, vineyards) correspond to people of lower status and more varied forums on a smaller scale. In Sahagún there are examples of accounts of dispute cases from the second half of the tenth century, especially the last third,[27] but the largest percentage of these cases were argued in royal assemblies especially during the eleventh century.[28] And lastly, the texts of these accounts, despite differences in style and content, have a similar narrative structure, which I have discussed at length in the study cited above. This narrative quality is common, though not exclusive, to all records of this type, irrespective of their provenance.

In the León cathedral collection of dispute records, accounts (9) are in third place behind judicial transactions (17) and non-judicial transactions (11) for number of documents. Significantly, as in Sahagún, most of these accounts date from the eleventh century, share a marked narrative quality, and are also records of disputes over *villae* between the bishops of León and other aristocrats that were likewise resolved in royal assemblies before Alfonso V (r. 999–1028), Fernando I (r. 1037–1065), and Alfonso VI (r. 1065–1109).[29] However, the narratives of these disputes have something in common that distinguishes them from Sahagún's accounts: the arguments made by the bishops before the kings are based on the claim that the properties in dispute had belonged to the see and that the latter had lost them as a result of different conflictual circumstances, and this is why their restitution is being requested. Thus, the long narrative found in a text dated 1026 tells how Bishop Nuño of León—after discovering from documents in the cathedral archive that the *villa* of Revelle, having belonged to the see of León, had been taken and depopulated by Count Diego Fernández during an earlier rebellion—sues for the *villa* before King Al-

27 S1 159 (958), 276 (974), 277 (974), 295 (978), 356 (998). Of these five accounts, none is a record of a truly criminal case; although the latter two could be interpreted in that way, since they use an accusatory formulation in what seem to be disputes over land. The forums are more varied, and all five records are about disputes over land in which we see tensions around priests' legacies between their relatives and Sahagún. These disputes are heard by assemblies presided over by the king (S1 276, most likely a forgery) or a count.

28 S2 401 (1013), 514 (1048), 588 (1057), 632 (1063) and 663 (1067), S3 727 (1073), 786 [1080], 867 (1090), 881 (1091), 900 (1092), 901 (1093), 919 (1094) and 993 (1096). Among the civil cases, only six were fought in non-royal forums: one before a court held by an aristocratic family in its proprietary monastery, S2 424 (1029); two before a count, S3 977 (1096) and 1015 (1097); and three before courts that were possibly held by lords, S3 853 (1089), 884 (1091) and 1036 (1099). These are all disputes over land, but, except for the first, they are between people of lower status than is the case in disputes brought before royal assemblies, and they involve properties that are also of lesser importance (plots of land instead of *villae*, for example).

29 CL3 829 (1026), CL4 1007 (1043), 1084 and 1085 (1052), 1183 (1072), 1244 (1089), 1279 (1093).

fonso v, his counts, and his whole household, in the city of Cea. The other party to the suit restored the *villa* to the cathedral in a solemn ceremony in accordance with a negotiated settlement.[30]

We find a more explicit emphasis on the recovery and reconstruction of the see's patrimony during tumultuous times in a text, dated 1043, about Bishop Cipriano's claim to the *villa* of Religos and all the rights over its inhabitants, presented to King Fernando I. It contains the strongest possible argument for a policy of royal restitution, since it reports that the king, who was accompanied by Queen Sancha, said "better is he who restores than he who builds" (*intelleximus quia melius est qui restaurat quam qui hedificat*) to legitimize the restitution he ordered after having made inquiries that showed the see's rights over the *villa*.[31] The judicial proceedings are barely touched upon in this diploma because the focus seems to be mostly to trace out the king's political discourse, since at the same time that he declares support for the see of León, he publicly affirms and legitimizes his own power.[32] There is no doubt that this support of the king and his entourage for the reconstitution of the bishopric's patrimony also has significant political connotations for the participants in such 'political-judicial' ceremonies as royal assemblies, since this is where the ties that bind them together are made visible and confirmed.[33]

Documents from the León cathedral make repeated reference to the Leonese bishops turning to the king's justice, and this not only in accounts but also in other kinds of dispute records. For example, Bishop Froilán, in an important charter of gift to the cathedral, explains—referring to information about a much earlier period—that the properties being transferred had been taken from Bishop Servando by a count, and the former had been able to recover them by presenting a claim to King Vermudo II (r. 985–999) and his council.[34] Simil-

30 CL3 829.

31 CL4 1007. The responses of the bishop's dependents in this *villa* are documented in CL4 899 (1032).

32 For a different interpretation of this discourse, see Pascual Martínez Sopena, "Aristocracia, monacato y reformas en los siglos XI y XII," in *El monacato en los reinos de León y Castilla (siglos VII–XIII)* (León: Fundación Sánchez-Albornoz, 2007), 67–99, at 81–82.

33 On legitimation practices in these assemblies, see Isabel Alfonso, "Judicial rhetoric and political legitimation in medieval León-Castile," in *Building Legitimacy: Political Discourses and Forms of Legitimation in Medieval Societies*, ed. Isabel Alfonso, Julio Escalona, and Hugh Kennedy (Leiden: Brill, 2004), 51–87.

34 CL3 629 (1002), an example of a non-judicial transaction. But already back in 985 (CL2 508), King Vermudo II had donated to Bishop Sabarico of León several *villae* located in the Tierra de Campos, after acknowledging—as recorded in "writings and *agnitiones*"—that they belonged to the see of León through royal grant and that, as the bishop had com-

arly, the Curueño castle is restored to the see of León by Alfonso v in a solemn assembly in Sahagún in 1012, though the record leaves out any reference to judicial court process. The king simply considers the bishop's claims, and by doing so affirms his own authority and ability to act in this capacity.[35] Clearly, the Leonese bishops seem to have been interested in underlining the patronage they received from the king by creating long narratives to illustrate how they encouraged this patronage. The most telling text in this regard is perhaps the one that was copied on the opening folios of the *Tumbo Legionense*. This is an extensive narrative by Bishop Pelayo, dated 1073, in which he recounts his own efforts to recover episcopal properties from the time he acceded to his post.[36] Among its acquisitions, he recalls, in what can be understood as an incidental allusion to King Alfonso vi's explicit protection, was the church of San Martín de la Fuente, which had been unjustly appropriated in Fernando I's time and returned by his successor, Alfonso, who acknowledged that it belonged legitimately to the cathedral.[37]

It would seem that under Alfonso vi, royal support for the bishopric of León increased. This impression is perhaps due to the larger number of extant documents. The nature of these documents certainly seems to have been more formalized. It is worth pausing to consider two other documents, in addition to the accounts, connected to Alfonso vi that have been described as orders or statutes. A document from 1072 attempts to impose restrictions on the actions of *saiones* in homicide cases where the perpetrator is unknown, by limiting collective liability and curbing the abuses associated with the collection of fines. It seems justified to deduce that this measure was taken in response to com-

plained, they had been violently appropriated during a rebellion by Count Gómez Díaz and other men. This is undoubtedly an important political act that, on the one hand, establishes the power of the cathedral and its bishop but, on the other, constitutes an affirmation of royal power, which delegitimizes its opponents, branding them as usurpers and "people without God".

35 CL3 707. The mid-tenth-century charter of gift is extant by which King Ordoño III (r. 951–956) donated this castle to Bishop Gonzalo, CL2 300 (956).

36 CL4 1190 = *Tumbo Legionense*, fols. 9v–12r: Bishop Pelayo of León convened King Alfonso vi, his sisters, and the province's other bishops and abbots to the consecration of the see. Together with many other important figures and churchmen, they signed the document. In this text, the bishop recounts his life story and the difficulties endured by the church now being restored, indicating its possessions and how it acquired or recovered them. Another indirect allusion to Alfonso vi restoring properties to the see which had been lost during his father's reign can be found in CL4 1191 (1073).

37 *conuocaui inprimis regem domnum Adefonsum, cuius patrocinio post Deum uiuimus et quo iuuante operatus sum et adquisiui hec omnia que iam dixi*, CL4 1190.

plaints around these issues.[38] The second document, a 1089 decree, is explicitly tied to the resolution of a suit brought by Bishop Pedro of León against none other than Infanta Urraca, the king's powerful sister, whom he accuses of appropriating tenants and properties belonging to the cathedral. A settlement is reached in a solemn ceremony in a royal curia at Villalpando and a general resolution is issued for the entire kingdom that prohibits the transfer of estates and men among different kinds of lordship with the declared objective of preventing the kind of conflict created by these transfers.[39]

The León cathedral's judicial narratives emphatically demonstrate, in a way unlike what we see in Sahagún, its bishops' contentiousness in defending themselves against what they characterize as attacks by often unidentified antagonists on their patrimony and their lordly power during tumultuous times. It also demonstrates the overwhelming royal support they enjoyed.[40]

2.2 *The Lay Collections of Otero de las Dueñas and San Antolín del Esla*

Let us now turn to two monastic institutions whose archives, in contrast with those of Sahagún and the León cathedral, contained mainly the family records of their lay patrons. Otero de las Dueñas, a Cistercian convent founded in the thirteenth century, preserved the archives of counts Fruela Muñoz and Pedro Flaínez, eleventh-century ancestors of its founder, who were the main recipients of most of the extant documents. But the Otero collection also preserves the memory of some of the counts' ancestors, who received many documents going back to the 980s: Flaín Muñoz and Justa, the parents of Pedro Flaínez; and Fruela Vímaraz and Adosinda, the maternal grandparents of Fruela Muñoz, with fewer records.[41] The uniqueness of this collection, which comprises more

38 CL4 1183 = *Tumbo Legionense*, fols. 72ᵛ–73ʳ. It should be recalled that, with this decree, Alfonso VI endorsed the immunity that his father, Fernando I, had granted in 1047 to the see from the interference of royal *saiones* in its *villae* and properties in cases of homicide and others, CL4 1048.

39 CL4 1244. For detailed commentary on this document, see Carlos Estepa Díez, "Formación y consolidación del feudalismo en Castilla y León," in *En torno al feudalismo hispánico. I Congreso de Estudios Medievales* (Ávila: Fundación Sánchez Albornoz, 1989), 157–256, at 206–207.

40 These kinds of justifications are thus much earlier than the chaotic situation that followed the death of Alfonso VI, a situation that Fernández Catón attributes these grievances to, CL5, p. xiv.

41 One of the lay dossiers of documents identified at Sahagún by Kosto, "*Sicut mos esse solet*," 276–280, belonged to Muño Flaínez and Froileba, the grandparents of Pedro Flaínez. The dossier supposedly came to this monastery with the donation made by their daughter Jimena in 985 (S1 328). This illustrates one of the detours in the transmission that I mentioned earlier in connection to the misleading notion of 'comital archive'.

than 300 diplomas from before 1100, lies largely in the fact that it has come down to us on small pieces of parchment, many of which contain more than one record and in some of which both sides of the skin is used for writing.[42]

The Benedictine monastery of San Antolín is believed to be the family archive of its founder, Countess Sancha Muñoz, who ceded both monastery and archive to the León cathedral in 1040. It too contains the records of some of its founder's relatives. This countess, a half-sister on her father's side of Count Fruela Muñoz, also preserved diplomas from common ancestors, not only from her paternal grandparents, Froila Vigilaz and Jimena, but also from her father, Munio Fernández. The archive contains a small group of only 60 documents dating from 937 up to the end of the eleventh century that supposedly must have also been passed down as single-sheet parchments that remained in the see's archive starting from the unknown date when they were added up until they were copied as a block into the *Tumbo Legionense* at the beginning of the twelfth century.[43] However, my guess is that the transmission of these documents was more complicated than this suggests, which raises some issues that are worth exploring.[44]

In both Otero and San Antolín the percentages of dispute records are among the highest in the region, exceeding 30 per cent,[45] and in the case of Otero the raw number of these records (95) is also the highest. But the most striking contrast has to do with document formats. Compared to the large number of accounts at Sahagún and the León cathedral archives, in Otero and San Antolín most judicial information has been preserved in the form of judicial transactions (almost 70 in Otero and 11 in San Antolín).[46] This is true for the entire period, though there is a notable increase in the first third of the eleventh century. These transactions have the same format as charters of gift or sale of landed property.[47] They benefit political authorities who only occasionally

42 These have been studied by José Manuel Ruiz Asencio, "Notas sobre el trabajo de los notarios leoneses en los siglos X–XII," in *Orígenes de las lenguas romances en el reino de León, siglos IX–XII* (León: Centro de Estudios e Investigación 'San Isidoro', 2004), 87–117, at 102–104.

43 On this transmission, see Gregorio Del Ser, "Un monasterio benedictino leonés olvidado: San Antolín," in *Semana de Historia del monacato cántabro-astur-leonés* (Oviedo: Monasterio de San Pelayo, 1982), 175–194.

44 On the problems concerning this transmission, see below.

45 Only the monastery of Guimarães in Portugal has a higher percentage (40.9 per cent).

46 In Otero there are barely any non-judicial transactions (4) and both the accounts (6) and formal commitments (5) are rare. In San Antolín non-judicial transactions (5) and accounts (2) have a greater importance, in terms of percentages, and there are records of formal commitments (2) as well.

47 On donations presented as sales, see Wendy Davies, *Acts of giving. Individual, Community*

appear to wield judicial power, and they are issued in response to different felonious acts—that is, they are mainly records of criminal cases. The texts of these transactions vary widely in their content and their length, and the information they contain is highly fragmented and uneven. Many are documents without any specific judicial information but that have expressions summarizing the conflict to which they allude, though they may not report on court proceedings, while others seem to be direct settlements or extrajudicial agreements. In the vast majority, however, the judicial nature of the transaction is very clear,[48] to the point that these documents share some of the formal features of the accounts of dispute cases.[49] The combination of procedural details that appear in these texts allows us to deduce that each text records different parts of the judicial process, but it is not easy to venture hypotheses about the reasons for these differences. What is clear is that the fact that formularies existed did not mean that they were followed to the letter. These texts convey different narratives about resolution practices without ever attempting to reproduce the whole judicial proceedings that we assume took place. However, scribes do use terms and phrases that refer to the social and judicial procedures for resolving disputes, thus showing a clear understanding of their audiences and of the purposes for which these documents were written. Apparently, in addition to recording the transfer of property, it was equally important to publicize the reasons for the transfer.[50]

Let us take a closer look at the judicial dimension of these transactions in each of the two collections. At Otero, beginning in 987 and up until the end of the century, the main beneficiaries are Flaín Muñoz and his wife, Justa,[51] the parents of Pedro Flaínez, and to a lesser extent Fruela Vímaraz and Adosinda,[52] the maternal grandparents of Fruela Muñoz. At San Antolín there are extant transactions dating from 963 that benefit the paternal grandparents of Fruela Muñoz and his half-sister Sancha, Froila Vigilaz and Jimena, and especially

and the Church in Tenth Century Spain (Oxford: Oxford University Press, 2007), 156–160 and 218–219.

48 Examples of transactions that report in detail on the court proceedings that led to the transaction settlement: OD 31 (991), 109 (1017), 163 (1022), 168 (1024), 177 (1027), 193 (1030), 195 (1030). It is true that, because the information recorded in accounts (six cases in Otero and two in San Antolín) is more detailed, it becomes essential for looking into judicial process.

49 E.g., OD 177 (1027), 256 (1061), 221 (1036).

50 On the timing of these texts' writing, see Wendy Davies *Windows on Justice in Northern Iberia, 800–1000* (Abingdon: Routledge, 2016), chs. 2–5, and esp. pp. 147–149.

51 OD 27 (987), 31 (991), 32 and 33 (992), 34 (993), 44 (998), 49 (1000).

52 OD 37 (994), 40 and 41 (995).

those that their father, Munio Fernández, received beginning in 994 and well into the eleventh century.[53]

These are mainly criminal cases for different crimes that appear to have been resolved in local forums (before judges and *saiones*) where the accused are obliged to swear an oath, and sometimes to reinforce it by undergoing an ordeal, or else to acknowledge their guilt and to accept the penalties established by law. These penalties were routinely reduced through the mediation of *boni homines* and settled through the transfer of lands to the aristocrats mentioned above, whose authority is not justified in the document; rather, it is simply assumed. I will not go into the debate about whether the nature of this power to mete out justice is inherited or delegated, since I doubt it is relevant for our purposes here.[54] Suffice it to say that by the final decades of the tenth century, comital authority and patronage seem to be well established, though this did not do away with local forums for resolving conflicts.[55] The litigants appeal to the "benefit" of a count's power so that their interests (their "truth") are recognized in the disputes they are involved in.[56] In accordance, they accept not only the count's judicial decision, but also his right to derive a significant amount of property from his judicial powers. The judicial information contained in some of these texts foreshadows the kind of details that can be found, in more concise form, in later texts.

It is in the first third of the eleventh century that the largest number of judicial transactions are documented, benefitting, particularly, two of the most important figures of the Leonese aristocracy, Pedro Flaínez and Fruela Muñoz, who were descendants of the aforementioned figures and related to each other through the marriage of their children.[57] The political circumstances of these

53 One referring to Froila Vigilaz: CL2 360 (963), and five to Munio Fernández: CL3 561 (994), 578 (997), 624 (1002), 632 (1003), 671 (1008); moreover, there are three non-judicial records that refer to Munio Fernández: CL3 596 (1000), 605 (1001), 630 (1003), as well as one formal commitment: CL3 694 (1011).

54 In the case of the monastery of Guimarães, André Marques suggests the possible overlapping of both roles, proprietary and judicial, in some cases shared between the monastery and the counts who are its patrons.

55 This can be seen in a civil suit between private individuals that was resolved *in colacione de nostros homines*, OD 4 (946). On the variety of functions performed by local assemblies, see Álvaro Carvajal Castro, "Local meetings and meeting places in early medieval León," *Early Medieval Europe* 25, no. 2 (2017), 186–207.

56 OD 27 (987): *Et damus uobis ipsa ratione in beneficia que mandedis et deatis mici ueridatem cum meos intentores que abeo, pro illo kanado uel ereditatem de Ermegildo, presbiter, unde nobis iscripto fecit Ermegildo*. This is an argument that we will find later only in the texts related to Count Fruela Muñoz.

57 For Pedro Flaínez, who seems to have inherited the position of his father, Flaín Muñoz,

two counts, who dominated two areas near the Leonese mountains, are well known and seem very similar to each other, both in their proximity to the monarchy and the overlap of their power with the local networks.[58] This group of documents, which does not differ substantially from the documents of their predecessors, also confirms the similarities between their powers, both in the way these counts administered justice and in the social, non-aristocratic contexts in which this took place. There are also similarities in the kinds of crimes that were tried and the penalties imposed, the normative references that were invoked, in the fact that not only judges and *saiones* but also *asertores* and guarantors were present, as well as in the collective rituals and methods of mediation and their consequences.

The large size of the judicial corpus from Otero concerning the two counts makes it possible to study it from different perspectives, some of which have already been taken by other scholars.[59] In order to suggest some questions that may help us deepen our knowledge of the social fabric in which the tensions and conflicts documented in this corpus were generated and of the relationship between this social context and the ways the counts intervened to resolve conflicts, what I propose to do in what follows is to combine a couple of variables: the types of crimes and the role played by the count who benefits from the penalties imposed for those crimes. In order to do this, it will be useful to

---

without any break in continuity, there are 27 extant texts with judicial information spanning the period 1001–1048, 22 of which are judicial transactions in his favour. Only one case is recorded as an account, a text which in the customary narrative style elaborates on the fragmentary information found in transactions, OD 116 (1019). There are two non-judicial transactions that nonetheless contain important information in that regard: OD 124 (1019) and 188 (1029); and two formal commitments issued in the name of individuals that stood as sureties for the count: OD 189 and 190 (1029). For Fruela Muñoz, whose position cannot be considered to be inherited, there are 31 texts documented from between 1017 and 1044, all of which are judicial transactions except three important accounts each of which brings together several previous records: OD 147, 150 and 151 (all dated 1022); and a formal commitment: OD 159 (1022). In the second half of the eleventh century there are only nine documents with judicial information (compared to the 69 from the first half), and in them Fernando Flaínez, Pedro Flaínez's brother, and his son Diego Petriz (who will go on to marry María Froilaz, Fruela Muñoz's daughter) start to show up as beneficiaries of the same type of transactions.

58 On the development of royal power in this area in connection to the building up of these counts' domains, see Carvajal Castro, *Bajo la máscara*, 165–206.

59 The way comital justice worked has been explained in detail by Pascual Martínez Sopena, "La justicia en la época asturleonesa: entre el *liber* y los mediadores sociales," in *El Lugar del Campesino. En torno a la obra de Reyna Pastor*, ed. Ana Rodríguez (Valencia: Universidad de Valencia, 2007), 239–260. For an exhaustive study of justice in northern Iberia before the year 1000, see Davies, *Windows on Justice*.

distinguish between (1) disputes that arise between and affect only private individuals (cases that involve sexual conduct, theft, assault, appropriation) and (2) those in which the counts are the 'victims' of the crimes committed against their authority and/or affecting their estates (especially disputes related to seigneurial claims).

As for disputes between private individuals, there are about ten cases related to infractions of a sexual nature,[60] and among them relations between close family members—which are explicitly declared to be illegal—are most frequently punished.[61] But these documents also clarify conflicts in which people living in close proximity are involved, or family groups from the same vicinity.[62] Those responsible for bearing the punishment are usually the men or women charged, but in some cases the responsibility falls on the family group, in resolutions that are frequently mediated by *boni homines* or whose penalties are mitigated directly through the count's mercy.[63]

Theft and/or assault, with greater or lesser violence, give rise to a similar number of judicial transactions as sexual infractions.[64] These are generally crimes committed by and against private individuals[65] and also manifest themselves as conflicts between people who live in close proximity, such as injuries done to a neighbour[66] or petty theft of animals and/or money, which, nonetheless, seem to lead at times to the extreme act of homicide.[67] In these cases as

60 In charters of gift to Pedro Flaínez: OD 71 (1006), 99 (1014), 125 (1020), 187 (1028); to Fruela Muñoz: OD 133 (1021), 163, 166, 168 (all dated 1024), 177 (1027).

61 E.g., a woman acknowledged having committed the crime of adultery "without law" (*que facea adulterio sine lege*) with her sister's husband, OD71 (1006); in another case, the adulterer confesses in a public assembly before the count's *vicarius* and a *salo* that he abandoned his wife (to whom he had given no morning gift) and left with his brother's wife with whom he *fecit conbosco que lex non manda*, OD 125 (1020); a man confesses to having gotten his first cousin pregnant, OD 177 (1027); another to having impregnated his child's godmother, OD 166 (1024).

62 E.g., a man confesses to adultery with another man's wife, OD 187 (1028); another to having left his wife and taken another's daughter, OD 133 (1021).

63 For example, the mediation of *boni homines* enabled in one case a daughter of one of the litigants to be set free from prison for having relations with a monk, and in another case mentioned above vouched for a man accused of having gotten his child's godmother pregnant, OD 99 (1014) and 166 (1024); the count's mercy kept a woman from being whipped, as she would have had the law been enforced, in exchange for a gift of a land made by her brother and mother to Fruela Muñoz, OD 177 (1027).

64 In charters of gift to Pedro Flaínez: OD 75, 76 (both dated 1008), 93 (1013), 113 (1018); to Fruela Muñoz: OD 119, 120 (both dated 1019), 132 (1021), 147 (1022), 193 (1030).

65 That is why we read of *intentione per furto* between two individuals, OD 120 (1019).

66 OD 75, 76 (both dated 1008), 193 (1030).

67 OD 93 (1013), 114 (1018).

well, those responsible for paying the penalty are either the guilty party (always men) or their parents or relations,[68] which they discharge with land. Again, there is often mediation by *boni homines*[69] or the count will intervene on the side of leniency.[70]

These crimes generated transactions that often record fines being handed over directly to the count, who appears as the simple receiver of the fine, while there is no record of a trial.[71] In other cases, however, judges and *saiones* seem to act with relative autonomy to resolve these matters in local assemblies. They rule on what happened and set the fines,[72] often with the mediation of *boni homines*, as we have seen, who attempt to reduce the fine and make it payable in land. It is in these assemblies, sometimes in the presence of the count's *vicarius*,[73] that the guilty confess, that is, acknowledge that the crime was committed,[74] and sureties pledge to pay the fines.[75]

According to the extant texts, these collective decisions became effective immediately. However, there are signs that there were short circuits between the court proceedings and the execution of the sentence that seem to have allowed time for the parties to resolve matters without fulfilling the penalties they had incurred. In these cases, it is not hard to see the facts leading to the accusation as part of more-prolonged conflicts and feuds.[76]

The scarcity of information about the hidden conflicts behind these disputes is worth highlighting, precisely because too often these conflicts are overlooked. In addition to pointing out the frequency, in sociological terms,

68 OD 75, 76 (both dated 1008), 193 (1030).

69 OD 119 (1019), 132 (1021).

70 OD 120, 123 (both dated 1019), 158 (1022), 195 (1030–1035).

71 OD 71 (1006), 133 (1021), 166 (1024), 187 (1028).

72 OD 163 (1024).

73 There is only one case heard by Fruela Muñoz himself and his judges, after the defendants had been brought in by his *saio*: the aforementioned case of a woman who had become pregnant by her cousin, described in a text that makes a point of underlining Fruela's mercy in heeding the pleas for pardon in order to keep the woman from being whipped, as the law required, OD 177 (1027).

74 OD 125 (1020).

75 OD 99 (1014).

76 This is how we can understand the concealment of sentence by two men, Vicente and Fredino, who were fined 100 *sueldos*, to be paid by halves, as a result of a fight between them that led to injuries, recorded in two documents: OD 75 and 76 (both dated 1008). Another example is the slanderous accusation of adultery out of enmity, narrated in OD 168 (1024): *et leuantarunt crimine super Aurelio, que erat mesco con mulier de Arkaio* [...] *aposuerunt super illo suo enemigos.*

of these crimes, as Pascual Martínez Sopena does, or ascribing them to a certain "sexual proclivity" by their authors, as José María Mínguez suggests,[77] we should give some thought to how the recourse to courts and the formalization of accusations in a judicial context might have been a way to publicly resolve more-prolonged conflicts underlying even minor issues.[78] This line of inquiry seems essential for deepening our understanding of the tensions and conflicts running through these highly differentiated local societies. But the common feature of this group of crimes is that, unlike with the group discussed next, in none of these cases is the comital authority a party to the suit.

As for crimes that did directly affect the counts, the majority of which are infractions involving seigneurial rights, there is an important fact that has not been duly appreciated perhaps because crimes of a violent or sexual nature tend to be more colourful. This is the fact that the number of crimes affecting the authorities exceeds those involving only private individuals.[79] These crimes can be divided into two groups: (a) fleeing from the counts' lordship and (b) failure to meet seigneurial obligations.

Count Pedro Flaínez first appears, significantly, in a document dated 1001 which does not mention a trial but refers to how, after a local group had broken a commitment to not leave Valdoré (the centre of Pedro Flaínez's domains),

---

77 Martínez Sopena, "Justicia," 253; José María Mínguez, "Justicia y poder en el marco de la feudalización de la sociedad leonesa," in *La giustizia nell'alto medioevo (secoli IX–XI)*, Settimane di studio del CISAM 44 (Spoleto: CISAM, 1997), 1:491–546, at 531. On the punishment of sexual offences and the associated mechanisms of social control, see Judith M. Bennet, "Writing fornication: medieval leyrwite and its historians: The Prothero Lecture," *Transactions of the Royal Historical Society*, Sixth Series, 13 (2003), 131–162; on the regulation of sexual behaviour, see Henry Ansgar Kelly, "Law and Nonmarital Sex in the Middle Ages," in *Conflict in Medieval Europe: Changing Perspectives on Society and Culture*, ed. Warren C. Brown and Piotr Góreck (Hampshire: Ashgate, 2003), 175–194.

78 The way that these texts describe the boundaries and the provenance of the land donated reflects a dense social fabric that illuminates the tensions that could arise as well as the kind of assistance that was requested from comital authorities, e.g. OD 178 (1027). On the judicial formalization of different sorts of social conflicts, see the classic studies by Simon Roberts, *Order and Dispute: An Introduction to Legal Anthropology* (Oxford: Martin Robertson, 1979), and John Comaroff and Simon Roberts, *Rules and Processes: The Cultural Logic of Dispute in an African Context* (Chicago: Chicago University Press, 1986).

79 Involving Pedro Flaínez: OD 56 (1001), 70 (1006), 116, 121 (both dated 1019), 128 (1020), 136 (1021), 149, 154, 155 (all dated 1019), 174 (1025), 227 (1039), 245 (1048). Involving Fruela Muñoz: OD 109 (1017), 147, 148, 150, 151, 159 (all dated 1022), and documents that do not mention any crime but nonetheless stress the nature of the count's patronage: OD 122, 123, 142, 158 (all dated 1019), 178 (1027), 192 (1030), 198 (1032).

nor to attach themselves to another lord, the sureties for that commitment had to answer for its violation.[80] Another, similar diploma more articulately explains that these actions constituted a breach of loyalty and, ultimately, a betrayal of the lord.[81] These two texts illustrate a widespread recording practice that established penalties for non-compliance with this kind of commitment, which sometimes even had to be ratified.[82] Precisely, the only record in account format among Pedro Flaínez's documents stipulated a punishment for anyone who pledged himself to another lord, and in this case the infringement was accompanied by the theft of livestock.[83] The prohibition against buying the lands of those who changed lordship undoubtedly helped to tighten the lord's control over his dependents.[84]

A lord's dependents must not only remain under his power but also fulfil the obligations that such a power requires. The fines for failure to fulfil these obligations are rendered as transactions benefitting the lord. We have documentation of fines, especially benefitting Pedro Flaínez, that show the difficulties the lords faced and the strategies they employed in exercising their power. The accused in some cases confess to having encroached on the lord's domains,[85] moved boundary markers, or broken ground illegally in the forest;[86] elsewhere, they have to answer for damage done to *villae* held in lease;[87] and in other more-

80 OD 56 (1001).

81 OD 154 (1022): *pro que exiuimus de uestro mandato et perflamamus nos ad altero dono et iuramus nos et mentimus et conpresestes nos infideles*. The accused were forced to hand over the livestock that had been taken from them as collateral.

82 There are abundant extant examples in the Leonese corpus of formal commitments. Less frequent is any evidence of their ratification, hence the interest in the text that records how Belito Gotínez and Munio Enéquez appear before two of Fruela Muñoz's *vicarii* in order to acknowledge the loyalty commitment that the former had made to the count when he came from Asturias, at which time Munio had guaranteed that Belito would have Fruela alone as his lord., In light of Belito's renewed attempts to flee from Fruela's lordship, as recorded in the text, Munio had to vouch for the commitment again by pledging 100 *sueldos*, OD 159 (1022).

83 OD 116 (1019): [...] *comodo sic teniente Pedru Flainiz mandacione de dado de reie domno Adefonso, ic in Lorma, in suo iure, cum ganado et omines quantum in sua nodicia resona, si se leuabit Zidi, gognomento Andrias, per uiuolencia e derubit ipsa mandacione et sakabit inde ganado de iure de Pedru Flainiz, quantum in nodicia ressona, et adflamauise Zidi ad alia podestade.*

84 OD 70 (1006). In this case, the transaction seems to be payment for the illegal purchase of land from people who left Pedro Flaínez's *mandatione*.

85 OD 121 (1019): *pro que disrupit eo Braolio contestos domnigos et grebantauit limites uerdes, gum aqua rapia* [...] *Et deuinit inde atiua, gum omnibus bonis, et dedit in iudicatu ipsa terra*; similar to OD 155 (1022): *pro que fui contestos domicos et cele suos terragos et sua macana.*

86 OD 149 (1022).

87 OD 128 (1020): *pro ipsa uilla de Aceueto que obemus adconmendata* [...] *et danabimus kasas*

serious situations, they have to answer for the mismanagement of territories under their charge, as in the case of the fraud in collecting judicial fines in several jurisdictional districts (*mandationes*).[88] There are only three documents recording crimes against Fruela Muñoz's lordly power, for theft in his vineyards, theft of his grains, and, more importantly, for the kidnapping of one of his serfs, who 'chooses' to remain with her captor, in a case that reflects how the social fabric was woven together with threads and relationships that transcended the normative frame of the domanial and seigneurial lordship.[89] As with the disputes between private individuals, the resolution of these latter cases takes place in local assemblies and/or before the count's *vicarii*, as if, in an attempt to gain legitimacy, the count's authority adhered to the local procedures for conflict resolution. Here, too, we see a preponderance of solutions explicitly negotiated through the mediation of *boni homines*.

Unquestionably, what we see in this cache of transactions preserved in Otero's collection is, on the one hand, a continuation of judicial practices in punishing crimes among private individuals, and on the other, a clear up-tick in crimes relating to seigneurial rights, a reflection of the increasing power of figures such as Pedro Flaínez and Fruela Muñoz in this area of the Esla basin. However, it should be noted that the deployment of patronage as judicial aid, which Martínez Sopena rightly sees as a means for developing the special kind of lordship that will become the *behetrías* (communities who had the right to choose their lord), involved a very different kind of intervention on the part of the counts in judicial disputes.[90] The political figure of Fruela Muñoz, the

---

et oritos et pane et introsigo, adpreciato in CC solidos argenteos; OD 245 (1048): *Et dauit ego Manœl ipsa ereditate a uobis Petrum Flainizi et uxor uestra Bronildi porque abuit adzomenda uestra ullla, cum pane et uino, et dannauit, inde, per niglentia in apreziatura de CC arienzios ariento solidos*, in this case a debt for homicide was added.

88 OD 136 (1021): *quomodo si abuit eo Frenando mandationes adconmendatas, de uobis Petru Flainizi, Curonio et Lorma et Fereras, pro inde recare et uestros iudicatos sagare. Si fecit eo Fredenando Braolizi de ipsos iudicatos menos ad uobis Petru Flainizi, boues et uacas et ariento et lencius, in pretio de CCC solidos*; OD 174 (1025): *pro que abuit eo Cidi uestras kausas adconmendatas et subcelauit uestras terras et uestros iudicatos*. In the first case a certain reciprocity in the agreement might suggest a strategy on the part of the count to keep the accused within his sphere of influence.

89 OD 109 (1017), 147–148, 150–151 (all dated 1022). The fact that the last two documents are preserved along with a text showing that the agreement reached in trial had been fulfilled (in the first, on separate parchments, and in the other, on the same parchment) is interesting for the light it sheds on questions about how judicial process was recorded in writing. Another, similar case of two related texts being written on the same parchment involves a confession and a charter of gift to Count Pedro Flaínez: OD 125 (1020).

90 Martínez Sopena, "Justicia," 260. Out of the extensive bibliography on *behetrías*, see

only one documented for this kind of intervention, is not the authority who receives the 'fines' or the authority who judges; rather, he takes part in the dispute, supporting one of the parties, and the donations made to him constitute recompense for this support. And even though he is not a party to the suit in any of these cases, his patronage is invoked in several situations in which seeking out his protection or *benefactoria* is a way of taking him on as patron and proclaiming oneself to be his client.[91] We have seen the important role he plays as a 'helper' in feuds,[92] which points to factional dynamics in local conflicts that are not usually acknowledged.[93] In any case, the increase in seigneurial rule in these areas seems beyond doubt. The documentation from San Antolín actually provides evidence along these lines that should be noted, however briefly.

The main authority represented in the San Antolín documentation, after Munio Fernández, to whom numerous documents refer,[94] is his daughter, Countess Sancha. As the founder of the monastery, she seems to have been the one who controlled the family archive, which included records pertaining to her three husbands. These were, first, Count Pedro Fernández, a member of the Flaínez family who, like them, was closely linked to the monarchy, then Count Pedro Muñoz, and finally, Rodrigo Galíndez.

In addition to the similarities mentioned above between the judicial transactions received by the lay patrons of San Antolín and those preserved in the Otero archive, the clearer evidence of the accretion of seigneurial rule and the difficulties in imposing it[95] would by itself justify a detailed commentary on San Antolín's documents. But together with these, there are further reasons for including this collection in this overview of Leonese dispute records.

Cristina Jular Pérez-Alfaro and Carlos Estepa Díez, eds., *Land, Power and Society in Medieval Castile. A Study of the Behetría Lordship* (Turnhout: Brepols, 2009).

91 On legal disputes as a form of political struggle, see Isabel Alfonso, "Resolución de disputas y prácticas judiciales en el Burgos medieval," in *III Jornadas Burgalesas de Historia. Burgos en la Plena Edad Media* (Burgos: Asociación Provincial de Libreros de Burgos, 1994), 211–243; regarding aid or patronage and the rhetoric of 'beneficence', see Isabel Alfonso, "Conflict in the Behetrías," in *Land, Power and Society*, ed. Jular Pérez-Alfaro and Estepa Díez, 275–316.

92 As in the case mentioned above of a false accusation of adultery resulting from a feud: *Pro que ⟨fuit⟩ Froila Moniz suo adiutatore et ahallaçabit ibso Aurelio de ibsa crimine sano*, OD 168 (1024).

93 For an example of what seems to be a resolution of a local war, because there are groups battling each other and a division of loyalties, see OD 180 (1027).

94 Munio Fernández appears in nine extant dispute records dated between 994 and 1011; see details above, n. 53.

95 CL3 851, 856 (both dated 1029); CL4 906 (1032), 1026 (1045).

These reasons have to do with the incorporation of San Antolín into the León cathedral, the transmission of its documents in the *Tumbo Legionense*, and the objectives and strategies involved in these two processes. In what follows, I will merely sketch out these issues in the hope of encouraging further research on them.

Even though it lacks the customary epigraph identifying the documentation from other monasteries included in León's cartulary, the group of documents attributed to San Antolín constitutes one of the blocks in the *Tumbo Legionense*. Chronologically, it spans the period from the year 937 up to the end of the eleventh century.[96] But in the *Tumbo*, where it occupies folios 176^{v}–198^{v}, the documents are not presented in chronological order. They begin with the splendid donation that Sancha and her third husband, Rodrigo Galíndez, made to San Antolín in 1038,[97] followed by two donations made in 1040, one by Countess Sancha to the León Cathedral and the other by her nephew Nuño Petriz to the monastery itself. These two charters of gift are closely connected to the two diplomas copied next, one dated 1043 and the other 1067.[98] These concern two lawsuits over Cimanes, the only *villa* that appears both in the aunt's donation to the cathedral and in the nephew's donation to San Antolín. The order in which these five documents were copied at the beginning of the San Antolín block in the *Tumbo* raises several questions about who was responsible for choosing this order. The answers to these questions can ultimately be sought only in the context in which the cathedral cartulary was produced and the features of the materials that were used to produce it.[99]

It has been suggested that the production of this cartulary, which was completed in 1124 by Juan Pérez, Bishop Diego's notary, seems to stem from the formal division of the see's patrimony between the bishop and the cathedral chapter.[100] In order to distribute the assets, a careful inventory of the different

96 The belief that this is above all a family archive is supported by the fact that the monastery is mentioned in only four documents, which were published by Del Ser, "Un monasterio," 175–194.

97 CL4 970 = *Tumbo Legionense*, fols. 176^{v}–178^{r} (1038).

98 CL4 992 = *Tumbo Legionense*, fols. 178^{v}–179^{r} (1 August 1040), 993 = fols. 179^{r-v} (12 November 1040), 1006 = fols. 179^{v}–180^{v} (1043), 1151 = fols. 181^{r}–182^{r} (1067).

99 On the role of cartularies as vehicles for preserving both the documents copied in them and the archives from which their sources came, as well as other collections, see the illuminating study by Julio Escalona, "Cartularios, memoria y discurso en la Castilla medieval," in *La memoria del poder, el poder de la memoria*, ed. Esther López Ojeda (Logroño: Instituto de Estudios Riojanos, 2017), 163–203.

100 José Antonio Fernández Flórez, "La huella de los copistas en los cartularios leoneses," in *Orígenes de las lenguas romances* (León: Centro de Estudios e Investigación 'San Isidoro', 2004), 159–227, at 172; Herrero de la Fuente, "Cartularios leoneses," 131–143.

monasteries that had been incorporated into the cathedral would have been taken. According to this hypothesis, this task must have been made easier by the fact that the records belonging to all of the monasteries had been brought together in the same archive, though the different collections were kept separated from each other, perhaps in different boxes. This physical separation is believed to be reflected in the organization of the *Tumbo* itself, in which the documents were grouped by monastery. Nonetheless, if we assume that the cartulary was produced using the original materials that were incorporated with the monasteries, and that "all batches of documents begin with the texts of greatest authority and interest",[101] the question again arises as to who was responsible for the internal organization of the block of texts from each monastery. Should we assume that this choice was made by the *Tumbo*'s copyist and that his criteria for what constituted the "greatest authority and interest" determined the arrangement of the documents? Cleary, individual studies on each block in the overall context of the cartulary's production are needed in order to propose hypotheses in answer to this question.[102] My observations regarding the group from San Antolín are intended merely to call attention to the need for such research. As I noted above, this research cannot be detached from questions relating to the processes involved in the incorporation of the documentation. We begin to see that these processes are more

101 Herrero de la Fuente, "Cartularios leoneses," 141. Fernández Flórez, "La huella," assumes it implicitly by emphasizing the copyist's reliability; and Herrero, explicitly when she affirms that "in the case of the *Becerro Gótico de Sahagún* and the *Tumbo* we can confirm that they were made directly from the originals" and following a pre-established order, Herrero de la Fuente, "Cartularios leoneses," 151.

102 This research would need to delve deeper into the conflictive context revealed by the very need to divide the see's patrimony between the bishop and chapter. One document dated 1120 (when the cartulary was being copied) illustrates this situation like none other, in my opinion. It contains the provisions given by Bishop Diego that establish the canonic procedure (*sicuti sancti canones*) of assigning resources to the canons in order to prevent the *iniustitiam et controversiam* created by the fact that the prebends received by the canons depended on the good will of the prelate, which was conditioned by *amicitia, seruicium, amor sui generis, uel ira, et odium*. On these structural conflicts within the church that affected relations with other, external networks, see Isabel Alfonso, "Litigios por la tierra y "*malfetrías*" entre la nobleza medieval castellano-leonesa," *Hispania* 197 (*Desarrollo legal, prácticas judiciales y acción política en la Europa medieval*) (1997), 917–955, at 933–936 and 955. On a similar conflict affecting the Worcester cathedral, the written testimonies of which can be found in Hemming's cartulary, see Francesca Tinti "*Si litterali memorie commendaretur*: memory and cartularies in eleventh-century Worcester," in *Early Medieval Studies in Memory of Patrick Wormald*, ed. Stephen Baxten et al. (Farnham: Ashgate, 2009), 475–497.

complex than what is suggested by assuming simply that the documentation was incorporated at the same time as the institution that supposedly housed it.[103]

The fact that San Antolín's block opens with the five documents mentioned above doubtless reflects certain objectives; it is difficult to guess what these objectives might have been or who established them. The fact that the block begins on folios 176^{v}–178^{r} with the joint endowment from Rodrigo and Sancha might be interpreted according to the usual logic of highlighting the foundational moment, which in this case is embellished with the account of the translation of the saint's relics that Rodrigo himself had gone to France in search of and had deposited in the monastery which he and his wife had founded. More surprising is the fact that in the first part of the *Tumbo*, where the documents ascribed to the cathedral are copied, there is another document that seems to duplicate the same endowment, though it records only Sancha's gift and not the one from her husband or the narrative about the relics that Rodrigo brought with him.[104] Gregorio del Ser's scepticism regarding the authenticity of the diploma that contains the joint endowment—which he believes must have been concocted out of this other document containing only Sancha's endowment at a time when there was conflict between the bishoprics of León and Palencia—might provide clues about the context in which the block of documents from San Antolín was arranged.[105]

Sancha's donation of San Antolín to the León cathedral in 1040, only two years after the endowment, has been interpreted within the framework of ecclesiastical reform, which prompted the incorporation of private monasteries into larger institutions.[106] Sancha would thus have been, in the opinion of Martínez Sopena, the embodiment of this new form of aristocratic piety that

103 It would perhaps be worthwhile to look into the different levels of agency that participated in the compilation of the *Tumbo*, along the ingenious lines proposed by Julio Escalona, "¿Un "cartulario milagroso"? Cronología y proyecto en los *Miraculos Romançados* de Santo Domingo de Silos," in *Histoires, femmes, pouvoirs. Mélanges offerts au Professeur Georges Martin*, ed. Jean-Pierre Jardin, Patricia Rochwert-Zuili, and Hélène Thieulin-Pardo (Paris: Classiques Garnier, 2018), 159–199.

104 CL4 971 = *Tumbo Legionense*, fols. 33^{r}–34^{v} (1038).

105 Del Ser, "Un monasterio," 186, n. 1, considers this document to be a forgery—and therefore does not publish it—because it includes the legend of San Antolín's relics at a time when the Palencia see had already been founded with the same dedication. Ruiz Asencio does not share Del Ser's opinion, however, and believes that the two documents are reconcilable by assuming (without proof) that Sancha would have wanted another document drawn up with her assets only while her husband was still alive; see Ruiz Asencio's comments in a note to CL4 970 (1038), p. 106.

106 Del Ser, "Un monasterio," 179, for example, attributes it to the fact that San Antolín ori-

was just beginning to develop, which was "based on the absolute renunciation of the enjoyment of ecclesiastical things, in a flagrant breach with family traditions".[107] However, the fact that Sancha's gift to the cathedral and her nephew Nuño Petriz's gift to San Antolín coincide chronologically allows these contradictory actions to be interpreted not so much, or not only, as different stances toward reform but as a sign of opposite family strategies with regard to the advantages that links to the episcopal circle might bring.[108]

Two accounts copied into the *Tumbo* after the charters of gift mentioned above describe complaints by some men from Cimanes, the only one among numerous *villae* that was included in both gifts, providing further information about these matters.[109] In them, the history of Cimanes is recounted beginning in the late tenth century, when Munio Fernández, Nuño's grandfather, received the *villa* from the king as a reward for his loyalty, and continuing up to when Nuño, still a minor, inherited it at the death of his father, Pedro Muñiz. A violent uprising by the people of Cimanes, who claimed to have hereditary rights to properties in the *villa*, occurred at this juncture, when in addition to the title passing from one member of the family to another, there was a transfer to two different ecclesiastical institutions. These changes in ownership required a renegotiation of the existing personal and material relationships that were affected. We ignore why Countess Sancha disposed of her nephew's properties, giving them to the cathedral, but the fact that Nuño does not follow her lead and instead gave the properties to the monastery, an act that is confirmed by the parties to the litigation, can be seen as an expression of an attempt by the monastery to maintain its autonomy vis-a-vis the see of León. If this hypothesis is correct, it would make sense that there were intra-familial tensions that united factions from the community of Cimanes around the young heir

ginated as a family monastery at a time when the tendency was toward concentration in larger institutions.

107 Martínez Sopena, "Aristocracia," 81.

108 The study by Martínez Sopena cited in the previous note contains information about opposing positions among the extended family that supports this interpretation. These positions are not only reactions to the carving up of the family's monastic properties; they are also indicative of different designs for connecting to the world beyond the family. On possible disputes within the family that owned Guimarães and their connection to the process of writing the monastery's cartulary, see André Evangelista Marques, "O cartulário: construção e transmissão," in *Livro de Mumadona: Cartulário do Mosteiro de Guimarães: Edição crítica*, ed. Luís Carlos Amaral et al. (Lisbon: Academia das Ciências de Lisboa, 2016 [2018]), xxxi–lxv, at li.

109 CL4 1006 = *Tumbo Legionense*, fols. 179^{v}–180^{v} (1043) and 1151 = fols. 181^{r}–182^{r} (1067). For a detailed analysis of these two suits, see Alfonso, "Litigios por la tierra," 920–924.

and against his aunt. The violent death of Sancha years later "at the hands of her nephew", as we read in the *Necrologio Legionense*, would support this hypothesis.[110] Moreover, the fact that these two accounts were brought before kings—the first one by Countess Sancha, before Fernando I, and the second by Bishop Pelayo, before Alfonso VI—seems to point to difficulties among the lay and ecclesiastical aristocracy in exercising their domanial and seigneurial power on the local level. The dynamics of the relationships that the aristocracy established with local notables are also made manifest in these disputes. We thus see the development of seigneurial power from a perspective that is reflected in the format of the documents: when the aristocracy is not able to impose their power upon local notables, they appeal to royal justice. This makes the accounts from San Antolín similar to those from Sahagún and the León cathedral.

By way of summary, let us say that the interest in examining these two collections of lay documents lies in observing, firstly, the preponderance of judicial transactions over other types of dispute records and the connection between this document format and the kinds of cases that are resolved and the social status of the parties. Everything indicates that we are dealing here with a forum of seigneurial justice, which allows us to get a closer look at the conflicts and tensions running through the fabric of local society. The few extant accounts in the two collections were dealt with at the same or higher social levels. Secondly, there is another important aspect suggested by these texts, which has to do with internal competition within the aristocratic family groups themselves. The foundation of monasteries by members of these aristocratic families is the result of individual rather than group strategies, and the different links that were forged in doing so allow us to trace this internal competition and thus to focus on aspects other than ecclesiastical reform, which has occupied such a

110 *VI^a kalendas a[u]gusti. Luna. Eodem die obiit famula Dei Sancia comitissa, que obtulit monasterium Sancti Antonini cum hereditatibus suis ecclesie Sancte Marie, et ideo a nepote sui interfecta fuit* [...], CL10, p. 448. Martínez Sopena mentions the murder of Countess Sancha, as a result of this donation, as one piece of evidence for the view that the conversion of family monasteries into Benedictine monasteries was accompanied by violence, which, along the lines mentioned before, he interprets as the "fruit of different notions about the relationship between the aristocracy and ecclesiastical institutions", Pascual Martínez Sopena, "Reyes, condes e infanzones. Aristocracia y *alfetena* en el reino de León," in *XXX Semana de Estudios Medievales de Estella* (Pamplona: Gobierno de Navarra, 2004), 109–154, at 132. On the death of Countess Sancha and the inclusion of her image along with those of the Leonese monarchs in the *Libro de las Estampas*, see Margarita Torres and Fernando Galván Fraile, "La condesa Sancha Muñiz. Una nueva aproximación a su figura," *Medievalismo* 5 (1995), 9–30.

central place in the historiography.[111] The case of San Antolín calls for further research on a topic that has received little attention: the conflicts within kinship groups.[112]

Bibliography

Abbreviations

CL1, CL2, CL3, CL4, CL5, CL10: *Colección documental del archivo de la catedral de León (775–1230)*. Vol. 1 (*775–952*), edited by Emilio Sáez; vol. 2 (*953–985*), edited by Emilio Sáez and Carlos Sáez; vol. 3 (*986–1031*) and vol. 4 (*1032–1109*), edited by José Manuel Ruiz Asencio; vol. 5 (*1109–1187*), edited by José María Fernández Catón; vol. 10 *Obituarios medievales*, edited by Mauricio Herrero Jiménez. León: Centro de Estudios e Investigación 'San Isidoro', 1987, 1990, 1987, 1990, 1990, 1994.

OD: Fernández Flórez, José Antonio, and Marta Herrero de la Fuente, eds. Colección documental del monasterio de Santa María de Otero de las Dueñas. Vol. 1 (*854–1108*). León, Centro de Estudios e Investigación 'San Isidoro', 1999.

S1, S3, S4: *Colección diplomática del monasterio de Sahagún (857–1230)*. Vol. 1 (*Siglos IX y X*), edited by José María Mínguez Fernández; vol. 2 (*1000–1070*) and vol. 3 (*1073–1109*), edited by Marta Herrero de la Fuente. León: Centro de Estudios e Investigación 'San Isidoro', 1976, 1988.

Other Primary Sources

Cavero Domínguez, Gregoria, and Encarnación Martín López, eds. *Colección documental de la Catedral de Astorga, I (646–1126)*. León: Centro de Estudios e Investigación 'San Isidoro', 1999.

Sanz Fuentes, María Josefa, et al., eds. *El "Liber Testamentorum" de la catedral de Oviedo*. Barcelona: Moleiro Editor, 1995.

111 Personal agency could play a major role in the foundation of monasteries, as shown by María Elida García García, "Aristocracia laica y monasterios familiares en Asturias (ss. X y XI)," in *Homenaje a Juan Uría Ríu* (Oviedo: Universidad de Oviedo, Servicio de Publicaciones: 1997), 253–274. On the other hand, Mariel Pérez, "Control," 815–817, suggests that, in the long run, Leonese aristocratic families tended to build their patronage networks around different foundations, in a strategy of self-promotion that would clash with the movement of ecclesiastical reform from the mid eleventh century.

112 Martin Aurell, ed., *La Parenté déchirée: les luttes intrafamiliales au Moyen Âge* (Turnhout: Brepols, 2010).

Secondary Works

Agúndez San Miguel, Leticia. *La memoria escrita en el monasterio de Sahagún (años 904–1300)*. Madrid: Consejo Superior de Investigaciones Científicas, 2019.

Alfonso, Isabel. "Resolución de disputas y prácticas judiciales en el Burgos medieval." In *III Jornadas Burgalesas de Historia. Burgos en la Plena Edad Media*, 211–243. Burgos: Asociación Provincial de Libreros de Burgos, 1994.

Alfonso, Isabel. "Litigios por la tierra y "*malfetrías*" entre la nobleza medieval castellano-leonesa." *Hispania* 197 (*Desarrollo legal, prácticas judiciales y acción política en la Europa medieval*) (1997), 917–955.

Alfonso, Isabel. "Judicial rhetoric and political legitimation in medieval Leon-Castile." In *Building Legitimacy: Political Discourses and Forms of Legitimacy in Medieval Societies*, edited by Isabel Alfonso, Hugh Kennedy, and Julio Escalona, 51–87. Leiden: Brill, 2004.

Alfonso, Isabel. "Conflict in the Behetrías". In *Land, Power and Society in Medieval Castile. A Study of the Behetría Lordship*, edited by Cristina Jular Pérez-Alfaro and Carlos Estepa Díez, 275–316. Turnhout: Brepols, 2009.

Alfonso, Isabel. "El formato de la información judicial en la Alta Edad Media peninsular." In *Chartes et cartulaires comme instruments de pouvoir. Espagne et Occident chrétien (VIIIe–XIIe siècles)*, edited by Julio Escalona and Helène Sirantoine, 191–218. Toulouse: Université de Toulouse-Le Mirail, 2013.

Aurell, Martin, ed. *La Parenté déchirée: les luttes intrafamiliales au Moyen Âge*. Turnhout: Brepols, 2010.

Bennet, Judith M. "Writing fornication: medieval leyrwite and its historians: The Prothero Lecture." *Transactions of the Royal Historical Society*, Sixth Series, 13 (2003), 131–162.

Calleja Puerta, Miguel. "La Catedral de Oviedo como centro de conservación de documentos en la alta Edad Media." In *Estudos em homenagem ao Professor Doutor José Marques*, vol. IV, 179–191 Porto: Faculdade de Letras da Universidade do Porto, 2006.

Carbajo Serrano, María José. "El monasterio de los santos Cosme y Damián de Abellar. Monacato y sociedad en la época astur-leonesa." *Archivos Leoneses* 81–82 (1987), 7–300.

Carvajal Castro, Álvaro. *Bajo la máscara del* Regnum. *La monarquía asturleonesa en León (854–1037)*. Madrid: Consejo Superior de Investigaciones Científicas, 2017.

Carvajal Castro, Álvaro. "Local meetings and meeting places in early medieval León." *Early Medieval Europe* 25, no. 2 (2017), 186–207.

Comaroff, John, and Simon Roberts. *Rules and Processes: The Cultural Logic of Dispute in an African Context*. Chicago: Chicago University Press, 1986.

Davies, Wendy. *Acts of giving. Individual, Community and the Church in Tenth Century Spain*. Oxford: Oxford University Press, 2007.

Davies, Wendy. *Windows on Justice in Northern Iberia, 800–1000*. Abingdon: Routledge, 2016.

Del Ser, Gregorio. "Un monasterio benedictino leonés olvidado: San Antolín." In *Semana de Historia del monacato cántabro-astur-leonés*, 175–194. Oviedo: Monasterio de San Pelayo, 1982.

Durany Castrillo, Mercedes, and María Carmen Rodríguez González. "Puntualizaciones sobre la datación de algunos documentos de la Catedral de Astorga del primer tercio del siglo XI. De Jimeno a Sampiro." *Estudios Humanísticos. Historia* 3 (2004), 275–302.

Escalona, Julio. "Antes de los cartularios: gestión de archivos y transmisión de los documentos de la Castilla condal (siglo IX-1038)." In *Chartes et cartulaires comme instruments de pouvoir. Espagne et Occident chrétien (VIIIe-XIIe siècles)*, edited by Julio Escalona and Hélène Sirantoine, 147–167. Toulouse: Université de Toulouse-Le Mirail, 2013.

Escalona, Julio. "Cartularios, memoria y discurso en la Castilla medieval." In *La memoria del poder, el poder de la memoria*, edited by Esther López Ojeda, 163–203. Logroño: Instituto de Estudios Riojanos, 2017.

Escalona, Julio. "¿Un "cartulario milagroso"? Cronología y proyecto en los *Miraculos Romançados* de Santo Domingo de Silos." In *Histoires, femmes, pouvoirs. Mélanges offerts au Professeur Georges Martin*, edited by Jean-Pierre Jardin, Patricia Rochwert-Zuili, and Hélène Thieulin-Pardo, 159–199. Paris: Classiques Garnier, 2018.

Estepa Díez, Carlos. "Formación y consolidación del feudalismo en Castilla y León." In *En torno al feudalismo hispánico. I Congreso de Estudios Medievales*, 157–256. Ávila: Fundación Sánchez Albornoz, 1989.

Fernández Catón, José María. "El Tumbo Legionense. Notas sobre su origen, reacción, estructura, contenido y utilización." In *Actas do IV Congreso Internacional de Latim Medieval Hispânico*, 415–435. Lisbon: Centro de Estudos Clássicos, 2007.

Fernández Flórez, José Antonio. "La huella de los copistas en los cartularios leoneses." In *Orígenes de las lenguas romances*, 159–227. León: Centro de Estudios e Investigación 'San Isidoro', 2004.

Fernández Flórez, José Antonio, and Marta Herrero de la Fuente. "Libertades de los copistas en la confección de cartularios: el caso del Becerro Gótico de Sahagún." In *Scribi e colofoni: le sottoscrizioni di copisti dalle origini all'avvento della stampa (Atti del Seminario di Erice: X Colloquio del Comité international de paléographie latine, 23–28 ottobre 1993)*, edited by Emma Condello and Giuseppe De Gregorio, 301–324. Spoleto: Centro Italiano di Studi sull'alto Medioevo, 1995.

Gambra, Andrés. *Alfonso VI, cancillería, curia e imperio*. Vol. 1 *Estudio*. León: Centro de Estudios e Investigación 'San Isidoro', 1997.

García García, Elida. "Aristocracia laica y monasterios familiares en Asturias (ss. X y XI)." In *Homenaje a Juan Uría Ríu*, 253–274. Oviedo: Universidad de Oviedo, Servicio de Publicaciones: 1997.

García Leal, Alfonso. *El archivo de los condes Fruela Muñoz y Pedro Flaínez: la formación de un patrimonio nobiliario en la montaña asturleonesa (854–1048)*. León: Universidad de León, 2010.

Herrero de la Fuente, Marta. "Cartularios leoneses: Del *Becerro Gótico de Sahagún* al *Tumbo Legionense* y al *Libro de las Estampas*." In *La escritura de la memoria: los cartularios*, edited by Elena E. Rodríguez Díaz and Antonio Claret García Martínez, 111–152. Huelva: Universidad de Huelva, 2011.

Jular Pérez-Alfaro, Cristina, and Carlos Estepa Díez, eds. *Land, Power and Society in Medieval Castile. A Study of the Behetría Lordship*. Turnhout: Brepols, 2009.

Kelly, Henry Ansgar. "Law and Nonmarital Sex in the Middle Ages." In *Conflict in Medieval Europe: Changing Perspectives on Society and Culture*, edited by Warren C. Brown and Piotr Góreck, 175–194. Hampshire: Ashgate, 2003.

Kosto, Adam J. "*Sicut mos esse solet*: documentary practices in Christian Iberia, c. 700–1000." In *Documentary Culture and the Laity in the Early Middle Ages*, edited by Warren Brown, Marios Costambeys, Matthew Innes, and Adam J. Kosto, 259–282. Cambridge: Cambridge University Press, 2013.

Marques, André Evangelista. "O cartulário: construção e transmissão." in *Livro de Mumadona: Cartulário do Mosteiro de Guimarães: Edição crítica*, edited by Luís Carlos Amaral et al., xxxi–lxv. Lisbon: Academia das Ciências de Lisboa, 2016 [2018].

Martínez Sopena, Pascual. "Reyes, condes e infanzones. Aristocracia y *alfetena* en el reino de León." In *XXX Semana de Estudios Medievales de Estella*, 109–154. Pamplona: Gobierno de Navarra, 2004.

Martínez Sopena, Pascual. "Aristocracia, monacato y reformas en los siglos XI y XII." In *El monacato en los reinos de León y Castilla (siglos VII–XIII)*, 67–99. León: Fundación Sánchez-Albornoz, 2007.

Martínez Sopena, Pascual. "La justicia en la época asturleonesa: entre el *liber* y los mediadores sociales." In *El Lugar del Campesino. En torno a la obra de Reyna Pastor*, edited by Ana Rodríguez, 239–260. Valencia: Universidad de Valencia, 2007.

Mínguez, José María. "Justicia y poder en el marco de la feudalización de la sociedad leonesa." In *La giustizia nell'alto medioevo (secoli IX–XI)*, Settimane di studio del CISAM 44, vol. 1, 491–546. Spoleto: CISAM, 1997.

Pérez, Mariel. "El control de lo sagrado como instrumento de poder: los monasterios particulares de la aristocracia altomedieval leonesa." *Anuario de Estudios Medievales* 42, no. 2 (2012), 799–822.

Roberts, Simon. *Order and Dispute: An Introduction to Legal Anthropology*. Oxford: Martin Robertson, 1979.

Rodríguez Fernández, Justiniano. *El monasterio de Ardón. Estudio histórico sobre los centros monásticos medievales de Cillanueva y Rozuela*. León, Centro de Estudios e Investigación 'San Isidoro', 1964.

Ruiz Asencio, José Manuel. "Notas sobre el trabajo de los notarios leoneses en los siglos x–xii." In *Orígenes de las lenguas romances en el reino de León, siglos ix–xii*, 87–117. León: Centro de Estudios e Investigación 'San Isidoro', 2004.

Sanz Fuentes, María Josefa. *El Tumbo Negro de la Catedral de Astorga: una aproximación a su historia*. Astorga: Centro de Estudios Astorganos Marcelo Macías, 2010.

Tinti, Francesca. "*Si litterali memorie commendaretur*: memory and cartularies in eleventh-century Worcester". In *Early Medieval Studies in Memory of Patrick Wormald*, edited by Stephen Baxten, Catherine Karkov, Janet L. Nelson, and David Pelteret, 475–497. Farnham: Ashgate, 2009.

Torres, Margarita, and Fernando Galván Fraile. "La condesa Sancha Muñiz. Una nueva aproximación a su figura." *Medievalismo* 5 (1995), 9–30.

Yañez Cifuentes, María del Pilar. *El monasterio de Santiago de León*. León: Centro de Estudios e Investigación 'San Isidoro', 1972.

CHAPTER 3

Documentary Production and Dispute Records in Castile before the Year 1100

Isabel Alfonso

1 Castilian Documents from the Ninth to the Eleventh Century

Julio Escalona has pointed out three main features of the Castilian documentation from the comital period (ca. 800–1038): the scarcity of original documents, the reliance on cartularies and other kinds of later copies, and the existence of a significant number of forgeries. These features are not unique to Castile, which reinforces the need for comparative analyses of regional corpora. Escalona remarks that the fact that historians are familiar with their material does not mean that there are no difficulties in using it. As in other geographical regions, we lack a systematic catalogue of the Castilian corpus compiled according to modern historical and diplomatic criteria. This has prompted Escalona to create a database that will make it possible to mine the whole corpus of Castilian documents up to 1038. Above all, this database will make it possible to answer some key questions about the documents' provenance, since we know that the collections kept by those monasteries that became major ecclesiastical institutions in the twelfth century or later are an "amalgam of documents of diverse origin", a phenomenon that is also not unique to Castile.[1]

The boundaries of Castile's territory shifted as a result of political developments during the tenth and eleventh centuries, both within the county of Castile itself and in the kingdom of Navarre. During the period of its greatest territorial extent, the county of Castile stretched from the Cantabrian Sea to

1 Julio Escalona, "La documentación de la Castilla condal: viejos problemas y nuevas perspectivas," in *Mundos medievales. Espacios, sociedades y poder. Homenaje al Profesor José Ángel García de Cortázar y Ruiz de Aguirre*, ed. Beatriz Arízaga Bolumburu et al., 2 vols (Santander: Universidad de Cantabria, 2012), 1:473–487; see also Julio Escalona, "Antes de los cartularios: gestión de archivos y transmisión de los documentos de la Castilla condal (siglo IX-1038)," in *Chartes et cartulaires comme instruments de pouvoir. Espagne et Occident chrétien (VIIIe-XIIe siècles)*, ed. Julio Escalona and Hélène Sirantoine (Toulouse: Université de Toulouse-Le Mirail, 2013), 147–167. The abbreviations used in this paper for editions of charters are listed in the bibliography.

 | DOI:10.1163/9789004683006_005

the Duero River and included the adjacent counties of Álava and Monzón; in the last quarter of the eleventh century, Castile expanded its territory with the incorporation of La Rioja.

The institutions that preserved 'Castilian' documents dated before 1100 are scattered among the coastal area (monasteries of Santa María del Puerto and Santillana), the northeast (monasteries of Santa María de Valpuesta and San Salvador de Oña), the central area (the Burgos cathedral, the collegiate church of San Cosme y San Damián de Covarrubias and the monasteries of San Pedro de Cardeña, Ibeas, San Pedro de Arlanza, and Santo Domingo de Silos),[2] and the western border (monasteries of Husillos, Cozuelos, and San Isidro de las Dueñas).[3] However, numerous documents concerning Castile come from institutions located outside its borders, as is the case with Cozuelos, San Isidro de las Dueñas, and especially San Millán de la Cogolla, a monastery within Navarre's sphere of influence up until the incorporation of La Rioja into Castile in 1076 but that had been gradually absorbing smaller monasteries in Castile from before that date (see above, Map 0.1).[4]

In quantitative terms, Castile has the smallest number of documents of any region in northern Iberia, with only approximately 1000 documents for the entire period before the twelfth century and with only seven centres that transmitted more than 60 documents (see above, Table 0.1). Silos, meanwhile, has fewer than 30 documents, and Covarrubias fewer than 20. Of the seven institutions with more than 60 documents, there are three with more than 100, and one of them, the monastery of Cardeña, has almost 400. The volume of this collection puts Cardeña in the same league as major institutions in other regions, such as the monastery of Santa María de Otero de las Dueñas and the León and Astorga cathedrals, in the Leonese region, while it is just behind the monastery of Celanova in Galicia and ahead of all institutions in Portugal, Aragon and Navarre, with the exception of San Millán de la Cogolla.

The chronological distribution of the Castilian corpus is quite balanced from one century to the next, though there is a slightly smaller number of documents before the year 1000, a marked concentration between 940–970, followed by

2 The fact that the Arlanza river was the backbone connecting the monastic scriptoria in the Burgos region has been remarked by José A. Fernández Flórez and Sonia Serna in BGC, p. 57.

3 Though these monasteries were within León's sphere of influence in the tenth century, a century later they were part of Castile's territory.

4 For an overview of documents from institutions outside of Castile's territory, also in the Leonese area, see Escalona, "La documentación de la Castilla condal," 478–479.

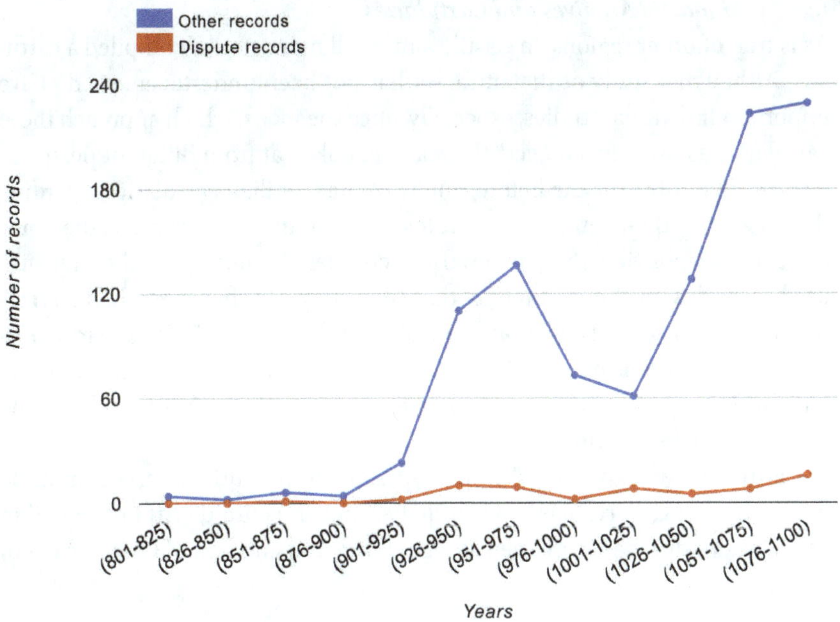

GRAPH 3.1 Proportion of Castilian dispute records before 1100, by quarter-century

a decrease until 1010 and a progressive increase during the eleventh century. In other words, the volume of documents from Castilian institutions does not seem to vary as widely from one century to the next as do, for example, the collections from Navarre, Aragon or Galicia (see above, Table 0.2 and Graphs 0.2 and 0.4). However, although the Cardeña collection is the largest overall, its volume decreases slightly in the eleventh century, whereas the numbers at other institutions such as Oña, Arlanza, and the Burgos cathedral increase during the same period.

As has already been mentioned, the scant number of originals is an important feature of Castile's documentation. Although this is a common phenomenon throughout northern Iberia (with the exception of Catalonia), it is starker in this region. What this means is that the transmission of the texts relied on later archival procedures and copying, basically in cartularies.[5]

5 For the comital period, originals represent a mere 1.5 per cent of the corpus, and these come mostly from Valpuesta, Oña, and Covarrubias; Escalona, "Antes de los cartularios," 133, and

1.1 *Monastic Archives and Cartularies*

As is true of other regions, in Castile almost all monasteries compiled a cartulary. Although a study of the entire set has not been undertaken, we do have important individual studies, especially since the 1990s, which approach these cartularies as historical objects that can be looked at from different perspectives. Escalona stresses the heterogeneity of the Castilian cartularies regarding the reasons for their compilation, the logic of their internal structure, their processes of composition, their material aspects, their discourse, and the strategies used to deal with the documents that they copy. He therefore characterizes them as not only "multifunctional" but also "multitemporal."[6] These cartularies vary widely in terms of their dates of compilation. The oldest (from Valpuesta and Cardeña) go back to the eleventh century, but the majority date from the twelfth to the fourteenth.

Cartularies were produced in many Castilian institutions: in Santa María del Puerto,[7] in Covarrubias,[8] in Santillana,[9] in San Pedro de Arlanza,[10] and in San Salvador de Oña.[11] However, as regards the transmission of Castilian docu-

---

Escalona, "La documentación de la Castilla condal," 481, also noting the decisive nineteenth-century documentary losses, especially in the aftermath of the expropriation of ecclesiastical property.

6 Julio Escalona, "Cartularios, memoria y discurso en la Castilla medieval," in *La memoria del poder, el poder de la memoria*, ed. Esther López Ojeda (Logroño: Instituto de Estudios Riojanos, 2017), 163–203, at 167. This provides a clear analysis of cartularies as vehicles for documentary transmission, as well as of the multiple archives and materials on which cartulary compilers drew. Escalona's remarks should also be borne in mind when assessing the cartularies compiled in other Iberian regional contexts.

7 Puerto; see also Rosa María Blasco Martínez, *Los cartularios de Cantabria (St. Toribio, Sta. María del Puerto, Santillana y Piasca): estudio codicológico, paleográfico y diplomático* (Santander: Estudio, 1986).

8 Covarrubias.

9 Santillana; Carmen Díez Herrera, Luis López Ormazábal and Rogelio Pérez Bustamante, eds., *Abadía de Santillana del Mar. Colección diplomática* (Santillana del Mar: Taurus Ediciones Fundación Santillana, 1983); see also Blasco Martínez, *Los cartularios de Cantabria*.

10 The whereabouts of Arlanza's cartulary since the Spanish Civil War are unknown, but a research group led by Julio Escalona has been working on its reconstruction. Their findings were published preliminarily in Julio Escalona and Pilar Azcárate, "Una fuente 'casi' perdida para la historia de la Castilla medieval. Notas en torno al Becerro de San Pedro de Arlanza," *Hispania* 208 (2001), 449–474; and a full edition will appear soon, Paloma Juárez, Julio Escalona and Pilar Azcárate, eds., *Documentación de Arlanza, siglos X–XI* (forthcoming).

11 Oña; Isabel Oceja Gonzalo, ed., *Documentación del monasterio de San Salvador de Oña (1032–1284)* (Burgos: Ediciones J.M. Garrido Garrido, 1983). The phenomenon of "multiple cartularization" is reflected in this monastery's scriptorium, which was particularly prolific in its production of all kinds of materials, Escalona, "Cartularios, memoria y discurso," 188.

ments, most noteworthy are the cartularies of San Pedro de Cardeña and of Santa María de Valpuesta. The existence in both cases of recent, reliable critical editions makes it possible to study them from different perspectives. In what follows, I will focus on these two cartularies.

According to its latest editors, the *Becerro Gótico de Cardeña* is the earliest major Iberian cartulary.[12] Produced in 1086, it contains a large number of texts and constitutes an extremely rich source of information for the study of history in general and the history of the county of Castile in particular. This is because 232 out of the 373 documents that can be dated to between 899 and 1085 deal with the comital period, which ended in 1038. This mass of documents is much larger than what all the other Castilian monasteries combined have for this period. Also noteworthy is the large size of the cartulary's parchment folios and the exquisite Visigothic script in which it is written, which indicates a sophisticated scribal culture at Cardeña. Unlike Arlanza's cartulary, this one seems to have been put together with a view to exhaustively reproducing all of the documents in the Cardeña archive.[13]

The 26 batches of documents identified by the editors in the cartulary lead them to wonder about the reasons for the documents being ordered this way, but they also make it possible to detect the origins and linguistic traits of some of these groups of documents. Geography is the most important criterion in the general organization of the cartulary and also within individual batches. These batches do not follow any chronological order, and their internal consistency is very uneven: in them, as in many other cartularies, we find traces of different archives where documents copied into the *Becerro* originated.[14] The editors' introduction has proven crucial for analyzing the information about disputes contained in Cardeña's cartulary, as will be seen below.

An edition of the as yet unpublished cartulary of the monastery of Froncea is currently being prepared by David Peterson and María Josefa Sanz Fuentes.

12 BGC. This recent edition by Fernández Flórez and Serna includes an exhaustive introductory study that, despite its main focus on diplomatics and linguistic issues, allows for different approaches to the cartulary's material. This cartulary—currently held at Madrid's Biblioteca Francisco de Zabálburu—was previously edited by Luciano Serrano, ed., *Becerro Gótico de Cardeña* (Valladolid: Cuesta Editor, 1910), and Gonzalo Martínez Díez: Cardeña. The latter edition is used in the PRJ database and is thus the one that I will be using here, although reference to the latest edition is made when necessary.

13 Escalona, "Antes de los cartularios," 141–142.

14 BGC, pp. 179–222. Focusing on the cartulary's structure and trying to understand the process of going "from the document to the cartulary", Escalona, "Cartularios, memoria y discurso," 180–183, has also asked how the monastery's archive was organized, noting that Cardeña's cartulary, unlike the *Becerro Galicano* of San Millán de la Cogolla, does not transmit the history of the archive from which it takes its materials.

Valpuesta's *Becerro Gótico* and *Becerro Galicano* were also recently published in a critical edition.[15] The *Becerro Gótico* is a composite codex made in the twelfth century that gathers together chronologically disparate quires and includes fragments of at least two different cartularies, written in Visigothic script, that are earlier than that of Cardeña.[16] The two *becerros* have an explicit connection, since the *Galicano*, produced in 1236, presents itself as a new version of its predecessor. It declares itself to be a copy of the "old book", which it does indeed reproduce with a high degree of faithfulness, at least in the order of the documents. This marks a striking contrast with the *Becerro Galicano* of San Millán de la Cogolla, which David Peterson's detailed analyses have shown to be completely different from its predecessor, the non-extant *Becerro Gótico*, in its ordering, the way it was put together, and its intentions. The *Galicano* incorporated new materials, many of them falsified documents intended to bolster the monastery's claims in some of the disputes that it was engaged in at the time.[17]

2 The Corpus of Castilian Dispute Records

Castile's corpus of dispute records, which comprises only 61 documents,[18] makes up less than six per cent of the region's total documentation, a ratio that is comparable only to those of Navarre, Aragon, and Catalonia,[19] and differs greatly from the ratios in León (11.2 per cent), Portugal (16.5 per cent), and especially Galicia (20.4 per cent) (see above, Table 0.1 and Graph 0.5).

15 José M. Ruiz Asencio, Irene Ruiz Albi, Mauricio Herrero, eds., *Los Becerros Gótico y Galicano de Valpuesta* (Madrid: Real Academia de la Lengua, 2010).

16 For a summary of the most important aspects of this codex compared to other cartularies, see Escalona, "Cartularios, memoria y discurso," 177.

17 Escalona, "Cartularios, memoria y discurso," 188. David Peterson, "El *Becerro Gótico* de San Millán. Reconstrucción de un cartulario perdido," *Studia Historica. Historia Medieval* 29 (2011), 147–173, and David Peterson, "Rebranding San Millán: the Becerro Galicano as a rejection of the monastery's Navarrese heritage (1192–95)," *Journal of Medieval Iberian Studies* 5, no. 1 (2013), 1–20. On San Millán, see also below, Chapter 4.

18 To put into perspective how small this corpus is, we should recall that some institutions in Galicia, León, and Catalonia surpass alone this number: Celanova (118 dispute records), Otero de las Dueñas (95), Sahagún (80), Barcelona, Vic, and Urgell cathedrals (120, 112, and 86, respectively), not to mention the archive of the counts of Barcelona (135).

19 The ratio of dispute records to the overall number in Catalonia is 6.5 per cent, but the Catalan materials in the PRJ database are still under review.

TABLE 3.1 Castilian institutions that preserved five or more pre-1100 dispute records

Institution	All records (n)	Dispute records (n)	Dispute records (%)	9th c.	10th c.	11th c.	Originals	Copies	Authentic	Suspect	False
S. Pedro de Cardeña	382	24	6.28	0	14	10	0	24	24	0	0
S. Salvador de Oña	139	12	8.63	0	2	10	1	11	11	1	0
Sta. María del Puerto	61	9	14.75	1	2	6	0	9	8	1	0
Sta. María de Valpuesta	96	6	6.25	0	4	2	4	2	6	0	0
TOTAL	678	51		1	22	28	5	46	49	2	0

In general, the chronological distribution of this corpus is less uneven than in other regions (see above, Table 0.2 and Graphs 0.8, 0.10 and 3.1). However, there is an uneven distribution of dispute records among institutions (see above, Maps 0.2 and 0.4). For the entire period, the only two monasteries with more than ten dispute records are Oña (12) and Cardeña (24), while institutions such as Valpuesta, Santa María del Puerto, and Santillana preserved very few, though the ones they do have are important (Table 3.1 and below, Graph 3.2). The rest of the thirteen Castilian institutions either have barely any records with this kind of information or lack them completely. Noteworthy examples are the monastery of Arlanza and the Burgos cathedral, whose collections preserve a large volume of documents but little or no direct or indirect information about the settlement of disputes.

The reasons for these differences are difficult to ascertain, but one should bear in mind that, although it is possible that documents were lost, it is also possible that their absence is the result of different strategies of record-making and/or record-keeping.[20] However, there are not only quantitative but also qualitative differences, and we must look for explanations for these. There are collections in which records of certain types of disputes predominate over others, and the form chosen for these records also differs from one institution to another.

20 Regarding the differences in the proportion of dispute records, and of specific types of dispute records, between different institutions and different regions, Wendy Davies, *Windows on Justice in Northern Iberia, 800–1000* (Abingdon: Routledge, 2016), 188, 257, believes that this may be less a matter of the volume of documentation being preserved than an indication of more proactive institutional strategies. On the influence that the criteria used in the compilation of the cartulary of Arlanza may have had on the documentation included in it, see Escalona, Azcárate, "Una fuente 'casi' perdida."

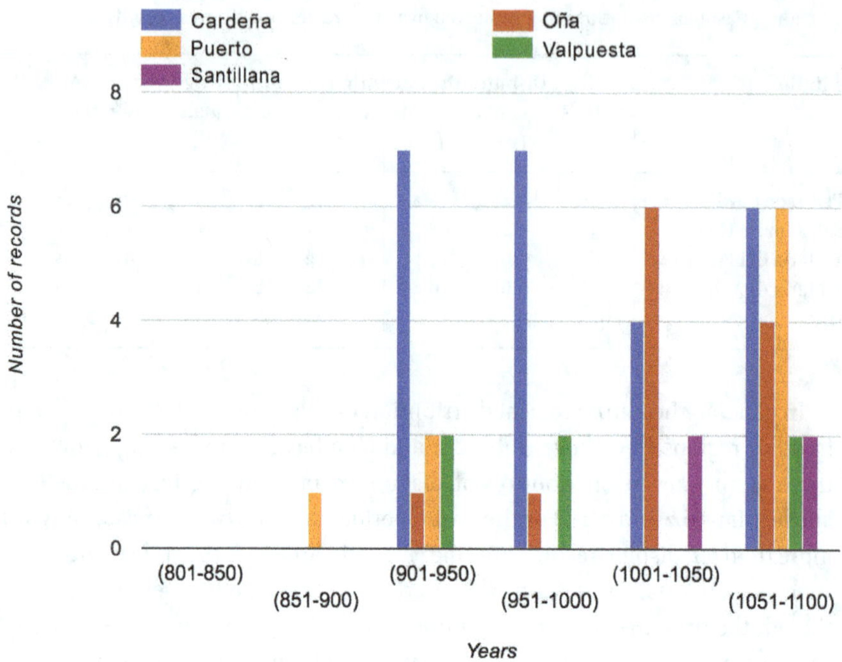

GRAPH 3.2 Largest Castilian collections of pre-1100 dispute records, by half-century

As is the case in Navarre, Aragon, and Galicia, this documentation is copied for the most part in cartularies, with hardly any single-sheet parchments,[21] and a sizeable number of dispute records are considered by their editors to be forgeries or to have been manipulated in some way to further the plans and objectives of the institutions which produced those cartularies (see above, Table 0.3 and Graph 0.6). How did these strategies affect dispute records? It is not possible to compare the frequency of falsification between these and other types of documents since the PRJ database only has information on the authenticity of the former. However, only two Castilian dispute records, from Santa María del Puerto and Oña, have raised suspicions regarding their authenticity.[22] This low number suggests that, again as in the case of Galicia, Navarre, and Aragon, falsifications are not numerous among dispute records.[23]

---

21 For the entire period there are only seven dispute records written on single-sheet parchments: four from Valpuesta, two from Covarrubias, and one from Santillana.

22 Puerto 2 (927) and Oña 12 (1011); for suspicions about the authenticity of the latter, see Manuel Zabalza Duque, ed., *Colección diplomática de los Condes de Castilla* (Valladolid, Junta de Castilla y León, 1998), no. 69, esp. pp. 503–506.

23 On the nature of Castilian judicial records, see Igor Santos Salazar, "Ruling through court:

Given the almost total absence of single-sheet parchments, it is difficult to address questions related to the material aspects of dispute records. It is worthwhile, however, to note the way the texts were ordered, dated, and copied into the cartularies in which they have come down to us,[24] not least because this has a bearing on the documents' form and typology. The importance of the transmission processes will be seen more easily as we proceed to analyse the form and content of these records.

3 Overview of the Types of Dispute Records Extant in Castile

The 61 Castilian dispute records are largely copied in the cartularies of six monasteries: Cardeña, Oña, Santa María del Puerto, Valpuesta, Santillana, and Covarrubias. These records have some features in common with the dispute records from other regions as well as some that set them apart. One can find information about disputes across different documentary formats, but these records are invariably monastic in their origin. Such information is, in general, very fragmentary. Only rarely is it more complete, in documents that we may describe as summary accounts of dispute settlement processes. These documents recount—generally in past tense and with more narrative detail than other texts—how the conflict began and how it evolved, presenting the parties involved and their respective claims, the forum before which the case was brought, and sometimes detailing the composition of the tribunal and the nature of its authority. Often, these documents mention the evidence—both oral and documentary—that was demanded by the court and how it was obtained, as well as the ruling handed down by the judge and, sometimes, how it was enforced and the guarantees and fines in place in case of failure to comply with the terms of the sentence.

The other types of dispute records fit into one of two groups. The first comprises documents that focus explicitly on one or more procedures in the course of court proceedings: in the case of confessions, the acknowledgement of guilt and/or of the other party's claim, or the oaths taken; in the case of judicial trans-

---

the political meaning of the settlement of disputes in Castile and Álava (ca. 900–1038)," *Al-Masāq: Journal of the Medieval Mediterranean* 29, no. 2 (2017), 33–50.

24 Julio Escalona, Cristina Jular Pérez de Alfaro and Anna Bellettini, "Two graphical models for the analysis and comparison of cartularies," *Digital Medievalist* 1 (2017), at http://journal.digitalmedievalist.org/articles/10.16995/dm.55/ (accessed 30 July 2020). However, as the authors rightly points out, this method can only be applied cartulary by cartulary, and this work is yet to be done.

actions, the way in which the court ruling, or sometimes the agreed-upon resolution, was carried out. The second group is made up of documents—mostly land conveyances—with indirect references to disputes, apparently incidental to the main purpose of the record.

Before looking into the different types of dispute records extant for Castile, one should recall what was said in the introduction to this volume about the need to dispense with standard, ideal diplomatic models, and take a perspective that combines, in the context of each documentary collection, the different pieces of information about disputes and the different formats in which this information is recorded. Ultimately, it is a matter of trying to contextualize as much as possible these records, which elude traditional diplomatic categories and for which we often ignore when, where, why, or under what circumstances they were written.[25] Furthermore, while examining the document forms through which information about disputes was mainly channelled in the collections of individual institutions, one must also keep in mind that the archives of major ecclesiastical houses came to incorporate those of smaller entities, as happened elsewhere in northern Iberia.

As in other regions, in the Castilian corpus much information about disputes is to be gained from judicial transactions, that is, charters of donation, sale, or exchange that record transactions following a court case. There are twice as many documents of this kind as accounts of disputes, which are the second most numerous format. The cartulary of Cardeña contains the largest number of records of both types; and Santa María del Puerto's cartulary has the second-highest number of judicial transactions but no accounts. Confessions are almost as numerous as accounts and they can be found in almost all the collections. An examination of the information provided by confessions, together with several oaths, will allow us to identify some of the most important issues in the Castilian corpus of dispute records, which in turn can be compared to other regional corpora.

Given that Cardeña's collection includes the largest volume of texts with references to conflicts, disputes, and their modes of resolution, the observations that follow will be based on this corpus, keeping in mind the caveat mentioned above about the miscellaneous provenance of these texts. Cardeña's corpus of dispute records is made up of 24 documents (14 from the tenth century and 10 from the eleventh), the largest number of which are judicial transactions (8), followed by accounts of disputes (5), confessions (3), non-judicial transactions

25 For a suggestive exploration of the different stages at which these documents were written, both during and after court proceedings, see Davies, *Windows on Justice*, chs. 2–5 and pp. 147–149.

(3), and pacts-agreements (2), in addition to two documents recording guarantees and pledges and one confirmation charter. In what follows, I will attempt to combine the form of these documents with the judicial variables that I consider the most important for analyzing the information they contain, making pertinent comparisons with dispute records from other Castilian institutions whenever this is possible.

3.1 *Accounts of Dispute Cases*

Three of the Cardeña accounts date from the tenth century and two from the eleventh. They are characterized by the fact that one party is always a monastic institution and by the narrative quality of the texts. They differ from one another as to the third parties[26] before which the suit is brought and as to the emphasis placed on other aspects of judicial process, such as the kinds of proof that are requested or presented and the resolutions that are reached. They also differ from one another in the status of the other party and the reason for the dispute: in three cases a monastery is engaged in a dispute with a group of lay people over water or pasture rights, whereas the other two are disputes with individual ecclesiastics over property.

The earliest of the conflicts over water use, dated from 932, is a dispute between the abbot of the monastery of San Torcuato and a group of *heredes* from several *villae* over the water being used by mills built along an irrigation channel running from Castañares to Burgos. The suit was brought before a comital assembly, and the document mentions the attendance not only of Count Fernán González, his *alferez*, Gómez Díaz, and other magnates, but also a large crowd including inhabitants of several places in the area. To prove the abbot's claim, the court ordered the document backing up his rights to be presented and a monk to take an oath to vouch for the document's authenticity. However, before this could be done, the *heredes* admitted their defeat (*cognouerunt se per iustitiam et non fecerunt illum iurare*) and acknowledged the monastery's claim, and fines were established for anyone who disregarded the claim.[27]

26 I borrow the term 'third parties' from anthropology, instead of the more usual 'tribunal' in order to avoid identifying the authority that rules on the case. I also use 'forum' and 'assembly' in the same way; see Julio Escalona, "Community meetings in early medieval Castile," in *Power and Place in Europe in the Early Middle Ages*, ed. Jayne Carroll, Andrew Reynolds, and Barbara Yorke (Oxford: Oxford University Press, for the British Academy, 2019), 216–237.

27 Cardeña 22 (932).

The other two accounts over productive resources date from 1073.[28] One, which was settled by King Alfonso VI of León-Castile (r. 1065–1109), is the well-known case in which the *infanzones* from the Orbaneja valley, who represented four out of the five *villae* in the valley, denied common pasture rights to the inhabitants of the fifth *villa*, who were dependents of Cardeña. It was ruled that, despite the pretensions of the rest of the valley, the monastery's dependents had an equal right to the common pastures. The other account from the same year was heard before an assembly made up of a judge, an aristocrat who had authority over the area, a *maiorinus*, and many others. It recounts how a group of *heredes* from Olmos de Pisuerga[29] sued the lay *tenente* of the monastery of Santa María de Rezmondo over a water channel for the mill that they had built on a farm belonging to the monastery, below the monastery's own mills. They maintained that it belonged to them *per foro*. In this case as well, the lay group's suit came to nothing.

As for property disputes between churchmen, in 945 a dispute between a priest by the name of Ariolfo, that another document connects to Cardeña, and a monk named Esteban, from Valeránica, over the inheritance of another priest, named Jimeno, was decided before an assembly made up entirely of ecclesiastics. The assembly investigated the documentary evidence presented by each party and found that one of the monk's documents was false. His claim was therefore denied, and in an act of self-humiliation he begged for forgiveness and threw the false document into the fire.[30]

In 966 a case was recorded in which a nun from the convent of San Julián repeatedly disobeyed the rule of her house. The forum in which the case was decided is not indicated in the document, but it was also probably an assembly of ecclesiastics. The ruling sentenced the nun to expulsion, though it seems that an agreement of some kind was reached.[31]

Before commenting in more detail on the information about judicial process provided by this small group of accounts, it will be worthwhile to pause briefly to consider how they are written, recalling that one of the features they have in common is their narrative character. With the exception of the first one, which is recounted in the first person by the abbot (*ego Stefanus abba sic*

28 Cardeña 340 and 342.

29 It is interesting that in 1072 a large group of men from this *villa*—among whom we are able to identify the judge and some of the *heredes* who are mentioned in this account—donated their own church in Olmos to Diego, a priest and abbot who that same day handed himself over to that church of Santa María, BGC 248 and 249.

30 Cardeña 55. See also below.

31 Cardeña 129. We should note that the nun's representative, a priest named Juan, acted on her behalf, and that, together with other witnesses, a surety confirmed the agreement.

abui iudicio cum ...),[32] all the others present impersonal accounts using similar formulas, typical of this format, alluding to the origin of the lawsuit: *sic abuerunt questionem et querellam, orta est intentio inter, altercatio que est orta inter, orta fuit contemptio inter*.[33] What meaning can we deduce from this? When, by whom, and in which scriptorium were these documents drawn up? What purpose were they intended to serve? To whom were they addressed when they were written? Who was their intended audience when they were copied into the cartulary of Cardeña? At what point did they acquire the narrative format in which they have been preserved?[34] Admittedly, these are difficult questions to answer, but by asking them we keep them within the framework of our analysis.

The texts of two accounts allow us to dig deeper into these questions and to imagine what strategies Cardeña was pursuing in writing down these cases and including them in the monastery's cartulary. The account from 945—a dispute over the property of the priest Jimeno—is a well-known text that is frequently used by historians wanting to show that in the Middle Ages the trustworthiness of a document was assessed on the basis of diplomatic criteria alone, which is tantamount to believing that these criteria are objective. The text's emphasis on the scrutiny of the documents that were presented in court to settle the dispute seems to back up this interpretation. It declares as false the *carta traditionis* that a monk from Valeránica presented to prove the transfer of the disputed properties to his monastery, and as authentic the *cartula comparationis* with which the priest Ariolfo—no connection to Cardeña is mentioned—defended his rights to the properties by virtue of having bought them.[35] The account of the dispute was copied in the cartulary after this record of sale. The two texts are treated as a single document by the editors of the *Becerro Gótico*, who hypothesize that this pairing of documents predates the cartulary. That is, they would have been written together on a single sheet of parchment that the cartulary scribe chose to reproduce. This hypothesis seems plausible enough, though it is difficult to prove.[36]

32 Cardeña 22 (932).

33 Cardeña 55 (945), 129 (966), 340 (1073) and 342 (1073).

34 This last question stems from the debate about the composite nature of many of the copies transmitted in cartularies. On all these questions, see Escalona, "Cartularios, memoria y discurso."

35 This is a sale by the priest Jimeno to the priest Ariolfo of a group of properties (not mentioned in the account) that make up the former's inheritance in Burgos—including lands, houses, and the church of Santa Cruz and San Julián—for 102 silver *sueldos* and six crimson *sayales*, BGC 69 (914).

36 Julio Escalona, "Antes de los cartularios," mentions other Castilian texts about one and

However, the placement of these two texts—neither of which mentions the monastery of Cardeña—on fols. 20^{v} A and 21 A of the cartulary obscures the pre-existing link between the buyer, the priest Ariolfo, and Cardeña. Only a few months before the dispute, Ariolfo had entered the monastery by means of a *traditio* that is copied many folios earlier in the cartulary.[37] This gap between documents, which dissociates the dispute and its outcome from the pre-existing link between Ariolfo and the monastery, reveals some of the strategies underpinning the compilation of Cardeña's cartulary. In my opinion, the priest Ariolfo's link to Cardeña helps us to better understand the reasons for his legal victory over the monk from Valeránica. One should not be misled by the impersonal style in which the text of the account is written, nor by the 'objective' criteria reportedly used to judge the value of the written evidence presented in court.[38] While it is true that Cardeña is not mentioned in this text, Cipriano and Esteban, two of the abbots who make up the judicial assembly, can be identified by other documents as successive abbots of Cardeña.[39] The fact that a document is declared authentic or false in court, therefore, also needs to be understood in light of the power relations between the different parties to the suit, since we do see a willingness on the part of the litigants to employ these standards of authenticity for their own strategic purposes. Moreover, it is perhaps not farfetched to imagine that Cardeña was interested in preserving in its cartulary—which was compiled in the last third of the eleventh century—a record of this 'diplomatic' victory over Valeránica, for reasons of competition. To be able to publicly demonstrate that a false document was presented by Valeránica, whose scriptorium possibly still enjoyed the great prestige it had earned a century earlier, might have increased Cardeña's own prestige.[40]

---

the same issue that were copied together on single-sheet parchments. He suggests this was done mostly for administrative reasons but does not rule out the possibility that legal disputes were also a reason for this practice.

37 BGC 23, fol. 8 (March 945).

38 On the ignorance on the part of historians of the criteria used in the Middle Ages to determine the authenticity of a document, see Julio Escalona, "Lucha política y escritura. Falsedad y autenticidad documental en el conflicto entre el monasterio de Santo Domingo y el burgo de Silos (ss. XIII–XIV)," in *Conflictos sociales, políticos e intelectuales en la España de los siglos XIV y XV* (*XIV Semana de Estudios Medievales de Nájera*) (Logroño: Instituto de Estudios Riojanos, 2004), 205–252.

39 Cipriano is documented as the abbot of Cardeña up to 944, while Esteban appears in that role from February 945. The reason why they are both present in this lawsuit is not clear, but it may be that one of the names belonged to a different figure.

40 On San Pedro de Valeránica and its famous scribe Florencio, see Manuel Díaz y Díaz, "El

We should also address Cardeña's motives in producing an account of the 1073 dispute that was mentioned above between the group of *heredes* from Olmos and the lay *tenente* of the monastery of Rezmondo, whose name was Vermudo Sendíniz.[41] This text is part of a group of documents that is believed to have come to Cardeña with the incorporation of the monastery of Rezmondo, also in 1073, by means of the *traditio* that Vermudo himself made a few months after the lawsuit.[42] Indeed, there are signs that the conflict prompted the compilers of the *Becerro Gótico* to include this dossier, among which is a false charter attributed to Count Fernán González that seems to have been drawn up in the same context.[43] The fact that Vermudo Sendíniz appears in the account of the dispute not as the owner but as the *tenente* of Rezmondo makes it reasonable to conclude that, in spite of the date on the *traditio*, the monastery was transferred to Cardeña before and not after the dispute.[44] This *traditio*, which is copied in the cartulary at the head of this group of documents, recounts how Vermudo Sendíniz had been given the Rezmondo monastery by King Sancho II of Castile-León (r. 1065–1072) as a reward for his services.[45] And, sure enough, this royal gift, from two years earlier, is copied into the cartulary after the *traditio* and before the account of the dispute.[46] In this case also, the ordering of documents obscures Vermudo Sendíniz's connection to Cardeña at the time of his dispute with the *heredes* from Olmos.

escriptorio de Valeránica," In *Codex Biblicus Legionensis. Veinte estudios* (León: Real Colegiata de San Isidoro, 1999), 53–72; and a brief summary in BGC, pp. 65–67. It is true that one should ask, as Julio Escalona suggested to me in a private communication, if the memory of Valeránica's splendour would still have aroused a competitive impulse in Cardeña, since more than twenty years had passed since Valeránica was annexed to the Burgos cathedral when Cardeña's cartulary was compiled.

41 Cardeña 342 (8 August 1073) = BGC 228, fol. 63v A-B.

42 BGC 226 (30 November 1073), fol. 62v A-B.

43 On this batch of 14 documents, which was part of a family/monastic archive, and its incorporation into Cardeña, where the 'false' 969 charter by Fernán González (BGC, 229) could have been drawn up, see BGC, pp. 204–207 and 225–245.

44 After commenting on King Sancho II's 1071 donation of Rezmondo to Vermudo Sendíniz, Fernández Flórez and Serna believe that this monastery was transferred to Cardeña in November 1073 because of difficulties arising from the conflict that had taken place a few months earlier, BGC, p. 319, n. 1054.

45 In appreciation of this gift, Vermudo Sendíniz, who is thought to work as a royal scribe, gave the king a *librum misticum* that, according to the editors of the *Becerro Gótico*, indicates a circulation of codices that we can barely guess at, BGC, p. 207.

46 BGC 227 (26 March 1071), fols. 62v B-63 B.

An exploration of these issues should, therefore, help us to understand some of the reasons why these lawsuits were recorded, and why such records were preserved and transmitted, which means delving deeper into the complexities of cartulary-making. Furthermore, it is important to consider the ways in which the different procedures and practices involved in the settlement of disputes were recorded in documentary formats other than the accounts looked at so far. Are we to surmise that the judicial information that has come down to us in other kinds of dispute records is the result of each step in the court process being written down in a document? Or is it simply that these records served other purposes or met other needs arising from different socio-political contexts? An examination of these other types of records conveying information about disputes at Cardeña will allow us to refine these hypotheses.

3.2 *Confessions*

There are three documents, all from the tenth century, that take this format. In the earliest one, a priest by the name of Gonzalo, in response to a claim by Cardeña, declared before Count Fernán González and many others that for three years he retained a *casa* in Pesquera de Ebro and (apparently) the church of Santos Justo, Pastor y Saturnino, which his uncle Alarico had given *per testamentum et scriptura* to the monastery. Therefore, in obedience to the orders of the count and of a Bishop Basilio, he restored these properties and guaranteed, by means of establishing a punishment for non-compliance, that no one in his family would claim them. Narrated in the first person, which is the main feature that documents in this format share (*manifestus sum egu Gundissalbo presbiter*), and containing several expressions regarding the truth of the statement (*uerum est quod negare non ualeo*; *sic me cognosco in ueritate*), this confession entails the explicit restitution of the disputed property, which is effected through the *saio* (*consigno et persolbio per manus sayone*), as is often the case.[47] No penalties are mentioned, only a punishment in the event that a dispute arises over the properties. The document refers to itself as *hanc manifestum* but also *hanc scedula restaurationis*, which seems to indicate a link between the two acts of confession and restitution.[48]

It is interesting to compare and contrast the lawsuit described in this confession with the dispute discussed above between the monk Esteban, from

---

47 On the judicial role of *saiones* in the different regions of northern Iberia, see Davies, *Windows on Justice*, 164–168.

48 Cardeña 35 (941).

Valeránica, and the priest Ariolfo, who was connected to Cardeña, which had a similar cause: the bequest of a priest. In both, the documentary evidence proves decisive for the outcome of the case, though in the case of Gonzalo Cardeña's possession of the disregarded charter of gift does not seem to have been sufficient, and the confession of the guilty party was needed.[49] But it is not only that these disputes were recorded in different formats: the forums in which they were resolved were also different. In one case, the dispute was brought before an assembly of ecclesiastics, and in the other a comital assembly. It is also interesting to note that the text of a confession, which would seem to be intended simply to record the losing party's acknowledgement of guilt or an admission of the truth of the winning party's claim, can contain as much information about the court proceedings as does a narrative account. Why were the different formats used, then? Is it perhaps the fact that the dispute recorded in a confession is criminal in nature, which determined how the event was consigned to writing? Or did the format depend more on the forum in which each of the two cases was tried?[50] It would be worthwhile to look at both factors together to determine how they affect the way similar disputes are recorded.

A second confession also refers to a conflict over the gift of a priest. In this case, someone named García is obliged by the representative of Cardeña's abbot to confess before Count Fernán González and many others that his brother, a priest by the name of Oveco, had donated the *casa* of San Pedro y San Pablo de Tobilla to the monastery when he entered it and that he, García, expelled the monks who were living there, until he was forced by an order from the count to restore it to them. García makes this confession because he is not able to present the charter of gift for the *casa* that, he alleged, his brother had given to him. The text, which is also in the first person (*manifestus sum ego Garsea*) and repeatedly refers to itself as a *manifestum*, which also took place before a comital assembly, contains a greater amount of information about judicial process than do other confessions. However, this information is a bit disorganized, in that it alludes to, among other things, a formal commitment to appear in court—a step that precedes the judgement—in which García promised to appear with the documents (*meas cartas*) to prove his alleged ownership, with a surety pledging to pay 300 *sueldos* to the count if he failed to comply. This

49 Fernández Flórez and Serna believe that the charter that priest Gonzalo is alluding to is the 917 *traditio*-donation by the priest Alarico, which is copied in the following folios of the *Becerro Gótico*, BGC 297.

50 According to Davies's hypothesis, mentioned above, the format is mostly associated with the stage at which the information was put into writing. She classifies confessions as "primary records", or texts written during court proceedings or shortly after.

guarantee does not seem to have taken effect because García did appear in court and admitted that he was not able to present proof; neither is there any mention of a restitution, which might have taken place before, and thus the confession closes the case. Again, it is the criminal formulation that requires the explicit confession of the guilty party. And this narrative 'disorganization' seems to be a reflection of the different stages of a far longer process than a one-off 'judicial confession' would suggest.[51]

The last confession preserved in Cardeña's collection is dated 972. It was likewise resolved in a comital assembly, this time before Count García Fernández and Burgos's *concilium*, in the presence of many *boni homines* across the social spectrum (*a minimo usque ad maximo*). It is also narrated in first person by one Iñigo and his brother the priest Galindo, who acknowledge that they are guilty (*manifesti sumus culpauiles nos ese*) of having denied in court, under oath, that they had received a loan of some wine from a monk of Cardeña.[52] This case might seem less important than the ones discussed above due to the lesser value of the disputed goods, but it is highly significant due to the emphasis placed on the act of perjury (*in uanitate* and *in falsitate*) and its implications. Both the judges and the men who had vouched for the truth in this deal ended up looking like untrustworthy men (*fallaciosos*). The crime of deceit is, thus, the background against which this confession was made and recorded. But the document, whose reiterative quality seems to suggest an attempt to combine two texts,[53] provides even more information, since the only possible resolution that the accused themselves can imagine is a *rogo et pacto*, in other words a negotiation process that is barely alluded to here but whose ritual is used in other procedures.[54] The agreement to hand over a vineyard to the count as a fine must have been the result of these negotiations, which may have involved a group of men who subscribe the record stating that they were present both at

51 Cardeña 90 (957). Igor Santos comments on this document in order to make the point that documentary evidence was essential in sustaining property claims by ecclesiastical bodies and laymen alike; see below, Chapter 10, p. 296.

52 Cardeña 151 (972).

53 Fernández Flórez and Serna point out the similarities between this document and earlier confessions, but they also say that "it was put together in a rather irregular, anarchic way", perhaps due to the desire to record in a single document two separate proceedings: the trial and the payment or fine (BGC, p. 259). However, both situations seem to be seamlessly combined in the 941 document commented on above (Cardeña 35).

54 This ritual is implicitly referred to in a number of judicial transactions for indicating the payment of fines: *rogauimus tibi cum una vinea*, Cardeña 263 (1050); in a document from Oña a portion of the fine is negotiated: *uenimus ad rogo*, Oña 52 (1067); *et pro rogo de omnes vonos pariabimus ipsa nostra ereditate*, Covarrubias 15 (1027).

the confession and at the payment of the fine (*sic in manifestatione qualiter et in pectatione*). It is noteworthy that in this case the evidence being put forward and questioned in the trial is the oath itself, instead of a document.

Beyond the repeated formulas that guide the narratives, there are several other features that one can observe both in the confession records from Cardeña and in the few that are extant from other Castilian collections: the frequent involvement of priests, or members of their families;[55] the fact that an inheritance is frequently the origin of the dispute; the judicial context in which they are made; the criminal nature of the suit; and the link between confession and restitution in cases related to property,[56] and between confession and payment of a fine in other kinds of cases.[57] To what extent did the fact that the cases were resolved in a comital forum influence the way the lawsuit was recorded? Doubtless, this variable should be kept in mind in order to broaden the scope of research.

3.3 *Oaths*

Before going on to discuss other document formats in Cardeña's corpus of dispute records, we should point out that the Valpuesta and Puerto collections, which contain no accounts of disputes, do have several documents recording verbatim oaths, which are lacking in Cardeña's collection. In 911, the scribe who recorded a lawsuit between the abbot of Valpuesta and two priests—who denied having previously made a gift to that institution—decided to include the statements of the abbot's witnesses, who swore that they had been present when the *traditio* was made and had even been involved in the delimitation

55 I mean as parties to the disputes, not in the tribunals or as witnesses, where we find them even more often. On priests, see Wendy Davies, "Local priests and the writing of charters in Northern Iberia in the tenth century," in *Chartes et cartulaires*, ed. Escalona and Sirantoine, 29–43.

56 Puerto 1 (863) is described as a *scriptura manifestationis uel consignationis*, because Rebelio's confession here clearly leads to the restitution of the disputed property. But the confession record most like the ones from Cardeña is Valpuesta 33 (956), in which the priest Sesvuto, as a party to a suit involving the monastery of Valpuesta, has to acknowledge before the judge that a house in Pando belonged to the monastery. The confession functions as a confirmation of Valpuesta's ownership, corroborated moreover by many witnesses, including several *saiones* and priests.

57 When Citi Pinioliz, who had a wife *dotata and arrata*, acknowledges having committed adultery and fornication with his daughter-in-law, the judges themselves corroborate that both the confession and the payment of the fine were made in their presence, Covarrubias 11 (979). Upon acknowledging (*cognosco me in ueritate*) that he has not been able to make good on a pledge, Falcón Falcones cedes other properties, and the document confirms and guarantees this, Oña 52 (1067).

of the disputed properties. Interestingly, in this text, described as a *iudicius uel manifestus*, the witnesses' oath (*condiciones sacramentorum*), which takes up most of the parchment sheet, is clearly distinguished from the confession, or *agnitio*, of the guilty parties (*cognouimus quod uerum testificauerunt*). This confession was prompted by the testimony given by the witnesses before the altar of the church of San Millán de Gabinea (Orduña) as ordered by Gonzalo Téllez, count of Lantarón. Thus, the evidence that was demanded and accepted in court—over an issue similar to the ones in the suits discussed above, and which, like them, involved priests—was, once again, an oath.[58]

There is a similar text that contains the sworn testimony for the monastery of Valpuesta in its suit against Puerto. The witnesses in this case swear an oath—as ordered by several judges, among whom three abbots are named—that they know for a fact that a priest by the name of Fenesterio donated the church of San Martín and all its property to Santa María de Valpuesta when he entered the monastery. They take the oath with their hands on the written statement itself, placed on the altar of the church. Unlike the previous document, this one lacks an *agnitio*, or confession, by the other party, perhaps because it records an earlier stage in the proceedings.[59]

In Puerto's collection there is a long text in which an oath is inserted into the narrative of a court case. The scribe uses the standard, first person *conditiones sacramentorum* formula to record the oath by which the various witnesses for the abbot swore that the *villa* of Carriazo, over which the monastery was suing a family group of *heredes* from Soario, had been donated to the monastery by the priest Elías.[60] After this sworn testimony has been given, next comes the confession, in the past tense, of the *heredes*, acknowledging the truth of what has been testified and restoring the disputed *villa* to the abbot, who received it through the *saio* and before *boni homines*. There is another document from the same year about this case which, in my opinion, can be classified as a formal commitment to appear in court, made by both parties before a *saio*.[61] In this *placitum*, an abbot by the name of Montano and a priest by the name of Cissela vow to a *saio* named Rodano to appear on the feast day of Saint Bartholomew, in August, before two priest-judges, Esnici and Dulcidio, or be fined five *sueldos*. The abbot appears with others to testify and swear that the *villa* of Carriazo, which is the disputed property, had belonged to one *domnus* Elías, a priest attached to the monastery of Puerto, who had inherited it from his family. For

58 Valpuesta 10 (911).
59 Valpuesta 11 (919).
60 Puerto 2 (927).
61 Puerto 3 (927).

his part, the priest Cissela would testify that he bought the property from Elías and his mother. This is not, then, a text containing the "execution of the sentence", as the editor has argued due to the fact that it is dated a few months after the trial. This commitment to appear in court is also of interest because it is the only one in the entire Castilian corpus that has been preserved as a separate text, although we have seen references to this practice in documents with other formats.[62]

These oaths share several features with confessions. They both allude to a similar social context, in which priests are engaged in conflicts, and both are performed in court, by order of the count or judges. However, the oaths have a specific ritual and a sacred space inside churches, which we do not see in the confessions. Moreover, none of the Castilian oaths is associated with a criminal case.

3.4 *Judicial and Non-judicial Transactions*

There is also relevant information about disputes to be derived from judicial transactions. These are mainly charters of gift and exchange in which the conflict is often formulated in criminal terms—that is, as the result of someone having committed a crime. Thus, a man by the name of Martín, who did not have the wherewithal to pay the fine of 400 *sueldos* for the robbery that he had been "guided by the devil" to commit at a church, is obliged to hand over his farm to Cardeña.[63] One can imagine that he handed over this property only after having pled—that is, negotiated—with the monastery to settle the case. Likewise, a man named Juan and his wife used their garden and vineyard to beg (*rogauimus tibi … cum*) to settle their default on certain obligations.[64] In an interesting *carta traditionis*, a nun declares that she is donating her own convent to Bishop Gómez, who will leave it to Cardeña upon his death, because she did not have the 100 *sueldos* to pay the bishop for the convent's consecration and could not cover the expenses for the food that was usually served at such celebrations.[65] Also interesting is the donation that someone named Fronilde made to her daughter Natalia in order to provide a bequest that was equal to that left to her sister Regina. It is possible that this transaction, which was done

62 Cardeña 90 (957). On account of the scarcity of these formal commitments, which have a standard format in first person present, Davies does not set them apart as a separate category of judicial documents. Moreover, in her opinion, these documents were never intended to be preserved. However, the use of similar formulas (though these are not included in the *Lex Visigothorum*) leads her to believe that very old conventions were being followed, Davies, *Windows on Justice*, 135.

63 Cardeña 374 (1083).

64 Cardeña 263 (1050).

65 Cardeña 247 (1045).

within the family but in the presence of Villafría's *concilium* and a priest named Cristóbal, who was also a *maiorinus*, is the result of a claim by the 'disinherited' or unequally settled upon sister.[66]

In addition to teaching us about judicial practice, these transactions shed light on the tensions and conflicts that arose in these local societies and how they were resolved. They barely refer to the forum before which the disputes were brought. Among the transactions in the Cardeña corpus, besides the case just mentioned, involving the division of the family estate before the local *concilium* and a *maiorinus*, we also know of a transfer that a family had to make to Cardeña to comply with a decision (*prouidentia*) by Count Fernán González and by judges *et seniorum turbam ex concilio* from Burgos.[67] More than a century later, the transfer of small gardens to the abbot of Cardeña by two men, Gonzalo and Alfonso, and their neighbours from Villariezo seems to settle a lawsuit that had been presided over by judges from Burgos. This transfer, which enlarged the monastery's orchard and made it more compact, seems to have been obtained in exchange for pardoning an unpaid debt.[68] Sometimes the text of a transaction includes the confession of wrong that gave rise to the transfer, and this provides much more information about the context of the lawsuit.[69]

The indirect information contained in non-judicial transactions in the Castilian corpus is almost negligible. There are only three documents of this kind from Cardeña and one from Oña which allude to the fact that the property being transferred had been the subject of previous lawsuits. From Cardeña there are documents about a group of *heredes* donating a church that they had disputed in court;[70] about Vermudo Godestioz and a *villa* he had acquired in a suit presided over by Count Fernán González;[71] and about some houses and farm that a man named Morello donated when he joined the monastery, adding that he had sued his lord over these properties.[72] From Oña we have a large gift by Munio Díaz de Caleruega and his family, who had received some of the valuable properties donated from an individual whom Munio had helped by paying

66 Cardeña 192 (984).

67 Cardeña 36 (950).

68 Cardeña 329 (1070).

69 In Camesa's *concilium*, Munio Leceniz and his wife Gotina restore to Abbot Juan of Santa Juliana (Santillana) the land they had in Villa Periedo, acknowledging (*cognobimus*) the monastery's claim to those lands together with others, Santillana 35 (1022). Also, Puerto 47 (1086).

70 Cardeña 54 (945).

71 Cardeña 59 (947).

72 Cardeña 332 (1071).

a judicial fine (a horse) for him.[73] It is noteworthy that some of these non-judicial transactions refer to judicial transactions the records of which seem to have been lost.[74]

3.5 *Documents Recording Guarantees and Pledges*

A different kind of information comes from documents recording guarantees. This is how I think we should understand the confirmation made by a man named Diego Ovecoz to his nephews and *heredes* and in the presence of *boni homines*—among whom there was a judge—of the sale of some water rights to the monastery of San Martín de Villabáscones, made fifteen days before the confirmation, and of which there is also an extant record.[75] The terminology used (*autorifico, roboro*) makes it likely that this confirmation is provided because such rights had been challenged or in order to prevent them from being challenged. It thus constitutes a kind of security. Somewhat different, but with a similar purpose, is a document in which a priest named Juan publicly promises to stand surety for a man named Daniel that he would comply with the court's ruling in a suit over a plot of land being disputed between Daniel and the abbot of Cardeña alongside a monk named Velasco.[76]

There are also some records of pledges in the Castilian corpus. As an example, there is a very short document from Valpuesta in which a man called Vermudo names sureties, before the abbot, Álvaro. In the event that he is unable to fulfil the agreement with the abbot, the sureties commit to hand over their cows to the monastery.[77] Even though we have little documentation on this issue, sureties seem to have had a frequent—sometimes even essential—role in the different stages of judicial process.[78] A good illustration of this practice comes from a confession record from Oña. In it, someone by the name of Falcón Falcones acknowledges that he was not able to pay the security of 200

73 Oña 84 (1084).

74 On references to *deperdita* in Castilian dispute records, see below, Chapter 10.

75 Cardeña 87 and 88 (both 995); they are published together in BGC 37.

76 Cardeña 103 (962). This is a *fidiaturia* signed before Abbot Sarrazino, the *maiorinus* of Poza, Álvaro Zianiz, and many others.

77 Valpuesta 43 (968?): *Ego, Uermudo, sic mito fidiatores ... Ego, Uermudo, qui hanc fidiatura feci et relege[ndo] audibi, manu mea roborabi.*

78 See Valpuesta 93 ([1049–1095]?); and Santillana 81 (1062), in which three men act as sureties in a case of penal enslavement of a woman who had committed adultery. On the topic of sureties, guarantees and pledges, see Wendy Davies, "On suretyship in tenth-century northern Iberia," in *Scale and Scale Change in the Early Middle Ages. Exploring Landscape, Local Society and the World Beyond*, ed. Julio Escalona and Andrew Reynolds (Turnhout: Brepols, 2011), 133–152.

sueldos in silver that he had pledged to Abbot Enneco for Gonzalo Díaz, and he therefore was obliged to give him double that amount, 400 *sueldos*, only part of which he was able to pay, and for the rest he agreed (*uenimos ad rogo*) to hand over his property in Petrapidonia and the plots of land that had belonged to his father's *palatium*. This document confirms and guarantees the transfer of these properties.[79]

3.6 *Pacts-Agreements*

Another important type of document containing information on disputes is that of pacts-agreements. Although few in number, these records are of great interest. There are two pacts that are separated by almost one hundred years, but they have in common the fact that in both of them an agreement is made between a monastery and a group of locals, as well as the fact that both attempt to regulate water use and the maintenance of channels and mills.[80] In the first one, a document from 956, an abbot named Iñigo, a priest by the name of Mancio and the monastic community of San Martín de Villabáscones come to an agreement, in the atrium of the monastery, with the local *concilium*. The latter are granted access to the amount of water that passes through the hole in a mill wheel for use in their gardens and other needs in exchange for them keeping the channel that brings the water from a dam clear. The penalties for breach of contract by any of the parties are specified, which is quite unusual. The document ends with a collective corroboration of the pact by the entire *concilium*.[81]

In the other document, from 1065, all the people from Villa de Urrez and Cabrera, from *minimo ad maximum*, state that they have voluntarily come to an agreement (*facimus tali cautum … de spontanea nostras uoluntas*) with Abbot Iñigo of San Julián de Bezares regarding the use and maintenance of the mills that they hold in common, one in Villa Herreros on the River Arlanzón and the other in the *villa* of Urrez.[82]

Despite the long lapse of time separating these two pacts, they have several similarities that are worth pointing out:

- the apparently informal, bilateral nature of these agreements, which seem to have been reached without any third parties (this contrasts with, for

---

79 Oña 52 (1067).

80 Fernández Flórez and Serna provide a commentary on these two pacts, which they include in the category "other documents", though they say that they could be considered agreements, BGC, p. 331.

81 Cardeña 89 (956).

82 Cardeña 314 (1065).

example, the pact that Count Sancho granted to or imposed on the people living in the neighbourhood of the monastery of Oña to regulate the use of pasturelands);[83]
- the identity of the parties: a monastery and a local community, in both cases;
- the contents of the agreements, both concerning the distribution of water rights from mill dams and the maintenance of such structures;
- the local codes (*fueros*) that are alluded to in both cases, where the taks of clearing the channel and taking care of the mills are established *per foro*;[84]
- the nature of the sanctions that are stipulated in case of violation of the agreements, which in the first case are reciprocal, though this is unusual (*Si quis ex undique ambobus partibus*);
- the fact that both documents come from monasteries that were later incorporated into Cardeña, along with their respective archives, which gave rise to specific dossiers in the cartulary. San Martín de Villabáscones was handed over by Abbot Mancio in 963,[85] only a few years after the agreement mentioned above, in which he had acted as priest. This text is transmitted in the *Becerro Gótico* along with other documents from the same institution that appear distributed across different sections.[86] As for San Julián de Bezares, we do not know when it was incorporated into Cardeña, but possibly in the 1080s, when this pact was copied into the cartulary. Its text was transmitted along with others that had been copied on a single-sheet parchment after a grant by Count Fernán González whose authenticity has been the subject of debate. This group of texts made up what has been referred to as a pre-cartulary or pancarta.[87]

83 Oña 13 (1011). Santos, "Ruling through court," 146, attributes the informal—and in his view exceptional—nature of the pact with the *concilium* of Villabáscones to the relationship that must have existed between this local community and the monastery of Cardeña, since the former had collectively donated their plots of land to the latter a few years before this agreement, Cardeña 42 (944–951).

84 For a study on peasants' struggles in the negotiation of local codes (*fueros*), see Isabel Alfonso, "Campesinado y derecho: la vía legal de su lucha (Castilla y León, siglos X–XIII)," *Noticiario de Historia Agraria* 13 (1997), 15–31.

85 Cardeña 108 (963).

86 On the group of documents from Villabáscones, see BGC, pp. 186–190.

87 The whole group of documents from Bezares, which is in the same hand that wrote most of the *Becerro Gótico*, must have been copied shortly before 1086; BGC, pp. 220–221. There is also a discussion of this group of documents in Escalona, "Cartularios, memoria y discurso," 175–176.

4 Final Considerations

In these pages I have used the exceptionally rich Cardeña collection as a sample for assessing the information yielded by dispute records from Castile. Throughout my analysis, I tried to show that the motives for recording information about disputes in different documentary formats are more complex than previously assumed. After all, records of disputes are not due only, or even principally, to the alleged legal obligation to make 'official' court records or to the beneficiaries' desire to preserve a written record of court decisions in their favour.

An analysis combining documentary form with other variables has shown that disputes between monastic institutions and local communities over landed resources and basic means of production, such as water and mills, have been recorded in the form of narrative accounts and pacts-agreements; that lawsuits over the inheritance of priests, opposing their alleged heirs (among whom there might be another priest) and the institutions claiming to be the beneficiaries of such inheritances, have come down to us in the form of records of confession and oath; and, finally, that records of judicial transactions arise primarily from the punishment of crimes.

It would certainly be worthwhile to look at other factors that doubtless influenced the form that records took, such as the different forums in which disputes were settled and the status of the main litigants. While such an analysis is beyond the scope of this study, it is to be hoped that the planned improvements to the PRJ database will facilitate it down the line.[88]

Bibliography

Abbreviations

BGC: Fernández Flórez, José A., and Sonia Serna, eds. *El Becerro Gótico de Cardeña: el primer gran cartulario hispánico (1086)*. Madrid: Real Academia Española. Burgos: Instituto Castellano y Leonés de la Lengua, 2017.

Cardeña: Martínez Díez, Gonzalo, ed. *Colección documental del monasterio de San Pedro de Cardeña*. Burgos: Caja de Ahorros y Monte de Piedad del Círculo Católico de Obreros de Burgos, 1998.

Covarrubias: Serrano, Luciano, ed. *Cartulario del Infantado de Covarrubias*. Valladolid: Cuesta Editor, 1907.

88 On such improvements, see above, n. 45 to the introduction.

Oña: Álamo, Juan del, ed. *Colección diplomática de San Salvador de Oña (822–1284)*. Vol. I *822–1214*. Madrid: CSIC, 1950.

PRJ: *PRocesos Judiciales en las sociedades medievales del norte peninsular*. Accessed 30 July 2020. http://prj.csic.es/.

Puerto: Abad Barrasús, Juan, ed. *El monasterio de Santa María del Puerto (Santoña) 863–1210*. Santander: Diputación Provincial de Cantabria, 1985.

Santillana: Josúe, Eduardo, ed. *Libro de Regla o Cartulario de la antigua abadía de Santillana del Mar*. Madrid: Centro de Estudios Históricos, 1912.

Valpuesta: Ruiz Asencio, José M., Irene Ruiz Albi, and Mauricio Herrero, eds. *Los Becerros Gótico y Galicano de Valpuesta*. Madrid: Real Academia de la Lengua, 2010.

Other Primary Sources

Díez Herrera, Carmen, Luis López Ormazábal, and Rogelio Pérez Bustamante, eds. *Abadía de Santillana del Mar. Colección diplomática*. Santillana del Mar: Taurus Ediciones, Fundación Santillana, 1983.

Juárez, Paloma, Julio Escalona, and Pilar Azcárate, eds. *Documentación de Arlanza, siglos X–XI* (forthcoming).

Oceja Gonzalo, Isabel, ed. *Documentación del monasterio de San Salvador de Oña (1032–1284)*. Burgos: Ediciones J.M. Garrido Garrido, 1983.

Serrano, Luciano, ed. *Becerro Gótico de Cardeña*. Valladolid: Cuesta Editor, 1910.

Zabalza Duque, Manuel, ed. *Colección diplomática de los Condes de Castilla*. Valladolid: Junta de Castilla y León, 1998.

Secondary Works

Alfonso, Isabel. "Campesinado y derecho: la vía legal de su lucha (Castilla y León, siglos X–XIII)." *Noticiario de Historia Agraria* 13 (1997), 15–31.

Blasco Martínez, Rosa María. *Los cartularios de Cantabria (St. Toribio, Sta. María del Puerto, Santillana y Piasca): estudio codicológico, paleográfico y diplomático*. Santander: Estudio, 1986.

Davies, Wendy. "On suretyship in tenth-century northern Iberia." in *Scale and Scale Change in the Early Middle Ages. Exploring Landscape, Local Society and the World Beyond*, edited by Julio Escalona and Andrew Reynolds, 133–152. Turnhout: Brepols, 2011.

Davies, Wendy. "Local priests and the writing of charters in Northern Iberia in the tenth century" In *Chartes et cartulaires comme instruments de pouvoir. Espagne et Occident chrétien (VIII*[e]*-XII*[e] *siècles)*, edited by Julio Escalona and Hélène Sirantoine, 29–43. Toulouse: Université de Toulouse-Le Mirail, 2013.

Davies, Wendy. *Windows on Justice in Northern Iberia, 800–1000*. Abingdon: Routledge, 2016.

Díaz y Díaz, Manuel. “El escriptorio de Valeránica.” In *Codex Biblicus Legionensis. Veinte estudios*, 53–72. León: Real Colegiata de San Isidoro, 1999.

Escalona, Julio, and Pilar Azcárate. “Una fuente ‘casi’ perdida para la historia de la Castilla medieval. Notas en torno al Becerro de San Pedro de Arlanza.” *Hispania* 208 (2001), 449–474.

Escalona, Julio. “Lucha política y escritura. Falsedad y autenticidad documental en el conflicto entre el monasterio de Santo Domingo y el burgo de Silos (ss. XIII–XIV).” in *Conflictos sociales, políticos e intelectuales en la España de los siglos XIV y XV* (*XIV Semana de Estudios Medievales de Nájera*), 205–252. Logroño: Instituto de Estudios Riojanos, 2004.

Escalona, Julio. “La documentación de la Castilla Condal: viejos problemas y nuevas perspectivas.” In *Mundos Medievales. Espacios, sociedades y poder*, edited by Beatriz Arízaga Bolumburu et al., 2 vols, vol. 1, 473–487. Santander: Ediciones Universidad de Cantabria, 2012.

Escalona, Julio. “Antes de los cartularios: gestión de archivos y transmisión de los documentos de la Castilla condal (siglo IX-1038).” In *Chartes et cartulaires comme instruments de pouvoir. Espagne et Occident chrétien* (*VIII*e*-XII*e *siècles*), edited by Julio Escalona and Hélène Sirantoine, 147–167. Toulouse: Université de Toulouse-Le Mirail, 2013.

Escalona, Julio. “Cartularios, memoria y discurso en la Castilla medieval.” In *La memoria del poder, el poder de la memoria*, edited by Esther López Ojeda, 163–203. Logroño: Instituto de Estudios Riojanos, 2017.

Escalona, Julio. “Community meetings in early medieval Castile.” in *Power and Place in Europe in the Early Middle Ages*, edited by Jayne Carroll, Andrew Reynolds, and Barbara Yorke, 216–237. Oxford: Oxford University Press, for the British Academy, 2019.

Escalona, Julio, Cristina Jular, and Anna Bellettini. “Two graphical models for the analysis and comparison of cartularies.” *Digital Medievalist* 1 (2017). Accessed 30 July 2020. http://journal.digitalmedievalist.org/articles/10.16995/dm.55/.

Peterson, David. “El *Becerro Gótico* de San Millán. Reconstrucción de un cartulario perdido.” *Studia Historica. Historia Medieval* 29 (2011), 147–173.

Peterson, David. “Rebranding San Millán: the Becerro Galicano as a rejection of the monastery’s Navarrese heritage (1192–95).” *Journal of Medieval Iberian Studies* 5, no. 1 (2013), 1–20.

Santos Salazar, Igor. “Ruling through court: the political meaning of the settlement of disputes in Castile and Álava (ca. 900–1038).” *Al-Masāq: Journal of the Medieval Mediterranean* 29, no. 2 (2017), 33–50.

CHAPTER 4

Documentary Production and Dispute Records in Navarre and Aragon before the Year 1100

Isabel Alfonso

1 Navarrese and Aragonese Documents from the Ninth to the Eleventh Century

Scholars of early medieval Navarre and Aragon have consistently noted the scarcity of extant sources for both regions and the fact that the available charter editions are scattered and vary widely in their quality and their editorial criteria. This will doubtless have an impact on the general survey attempted here.[1]

Like the other regions in northern Iberia, the Navarre-Aragon area has poorly defined borders that shifted throughout the period considered here. Not only were they pushed southward, but there were also changes in the hegemonic relationship between the two political entities: the kingdom of Pamplona/Navarre and the county of Aragon, which became an independent kingdom under Ramiro I (r. 1035–1063). For the entire period before the year 1100, there are fewer than 3000 extant documents (1408 from Navarre and 1357 from Aragon). While this figure is almost three times that of the corpus in Castile and more than twice that of Portugal or Galicia, it is much lower than that of León and, of course, Catalonia (see above, Table 0.1).[2]

Both in Navarre and in Aragon, from the early decades of the ninth century and up to the last decade of the eleventh, the number of documents follows an upward trend that has several noteworthy peaks. In Navarre, the first of these peaks takes place in the middle of the tenth century, and another in 1060–

---

1 Carlos Laliena Corbera, "Problemas historiográficos de la Alta Edad Media Aragonesa: una revisión crítica," *Argensola* 113 (2003), 13–36, at 15–17; Juan J. Larrea, "La condición del campesinado navarro-aragonés entre los siglos IX y XII: una revisión crítica," *En la España Medieval* 29 (2006), 383–409, points out that, for the western Pyrenees, the sources are scarce and problematic before the second or third decade of the eleventh century. The abbreviations used in this paper for editions of charters are listed in the bibliography.

2 This comparison does not take into account the varied sizes of the regions compared; cf. above, Map 0.1.

 | DOI:10.1163/9789004683006_006

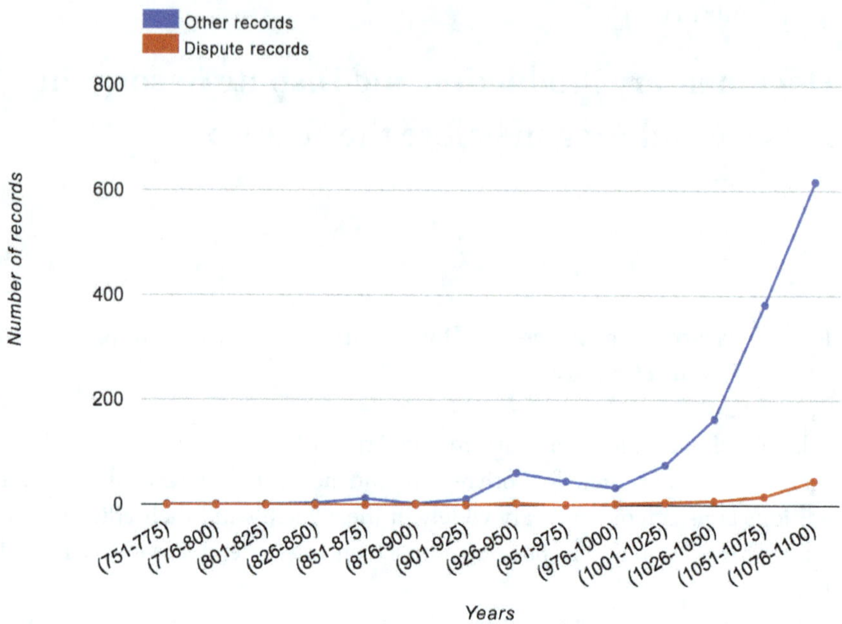

GRAPH 4.1 Proportion of Navarrese dispute records before 1100, by quarter-century

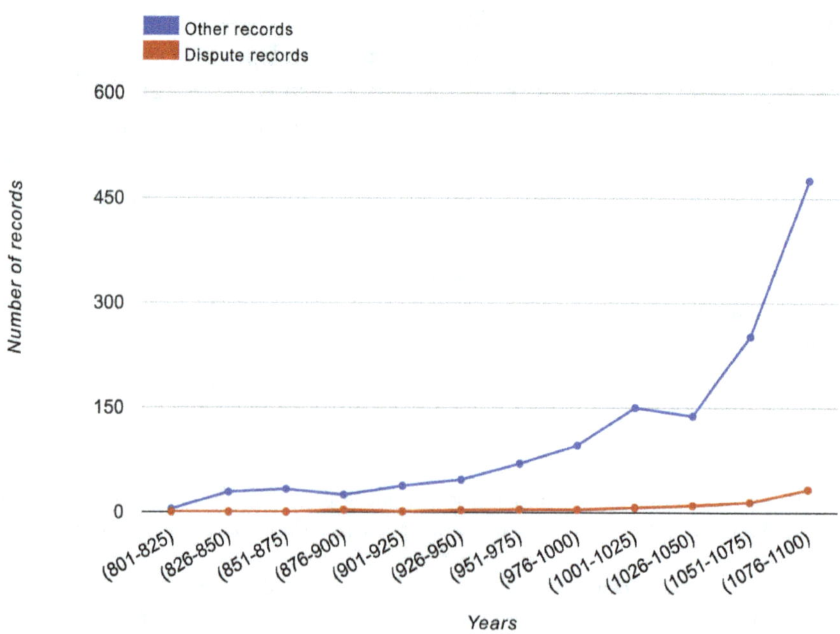

GRAPH 4.2 Proportion of Aragonese dispute records before 1100, by quarter-century

1090, with a significant decline in the 1090s. In Aragon, however, the biggest peaks correspond to the 970s, and then the 1010s, with a notable increase in 1080–1100 (see above, Table 0.2 and Graphs 0.2 and 0.4).

Of course, the unequal distribution reflects vicissitudes in the monastic scriptoria and archives that produced and/or preserved the documents. Thus, the large increase in documents from Navarre and Aragon in the eleventh century—2253 extant documents as against 401 in the tenth—is associated with the founding or strengthening (by way of royal or aristocratic patronage) of the religious institutions that produced them, and also with the process by which smaller monasteries were absorbed by some major houses. The latter came to incorporate not only the properties but also the archives of the former, after which many documents were copied into cartularies that began to be compiled in the last third of the eleventh century.[3] In any case, both in Navarre and in Aragon, the bulk of the extant documents are concentrated in the second half of the eleventh century (in Aragon there are twice as many from the second half of the century compared to the first, and in Navarre, three times as many), and in this same period dispute records are also more numerous. This increase in the volume of documents in the second half of the eleventh century, especially in the last two decades, contrasts with the situation in Galicia—where there is a concentration of documents from the first half of the century—and is more in line with what we see in León, Portugal and Castile (see above, Graphs 0.3 and 0.4).

The institutions which preserved pre-1100 records are distributed geographically among several areas (see above, Map 0.1). In the area of the western Aragonese Pyrenees, although the main institutions transmitting pre-1100 documents are the monastery of San Juan de la Peña and the Huesca-Jaca episcopal see, a large part of their documentary collections comes from monasteries that were absorbed by these institutions. Thus, San Pedro de Siresa, which in the mid-ninth century was the most important monastery in this area, being one of the main centres of power associated with the counts of Aragon, ended up becoming a priory belonging to the bishopric of Huesca-Jaca in

3 It is necessary to bear in mind the possibility, noted by Nuria Grau regarding the Roda cathedral, that there was a distortion in the type and quantity of documents that were actually being generated during this period, since the decision whether to include certain documents in the cathedral cartulary was a choice on the part of the institution; Nuria Grau Quiroga, *Roda de Isábena en los siglos X–XIII. La documentación episcopal y del cabildo catedralicio* (Zaragoza: Institución "Fernando el Católico" (CSIC), Diputación de Zaragoza, 2010), 284, at http://ifc.dpz.es/publicaciones/ver/id/3036 (accessed 30 July 2020).

1145.[4] In the eleventh century, however, the most important monastery in the kingdom of Aragon was San Juan de la Peña, which by royal order had incorporated as priories a series of lesser monasteries, including San Martín de Cillas, Santa María de Fuenfría, San Martín de Cercito and San Julián de Navasal, located in the upper valleys of this region.[5]

In the Ribagorza and Sobrarbe area of the eastern Pyrenees, the network of monasteries that was dominant until the middle of the eleventh century began to lose its ascendancy, once again due to royal intervention. Most of these monasteries were ultimately incorporated into either the episcopal see of Roda or the monastery of San Victorián de Sobrarbe.[6] Prominent among them were the monasteries of Santa María de Alaón, in the Noguera Ribagorzana valley, and Santa María de Obarra, in the Isábena valley. Alaón, the most important of these monasteries in terms of extant documents from the ninth and tenth centuries, was incorporated into the bishopric of Roda in the second half of the eleventh.[7] Obarra became a priory dependent on San Victorián at the end of the eleventh century.[8] However, unlike what happened in San Juan de la Peña, which included the documents from its incorporated monasteries in its cartulary, documents from Alaón and Obarra have come down to us through their own cartularies, since monastic life continued in both of them under the control of other institutions.

In the pre-Pyrenean area is the monastery of San Andrés de Fanlo, a modest aristocratic foundation that flourished in the middle of the eleventh century, before becoming a priory of Montearagón at the end of the century. Its documents have come down to us in a thirteenth-century cartulary.[9]

In central Navarre, the institution that transmitted most documents is the monastery of San Salvador of Leire, located in the Sierra de Leire, 50 km east

4 Antonio Ubieto Arteta, ed., *Cartulario de Siresa* (Valencia: Anubar, 1986).

5 Ana Isabel Lapeña Paúl, *El monasterio de San Juan de la Peña en la Edad Media (desde sus orígenes hasta 1410)* (Zaragoza: Caja de Ahorros de la Inmaculada Aragón, 1989). For further information, see below.

6 Grau, *Roda de Isábena*; Ángel J. Martín Duque, ed., *Colección diplomática del monasterio de San Victorián de Sobrarbe (1000–1219)* (Zaragoza: Universidad de Zaragoza, 2004).

7 Alaón.

8 Antonio Ubieto Arteta, ed., *Documentos del monasterio de Obarra (Huesca) anteriores al año 1000* (Zaragoza: Anubar, 1988); Obarra.

9 The manuscript disappeared during the Spanish Civil War and reappeared at a public auction in London in 1971. It was acquired by the University of Pennsylvania, where it is currently held at the Library of Rare Books and Manuscripts, and has now been edited: Fanlo.

of Pamplona, the episcopal see. Leire's importance is comparable to that of San Juan de la Peña.[10] To the west of Pamplona, near Estella, is located another important monastery, that of Santa María de Irache.[11]

In western Navarre, near the border with Castile, three monasteries deserve special mention: San Martín de Albelda (a royal foundation dating back to the tenth century, it served as one of the residences of the bishops of Calahorra-Nájera between 1033 and 1092);[12] San Millán de la Cogolla (another residence of the bishops of Calahorra-Nájera, located at the foot of the Sierra de la Demanda on the eastern slope separating the Meseta from the Ebro Valley);[13] and Santa María de Valvanera, in the Sierra de Cameros, not far from San Millán.[14] Also located in this area are the monastery of Santa María de Nájera and the Calahorra cathedral.[15]

1.1 *Monastic Archives and Cartularies*

Like in other regions, monasteries were the main institutions responsible for transmitting early medieval documents in Navarre and Aragon; indeed, episcopal archives have little importance here.[16] It has been pointed out, for instance, that the scarcity of documents from before 1000 makes it necessary for

10 Leire; Luis Javier Fortún, *Leire, un señorío monástico en Navarra (siglos IX–XIX)* (Pamplona: Gobierno de Navarra, 1993).

11 José María Lacarra, ed., *Colección diplomática de Irache. I. 958–1222* (Zaragoza: Instituto de Estudios Pirenaicos (CSIC), Universidad de Navarra, 1965).

12 Albelda; Eliseo Sáinz Ripa, ed., *Colección diplomática de las Colegiatas de Albelda y Logroño*, vol. 1 (*924–1399*) (Logroño, Diputación Provincial, 1981).

13 Fernando García Andreva, ed., *El Becerro Galicano de San Millán de la Cogolla. Edición y estudio* (San Millán de la Cogolla: Cilengua, 2010); a digital edition (BGD, based on the former) is now available, at www.ehu.eus/galicano (accessed 30 July 2020); Manuel Zabalza Duque, ed., *Colección diplomática de los Condes de Castilla* (Valladolid: Junta de Castilla y León, 1998).

14 Francisco Javier García Turza, ed., *Documentación medieval del monasterio de Valvanera (siglos XI–XIII)* (Zaragoza: Anubar, 1985).

15 Margarita Cantera Montenegro, ed., *Colección documental de Santa María la Real de Nájera*, vol. 1 (*Siglos X–XIV*) (San Sebastián: Sociedad de Estudios Vascos, 1991); Ildefonso Rodríguez R. de Lama, ed., *Colección diplomática medieval de La Rioja (923–1225)*, vol. II *Documentos (923–1168)* (Logroño: Gobierno de la Rioja, Instituto de Estudios Riojanos, 1976). José Ángel García de Cortázar, *La construcción de la diócesis de Calahorra en los siglos X a XIII: la Iglesia en la organización social del espacio* (Logroño, Instituto de Estudios Riojanos, 2018), 69–73, 96–107.

16 The ratio of documents preserved in episcopal archives to the overall number of records is similar in Navarre and Castille (6 per cent), whereas the figure for Aragon (14 per cent) is closer to that of Galicia (17 per cent); see above, Chapter 1.

scholars researching the bishopric of Roda, its organization, or any other subject connected to Ribagorza, to rely on records from the different monasteries in the area.[17]

The monastery of San Millán de la Cogolla stands out, with 742 documents, among the institutions that preserved early medieval records in Navarre.[18] In fact, the shape of the line graph for the region's extant documents (see above, Graph 4.1) is almost identical to that of San Millán's. Next in line, with much lower numbers, are the monasteries of Leire (184 documents) and Valvanera (189, for the eleventh century only). Three other institutions have preserved only just over 70 documents; the rest have 20 or less.

In Aragon, the archives with the greatest volume of extant documents before 1100 belong to three monasteries with more than 200 records each: Alaón (285), San Juan de la Peña (252) and Obarra (201), followed by three others that each have more than 100: San Victorián (136), Fanlo and the Roda cathedral (104 each); the rest, with the exception of the Huesca cathedral (68), have barely 20 a piece.

Another general feature of the documentation from Navarre and Aragon is the dependence on cartulary copies. There is at least one cartulary from practically every ecclesiastical institution. We know that there were two crucial periods of documentary compilation and reorganization: one that began in the final decades of the eleventh century and the early decades of the twelfth, and another in the eighteenth century.[19] Even though there is as yet no comprehensive study on the processes and contexts underpinning cartulary-making in both regions, and the existing editions are of variable quality, it is clear that some Navarrese and Aragonese cartularies, such as those from San Millán de la Cogolla, Leire and San Juan de la Peña, are amongst the most important ones produced in northern Iberia during the eleventh to thirteenth centuries.

San Millán's *Becerro Galicano* stands out not only because of the number of documents it includes, which is a clear indication of the importance that this monastery assumed during the central Middle Ages, but also because of the

17 Grau, *Roda de Isábena*.

18 This exceptional material has attracted much scholarly attention, e.g. the classical book by José Ángel García de Cortázar, *El dominio del monasterio de San Millán de la Cogolla (siglos X a XIII): Introducción a la historia rural de Castilla altomedieval* (Salamanca: Universidad de Salamanca, 1969).

19 A highly interesting and detailed study of the vicissitudes of Leire's archive appears in Fortún, *Leire*, 37–51. For the archive of the Roda cathedral, see Grau, *Roda de Isábena*, 281–284.

sound scholarship it has attracted, which helps us to better understand how the cartulary was created. The scribe who began to write the *Galicano* in about 1195 would have made use of the material in another important cartulary from the beginning of the twelfth century, the now lost *Becerro Gótico*, whose contents we know from the detailed references made to them by one of the monastery's archivists in the eighteenth century. David Peterson's reconstruction of this earlier cartulary is essential for understanding both how San Millán's scriptorium functioned and how the *Galicano* was made. He shows how this codex reorders the contents of the *Gótico* but also introduces new material, including abundant falsifications. These falsifications were, however, inserted at different times, in different styles, and for different reasons.[20]

The 'jewel' of the Leire archive is the *Becerro Antiguo*, which must have begun to be written at the end of the eleventh century. It seems to combine the *Cartulario del abad Raimundo*, expanded between 1111 and 1120, a brief *Cuaderno de privilegios reales*, also begun during the abbacy of Raimundo but later interrupted and then resumed in the following generation, and finally the *Cartulario de los abades García y Pedro*, which was compiled between 1120 and 1150.[21] However, just as in other monasteries, earlier stages of compilation have been identified in Leire, as can be seen in a *pancarta* whose documents were not included in the *Becerro Antiguo*.[22] The decision not to include these documents might have been due, as Juan José Larrea speculates, to the rejection by the new French abbot (Raimundo, the cartulary's sponsor) of the earlier plan adopted by the monastery's scriptorium, or possibly it was thought that the oldest records were already preserved in the *pancarta* as well as in a kind of royal chronicle.[23] As in so many other monasteries, in the eighteenth century there

20 The *Becerro Galicano* is held in the monastery library at San Millán. David Peterson, "Reescribiendo el pasado. El Becerro Galicano como reconstrucción de la historia institucional de San Millán de la Cogolla," *Hispania* 233 (2008), 653–682; David Peterson, "El *Becerro Gótico* de San Millán. Reconstrucción de un cartulario perdido," *Studia Historica. Historia Medieval* 29 (2011), 147–173; David Peterson, "Mentiras piadosas. Falsificaciones e interpolaciones en la diplomática de San Millán de la Cogolla," in *Las donaciones piadosas en el mundo medieval*, ed. Alfonso García Leal (Oviedo: Universidad de Oviedo, 2012), 295–314; David Peterson, "Rebranding San Millán: the Becerro Galicano as a rejection of the monastery's Navarrese heritage (1192–95)," *Journal of Medieval Iberian Studies* 5, no. 1 (2013), 1–20.

21 The *Becerro Antiguo* is currently held at the Archivo General de Navarra; Fortún, *Leire*, 40.

22 The only exception being Leire 1 (842). The published edition of Leire's documents organizes the material by date of each text rather than in cartulary order, and the same applies to the documents copied in the *pancarta*.

23 I owe this information to Juan José Larrea, who is currently supervising a Ph.D dissertation at the University of the Basque Country on the circumstances in which these sources were produced and transmitted.

was a thorough review of Leire's collections, which were reordered and copied into the *Becerro Menor* and other codices.[24]

The *Libro Gótico* is San Juan de la Peña's most important cartulary. Its earliest nucleus of texts dates from 1060, with new sections added in subsequent decades. Documentation from incorporated monasteries was either copied into the *Libro Gótico* or added in the form of quires as part of the process of monastic reorganization that took place in the last third of the eleventh century.[25] In spite of the fact that there is no modern critical edition,[26] we know about its complex history and the multiple falsifications that it contains, but above all we have important studies about the transmission and development of the texts from some of the Pyrenean monasteries absorbed by San Juan de la Peña.[27] For example, Larrea has done an exemplary analysis of documents from San Martín de Cillas that sheds light both on San Juan de la Peña's archive and, more broadly, on the monastery's evolution.[28] Our knowledge of San Juan de la Peña's documentation as a whole remains, however, pretty much blurred.

Although we are still lacking a systematic and comprehensive analysis of the socio-political profile of the ecclesiastical institutions that produced and/or transmitted documents in Navarre and Aragon, specific studies allow us to identify what seems to be a prominent feature of these institutions: the link between them, or at least the most important of them, and the political authorities around whom these institutions chose to anchor their memory in the eleventh century. To name but a few Aragonese examples, the monastery of

24 *Leire*; Fortún, *Leire*.

25 Ángel Canellas López, "El Cartulario visigótico de San Juan de la Peña," in *Homenaje a Don Agustín Millares Carlo*, 2 vols (Gran Canaria: Confederación española de Cajas de Ahorros, 1975), 1:205–239; María José Bádenas Población, "El índice del Libro Gótico de San Juan de la Peña ¿Ordenar para administrar?," in *La escritura de la memoria: los cartularios*, ed. Elena E. Rodríguez and Antonio C. García (Huelva: Universidad de Huelva, 2011), 335–358. The cartulary was acquired in 1906 by the University of Zaragoza, where it is currently held. It is accessible online at https://zaguan.unizar.es/record/717 (accessed 20 June 2023).

26 SJP. This edition has some flaws, which have been pointed out by Carlos Laliena Corbera, "Documentos sobre la servidumbre en la sociedad navarro-aragonesa del siglo XI," *Príncipe de Viana* 211 (1997), 371–392; the author edits 22 eleventh-century documents from San Juan de la Peña, most of which undated, and offers hypothetical dates for quite a few. Other documents were printed in José María Lacarra, "'Honores' et 'tenencias' en Aragon (XIe siècle)," *Annales du Midi* 80, no. 89 (1968), 485–528, at 516–518 (appendixes nos. 1 and 2).

27 Lapeña Paúl, *El monasterio de San Juan de la Peña*.

28 Juan José Larrea, "La documentación de San Martín de Cillas. Un ensayo de crítica de las fuentes altomedievales," *Revista de Historia Jerónimo Zurita* 61–62 (1990), 7–74.

Siresa and the see of Roda had close ties with the counts of Aragon, whereas San Juan de la Peña was itself a royal foundation. Royal power was also decisive for the incorporation of the lesser monasteries in the Pyrenees into other institutions from the mid eleventh century. In fact, the monastic reorganization of the Ribagorza area has been attributed to the monarchy.[29]

Ultimately, the competition for royal favour was crucial for the development of medieval religious centres in general. Leire, which had a contentious relationship with the kings of Pamplona (it served as their pantheon), had to compete with the powerful monasteries of San Millán and San Martín de Albelda after the conquest of La Rioja (920) to attract the attention and the favour of the king. Links to the aristocracy seem to be a phenomenon more of the eleventh century, which can be seen clearly in the case of San Andrés de Fanlo.[30]

1.2 *The Documents as Historical Sources*

Three main issues must be borne in mind when considering the problems and possibilities of the Navarrese and Aragonese documentary corpora from before 1100.

First, most of the information for this period comes from cartularies written in major monastic houses in the twelfth century, as shown in the previous section.

Second, the copying of documents originating in lesser monasteries into these cartularies was a more complex process than has often been assumed; many forgeries purportedly dating from the eighth, ninth and early tenth centuries were included. Peterson has studied San Millán's falsifications and warns about these problems, given how important this information is for the general history of early medieval Iberia and especially for the early history of the two kingdoms that would become the most important ones in central Iberia, Navarre and Castile.[31]

Finally, the information contained in the extant documents from Navarre and Aragon often, or in general, transcends the territory of a single kingdom.

---

29 Grau, *Roda de Isábena*, 37; and Guillermo Tomás Faci, *Montañas, comunidades y cambio social en el Pirineo medieval. Ribagorza en los siglos X–XIV* (Toulouse: Presses Universitaires du Mirail-Prensas de la Universidad de Zaragoza, 2016), 142–154. On charter production and, especially, transmission in the Pyrenean area, see Guillermo Tomás Faci, "La construcción de la memoria escrita en los archivos eclesiásticos de Ribagorza (ss. XI–XIII)," *Edad Media: Revista de Historia* 16 (2015), 89–105.

30 Fanlo, p. 30.

31 Peterson, "Mentiras piadosas."

This is not only because the political unit to which some particular monasteries belonged changed during the period considered here but, more importantly, because their location on the frontier between two political units meant that the expansion of their domains would necessarily transcend political boundaries. Martín Duque says, regarding Navarre before 1004, that only one-fourth of its documents—mostly from Leire—deal with Navarre itself, while three-fourths have to do with external areas (the 'kingdom' of Nájera, 'Old' Aragon) that at some point were linked to the Pamplona kings.[32] Something similar could be said of the documentation from San Millán, whose properties were divided between Castile and Navarre, thus being particularly affected by the fluctuations in political geography during this period.[33]

2 The Corpus of Navarrese and Aragonese Dispute Records

The information on the settlement of disputes that is to be found in Navarrese and Aragonese records varies a great deal both over time and from one institution to another, and also according to document type. In what follows, I will examine some of this variety, both in the corpus of dispute records as a whole and among the dispute records preserved by some particular institutions.

As with the overall number of documents, the corpus of dispute records from Navarre and Aragon is very unevenly distributed from one century to the next. Of the 163 dispute records dated before 1100, only 21 (13 per cent) come from the ninth and tenth centuries, while 142 (87 per cent) are from the eleventh (see above, Graphs 0.8, 0.10, 4.1 and 4.2). Before 1000, the ratio of dispute records to the total is barely four per cent, and during the eleventh century it rises to six per cent only. This proportion is similar to that of Castile, but lower than those of León (11.2 per cent), Portugal (16.5 per cent) and especially Galicia (20.4 per cent) (see above, Table 0.1 and Graph 0.5).

The distribution of dispute records among institutions in Aragon and Navarre is also very unequal (see above, Maps 0.2 and 0.4). In Aragon, only two institutions managed to transmit through their respective cartularies a

32 *Leire*, p. xi.

33 The richness of this documentation for La Rioja Alta is highlighted by Juan José Larrea, "Obispos efímeros, comunidades y homicidio en La Rioja Alta en los siglos X–XI," *Brocar* 31 (2007) 177–199, at 188. Peterson also insists throughout his scholarship on the importance of the fact that San Millán is located near the border.

TABLE 4.1 Aragonese institutions that preserved five or more pre-1100 dispute records

Institution	All records (n)	Dispute records (n)	Dispute records (%)	9th c.	10th c.	11th c.	Orig-inals	Cop-ies	Authen-tic	Sus-pect	False
S. Juan de la Peña	252	32	12.7	1	8	23	6	26	27	2	3
Catedral de Roda	104	14	13.46	0	1	13	0	14	14	0	0
Sta. María de Obarra	201	9	4.48	0	0	9	0	9	9	0	0
S. Andrés de Fanlo	104	8	7.69	0	0	8	0	8	8	0	0
Sta. María de Alaón	285	6	2.11	1	3	2	0	6	6	0	0
TOTAL	946	69		2	12	55	6	63	64	2	3

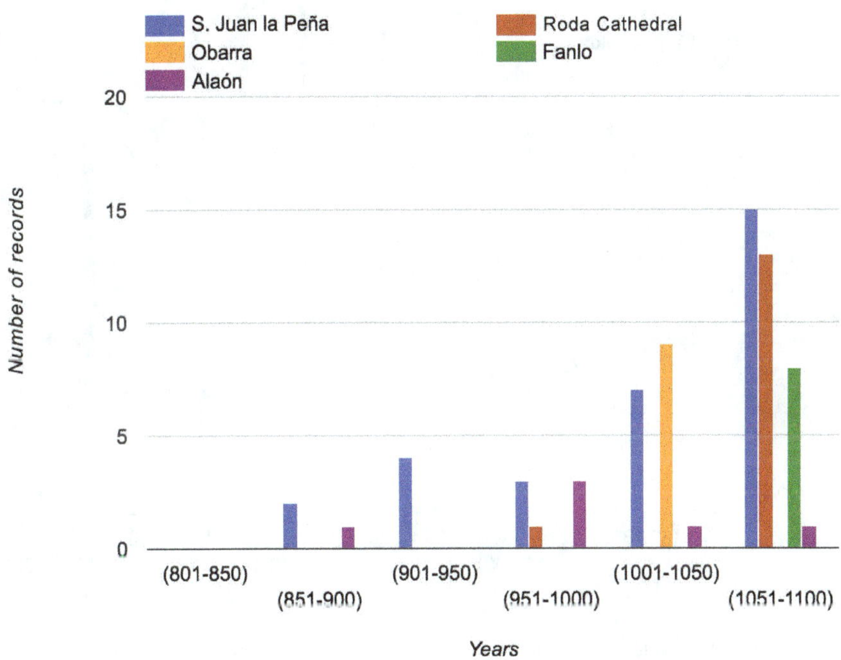

GRAPH 4.3 Largest Aragonese collections of pre-1100 dispute records, by half-century

good number of dispute records dated across the period considered here: San Juan de la Peña, with 32 texts (12.7 per cent of its total documentation), and the Roda cathedral, with 14 (13.5 per cent), although these figures need to be put into chronological context.[34]

34 The only institutions that preserved pre-1000 dispute records are San Juan de la Peña and

TABLE 4.2 Navarrese institutions that preserved five or more pre-1100 dispute records

Institution	All records (n)	Dispute records (n)	Dispute records (%)	9th c.	10th c.	11th c.	Originals	Copies	Authentic	Suspect	False
S. Millán de la Cogolla	742	46	6.2	0	4	42	1	45	45	1	0
S. Salvador de Leire	184	18	9.78	1	0	17	0	18	15	2	1
S. Saturnino de Artajona	16	7	43.75	0	0	7	2	5	7	0	0
Pamplona Cathedral	74	5	6.76	0	0	5	0	5	5	0	0
TOTAL	1016	76		1	4	71	3	73	72	3	1

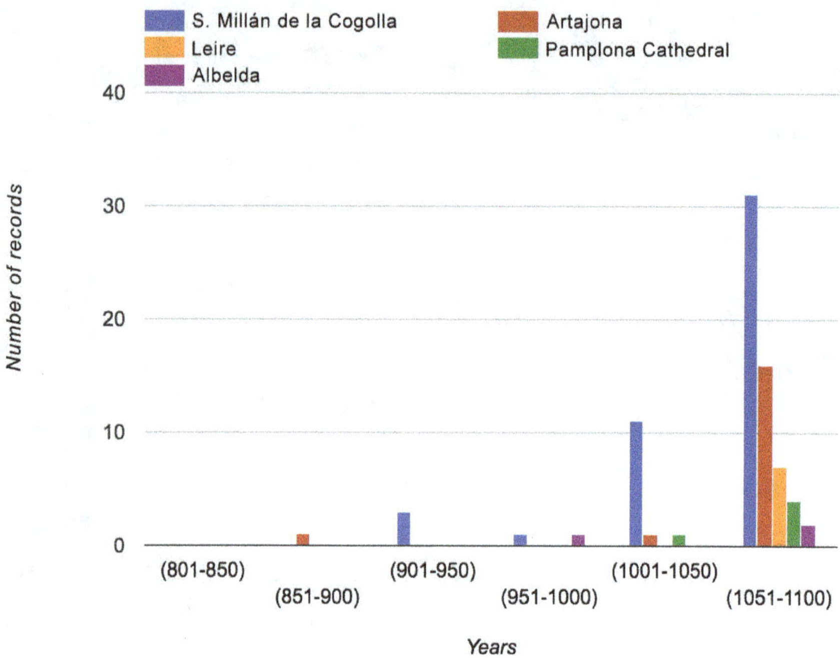

GRAPH 4.4 Largest Navarrese collections of pre-1100 dispute records, by half-century

The same is true of the dispute records from Navarre, which are concentrated in Leire (18/9.8 per cent of its total documentation) and San Millán (46/6.2 per cent). The remaining institutions have hardly preserved any dispute records or lack them completely. It is noteworthy, for instance, that there are some

Alaón. In the eleventh century, the picture is quite different: in addition to San Juan de la Peña we also have Roda, Obarra and Fanlo.

institutions with a large volume of documents but barely any that yield information, whether direct or indirect, about disputes: Albelda has only three dispute records out of a total of 70 documents; San Victorián has two out of 136; Alaón, six out of 285; and Valvanera only one out of 189.

The reasons for these differences are virtually impossible to ascertain, but one should bear in mind that the low percentages could be due to the loss of documents, or are possibly the result of different strategies of record-making and/or record-keeping.[35] However, there are not only quantitative but also qualitative differences, and we must look for explanations for these. There are collections, as will be discussed in detail below, in which records of certain types of disputes predominate over others, and the form chosen for these records also differs from one institution to another.

As is the case in Castile and Galicia, this documentation is copied for the most part in cartularies, with hardly any single-sheet parchments, and a sizeable number of dispute records are considered by their editors to be forgeries or, rather more frequently, to have been manipulated in some way to further the plans and objectives of the institutions which produced those cartularies (see above, Table 0.3 and Graph 0.6). How did these strategies affect dispute records? It is not possible to compare the frequency of falsification between these and other types of documents since the PRJ database only has information on the authenticity of the former. However, only three Navarrese dispute records, from Leire and San Millán, and twice that number in Aragon, from San Juan de la Peña and Somport, have raised suspicions about their authenticity.[36] These numbers seem to suggest that, again as in the case of Galicia and Castile, falsifications are not numerous among dispute records.

Given the almost total absence of single sheets, it is difficult to address questions related to the material aspects of dispute records. However, it is important

35 Regarding the differences in the proportion of dispute records, and of specific types of dispute records, between different institutions and different regions, Wendy Davies, *Windows on Justice in Northern Iberia, 800–1000* (Abingdon: Routledge, 2016), 188, 257, believes that this may be less a matter of the volume of documentation being preserved than an indication of proactive institutional strategies (or the lack thereof).

36 Leire 3 (880), 17 (1015) and 131 (1090); Fortún, *Leire*, 49, includes a table showing the authenticity of documents from Leire dated before 1083. San Millán: BGD 1* (1063), though there are differences of opinion regarding the authenticity of this document. San Juan de la Peña: SJP 7 (893/), 16 (947), 20 (964), 155 and 156 (both 1060). Santa Cristina de Somport: Jukka Kiviharju, ed., *Colección diplomática del Hospital de Santa Cristina de Somport I (Años 1078–1304)* (Helsinki: Academia Scientiarum Fennica, 2004), no. 1 (1078).

to note the way in which documents were ordered, dated, and copied into the cartularies in which they have come down to us,[37] not least because this has a bearing on the documents' form and typology. The importance of the transmission processes will be seen more easily as we proceed to analyse the form and content of these records.

3 Best-Documented Judicial Processes in Navarre and Aragon

Among the records of dispute settlement processes from Navarre and Aragon, those that relate to disputes about ownership of land, productive resources, or the boundaries of productive areas (pasturelands, salt deposits, waterways) are either the most noteworthy or the most numerous. These types of conflicts are sometimes clearly distinguished from one another, but in other cases they are presented as overlapping. An analysis of all of their nuances would require a detailed study, which is not possible here, but it is worthwhile to point out some general features.

Boundary disputes are actually disputes over the control of land, either agricultural or pastoral (or silvopastoral), and in Aragon, unlike Navarre, these disputes constitute a large portion of the available documentary corpus.[38] Major Navarrese institutions like San Millán and Leire lack information about boundary disputes for the period prior to the eleventh century,[39] while San Juan de la Peña's *Libro Gótico* includes a large number of texts about this kind of dispute, most of which were manipulated (when not outrightly forged) upon the annexation to San Juan de la Peña of the smaller Pyrenean monasteries where these texts originate.

In fact, as Larrea shows in his chapter in this volume, the earliest records from these small monasteries have to do with the delimitation of their own

37 Julio Escalona, Cristina Jular Pérez-Alfaro and Anna Bellettini, "Two graphical models for the analysis and comparison of cartularies," *Digital Medievalist* 1 (2017), at http://journal.digitalmedievalist.org/articles/10.16995/dm.55/ (accessed 30 July 2020). However, as the authors rightly points out, this method can only be applied cartulary by cartulary, and this work is yet to be done.

38 Larrea, "La condición del campesinado," 390.

39 Leire 3 (880), which records the drawing of boundaries to put an end to the ongoing *magna contentio* between the people of Filaria and those of Lerda and Añués, is considered problematic. According to its editor, this part of the text, which he prints in a footnote, is an interpolation included in a later copy. Fortún, *Leire*, 49, likewise includes this document among Leire's forgeries.

territories.[40] By looking into the judicial processes often associated with such demarcations and the documents that they generated, Larrea could gain some insight into the relationship between the practice of drawing boundaries and the discourses used to represent this practice. These are narrative texts that, by emphasizing the king's or the count's intervention in the peace-making ritual of drawing the disputed boundaries between monastic institutions and peasant communities, or between different peasant communities, help to establish the king's or the count's political power. The logic of these monastic narratives, Larrea suggests, should be understood in relation to the discourse about these institutions' past, because of the value these rituals had in the process of constructing political power in Navarre and Aragon.[41]

During the eleventh century one sees certain changes in the records of boundary disputes. They practically disappear from San Juan de la Peña's cartulary, where disputes over the ownership and control of productive resources come to predominate. On the other hand, in Leire's cartulary two different dispute processes involving monasteries and local communities are recorded. In one, from the 1050s, the boundaries of a monastic territory are contested by a neighbouring community and the dispute is settled through a royal perambulation; this resembles the disputes recorded in San Juan de la Peña's cartulary.[42] In the other, from the end of the century, the plaintiff is again a community, here a community of dependents (Eguillor's *homini rustici* or *meschini*), that is suing before the king for the monks to cede croplands and woodlands that, according to the monastery, the people of the community had occupied illegally.[43]

It is San Millán's cartulary that most fully documents these boundary disputes throughout the eleventh century. The importance that this information had for the monks—in that it protected their livestock and pasturelands—is

---

40 See below, Chapter 12.

41 Grau, *Roda de Isábena*, 37, also points out the link between the appearance of the Roda bishopric and the political interests of the counts of Ribagorza. One noteworthy document that is included in Roda's cartulary is the judicial demarcation of San Pedro de Lastonosa by Count Unifredo (971–981), ibidem, no. 7.

42 This is the dispute between the monastery of Larraún, which was later absorbed by Leire, and the people of Rasa, which was resolved by King Sancho Garcés IV of Pamplona through a linear demarcation ritual similar to the ones described by Larrea. Information about this dispute is preserved in a royal donation charter by which Larraún is granted to a lay aristocrat, Leire 50 (1056).

43 This is a *Carta rememoriationis atque definicionis* from King Pedro I of Aragon and Pamplona (r. 1094–1104) certifying a gift from his father, Sancho Ramírez (r. 1063–1094), Leire 169 (1099)—note the highly interesting narrative.

reflected in the fact that many of these documents, which are from different dates and refer to different locations, are copied on the first few folios of the cartulary, and one document may even have been forged. On folio IV^{v}, at the end of the *Privilegio de los Votos*, the cartulary introduces, in a different hand, a pact that the abbot of San Millán reached in 1063 with the people of Ojacastro regarding the terms of their access to pastures and woods.[44] On folios 1^{v}–2^{v}–3 are copied two false royal privileges dated 929 that protect the monastery's rights and its pasturelands. They precede the 1050 royal resolution, copied on folio 3–3^{v}, in which King García Sánchez III of Pamplona (r. 1035–1054) and Queen Estefanía established an agreement between the monks of San Millán and the inhabitants of Madriz, who, "spurred by the devil," gave rise to a dispute over certain boundaries and the use of pasture and woodland. The charter fixed the borders of the area belonging to San Millán, establishing that the monastery's animals and livestock were allowed to graze throughout Madriz's territory, thus confirming, defining, and stabilizing the boundaries disputed by the monks and the inhabitants of Madriz.[45] On folios 4^{v}–5 is recounted the *querimonia* that the monks brought before King Sancho Garcés IV of Pamplona (r. 1054–1076) against the people of Pazuengos because they did not recognize San Millan's right to pasture its cows in Losillas. This time the king confirmed the privileges that he had previously granted to the monastery.[46]

We have information of a different sort about a late-eleventh century dispute between the communities of Tobía and Matute, on the one hand, and the small village of Coja, on the other. The former had denied the latter access to the surrounding area that together they had exploited *tam in erbis quam in montibus et terminis*. In this case, unlike the ones mentioned above, it was not the king who settled the dispute; rather, the people from these villages arranged to resolve their differences in a duel, and the representative from Coja emerged victorious. The large gathering that apparently attended the event, however, also included powerful local figures: *senior* Lope López, *dominante* in Tobía, *senior* García Garceiz, *merino* in Nájera and Río de Alesanco, Sancio Garceiz, *merino* in Río de Tobía, and Count García of Nájera. And although the text does not name San Millán, it is easy to imagine that the monastery supported Coja,

---

44 This can be considered a *pacto foral* that grew out of conflicts over keeping livestock. It was established by San Millán, and the community of Ojacastro accepted it and promised to abide by it, BGD 1* (a note in the digital edition expresses doubt about the document's authenticity, but García Andreva, *El Becerro Galicano*, 57, takes it as authentic).

45 BGC 1 and 2 (929), 3 (1050). Regarding these false documents, see Peterson, "Mentiras piadosas," 267–268.

46 BGD 6 (1070). This is a very short document that, nonetheless, alludes to an *altercatio* within the community of Pazuengos, in which one faction supported the monks.

since this village had long been part of its domain.[47] In fact, Sancho III of Pamplona had had to intervene previously, in 1014, with a formal donation to certify the monastery's possession of this village and the pasturelands it held in common with Tobía and Matute, both during the day and at night, as the oldest villagers had testified. This is an implied but, in my opinion, clear allusion to disputes surrounding the control of the village territory, as well as to the use of perambulation to establish its boundaries.[48]

The records of property disputes provide a different picture for several reasons. First, these records are predominantly from the eleventh century, especially its second half. Second, they are about conflicts between monasteries and lay people of high social rank. Third, inheritance rights are used as an argument in the suits brought by these lay people. Fourth, the disputes were resolved predominantly through compromise.[49] However, these documents have other aspects in common with boundary disputes, such as the narrative framing of judicial process and the royal intervention to resolve the disputes. As for their institutional distribution, they predominate at San Juan de la Peña,[50] Leire,[51] and also San Andrés de Fanlo,[52] but are virtually non-existent at San Millán.

In the corpus of dispute records from Navarre and Aragon, there is also information about conflicts that can be grouped under the rubric of disputes over the status of dependents and/or the rents and exactions due by or claimed from them, though these disputes are much less numerous. They come mostly from San Juan de la Peña and San Millán. In general, they are very short texts in which there is significant royal intercession on behalf of the monasteries, as in the other judicial processes. The monks at San Juan de la Peña entered into

47 BGD 473 (1097), on fol. 152. The placement of this document after the 1044 *Fuero de Madriz* is also not surprising, since one of its provisions says: *Tovia et Cogga semper I⟨a⟩ dẹfesa ovieron*, BGD 472, on fols. 151v–152. The dispute over this area, formulated as a criminal case, can also be seen in the enquiry into whether the people of Coja should have to pay along with those from the other two villages for the murder of a man that took place within Matute's territory, BGD 62 (1089). On the criminal framing of disputes over commons, see below.

48 BGD 57.

49 On disputes resolved through compromise in eleventh-century royal tribunals, see Takashi Adachi, "Documents of dispute settlement in eleventh-century Aragón and Navarra: King's tribunal and compromise," *Imago Temporis. Medium Aevum* 1 (2007), 71–85. According to Adachi, these settlements do not mean that there was a breakdown in public justice—as the mutationist school maintains; rather, they were the Crown's strategy for widening its range of action in accordance with the needs of society.

50 E.g., SJP 73 (1039), 85 (1044), 113 (1054) and 167 (1061).

51 E.g., Leire 52 (1057), 110 (1083), 127 (1088), 157 (1097) and 171 (1099).

52 E.g., Fanlo 144 ([1055]) and 51 ([1080–1090]).

disputes with high-ranking figures over the right to keep or recover dependents. But they also disputed with the dependents themselves to force them to acknowledge their status and, consequently, the rents or dues that they owed.[53]

It is worth noting that, in some cases, the texts resemble the *fueros* that grew out of disputes over rents or the status of dependents.[54] Although few in number, the documents from San Millán demonstrate above all the peasants' resistance to their state of servitude and the obligations that it entailed, both in terms of labour and rents. The holding of *hereditates* seems to have been linked, at least from the monastery's point of view, with dependent status: if this was not acknowledged by the peasant, he had to leave the land; in these texts violence also seems to be linked to these contending views.[55] Thus, in spite of the fact that information on this kind of dispute is scant, at least compared to the abundant documentation in Galicia, it does show the dependent status of large

---

53 E.g., SJP 72 (1038), a restitution by the king of a monastic dependent; SJP 79 (1042), a royal confirmation of properties and serfs (*mezquinos*) in Biniés and Beralevilla that had been donated to San Juan de la Peña and over which the monastery brough one of the donor's heirs to court; Laliena Corbera, "Documentos sobre la servidumbre," no. 6 ([1076–1080]), also about the Biniés serfs.

54 It is possible to guess at the conflicts leading to the agreement (*comenenza*) regarding the exactions due from the people of Legriso, which was formalized in a sort of *fuero*, Laliena Corbera, "Documentos sobre la servidumbre," no. 8 (1092); along the same lines is the *karta ingenuationis* by which the abbot freed the inhabitants of Badagüás from *malos censos*, indicating how this *placuit hominibus illius ville*, ibidem, no. 9 (1096). This is made more explicit in the text wherein the abbot exempts the inhabitants of Sangorrín from paying the *carneratura*, about which *eratis querelantes quod foro malo posuerant super vos quod non* [*solebatis*] *habere*, ibidem, no. 10 (1099). On the 'legal' dimension of peasant resistance, see Isabel Alfonso, "Campesinado y derecho: la vía legal de su lucha (Castilla y León, siglos X–XIII)," *Noticiario de Historia Agraria* 13 (1997), 15–31; and Isabel Alfonso, "La contestation paysanne face aux exigences de travail seigneuriales en Castille et León. Les formes et leur signification symbolique," in *Pour une anthropologie du prélèvement seigneurial dans les campagnes médiévales (XIe–XIVe siècles). Réalités et représentations paysannes*, ed. Monique Bourin and Pascual Martínez Sopena (Paris: Publications de la Sorbonne, 2004), 291–320.

55 A well-known case is that of a peasant woman from Terrero, a village belonging to San Millán. According to the bishop who ruled on her case, she did not want to perform the mandatory labour in the fields because she considered herself to be above her neighbours, but an inquiry showed that, like them, she had been born of *tribu servili*, BGD 51 (1043). Another text recounts the complaint that San Millán brought before King Alfonso VI of León-Castile (r. 1065–1109) against the Sarraciniz brothers, who claimed to be freeborn, but could not prove it, and refused to do any service; an order was given that, if they persisted in their refusal, they should give their plots of land back to the monastery and go wherever it suited them; then, a short *notitia* recounts how one of the brothers had killed a royal *merino* and had not yet paid the fine of 500 *sueldos* for the homicide, so the monks persisted in their complaint, BGD 215 (1077). A third example is BGD 202 (1086).

sectors of the peasantry in this part of northern Iberia, as well as the existence of disputes over who should profit from it.[56]

The same can be said of the kind of tension around credit practices and debts. The small number of documents from Navarre and Aragon about these matters, far fewer than in Galicia or Catalonia, is itself significant. Still, it is worth mentioning two cases from San Millán that are interesting for several reasons: they are copied together on a single folio of the *Becerro Galicano*; they are both disputes between lay people; they are similar, even in their terminology (*renovo*), to Galician documents; the creditors in both cases are a married couple, and the properties handed over to them by the debtors are located in the same village; and the fact that the monastery is not mentioned leads one to think that both documents came originally from a lay archive.[57]

Lastly, another extremely interesting group of documents—though relatively unimportant in terms of numbers—has to do with disputes that, in contrast to the civil nature of the disputes mentioned above, we might call criminal. Although these kinds of disputes are present in the collections of Alaón,[58] San Juan de la Peña,[59] Leire,[60] and Albelda,[61] the institutions with the largest numbers of such records—all from the eleventh century—are the monasteries of Obarra (6), in Ribagorza, and San Millán (9), in La Rioja. However, the documents with this information differ both in form and content from one collection to the next.

56 The number of dependents and the implications of their status are still a matter of historiographical debate, though. See the critical review by Larrea, "La condición del campesinado;" and, more recently, Carlos Laliena Corbera, *Siervos medievales de Aragón y Navarra en los siglos XI–XIII* (Zaragoza: Prensas Universitarias de Zaragoza, 2012).

57 BGD 190 (1045) and 189 (1051). It is known that monastic archives incorporated documents from lay individuals by different means, and this issue is explored in several other chapters in this volume. The identification of lay archives, with all that their existence implies, is turning out to be one of the most productive avenues for research on medieval records, also in northern Iberia. For a good overview with an updated bibliography, see Julio Escalona, "Cartularios, memoria y discurso en la Castilla medieval," in *La memoria del poder, el poder de la memoria*, ed. Esther López Ojeda (Logroño: Instituto de Estudios Riojanos, 2017), 163–203. More generally, see Warren Brown et al., eds., *Documentary Culture and the Laity in the Early Middle Ages* (Cambridge: Cambridge University Press, 2013).

58 Alaón 71 (899) and 132 (964).

59 SJP 81 (1043), 165 (1061); Lacarra, "'Honores' et 'tenencias'," 517–518, no. 2 (1090).

60 Leire 142 (1094), a jurisdictional dispute between the monastery and an aristocrat formulated in criminal terms as a dispute about the death of a horse and other mutual offences. The record takes the form of a *carta rememoracionis uel concordie*, a formula which Adachi, "Documents of dispute settlement," believes to be distinctively Navarrese.

61 Albelda 20 (978) and 60 (c. 1082).

The documents from Obarra tend to be framed as a judicial transaction presented as a *carta emendacionis* by which real properties (arable plots, vineyards, houses, etc.) are given as compensation for some misdemeanour, often unspecified (*emenda per illas foras factura*). They are very short documents that have come down to us in two *rotuli* on wooden cylinders with a strip of stitched parchments that together make up the cartulary related to the properties of a family from Ribagorza: the *rotuli* of Ballabriga and Benasque.[62] This cartulary's secular nature and the documents it contains about the punishment of misdemeanours are highly reminiscent of the aristocratic archive preserved at the monastery of Otero de las Dueñas in León.[63]

The records from San Millán—all save two of which are preserved in cartulary form—are of another kind entirely. They are all about punishments or fines resulting from homicide. There is indirect information from non-judicial transactions, such as King Sancho Garcés IV's donation to the monastery of an estate that he had confiscated as a fine for sedition and homicide;[64] and direct information from judicial transactions, such as the sale of two vineyards in Bobadilla to pay fines for homicides.[65] But the most interesting documents are those in which issues of jurisdiction, homicide, and access to communal resources are combined. In these cases, the legal prosecution of a homicide is used as a pretext to protect jurisdiction over areas that are being disputed by different parties.[66] This happens, for example, in the case of the six mills that were confiscated by a royal court from the inhabitants of Alesanco and confirmed to San Millán, along with Terrero's whole territory, at the same time as San Millán paid the king a fine for the killing of a man in the mills.[67] It also happens in the case, mentioned above, where San Millán used a fine for a homicide that took place within the boundaries of the village of Matute as a strategy to preserve the rights of its village of Coja over communal spaces.[68] It is interesting to point out how the monks of Albelda, in an opposite move, chose to

62 Obarra 81 ([c. 1015–1019?]/), 94 ([c. 1020]), 95 ([c. 1020]), 101 ([c. 1020]) and 125 ([c. 1043–1045]), many of which are opisthographs, described by the editor (p. xv).

63 On this collection, see above, Chapter 2.

64 BGD 46 (1074).

65 BGD 76 (1081) and 71 (1082).

66 See below, Chapter 13, for a perceptive analysis of a similar judicial case through which the monastery of Sahagún tried to assert its lordly authority over a local community.

67 BGD 141 (1076). The confirmation is the final ruling on a dispute that the king himself ruled on.

68 BGD 62 (1089); also BGD 536 (1085). On the relationship between homicide and jurisdiction in the documents from San Millán, see Juan José Larrea, "Obispos efímeros," where these texts are commented on in detail.

assert their immunity and set the boundaries within which this immunity was in force by claiming that they had never paid fines for homicides committed or victims found within their territory.[69]

Bibliography

Abbreviations

Alaón: Corral Lafuente, José Luis, ed. *Cartulario de Alaón (Huesca)*. Zaragoza: Anubar, 1984.

Albelda: Ubieto Arteta, Antonio, ed. *Cartulario de Albelda*. Valencia: Anúbar, 1960.

BGD: *Becerro Galicano Digital*. Accessed 30 July 2020. www.ehu.eus/galicano.

Fanlo: Laliena Corbera, Carlos, and Eric Knibbs, eds. *El cartulario del monasterio aragonés de San Andrés de Fanlo (siglos X–XIII)*. Zaragoza: Universidad de Zaragoza, 2007.

Leire: Martín Duque, Ángel J., ed., *Documentación medieval de Leire (siglos IX a XII)*. Pamplona: Diputación Foral de Navarra, Institución Príncipe de Viana, 1983.

Obarra: Martín Duque, Ángel J., ed. *Colección diplomática de Obarra (siglos XI–XIII)*. Zaragoza: CSIC, 1965.

PRJ: *PRocesos Judiciales en las sociedades medievales del norte peninsular*. Accessed 30 July 2020. http://prj.csic.es/.

SJP: Ubieto Arteta, Antonio, ed. *Cartulario de San Juan de La Peña*. 2 vols. Valencia: Anubar, 1962–1963.

Other Primary Sources

Cantera Montenegro, Margarita, ed. *Colección documental de Santa María la Real de Nájera*. Vol. I (*Siglos X–XIV*). San Sebastián: Sociedad de Estudios Vascos, 1991.

García Andreva, Fernando, ed. *El Becerro Galicano de San Millán de la Cogolla. Edición y estudio*. San Millán de la Cogolla: Cilengua, 2010.

García Turza, Francisco Javier, ed. *Documentación medieval del monasterio de Valvanera (siglos XI–XIII)*. Zaragoza: Anubar, 1985.

Kiviharju, Jukka, ed. *Colección diplomática del Hospital de Santa Cristina de Somport I (Años 1078–1304)*. Helsinki: Academia Scientiarum Fennica, 2004.

Lacarra, José María, ed. *Colección diplomática de Irache. I. 958–1222*. Zaragoza: Instituto de Estudios Pirenaicos (CSIC), Universidad de Navarra, 1965.

69 Albelda 60 (c. 1082) is a *notitia* of deaths that took place in Albelda's territory for which the monastery did not pay any fines: *Hec est noticia de homines qui mortui fuerunt in terminos de Albaida; et non pectaverunt pecta nec ullo homicidio*. The text ends by saying *Et de hodie in antea nullus sit ausus nobis inquietare homicidio pro termino*.

Martín Duque, Ángel J., ed. *Colección diplomática del monasterio de San Victorián de Sobrarbe (1000–1219)*. Zaragoza: Universidad de Zaragoza, 2004.

Rodríguez R. de Lama, Ildefonso, ed. *Colección diplomática medieval de La Rioja (923–1225)*. Vol. II *Documentos (923–1168)*. Logroño: Gobierno de la Rioja, Instituto de Estudios Riojanos, 1976.

Sáinz Ripa, Eliseo, ed. *Colección diplomática de las Colegiatas de Albelda y Logroño*. Vol. 1 *(924–1399)*. Logroño: Diputación Provincial, 1981.

Ubieto Arteta, Antonio, ed. *Cartulario de Siresa*. Valencia: Anubar, 1986.

Ubieto Arteta, Antonio, ed. *Documentos del monasterio de Obarra (Huesca) anteriores al año 1000*. Zaragoza: Anubar, 1988.

Zabalza Duque, Manuel, ed. *Colección diplomática de los Condes de Castilla*. Valladolid: Junta de Castilla y León, 1998.

Secondary Works

Adachi, Takashi. "Documents of dispute settlement in eleventh-century Aragón and Navarra: King's tribunal and compromise." *Imago Temporis. Medium Aevum* 1 (2007), 71–85.

Alfonso, Isabel. "Campesinado y derecho: la vía legal de su lucha (Castilla y León, siglos X–XIII)." *Noticiario de Historia Agraria* 13 (1997), 15–31.

Alfonso, Isabel. "La contestation paysanne face aux exigences de travail seigneuriales en Castille et León. Les formes et leur signification symbolique." In *Pour une anthropologie du prélèvement seigneurial dans les campagnes médiévales (XIe–XIVe siècles). Réalités et représentations paysannes*, edited by Monique Bourin and Pascual Martínez Sopena, 291–320. Paris: Publications de la Sorbonne, 2004.

Bádenas Población, María José. "El índice del Libro Gótico de San Juan de la Peña ¿Ordenar para administrar?" In *La escritura de la memoria: los cartularios*, edited by Elena E. Rodríguez and Antonio C. García, 335–358. Huelva: Universidad de Huelva, 2011.

Brown, Warren, Marios Costambeys, Matthew Innes, and Adam J. Kosto, eds. *Documentary Culture and the Laity in the Early Middle Ages*. Cambridge: Cambridge University Press, 2013.

Canellas López, Ángel. "El Cartulario visigótico de San Juan de la Peña." In *Homenaje a Don Agustín Millares Carlo*. 2 vols. Gran Canaria: Confederación Española de Cajas de Ahorros, 1975.

Davies, Wendy. *Windows on Justice in Northern Iberia, 800–1000*. Abingdon: Routledge, 2016.

Escalona, Julio. "Cartularios, memoria y discurso en la Castilla medieval." In *La memoria del poder, el poder de la memoria*, edited by Esther López Ojeda, 163–203. Logroño: Instituto de Estudios Riojanos, 2017.

Escalona, Julio, Cristina Jular Pérez Alfaro, and Anna Bellettini. "Two graphical models for the analysis and comparison of cartularies." *Digital Medievalist* 1 (2017). Accessed 30 July 2020. http://journal.digitalmedievalist.org/articles/10.16995/dm.55/.

Fortún, Luis Javier. *Leire, un señorío monástico en Navarra (siglos IX–XIX)*. Pamplona: Gobierno de Navarra, 1993.

García de Cortázar, José Ángel. *El dominio del monasterio de San Millán de la Cogolla (siglos X a XIII): Introducción a la historia rural de Castilla altomedieval*. Salamanca: Universidad de Salamanca, 1969.

García de Cortázar, José Ángel. *La construcción de la diócesis de Calahorra en los siglos X a XIII: la Iglesia en la organización social del espacio*. Logroño, Instituto de Estudios Riojanos, 2018.

Grau Quiroga, Nuria. *Roda de Isábena en los siglos X–XIII. La documentación episcopal y del cabildo catedralicio*. Zaragoza: Institución "Fernando el Católico" (CSIC), Diputación de Zaragoza, 2010. Accessed 30 July 2020. http://ifc.dpz.es/publicaciones/ver/id/3036.

Lacarra, José María. "'Honores' et 'tenencias' en Aragon (XIe siècle)." *Annales du Midi* 80, no. 89 (1968), 485–528.

Laliena Corbera, Carlos. "Documentos sobre la servidumbre en la sociedad navarro-aragonesa del siglo XI." *Príncipe de Viana* 211 (1997), 371–392.

Laliena Corbera, Carlos. "Problemas historiográficos de la Alta Edad Media Aragonesa: una revisión crítica." *Argensola* 113 (2003), 13–36.

Laliena Corbera, Carlos. *Siervos medievales de Aragón y Navarra en los siglos XI–XIII*. Zaragoza: Prensas Universitarias de Zaragoza, 2012.

Lapeña Paúl, Ana Isabel. *El monasterio de San Juan de la Peña en la Edad Media (desde sus orígenes hasta 1410)*. Zaragoza: Caja de Ahorros de la Inmaculada Aragón, 1989.

Larrea, Juan José. "La documentación de San Martín de Cillas. Un ensayo de crítica de las fuentes altomedievales." *Revista de Historia Jerónimo Zurita* 61–62 (1990), 7–74.

Larrea, Juan José. "La condición del campesinado navarro-aragonés entre los siglos IX y XII: una revisión crítica." *En la España Medieval* 29 (2006), 383–409.

Larrea, Juan José. "Obispos efímeros, comunidades y homicidio en La Rioja Alta en los siglos X–XI." *Brocar* 31 (2007) 177–199.

Peterson, David. "Reescribiendo el pasado. El Becerro Galicano como reconstrucción de la historia institucional de San Millán de la Cogolla." *Hispania* 233 (2008), 653–682.

Peterson, David. "El *Becerro Gótico* de San Millán. Reconstrucción de un cartulario perdido." *Studia Historica. Historia Medieval* 29 (2011), 147–173.

Peterson, David. "Mentiras piadosas. Falsificaciones e interpolaciones en la diplomática de San Millán de la Cogolla." In *Las donaciones piadosas en el mundo medieval*, edited by Alfonso García Leal, 295–314. Oviedo: Universidad de Oviedo, 2012.

Peterson, David. "Rebranding San Millán: the Becerro Galicano as a rejection of the monastery's Navarrese heritage (1192–95)." *Journal of Medieval Iberian Studies* 5, no. 1 (2013), 1–20.

Tomás Faci, Guillermo. "La construcción de la memoria escrita en los archivos eclesiásticos de Ribagorza (ss. XI–XIII)." *Edad Media: Revista de Historia* 16 (2015), 89–105.

Tomás Faci, Guillermo. *Montañas, comunidades y cambio social en el Pirineo medieval. Ribagorza en los siglos X–XIV*. Toulouse: Presses Universitaires du Mirail-Prensas de la Universidad de Zaragoza, 2016.

CHAPTER 5

Documentary Production and Dispute Records in Catalonia before the Year 1100

Josep M. Salrach

1 Catalonian Documents from the Ninth to the Eleventh Century

The overall number of documents from the Catalan counties dated before 1100 is possibly as many as 15,000, though we still do not know how many of the eleventh-century documents remain unpublished. The PRJ database lists over 12,000 published documents, and this figure makes Catalonia by far the leader in volume of extant documents among the regions of northern Iberia (see above, Table 0.1).[1]

The distribution of these documents from one century to the next is highly uneven but shows a clear and steady increase beginning in the tenth century, with nearly twice as many documents being produced in the eleventh century as in the tenth (see above, Table 0.2 and Graphs 0.2 and 0.4). Among this corpus, there are 4756 documents from the ninth and tenth centuries (also including three from the end of the eighth century), of which 175 (3.7 per cent) are dispute records, and 7349 from the eleventh century, of which 611 (8.3 per cent) are dispute records.

1 A recent edition of 557 Catalonian dispute records from the ninth to eleventh centuries (JRC) will be used throughout this chapter for easier referencing of documents that are scattered among several editions. Being the only compilation of its kind to the present, JRC was put together as a representative sample of the Catalonian material surveyed in the PRJ database at http://prj.csic.es (accessed 30 June 2020), making it possible to illustrate many of the points discussed here. It should be kept in mind that this edition excludes a relatively large number of documents that are presented formally as *definitiones et recognitiones*, as it is not clear that they were the result of judicial rulings or transactions. It also excludes documents that are not preserved in their entirety (whether as originals or copies) and documents that are known only through summaries or *regesta*. The abbreviations used in this paper for editions of charters are listed in the bibliography.

 | DOI:10.1163/9789004683006_007

TABLE 5.1 Catalonian records before 1100, by half-century

Dates	All records (n)	Dispute records (n)	Dispute records (%)
780–900	486	53	10.91
901–950	1249	33	2.64
951–1000	3021	89	2.95
1001–1050	3201	254	7.94
1051–1100	4148	357	8.61
Total	12105	786	

1.1 *Ecclesiastical Archives and the Archive of the Counts of Barcelona*

Most of the documents survive in their entirety, as originals or copies, though some came down to us as partial copies, summaries, and notices. They have been transmitted essentially by ecclesiastical institutions, whether bishoprics or monasteries (see above, Map 0.1). There is scant documentation from the episcopal see of Elne, in Roussillon, but the bishoprics of Barcelona, Urgel, Vic, and Girona each have their own archive containing abundant documentation. The monasteries that were most important for transmitting documents are Sant Cugat del Vallès, Sant Benet de Bages, Sant Llorenç del Munt, Sant Joan de les Abadesses, Sant Miquel de Cuixà, and Santa Maria de Ripoll. However, there is also a relatively large number of monastic institutions that have passed down small collections, sometimes as small as a single document. The PRJ database lists a total of 54 monastic institutions, though the list might well be longer than that. Among the monasteries with published cartularies and diplomatic collections, we find Sant Cugat del Vallès, Sant Daniel de Girona, Sant Esteve de Banyoles, Sant Llorenç del Munt, Sant Pere de Casserres, and many more. Although some of these institutions were founded after the eleventh century, their archives were used to store documents from earlier periods that came from either private individuals or other institutions.

In spite of the fact that ecclesiastical institutions kept the largest number of documents, there is one lay institution that has passed down to us one of the most important early medieval archives in Catalonia, that of the counts of Barcelona. Being now preserved in the Archive of the Crown of Aragon, it consists of more than 1300 documents from the years 844–1100, among them 137 dispute records (10.4 per cent).[2] This is a patrimonial archive that is not

2 Documents from the monastery of Sant Joan de les Abadesses that were incorporated into the

altogether different in its document typology from other aristocratic archives. The largest group of documents are private records of land purchases/sales, gifts, loans, and exchanges; these are followed in number by documents that are truly feudal—*convenientiae* and oaths of fidelity. Of course, in addition to these there are also a number of documents of a distinctly political nature, such as treaties and alliances between sovereigns.

Most of the private documents do not concern the comital family directly but rather other private individuals, whose identities are mostly unknown. This is explained by the custom—we might even consider it the norm—of transferring documents along with the transfer of real property. The archive of the counts of Barcelona also included the archival collections of the comital families that merged with that of Barcelona. Thus, the original collections of the counts of Barcelona were added to over time and came to include records of the counts of Besalú, Cerdanya, and Pallars, as well as others associated with the Occitan expansion to Carcassonne and Provence and with the rise of the Crown of Aragon.[3]

The main centres of document production—the cathedrals, major monasteries and the comital court of Barcelona—were particularly concerned with preserving the documents that bore witness to these institutions' property rights. This concern is not only voiced by the texts themselves but can also be seen in the fact that copies were made, lost documents were reconstructed, and cartularies were produced. The largest number of cartularies—as well as the most important ones—are from the twelfth, thirteenth and fourteenth centuries.

The best-known and most original Catalan cartulary is the *Liber feudorum maior*, produced between about 1187 and 1192 on the orders of Alfonso II (the Chaste), king of Aragon and count of Barcelona (r. 1164–1196). The objective

---

Archive of the Crown of Aragon at the beginning of the seventeenth century are not included in these figures. Regarding this incorporation of documents, see Rafael Conde, "Estudi arxivístic," in PAC 1:17–62; Miquel S. Gros, "L'arxiu del Monestir de Sant Joan de les Abadesses. Notícies historiques i regesta dels documents dels anys 995–1115," in *II Col·loqui d'història del monaquisme català* (Poblet: Abadia de Poblet, 1974), 2:87–128; and the introduction to CCVII.

3 The parchments from the archive of the counts of Barcelona dated between the ninth to eleventh centuries have been published in Federico Udina Martorell, ed., *El archivo Condal de Barcelona en los siglos IX–X* (Barcelona: CSIC, 1951), 242 documents; PAC, 963 documents; and Ignasi J. Baiges, Gaspar Feliu and Josep M. Salrach, eds., *Els pergamins de l'Arxiu Comtal de Barcelona de Ramon Berenguer II a Ramon Berenguer IV*, 4 vols (Barcelona: Fundació Noguera, 2010), 1149 documents (324 dated before 1100).

was to bring together correct and proper copies of the documents that established the material, juridical and political foundations of the counts' authority as sovereign in Catalonia and Occitania, as well as the documents that attested to the dynastic union with the kingdom of Aragon. In essence, it included *convenientiae*, oaths of fidelity, documents granting possession of castles, treaties, and wills. Though parts of it have been lost, the *Liber feudorum maior* originally consisted of two volumes, 867 folios and 930 documents. The count-kings, who were direct descendants of Alfonso II, knew the testimonial value of the cartulary and carefully preserved it. Following the extinction of the direct line of the House of Barcelona-Aragon (1410) and the incorporation of the Crown of Aragon into the Spanish monarchy, this cartulary was kept for centuries by the archivists of the Royal Archive of the Crown of Aragon. Today, only 88 folios, containing 183 pieces of writing and 79 miniatures, remain. However, thanks to an index that was created in the fourteenth century and the fact that the Archive of the Crown of Aragon retains almost all the originals and copies that had been reproduced in the *Liber feudorum maior*, Francesc Miquel Rosell was able to recreate it almost in its entirety for his 1945 edition.[4]

Another cartulary called *Liber feudorum Ceritaniae et Rosilionis*, which was produced at the beginning of the thirteenth century, contains the same documents from the counties of Cerdanya and Roussillon that had been included in the *Liber feudorum maior*, plus another six documents.

Apart from these two, all the other known cartularies in Catalonia come from ecclesiastical institutions. All the large bishoprics that existed around the year 1000 compiled cartularies. The cartulary of the cathedral of Elne (Roussillon), produced in the twelfth century, was lost at the beginning of the nineteenth, but in the seventeenth and eighteenth centuries many of its documents had been copied.[5] All the original documents from the see of Elne have been lost.

4 Francisco Miquel Rosell, ed., *Liber feudorum maior*, 2 vols (Barcelona: CSIC, 1945–1947), 902 documents. Among the studies on this cartulary, I would highlight Adam J. Kosto, "The *Liber Feudorum maior* of the counts of Barcelona: the cartulary as an expression of power," *Journal of Medieval History* 27, no. 1 (March 2001), 1–22. On the iconography in this manuscript, see Josep M. Salrach, "Imatges de la historia del poder en la pintura catalana medieval. Les miniatures del *Liber feudorum maior*," in *Le plaisir de l'art du Moyen Âge. Commande, production et réception de l'oeuvre d'art* (Paris: Piccard, 2012), 854–864.

5 CCVI 1:58–60. This edition includes all the ninth- and tenth-century documents from the see of Elne and from the counties mentioned in the title, with a description of the archives and of the extant document collections.

The cartulary of the Urgel cathedral, titled *Liber Dotaliorum Ecclesiae Urgellensis*, which is preserved in the chapter archive today, contains some 1200 documents. It was produced in the thirteenth century, though it has additions from as late as the eighteenth. This archive contains many original parchments from the ninth to eleventh centuries, among them the oldest extant parchment in Catalonia, which originated at the monastery of Sant Climent de Codinet and dates from 815.[6]

The chapter and episcopal archives of Vic preserve a large number of original parchments from the ninth to eleventh centuries, in addition to a cartulary produced in the thirteenth century, titled *Liber dotationum antiquarum*, in which 272 documents from the chapter archive are copied.[7]

Girona's chapter and episcopal archives preserve many documents from before 1100, as well as three later cartularies: the *Llibre Gran de la Sagristia Major*, the *Llibre Verd* and, most importantly, the *Cartoral de Carlemany*. This third cartulary combines two earlier ones, the first written at the beginning of the thirteenth century and the second in the 1310s. It contains 625 documents from the ninth to eleventh centuries.[8]

The Barcelona cathedral archive is, without a doubt, the most important archive in Catalonia. It has more than 40,000 parchments, many of which are originals.[9] It also has the largest cartulary in Catalonia, the four-volume *Libri Antiquitatum*. This work from the mid-thirteenth century copies a selection of the parchments that are preserved and stored in the Barcelona cathedral.[10]

---

6 Cebrià Baraut, "Els documents conservats a l'Arxiu Capitular de la Seu d'Urgell. I. Segles IX–X," *Urgellia* 2 (1979), 7–145; "Els documents, dels anys 981–1010," *Urgellia* 3 (1980), 7–166; "Els documents, dels anys 1010–1035," *Urgellia* 4 (1981), 7–186; "Els documents, dels anys 1035–1050," *Urgellia* 5 (1982), 7–158; "Els documents, dels anys 1051–1075," *Urgellia* 6 (1983), 7–243; "Els documents, dels anys 1076–1092," *Urgellia* 7 (1984–1985), 7–218; "Els documents, dels anys 1093–1100," *Urgellia* 8 (1986–1987), 7–149. A good description of the early medieval collections of the Urgel chapter archive can be found in the introduction to CCVIII, 1:65-83.

7 On the collections of the Vic cathedral, see the introduction to CCIV, 1:33–35.

8 For the collections of the church of Girona, see the introduction to CCV, 1:31–32. Josep Maria Marquès i Planagumà edited the *Cartoral, dit de Carlemany, del bisbe de Girona (segles IX–XIV)*, 2 vols (Barcelona: Fundació Noguera, 1993).

9 The 350 documents from the ninth and tenth centuries were published by Àngel Fàbrega i Grau, ed., *Diplomatari de la catedral de Barcelona. Documents dels anys 844–1000* (Barcelona: Arxiu Capitular de Barcelona, 1995). The 1715 documents from the eleventh century were published by Josep Baucells i Reig et al., eds., *Diplomatari de l'Arxiu Capitular de la Catedral de Barcelona. Segle XI*, 4 vols (Barcelona: Fundació Noguera, 2000).

10 Josep Mas i Domènech, *Rúbrica dels "Libri Antiquitatum" de la seu de Barcelona*, vols. 9,

Catalonia's monastic scriptoria produced as many or perhaps even more documents than did the episcopal sees. There were many monastic communities scattered throughout Old Catalonia, that is, the lands belonging to the Elne, Urgel, Girona, Barcelona and Vic dioceses, during the early Middle Ages. The smallest of them were absorbed by the larger ones, which also integrated their properties and archives. Major houses such as Sant Miquel de Cuixà, Santa Maria de Ripoll, Sant Benet de Bages, Sant Cugat del Vallès, and the aforementioned Sant Joan de les Abadesses, are among the monasteries with the largest documentary output.

The oldest records from Sant Miquel de Cuixà, in Conflent, were lost in the year 878 due to a flood and had to be reconstructed in four judicial sessions through testimony from witnesses. Copies of this monastery's medieval documentation were made during the early modern period, before it was definitively lost in 1793 when the monastery was attacked and pillaged. Also lost at that time was the twelfth-century *Cartoral Major* o *Llibre Verd* and the fourteenth-century *Cartoral Menor*, although there are extant transcriptions, summaries and annotations of both.[11]

The documentation from the monastery of Ripoll, in the pre-Pyrenean region, which was the most important cultural centre during the period when Catalonia was ruled by counts, suffered a similar fate: the monastery and its archive were attacked and burned in 1835. Thousands of parchments and seven cartularies were lost. Fortunately, in the seventeenth to nineteenth centuries, scholars and archivists had copied and summarized many of Ripoll's documents, making possible the recent publication of all the documents from the ninth to eleventh centuries that could be gathered and reconstructed.[12]

In terms of extant medieval parchments, the monastery of Sant Benet de Bages, in central Catalonia, is the richest of all Catalan collections. It is estimated to have kept some 5000 documents, which were scattered when the monastery was expropriated in 1835. Out of this enormous group of documents,

10, 11 and 12 of the collection *Notes històriques del bisbat de Barcelona* (Barcelona: La Renaixensa, 1914–1915)—includes summaries of the 2790 documents from this cartulary, presented in chronological order, beginning in 844 and going up to 1260.

11 Paris, Bibliothèque nationale de France, Collection Baluze, vol. 107 (Documents relatives à la Marche d'Espagne), fols. 366–404. Département des manuscrits, cote: Baluze 107, available at https://gallica.bnf.fr/ark:/12148/btv1b9002786v/f1.image (accessed 30 June 2020); CCVI, 61–66.

12 Ramon Ordeig i Mata, ed., *Diplomatari del monestir de Ripoll (segles IX–X); Diplomatari del monestir de Ripoll (segle XI)* (Vic: author's edition, 2015–2016), total of 780 documents.

only those from the tenth century have been published to date.[13] However, there is an unpublished dissertation focused on identifying, editing and analysing the records from the former archive at Sant Benet, beginning in the year 898 (the date of the oldest document) and going up to 1123.[14]

Sant Cugat del Vallès, the most important monastery in the county of Barcelona, has one of the best-preserved monastic collections in Catalonia. This is due to the fact that, at the time of the expropriation, its collections went directly to the Archive of the Crown of Aragon. As in other ecclesiastical archives, there are original parchments and copies (the ratio is one to three for documents from the ninth and tenth centuries: about 100 originals and slightly more than 300 copies).[15] This monastery also produced a valuable thirteenth-century cartulary.[16]

1.2 *The Documents as Historical Sources*

The Catalonian documents provide invaluable information about political power, society, the family, the economy, and culture. Regarding political power, the ninth-century documents—especially the Carolingian precepts, plus the Frankish narrative sources—tell us about the political geography (counties and *pagi*) and the fiscal organization of what some chroniclers called the *Marca Hispanica*, the counts subject to the Carolingian monarchy and the vicissitudes they underwent. The tenth-century documents clearly show the distancing of the Catalan counties from the Frankish sphere of influence, with the establishment of comital hereditary succession; the internal struggles for hegemony between different comital lineages or different branches of the same lineage; the at times fraught relationship between lay and ecclesiastical power; and the history of the ecclesiastical institutions and their leaders. The documentation from the eleventh century illustrates the institutional changes in the political system through the appearance of three new kinds of documents: *convenientiae*, grants of fiefs, and oaths of fidelity.[17]

---

13 In the introduction to CCIV, 1:41–43, there is a brief description of the former archive of the Sant Benet monastery, the difficulties its collections have faced and their current status.

14 Joan Salvadó i Montoriol, "El monestir benedictí de Sant Benet de Bages. Fons documental: identificació, edició i estudi. Segles X–XI" (Ph.D. dissertation, Universitat de Lleida, 2012), at https://www.tdx.cat/handle/10803/95946#page=2 (accessed 30 June 2020).

15 For more information about the collections of the old archive at Sant Cugat, see the introduction to CCVII.

16 José Rius Serra, ed., *Cartulario de Sant Cugat del Vallés*, 3 vols. (Barcelona: CSIC, 1945–1947): publishes 800 documents dated up to 1108.

17 Josep M. Salrach, "Estudi històric i documental," in PAC, 1:216–257.

Documents from the ninth to eleventh centuries do not specify the social status of individuals, but they do indicate, when appropriate, the functions that individuals perform in society: whether they are counts, bishops, abbots, viscounts, priests, *vicarii*, *saiones*, etc. This information allows us to distinguish to a certain extent between those who govern and those who are governed, the powerful and the lowly, superiors and inferiors, but it does not allow us to go beyond these dichotomies. Some documents, especially from the ninth century, reveal that there were people who we might call slaves, legally speaking (*servi*, *mancipia*). There are records as well of *servi fiscales*, but we do not know what their obligations were. There is less information in the ninth- and tenth-century documents about the system of land ownership. Although it is clear that both large estates and small landholdings existed, we do not know what their size was or how the labour system on the large estates functioned; even if the eleventh-century documents provide more information about all of this than do the documents from the ninth and tenth centuries. The extant records offer, however, greater clarity about how the clergy was organized and its hierarchies.[18]

The documents from these centuries also provide useful information about the history of the family. The hundreds of extant wills tell us a good deal about how testators thought and felt, and about the norms of succession, especially as regards the issue of inheritance; this information is complemented by what we learn from records of sale and gift. All these documents teach us about family properties, about the rights of married women to the tenth part of their husbands' properties, about the division (or lack thereof) of the family estate according to the provisions of succession, etc.[19]

The documents also provide information regarding the activities that we rather improperly call economic activities, since a relative majority of them are records of land purchases/sales or gifts. The former allow us to analyse the beginnings of the pre-capitalist stage of the land market in all its complexity, especially as it relates to the use and circulation of money. Land gifts, especially to ecclesiastical institutions, are generally attributed to religious motiv-

18 Many valuable studies on social history have been based on this documentation. For example, Pierre Bonnassie, *La Catalogne du milieu du Xᵉ à la fin de XIᵉ siècle. Croissance et mutations d'une société*, 2 vols (Toulouse: Université de Toulouse-Le Mirail, 1975–1976).

19 On testate succession, see Antoni M. Udina i Abelló, *La successió testada a la Catalunya altomedieval* (Barcelona: Fundació Noguera, 1984). On the family in general, see Lluís To Figueras, *Família i hereu a la Catalunya nord-oriental (segles X–XII)* (Barcelona: Publicacions de l'Abadia de Montserrat, 1997).

ations, but in many cases they could have been ways to liquidate debt. Fewer in number but of no less significance are the documents recording pledges. These documents tell us about the people who extended credit and those who incurred debt, about the value of the loans, the terms, interest, in-kind and cash loans, etc. There do not seem to have been individuals who specialized in lending; rather, many different kinds of people were involved, including clergy. Loans were typically short-term; the debtor usually offered land as security; people who had run out of food reserves and were suffering from hunger would often apply for in-kind loans of grain, generally shortly before the harvest, to be repaid shortly after. Unpaid loans, which resulted in the forfeiture of the land used as collateral, also fuelled the land market in its own way, as we will see below.

2 The Corpus of Catalonian Dispute Records

The 786 documents that comprise Catalonia's corpus of dispute records make it by far the largest in northern Iberia in absolute terms. However, the ratio of dispute records to the overall number of extant documents (6.5 per cent) is similar to that in Castile and Navarre-Aragon, smaller than that of León (11.2 per cent) and far smaller than that of Portugal (16.5 per cent) and especially Galicia (20.4 per cent) (see above, Table 0.1 and Graph 0.5).

As we saw with the overall Catalan corpus, there is a highly uneven distribution of dispute records between different centuries (see above, Graph 0.8). Up to the middle of the tenth century, there are fewer than one hundred dispute records. After this, when the political situation becomes more stable (under the grandsons of Count Guifré I, that is, the second generation of independent counts), the overall number of records produced and preserved, as well as that of dispute records, largely increases. It might be useful to look at short, 25-year periods, which is about the duration of a generation (see below, Graph 5.1).

It is tempting to speculate on the degree of social conflict at different points in time as indicated by the number of dispute records and their contents. However, meticulous and painstaking research would be necessary to overcome the difficulties involved in extrapolating conclusions from simple ratios of dispute records to the overall number of documents, and this research would need to take into account, among other factors, issues connected to the production and transmission of records (see above, Maps 0.1 and 0.5).

It should be pointed out that, while most known documents from the ninth century have been preserved in later copies, most documents from the tenth

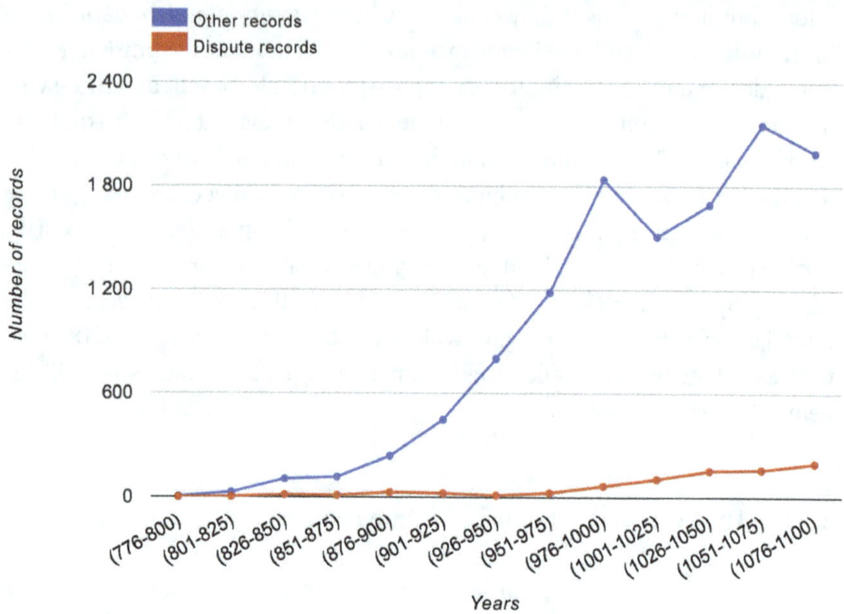

GRAPH 5.1 Proportion of Catalonian dispute records before 1100, by quarter-century

TABLE 5.2 Catalonian institutions that preserved ten or more pre-1100 dispute records

Institution	All records (n)	Dispute records (n)	Dispute records (%)	9th c.	10th c.	11th c.	Originals	Copies	Authentic	Suspect	False
Counts of Barcelona	1322	135	10.21	0	4	131	126	9	134	1	0
Barcelona Cathedral	2081	120	5.77	0	20	100	69	51	120	0	0
Vic Cathedral	1604	112	6.98	2	10	100	99	13	112	0	0
Urgell Cathedral	1216	86	7.07	3	13	70	49	37	86	0	0
S. Cugat del Vallès	789	55	6.97	0	4	51	9	46	55	0	0
Girona Cathedral	460	41	8.91	15	7	19	12	29	41	0	0
S. LLorenç del Munt	503	23	4.57	0	1	22	22	1	23	0	0
S. Joan de les Abadesses	344	15	4.36	0	8	7	10	5	15	0	0
Sta. Ana de Barcelona	151	15	9.93	0	0	15	12	3	15	0	0
S. Miquel de Cuixà	268	14	5.22	11	3	0	0	14	14	0	0
Sta. María de Serrateix	130	12	9.23	0	2	10	5	7	12	0	0
Villa de Cardona	117	12	10.26	0	0	12	5	7	12	0	0
Sta. María de Gerri	107	12	11.21	0	1	11	2	10	12	0	0
TOTAL	9092	652		31	73	548	420	232	651	1	0

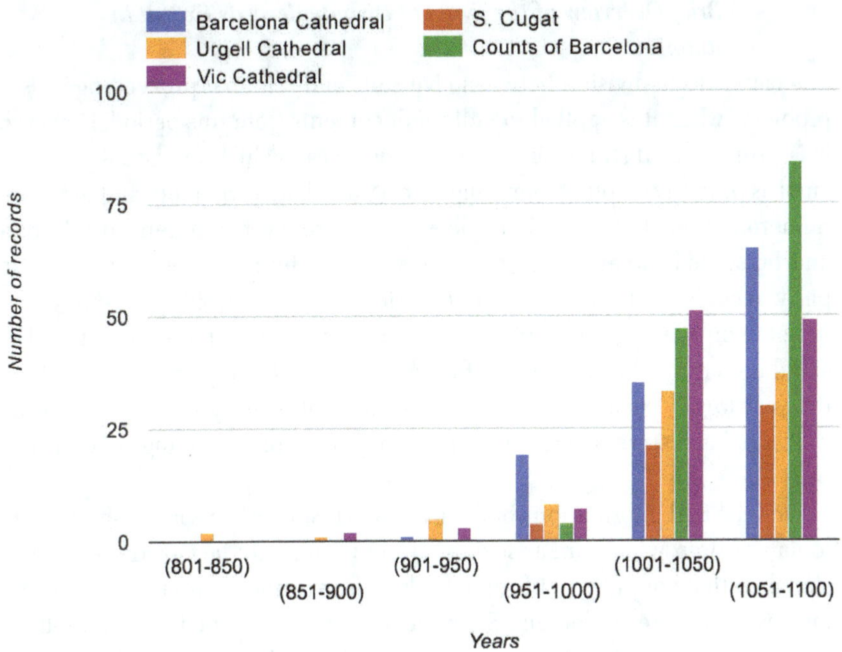

GRAPH 5.2 Largest Catalonian collections of pre-1100 dispute records, by half-century

and eleventh centuries are single-sheet originals (see above, Table 0.3 and Graph 0.6).

As in other regions, there is also evidence in Catalonia of document falsification.[20] However, rather than plainly false documents, what we find in the Catalonian corpus from the ninth to eleventh centuries are documents that have been manipulated; in other words, copies of documents with interpolated material.[21] In general, documents copied into cartularies seem to have been manipulated more than were single-sheet copies. The latter are often closer in time to their originals, and they were made mostly because of the need to preserve writing that was deteriorating and in danger of being lost. Thus, more often than not it was the scribe's duty to reproduce the document as accurately as possible. In the twelfth and thirteenth centuries, when notarial copies first appeared, accuracy became the norm.

20 JRC 89; and Josep M. Salrach, *Justícia i poder a Catalunya abans de l'any mil* (Vic: Eumo Editorial, 2013), 61–67.

21 On the manipulation of documents, see Gaspar Feliu, "Alguns exemples de manipulacions falsificadores en documents altmedievals," *Acta Historica et Archaeologica Mediaevalia* 23/24 (2002–2003), 51–68.

2.1 *A Brief Overview of the Types of Dispute Records Extant in Catalonia*

The classic legal division between civil suits and criminal proceedings raises problems when it is applied to judicial documents from this period. However, it is possible to distinguish between civil cases—which are usually formulated as property disputes over inheritances and land ownership and are more numerous, though they might involve litigants from very different social strata and be settled in very different forums—and criminal cases, in which one party accuses another of a crime (homicide, adultery, robbery, using counterfeit money, usurpation).[22] It is along these lines that we should understand the criminal formulation of a suit brought by a peasant community in the year 1013, accusing the count of Barcelona of illegally selling to a private individual a pasture where the community had a long-standing right of usufruct.[23]

One can find information about justice and disputes in a wide range of Catalonian records, which can arise either from what might be called the "professional" activity of judges in formal trials or from rather more informal mechanisms of dispute settlement. Such records can be grouped into the following types: trial records, testamentary publication charters, records of sworn oaths of witnesses, bipartite agreements (*convenientiae*), quitclaims (*definitiones*), procedural guarantees, memorials of complaint (*querimoniae*), settlements (*pacificationes*), reconstructions of lost documents (*reparationes scripturarum*), judicial sentences, and records of arbitration.

In the trial records, which the *Liber iudiciorum* calls *iudicati* (singular *iudicatum*),[24] four different parts can be distinguished. First, there is a heading that states the authority presiding over the proceedings or in whose name justice is being administered; the judge or judges assigned to resolve the case; the eyewitnesses or good men (*boni homines*) who were supposed to guarantee that the court followed correct procedure; and the *saio*, an officer responsible for bringing the accused before the court and enforcing the sentence. Second, the claim or accusation, formulated by an agent of the plaintiff, is presented and then answered by the respondent party, thus establishing the two parties' posi-

22 See the remarks on different types of criminal cases in Salrach, *Justícia i poder*, 160–173, and the documents in JRC 31, 112, 115 and 131. At some point before 1028 the comital court punished the theft of a golden chalice from the see of Barcelona by confiscating an allodial property belonging to the guilty party, JRC 221.

23 See the analysis of the case in Salrach, *Justícia i poder*, 114–118, and the text in JRC 162.

24 Karl Zeumer, ed., *Leges Visigothorum*, MGH LL nat. Germ. 1 (Hanover: Hahn, 1902), II.3.2.

tions. Third, we have the evidentiary part—that is, at the request of the judges, documents and witnesses are presented, the former are examined, and the latter deposed; for this phase, the judges, if necessary, give each party one or more deadlines. At the end of the tenth century, and especially during the eleventh, new forms of proof were introduced: the trial by ordeal, or "judgment of God," and the trial by combat.[25] Fourth and last, the sentence or its equivalent is given, as when the losing party renounces their right or the right that they were defending.

For many suits, the complete trial record has not been preserved and we have only some documents corresponding to parts three and four of the trials—that is, the sworn oaths or witnesses' statements and the sentence or quitclaim. The records of sworn oaths mention the authority (a judge and a priest, at the minimum) and the auditors before whom the witnesses take the oath and testify. The procedure takes place inside a church in front of the altar. Before testifying, the witnesses swear with their hands on the altar that they will tell the truth, then they testify, and finally they swear again on the truth of what they have said. Normally, the opposing party is present at the testimony and accepts it. But it is not uncommon for the opposing party to refuse to accept the testimony and withdraw from the trial, which forces the judges to accept the testimony themselves and to hand down a default judgment.

The largest number of extant judicial documents from Catalonia are quitclaims, called *definitiones*, *recognitiones* and *evacuationes*, which generally take the place of judicial sentences and even of *iudicati*. The text of these documents presents, first, the names and functions (judge, *saio*, *boni homines*) of the members of the tribunal; then, the parties to the conflict, often with their representatives and lawyers; next, it includes an explanation of the suit; and finally, the most important part: the statement of the losing party acknowledging that the opposing party has a superior right and renouncing its own, in some cases acknowledging that this is done at the behest of the judges. It is highly significant that in the 1010s these documents start to include not only the words *definitio*, *recognitio*[26] and *evacuatio* but also *pacificatio*. This period is also when we see the appearance of a kind of document, the simple *definitio*, from which all reference to a legal suit has disappeared, leaving only the renunciation of a

25 The earliest ordeal recorded in Catalonia, a *iudicium per examine caldaria* from the year 988, involved a private individual accused of hiding his brother's will, which benefitted the monastery of Sant Cugat, JRC 106. The oldest known case of the *iuditium Dei in aqua frigida* is from 1036, JRC 256. The judicial duel appears in Catalonian documents beginning in the second half of the eleventh century, JRC 398 (1072).

26 Similar to the term *agnitio*, used in the documentation from north-western Iberia.

property or a right. Remunerated renunciations also become very common in this period. These arise from civil suits that are settled through negotiation and pacts involving transactions and compensations. However, there are so many extant *definitiones*, and they become so standardized, that one often wonders whether they are truly the result of conflicts and lawsuits or simply commercial negotiations and sales.

There are few extant judicial sentences, if we understand the term to mean specific documents that contain sentences pronounced by judges. The most emblematic document of this sort is perhaps the record of the sentences that a tribunal of prelates and magnates, acting as judges, handed down for each of the complaints presented by Count Ramón Berenguer I against Mir Geribert in about 1058.[27]

It is impossible to know how numerous extrajudicial settlements were compared to judicial rulings. In the tenth century and at the beginning of the eleventh, it is already clear that some cases, which are formally judicial cases, were resolved without the need for judges through negotiation between the parties and the mediation of *boni homines*.[28] The documents called *pacificationes* are generally the result of these types of agreements reached by the opposing parties, with the assistance and advice of friends and third parties to whom the opposing parties often assign an almost arbiter-type role.[29] In other suits, especially those that have most to do with specifically feudal issues, the parties refuse to submit their case to ordinary justice and entrust it to respectable persons from their own sphere, for them to settle the dispute and issue a sentence that the parties promise to abide by. Normally, the only thing that has been preserved out of this entire process is the arbitral decision.[30] Over the course of the eleventh century, there are more and more conflicts, especially feudal ones, that are resolved by assemblies of nobles and prelates, sometimes with the assistance of a judge. In these cases, the opposing parties negotiate and reach an agreement through the mediation and advice of friends and other trusted individuals in attendance.[31]

---

27 JRC 330.

28 This happened in the year 1000, in a conflict between some private individuals and a vassal of the count of Barcelona over rights and lands of a fiscal nature, JRC 136.

29 This was the case of a *pacificatio* dated 993, arising from a land dispute which was resolved through the payment of a fine, or compensation, JRC 122.

30 See, for example, the decision rendered in 1052 by the bishops of Vic and Barcelona in a dispute over the Begur castle between the count of Barcelona and a magnate, JRC 310. It was perhaps in disputes within families over inheritances where arbitration was used most frequently, JRC 103 and 150.

31 See some of the documents with resolutions or settlements that were reached in these

3 Best-Documented Judicial Processes in Catalonia

An examination of the documents reveals that judges dealt primarily with five issues, which can be grouped into two spheres: the sphere of conflict that includes suits involving violent acts and simple disputes, and the sphere of the administration of ordinary justice, which includes probate, *reparationes* of lost documents, and foreclosures or enforcement proceedings against collateral.

3.1 *Accounting for Violence*

Although acts of violence are not absent from lawsuits prior to the year 1000,[32] later documents seem to make much more frequent reference to violent acts, destruction of property, coercion, abuse, assault, mutilation, murder, and robbery. True, the larger number of documents from the eleventh century, compared to before then, might distort our perception of reality. And it is also true that the clergy, which had a grip on writing, and especially its preservation, disputed the ownership of churches and control over tithes with lay aristocrats, which doubtless led to an exaggeration of the violence attributed to the nobility, a kind of demonization or criminalization of the nobleman.[33] In any case, the documentation from the eleventh century has its own lexicon of violence. If we grant that this is surely more than an illusion and try to find some explanation, we might surmise that the increase in conflict was due to disputes among the powerful, including clerical magnates, over control of land, men and rents, against the backdrop of a growing pressure exerted on the peasantry in order to increase its subjugation and exploitation. This supposition is based on numerous suits over acts of violence that all different kinds of courts had to rule on or mediate.[34]

---

assemblies, all from the year 1100: JRC 545, 548, 550 and 551. Josep M. Salrach, "Les modalités du règlement des conflits en Catalogne aux XIe et XIIe siècles," in *Le règlement des conflits au Moyen Âge. XXXIe Congrès de la SHMES (Angers, juin 2000)* (Paris: Publications de la Sorbonne, 2001), 117–134, in which an attempt is made to create a typology to characterize the different kinds of non-judicial (meaning extra-judicial) conflict resolution.

32 See, for example, a trial from 872 for physical aggression and illegal arrest in JRC 17; and the imposition of slavery as a punishment for murder, JRC 96 (987).

33 On the rhetoric of violence used by ecclesiastical scribes in the documentation from León, see Isabel Alfonso, "Litigios por la tierra y "*malfetrías*" entre la nobleza medieval castellano-leonesa," *Hispania* 197 (*Desarrollo legal, prácticas judiciales y acción política en la Europa medieval*) (1997), 917–955.

34 In some Catalonian sources, the lexicon of violence is very much present. See Josep

It then became common for the parties in these suits to draw up complaints (*querimoniae, rancuras*), and we have quite a few examples of these from the eleventh and twelfth centuries. These normally contain the complaints of counts, prelates and nobles, and sometimes peasant communities, against third parties whom they accuse of acts of violence.[35] These documents were drawn up as memoranda and perhaps as instruments of proof in a lawsuit. And they seem to suggest that judges, arbitrators and third parties read them and either passed down sentences and resolutions or proposed agreements based on them.[36] Such documents constitute an inventory, and at times almost a narrative, of the violent acts employed by the powerful and their warriors. These inventories constitute something of a relic because their function was circumstantial: they were used to calculate damages during settlement negotiations or during trials over acts of violence. Once the dispute had been resolved, it did not make sense to keep these documents (which, moreover, are not legal instruments, since they do not include the date or the names of the notary or scribe, or of witnesses). Nonetheless, as has been said, many of these documents were preserved. They tend to include more text in Catalan than do other types of records, and not only single words but whole sentences and parts.[37]

M. Salrach, "*Multa placita et contenciones*: conflictos de los siglos X–XII en el *Cartulario de Sant Cugat del Vallès*," in *Les origines de la féodalité. Hommage à Claudio Sánchez Albornoz*, ed. Joseph Pérez and Santiago Aguadé Nieto (Madrid: Casa de Velázquez, Universidad de Alcalá, 2000), 197–228.

35 Up to now, the only monograph on sources of this kind—though it focuses on peasant grievances in the twelfth century—is Thomas N. Bisson's study *Tormented Voices: Power, Crisis, and Humanity in Rural Catalonia, 1140–1200* (Cambridge, MA: Harvard University Press, 1998). Criticism of Bisson's interpretation of these sources can be found in Isabel Alfonso, "Los nombres de la violencia y el control de su legitimación," *Hispania* 208 (2001), 691–706.

36 As pointed earlier, the court that ruled on the complaints presented by Count Ramón Berenguer I against Mir Geribert in about 1058 heard and rendered a verdict on each complaint; see above, n. 27. For eleventh-century memorials of complaint, the oldest of which is from about 1057, see JRC 324, 330, 331, 341, 393, 404, 435, 439, 503, 507, 511 and 519.

37 See the philological study of one of these documents in Joan Anton Rabella, "Greuges de Guitard Isarn, senyor de Caboet (1080–1095)," in *Estudis de Llengua i Literatures Catalanes XXXV (Homenatge a Arthur Tierry)* (Barcelona: Publicacions de l'Abadia de Montserrat, 1997), 9–49. This is one of the oldest extant texts written in Catalan. It has been seen as being written between 1080–1095, although it is now clear that this did not happen before late 1105-early 1106, Josep M. Salrach, "Els greuges de Guitard Isarn, señor de Caboet (Alt Urgell). Traducció, datació i lectura," *Butlletí de la Societat Catalana d'Estudis Històrics* 31 (2020), 503–517.

The feudal pact in itself, referred to as *convenientia* in the Catalonian documents, was sometimes a peace agreement between former enemies that entailed a review of the respective grievances and of the compensation paid for each grievance.[38] Sometimes these pacts—whether they were resolutions of conflicts or alliances—were accompanied by documents in which both parties provided guarantees of compliance. When disputing parties decided to take a case before a court, the latter demanded written and sometimes even material guarantees that the parties would appear at the trial and would accept the ruling. This practice is called *firmare directum*, and it is referred to in many documents.[39] There is even an extant *convenientia* that was signed by the counts of Pallars Sobirà and Pallars Jussà in which they provide mutual guarantees that they will take their complaints to court.[40]

3.2 *Disputes over Land and Rights*

Most conflicts settled by courts would seem to be disputes over property and, therefore, correspond to the sphere that today we would call civil suits, but the situation is actually more complicated than that would suggest. There are many conflicts of this type: for example, complaints by bishops and abbots against private individuals, demanding the restitution of lands that belong to their institutions;[41] disputes between private individuals;[42] inheritance disputes between members of the same family;[43] boundary disputes;[44] conflicts between communities or private individuals over salt deposits[45] and waterways;[46] lawsuits over the illegal sale or gift of land;[47] among others.

However, it is equally true that in the ninth and tenth centuries, many of the conflicts over property and rights, even when they seem to have to do with

38 Adam J. Kosto, *Making Agreements in Medieval Catalonia: Power, Order, and the Written Word, 1000–1200* (Cambridge: Cambridge University Press, 2001), is devoted entirely to the study of *convenientiae*. See, in a single document, the record of breaking an oath of fidelity, rebellion, complaints and the reconciliation agreement, with compensations, that the viscount and count of Cerdanya reached in 1061, JRC 341.

39 Some widows, who on the advice of *boni homines* agree to withdraw their claim to a disputed mill, attempt in vain to recover the pledge they had put down for the suit, according to a document from the year 1089, JRC 472.

40 On an unknown date between 1049 and 1081, JRC 438.

41 Among the many possible examples, see three from 1025–1029: JRC 212, 221, 225.

42 JRC 122 (993).

43 JRC 213 (1025) and 223 (1028).

44 JRC 123 (993).

45 JRC 98 (987).

46 JRC 218 (1027) and 224 (1029).

47 JRC 42 (898) and 135 (999).

land and thus to belong to the private sphere (civil suits), also concern what we would today call the public sphere. This is not because one of the parties in the suit is an authority, which often happens, but because the thing in dispute is a piece of property or a right that we might consider to be of public origin. In fact, a close examination of this kind of suit leads to the conclusion that the large estates in the counties of Catalonia during the Carolingian period were partly of a public nature, in the sense that such estates included public lands and rights that had been awarded first by the Carolingian monarchs and then by the Catalan counts to their loyal followers and delegates. An examination of these suits also suggests that the ultimate goal of the dispute was often not the land itself but the income that could be derived from it and its inhabitants. Let us take a look at some examples.

The numerous conflicts that arose in the ninth century between the bishops of Girona and private individuals in certain *villae* belonging to the cathedral's patrimony are understandable not only because some or many of these individuals were *hispani*, who enjoyed the count's or the king's protection, but also because such patrimony was made up of lands granted or confirmed by the Carolingian monarchs, who apparently were not able to give anything in the Catalan counties except public lands and rights.[48] The *villae* that Charlemagne and his successors gave to the bishops, which were separate from the lands ceded to the counts, were used by the inhabitants for their own sustenance. But they were also public or fiscal areas where any lands not privately owned were considered *fisci*, and where the inhabitants had to pay tributes or taxes and perform services for the bishop and his agents.

It is easy to imagine that, after the political vicissitudes of the eighth century and the changes introduced by the Carolingians in the ninth century, the bishops turned to the law in order to consolidate their sphere of authority and affirm their rights. There were disputes over the drawing of boundaries. There were also disputes with *aprisiatores*, who were using uncultivated lands without authorization, which was required because, in the Carolingian tradition, uncultivated lands were public assets that were dependent on the public authorities and their agents and beneficiaries. Local communities had a right to use uncultivated lands, if they paid a specific tribute called the *pasquarium*, but not the right of *aprisio* and appropriation. The central issue in these suits—besides setting the boundaries of the *villae* belonging to the see of Girona and determining if the *aprisiones* were being done inside or outside of these

48 JRC 2 (817), 5 (841), 12 (850), 32 (881), 35 (888), 37 (892), 38 (892), 39 (892), 40 (893), 41 (893), 47 (900), 64 (921) and 65 (921).

villae—was whether to accept the conversion of the *aprisiones* into the private property of the *aprisiatores*, which would happen by default if a ruling was not handed down on time to prevent it, or to gain judicial recognition of the bishop's superior right to the lands occupied by the *aprisiatores*, thus allowing him to let them out to tenants.[49]

Another example that illustrates an estate of public origin is the well-known lawsuit dated 913 in which some 500 families from Ripollès acknowledged that the land where they lived and worked was not their own but belonged to the monastery of Sant Joan de les Abadesses, because Count Guifré I had delimited what had been an uncultivated tract of land and settled the families on it to bring it into cultivation. Once the uncultivated land had been made productive in this way, the count handed it over to the abbess at the end of the ninth century. When the count died, his children brought a suit against the peasants, and they were forced to acknowledge the abbess's dominion and their obligation to pay her the *servitium* or *servitium regis*. These were the terms used in the Catalan counties during the period to designate the group of payments and services due from the heads of households in the *villae* and *villares* to the public authority.[50]

Other suits provide a clear illustration of this relationship between *villa*, *fiscum* and *servitium*.[51] Perhaps the most illuminating of all the lawsuits over public lands and rights is the one from Vilamacolum, in the county of Empúries, also from the year 913. There, the count's *asertor et mandatarius* demanded from the inhabitants of the *villa* a combination of all the public burdens and taxes (military service, public works, lodging, tributes) referred to in the trial record with the formula *censum, functionem, tributum et servitium* and also with the generic term *servitium*.[52]

3.3 *Testamentary Publication Charters*

One of the most common types of documents in Catalan cartularies and collections of diplomas are testamentary publication charters.[53] We cannot ignore them if we want a full accounting of the activities of judges in the ninth to eleventh centuries. In fact, from the perspective of the people who lived in the Catalan counties one thousand years ago, testamentary publication charters

49 Salrach, *Justícia i poder*, 69–83.

50 JRC 60 and 61.

51 JRC 20, 70, 73 and 136.

52 JRC 59.

53 In addition to the 786 dispute records taken into consideration in this chapter, the Catalonian documentation includes 416 testamentary publication charters. This is a very high

were records of legal proceedings in which, by means of witnesses' statements, judges confirmed and vouched for the authenticity of the last wishes of the deceased.[54]

Judging by extant wills, we can say that testators expressed their last wishes when they were ailing and thought that the end of their earthly days was near but still had the capacity to make decisions and communicate. A scribe, usually a cleric, would take down the dying person's wishes, *pro anima* provisions, burial instructions, bequests to the Church and to the family, and the names of the executors. The witnesses who were present would add their signatures to that of the testator on the document. Frequently, any executors who were present would also sign.

Within a period of no more than six months after the testator's death, the executors would go to the judge and proceed to read the will. The judge would then call the executors and witnesses to a judicial session that usually took place in the church that was closest to the place where the deceased had lived, had the most family and local ties, or where most of his or her properties were located. In the presence of the deceased's neighbours, friends and family, the judge and a priest or several judges and priests would administer oaths to executors and witnesses, who would swear with their hands on the altar that the wishes expressed in the will were true, which they were able to recite from memory in great detail. The purpose of this session was not only to certify the authenticity of the will and demonstrate that it was the last of possibly several versions but to do so publicly and make the will known. This is why it was read in the most suitable place, before an audience of neighbours, friends and family who might have an interest in the contents. And it is also the reason behind the requirement that the will be read no later than six months after the testator's death. In fact, there was another reason for the probate process: the judge's order that it produced gave the force of law to the commission that the executors had received from the testator. In this entire process, there was strict adherence to the dictates of the *Liber iudiciorum* or *Lex visigothorum*.[55]

---

ratio, which is why the latter documents were originally included in the PRJ database. The fact that they were not—despite their judicial context—necessarily linked to conflicts is the reason why they have been excluded from the statistical material presented in this volume. It is also the reason for creating a separate category in the PRJ database that will soon allow searches to include or exclude this kind of document.

54 Antoni M. Udina i Abelló, "La adveración sacramental del testamento en la Cataluña altomedieval," *Medievalia* 12 (1995), 51–64; see also above, n. 19.

55 Zeumer, *Leges Visigothorum*, II.5.12 and II.5.14.

In all cases, after obtaining a testamentary publication charter, the executors would proceed to draw up the documents disposing of the estate according to the testator's instructions. These documents were usually charters of gift to private individuals and institutions, and sometimes charters of sale as well. In the documents, the executors say they are acting in accordance with the orders of the testator, as expressed in his/her will, for which they rely upon the mandatory deposition proceedings that were carried out within the legal timeframe. In a somewhat clichéd way, though with some variations, the executors begin these documents with the formula: *Certum quidem et manifestum est enim quia precepit nobis condam … per suum testamentum, unde iudicium obligatum tenemus infra metas temporum a serie condicionis editus*.[56] In other words, everything was done in accordance with a strict observance of the law.

3.4 Reparationes *of Lost Documents*

The law provided a reminder of the social obligation to draft documents and the way it should be done so that the document might guarantee the permanence of the legal act by making it a matter of public record. For this reason, it was said that writing "opened a present act to the eternity of future time."[57] As time passed—and humidity, insects and rodents took their toll on a document, threatening its destruction—a *translatio* would need to be created: a copy identical to the original made by a scribe in the presence of witnesses and sometimes a judge. The *translatio* would have the same value as the original.[58]

It also sometimes happened that a document would be removed or destroyed by someone with an interest in voiding the legal act recorded therein. This constituted a crime, punishable by law. An example comes from the year 988, when an agent of Sant Cugat's abbot accused an individual named Sentemir of having hidden his deceased brother's will, which according to the statement of a witness had been kept in a *cartatario* and included a bequest of half the brother's property to the monastery. Sentemir denied the accusation. When the court insisted that he confess, he asked for a trial by ordeal *per examine caldaria*, saying that he would put his hand into boiling water and would not get burned. When this did not happen, the text says that Sentemir's evil deed was discovered and he confessed that he had ordered his wife to

56 PAC 74 (1004). Salrach, *Justícia i poder*, 157.

57 See the laws on the obligation to create records and how to do so in Zeumer, *Leges Visigothorum*, II. 5 and V.4. Michel Zimmermann, *Écrire et lire en Catalogne* (*IX*[e]*–XII*[e] *siècle*), 2 vols (Madrid: Casa de Velázquez, 2003), 1:11 and 19.

58 Ibid., 1:71–73.

burn the will. Once culpability had thus been acknowledged, the court granted Sentemir's appeal for clemency and, instead of condemning him to slavery, as required by law, imposed a fine amounting to a substantial portion of his property. In this case, the judicial document took the place of the will as the deed that legitimized the transfer of property from the deceased to Sant Cugat.[59]

When a document was lost for any reason (flood, fire, pillage), its owner went to a judge to have it remade. Thus would begin a process whose roots went back to Roman law, which had been recovered or, in this case, adapted by Visigothic lawmakers. In effect, according to Roman constitutions compiled in the Justinian Code (IV.20.18 and IV.21.4–8), the destruction of documents should not negatively affect their owners because the lost documents could be replaced by witnesses' statements (*testatio amissorum instrumentorum*) before the public authorities.[60] The *Liber iudiciorum* adopts the heart of the Roman procedure, with perhaps the sole difference that in the Roman period the magistrates of the municipal *curia* took the lead role in acknowledging the report of the loss and taking statements from witnesses, while in the Visigothic period and later this role belonged to judges.[61]

In effect, the *Liber* established a procedure called *reparatio scripturae*, according to which a person whose documents are destroyed should go to a judge and report the loss. At that point, the judge would take a statement about the circumstances of the loss and the contents of the document or documents that were destroyed. Then, the judge would ask for witnesses to be called—if possible, the same people who were present when the original documents were drafted and who signed them (if they were indeed signed). Finally, the claimant would present to the judge these eyewitnesses, if they were still living, or other individuals who were familiar with the contents of the documents, and the judge would take sworn statements regarding everything that they knew about the documents (date, parties, witnesses, description and location of the properties, etc.), and the corresponding record would be drawn up. When the legal mechanism of the *reparatio* was scrupulously complied with in this way, it gave weight to the public act and transformed the sworn statement into a reconstruction of the lost document, made it a replica of the lost original.[62]

59 JRC 106.

60 Karl Zeumer, "Ueber den Ersatz verlorener Urkunden im fränkischen Reiche," *Zeitschrift der Savigny-Stiftung für Rechtsgeschichte, Germanistiche Abteilung* 1 (1880), 89–123.

61 Zeumer, *Leges Visigothorum*, VII.5.2.

62 Salrach, *Justícia i poder*, 185–194. See also Josep M. Salrach, "*Ad reparandum scripturas perditas*. El valor del documento en la sociedad de los condados catalanes (siglos IX y X)," *Territorio, Sociedad y Poder: Revista de Estudios Medievales* Anejo no. 2 (2009), 309–330.

Reparationes are quite numerous in the Catalonian corpus. Some examples are: four that were made in Conflent in 879 to replace documents from the Cuixà monastery that were destroyed during flooding of the Tet River in the summer of 878;[63] one made in Vic in 898 to replace documents from the year 893 belonging to private individuals;[64] another that was made on the request of Countess Garsenda in 930 of a record of sale dated 921, in the church of Sant Segimon del Bosc, in the region of Selva;[65] and some that were made in 987, 992 and 994 in Barcelona, of documents that were lost when the city was sacked by al-Manṣūr in July 985,[66] etc.

3.5 *Foreclosures or Enforcement Proceedings against Collateral*

Among Catalonian documents from the ninth to eleventh centuries, there are also documents recording pledges, in which one of the parties acknowledges having received a loan or incurred a debt—the amount is specified—and offers an asset, generally a piece of land, as security for the repayment of the loan or cancellation of the debt. These documents specify the makeup, the location, the boundaries and the property rights of the piece of land being offered as security. They also set the deadline for repayment of the loan or cancellation of the debt, generally for a few months or a year. And sometimes they state the consequences of default and the legal actions that will ensue in that eventuality, including the seizure of the property offered as security. It was precisely in this kind of situation when the debtor was in breach of contract, and a financial dispute arose between the creditor and the debtor—that the judicial authorities intervened.[67]

In effect, as can be deduced from many records of sale for pledged lands, one of the principal functions of judges during this period was the enforcement of the rights of the parties involved in the sale of property given as security, which was done according to the law. In these documents, the sellers specify the land that they are selling, the price and the source of their right to the land, stating that they hold it as security for credit extended to the original owner. Next, they specify the amount of the debt or credit and affirm that the agreed-upon repayment period has expired, that the debtor failed to repay and that, after waiting

63 JRC 25, 26, 27 and 28.

64 JRC 43 and 44.

65 JRC 68.

66 JRC 100, 119 and 125. Other examples: JRC 137 and 187; PAC 175.

67 After Pierre Bonnassie wrote a chapter of his thesis on the evolution of credit in the counties of Catalonia in the tenth and eleventh centuries, many more studies on this topic were published. See Bonnassie, *La Catalogne*, 399–408.

ten days (the grace period established by law[68]), they unsuccessfully demanded payment before witnesses. Lastly, based on what we see in many records of sale, the judges directed—possibly on the request of the debtors themselves—the creditors to sell the property, usually land, which was done by naming people to be in charge of setting the sale price.[69]

Considering that the value of the properties given as collateral must have been greater than the amount of the debts, the mediation of the sale of the properties by a judge was all but necessary. This is because, once the debts had been paid off using the proceeds from the sale, the law required that any remaining amount be given to the debtors, who had been deprived of their property.[70] However, the judges could exempt the creditors from this obligation, or this moral duty, to sell the property and instead grant them ownership of the pledged property. We do not know if this happened with any frequency, but there are documents showing that such a practice existed.[71]

4 Law and Justice

I will end this overview of early medieval Catalonian judicial records by looking at the interaction between the law and the judicial authorities.

The judges responsible for administering justice were individuals who had learned to read and write in church schools. There they had familiarized themselves with the *Liber iudiciorum* by studying manuscripts and later, in exercising their profession, consulted and applied the *Lex* to concrete cases, often copying laws or *aeras* from the *Liber* when necessary to support their decisions. As the documents make clear, the judges were appointed by the authorities—counts, certainly, but also very likely prelates—and they heard cases at sessions that took place periodically at established public sites.

Each judge had to take his copy of the *Liber* to hearings, and as described in many different documents, he would consult the text in search of the law or laws that he believed applied to the case before him. It was his duty to apply the law, which he could do by tempering its severity, which the law itself advised. This is what the court did in the trial of Sentemir that we looked at earlier. This

68 Zeumer, *Leges Visigothorum*, v.6.3.

69 See the many examples of the sale of lands used as security in JRC 84, 95, 108, 109, 110, 111, 134, 160, 173, 176, 181, 189, 235, 236, 249, 250, 257, 280, 365, 373, 403, 408 and 521.

70 Zeumer, *Leges Visigothorum*, v.6.3.

71 JRC 200 and 245.

also happened in a trial presided over by the bishop of Girona in the year 980, when the peasants from Palau de Santa Eulàlia attempted to break away from the bishopric's control. They claimed to hold their land in allod and presented a record to that effect that the court considered to be clearly false.[72] The bishop at that time, who was both the judge in the case and a party to it, ruled to give the *villa* to its inhabitants by way of a good deed (*ipsum alodem quem de potestate prefate sedis evaserunt eis beneficiamus*), in accordance with a law that advised moderation.[73]

Among the 557 dispute records included in the recent edition mentioned at the beginning of this chapter (JRC), one finds no fewer than 15 general references to the *Liber*, that is, with no indication of the book, title or *aera*; four specific references but without any text copied from the *Liber*; and 82 excerpts copied from the *Liber*. This is noteworthy. Adding together the general and specific references and copied excerpts, we find that the *Liber* is explicitly mentioned 101 times in the 557 documents. This says much about the legal knowledge of the judges, who also cited the Bible, canon law and Carolingian precepts.

Moreover, the references to the *Liber* are in themselves indicative of the kinds of cases that the judges ruled on. The fact that the records of their trials include some 22 quotes copied from Book II ("Concerning the Conduct of Causes") indicates that the judges faithfully followed the procedural rules governing lawsuits and, citing the *Liber* as a source of authority, demanded written proof, verified the validity of the documents, took statements from witnesses and confirmed the validity of last wills and testaments. The fact that they copied no fewer than 25 excerpts from Book V ("Concerning Business Transactions") is explained by the fact that most of the cases were disputes over property rights arising from gifts, sales, or exchanges, or over debts. And the fact that they included ten quotes from Book X ("Concerning Partition, Limitation, and Boundaries") is understandable given that the judges had to rule on cases in which people or communities either lost or gained rights as a consequence of the prescription periods determined by law (thirty or fifty years) and because they often had to rule on boundary disputes.

In short, judges during this period—whose function at least in theory was to apply the law with the goal of keeping the peace and ensuring the continuation of the established order—had to adjudicate many different kinds of cases and do so with authority and full knowledge of the facts. For this to be the case they

72 JRC 89.

73 Zeumer, *Leges Visigothorum*, XII.1.1.

needed knowledge of the law, a knowledge that is demonstrated by the quotations from the *Lex* that the judges included in the documents that they issued and signed.

Bibliography

Manuscripts

Paris, Bibliothèque nationale de France, Collection Baluze, vol. 107 (Documents relatives à la Marche d'Espagne), fols. 366–404. Département des manuscrits, cote: Baluze 107. Accessed 30 June 2020. https://gallica.bnf.fr/ark:/12148/btv1b9002786v/f1.image.

Abbreviations

CCIV: Ordeig i Mata, Ramon, ed. *Catalunya Carolíngia*. Vol. IV *Els comtats d'Osona i Manresa*. 3 vols. Barcelona: Institut d'Estudis Catalans, 1999.

CCV: Sobrequés i Vidal, Santiago, Sebastià Riera i Viader, and Manuel Rovira i Solà, eds. *Catalunya Carolíngia*. Vol. V *Els comtats de Girona, Besalú, Empúries i Peralada*. 2 vols. Barcelona: Institut d'Estudis Catalans, 2003.

CCVI: Ponsich, Pere, ed. *Catalunya Carolíngia*. Vol. VI *Els comtats de Rosselló, Conflent, Vallespir i Fenollet*. 2 vols. Barcelona: Institut d'Estudis Catalans, 2006.

CCVII: Baiges, Ignasi J., and Pere Puig, eds. *Catalunya Carolíngia*. Vol. VII *El comtat de Barcelona*. 3 vols. Barcelona: Institut d'Estudis Catalans, 2019.

CCVIII: Ordeig i Mata, Ramon, ed. *Catalunya Carolíngia*. Vol. VIII *Els comtats d'Urgell, Cerdanya i Berga*. 2 vols. Barcelona: Institut d'Estudis Catalans, 2020.

JRC: Salrach i Marès Josep Maria, and Tomàs Montagut i Estragués, eds. *Justícia i resolució de conflictes a la Catalunya medieval. Col·lecció diplomàtica. Segles IX–XI*. Barcelona: Generalitat de Catalunya, Parlament de Catalunya, 2018. Accessed 30 June 2020. https://www.parlament.cat/web/documentacio/cataleg/fitxes/index.html?p_fw=16663218.

PAC: Feliu, Gaspar, and Josep M. Salrach, eds. *Els pergamins de l'Arxiu Comtal de Barcelona de Ramon Borrell a Ramon Berenguer I*. 3 vols. Barcelona: Fundació Noguera, 1999.

PRJ: *PRocesos Judiciales en las sociedades medievales del norte peninsular*. Accessed 24 June 2020. http://prj.csic.es/.

Other Primary Sources

Baiges, Ignasi J., Gaspar Feliu, and Josep M. Salrach, eds. *Els pergamins de l'Arxiu Comtal de Barcelona de Ramon Berenguer II a Ramon Berenguer IV*. 4 vols. Barcelona: Fundació Noguera, 2010.

Baraut, Cebrià. "Els documents conservats a l'Arxiu Capitular de la Seu d'Urgell. I. Segles IX–X," *Urgellia* 2 (1979), 7–145; "Els documents, dels anys 981–1010" *Urgellia* 3 (1980), 7–166; "Els documents, dels anys 1010–1035," *Urgellia* 4 (1981), 7–186; "Els documents, dels anys 1035–1050," *Urgellia* 5 (1982), 7–158; "Els documents, dels anys 1051–1075," *Urgellia* 6 (1983), 7–243; "Els documents, dels anys 1076–1092," *Urgellia* 7 (1984–1985), 7–218; "Els documents, dels anys 1093–1100," *Urgellia* 8 (1986–1987), 7–149.

Baucells i Reig, Josep, Àngel Fàbrega i Grau, Manuel Riu i Riu, Josep Hernando i Delgado, and Carme Batlle i Gallart, eds. *Diplomatari de l'Arxiu Capitular de la Catedral de Barcelona. Segle XI*. 4 vols. Barcelona: Fundació Noguera, 2000.

Fàbrega i Grau, Àngel, ed. *Diplomatari de la catedral de Barcelona. Documents dels anys 844–1000*. Barcelona: Arxiu Capitular de Barcelona, 1995.

Marquès i Planagumà, Josep Maria, ed. *Cartoral, dit de Carlemany, del bisbe de Girona (segles IX–XIV)*. 2 vols. Barcelona: Fundació Noguera, 1993.

Miquel Rosell, Francisco, ed. *Liber feudorum maior*. 2 vols. Barcelona: CSIC, 1945–1947.

Ordeig i Mata, Ramon, ed. *Diplomatari del monestir de Ripoll (segles IX–X)*; *Diplomatari del monestir de Ripoll (segle XI)*. Vic: author's edition, 2015–2016.

Rius Serra, José, ed. *Cartulario de Sant Cugat del Vallés*. 3 vols. Barcelona: CSIC, 1945–1947.

Udina Martorell, Federico, ed. *El archivo Condal de Barcelona en los siglos IX–X*. Barcelona: CSIC, 1951.

Zeumer, Karl, ed. *Leges Visigothorum*. Monumenta Germaniae Historica, Leges nationum Germanicarum 1. Hanover: Hahn, 1902.

Secondary Works

Alfonso, Isabel. "Litigios por la tierra y "*malfetrías*" entre la nobleza medieval castellano-leonesa." *Hispania* 197 (*Desarrollo legal, prácticas judiciales y acción política en la Europa medieval*) (1997), 917–955.

Alfonso, Isabel. "Los nombres de la violencia y el control de su legitimación." *Hispania* 208 (2001), 691–706.

Bisson, Thomas N. *Tormented Voices: Power, Crisis, and Humanity in Rural Catalonia, 1140–1200*. Cambridge, MA: Harvard University Press, 1998.

Bonnassie, Pierre. *La Catalogne du milieu du Xᵉ à la fin de XIᵉ siècle. Croissance et mutations d'une société*. 2 vols. Toulouse: Université de Toulouse-Le Mirail, 1975–1976.

Feliu, Gaspar. "Alguns exemples de manipulacions falsificadores en documents altmedievals." *Acta Historica et Archaeologica Mediaevalia* 23/24 (2002–2003), 51–68.

Gros, Miquel S. "L'arxiu del Monestir de Sant Joan de les Abadesses. Notícies historiques i regesta dels documents dels anys 995–1115." In *II Col·loqui d'història del monaquisme català*, vol. 2, 87–128. Poblet: Abadia de Poblet, 1974.

Kosto, Adam J. "The *Liber Feudorum maior* of the counts of Barcelona: the cartulary as an expression of power." *Journal of Medieval History* 27, no. 1 (March 2001), 1–22.

Kosto, Adam J. *Making Agreements in Medieval Catalonia: Power, Order, and the Written Word, 1000–1200*. Cambridge: Cambridge University Press, 2001.

Mas i Domènech, Josep. *Rúbrica dels "Libri Antiquitatum" de la seu de Barcelona*, 4 vols. *Notes històriques del bisbat de Barcelona*, 9–12. Barcelona: La Renaixensa, 1914–1915.

Rabella, Joan Anton. "Greuges de Guitard Isarn, senyor de Caboet (1080–1095)." In *Estudis de Llengua i Literatures Catalanes* XXXV (*Homenatge a Arthur Tierry*), 9–49. Barcelona: Publicacions de l'Abadia de Montserrat, 1997.

Salrach, Josep M. "*Multa placita et contenciones*: conflictos de los siglos X–XII en el *Cartulario de Sant Cugat del Vallès*." In *Les origines de la féodalité. Hommage à Claudio Sánchez Albornoz*, edited by Joseph Pérez and Santiago Aguadé Nieto, 197–228. Madrid: Casa de Velázquez, Universidad de Alcalá, 2000.

Salrach, Josep M. "Les modalités du règlement des conflits en Catalogne aux XIe et XIIe siècles." In *Le règlement des conflits au Moyen Âge. XXXIe Congrès de la SHMES (Angers, juin 2000)*, 117–134. Paris: Publications de la Sorbonne, 2001.

Salrach, Josep M. "*Ad reparandum scripturas perditas*. El valor del documento en la sociedad de los condados catalanes (siglos IX y X)." *Territorio, Sociedad y Poder: Revista* Anejo no. 2 (2009), 309–330.

Salrach, Josep M. "Imatges de la historia del poder en la pintura catalana medieval. Les miniatures del *Liber feudorum maior*." In *Le plaisir de l'art du Moyen Âge. Commande, production et réception de l'oeuvre d'art*, 854–864. Paris: Piccard, 2012.

Salrach, Josep M. *Justícia i poder a Catalunya abans de l'any mil*. Vic: Eumo Editorial, 2013.

Salrach, Josep M. "Els greuges de Guitard Isarn, señor de Caboet (Alt Urgell). Traducció, datació i lectura." *Butlletí de la Societat Catalana d'Estudis Històrics* 31 (2020), 503–517.

Salvadó i Montoriol, Joan. "El monestir benedictí de Sant Benet de Bages. Fons documental: identificació, edició i estudi. Segles X–XI." Ph.D. dissertation, Universitat de Lleida, 2012. Accessed 30 June 2020. https://www.tdx.cat/handle/10803/95946#page=2.

To Figueras, Lluís. *Família i hereu a la Catalunya nord-oriental (segles X–XII)*. Barcelona: Publicacions de l'Abadia de Montserrat, 1997.

Udina i Abelló, Antoni M. *La successió testada a la Catalunya altomedieval*. Barcelona: Fundació Noguera, 1984.

Udina i Abelló, Antoni M. "La adveración sacramental del testamento en la Cataluña altomedieval." *Medievalia* 12 (1995), 51–64.

Zeumer, Karl. "Ueber den Ersatz verlorener Urkunden im fränkischen Reiche." *Zeitschrift der Savigny-Stiftung für Rechtsgeschichte, Germanistiche Abteilung* 1 (1880), 89–123.

Zimmermann, Michel. *Écrire et lire en Catalogne (IXe–XIIe siècle)*. 2 vols. Madrid: Casa de Velázquez, 2003.

CHAPTER 6

From Written Sources to Digital Tools: The PRJ Database of Iberian Judicial Records in Context

Francesca Tinti

1 Introduction

It is with mixed feelings of gratitude and apprehension that I have accepted to contribute to this volume. The gratitude element is easy enough to explain. This chapter is a revised and updated version of the talk I gave in Santiago de Compostela in November 2015 at the conference on early medieval judicial proceedings that the volume's editors organized to mark the launch of the PRJ database. I am grateful to Isabel Alfonso and her team for asking me to provide an assessment of the database itself, bearing in mind recent work on other collections of medieval sources that rely on comparable digital tools. At the same time, however, the task feels daunting for a variety of reasons. Firstly, Digital Humanities have become such a wide and complex research area that it is difficult for anyone to define exactly what they are or do, let alone feel in control of their many and varied developments.[1] Secondly, because of the speed with which the field evolves, technologies also age quickly and publishing about projects that rely on such technologies often feels like an ephemeral effort. Thirdly, and perhaps more importantly, Digital Humanities have begun to attract criticism questioning their actual intellectual accomplishments as well as their ethics.[2]

1 Several scholars in the past twenty years or so have tried to define Digital Humanities but the field is difficult to pin down into exact descriptions or definitions. Interestingly, such efforts are also difficult to follow because several of the websites and blog posts which hosted those attempts at defining the field are no longer available. For a list of milestones in the development of this important research area, originally posted onto a blog post of Brandeis University by John Unsworth, see now the web page of Duke University Libraries, revised and updated by Julia Glaubermann in spring 2016 at https://guides.library.duke.edu/digital_humanities (accessed 10 July 2018).

2 For recent strong criticism see Timothy Brennan, 'The Digital Humanities Bust,' *The Chronicle of Higher Education*, 15 October 2017, at http://www.chronicle.com/article/The-Digital-Humanities-Bust/241424 (accessed 10 July 2018). For a response to Brennan see Eric Weiskott, 'There is no Such Thing as "the Digital Humanities",' *The Chronicle of Higher Education*, 1 November 2017, at https://www.chronicle.com/article/There-Is-No-Such-Thing-as/241633 (accessed 10 July 2018).

 | DOI:10.1163/9789004683006_008

This is obviously not the place to address directly any of these issues, but it is important to bear them in mind when assessing and comparing research projects whose output falls within the remit of Digital Humanities.

In this chapter I shall first present the main features and general functioning of the PRJ database from the point of view of an external user who has not participated in its creation;[3] subsequently, I shall try to put the PRJ project in context by comparing it with other initiatives with similar goals. In the process I hope to highlight the many merits of this database and the avenues that it is likely to open for future research, as well as possible areas of improvement which may become more apparent thanks to this comparative exercise.

2 The PRJ Database's Main Features

The PRJ database aims to furnish scholars with the tools necessary for studying dispute settlements and the exercise of justice in Northern Iberia from the ninth century to the end of the eleventh.[4] In order to provide such tools, the project's team have had to gather and analyse all the published collections of documentary sources that survive for that period. The reason for this maximalist approach can be explained bearing in mind that one of the researchers' primary objectives in devising the project was eminently quantitative, in that they first wanted to establish how many of the surviving documentary sources from Northern Iberia contain materials dealing with the settlement of disputes and the exercise of justice. This could only be done by examining the contents of collections of sources published with differing editorial criteria in Spain and Portugal across a period of time stretching from the late nineteenth century to the present day.[5] Counting these documents is no easy business, as the researchers explain on their website by pointing out that scholars often disagree on what constitutes a 'text unit', especially when dealing with records contained in medieval cartularies.[6] In spite of these difficulties, however, the

3 It should be stressed that this description will obviously reflect the status of the website and database at the time of writing in spring-summer 2018 and subsequent revision in summer 2020. Future readers are likely to detect differences between what is flagged here and possible later versions of the database.

4 For a brief introduction see the project's website at http://prj.csic.es/ (accessed 24 June 2018).

5 For a full list of the editions examined by the PRJ researchers see http://prj.csic.es/bibliografia_en.php?c=4.

6 http://prj.csic.es/base_documentos.php?m=4&c=6&s=3.

PRJ project has so far examined a total of circa 22,000 documents, of which approximately 10 per cent contain information on disputes and the exercise of justice. In the database such records are referred to as 'judicial documents', even though the PRJ researchers are well aware that not all of them refer to court-cases. Both here and in the database, therefore, the adjective 'judicial' must be understood as an umbrella term referring to all documents dealing with some type of dispute, irrespective of whether this was settled in a public court-case. The total number of such records will increase noticeably when the Catalan materials, which are currently not included, are also covered. All documents have been classified both geographically and chronologically, so that users have access to a notable range of searching possibilities. The simplest searches are those conducted on the documents of a specific institution (normally ecclesiastic). For instance, if one wants to find out how many documents from the cathedral of Huesca in Aragon contain 'judicial' information, one can go to the relevant search page by clicking on 'Search by Institutions', choose 'Aragon' as a region, 'Huesca cathedral' as an institution, click on 'search', and obtain a table (shown in Figure 6.1) indicating that out of a total of 1357 surviving records for Aragon, 80 provide information on disputes or related matters. Of these 1357 total records, 68 documents proceed from Huesca, of which four are classified as 'judicial'.

Users can also choose to widen their searches by investigating the documents proceeding from one of the seven regions into which Northern Iberia has been divided for the purposes of this project (North Portugal, Galicia, Castile, León, Navarre, Aragon and Catalonia). This can be done by clicking on 'Search by region' and choosing the relevant region or regions. This tool also allows for a certain degree of comparison when choosing more than one region in the list. For instance, if one clicks on both Galicia and Castile, after providing a date range of 800–1100, one obtains the table shown in Figure 6.2.

This shows that for the period between the start of the ninth and the end of the eleventh century there survive more documentary sources from Galicia (1290) than Castile (999). Moreover, a higher percentage of those from Galicia contain 'judicial' information (20.62 per cent vs 6.11 per cent).

More complex searches allow for comparisons among a number of different institutions. In all cases users can decide the chronological range of their searches and choose whether they want the system to retrieve just the number of documents containing 'judicial' information and/or the proportion of 'judicial' documents over the total of surviving documents for a given period of time. The searching possibilities are therefore remarkably numerous, opening the way to hitherto uncharted comparative analyses.

FIGURE 6.1 Results of a search by institution through the PRJ database

Beyond the markedly quantitative character of the project, one can note that the database also allows users to get direct access to the text of all the records from Northern Iberia that contain materials related to disputes and justice. This access is provided in two different ways, either as the result of a search through the institutions of a given region, or via a wider search through the entire corpus by simply inserting a string of characters or words. In the first case, users will be provided with a list detailing for every institution the total number of documents from a given period that can be classified as 'judicial'; by clicking on that number it is possible to obtain a list of texts that can then be downloaded. For instance, after clicking on 'Search by institutions', one can choose Navarre as a region. The resulting list of 11 institutions, shown in Figure 6.3, provides the number of total documents surviving for each of them as well as the percentage and exact number of records among the surviving ones which

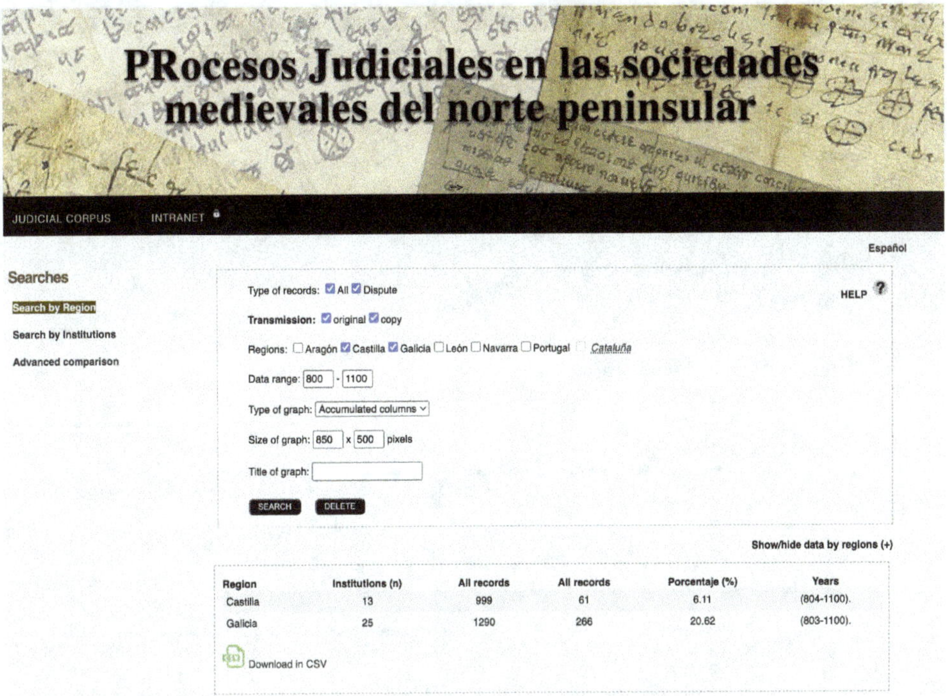

FIGURE 6.2 Results of a search for judicial documents from Galicia and Castile in the PRJ database

deal with disputes and judicial matters. In the case of San Millán de la Cogolla, the database tells us that 46 out of a total of 742 records have 'judicial' contents. By clicking on number 46 the system will generate another list which provides access to the relevant texts.

For the second type of search, it is necessary to move to the section of the website called 'Judicial corpus'. Here by simply entering a string of characters or words, the list of results will provide snippets of all the records containing those characters or words. In this case too, it is possible to download the entire text of all retrieved documents.

All descriptions of database functioning run the risk of sounding dull and dry, and the one just provided is no exception. Those readers who have not already left this chapter in order to access the website and play with the database are encouraged to do so. While surfing through the methodology section, they will notice that in their efforts to identify all the records that contain information on disputes or the exercise of justice, the PRJ team members have also devised a list of documentary typologies which includes the following categories: judicial transactions, lawsuits, *placita*/*pacta*/agreements, judicial confirmations, confessions, *notitiae* and inventories, and non-judicial transac-

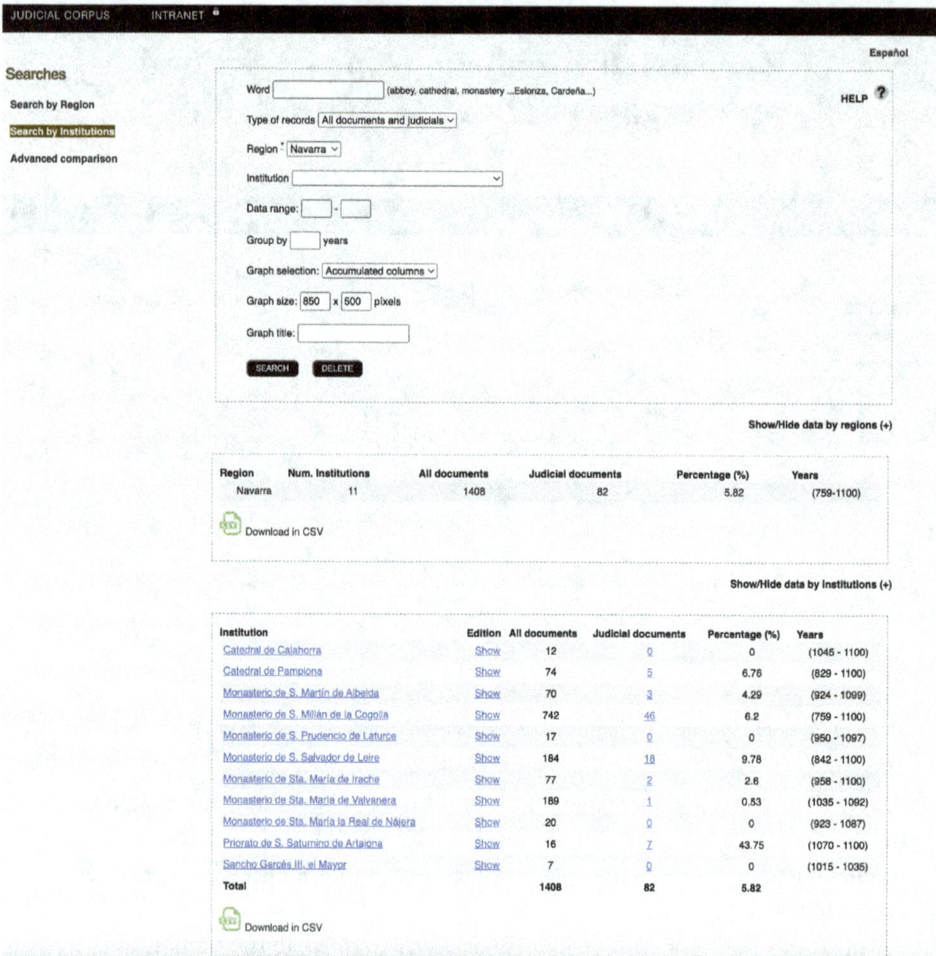

FIGURE 6.3 Judicial documents from institutions in Navarre, as displayed in the PRJ database

tions.[7] For each of them they provide a useful description and definition aiming at determining the amount and nature of 'judicial' information that each type of document may provide. Interestingly, however, this very categorization is not applied to the records themselves, either in the lists generated when searching through the collection of a given institution, or in the summaries provided with the edited texts. Admittedly, in the Spanish version of the database methodology, the list of documentary typologies is described just as a 'proposal': a systematic categorization of all documents according to these criteria would have probably been too demanding at this stage, but could perhaps be added in the future, following more specific case studies.

7 http://prj.csic.es/criterios_en.php?m=5&c=6&s=4.

3 An Excursus across Select Comparable Initiatives

After having briefly described the features of the PRJ database, I would like to put it in context by comparing its rationale and characteristics with those of other digital initiatives dealing with medieval documents. A first example that comes to mind is that of the *Codice Diplomatico della Lombardia Medievale* (CDLM).[8] This seems to share with the PRJ project two main features; the first one has to do with the modern regional approach, as in both cases documents are assigned to a region or area on the basis of modern administrative boundaries. The PRJ researchers are very well aware of the limits and possible problems arising from their geographical classification and devote a section of their introduction to explaining the relationship between the geographical organization of the materials and the boundaries of modern Spanish *comunidades autónomas*, which historians all too easily tend to project backwards to the Middle Ages.[9] They clarify that the 'historical regions' into which all documents in the database have been classified rely on, but do not correspond to, modern administrative regions, as Asturias has been included in the León region; Cantabria in Castile; and La Rioja in Navarre. The fluid borders of the polities which existed in these regions in the early and high Middle Ages shifted during the period covered by the PRJ project; nonetheless, in order to be able to structure the database and allow for comparisons between documentary collections form different areas, it was understandably necessary to apply some type of geographical organization, even though the PRJ team rightly refrained from furnishing borders for these hypothetical regions in the distribution map provided on the relevant page of their website. The CDLM website, by contrast, deliberately gathers documentary collections from institutions located within the modern administrative borders of *Regione Lombardia* (for which a map is also provided),[10] and the website itself is hosted on the official server of the region's *Beni Culturali* department. In this case the modern administrative unit provides a framework for the materials collected and a useful point of access to the records' repository, without engaging with issues of medieval territorial boundaries. The 'Lombardia Medievale' in the

8 http://www.lombardiabeniculturali.it/cdlm/ (accessed 10 July 2018). It should be noted that after several years of intense production, the activities of this project have been suspended because of lack of funding, as stated on the web page of its director, Prof. Michele Ansani of the University of Pavia at http://studiumanistici.unipv.it/?pagina=docenti&id=5 (accessed 10 July 2018).

9 http://prj.csic.es/base_regiones_en.php?m=2&c=6.

10 http://www.lombardiabeniculturali.it/cdlm/edizioni/mappa.

name of the project, therefore, is not to be intended literally, as if it referred to a defined medieval geopolitical entity, but rather as a modern container of medieval records. Within this regional container, editions of documents are also assigned to more specific areas revolving around the main urban centres in the region (*area bergamasca, bresciana, comasca, cremonese, lodigiana, milanese* and *pavese*).

The second feature that the PRJ project shares with CDLM is the way in which earlier editions of documentary sources have been acquired digitally and codified so that the visual rendering of collections which were published across many decades by several different publishers is given a uniform and web-friendly layout. It must be stressed, however, that while the aim of CDLM is the provision of a corpus of editions as comprehensive as possible, including introductions to the various documentary collections, PRJ clearly has different goals, as it does not aim at providing access to all the published sources of ninth- to eleventh-century Northern Iberia, but just to those deemed to contain relevant 'judicial' materials. Moreover, as was mentioned above, one reaches such records only after having launched specific searches, either within the collection of a specific institution or by typing in a string of characters for a search through the entire corpus.

One of the areas in which one may wish to see further or clearer information concerns the degree of authenticity that has been assigned to each of the documents containing 'judicial' materials, which are currently described as authentic, forged or suspect. Expressing possible degrees of charters' authenticity within a database can be fairly tricky, and several other projects have had to deal with similar questions without necessarily finding an ideal solution, given the variety of issues that may arise from the analysis of medieval documents.[11] It may be worth considering, however, whether the database should at least include one more category such as 'interpolated' to cater for those documents which preserve an authentic basis but were subsequently modified or augmented. These are currently included in the 'suspect' category.

Other projects, which like PRJ focus on a corpus of medieval administrative and legal records, stand out for contemplating a more explicit interest in the manuscript context within which those records have been preserved. For

---

11 Cf., for instance, the options offered in terms of charters' possible authenticity by *The Making of Charlemagne's Europe* at http://charlemagneseurope.ac.uk/browse/charters/ (accessed 10 July 2018), and those included by the *Chartae Galliae* project at http://www.cn-telma.fr//chartae-galliae/recherche/?q=*&rows=10 (accessed 10 July 2018). The latter has five categories under *Authenticité*: *oui* (meaning authentic), *douteux*, *faux*, *non suspecté*, *suspect*.

instance, the *Early English Laws* project, whose main aim is to 'publish online and in print new editions and translations of all English legal codes, edicts, and treatises produced up to the time of Magna Carta 1215', allows users to access the relevant portions of the manuscripts in which those texts survive. This can be done by clicking on 'Laws' in the horizontal menu bar of the project's website and then choosing 'Manuscripts', or via the Text Indices, as for each legal text it is possible to access both a list of print editions and a list of the manuscripts in which the relevant legal text has been preserved.[12] The development of similar tools for the PRJ project would be probably too demanding, given the numerous repositories of single sheets and manuscripts from which one should obtain permission in order to reproduce images of codices which, in many cases, will have probably not been digitized yet. Comprehensiveness in this respect would therefore be a very ambitious goal, requiring several further years of activity and substantial funding. It may be worth considering, however, whether links could be provided for at least those manuscripts and single-sheet charters which have already been digitized and are available online. This would be the case, for instance, for the *Becerro Galicano de San Millán de la Cogolla*, which was the object of a pioneering project aiming at providing the first digital edition of a medieval cartulary from the Iberian Peninsula. As this is the edition that has also been used by the PRJ project to provide the text of most 'judicial' records preserved by the monastery of San Millán, it would be relatively easy to link the text of each of the relevant documents to the images of the folios in which these appear in the cartulary.[13] Images from other cartularies which contain records identified by the PRJ project as relevant for their 'judicial' contents, have already been digitized and are available online. These include the *Libro Gótico de San Juan de la Peña*, from the homonymous monastery in Aragon, made available online by the University of Zaragoza,[14] and several others that can be accessed via the PARES (*Portal de Archivos Españoles*) website, maintained by the Spanish Ministry of Education.[15] Among the earliest manuscripts that can be visualized thanks to this website there is the *Becerro Gótico de Santa María de Valpuesta*, from which the PRJ project has identified a number of relevant tenth-century records by relying on a recent important edition.[16]

12 http://www.earlyenglishlaws.ac.uk/ (accessed 11 July 2018).

13 www.ehu.eus/galicano (accessed 11 July 2018).

14 https://zaguan.unizar.es/record/717 (accessed 11 July 2018).

15 http://pares.culturaydeporte.gob.es (accessed 20 April 2020).

16 José M. Ruiz Asencio et al., eds., *Los Becerros Gótico y Galicano de Valpuesta* (Madrid: Real Academia de la Lengua, 2010).

A possible example to follow in this respect is that provided by the *Bibliotheca Legum*, a project led by Karl Ubl at the University of Cologne, whose website contains a database of Carolingian secular law texts.[17] Through its horizontal bar menu it is possible to access a list of relevant manuscripts ordered alphabetically by their shelf mark, and by clicking on any one of them, a detailed description of each manuscript (covering origin, provenance and contents) is obtained. Whenever digital images are already available online, a link is provided. The *Bibliotheca Legum* website is also interesting for the bibliographical information it provides on each of the legal codes it describes through a list of recommended readings. One wonders whether a possible future area of development for the PRJ database could be the provision of updated bibliographical references for each of the 'judicial' records identified by the research team. Admittedly this would be a noticeable effort, in some respects similar to that undertaken for the creation of the *Electronic Sawyer* database.[18] This is an online catalogue of Anglo-Saxon charters based on the fundamental register first published in book format by the late Peter Sawyer in 1968.[19] The book itself aimed at providing for each of the 1875 records listed (including lost and incomplete texts) bibliographical references to all known published studies which discuss or at least mention the corresponding charter. The volume revolutionized the field, making it possible for scholars and students to find their way much more easily among Anglo-Saxon documentary sources. The bibliographical section, however, was bound to age quickly and to be in need of continuous updating. For several years in the 1990s scholars debated what format a revised version of Sawyer's list should take until a project proposal fronted by Simon Keynes was funded by the British Arts and Humanities Research Council. This allowed, among other things, for the conversion of Sawyer's list into a database, first released online in 2008, and the insertion of the more recent bibliographical references collected by Susan Kelly, Rebecca Rushforth and others up until ca. 2005. Thanks to this project it was thus possible to augment and update the bibliographical references which accompany each charter. But, of course, 18 years later the database is in need of further updating which would require institutional funding.[20] It is therefore with a sense of uneasiness and uncertainty that I suggest the addition of bibliographical references to the 'judi-

17 http://www.leges.uni-koeln.de/en/ (accessed 11 July 2018).

18 https://esawyer.lib.cam.ac.uk/about/index.html (accessed 24 June 2020).

19 P.H. Sawyer, *Anglo-Saxon Charters. An Annotated List and Bibliography* (London: Royal Historical Society, 1968).

20 On the website of the Electronic Sawyer an entire section called 'Development' lists the aspects of the website and database that its creators would like to develop further. Num-

cial' records appearing in the PRJ database, as I am aware that even if the resources necessary to face such a challenge were made available, how can one guarantee continued and regular uploading of references to new publications?

Online publications are normally praised for their flexibility and the advantages that they offer in terms of possible continuous amendments and improvements, especially when compared to traditional printed publications.[21] In fact, when surfing through the websites of the various projects that have been mentioned in this chapter, I have been struck by the frequent references to incomplete data-entry, lack of funding and lists of desiderata. One thus has the impression that ambitious digital projects often end up not achieving everything that was promised in the initial application for funding. Researchers often find it difficult to strike a balance between presenting proposals that are ambitious enough to obtain funding and setting reasonable goals which can be achieved within the timeframe of the duration of the project. If those goals are then not reached for whatever reason, it is close to impossible to find the financial resources necessary to complete the project. Major funding bodies are typically not interested in incremental results, and digital humanities projects, because of their very nature, normally necessitate multidisciplinary team-work and, consequently, substantial funding.[22] In other words, the completion of many such projects cannot be left to the principal investigator's will, time and determination to accomplish their goal, something which, by contrast, is more often the case with traditional print publications. Digital Humanities projects have to face numerous challenges from their inception to their completion and beyond, with structured systems of evaluation and peer-reviewing often finding it difficult to assess such projects or the CV of those researchers who have

ber 1 on the list is the 'Collection and processing of references to charters in books and articles which have appeared since c. 2005, and regular uploading of this information to the Electronic Sawyer'.

21 It should be noted, however, that such characteristics of online publications are not necessarily or not always perceived as positive features. See further Francesca Tinti, 'Fuentes escritas: transcripción, digitalización, historia social de la escritura,' in *Nuevos temas, nuevas perspectivas en Historia Medieval: XXV Semana de Estudios Medievales Nájera, del 28 de julio al 1 de agosto de 2014*, ed. Esther López Ojeda (Logroño: Instituto de Estudios Riojanos, 2015), 59–81, esp. 78–79.

22 It is mostly thanks to the so-called 'Digital Turn' that scholars of the humanities in general, and medieval studies in particular, have begun to approach, value and engage more actively than ever before in collaborative work, something that used to be exceptional in our field. The PRJ project is certainly a valuable example of such collaborative work.

invested much of their time and energies in digital enterprises.[23] These are, however, challenges that are worth facing and problems that the scholarly community must be able to address and, as far as possible, solve.

4 Conclusion

From the excursus which has been conducted here it is possible to conclude that the PRJ project presents some distinctive features which set it apart from other enterprises aiming at gathering and analyzing the contents of (early) medieval legal and administrative records. In particular, what appears to stand out primarily is the eminently quantitative nature of the main searches that can be carried out through the database search tools. The amount of data accumulated is remarkable and allows for diverse research questions to be addressed, especially in comparative terms. A few further possible avenues for development have been suggested here as ways to make the database even more profitable for its users. These include direct links to manuscript images of relevant judicial records, especially when digitized manuscripts are already available online, and the development of detailed bibliographical references for each of the 'judicial' records for which an edited text is also provided through the PRJ database. The development of possible new tools will obviously depend on the availability of further funding, given the collaborative, multidisciplinary efforts that projects like this one require.

Ultimately, the PRJ project's impact, as is often the case with these types of enterprises, will only be assessed with time, when and if scholars of early and high medieval justice in Northern Iberia will consult this tool as the main reference for their own research. What is to be especially hoped is that the wider cross-regional vocation of PRJ will stimulate research projects which go beyond and across the borders of the modern *comunidades autónomas*. Far too often in Spain, but also elsewhere in Europe, the geographical limits of medieval historical research are dictated by modern political and administrative boundaries, which, needless to say, often also determine the availability of research funding. The PRJ research team have created a database which bridges across such divi-

23 For more detailed observations on the difficulties that medieval historians often encounter to develop Digital Humanities projects in Spain, see Tinti, 'Fuentes escritas,' 78–81. Cf., more generally, *A Short Guide to the Digital_Humanities*, accessible as a stand-alone publication at http://jeffreyschnapp.com/wp-content/uploads/2013/01/D_H_ShortGuide.pdf (accessed 16 July 2018). This was originally published as the closing section of Anne Burdick et al., *Digital_Humanities* (Cambridge, MA: MIT Press, 2012).

sions, thus providing scholars with a tool which will allow them to pursue novel research questions on the settlement of disputes and the exercise of justice in medieval Northern Iberia.

Bibliography

Ansani, Michele, ed. *Codice diplomatico della Lombardia Medievale*. Accessed 10 July 2018. http://www.lombardiabeniculturali.it/cdlm/.

Becerro Galicano Digital. Accessed 11 July 2018. www.ehu.eus/galicano.

Brennan, Timothy. 'The Digital Humanities Bust.' *The Chronicle of Higher Education*, 15 October 2017. Accessed 10 July 2018. http://www.chronicle.com/article/The-Digital-Humanities-Bust/241424.

Burdick, Anne, Johanna Drucker, Peter Lunenfeld, Todd Presner, and Jeffrey Schnapp. *Digital_Humanities*. Cambridge, MA: MIT Press, 2012.

Chartae Galliae. Accessed 10 July 2018. http://www.cn-telma.fr//chartae-galliae/index/.

Early English Laws. Accessed 11 July 2018. http://www.earlyenglishlaws.ac.uk/.

Electronic Sawyer. Accessed 24 June 2020. https://esawyer.lib.cam.ac.uk/about/index.html.

Glaubermann, Julia, ed. *Digital Humanities*, spring 2016. Accessed 11 July, 2018. https://guides.library.duke.edu/digital_humanities.

Libro gótico de San Juan de la Peña. Accessed 11 July 2018. https://zaguan.unizar.es/record/717.

The Making of Charlemagne's Europe. Accessed 10 July 2018. http://charlemagneseurope.ac.uk/browse/charters/.

Pares. Portal de Archivos Españoles. Accessed 20 April 2020. http://pares.culturaydeporte.gob.es.

PRJ: *PRocesos Judiciales en las sociedades medievales del norte peninsular*. Accessed 24 June 2020. http://prj.csic.es/.

Ruiz Asencio, José M., Irene Ruiz Albi, and Mauricio Herrero Jiménez, eds. *Los Becerros Gótico y Galicano de Valpuesta*. Madrid: Real Academia de la Lengua, 2010.

Tinti, Francesca. 'Fuentes escritas: transcripción, digitalización, historia social de la escritura.' In *Nuevos temas, nuevas perspectivas en Historia Medieval: XXV Semana de Estudios Medievales Nájera, del 28 de julio al 1 de agosto de 2014*, edited by Esther López Ojeda, 59–81. Logroño: Instituto de Estudios Riojanos, 2015.

Ubl, Karl, ed. *Bibliotheca legum regni Francorum manuscripta* (Cologne, 2012). Accessed 11 July 2018. www.leges.uni-koeln.de

Weiskott, Eric, 'There is no Such Thing as "the Digital Humanties".' *The Chronicle of Higher Education*, 1 November 2017. Accessed 10 July 2018. https://www.chronicle.com/article/There-Is-No-Such-Thing-as/241633.

PART 2

Recording Disputes: The Textual Construction of Judicial Process

CHAPTER 7

Disputing and Dispute Records in the *Formulae Visigothicae*

Warren C. Brown

1 Introduction

In this essay, I will discuss, from the perspective of the questions that frame this volume, five early Spanish judicial records. These appear in the collection of document models that are traditionally said to come from the Visigothic kingdom and are now called the *Formulae Visigothicae* (FV).[1] I will explore what they say about how people in the world that produced them handled conflict. More than this, however: I want to explore the interplay between the disputing processes that the texts describe, the texts themselves, and the contexts in which the texts were created and transmitted to us. To be specific, I want to look not only at what these texts say about conflict, but at what kinds of texts they are, how they came to be part of the FV, how they came to us, and, finally, what we can actually learn from them. The five dispute formulas in the FV are the farthest thing imaginable from transparent records of Visigothic disputing processes. The FV has a complicated origin and transmission that reaches from the seventh (possibly the late sixth) century through the high Middle Ages into the early modern period. Its story was shaped not only by the practical decisions of those who wanted to collect and pass on useful models for documents, but also by the larger history of Spain itself and the ideological needs of some of the people involved. If this volume is concerned with the complex relationship between our sources, the disputes they depict, and the contexts in which they were written and transmitted, in the FV this complexity reaches an extreme. At

1 "Formulae Visigothicae," in Karl Zeumer, ed., *Formulae Merowingici et Karolini Aevi*, MGH LL 5 (Hanover: Hahn, 1886), 572–595; "Formulae Wisigothicae," in Juan Gil, ed. *Miscellanea Wisigothica* (Seville: Publicaciones de la Universidad de Sevilla, 1972), 69–112. I would like to thank 1) Caroline Howard, who in 2016 as a Caltech Summer Undergraduate Research Fellow helped me explore the manuscript of the FV and its commissioner Ambrosio de Morales, and 2) my Caltech colleague George W. Pigman, whose patient efforts to help me untangle the sometimes difficult Latin of the FV have been invaluable.

 | DOI:10.1163/9789004683006_009

the end, we will have to ask ourselves whose ways of handling conflict we have been looking at, and whether we can even know.

I face these early Spanish texts from the perspective of an outsider, that is, someone who up to now has never worked on Spain or with Spanish sources. I have spent most of my career studying conflict resolution and judicial processes on the other side of the Pyrenees, in the kingdoms of the Merovingian and Carolingian Franks. I started out studying the judicial records and other accounts of conflict contained in ecclesiastical and monastic charter collections and cartularies. Most recently, I have been working intensively with the same kind of texts I will be looking at here, namely documentary formulas. These sources, both because of their content and because of their manuscript survival patterns, have kept me focused above all on the eighth and ninth centuries, that is, the Carolingian period.[2] So as I approach the Visigothic formulas, I will be trying to make sense of them from the perspective of someone experienced in working with similar kinds of texts, but from a different place and later time (though as we will see below, the time may not be as different as it seems at first glance). I have been conditioned by my Franks, with their often colourful ways of handling disputes, and by the particular problems posed by the texts that they left behind.

2 Formulas

Formulas are templates for documents, which have had all specific information, such as names, dates, places, and other details, removed. They served their users, mainly clerical and monastic scribes and students, as models or sources of language to use when they had to write documents, or when they had to learn how to write them.[3] The following is Frankish; it originated in or around Tours in the middle of the eighth century and survives in four ninth-century

2 See inter alia *Unjust Seizure: Conflict, Interest and Authority in an Early Medieval Society* (Ithaca, NY: Cornell University Press, 2001); "When Documents Are Destroyed or Lost: Lay People and Archives in the Early Middle Ages," *Early Medieval Europe* 11, no. 4 (2002): 337–366; "Conflict, Letters, and Personal Relationships in the Carolingian Formula Collections," *The Law and History Review* 25, no. 2 (Summer 2007): 323–344; "Lay People and Documents in the Frankish Formula Collections," in *Documentary Practices and the Laity in the Early Middle Ages*, ed. Warren C. Brown et al. (Cambridge: Cambridge University Press, 2013), 125–151; *Beyond the Monastery Walls: Lay Men and Women in Early Medieval Legal Formularies* (Cambridge: Cambridge University Press, 2023).

3 See Alice Rio, *Legal Practice and the Written Word in the Early Middle Ages: Frankish Formulae, c. 500–1000* (Cambridge: Cambridge University Press, 2009).

manuscripts. It represents a sales contract (in the translations here and below, the letters A and B always refer to the two principal actors):

> Another Document of Sale
> To the magnificent brother B (*illo*) I A (*ille*). It was agreeable to me to sell to you, and thus I have sold the field N, or vineyard, belonging to me within the boundaries of Saint C (*illius*) [i.e., a monastery] in the place called N (*illo*), having so-and-so many (*tantos*) *aripennos* [a unit of dimension]; that is on the one side fronting the land of D (*illius*), on the other side the land of E (*illius*); whence I have accepted from you a price that was acceptable to me, valued at so-and-so many (*tantos*) *solidos*, so that from this day, you should have free power to do with the above-named property whatever you wish, saving the rights of Saint C (*ipsius*). And if I myself or any of my heirs or any person whatever shall presume to raise any calumny or objection against this sale, let him pay to him against whom he raised the quarrel 15 *solidos*, and let this sale remain firm.[4]

This second example is from the FV; it is a formula for the opening lines of a charter recording a property exchange:

> To the honourable lord brother B (*ill.*), [I] A (*ill.*). That which is the common wish of both parties ought to be preserved by mutual consent, but the testimony of writing is required to preserve the memory for posterity. Therefore, it agrees and coincides with our wish, that we ought to give to each other this and that (*hoc et illud*) in exchange; and this has been done. Which properties, therefore ....[5]

A surprising number of such formulas survive from early medieval Europe. By far the majority are Frankish; about forty Frankish manuscripts containing formulas survive from the eighth through the tenth century, with most coming from the ninth.[6] Two collections survive from Spain: a tenth century collection

4 "Formulae Turonenses," in Zeumer, *Formulae*, no. 8, 140.

5 FV 28: ed. Zeumer, 588; ed. Gil, 100.

6 "About forty": the number here depends on what one counts as a formula collection and indeed on what one counts as a formula. Rio, *Legal Practice*, 241–271, in her "A Handlist of Manuscripts," lists thirty-six manuscripts. A few of these, however, contain only one or two formulas. There are other manuscripts that she does not list that also contain one or a few formulas, written in empty spaces between texts, in margins, etc. In addition, some collections of actual document or letter texts that survive from the period may have been intended to serve the same purpose as formulas.

from the abbey of St. Mary at Ripoll in Catalonia,[7] and the FV. The formulas are therefore—for early medieval sources—numerous. However, they are not easy to use; they are by nature abstracted, conservative, and hard to anchor in time and space. They lack the specific information about people, properties, and institutions contained in the surviving ecclesiastical and monastic records. They preserve language, descriptions of procedure, and document types that predate the time in which they were written down—often by centuries (this is especially true, as we will see, of the FV). It is therefore easy to see the formulas as ahistorical, that is, as disconnected from a world in which what they said no longer applied and may not have even been understood.[8]

It is not in the formula texts per se, however, but rather in the manuscripts in which they survive that we can find an anchor. If we look at the collections as they actually stand in the manuscripts, we can tell that their compilers deliberately gathered, selected, and adapted texts that ranged from old to contemporary and organized them into logically coherent groups for easy reference. Sometimes they took them from their own archives or libraries and anonymized them. Sometimes they took them from other formula collections that visitors or newcomers had brought, often over very long distances. They selected some formulas and abandoned others, modified them and reordered them, and combined them with pieces of other formula collections or with texts of their own according to their own particular needs. In many cases they inserted notes about how to use the formulas for students or less experienced scribes. The results were collections of models that were intended for both practical use and education. Though they might contain document texts that were older, even far older, than the time in which they were copied and that came from several different places, as a whole they reflected their compilers' sense, in their own times and places, of what the people around them did—or might possibly do, or had done that was interesting—that might require documents.[9]

In the case of the Frankish collections, we can say something about what those times and places were because we can usually date and place the manuscripts, e.g., "Tours, first half of the ninth century" or "in or near Salzburg, end of the ninth century".[10] Even for those that we cannot, the handwriting still

7 Michel Zimmermann, "Un formulaire du xème siècle conservé à Ripoll," *Faventia* 4 (1982), 25–86.

8 Rio, *Legal Practice*, 27–30.

9 Brown, "When Documents are Destroyed or Lost," esp. 354–362; Warren Brown, "Die karolingischen Formelsammlungen—warum existieren sie?" in *Die Privaturkunden der Karolingerzeit*, ed. P. Erhart, K. Heidecker, and B. Zeller (Dietikon-Zurich: Urs-Graf Verlag, 2009), 95–101; Rio, *Legal Practice*, 63–66.

10 Warsaw, Biblioteka Uniwersytecka, 1; Munich, Bayerische Staatsbibliothek, Clm 4650; Rio, *Legal Practice*, 247–248, 270.

lets us put them in Carolingian Francia. Not the FV, however. We have no way to anchor this formula collection in time and place because it lacks that final piece: the manuscript witness. The FV's manuscript tradition is an early medievalist's worst nightmare. All that we have is a codex commissioned in the late sixteenth century by one Ambrosio de Morales, an antiquary and historian in the employ of King Philip II of Spain (see Figure 7.1).[11] Comprising III + 252 folia, it contains an eclectic mix of texts, drawn from several sources, that range in date from late antiquity into the thirteenth century. These include genealogies and lists of bishops and kings, legal and school texts, annals, chronicles, histories and hagiography, and letters to and from kings and other important persons. By and large, however, the contents seem to concentrate on the Visigothic and Asturian/Leonese kings from ca. 600–900. Morales drew his texts from several sources. The first and most important of these was a now-lost manuscript written out in Oviedo sometime in the first half of the twelfth century, at the orders of Oviedo's bishop, Pelagius.[12] Among the texts that Morales took from the Pelagius manuscript are the FV.[13] This copy of the FV in the Morales codex is our only witness to them. It gives us two anchor points: the scholarly circle surrounding the Spanish royal court towards the end of the sixteenth century and Oviedo in the first half of the twelfth. Neither of which helps us identify the world of the FV.

So what makes the FV Visigothic? The conventional wisdom has them originating in Córdoba during the reign of the Visigothic king Sisebut (r. 612–621).[14] The dating is based on one formula—a spectacular verse text for a marriage gift—in which the scribe left in a reference to King Sisebut's third regnal year. The location rests on another that describes the submission of a document to

---

11 Madrid, Biblioteca Nacional de España, 1346; Roger Collins, "Ambrosio de Morales, Bishop Pelayo of Oviedo and the Lost Manuscripts of Visigothic Spain," in *Wisigothica. After M.C. Díaz y Díaz*, ed. Carmen Codoñer and Paulo Farmhouse Alberto (Florence: SISMEL—Edizioni del Galluzzo, 2014), 609–632.

12 In the most recent work on this question, Roger Collins suggests that this lost manuscript was compiled for King Alfonso VII of Castille (r. 1127–1157), rather than for his grandfather Alfonso VI (d. 1109), as has been commonly assumed; see "Ambrosio de Morales and the *Codex Vetustissimus Ovetensis*", in *Italy and the East Roman World in the Medieval Mediterranean: Empires, Cities, and Elites 476–1204*, ed. Thomas J. MacMaster and Nicholas S.M. Matheou (Abingdon: Routledge, 2021), 49–69.

13 Madrid, BNE, 1346, fols. 75^r–90^r.

14 Edorta Córcoles Olaitz, "About the Origin of the Formulae Wisigothicae," *Anuario da Facultade de Dereito da Universidade da Coruña* 12 (2008), 199–221, at 202–204, and *Las Formulae Wisigothicae. Aproximación a la práctica jurídica visigoda* (Lecce: Edizione Grifo, 2010), 12–17.

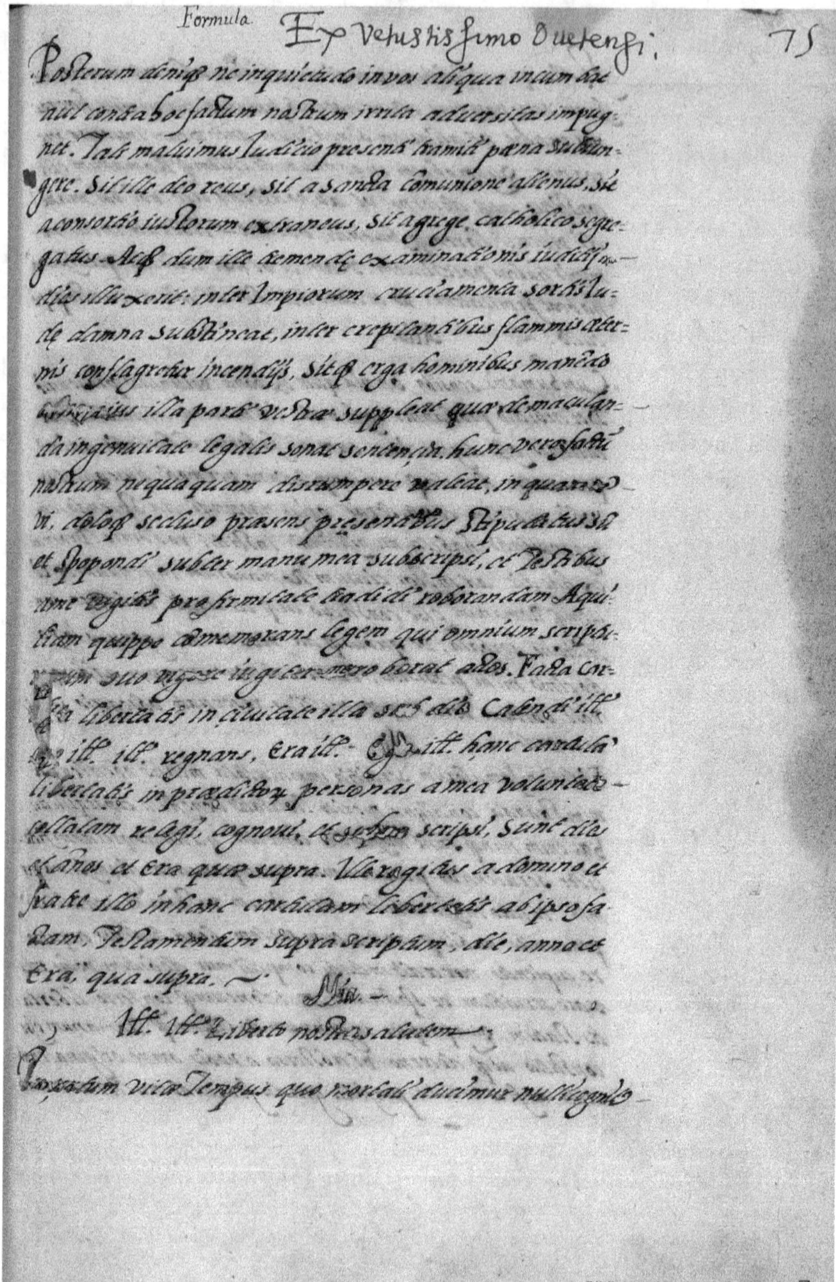

FIGURE 7.1 Madrid, Biblioteca Nacional de España, 1346, fol. 75r: the beginning of the sixteenth-century copy by Ambrosio de Morales of the *Formulae Visigothicae*
BNE

an assembly in Córdoba for validation and recording in the city's *gesta publica*.[15] Using these two bits of information to date and localize the collection this precisely requires one to assume, as some of the older scholarship has in fact done, that the FV were compiled when and where the documents on which these two formulas were based were originally composed. This seems dangerous in the extreme. However, it is safe to say that the formulas are Visigothic. A number of them refer to Goths; they were plainly written by or for Goths, or under a Gothic regime. Moreover, several use orthodox-catholic religious language, which puts them after the conversion to orthodox Christianity in 589 of King Reccared (r. 586–601).[16] So we can say with some certainty that at least the documents on which the FV were based were written in the Visigothic kingdom sometime after its kings became orthodox at the end of the sixth century. At least one of them was written during the reign of Sisebut, and another was composed in Córdoba.[17]

So far we have a collection of Visigothic-era document texts. What makes the FV a formula collection, in the sense of a collection of model documents deliberately intended for reference, reuse, and/or study?[18] To begin with, not only has all (or most) specific information been removed from the individual texts, at some point they were deliberately organized to make it easier to find examples of particular kinds of documents. The FV as we have it contains forty-

15 FV 20, 25.

16 Córcoles Olaitz, "About the Origin," 210–218 and *Las Formulae Wisigothicae*, 28–34. Córcoles Olaitz suggests here that the texts could in fact have been written after the time of Leovigild (573), the king who started to consider the religious unification of the kingdom.

17 Cf. Ángel Canellas López, *Diplomática hispano-visigoda* (Zaragoza: Institucion "Fernando el Catolico," 1979), 16–17, 21–29; Rosa Mentxaka, "En torno a 'formulae visigothicae' 44," in *Scripta Antiqva: in honorem Angel Montenegro Duque et José María Blázquez Martínez*, ed. Ángeles Alonso Ávila and Santos Crespo Ortiz de Zárate (Valladolid: s.n., 2002), 827–840, at 828–829.

18 Here I must differ with Collins, "Ambrosio de Morales," 626, when he suggests that the FV might not have been a "proper formulary" in this sense because it contains more examples of certain kinds of documents than such a formulary would require and others that would have been of little use to working notaries (in particular the verse formula for a dotal gift FV 20). While we cannot know for certain why the FV was ultimately put together in the form in which we have it, its contents per se do not preclude a practical intent. A number of the Frankish formula collections are similarly uneven or biased in their contents, and several contain apparently random but deliberately anonymized verse texts (which has in some cases have been masked in the MGH edition by Zeumer's editorial decisions about what constituted a formula or what properly belonged to a given collection). Nevertheless, from their arrangement and manuscript contexts, these collections appear to have been compiled for practical use or at least reference or study.

six formulas.[19] It may be incomplete. The first formula, FV 1, lacks a title and starts in the middle of a document text, so it is possible that what we have is not all of what there once was and that there were other formulas that preceded it. On the other hand, the text as it stands in the Morales codex starts at the top of a page, with a capital letter. Moreover, only six of the FV represent complete documents; fourteen more are substantially complete, while twenty-six are document fragments. Given the number of fragmentary documents in the collection it is at least possible that FV 1 is not incomplete and that it was the in fact intended to be first text of the collection; we will never know for certain. Be that as it may: in the surviving corpus, the first thirty formulas are grouped by subject: manumissions, the foundation or endowment of churches, sales of unfree, marriage gifts, testaments or other documents of succession, exchanges, and donations. Someone clearly wanted to create an accessible reference or teaching collection. The remaining sixteen, however, are different. They appear to be a random mix of unrelated document texts, with no discernible logic to their arrangement, save that two formulas for precarial arrangements and three formulas for mandates are placed together. Without being able to say for sure, it looks like someone took a pre-existing and organized collection of formulas, copied it, and then added some more formula texts onto the end.[20] As for when either of these steps took place (i.e., the creation and organization of the first collection of formulas or the possible addition of the final sixteen), we cannot say. It is entirely possible that one or the other step took place sometime during the Visigothic period. It is also possible, however, that the collection was created and/or modified after the Visigothic period, even well afterwards.[21] Similar processes are visible in Francia. For example: the group of formulas from Angers commonly known as the *Formulae Andecavenses* is frequently called the oldest of the Frankish formula collections because the language in some of the texts goes back as early as the sixth century. However, the manuscript in which the formulas sur-

19 Following Zeumer. Gil edits only forty-five; he leaves out a block of text that on fol. 90r of the Morales codex lies between the *factum placitum* at the end of FV 45 and the beginning of a letter of Pope Gregory I.

20 Miguel Calleja Puerta, "Ecos de las Fórmulas Visigóticas en la documentación altomedieval Astur-Leonesa," in *Les formulaires. Compilation et circulation des modèles d'actes dans l'Europe médiévale et moderne*, ed. O. Guyotjeannin, L. Morelle, and S.P. Scalfati (Paris: Éditions en ligne de l'École des chartes, 2016), section I: "El manuscrito de las *Fórmulas visigóticas*," at http://elec.enc.sorbonne.fr/cid2012/part4 (accessed 4 September 2017).

21 Córcoles Olaitz goes so far as to suggest, quite plausibly, that the FV in their present form were not known in the Visigothic period: "About the Origin," 218 and *Las Formulae Wisigothicae*, 34–35. Cf. Mentxaka, "En torno," 829.

vive stems from the second half of the eighth century, and some of the formulas fit both in language and in content perfectly well with documents of this period.[22] The Angers formulas as they actually stand in the manuscript thus appear to represent a collection compiled and copied out not during the early Merovingian period but rather in the early Carolingian, by members of an ecclesiastical scriptorium who gathered up the examples they had around them, many of which were very old.[23] Other Carolingian-era collections similarly picked up texts of Merovingian or even late antique origin as their compilers combined pieces of pre-existing formula collections with material from their own archives to create the collections they wanted from the resources they had available.[24] I will return to this question of when the FV might have been compiled at the end of this essay.

3 Judicial Practices in the FV

At the very least, we can say this: we have in front of us a collection of formulas that derive from documents written in the Visigothic period. What do these formulas say about conflict resolution? Very little. Of the forty-six formulas in the FV, only five deal with disputes. Nevertheless, these five formulas show us some of the different ways that people in their world handled disputes, some of the roles that judicial assemblies and judicial officials could play in disputes, and some of the different ways that information about disputes could be recorded and transmitted.

All of our dispute formulas deal with disputes among lay people. One deals with a property dispute (FV 35). A second records a dispute over the ownership of *servi* (FV 40). The third has someone asking someone else to handle a specific dispute for him; what the dispute is about is left blank (FV 41). The fourth deals with someone who has failed to pay back a debt (FV 42), while the fifth concerns a runaway *servus* (FV 43).

As for how the disputes they record were handled: one, FV 40, records a dispute that was brought before a formal judicial court:[25]

---

22 Fulda, Landesbibliothek D 1; Rio, *Legal Practice*, 244.

23 Rio, *Legal Practice*, 67–80; *The Formularies of Angers and Marculf: Two Merovingian Legal Handbooks*, trans. Alice Rio (Liverpool: Liverpool University Press, 2008), 39–46, 248–254.

24 See e.g. Brown, *Beyond the Monastery Walls* on Paris, Bibliothèque nationale de France, ms. lat. 2123 and the formula collection from Flavigny.

25 FV 40: ed. Gil, 108–109; ed. Zeumer, 593–594. Here and throughout I follow Gil's text.

> Diiudicatio.
> Tunc enim veritas ex consequenti ratione colligitur, cum in examinatione partes litigantium veniunt. Ergo cum inter illum (A) et illum (B) arbitres sedissemus, vicisim se multis iurgiis impugnare coeperunt; cumque diutissime contendendo et se mutuo iniuriando crebris conviciis lacessirent, legis autoritate illis praecepimus, ut, remota iurgiorum controversia, propria in conspectu nostro propalarentur negocia.

Appropriately titled "Judgment", the formula starts by saying that the truth is found in a logical fashion when the quarrelling parties come to a hearing. Then we hear the first-person voice of the judges. They describe how two men A and B came before them and began to attack and insult each other. After the judges had had enough, they ordered the parties to stop quarrelling and present their cases to them.

> Tandem ille (A) contra illum (B) asseruit, dicens: 'Rem illam, quae iure patris mei debitam mansit, cur eam in tuo servitio habeas, edicito'. E contra ille (B) ait: 'Rem istam, quam a nobis reposcere conaris, per ill. et ill. capitulo nobis collata sunt, et per tot annos nominata res iure patris[26] mei ill. et nostro servitio mansit'.

Man A stepped forward and demanded to know why man B was holding property in his service that belonged to his father—we learn later on that the property was a pair of *servi*. B responded that the property had been transferred to his family by two other men, and that it had belonged to his father and been in their service for x number of years.

> 'Sed si iuxta quod asseris, res illa esse patris tui ill. iure fuisse debita affirmas, convincere te oportet'. Tunc ille (A) petitor secundum ill. (B) responsum se talem probationem manifestus est habere; quam etiam in nostro iuditio proferens, id est, illum (A) et illum (B), iuxta legum decreta sagaci intencione eos segregatim percontari decreuimus. Quorum dum testimonium liquide discutere conaremus, invenimus illum et illum servos esse illius (A)[27] et consanguineos fratres eorum in servitio originali

26 Gil gives *patres*, Zeumer *patris*. The manuscript (fol. 88ʳ) has a somewhat smudged "e" with a dot over it; it is possible that the scribe wrote an "e" and then hurriedly corrected it to an "i". Since *patris* makes more sense, I have chosen to follow Zeumer's reading.

27 I assume that both *illius* here and the *ill.* that follows refer to A because of B's immediate opposition to this finding in the next section of the text.

> esse ill. (A); et ill. et ill. de ea, quae testificare conabantur, bifarios eos testificare deprehendimus: ill. dixit sic et alius dixit hoc et illud se scire.

Then things get really interesting: B went on to say that if A wanted to claim that the property was his, he should prove it. A (now identified as the plaintiff—*petitor*) replied that he had proof and produced it. The judges then interrogated each of the parties separately. The judges found that the two *servi* in question had originally belonged to A and that their brothers had also been in A's service. In other respects, however, the two men gave contradictory testimony: "this one (A) said thus, and the other (B) said that he knew this and that."

> Proinde nec mora obsistit et ille (B) in nostro conspectu, sententias legis libri ill. protulit, legem illam qui est sub titulo illo, era illa, ubi dicit hoc et illud.

But the dispute was not yet settled. B did something here that I have never seen in a Frankish formula: he cited the law. When a Frankish formula cites or quotes the law, it is the formula text itself that does so. For example, this formula from the mid-eighth century Tours collection, describing the settlement of a case of bride theft, begins:

> Viventibus patribus inter filios familias sine voluntate eorum matrimonia non legitime copulantur, sed contracta non solvuntur. Idcirco ego in Dei nomine ille dulcissima coniux mea illa. Dum et te sine voluntate parentum tuorum rapto scelere in meo sociavi coniugio ....[28]

The first sentence is a verbatim quotation from one of the versions of the Roman Law of the Visigoths (*Lex Romana Visigothorum*) that circulated in Francia, the so-called Epitome Aegidius.[29] In FV 40, in contrast, the formula describes the individual himself citing the law in the middle of a court debate; it assumes that a lay person involved in a dispute would have known the law well enough to use it in court. The formula also provides spaces for a scribe to say exactly which law: B cited the law in Book x, title x, number x, "where it says this and that". The formula does not, unfortunately, tell us what body of law was being used. The editor of the formulas for the *Monumenta Germaniae*

28 "Formulae Turonenses," ed. Zeumer, no. 16, 143–144.

29 Gustav Haenel, ed., *Lex Romana Visigothorum*, (Aalen: Scientia Verlag, 1962), Pauli Sententiarum II, 20, 2, Interpretatio (Epit. Aeg.), 368.

Historica, Karl Zeumer, suspected that it was the Visigothic laws rather than the *Lex Romana Visigothorum*, because references to the law of the Goths in ninth century documents cite the law in the same way, by book, title and number.[30] But the *Lex Romana Visigothorum* is also organized that way, so the formula could just as easily be referring to this.

In any case, returning to FV 40:

> His expletis sermonibus, ille petitor (A) contra illum (B) asseruit, dicens hoc et illud. Tunc ill. (B) hoc, quod ill. (A) petitor sermone professus est, per idoneum testem firmari expetit. Ad haec ille (A) petitor adiecit praeter se et illum (B) nullam tertiam personam interfuisse.

In response to B's statement of the law, A said "this and that". B fired back, saying that A should back up what he said with a suitable witness. A replied that except for himself and B, there was no third person present.

> Sed tunc ill. (B) suo sermone professus est hoc et illud. Cumque illi (B)[31] imperatum a nobis fuisset ut iuxta quod locutus est pro rem illam et illam sacramentum redderet, ipse illud iuramentum reddere non ausauit. Tunc nos decreuimus hoc et illud. Quam rem ad singula decernentes in hanc iuditii paginam inseruimus, quatenus futuris temporibus iustitiam habens congaudeat et calumniantis adversa vox spe facta conticescat. Facta iuditii pagina in ciuitate illa, sub die Calendis illis, anno illo regno illo, era illa. Ille hanc iuditii paginam nostro in iuditio latam subscripsit ….

In reply, B said "this and that". The judges ordered B to swear an oath to what he had said. But he did not dare to, and backed down. So the judges decreed "this and that" and ordered a document drawn up listing all the steps taken, that is, this formula.

This formula can only have been drawn from a real document that dealt with a real situation. It is very lively, and describes the parties' manoeuvring in great detail; I even get the feeling that emotions were running high. It describes a very structured procedure: each party makes its case, witnesses are summoned, an oath is requested and refused, and the judges make their decision. Nevertheless, the formula, with all of its "ille"s and "hoc et illud"s, provides its users with plenty of room to adapt it to their own specific needs.

30 FV 40, ed. Zeumer, 593, n. 3.

31 This appears to be the defendant B; cf. Zeumer, note 1 to his edition of FV 40, 594.

We learn several things from FV 40. First, property disputes like this could land before judges. Second, judges played an active role in the proceedings they were overseeing, to the point here of enforcing discipline on a pair of very angry litigants and interviewing them separately to allow each to make his case. Third, laws were available and people in conflict considered them to be important, even binding; at least some lay landowners knew them well enough to cite relevant passages in court. Fourth, when testimony and/or the law failed to end the case, judges could try to resolve the "he said, he said" by forcing one of the parties to take an oath. Fifth, oaths were taken very seriously; here the person who was supposed to take the oath refused to—it seems that he did not want to risk God's wrath by perjuring himself.[32] So the judges stepped in and made a judgment. Finally, the process resulted in a document designed to prevent future challenges.

Others of our formulas tell us indirectly that judicial processes like this took place. FV 41 refers tangentially to a process like the one we just went through.[33] It is what we would call a power of attorney:

> Iniuncto.
> Domino mihi indiuiduo fratri ill. (B) ill. (A). Rogo atque iniungo tuae fraternitati ut ad vicem personae meae peragere iubeas et intentio, quae inter me et illum per hoc et illud uertitur, in praesentia iudicum secundum ordinem legum negotium meum prosequi procures, ita ut quicquid de lege et iustitia egeris, ratum me in omnibus esse policeor. In quo iniuncto praesens praesentibus stipulatus sum et spopondi, subter manu mea subscripsi et testibus bene natis viris a me rogitis tradidi roborandum. Facto iniuncto sub die…

A man A writes to a *dominus* B (whether his lord or a patron is not clear). He asks B to go in his place before judges and prosecute a matter between him and another "over this and that", and that he pursue his lawsuit (*negotium*) according to the dictates of the laws. A agrees to ratify whatever B did. This text anticipates the same sort of procedure as the previous one: a dispute over "this and that" to be taken before judges who would judge the case according to the laws. Unfortunately, it does not tell us what the dispute was about.

32 The horrible things that God might do to someone who swore falsely are spelled out in great detail in FV 39, *Conditiones sacramentorum*: ed. Gil, 106–108; ed. Zeumer, 592–593.

33 Ed. Gil, 109–110; ed. Zeumer, 594.

The next one, FV 42, is similar, except this time it does tell us what the dispute was about, namely a quarrel between brothers over an unpaid debt:[34]

> Alio iniuncto.
> Spero (A) iniungoque tuae charitati (B) propter apicem personae meae ut fratrem nostrum illum (C) pulsare debeas propter auri solidi num. tot, quos nos ei praestitimus, unde et placitum ipsius apud nos tenemus, ut solidos ipsos iuxta placiti sui tenorem perpetua intentione recipere debeas. Quod si contempserit et saepe dictos solidos uobis restituere distulerit, eum in praesentia iudicis compellere facias et secundum legis tramitem uobis per iudicis imperium seu iuditium satisfacere debeat. Quicquid egeris ....

One man A enjoins another man B to prosecute his brother C.[35] The suit concerned some number of gold *solidi* that A had loaned to C. The writer asks the recipient to get the money back. If his brother should delay in repaying the money, the recipient was to force him to come before judges and to give satisfaction by the judges' command according to the laws. The text is supposed to end with the formulaic tag promising that whatever B did, A would consider binding.

One formula among our five, FV 35, is very interesting not only because of the conflict that it describes, but also because the agreement it records does not end the conflict; instead, it regulates it.[36] The formula also tells me at least something new about the role documents could play in an early medieval judicial process; I have never seen anything like it among the Frankish formulas. The text is incomplete; the story picks up in the middle of a sentence:

> [...] quia rem iuris mei (A) debitam, quam ille (B) sua [aua]ritia[37] extra discusionem iudicantis uiolentius usurpatione de meo dominio abstulit, nullos in eodem loco profligat labores certe nec quicquam inibi augmentat, dum interim manente iustitia per legum statuta appetendo iuditiariam potestatem inter partes de ueritate silentium imponatur. Quod

34 Ed. Gil, 110; ed. Zeumer, 594.

35 This text, like some formula texts from north of the Pyrenees, promiscuously mixes singular and plural forms of the first and second person pronouns to refer to both the actor and the addressee as individuals. I think it is safe to assume that the accused is brother to the plaintiff only.

36 Ed. Gil, 103–104; ed. Zeumer, 590–591; Córcoles Olaitz, *Las Formulae Wisigothicae*, 130–134.

37 Ms. and Zeumer: *suo vitio*.

si transcen[den]s hanc coniurationem nostram hoc quod in iure nostro pertinet in aliquod augmentauerit, sciat se, per iustitia dum nostro dominio hoc ipsum probauerimus, debere secundum legum instituta de inuasione uel singulis annis frugum collectione ac sumptus per litis expensas nobis satisfacere et hoc quod inibi profligauit amittere. Factum labellum ....

This is an interim agreement, between two parties to a dispute, about how to regulate their relationship while they were (or while at least one of them was) waiting for a court hearing. The first-person narrator A claims that another man B had taken property from him without a judicial hearing. He states that while they were waiting for a hearing, both sides were to remain silent about the matter. The man B was not to take any produce from the property, nor was he to add to it in any way. If he did, he would be required, once a hearing had proven A's rights, to make amends and pay for A's legal costs.

Since we lack the beginning of the text, we have no idea how this agreement was arranged. It could have been negotiated by the two parties directly; it could equally have been imposed by whatever judicial authority was going to ultimately decide the case.[38] What is new and interesting for me is that this text records an interim and therefore temporary arrangement designed to manage the relationship between two people in conflict until a judicial hearing can resolve the dispute. It tells us that documents could be generated at various stages of a dispute process, not just at the end. Of course, the text only presents one side's view of the matter; we have to assume that the document would only have been written if the other side had agreed.

The last formula of our five, I must confess, may not even qualify as a dispute record. FV 43 is quite short; like FV 42, it has one man giving another the authority to take care of a legal matter for him:[39]

Alio iniuncto.

Domino et in Christo fratri ill. (B) ill. (A). Iniungo tuae charitati, ut ad uicem personae meae, dum te Deus in locum illum cum salute perduxerit, seruum iuris mei nomine ill., qui de seruitio meo se subtraxit, perquirere debeas et dum eum inueneris conscriptum meo dominio reuocare studeas. Quicquid egeris gesserisue ....

38 A suggestion buttressed by the reference to the laws and the statement "let silence be imposed"; I thank André Marques for the suggestion.

39 Ed. Gil, 110; ed. Zeumer, 594.

It is addressed by a man A to a *dominus* B. A asks B—“since God has led you in good health to the place X”—to search for a *servus* of his who had run away. When he found him, he was to try to have him returned to A’s service. If I want to call this a dispute, then the dispute is between the person A and his runaway *servus*. Beyond this, we learn nothing about how B would have gone about fulfilling his commission. The formula is interesting, however, insofar as we see someone taking advantage of the fact that someone he knew (from the title *dominus* his patron, perhaps?) happened to be in the area where his *servus* had disappeared to have him go look for him.

Now to back up and look at these five formulas as a group. Each of them deals with a different kind of dispute. They also deal with different parts or stages of extended dispute processes, revealing that the search for justice could end up producing not one but rather a series of documents. FV 40 concerns a property dispute, over rights to *servi*, that is handled in a judicial forum. The court process generates a document that records what happened and what the judges decided. FV 41 does not tell us what the dispute it records was about; it could be used for any kind of dispute that was headed for a judicial hearing. FV 42 deals specifically with a dispute within a family over an unpaid debt. But both are what we would call powers of attorney, written up in advance of a judicial hearing. They tell us, therefore, about a possible preliminary step: if you have to go to court, you might try to get a patron or a representative who is more powerful or better skilled at such things to handle the case for you. FV 35 concerns a charge of unjust property seizure; it records a temporary agreement over products from and improvements to the disputed property until a hearing can take place. FV 43, about the runaway *servus*, is an outlier. It too is a power of attorney, recorded in a document that was presumably given to the author’s patron and proxy. It does not tell us how the proxy would have gone about reclaiming the *servus*. It is possible that he would have gone to a court. It is also possible, however, that he would have hired a gang of thugs to seize the *servus*. We will never know.

None of these formulas show any sign of a distinction between different kinds of wrongs (such as the one in both Roman and in modern western laws between civil and criminal offenses),[40] which is in the Frankish north also completely absent. The compiler of the FV apparently thought that all kinds of disputes could come before judges (an attitude highlighted by the power of attorney formula FV 41 that leaves the subject of the dispute to be filled in). Or

40 A distinction that was picked up in the *Liber iudiciorum*: Karl Zeumer, ed., *Leges Visigothorum*, MGH LL nat. Germ. 1 (Hanover: Hahn, 1902), e.g. II.1.17, p. 63: *Ut iudices tam criminales quam communes terminent causas*. I thank André Marques for the reference.

he was only interested in formulas for disputes that would come before judges. I am struck by his particular interest in powers of attorney; he copied three of them. Perhaps he thought that he was more likely to need models for these. If so, this would suggest a world in which people frequently sought help with their judicial affairs from others.

Do we have enough information here to generalize about the legal culture of the FV's world? The answer is: no, of course not. The FV does not offer us a broad enough spectrum of different kinds of disputes. It would be very helpful to see a good killing, or a theft or a robbery; these appear quite commonly in the Frankish formulas. But the compiler of the FV did not choose to include documents that dealt with such matters. Or perhaps, if FV 1 is in fact incomplete rather than a deliberately truncated fragment, formulas concerning homicide, robbery, etc. were in an earlier section of the collection that was lost before it reached twelfth-century Oviedo. In any case, their absence from the FV does not mean that homicides, thefts, or robberies did not occur. Any differences between the kinds of documents that appear in the FV and in the Frankish formulas have in my opinion little or nothing to do with different legal cultures, or different landscapes of conflicts and ways of handling them. They are entirely an artefact of the formula collections, that is, how and why the collections were put together, and what their compilers chose to copy and what they did not—or what was lost when part of the collection went missing.

4 So What?

Now we get to a question that I alluded to at the beginning of this essay but have avoided for most of it: what society have we actually learned anything about? That of the Visigothic kingdom? Twelfth century Oviedo? The Spanish court at the turn of the seventeenth century? Given the actual physical object that we have in hand, the Morales codex, all are possible.

There is no argument that the documents on which the FV were based were Visigothic in origin. Looked at from this perspective, then, we can say that they tell us something about disputes among laymen in the Visigothic kingdom as a whole (possibly but far from certainly in the region around Córdoba, from the single reference in FV 25) within a very broad span of time: from the late sixth century through the end of the kingdom at the beginning of the eighth.

Another anchor point would be that unknown time at which someone gathered these documents of most likely different origins together, anonymized them, and organized them into a formula collection. We know from the reference in FV 20 to King Sisebut that this was done sometime after 612–621.

And I am going to suggest that this was done before the formulas were copied in the twelfth century into the Pelagius manuscript, because the FV as Morales found them appear to have been modified already at least once: though we cannot be certain, it looks very much like an original, organized collection of formulas was supplemented at some later time with an additional, less well-organized group of texts. Interestingly, this is where all of our dispute formulas are.

Even if all of the documents that were taken up in the FV are of Visigothic origin, there is no reason to assume that the formula collection *qua* formula collection is Visigothic; as noted at the beginning of this essay, it could easily have been put together later, as a product not of Visigothic but rather post-Visigothic needs. If we decide that this was so, then we could apply what we have learned about conflict resolution and judicial processes to this later period. It takes effort to gather, anonymize, and organize a formula collection, or to gather up more documents and add them to a pre-existing formula collection that you have decided to copy. Whoever put in the effort thought that the documents he was gathering, choosing, and copying were useful; they had, therefore, to bear some resemblance to what went on in his world.

So when and where was "his world"? A good place to look would be when and where we can find documents using language that echoes the FV. Having this kind of language show up in actual documents would suggest that either the FV or some similar dossier of formulas based on Visigothic models had been compiled and was in circulation. To start with the 'when': phrases that also appear in some of the FV begin to appear in documents from the middle of the ninth century.[41] Here is a plausible starting point. Echoes of the FV become more and more common as we move into the tenth century, and they continue to be visible into the twelfth. As for the 'where', this should come as no surprise: the Christian north of Spain, specifically the churches and monasteries of Asturias/León and what later became Castile.[42]

Early examples use phrases very similar or even identical to phrases in the FV. Among the earliest is a charter from the cathedral church at León of 864. It begins:

41 Gil, "Formulae Wisigothicae," notes later documentary echoes of the FV in the apparatus to each formula; the earliest, from FV 30, is from 858.

42 See, in addition to Gil's apparatus: Calleja Puerta, "Ecos de las Fórmulas Visigóticas," esp. section III: Les documentos astur-leoneses del siglo IX, and IV: Las donaciones a iglesias en los siglos X–XI; Ernesto Pastor Díaz de Garayo, "Los testimonios escritos del sector meridional de Castilla (siglos X–XI). Ensayo de crítica documental," *Historia, Instituciones, Documentos* 24 (1997), 355–380, esp. the chart on p. 379 showing uses of language from the FV in documents of the tenth and eleventh centuries.

> In Dei nomine. Uobis domno Nunno, ego seruus uester Ausonius in Domino salutem. Magnus est donationis titulis in co (*sic*) nemo potest actum inrumpere largitatis sed quicquid grato animo et prona uolumtate offertur oportet semper libenter amplecti ….

This is substantially the same as the language that opens FV 30: *Domino et fratri ill. ill. Magnus donationis est titulus in quo nemo potest actum largitatis inrumpere. Et ideo quod prona largitate offertur, libenter semper debet amplecti ….*[43]

By the time we get to the tenth and eleventh centuries, we can see scribes doing exactly the same thing that their Frankish counterparts did when they drew on formulaic models, whether to draft charters, or the forge them: they used a formula as a basic framework, but took it apart, adapted it to their own needs, and filled it in with situation-specific information.[44] Ernesto Pastor Díaz de Garayo has identified a number of tenth and eleventh century documents that use in this way major pieces of texts matching formulas in the FV, especially (but not exclusively) FV 8, a formula for a gift of property to a church.[45] The following example comes from the beginning of text purporting to be a charter of 954, from the monastery of San Sebastián de Silos, but that has been identified as a forgery of the eleventh century. The passages in bold echo FV 8:

> In nomine Sancte et individue Trinitatis. **Dompnis sanctis invictissimis ac triumphatoribus martiribus gloriosis atque venerandis nobisque post Deum fortissimis patronis** Sanctorum Sebastiani et Sanctorum apostolorum Petri et Pauli et Sancti Emiliani fidelissimi testis Christi, **quorum reliquie condite requiescunt, et in quorum honore baselica fundata est** in suburbio que vocitant Tablatello super crepidinem fluminis quem dicunt Ura, nobisque indignis Fredenando Gundisalviz et uxor mea Sancia; licet primordia bonorum operum, que inspirante Deo in mente gignitur, iusticie operibus deputetur, tamen ea que maiori cumulo et pociori crescunt, ampliori remuneratione espectetur in premio. Digne

43 Antonio C. Floriano, ed., *Diplomática española del periodo astur. Estudio de las fuentes documentales del Reino de Asturias (718–910)*, vol. 1 *Cartulario crítico: primera parte (desde Pelayo a Ordoño I)* (Oviedo: La Cruz, 1949), no. 81, 324–326. FV 30: ed. Gil, 100–101; ed. Zeumer, 589.

44 See, for example, a Bavarian charter of the year 816, which draws its general structure from a formula whose text originated in the region of the Salian Franks: Gebhard Rath and Erich Reiter, eds., *Das älteste Traditionsbuch des Klosters Mondsee* (Linz: Oberösterreichisches Landesarchiv, 1989), no. 52/2, 155–156; "Formulae Salicae Lindenbrogianae," in Zeumer, *Formulae*, no. 2, 267–268.

45 Pastor Díaz de Garayo, "Los testimonios escritos," 359–360 and 379.

> igitur iam sue spei vota in domo celica mansionum multarum colocat, qui domum sancta ecclesie restaurat vel in melius contruere provocat. Nos igitur Fredenando et Sancia, **piacolorum nostrorum honeris pro gravatione cupientes expiare flagicia et peccatorum nostrorum mole, propterea orationes vestras desiderantes adiutorium sublevare, inde parva pro magnis offerimus hunuscula (sic). Nullius quidem in hoc seculo hominum vos indigeret censum scimus, quia iam pro sanctificatione Dominus noster in suo vos regno proprio ditatus munere cumulavit.** Ideo **pro luminaria ecclesie vestre atque stipendia earum vel pauperum, aut qui in altaria beatitudinis vestre et reliquias iam nominati deservire cotidianis diebus videntur** monachorum omnium ibidem degentium cunctorumque obediencium, **id offerimus sacrosancto altario vestro ad integro, sicut a nobis dignoscitur nunc usque fuisse possesum.** In primis, fundamentum ipsius locum, in quo hec eadem ecclesia sita est ….[46]

Examples like this strongly suggest that the scribes concerned had dossiers of models available to them that they were using to help them draft their documents.

Careful readers will perhaps have noticed that I am trying hard not to say that scribes in the ninth, tenth, and eleventh-century Christian north were 'using' or 'drawing on' the FV. I do not think that it is safe to do so. Was there by this point a discreet 'FV' that had a unitary and coherent form and that all of these churches and monasteries had access to, such that we can talk about 'using' the FV? I doubt it; the *Formulae Visigothicae* as a discrete object is a creation first of Morales and then of Karl Zeumer and the *Monumenta*. Many if not most of the formula collections produced on the Frankish side of the Pyrenees, in the same period we are discussing here, contain copies or versions of older formulas or formula collections that their compilers got from somewhere else. Formula collections, pieces of formula collections, and even individual formulas travelled; they were carried from place to place, broken up, selected from, reorganized,

46 Miguel C. Vivancos Gómez, ed., *Documentación del monasterio de Santo Domingo de Silos (954–1254)* (Burgos: Ediciones J.M. Garrido Garrido, 1988), no. 1, 3–5. FV 8: ed. Gil, 80–81; ed. Zeumer, 579. For the identification of this charter as a forgery see Manuel Zabalza Duque, *Colección diplomática de los condes de Castilla: edición y comentario de los documentos de los condes Fernán González, García Fernández, Sancho García y García Sánchez* (Valladolid: Junta de Castilla y León, 1998) no. 29, 271–273, and pp. 115–130. Zabalza Duque bases his identification in part on a comparison of this text with other, genuine, Castilian charters of the tenth and eleventh centuries, several of which likewise contain language matching formulas in the FV. I thank André Marques for the reference.

combined with other formulas, etc., as scribes created the collection of models that they wanted. The results were unique collections of various sizes and shapes. There were a few core collections that do seem to have maintained some kind of coherent identity as they moved. The famous seventh-century formula collection of Marculf, for example, and the mid-eighth century collection from Tours, were both picked up and copied more or less whole in the Carolingian period into a number of manuscripts. More numerous, however, are the manuscripts in which they and other earlier formula collections were copied selectively and combined with texts from other sources.[47] It is very likely, I would argue, that the same was going on in ninth and tenth century northern Spain; several dossiers of formulas were in circulation, that were copied and recopied, selected from, and supplemented with additional texts at need. Especially popular or useful formulas must have been copied several times in several places. In the specific regions where scholars have looked closely, for example, it appears that a great number of churches and monasteries had access to the text of FV 8; this is the most commonly echoed formula from the collection.

Why does this Visigothic-style language appear in the north when and where it does? There are several reasons, I suspect. The middle of the ninth century saw unrest in the Christian communities of Al-Andalus provoked by radicals as they fought the creeping assimilation of Christians into Muslim society—the most visible manifestation of this struggle being, of course, the martyrs of Córdoba. Starting at about the same time, and increasing in the tenth century, an exodus of Mozarabic monks, many if not most of whom came from in or around Córdoba, streamed into the Christian kingdoms of the north. Some of this exodus may have been sparked by the hostility to Christians in the south that the martyrs of Córdoba had provoked, some by the civil wars in Al-Andalus that led to the birth of the Umayyad caliphate. Finally, it is from the first half of the ninth century that northern Christian rulers began to present themselves consciously as heirs to and restorers of the Visigothic kingdom.[48] It is only natural that people from the south would carry old documents northwards, where they would find a ready audience among scribes looking for authority bearing documentary forms and language.

I have not found any real documents from this period that use language directly matching language from the five dispute formulas I discussed above. This

47 On the Marculf and Tours collections, and their copying and transmission history, see Rio, *Legal Practice*, 81–101, 112–117.

48 Roger Collins, *Early Medieval Spain: Unity in Diversity, 400–1000*, 2nd ed. (New York: St. Martin's Press, 1995), 211–221, 229.

is not at all surprising. What real documents we do have come from church and monastic archives and cartularies. Even if scribes at these churches and monasteries had used our dispute formulas to help them produce documents, these would not have been documents that they would likely have kept in their own archives. But we do know that the dispute formulas were circulating in the north, because they survived in the dossier that was copied in Oviedo in the twelfth century into the Pelagius manuscript and that became the FV. I would suggest, then, that they still bore some resemblance to what people in northern Spain in the ninth and tenth centuries might have done.[49] At the very least, to the one person who chose to gather and copy them into his formula collection, or perhaps tack them onto the end of an already-existing formula collection, they were still recognizable descriptions of conflicts that could have taken place and ways that these conflicts could have been handled.

By the time we get to the eleventh century, we can still see hints of the FV, but they are less clear and harder to find. The older language had been combined with newer formulaic traditions that had developed in their own contexts, to form a new pool of formulas and formulaic language. It is possible that by this point some scribes who used language like that in the FV no longer even knew that they were drawing on Visigothic tradition. But we know that at least one dossier of Visigothic formulas had survived in Oviedo because it was there when Bishop Pelagius put together his collection of old texts in the twelfth century. What is interesting is that in the entire period from the mid-ninth century up to this point, it is hard to find traces of the FV in this one place that we know this actual collection of formulas showed up: the cathedral church at Oviedo.[50] If they were not used there, why were they brought there, to be found by Pelagius and incorporated into his manuscript? To answer these questions, we would need to reconstruct the manuscript as best we can from the Morales codex, to get a sense for why it was put together and what it might have been used for. This exercise would tell us nothing, however, about how the images of conflict in the FV connect to the realities of Oviedo in the first half of the twelfth century; we would learn something instead about how our handful of dispute formulas, and the larger dossier of Visigothic-era texts in which they were included, fit Pelagius's own purposes.

---

49 See most recently Wendy Davies, *Windows on Justice in Northern Iberia, 800–1000* (Abingdon: Routledge, 2016), who argues for strong continuities in the formulaic language used by scribes writing judicial records across this period.

50 Calleja Puerta, "Ecos de las Fórmulas Visigóticas," section IV: Las donaciones a iglesias en los siglos X–XI, and Conclusion.

There is one further step that we could take, to the one physical, tangible object that we actually have: the Morales codex. Why was Morales sent out by King Philip II to search for old texts, and why once he found the Oviedo manuscript did he choose to copy its contents? Did he have the FV copied wholesale with the other contents of the Oviedo manuscript, or did he expressly ask for them to be included? Here too we could get some valuable historical information out of the FV; we would be using them to learn something about the priorities and worldviews of the royal court and its intellectual servants in late sixteenth century Spain.[51]

But this carries us a long way from the specific conflicts and judicial processes with which we started. Here at the end, I am going to return to them, and hazard some optimistic conclusions. The formulas we have looked at tell us some general things about the kinds of disputes that could occur among laymen in the Visigothic kingdom and how they could be handled.[52] Our selection of disputes is limited; they deal only with property, both landed and human. But they are enough to give us some evidence that this was a world that, in practice at least, did not differentiate between different kinds of wrong, as we do between civil and criminal offenses. Disputes could take some time to resolve. People in conflict went through several steps along the way, each of which could generate a different kind of document; it appears in fact that disputing processes usually ended up producing not one but rather a series of documents. Always in the picture is a judicial assembly with its judges and its law: disputants are either at court or are in the process of going to one; they are arranging for others to go to courts on their behalf, or they are threatening people with court action to get them to surrender. Once we arrive at a court, we find the law, not only in the text of the document but in the mouths of the disputants. Laws were a clear normative reference point for these disputes; people were aware of them and considered them important. It was not, however, simply the authority of the law that constrained people's behaviour. Negotiation may have worked alongside judicial processes or helped to manage them. Patrons with unspecified powers could be very useful. And above all was God, whose ability to punish false testimony was sufficiently frightening that one might refuse to swear an oath, even if it meant losing the case.

---

51 See esp. Collins, "Ambrosio de Morales and the *Codex Vetustissimus Ovetensis*."

52 I can only echo with approval the subtitle to Córcoles Olaitz, *Las Formulae Wisigothicae*, which captures the situation perfectly: *Aproximación a la práctica jurídica visigoda*.

Bibliography

Manuscripts

Madrid, Biblioteca Nacional de España, 1346, Tratados y epístolas varios, s. XVI, fols. 75r–90r.

Primary Sources

Floriano, Antonio C., ed. *Diplomática española del periodo astur. Estudio de las fuentes documentales del Reino de Asturias (718–910)*. Vol. 1 *Cartulario crítico: primera parte (desde Pelayo a Ordoño I)*. Oviedo: La Cruz, 1949.

Gil, Juan, ed. *Miscellanea Wisigothica*. Seville: Publicaciones de la Universidad de Sevilla, 1972.

Haenel, Gustav, ed. *Lex Romana Visigothorum*. Aalen: Scientia Verlag, 1962.

Rath, Gebhard, and Erich Reiter, eds. *Das älteste Traditionsbuch des Klosters Mondsee*. Linz: Oberösterreichisches Landesarchiv, 1989.

Vivancos Gómez, Miguel C., ed. *Documentación del monasterio de Santo Domingo de Silos (954–1254)*. Burgos: Ediciones J.M. Garrido Garrido, 1988.

Zabalza Duque, Manuel, ed. *Colección diplomática de los condes de Castilla: edición y comentario de los documentos de los condes Fernán González, García Fernández, Sancho García y García Sánchez*. Valladolid: Junta de Castilla y León, 1998.

Zeumer, Karl, ed. *Formulae Merowingici et Karolini Aevi*. Monumenta Germaniae Historica, Legum Sectio v. Hanover: Hahn, 1886.

Zeumer, Karl, ed. *Leges Visigothorum*. Monumenta Germaniae Historica, Leges nationum Germanicarum 1. Hanover: Hahn, 1902.

Secondary Works

Brown, Warren. *Unjust Seizure: Conflict, Interest and Authority in an Early Medieval Society*. Ithaca, NY: Cornell University Press, 2001.

Brown, Warren. "When Documents Are Destroyed or Lost: Lay People and Archives in the Early Middle Ages." *Early Medieval Europe* 11, no. 4 (2002), 337–366.

Brown, Warren. "Conflict, Letters, and Personal Relationships in the Carolingian Formula Collections." *The Law and History Review* 25, no. 2 (Summer 2007), 323–344.

Brown, Warren. "Die karolingischen Formelsammlungen—warum existieren sie?" In *Die Privaturkunden der Karolingerzeit*, edited by Peter Erhart, Karl Heidecker, and Bernhard Zeller, 95–101. Dietikon-Zurich: Urs-Graf Verlag, 2009.

Brown, Warren C. "Lay People and Documents in the Frankish Formula Collections." In *Documentary Practices and the Laity in the Early Middle Ages*, edited by Warren C. Brown, Marios Costambeys, Matthew Innes, and Adam J. Kosto, 125–151. Cambridge: Cambridge University Press, 2013.

Brown, Warren C. *Beyond the Monastery Walls: Lay Men and Women in Early Medieval Legal Formularies*. Cambridge: Cambridge University Press, 2023.

Calleja Puerta, Miguel. “Ecos de las Fórmulas Visigóticas en la documentación altomedieval Astur-Leonesa.” In *Les formulaires. Compilation et circulation des modèles d'actes dans l'Europe médiévale et moderne*, edited by Olivier Guyotjeannin, Laurent Morelle, and Silio P. Scalfati. Paris: Éditions en ligne de l'École des chartes, 2016. Accessed 4 September 2017. http://elec.enc.sorbonne.fr/cid2012/part4.

Canellas López, Ángel. *Diplomática hispano-visigoda*. Zaragoza: Institucion “Fernando el Catolico,” 1979.

Collins, Roger. *Early Medieval Spain: Unity in Diversity, 400–1000*. 2nd ed. New York: St. Martin's Press, 1995.

Collins, Roger. “Ambrosio de Morales, Bishop Pelayo of Oviedo and the Lost Manuscripts of Visigothic Spain.” In *Wisigothica. After M.C. Díaz y Díaz*, edited by Carmen Codoñer and Paulo Farmhouse Alberto, 609–632. Florence: SISMEL—Edizioni del Galluzzo, 2014.

Collins, Roger. “Ambrosio de Morales and the *Codex Vetustissimus Ovetensis*.” In *Italy and the East Roman World in the Medieval Mediterranean: Empires, Cities, and Elites 476–1204*, edited by Thomas J. MacMaster and Nicholas S.M. Mathcou, 49–69. Abingdon: Routledge, 2021.

Córcoles Olaitz, Edorta. “About the Origin of the Formulae Wisigothicae.” *Anuario da Facultade de Dereito da Universidade da Coruña* 12 (2008), 199–221.

Córcoles Olaitz, Edorta. *Las Formulae Wisigothicae. Aproximación a la práctica jurídica visigoda*. Lecce: Edizione Grifo, 2010.

Davies, Wendy. *Windows on Justice in Northern Iberia, 800–1000*. Abingdon: Routledge, 2016.

Mentxaka, Rosa. “En torno a ‘formulae visigothicae’ 44.” In *Scripta Antiqva: in honorem Angel Montenegro Duque et José María Blázquez Martínez*, edited by Ángeles Alonso Ávila and Santos Crespo Ortiz de Zárate, 827–840. Valladolid: s.n., 2002.

Pastor Díaz de Garayo, Ernesto. “Los testimonios escritos del sector meridional de Castilla (siglos X–XI). Ensayo de crítica documental.” *Historia, Instituciones, Documentos* 24 (1997), 355–380.

Rio, Alice, trans. *The Formularies of Angers and Marculf: Two Merovingian Legal Handbooks*. Liverpool: Liverpool University Press, 2008.

Rio, Alice. *Legal Practice and the Written Word in the Early Middle Ages: Frankish Formulae, c. 500–1000*. Cambridge: Cambridge University Press, 2009.

Zimmermann, Michel. “Un formulaire du xème siècle conservé à Ripoll.” *Faventia* 4 (1982), 25–86.

CHAPTER 8

Creating Records of Judicial Disputes in Northern Iberia before the Year 1000

Wendy Davies

1 Introduction

This paper is about making records of judicial disputes, throughout ninth- and tenth-century northern Iberia, excluding Catalonia; Catalonia is excluded because of its different socio-political contexts and strong Frankish background.[1] Records of disputes that were handled in judicial assemblies survive in many forms, as is clear from the PRJ database, and have different kinds of content. I have used a ten-fold classification of the content of these records. This is different from the PRJ classification system, because it was devised independently and started long before my awareness of PRJ. Since the scheme deals with records up to the year 1000 only, this means that recording practice is less wide-ranging than that detailed by PRJ, although there is plenty of overlap.[2] I originally identified 289 cases in 257 records, in an analysis based on numbers of events rather than on numbers of documents, although it is now clear that eight cases in eight additional records should be added.[3] The essential characteristics of each category are as follows: Accounts are retrospective narratives, constructed after the events; Incidental records are just that—brief incidental references to judicial proceedings in a record whose purpose was to record something else, such as a sale or gift; Fines are records of payment of penalties consequent on judicial proceedings; Confessions and Oaths appear to be verbatim statements made during court proceedings, although their origin is more complicated than that; Agreements cover several categories of agreement, some immediately consequent on confessions and some subsequently constructed (with the benefit of hindsight, this category would probably have been better split); Mixed and Implied are, I hope, obvious, and in any case are tiny groups; Debts and Confiscations are for the most part

1 The abbreviations used in this paper for editions of charters are listed in the bibliography.

2 For detailed discussion, see my *Windows on Justice in Northern Iberia, 800–1000* (Abingdon: Routledge, 2016); ch. 2 for full exposition of the classification system.

3 I am very grateful to André Marques and Bernardo Cañon for this update.

 | DOI:10.1163/9789004683006_010

not consequent upon court cases, but need taking into account as indicators of non-judicial mechanisms of dispute resolution. Some types are very common (Accounts, Incidental, Fines) and others rare (Oaths especially, Confessions).

Understanding how these texts were constructed is important if we want to use them to illuminate events, relationships and processes in the ninth and tenth centuries and if we want to assess their levels of credibility. This is not as simple as supposing that there was a court reporter recording what happened in court, or a public notary constructing an 'official' document, or even a scribe in a monastery producing a record for monastic consumption, because the processes behind the creation of these records were much more complicated. It is the purpose of this paper to unravel some of these processes. I will begin by drawing attention to four different elements of format, across the whole corpus; and then indicate some regular stages in the construction process, before deconstructing some of the more complicated texts.

2 Significant Elements of Format

Firstly, formulaic framework. As it was everywhere in early medieval Europe, charter writing was highly formulaic, a point highlighted elsewhere in this volume by Warren Brown. Favourite formulas recur over and over again, like *ut de odierno die uel tempore ipsa uinea de nostro iure abrasa et in uestro iure sit traditam uel confirmata*, an example of a standard formula transferring title in regular charters of gift and sale.[4] Dispute records are much less formulaic than gift and sale charters, but there are nevertheless recurrent formulas in most categories. Hence, as many people have pointed out, *orta fuit intentio/contentio* is a standard way to begin an Account;[5] *cognosco/cognoui in ueritate* is a standard way to summarize a confession, although *que manifesto uerum esse fateor* is the way to introduce an actual Confession; *conditiones sacramentorum* is the standard introduction of an Oath and *nostrum placitum tibi compromittimus* the

4 CLI 143 (941). See my "Regions and micro-regions of scribal practice," in *Polity and Neighbourhood in Early Medieval Europe*, ed. J. Escalona, O. Vésteinsson and S. Brookes (Turnhout: Brepols, 2019), 305–324, for more detailed discussion.

5 See Agustín Prieto Morera, "El proceso en el reino de León a la luz de los diplomas," in *El reino de León en la alta edad media, II: Ordenamiento jurídico del reino* (León: Centro de Estudios e Investigación 'San Isidoro', 1992), 381–518, at 390; Isabel Alfonso, "El formato de la información judicial en la alta edad media peninsular," in *Chartes et cartulaires comme instruments de pouvoir. Espagne et Occident chrétien (VIIIe–XIIe siècles)*, ed. Julio Escalona and Hélène Sirantoine (Toulouse: Université de Toulouse-Le Mirail, 2013), 191–218, at 205.

standard introduction of one kind of Agreement; *presentemus nostras personas in presentia N* is the standard formula for expressing a commitment to appear in court;[6] while the sanctions of Incidental records, Fines and Debts, as also of gifts and sales on the *meseta*, frequently include the formula *Si quis contra hanc cartulam donationis aliquis homo ad disrumpendum uenerit uel uenero an ego uel quelibet subrogata persona*. Those who wrote dispute records, of whatever kind, wrote within an established formulaic framework. That means that the redactors will have drawn on a learned tradition, applying words deriving from much earlier practice, handed down through skilled families, as well as in some cases using formularies and model charters as well as the varied resources of the scriptoria of major monasteries and cathedrals. While some dispute records will have been produced in the context of a monastic or episcopal household, others will have been produced by people working in the inherited learned legal tradition; and others seem to have come from scribes working for aristocratic households (Braolio for Flaino Muñoz, Sendino for Munio Fernández, for example).[7]

The second element is narrative. Many records include an element of narrative, although this can be very brief. Some records include lengthy, detailed free-flow narrative of events leading up to judicial proceedings, then detail of the hearings themselves, and then the outcome. Lengthy narrative is especially characteristic of the type I call Accounts, which use the third person and past tense and are explicitly retrospective.

The third element is that of ritual words. In contrast with the narratives, some records are cast in the first person and present tense. These records tend to be much briefer and they represent a single aspect of judicial proceedings, not a whole story—for example, the words of evidence from witnesses or the moment of a confession. Such records include formulas as well as circumstantial detail. These formulas are so distinctive, their repetition so precise (with variants sometimes explained by oral transmission) and they are used at such widely distant locations, hundreds of kilometres apart, that I think it likely that these were ritual words uttered in court, words that everyone knew, characteristically invoked when a given part of the proceedings was reached—just as ritual words are used to introduce the oath in a modern English court.

6 Since they are rare, I did not include commitments as one of my ten classes of dispute text, but see Davies, *Windows on Justice*, 135–137. With hindsight, I might usefully have done so; in what follows I treat them as a distinctive type of text.

7 For the latter, see my "Local priests and the writing of charters in northern Iberia in the tenth century," in *Chartes et cartulaires comme instruments de pouvoir*, ed. Escalona and Sirantoine, 29–43.

The fourth element is verbatim reporting. It is extremely rare to encounter anything which looks like verbatim reporting. However, there are one or two records which suggest negotiated Agreements, that is, negotiated between two parties with assistance from reputable members of the court. These records seem to contain an attempt to represent what each party said. The short sentences read like speech: a series of events recounted by the party who initiated the case, sometimes repetitively, without formulas; then the voice shifts to the other party, outlining what was agreed.[8] This really is rare. If such records were common, they were not normally kept. But it does show that it is possible to conceive of a kind of court reporting, not necessarily written during court session, for records could be constructed immediately afterwards, in conversation with one or both parties. But these must be records that were made close to the meeting of the court.

3 Stages of Construction

Looking at the structures and contents of the entire corpus of dispute records makes it clear that the records we now have were created at different stages in relation to court cases. In the Agreements just mentioned, as in Oaths and Confessions and commitments, there is material that derives directly from the activity of the court—this is what might be termed a primary record. Here is an example, surviving as a separate record on a single sheet:

> In iudicio Flacenti, Carcia Ordonizi uel cetero concilio, manifestum sum, ego Flaino, ad peticione Elias, qui asere uoce de comite Flaino Monizi, uerum est, cot necare non ualeo, quia peccato inpidiente et diauolo inmitente sic toliuit, ego Flaino, muliere aliena ad suo marito et fecit qum ea adulterio et post ec sic fecit qum sua filia, qum matre et filia. Et que manifesto uerum est factore et manifestu nicili abeo que opona.
>
> Facto manifesto XI kalendas madias, era XXXIII. Flaino in hoc manifesto rouorabit.[9]

Secondly, there are cases in which such material, and/or more, has been worked up into a charter of conveyance: a raw confession becomes the reason for a transfer of property and so the transfer is recorded, with the usual formulas of

8 OD 4 (946), OD 43 (997), CL3 597 (1000).

9 OD 38 (21 April 995).

conveyance and an allusion to the fact of confession, but not a quotation of the words of confession. This might be termed a secondary record. Here is an example, surviving in a cartulary copy:

> Nos homines qui sumus habitantes in uilla Zacoys. Id sumus prenominati, Hordonio, Ueremudo, Habze, Abdella et Timimi, uobis domni Manillani abbati et domni Didaci et fratrum uestrorum monasterio Cellenoue. Plerisque manet cognitum quod obtinuimus quandam partem uillule sancti Felicis iuri nostro de dato pontificis domni Rudesindi episcopi beate memorie quod nobis dederat ad stipendium usufructuario. Et peccato nobis inpediente misimus illam in contemptionem ad fratrem uestrum frater Oduario qui ipsam deganeam sancti Felicis obtinebat pro que peruenimus in ipsam uillam in presentia iudicum Froyla Monniiz, Abraham abba, Pelagius Aspasandiz, Oduario Tetoniz, Gemondo Froylaiz, Alfidio Gulderes, Pelagius Tructesendiz, Fagildus confessus, Hoduario confessus, Uimara Froylaiz et aliorum multorum filii benenatorum turba non modica qui ipsos terminos preuiderunt secundum in uestra diuisione resonat. Et cuncti dixerunt quia uestra est ueritas.[10] Proinde causatus fuit nobis mandator uester nomine Saluator et roborauimus manifestum et placitum ut fuissemus ad legem, et quod nobis ordinasset adimplessemus.[11] Obinde agnouimus nos in ueritate et adsignauimus uobis in uestra uilla per textum scripture placiti et per saionem Gudesteo,[12] et fecimus uobis ligali placiti ut si in quacumque tempus, an nos an filii, neptis uel bisneptis nostris uobis aut fratribus uestris qui ipsam deganeam contenuerint aliquam calumpniam in ipsam uillam uobis inferre uoluerint pro ipsis terminis sicut in istam diuisionem resonat, quomodo pariemus uel tam nos quam qui hoc ausus fuerit infringere ipsam uillam duplatam et insuper per singula capita xx xx boues.
>
> Notum die v ydus Magii. Era xxv post Millesima.
>
> Hordonius in hoc placitum manu mea (*signum*). Ueremudo manu mea (*signum*). Habze manu mea (*signum*). Abdella manu mea (*signum*). Timimi manu mea (*signum*).
>
> Qui presentes fuerunt: Didacus presbiter. Crizila presbiter. Timimi presbiter. Melhe presbiter. Gudesteo presbiter. Nouidius presbiter. Teo-

---

10 A typical second-stage formula.

11 Reference to confession but not the actual words of confession, followed by another typical second-stage formula.

12 Reference to the actual handover of the property, but not the commitment to consign as in a primary record.

> demirus diaconus. Geodesindus Pepizi. Froyani Gaudio. Berosindus Iohanniz. Ero Audinizi. Azo Uimarizi. Fonso Sunilla et alii plures.[13]

Thirdly, there are the narrative Accounts, retrospective constructions which might refer to confessions, oaths and agreements but rarely quote them. The purpose here is to provide some explanatory background, preferably involving a legitimizing figure like a king, as also to focus on outcome and consequent confirmation of rights and/or conveyance of property—this might be termed a tertiary record, for an example of which, see the conclusion below (S 356).

There were, then, at least three distinct stages of creating records and three different types of context for their creation: brief documents written in or shortly after court sessions, arising from court procedure; longer documents of conveyance arising from the consequences of a court session, written subsequently; narrative Accounts of background, court proceedings and outcomes, written at some distance from proceedings. The best demonstration of first and second stages is, as Roger Collins pointed out thirty years ago, the Confession in the Celanova cartulary quoted above, which has four separate texts attached (not quoted).[14] Since I have discussed this text elsewhere, I will not do so at length here. However, the essentials are that the initial Confession is a retrospectively constructed text, referring to the fact of confession and recording the conveyance that was a consequence. The appended documents are a raw Confession, as made in court, a commitment by the representatives of both parties to appear in court, another commitment by the parties to appear in court with their evidence before a different judge, and a final commitment to hand over the disputed property. All four of these appended documents have the *signa* of one or both parties but no witnesses. Now, since there is another copy of the initial charter of conveyance later in the cartulary, which is almost identical but does not have the four additional appended documents,[15] it looks as if the retrospective record was the one for keeping and the four additional documents were the short-term outcome from the proceedings of the court case, not intended for the long-term archive. This set of texts is extremely

---

13 Cel 94 (11 May 987); fol. 38v.

14 See Roger Collins, "Visigothic law and regional custom in disputes in early medieval Spain," in *The Settlement of Disputes in Early Medieval Europe*, ed. Wendy Davies and Paul Fouracre (Cambridge: Cambridge University Press, 1986), 85–104, at 89–90. My interpretation of detail differs, but his main point that a single case might generate "a plethora of documents" must be right. See Davies, *Windows on Justice*, 44–48.

15 Cel 150; fol. 54r.

important in indicating the existence of brief texts (which not surprisingly do not survive in large numbers) generated in the course of a court case.

Recognition of these stages of construction allows us to differentiate the evidential value of 'complete' texts; it also allows us to disentangle some composite texts which are at the distance of some eleven hundred years difficult to comprehend. In what follows I will demonstrate what can be understood about the construction of some of these difficult texts by following the principles outlined above.

4 Deconstruction of Composite Texts

4.1 *CL1 192*

There is a set of related records in the early twelfth-century Tumbo de León, published by Emilio Sáez as a single record, and laid out in the cartulary as one record—although separate sections are very clearly differentiated; the fact that the twelfth-century scribe considered all of this to be one record is indicated by the space for a single large initial capital, which has faded or was never added.[16] Since the sections are indeed differentiated, and since each section is intrinsically coherent, it looks as if these sections originated at different times and that they or their exemplar may have been copied from a set of separate sheets, perhaps clipped or folded together. The texts relate to a dispute between the monastery of Santos Justo y Pastor (which lies in Ardón, to the south of León) and one Mateo who in 946—according to the monastery—had attempted to appropriate the church of San Esteban and surrounding land and had attacked the attached dependents; the case was prosecuted on behalf of the monastery by the priest Berulf, who acted as advocate in other cases in this area. The case, and the records, look relatively straightforward, although there was clearly some uncertainty about the monastery's title to the church, since two separate occasions of making the gift are recorded by two different sets of donors, a year apart in 943–944, in near identical charters.[17] Most of these ori-

16 Fols. 39v–40v.

17 CL1 176 (27 August 943), CL1 186 (24 September 944); these charters are essentially the same, although there are a few, but not many, variations in the formulas and CL1 176 has corrupt elements. Both of these texts, like CL1 192, survive as cartulary copies. Since the texts of CL1 176 and CL1 186 are so very close, it looks as if a single record of donation has been duplicated to provide for two sets of donors, perhaps different branches of one family as there is some repetition of personal names. Since CL1 176 cites Godesteo son of Mazaref as father of the donors, as does the witness evidence of CL1 192 (see parts 2 and 3 below); and since CL1 176 has a long witness list which appears to be a representation

ginal donors appear to have witnessed the transfer of property resulting from the court case recorded here, as also three (perhaps four) of the witnesses of the second donation.[18]

1. The first document is a commitment made to the *saio* (legal officer) Sando that the representatives of both parties (Berulf for the deacon Sisebut and the monastery, Reuelle for Mateo (his relation, perhaps, or a neighbour)) will appear in León, where Berulf will produce evidence of the monastery's title to the church and of the wounds inflicted by Mateo, and Mateo will receive the evidence; a very high 100-*solidi* sanction to the *saio* and court holder, in the event of default, is attached. It is dated 26 March 946 and ends with confirmation and *signa* of Berulf and Mateo, but no witnesses, as is common in primary records.[19] It seems odd that although Reuelle is named as spokesman for Mateo, it is Mateo's *signum* that is recorded and Mateo who agrees to appear (compare ACO B.1.11, parts 11–13, below);[20] and it is odd that the sanction is extremely high (again, compare ACO B.1.11 below):

> [B]erulfus presbiter, qui asseret in sua uoce[21] et de Siseuuto diacono uel de parte ecclesie uel monasterio, contra isto Riuelli, qui asseret in uoce Matheo, tibi saioni nostro Sando. Per hunc nostrum placitum, tibi conpromittimus qualiter die quod erit in alio die, post intrata dominica, in Legione de Galletia, presentem, ego Berulfus presbiter, mea persona et mea testimonia per quos firmem super isto Matheo, in cuius uoce asseret Reuelle, qualiter tenente in nostro iure uel post parte ecclesie ipsa ecclesia Sancti Stephani, cum suos dextros, ab integro, per istum testamentum et per auctores qui in ipso testamento resonant, et sic se leuauit[22] iste Matheo et suos minores, una et alia uice, et maliarunt nostros minores

of the León episcopal household (cf. CL1 201 (948), CL1 217 (950), CL1 220 (950)), whereas CL1 186 has a short and simple witness list which looks more local, I could believe that CL1 176 was created in the context of the court case of CL1 192, particularly since parts 2 and 3 of CL1 192 refer to the *testamentos* (i.e. documents) handed over to the monastery's representatives by the original donors.

18 The witnesses Vincepti and Braelio had participated in the first donation, sons of Godesteo iben Mazaref; the witnesses Siseuuto, Godesteo and Valerio had participated in the second donation, which had been witnessed by the CL1 192 witnesses, the priests Kacem, Andreas and Mantelli, and perhaps the *saio*'s representative Salomon.

19 See Davies, *Windows on Justice*, 55, 136.

20 A man called Reuelli appears as witness to the final transfer.

21 *qui asseret in sua uoce*; *qui asseret in uoce N*; *Per hunc nostrum placitum, tibi conpromittimus qualiter die* are all standard formulas.

22 For *sic se leuauit*, see also ACO B.1.11, parts 2, 4 and 6, and S 356, below at nn. 51, 57; it looks as if it was a standard way to make an accusation of intrusion.

> et fecerunt plagas in solidos LXXII, et promiserunt ipsa ecclesia cum suos dextros de nostro iure. Et ego Matheo, mea persona, pro ipsas testimonias accipere, et qui minime fecerit pariet saioni nostro uel post parte dominica solidos C.
>
> Factus placitus[23] VII kalendas aprilis, era DCCCCLXXXIIII.
>
> Berulfus presbiter et Matheo, in hoc placito manus nostras ++ roborauimus.

2. The second document is a statement of the witness evidence produced in favour of Berulf, Sisebut and the monastery by Gualamir and the priest Flaino, as prefigured in part 1:

> Verbo testis quod testificauerunt testimonias, de parte Berulfo et Siseuuto, id sunt: Gualamiro et Flaino presbitero, quia occulis uidimus et aures audiuimus et de presente fuimus quando[24] habebat ipsa ecclesia Godesteo iben Mazaref, cum suos dextros, ab integro, et sic fecerunt Bani Electa et filii domni Godestei inde testamentos ad isto Berulfo et Siseuuto; et sic se leuauit iste Matheo et expulsauit inde suos minores, de Berulfo et de Siseuuto, et fecerunt plagas in solidos LXXII. Et ec que testificamus et iurare debemus.

3. The third is the formal Oath of the witnesses, of one of the two standard types, with standard introduction.[25] It repeats the evidence cited in parts 1 and 2, and adds the names of the four judges; it concludes with a curse, which is unusual:

> Conditiones sacramentorum atque ex ordinatione[26] Furtunio, Aurelius, Teodela Gutiniz seu et Domnon Uimaraniz. Iuraturi sumus nos testes prolati, qui sunt de parte Berulfo et Siseuuto, id sumus, Gualamiro et Flaino presbitero. Iuramus inprimis per Deum Patrem omnipotentem qui fecit celum et terram, mare et omnia que in eis sunt; iuramus per XII Prophetas et XII Apostolos et sancta quatuor Euangelia, id sunt, Marcus, Matheus, Lucas et Iohannes; iuramus per reliquias Sancte Marie Uirginis et genetricis Domini nostri Ihesu Christi; iuramus per reliquias Sancti Claudii uel

23 Use of the nominative case here is extremely unusual.

24 *occulis uidimus et aures audiuimus et de presente fuimus quando* is a standard formula used in declaring evidence.

25 See Davies, *Windows on Justice*, 124–126.

26 Cf. *adque ex ordinatione* in the Oath of ACO B.1.11, part 5, below.

> per diuina omnia que sunt sancta; iuramus quia occulis uidimus et aures audiuimus et de presente fuimus quando habebat ipsa ecclesia Gudesteo iben Mazarref, cum suos dextros, ab integro, et sic fecerunt Uani Electa et filii domni Godestei inde testamentos ab istos Berulfo et Siseuuto; et sic se leuauit iste Matheo et expulsauit inde ipsos homines de Berulfo et de Siseuuto, et fecerunt plagas in solidos LXXI.[27] Et ec que iuramus, recte et fideliter iuramus, et si mentimus et nomen Domini in Filio[28] tangimus,[29] conprehendat nos iuditius quod sic conprehendit Dathan et Abiron, uiros sceleratissimos, qui propter eorum scelera uiuos et terra obsorbuit.

4. The fourth is not standard and is a separate confirmation of the sworn evidence by the accused, Mateo, with his *signum*:

> Quod testes testificauerunt et iudices iudicauerunt, et ego Matheo me in ueritate te agnosco, et iura et pena illis perdimitto et hanc conditionem manu mea confirmo +.

5. The fifth text is a commitment by Mateo to Berulf and Sisebut to hand the church over to the monastery by a Friday, with another very large sanction in *solidi*, to be paid to the court holder, completed with Mateo's *signum*; it has a non-standard form, for it would be more usual to make the commitment to the *saio* and to agree to appear on a given day in order to consign the property, rather than express the intention as a condition:

> Matheo uobis Berulfo et Siseuuto. Facio uobis placitum, ut die VI feria, si non consignauero ipsa ecclesia cum suos dextros, ab integro, post uestra parte uel de monasterio, quomodo pariem post parte dominica solidos C.
> Matheo in hoc placito manu mea +.

6. The sixth is a list of confirmers and witnesses of Mateo's preceding confirmation, including four judges and the *saio*, set out in two columns; it adds one judge to those named in part 3 but does not include Fortún García among them, as before. Fortún García and Pelayo González were high aristocrats, who attended the royal court, and there is at least one deacon from the cathedral church:

---

27 Note the minor variants from the last citation: *LXXII/LXXI, Bani/Uani, Mazaref/Mazarref, minores/homines.*

28 *in Filio* is perhaps an error for *in falso*; see n. 29.

29 For *et si mentimus et nomen Domini ... tangimus*, cf. *in falso* of ACO B.1.11, part 6, below; cf. also *nomen Domini falsamus* of Sob 109.

> In cuius copresentia roborauit ipsa conditione, id sunt:
>
> Furtunius Garseani cubiculari conf (monogram). Oueccus Nepotiani ts (*signum*).[30] Felix, diaconus de Sancta Maria, ts. Bonellus diaconus ts. Mirabiles diaconus ts.
>
> Sando, ubi saio fuit, conf. Aurelius quos iudicaui conf.[31] Pelagius Gundisaluiz quos iudicaui conf. Teoda Gutiniz quod iudicaui conf. Domnon Uimarani quod iudicaui conf.

7. The seventh document is a commitment by Mateo, made on 7 May to Berulf and Sisebut, that there will be no more and no worse assaults on the church, property nor dependents of San Esteban; it concludes with a very high sanction of 200 *solidi* payable to the monastery and the court holder in the event of default:

> Matheo uel filiis meis tibi Berulfo et Siseuuto, per hunc meum placitum uobis conpromittimus, ut de eodem die uel tempore,[32] si ego Matheo uel filiis meis uos Berulfo et Siseuuto in ipsos dextros de Sancti Stephani uel in omnem prestariam eius aliquam inquietationem fecerimus uel ad uestros minores aliquam disturbationem fecerimus, plus quam fecimus, quomodo pariemus uobis uel post parte dominica solidos CC.
>
> Factum placitum ipsas nonas maii, era DCCCCLXXXIIII.

8. The last document might arguably be seen as intrinsic to part 7; however, I have separated it because it relates to a further, subsequent event. This is a list of witnesses of the moment of consigning the church to Berulf by Mateo and his children, through the agency of the court holder's (Fortún García's) *saio*,[33] recorded in columns:

> Qui presentes fuerunt quando Matheo et filii eius consignarunt Sancti Stephani, cum suos dextros, ab integro, ad Berulfus presbiter, per manu saioni de Furtunio Garceiz cubiculari, id sunt:

---

30 Here, as elsewhere, I indicate by the word (*signum*) the *signa* that were more elaborate than simple crosses, which are represented by +.

31 *quos/quod iudicaui* is a standard way to represent the subscriptions of the judges of a court case.

32 *per hunc meum placitum uobis conpromittimus, ut de eodem die uel tempore* are standard formulas of commitment.

33 Or perhaps, in practice, through his representative, since it is the representative not the *saio* who is noted in the witness list.

Hacem presbiter. Teouigildus presbiter. Adrias presbiter. Mantelli presbiter. Alamiro presbiter. Mutarraf presbiter. Celso presbiter. Micael presbiter.

Abonazar presbiter. Titon presbiter. Gondemarus presbiter.[34] Siseuuto ts. Azfon ts. Godesteo ts. Fedzu ts. Vincepti ts.

Braelio ts. Baltasari ts. Reuelli ts. Melic ts. Abdelmelchi ts.

Peppi ts. Valit ts. Hazmo ts. Valerio ts. Fatta ts.

Fofo ts. Besuleo ts. Gaudio ts. Salomon, qui fuit uigarius de Sando, saioni.

There is no reason to suppose that this court case did not happen. It has many intrinsically credible features—the royal officer as court holder, the actions of his *saio* and the *saio*'s representative, the six-week period from accusation to final settlement, the use of standard formulas and standard procedures. Mateo and Reuelle appear to have been based in Marialba, just to the south of León and not far from Ardón, and they feature as witnesses to other charters in the 940s and 950s.[35] Álvaro Carvajal has pointed out that Fortún García, who was in any case a royal chamberlain, appears to have had considerable personal properties in the Tierra de Campos, one of which territories—*Mazules*—seems to be the "Villa de Mazul" which included the church of San Esteban.[36] It is not surprising, then, that it was his *saio* who handled the case and that Fortún was the court holder.

This text has a number of surprising features. These include the naming of a representative for Mateo, who does not appear to act for him; the background donation of the church to the monastery of Santos Justo y Pastor apparently by two different sets of donors; and the unusually high penalty clauses of 100 and 200 *solidi*—five *solidi* was the usual penalty for contravention of a commitment.[37] This suggests that the penalties, which lie in texts that were probably constructed for the beneficiary, may have been framed by the monastery to serve as a severe warning to other would-be intruders—perhaps an example of methods used by a monastery to warn local people to keep off its property, particularly when the title was recently acquired and somewhat uncertain. Here

34 Perhaps the protagonist of CL1 128 (938), recording a dispute in the same area.

35 CL1 187 (944), CL1 209 (950); see Álvaro Carvajal Castro, "La construcción de la monarquía asturleonesa en la meseta del Duero. Estudio de los procesos de integración territorial (s. IX–XI)," Universidad de Salamanca, Tesis Doctoral, 2013, 603.

36 CL2 482 (981); cf. CL3 749 (1017). Carvajal Castro, "La construcción de la monarquía," 366–368.

37 Cf. ACO B.1.11, parts 3, 11, 12, 13, below.

we see a representation of an intruder's mark at least three times on different documents, presumably presented to him in public, in an extremely high-level court in which there was an element of royal interest; once his capitulation had been secured, he was threatened with a gigantic sanction in the event of default. Whatever the politics of the situation, this text offers a very clear example of the existence of at least six separate, coherent, credible texts deriving from a single court case.

4.2 *T 66*

This record occurs in the early fourteenth-century cartulary of Santo Toribio in the Liébana, although it is clear that its ninth- and tenth-century material was collected earlier at the monastery of San Martín, Turieno, in the valley below Santo Toribio. It is quite difficult to comprehend this text; as it stands, the syntax is extremely misleading and there seem to have been errors and omissions in transmission. There is an occasional emendation of the cartulary text, which suggests that the scribe had some difficulty with his exemplar; and the extant cartulary does not differentiate between the constituent parts of the record; that, and the character of the record, suggests that it was copied from a copy and not from the original texts. However, there is enough to see that this composite document details the consequences of a dispute between two lay people, Siseguto and Fredinando, over control of a vineyard at Mieses, close to Turieno, in 962.

1. The first document is a first-person Confession by Siseguto in response to Fredinando's petition, using the standard formulas of Confession records; it was made on 7 May 962 in a court in the monastery of San Martín, witnessed by three judges, a *saio* and one other person. Siseguto had asked Fredinando to transfer a vineyard to him by charter. When this had been done, Fredinando was taken to court by Tellu Romanit, questioning his authority to deliver the charter (the text is ambiguous here—Tellu may have acted for the original owner or perhaps Tellu was himself the original owner). As a result Siseguto retracted his part in the transaction and Fredinando paid a fine of 50 *solidi* (also ambiguous):

> In iudicio Hopila abbas, Uermudi Allefonsiz, Gotini et Martinus, puerum regis, uel aliorum multorum iudicium (*sic*) et in conuentum ecclesie Sancti Martini, manifestus sum ego Sesecutus ad peticionem Fredinandi, qui asserit in sua uoce. Uerum est quod negare non ualeo,[38] qui fui ad

38 *Uerum est quod negare non ualeo* and *quod ego manifesto uerum esse factum, et in iudicio nihil abeo que hoponam* several lines below are the standard Confession formulas.

casa de Fredinando cum Froila et rogauimus illum per cartam traslatare de uinia qui est in Mesas cum suos arbores et translatauit uobis[39] Fredinandus ipsam cartam et prendibit illum Tellu Romanit ad iudicium, et litabit ipsa carta placitum pro autore, et recesamus nos de atorgatione,[40] et pariauit[41] Fredinandus quinquaginta sollos; et quod ego manifesto uerum esse factum, et in iudicio nihil abeo que hoponam. Ego Sesecutus in hoc manifesto manus mea + feci et in conuentum ecclesie roboraui.

Factus istus manifestus die II feria, ipsas nonas magias, Era M. Ego Hopila abbas, quod iudicaui manus mea + feci. Ueremudus Allefonsiz (*signum*). Gotinus quod iudicaui testis (*signum*). Alloritus ubi testis fui +. Sisinandus +.

2. The second document is a formal commitment by Siseguto and Fredinando, to the *saio*, that Siseguto will consign the vineyard to Fredinando on 15 May, together with another vineyard and some apple trees near Fredinando's house, with a sanction of five *solidi* payable to the *saio* in the event of default. It is not witnessed but has the *signa* of both parties:

Fredinandus et Sesegutus tibi Sanino[42] Allorito per hunc nostrum placitum,[43] qualiter die II feria quod est ipsos idus magias Era millesima consignem ego Sisecutus tibi Fredinando de uinea que est in Mus, iusta uinia Sancti Iuliani, et alia in Befares, iusta flumen Deua et pomares ad illa Cabella subtus tua casa;[44] et ego Fredinandus pro accipere ipsas uinias

---

39 *Recte nobis*? This abbreviated word could be read as *nobis*, but the minims are unclear on the scan of the microfilm of the manuscript.

40 A technical term; see Luis García de Valdeavellano, "Escodriñamiento y otorificación (contribución al estudio de la reivindicación mobiliaria en el derecho español medieval)," in *Centenario de la ley del notariado. Sección primera: estudios históricos*, 2 vols (Madrid: Junta de Decanos de Los Colegios Notariales de España, 1965), 2:125–335, at 274–324, who demonstrates unambiguously that the meaning of *autorigare* is to provide guarantees of the legitimate possession of a thing purchased.

41 The standard term for 'pay a fine' in charters of this period.

42 *Recte sayono* (i.e. *saio*)?

43 *per hunc nostrum placitum* is part of the standard formula of commitment; compare parts 11, 12, 13 of ACO B.1.11 below and parts 1 and 7 of CL1 192 above. Part 13 also has *ego N pro accipere NN per manum sayonis* and the 5-*solidi* sanction is characteristic of all four commitments in ACO B.1.11.

44 The form of the placename of the contested vineyard here and in part 4 is *Mus*, whereas in part 1 it is *Mesas*. It is clear from the detail of the location here that *Mus* must refer to *Mesas*, modern Mieses.

> et ipso pomare per manum sayonis et qui minus facerit pariet tibi sayoni nostro v sollos. Fredinandus in hoc pactum + feci. Sesegutus in hoc pactum + feci.

3. The third text is a guarantor document in which the guarantor Allorito undertakes to Fredinando, in the monastery's court, that if—three days after the due date—Siseguto should have defaulted on the preceding commitment, then Allorito himself will give Fredinando some comparable properties. There are no witnesses but the document has the *signum* of Allorito, who is clearly a different person from the *saio* Allorito since both are mentioned in the final sentence. There are very few surviving guarantor documents, but there are examples from Castile and the *meseta*:[45]

> Alloritus qui sum fiator de seguro contra Fredinandum usque ad diem v feria ipsus idus magius Era M, si non consignarem ego Sesegutus tibi Fredinando ipsas uineas que in pacto resonat, quomodo dem tibi ego Alloritus similes tales uinias et pomares; ego Alloritus in anc fiatura manus mea + feci in presencia Hopila abbas et sagoni Allorito uel aliorum multorum testibus.

4. The fourth document is a donation charter, which begins with a short passage of narrative detailing the events which preceded the donation. I will take these two sections separately.

a) A third-person narrative describes how Siseguto defaulted on the agreement, so that Allorito carried out the guarantee to Fredinando, giving him two substitute properties. Allorito then took Siseguto to a different court where he (Siseguto) confirmed the guarantee agreement, which carried a double penalty:

> mentiuerit Sesegutus placitum et fidiatura que roborauit Alloritus ad Fredinandum ipsa fiatura uinia in Befares et pomare in balle de Bosita et prendebit Alloritus Sesegutus ad iudicium ante Monio Uelasco et roborauit pactum pro ipsa fiatura uinia duplare et duplauit illa.[46]

b) Most of this document is a first-person donation charter, of 26 May, from Siseguto to the abbot of San Martín and to Allorito, through the agency of a different *saio*, concerning four properties; these properties are the two which

---

45 C 103 (962), V 43 (968–975), CL2 464 (979).
46 The *t* of *duplauit* has been erased.

had originally been specified in the commitment from Siseguto to Fredinando (that is in part 2), together with two additional properties. It concludes with sanction, dating clause and witness list (including the two *saiones* and three priests) of standard type; and the disposition includes a transfer formula of standard type:

> Ego Sesegutus per manum sagoni nostro Albiniano et consignaui uiniam in Toreuno, iusta uiniam regis et de alia parte iusta uiniam in Mus, iusta uinia Sancti Iuliani; et alia in Befares iusta flumen Deua; et pomare in Mus iusta flumen Deua, et alium ad illa Cabella. Consigno uobis ipsas uinias per manum sagonis et roborauit uobis carta et iudicium ut de odie die de meo iure sit abrasum et in iure de abbati nostro Hopila et Allorito sit confirmatum. Si quis tamen, aliquis uos ad disrumpendum pacta uel testamentum, an ego Sesegutus an germanis meis an aliquis subrogita persona, quomodo pariet uobis ipsas uinias duplatas et ipsum dictum uel quantum ad uos fuerit melioratum et hec scriptura ista firmiter abeat firmitatem.
>
> Facta pacta uel testamenta VII kalendas iunias Era M, principe sedente Sanzio in Legione. Ego Sesegutus in anc scriptura ista pacta uel testamenta manus mea + feci et testibus[47] quos iudicaui +. Gotinus quos iudicaui testis. Alloritus ubi sago fui testis (*signum*). Albinianus ubi sago fui +. Danus testis (*signum*). Lemicius presbiter (*signum*). Egerius presbiter testis (*signum*). Teodarius presbiter +. Iohannis testis.

There are clearly parts of the story that cannot be reconstructed and some parts remain ambiguous, but the process described is credible, especially with its several meetings on different dates in May 962 and with the involvement of two *saiones* and two different courts. All of the identifiable properties are very close together (within three km of each other) and they appear to be of rather small scale. It must be likely that the Allorito who benefitted from the final donation was Allorito the guarantor, since he had suffered a loss in making good his guarantee to Fredinando; the abbot benefitted as original court holder, to whom part of the penalty for default would be due. Whether or not any of the parties were tenants or clients of the abbot is not clear; it is possible, although this does not have to have been the case. Whether or not the guarantor came from the monastery is not stated but it is also possible. Despite the many difficulties of this text, it is very important for showing explicitly how a guarantor

47 There must be a name missing here.

carried out his responsibility and what he might do if the person he guaranteed defaulted. The text also suggests that a 50-*solidi* fine was at one stage paid—these sanctions were not just unrealisable pious hopes; and, very interestingly, the text explicitly shows the payment of the double penalty, as required by the sanction, in the final settlement. The form of the documents, the use of standard formulas and the circumstantial detail of the text make it perfectly clear that this record was constructed from four or more related but independent texts.

4.3 *ACO B.1.11*[48]

This very large, and very long, document, which survives on a single sheet in Oviedo cathedral archive, has the appearance of being an account of a court case between Pedro and Victino, heard in Gordón, ending up in favour of Pedro, confirmed in the royal court of the kings of León in 953, and witnessed by several people of very high status. If we look at it in detail, we can see that the basic story is stated no fewer than three times,[49] in association with eleven separate documents. The charter is very worn in parts and hence sometimes illegible.

1. The first document is a commitment by both parties (Victino represented by Vilifred) to the *saio* Karoso to appear in the court of Teodoredo and Felix on the 8th of the Ides of November (6 November), using the standard formula of commitment; Pedro also commits to bring witnesses:

> (Chrismon) Petrus frater qui acsere, in sua uoce, et Uilifredus frater qui respondet, in uoce de Uictino, tibi saionni nostro Karoso per unc nostrum placitum tibi conpromitimus qualiter die quod est die [...] viiio idus nobembris sic presentemus nostras personas in presentia Teoderedo Iustizi et Felix iudigum presentem ego Petrus mea persona et mea testimonia per quos firmetur super Uilifredo qui est uigarios de Uictino.

48 See Davies, *Windows on Justice*, 1–5, 146–151, for some discussion and photographs, where I used the text of Santos Agustín García Larragueta, ed., *Colección de documentos de la catedral de Oviedo* (Oviedo: Instituto de Estudios Asturianos, 1962), no. 26. The most recent published edition is Andrea M. Miranda Duque and Xosé Lluis García Arias, eds., *Documentos orixinales de los sieglos IX–X de los archivos del monesteriu de San Pelayo y de la catedral d'Uviéu* (Oviedo: Academia de la Llingua Asturiana, 2011), 61–67, no. 18; this diplomatic edition is a real improvement but my readings occasionally differ.

49 Note that the case is stated three times in the separate documents of CL1 192 above, as it is also in CL1 34 (915). This may have been standard practice. These documents were not intended to be kept and hence such repetition is not a feature of most texts that are preserved.

2. The second document is Pedro's statement of his evidence, in other words the story: how Victino invited him to dinner, gave him land to build a monastery and confirmed it on pain of a sanction of 100 *solidi* if he should default; the monastery was built but then Victino took it back, on the advice of his wife and Teodevera and Sister Gogina, and Victino also took a monastery that Pedro had acquired from his ancestors and a vineyard which Sister Gogina and Abbot Severo had given him; and then Abbot Severo confirmed Pedro's legitimate possession in a meeting in Gordón before Teodoredo and Felix:

> quomodo *segdente*[50] *se Petrus in suo monasterio de Seuero de Seuero abba sic se leuauit*[51] *Uictinus* et inuitauit Petrum ad sua mensa et in alio die accessit ad illo uolumtas animo karo et spontania sua uolumtate et donauit ad Petrum terra uagua sua ratione et de sua muliere Fredildi et de Teodeuera uno consilio aderato et terra donada et assinada super placito et iuramentum que fecissent ibidem monesterio ita et fecerunt et roborabit placito Uictinus in solidos c et monesterio facto et eglesia et kasas et corte clusa et ortum et pomare postum et aqua metuta que ipso monesterio regat syc se leuauit Uictinus per consilio de Uilifredo qui ipsa uoce autorigauit ad integritate et per consilio de serore Gugina et de Teouera et de Fredildi bracio forcioso animo orrido et tullerunt ad frater Petrum ipso monesterio et ipsa ereditate unde placito rouoraberunt et tulliuit mici alia eglesia quem abeba de auios meos et uinia que donauit Seuero appa et serore Gogina ad Petrum et autoriauit Seuero appa ad Petrum in concilio de Gordone ante Teoderedo Iustiz et Felix iudigum in conuentum eglesie Sancte Marine. Si se leuauit Uilifredus et Uictinus et tullerunt mici ipsa uinia et ipso uino.

3. The third document, which is a statement by Vilifred (the spokesman for Victino and his sisters) that he will receive [Pedro's] evidence, with a sanction of five *solidi* for detractors, is incomplete. It is in fact the end of the first document; together parts 1 and 3 represent the commitment of both parties to present and receive evidence in court, with that evidence (i.e. part 2) inserted between the commitments of each party:[52]

50 Italics indicate the start of the repeated passage.
51 For this expression see also n. 22 above and n. 57 below.
52 Cf., with a much larger penalty, CL1 192, part 1, above, where commitment to present and receive evidence is part of a single document.

et ego Uilifredus qui sum uigarius de Uictino et de suas sorores mea persona pro ipsas testimonias accipere et qui minime fecerit pariet solidos v que Petro et Uilifredo in oc placito manus nostras ++ fecimus.

4. The fourth is a witness statement for Pedro by thirty-three people, three of whom are named, the words of their statement being introduced by the standard formula for such cases. Their statement is in fact a repetition of Pedro's statement (part 2), with some very slight variants, adding the location of the land and ending with the *signa* of the three named witnesses:

> Ueruum testium que testifigaberunt testimonias de parte Petrum contra Uilifredo qui est uigarius et mantator de Uictino et de suas sorores id est Felix, Agila, Onorigus et alios plures numeros xxxa. Quia occulos uidimus et presente fuimus quando adduxo Uictinus frater Petrum ad sua mensa et *sedente se Petro in suo monesterio su mano de Seuero appa si se leuauit Uictinus* et accesit ad illum uolumtas animo karo et espontania sua uolumtate consilio aderato quum Teodeuera et Fredildi et rouorauit placito ad fratrem Petrum in solidos c de ipsa ereditate de Teodeuera et de Fredildi que donaberunt ad frater Petrum et donaberunt et assinaberunt ipsa ereditate que abebant in Paragiao terra uagua que fecisset ibidem monesterio, ita et fecerunt, et monesterio facto eglesia et kasas et coorte clusa et ortum et pomare postum et aqua que ipso monesterio regat si se leuauit Uitinus per consilio de Uilifredo et de sorore Gugina et de Teodeuera et de Fredildi bracio fortioso et animo orrido et tulliuit ad Petrum ipsa ereditate et ipso monesterio et alia eglesia quam abebat de suos auios et uinia que donauit Seuero appa et sorore Gugina ad Petrum et autogauit illa Seuero appa in concilio de Gordone ante Teoderedo Iustizi et Felix iudigum et si se leuauit Uictinus et Uilifredus et tullerunt ipsa uinia et ipso uino ad Petrum et que testifigamus et iurare deuemus Felix + Agila + Onorigus +.

5. The fifth is the Oath, of one of the two standard types, introduced by the standard formula:

> (Chrismon) Conditiones sagramentorum adque ex ordinatione Teoderedo Iustizi Felix iudigum iuraturi sumus nos testes prolati qui sumus de parte de frater Petro testifigantes contra Uilifredo qui est uigarius de Uictino, id est Felix et Agila et Onorigo, iuramus inprimis … Deum Patrem omnipotentem qui fecit celum et terra, mare et omnia qui in ei sunt, iuramus pro xii profetas et pro xiim apostolos et sancta iiiior Euangelia, id est, Marcus, Mahteus, Lugas et Ioannes, iuramus pro reliquias

> Sancta Maria uirginis et genetrix Domini nostri Ihesu Christi, iuramus pro reliquias Sancte Marine uirginis in cuius loco as conditiones manus nostras tenemus sibe et pro diuina omnia que sunt sancta, quia occulis uidimus et presentes fuimus et bene nobis cognitus manet in ueritatem.

6. And the sixth is the sworn evidence within the Oath, which is another repetition of Pedro's statement (part 2), with the location of the property (and is in fact the best—that is, the most coherent—version of this story). It ends with a slightly longer version of the ending of part 2, followed by a long sanction against anyone who should contravene the Oath or swear falsely, in which event he/she should submit to the judgment of God and the ordeal of hot water:

> quanto aduxo Uictinus Petrum ad sua mensa et *sedente se Petrum in suo monesterio sub mano de Seuero appa et si se leuauit Uictinus* cuius uigarius est Uilifredus pro consilio de Teodeuera et de Fredildi et accessit ad illos uolumtas animo karo spontania sua uolumtate et donaberunt et assinaberunt suas raciones quem abebunt in Paragiao sic Uictino quomodo etiam et Teodeuera et Fredildi ad frater Petrum spontania sua uolumtate et rouoraberunt placitum ad frater Petrum de omnia sua ereditate quem abebant in Paragiao ad integritate et roboraberunt placitum in solidos c et donaberunt et assinaberunt ipsa terra uagua quo fecissent monesterium ita et fecerunt et monesterio facto et eglesia et kasas et corte clusa et ortum et pomare postum et aqua mittuta qui ipsum monesterium inregat et ipso lauore facto sic se leuauit Uictinus pro consilio de Uilifredo qui ipsa uoce autorcauit ad integritate in concilio et pro consilio de sorore Gugina et de Teodeuera et de Fredildi et tulliuit ipsum monesterium ad Petrum et alia eglesia quam abebat Petrus de suos auios et uinia que donaberat Seuerus appa et serore Gugina ad Petrum et autorcauit illa Seuero abba ad Petrum in concilio de Gordone ante Teuderedo Iustiz et Felix iudigum in conuentum eglesie Sancte Marie et si se leuauit Uictinus et Uilifredus et tullerunt ipsa uinia et ipso uino ad frater Petrum et abent illo contra se et mentiuit ipsum placitum et abet et ereditate et placito contra se et qui iuramus recte et fideliter iuramus et in anc iuramento nunllo qui fraudis ingenio non interponimus et si mentimus et nomen Domini in falso tangimus conprendat nos iudicius Dei et pena kaldaria.

7. Part 7 is a statement that the oath was sworn in the church of Santa María at the gate of Gordón, and thereafter an innocent was taken to the ordeal. The

statement continues that the innocent's hand was clear three days later, the 12th of the Kalends of December (20 November) 923,[53] with confirmation of this by three special witnesses (of whom the third appears to have guarded the innocent during the three days of waiting), the two judges, another person, the innocent and the *saio*:

> Iuraberunt istas testimonias in eglesia Sancte Marie qui exitata est ad porta Gordonens et pro eorum iuramentum ingresus est innocens ad pena kaldaria nomine Fredenandus qui in tercio die limpidus apparuit coram multorum testium qui II sunt conscripti uel signa facturi late conditiones, notum die XIImo kalendas dicembris era DCCCCLXIa. Monnisso ubi fidelis fuit de amborum partibus et rogitus de frater Petrum manum mea roborabit (*signum*). Assuri ubi fidelis fuit de amborum partibus et rogitus de frater Petrum manu mea +. (Long Chrismon) Furakasas ubi fidelis de amborum partibus rogitus de frater Uilifredo manum mea et nocentem sub custodia tenuit et in IIIo die limpidum presentabit mea +. Teoderedus Iustizi quos iudicabi (*signum*). Felix quos iudigaui +. Gaudemiro … (Chrismon) Fredenandus ubi innocens fuit et aserias conditiones iurauit et manum in kaldaria misit et … eiecit et in IIIo die in concilio limpidus apparuit manum mea + (Chrismon) Karosus ubi saio fuit.

8. The eighth document is a list of witnesses of the oath, perhaps including the *saio*, in the church of San Martín:

> Qui preses fuerunt ad iuramentum id est Roderigus presbiter (*signum*). Sunliam presbiteri (*signum*). (Long Chrismon) … relius Cenderigus Taurellus Gello … Karosus Pepinus Placinus … in conuentum eglesie Sancti Martini episcopi.

9. The ninth is a (different) list of witnesses of the innocent's entry to the ordeal, including Vilifred:

53 The date is clearly problematic and does not match the *floruit* of the subscribers. The text appears to read 923, although the diplomatic edition can see an additional *v*, and hence reads 928; the subscriptions of the king and his court are consistent with 953, García Larragueta's preferred date. See the discussion of Miranda Duque and García Arias, *Documentos orixinales de los sieglos IX–X*, 61, who note an Abbot Severo recorded elsewhere in 932. A date for the court case in the 920s or early 930s seems more likely than the projected 953.

> Qui preses fuerunt quando innocens ingressus est ad pena kaldaria id est Furakasas, abba Romanus confirmat. Ioannes confirmat. Uilifredus confirmat. Quintila confirmat. Tedisclus.

10. The tenth is a list of witnesses of the emergence of the innocent with a clear hand; it is for the most part different from the confirmers of part 7, although it includes the two judges:

> Qui ipsum nocente limpidum uiderunt id est Teoderedo Iustizi. Felix Rubio. Maximynus Nikeiti. Aurelius Ualerianus. Azmon Nunillani presbiter. Donnellus. Sabgildus. Seuero.

11. The eleventh is the formal commitment of the two parties to the *saio* to appear in Gordón before judges with evidence to be sworn, with a sanction of five *solidi* for default but no witnesses; the formulas are standard commitment formulas:[54]

> Petrus et Uilifredus tibi sayonni nostro Karoso per unc nostrum placitum tibi compromitimus qualiter die quod erat die va f ... sic presentemus personas nostras ic in Gordone in presentia iudigum presentem ego Petrum mea persona ... ipsa testimonia pro ad iuramentum et ego Uilifredus mea persona per ipsas testimonias a iuramenture et qui minime fecerit parie solidos v que Petrus et Uilifredus in placito manus nostras (*signa*).

12. Part 12 is the formal commitment of the two parties to the *saio* to appear in Gordón before judges, on which occasion Vilifred will formally concede to Pedro, with a sanction of five *solidi* for default but no witnesses; the formulas are standard commitment formulas:

> Petrus et Uilifredus tibi saionni nostro Kaoroso per unc placitum tibi conpromitimus qualiter die quod sabbato sic presentemus personas nostras in presencia iudigum in Gordone presentem ego Uilifredus mea persona et meum pactum quantum lex mandat[55] per sentencia et ego Petrus mea persona pro accipere ipsum pactum per manum saionis et qui unc placitum exserserit pariet soldos v que et insuper conpleat ipsu pactum. Petrus et Uilifredus in placitu manus nostras + + fecimus.

54 Cf. CLI 192 and T 66 above.
55 Cf. *que les mantare* in the Agreement consequent on a confession, OD 39 (995).

13. The thirteenth is the formal commitment of the two parties to the *saio* to go to Erias and Paragiao, where Vilifred was to consign the property, with a sanction of five *solidi* for default but no witnesses; the formulas are standard commitment formulas:

> Petrus et Uilifredus tibi sayonni nostro Karoso per unc nostrum placitum tibi compromitimus qualiter die quod quo die va feria sic presentemus nostras personas ic in Ayrias pres (*sic*) in Paragiao presentem ego Uilifredus mea persona et assinnem ipsa uilla que in iudicio resonat per manum saionnis et ego Petrus mea persona pro ipsa uilla accepere et qui minime fecerit pariet solidos v que Petrus et Uilifredus in placito manus nostras + … fecimus.

14. The fourteenth is a list of witnesses and subscriptions of King Ordoño III and lay and clerical members of his court:

> Sub Christi nomine Gundesalbus aepiscopus sedis Legionensis confirmat (*signum*). Gundesindus comes palatii confirmat. Uermudus Nunnizi comes palatii. Fortes Iustizi confirmat. Dextera uirtus [*sic—recte* In Christi virtute?] Armentarius Dumiense sedis aepiscopus (*signum*). (Long Chrismon) Serenissimus princeps Hordonius (*signum*). Altissimi manu protectus Gudesteus Ouetense sedis aepiscopus (monogram). Sanctius serenissimus princeps confirmat (monogram). Geluira prolis Ranemiri confirmat (*signum*). Nebutianus presbiter (*signum*).

15. The fifteenth is an endorsement of 981, by a woman on behalf of Gogina, that the judgment was true, with confirmation and three witnesses:

> (Chrismon) In era XVIIII post millesima auidante domna Florentina in Sancta Eulalia in Lena anouit me ego Florentina comodo iste iudicio super Uictino est ueriuigo et de sua mano rouorado et ego in persona de domna Gogina et mea manum mea confirmo et autorigo manum mea. Qui preses fuerunt id est Neboziano presbiter (*signum*), Ranmondo presbiter (*signum*), Donnido presbiter cos noduit (*signum*).

Both part 14, the royal witness list, and part 15, the 981 endorsement, are added by different hands from the main hand. The contents of the three columns below the body of the text (which are not laid out in strict columns) are as follows: in the righthand column are parts 9 to 13, that is, the 4th and 5th witness lists and the last three commitments, still in the main hand; the chrismons indicate that this was part of the main design of the charter. The middle column and upper part of the left column contain the royal and aristocratic subscriptions, the king being focal. At the bottom left lies the 981 endorsement. This is clearly a retrospectively constructed document, intended to impress (by size and length, and royal and aristocratic *signa*). It equally clearly has corrupt elements; for example the split of parts 1 and 3 is very odd, the dating is inconsistent, while some of the witnesses of part 14 cannot be pre-981, the date of the endorsement below it (Gudesteo went to his bishopric ca. 992 and Armentario in 985); and it is clearly partly garbled: the repetitions of the long statement of Pedro's case include errors, omissions and nonsense. However, the text has equally clearly been constructed from something. It includes seven different witness or confirmer lists; it includes four different commitments, in standard form, using standard formulas; it includes a witness statement of evidence, introduced by the standard formula, an Oath of standard type, and an account of an ordeal of standard type, using standard wording. The arrangement of the fourth and fifth witness lists and the last three commitments in a separate appendix to the main charter, bottom right, in itself suggests that these were independently existing elements that were available to the redactor; and the main story, given the nature of its variants, must have been copied from a written text—the wording of the introduction to the story that Pedro was in his monastery under Abbot Severo is a good example of this.[56]

So, this extremely important charter shows us both that at tertiary stage a redactor could use different strategies to create a credible-looking charter—from invoking standard formulas to copying old documents to repeating them; but also that shorter, closer-to-court documents must have existed: someone must have been making notes of different sets of witnesses and someone must have been drawing up the commitments. There is in fact no reason to suppose that such a court case did not happen.

5 Conclusion

The above examples demonstrate that composite texts have been preserved which are essentially composed of primary, close-to-court, records. These have been brought together more or less coherently. Hence CL1 192 is still coherent; T 66 much less so, although since it survives in a late copy it is impossible to

56 See Davies, *Windows on Justice*, 150–151, for a detailed comparison of the three versions.

assess the original compiler's intention; and ACO B.1.11 looks coherent at first sight but is less so on perusal. Together, however, they make it abundantly clear that there was some element of court recording in the ninth and tenth centuries, although it looks as if these records were not intended for long-term preservation. Most of the judicial dispute records that are still preserved are post-court constructions, sometimes using primary records and at others not. This is particularly well demonstrated by Accounts. For example, the tertiary-stage Account that follows has some narrative background on the disputed properties, a brief indication of the court case, a reference to the oath taken, a reference to the subsequent confession and a solid conveyance with a guarantor and sanction:

> Hec est agnicio ueritatis facta sub era MXXXVIa, anno imperii domni nostri Garseani Gomiz comite et Zahbascorta ven Abolhauz sedente in Toro ipsas kalendas marcias.
>
> Denique orta fuit intemptio inter fratres de Domnos Sanctos, domno Uincentio abbate uel suos fratres contra Uela Uelaz pro Uilla de Petro qui est inter flumen Ceia et riuo Aratoi quia sic tenete fratres de Domnos Sanctos ipsa Uilla de Petro de testamento de Ansur maiordomo qui habuit ipsa uilla comparata de domna Salomona in La solidos et tenentes fratres de Domnos Sanctos ipsa uilla in suo iure sic se leuauit[57] Uela Uelaz et sacauit ipsa uilla de iure de fratres et presumpsit ipsa uilla et suas herencias;[58] et deuenerunt inde ad iudicium ante Garsea Gomiz et Zahbascorta in Uilla quam uocitant Alpando et dederunt fratres de Domnos Sanctos suo mandatore Andreas;[59] et petiuit ipse Uela Uelaz pro sua erencia et pro ipsa uilla iudicium et ordinarunt ad comite Garsea Gomiz et Zahbascorta uel omni concilio quia sic dederunt fratres de Domnos Sanctos suos iuratores;[60] et cognouit se Uela Uelaz in ueritate[61] qui duplare uel componere quantum per mendacium presumpserat sane constricti in iudicio; et non habente Uela Uelaz unde componeret ipsa uilla cum sua erentia et tradidit illa uilla per manu fidiatoris Gelmiro presbiter; et firmauerunt ipsa uilla cum sua erencia ad fratres de Domnos Sanctos secundum quod in concilio habuerunt.[62]

57 For this expression, see also CL1 192 and ACO B.1.11, nn. 22 and 51 above.

58 The background.

59 The court case.

60 Reference to the oath.

61 Reference to the confession.

62 The conveyance.

Ita tamen ut si deinceps ausus fuerit talia comittere ipse Uela Uelaz aut filiis uel neptis uel aliquis homo qui hoc destruere uoluerit quomodo pariat uobis uel uoci uestre ipsa hereditate duplata uel quantum uobis fuerit meliorata.[63]

Notum die quod erit ipsas kalendas marcias, era suprascripta.

Garsea Gomiz confirmat; Zabascorta confirmat; Ouecco Telliz confirmat; Fredenando Monniz confirmat; Garsia Fortuniz confirmat; Scape Pepiz confirmat; Argeuado confirmat.

Felix diaconus exarauit.[64]

The difference between close-to court and post-court construction has a bearing on the veracity of the record. Deconstruction of T 66 and ACO B.1.11 made clear that it was easy for corruption to enter copied text, whether intentional or not, just as the corpus of single sheets that might be regarded as 'originals' contains plenty of additions, corrections and mistakes. Corruption is common and does not have to invalidate the content of a text. That is not the same point as bias. Most of the surviving records of judicial disputes were very obviously constructed by or for the principal beneficiary; and even the closer-to-court records must for the most part have been constructed by representatives of the victors. Even where a record was drawn up by order of the *saio* (as we know some were, for example oaths[65]) or by a judge (as a few could have been[66]), there still may have been beneficiary influence. Would that we could unpack the complex of local relationships that influenced the redactors; but we cannot, and there are inevitable unknowns. Plenty of bias is nevertheless clear. Two thirds of retrospective Accounts have a monastic beneficiary and most appear to have been written to record a real or imagined ecclesiastical victory. They are inevitably biased in favour of the ecclesiastical body that produced them. On the other hand, deliberate falsification is a different matter and is much more difficult to spot in dispute records of pre 1000. While one might identify, on palaeographic grounds, a pseudo-original which claims to be a document fashioned much earlier than it actually was, it does not follow that the content of such documents was fabricated or invented. For the most part we have to depend on accumulation of glaring anachronisms to identify the deliberate falsification.

Most of the content of early medieval Iberian dispute records is beyond proof of any kind. Given the opportunities for inadvertent corruption and the

---

63 The sanction.

64 S 356 (1 March 998).

65 For example, the explicit reference to this in Sob 109.

66 For example, OD 31 (991), OD 43 (997).

straightforward bias of many of these texts, we need to retain a healthy scepticism about their contents. That means that in making our assessments we have to deal in terms of greater or lesser credibility, not proof. However, understanding the construction of the records makes it perfectly clear that elements of those texts reflect record-making that was itself part of judicial process and that even the most retrospective of records has a relationship, though complicated, with actual events.

Bibliography

Abbreviations

C: Martínez Díez, Gonzalo, ed. *Colección documental del monasterio de San Pedro de Cardeña*. Burgos: Caja de Ahorros y Monte de Piedad del circulo católico de obreros de Burgos, 1998.

Cel: Andrade Cernadas, José Miguel, with Marta Díaz Tie and Francisco J. Pérez Rodríguez, ed. *O Tombo de Celanova: estudio introductorio, edición e índices (ss.* IX–XII). 2 vols. Santiago de Compostela: Consello da Cultura Galega, 1995.

CL1, CL2, CL3: *Colección documental del archivo de la catedral de León (775–1230)*. Vol. 1 (*775–952*), edited by Emilio Sáez; vol. 2 (*953–985*), edited by Emilio Sáez and Carlos Sáez; vol. 3 (*986–1031*), edited by José Manuel Ruiz Asencio. León: Centro de Estudios e Investigación 'San Isidoro', 1987, 1990, 1987.

OD: Fernández Flórez, José Antonio, and Marta Herrero de la Fuente, eds. *Colección documental del monasterio de Santa María de Otero de las Dueñas*. Vol. 1. León: Centro de Estudios e Investigación 'San Isidoro', 1999.

S: Mínguez Fernández, José María, ed. *Colección diplomática del monasterio de Sahagún (857–1230)*. Vol. 1 (*Siglos* IX *y* X). León: Centro de Estudios e Investigación 'San Isidoro', 1976.

Sob: Loscertales de García de Valdeavellano, Pilar, ed. *Tumbos del monasterio de Sobrado de los Monjes*. 2 vols. Madrid: Dirección General del Patrimonio Artístico y Cultural, Archivo Histórico Nacional, 1976.

T: Sánchez Belda, Luis, ed. *Cartulario de Santo Toribio de Liébana*. Madrid: Archivo Histórico Nacional, 1948.

V: Ruiz Asencio, José Manuel, Irene Ruiz Albi, and Mauricio Herrero Jiménez, eds. *Los becerros gótico y galicano de Valpuesta*. 2 vols. Madrid: Real Academia Española—Instituto Castellano y Leonés de la Lengua, 2010.

Other Primary Sources

García Larragueta, Santos Agustín, ed. *Colección de documentos de la catedral de Oviedo*. Oviedo: Instituto de Estudios Asturianos, 1962.

Miranda Duque, Andrea M., and Xosé Lluis García Arias, eds. *Documentos orixinales de los sieglos IX–X de los archivos del monesteriu de San Pelayo y de la catedral d'Uviéu.* Oviedo: Academia de la Llingua Asturiana, 2011.

Secondary Works

Alfonso, Isabel. "El formato de la información judicial en la alta edad media peninsular." In *Chartes et cartulaires comme instruments de pouvoir. Espagne et Occident chrétien (VIIIe–XIIe siècles)*, edited by Julio Escalona and Hélène Sirantoine, 191–218. Toulouse: Université de Toulouse-Le Mirail, 2013.

Carvajal Castro, Álvaro. "La construcción de la monarquía asturleonesa en la meseta del Duero. Estudio de los procesos de integración territorial (s. IX–XI)." Universidad de Salamanca, Tesis Doctoral, 2013.

Collins, Roger. "Visigothic law and regional custom in disputes in early medieval Spain." In *The Settlement of Disputes in Early Medieval Europe*, edited by Wendy Davies and Paul Fouracre, 85–104. Cambridge: Cambridge University Press, 1986.

Davies, Wendy. "Local priests and the writing of charters in northern Iberia in the tenth century." In *Chartes et cartulaires comme instruments de pouvoir*, edited by Julio Escalona and Hélène Sirantoine, 29–43. Toulouse: Université de Toulouse-Le Mirail, 2013.

Davies, Wendy. *Windows on Justice in Northern Iberia, 800–1000*. Abingdon: Routledge, 2016.

Davies, Wendy. "Regions and micro-regions of scribal practice." In *Polity and Neighbourhood in Early Medieval Europe*, edited by Julio Escalona, Orri Vésteinsson, and Stuart Brookes, 305–324. Turnhout: Brepols, 2019.

García de Valdeavellano, Luis. "Escodriñamiento y otorificación (contribución al estudio de la reivindicación mobiliaria en el derecho español medieval)." In *Centenario de la ley del notariado. Sección primera: estudios históricos*, 2 vols, vol. 2, 125–335. Madrid: Junta de Decanos de Los Colegios Notariales de España, 1965.

Prieto Morera, Agustín. "El proceso en el reino de León a la luz de los diplomas." In *El reino de León en la alta edad media, II: Ordenamiento jurídico del reino*, 381–518. León: Centro de Estudios e Investigación "San Isidoro" (CSIC-CECEL), Caja de Ahorros y Monte de Piedad, Archivo Histórico Diocesano, 1992.

CHAPTER 9

Documentary and Procedural Engineering of Judicial Records in Italy (Ninth-Eleventh Centuries)

François Bougard

1 Introduction

Italian judicial sources,[1] included for the most part in the category of *notitiae iudicati*, are well known thanks to the corpus assembled and edited by Cesare Manaresi (1880–1959) in the 1950s and completed by Raffaello Volpini in 1975. The corpus stretches the period running from the conquest of Italy by Charlemagne (774) to the end of the eleventh century, and covers the geographic space of the kingdom.[2] For the earlier period, they have been edited in the *Codice diplomatico longobardo*, which also covers the duchy of Benevento.[3]

In 1887 the Monumenta Germaniae Historica projected a *Corpus placitorum* concerning the territories that were part of the Carolingian empire. Work was entrusted to Rudolf Hübner (1864–1945), then to Michael Tangl (1861–1921). But the project was never completed, and only preparatory lists—Italy until 1150, and France, Germania and Septimania until 1000—were published based on material already available in print.[4] The work of Manaresi, even if it is based on other scientific premises, is indirectly the fruit of the initial MGH project.

1 I thank Patricia Stirnemann for the translation of this article and the exchange of stimulating remarks that accompanied it. This paper cannot avoid being largely self-referential, but I will try to avoid repetition and incorporate the critical reflections in recent work. A selection of my publications can be found in the bibliography. The abbreviations used in this paper for editions of charters and of legal texts are also listed in the bibliography.

2 Cesare Manaresi, ed., *I Placiti del "Regnum Italiae"*, 3 t. in 5 vols (Roma: Tipografia del Senato, 1955–1960); Raffaello Volpini, "Placiti del *Regnum Italiae* (secc. IX–XI). Primi contributi per un nuovo censimento," in *Contributi dell'Istituto di storia medioevale [dell'Università cattolica del Sacro Cuore]*, ed. Paolo Zerbi, III (Milan: Vita e pensiero, 1975), 245–520.

3 *Codice diplomatico longobardo*, vol. III/1, ed. Carlrichard Brühl (Rome: Istituto storico italiano per il medio evo, 1973); vol. IV/1, ed. Brühl (Rome, 1981) for the duchy of Spoleto; vol. IV/2, ed. Herbert Zielinski (Rome, 2003) for the duchy of Benevento. See François Bougard, "*Tempore barbarici*? La production documentaire publique et privée," in *774. Ipotesi per una transizione*, ed. Stefano Gasparri (Turnhout: Brepols, 2008), 331–351, at 336–337.

4 Rudolf Hübner, "Gerichtsurkunden der fränkischen Zeit" [1891–1893] (Aalen: Scientia, 1971).

 | DOI:10.1163/9789004683006_011

The database *Procesos Judiciales en las sociedades medievales del norte peninsular* (*siglos* IX–XI), which furnishes the pretext for the present volume, is a comparable undertaking.

If Manaresi was able to finish his project, it is because the judicial sources produced in the kingdom of Italy benefitted from a homogeneity that did not exist elsewhere. During the Lombard period, the documentary production for the royal court or that of the dukes of Spoleto and Benevento can be compared to that of the kings and mayors of the Merovingian palace, but Merovingian Gaul had no ducal *placita*.[5] The Carolingian conquest signalled the end of the ducal courts at Spoleto (after 787) and the promotion of hearings presided over either by the king's *missi*, or by the count, the bishop or their representatives, as was the custom north of the Alps. As in the north, this more hierarchical structure depends upon a theoretical calendar: within the county, there were three *placita* each year, which lasted several days and were also the occasion for a gathering of free men. However, the sessions were in reality spread throughout the entire year, because one could request an independent hearing outside the three prescribed sessions, and there were also meetings presided over by the *missi* autonomously or by the king himself on his itinerary.

The Italian homogeneity is less a question of the general institutional framework than of the sources, at least in the way Manaresi considered it. He decided to limit his corpus to the assemblies held by those whom he called "the authorities of the realm". The Italian judicial institution was, in fact, equipped from an early date with professional, lay notaries who were often professional judges. These were the *scabini*, who appear from 780 on, then the *iudices*, who were attached to the palace in Pavia, whose activity can be followed from the closing years of the eighth century, but who became a properly structured group during the reign of Louis II (840–875). In the tenth century, the names *scabinus* and *iudex* become fused into a single title, that of *iudex domini regis/imperatoris*, a way of emphasizing their link with the central authority, even if it is not always sure that their nomination came from above.[6] These are the judges and notaries responsible for the relative uniformity of court records.

Unlike Hübner, Manaresi excluded the cases that pertained to ecclesiastical power when they only settled a dispute between two ecclesiastics, as well as

5 François Bougard, "*Tempore barbarici?*," 336–337; W. Bergmann, "Untersuchungen zu den Gerichtsurkunden der Merowingerzeit," *Archiv für Diplomatik* 22 (1976), 1–186.

6 François Bougard, *La justice dans le royaume d'Italie de la fin du* VIII*e siècle au début du* XI*e siècle* (Rome: École française de Rome, 1995); Andrea Castagnetti, *Note e documenti intorno alla caratterizzazione professionale dei giudici* (*secoli* IX-*inizio* X) (Verona: Università degli studi di Verona, 2008).

the 'feudal' pleas, that is, those pertaining to seigneurial justice.[7] These are limits that would not be fixed today between the 'public' and 'private' spheres. With such a selection of sources, how are we to understand clearly when and why the clergy resorted to secular courts or to episcopal or synodal tribunals for conflicts of similar nature, or during the progression of the settlement of a conflict?[8] In addition, these barriers are even less justified with regard to diplomatic form, because the records associated with different types of courts are virtually indistinguishable from one another.

In order to improve our notions concerning the judicial settlement of disputes, the corpus ought to be enlarged, and encompass assemblies of all kinds, regardless of the presiding authority. The enquiry undertaken for Tuscany, which is by far the most richly documented region in the kingdom, augmented the number of records concerned by almost a third, bringing the total number to nearly 600.[9] To widen the perspective, the dispute records written in Rome and the Papal States should be included, if they pertain to sessions excluded by Manaresi on the grounds that the emperor or his representative was not present.[10] And finally, we should add the records of the Lombard principalities of Salerno and Capua-Benevento, as well as those in Latin from Byzantine Puglia (around 200 documents for these three regions).[11]

As elsewhere, Italian judicial records concern disputes over ownership and property—land, rights, and persons. Conflicts concerning liberty are characteristic of the ninth and early tenth centuries, but rarely surface later.[12] Criminal justice is only indirectly present, appearing essentially when the sanctioning

---

7 Manaresi, 1: Introduction.

8 See Michael W. Heil, "Clerics, Courts, and Legal Culture in Early Medieval Italy, c. 650–c. 900" (PhD dissertation, Columbia University, 2013).

9 François Bougard, "Les plaids pour destinataires toscans," In *Europäische Herrscher und die Toskana im Spiegel der urkundlichen Überlieferung—I sovrani europei e la Toscana nel riflesso della tradizione documentaria (800–1100)*, ed. Antonella Ghignoli, Wolfgang Huschner, and Marie Ulrike Jaros (Leipzig: Eudora, 2016) 165–210.

10 Pierre Toubert, *Les structures du Latium médiéval: le Latium méridional et la Sabine du début du IXe siècle à la fin du XIIe siècle*, 2 vols (Rome: École française de Rome, 1973), 2:1191–313; Chris Wickham, *Roma medievale. Crisi e stabilità di una città, 950–1100* (Rome: Viella, 2013), 442–452; Giovanni Chiodi, "Roma e il diritto romano," in *Roma fra Oriente e Occidente*, Settimane di studio del CISAM 49 (Spoleto: CISAM, 2002), 1149–254; Francesca Santoni, "*Orta fuit intentio et litis calumpnia.* Processi e documenti nella Roma medievale," in *Roma e il suo territorio nel medioevo. Le fonti scritte fra tradizione e innovazione*, ed. Cristina Carbonetti, Santo Lucà, and Maddalena Signorini (Spoleto: CISAM, 2015), 365–394.

11 Paolo Delogu, "La giustizia nell'Italia meridionale longobarda," in *La giustizia nell'alto medioevo (secoli IX–XI)*, 257–308.

12 Antonio Padoa-Schioppa, "Processi di libertà nell'Italia altomedievale" [2011], in idem, *Giustizia medievale italiana. Dal* regnum *ai comuni* (Spoleto: CISAM, 2015), 93–136; Giu-

for murder, theft, or adultery entails consequences affecting possessions and must be documented. But the criminal procedure itself, for which we have very little information except for the Iberian Peninsula and Anglo-Saxon England,[13] was not documented by a written record at that time.

In order that the Italian corpus be fully comparable to that assembled by the PRJ project, we should include all the indirect information pertaining to the exercise of justice and the resolution of conflicts present in the many private charters. But most importantly, it must be remembered that a judicial document speaks to a specific moment, and only one, in the unfolding of the conflict: the moment when the case is submitted to an assembly *ad* (*iustitias*) *deliberandas*. A limitation of our different corpuses, whatever they include, is the extraction of these pieces from their more general documentary context. When consulting these ensembles, and when the sources lend themselves, it is not only a question of hoping to reap a better understanding of the actors and places. The aim is to reconstruct the entire documentary chain engendered by a single affair.

2 What's in a Judicial Dossier?

If one mixes, a bit artificially, the elements belonging to the ninth century and others that are not attested before the eleventh century, a judicial dossier would thus be likely to present all or some of the following elements:

(a) Before the court is assembled, it is not rare for a written complaint to be submitted to the authority. These *querimoniae*, characteristic of the eleventh century, emanate most often from monastic communities, and sometimes from canonical chapters.[14] Usually they take the form of a letter. Some are styled as a lamentation and a call for justice more or less rhetorically couched, others already furnish detailed legal arguments, as in a letter of around 1000 addressed by the abbot of S. Salvatore al Monte Amiata to the local count, Ildebrandus, denouncing the tithing abuses of the bishop of Chiusi. In an effort to convince

seppe Albertoni, "Law and the peasant: rural society and justice in Carolingian Italy," *Early Medieval Europe* 18 (2010), 417–445. For a late example, Manaresi, 3/1: no. 323 (Lucca, 1025).

13 Wendy Davies, *Windows on Justice in Northern Iberia 800–1000* (Abingdon: Routledge, 2016), 235.

14 Paolo Cammarosano, "Carte di querela nell'Italia dei secoli X–XIII," *Frühmittelalterliche Studien* 36 (2002), 397–402; Bougard, *La justice*, 241–242; François Bougard, "*Falsum falsorum judicum consilium*: l'écrit et la justice en Italie centro-septentrionale au XIe siècle," *Bibliothèque de l'École des chartes* 155 (1997), 299–314.

the count to intervene, the abbot of this royal monastery invokes pontifical privileges and imperial diplomas carefully reminding of the clauses mentioning spiritual and pecuniary sanction, as well as Lombard and Frankish legislation.[15] Likewise, in 1026–1027, a complaint addressed by the abbey of Farfa to Conrad II is studded with a series of legal axioms in praise of written contracts.[16] The grievances can also take the form of lists in *brevia*, like the "polyptych of misdeeds" drawn up around 1040 by the canons of Reggio Emilia in support of a complaint against the vassals of the marquis of Canossa.[17] In this last case, one imagines that the document was submitted in support of an oral declaration, along with the pieces justifying the rights of the canons over the lands and prerogatives that had been usurped. Such lists could also be drawn up at the suggestion of the authority, when a change in regime is marked by an initiative meant to show the new prince's commitment to his judicial duties. Such was the case in 1014 when Henry II was crowned emperor, according to the testimony of Abbot Hugh of Farfa.[18]

Certain abbots used other means. The abbot of S. Antimo in Val di Starcia, who brought suit in the same affair as the abbot of Monte Amiata, resorted to a more prosaic and costly procedure. According to the terms of a settlement made in 1005 with the same count Ildebrandus, he surrendered by *libellum* half of a monastery and its appurtenant assets, amongst which a castle, and in exchange the count was to escort the abbot and his successors on horseback in the dioceses of Florence, Lucca and Pistoia and provide assistance when necessary before the royal *curia*.[19] The formulation of the terms is general, without

15 Wilhelm Kurze, ed., *Codex diplomaticus Amiatinus*, 2 vols (Tübingen, Max Niemeyer, 1974–1982), 1: no. 225; Armando Petrucci et al., eds., *Lettere originali del Medioevo latino (VII–XI sec.)*, 1. *Italia* (Pisa: Scuola Normale Superiore, 2004), 33–47 (Ernesto Stagni). François Bougard, "Jugement divin, excommunication, anathème et malédiction: la sanction spirituelle dans les sources diplomatiques," in *Exclure de la communauté chrétienne: Sens et pratiques sociales de l'anathème et de l'excommunication*, ed. Geneviève Büher-Thierry and Stéphane Gioanni (Turnhout: Brepols, 2015), 215–238, at 215–216.

16 Ugo Balzani, ed., *Il Chronicon Farfense di Gregorio di Catino*, 2 vols (Rome: Istituto storico italiano per il medio evo, 1903), 1:73–77. Bougard, *"Falsum falsorum judicum consilium,"* 310–311.

17 Gloria Casagrande, "Il ritrovamento del testo completo del 'polittico delle malefatte', anno ca. 1040," in *Reggiolo medievale. Atti e memorie del Convegno di studi matildici, Reggiolo, 9 aprile 1978*, ed. Gino Badini (Reggio Emilia: G. Bizzocchi, 1979), 101–132.

18 Balzani, *Chronicon Farfense*, 1:68; Bougard, *"Falsum falsorum judicum consilium,"* 306.

19 Lucca, archivio arcivescovile, ++ I 72, printed at Simone Collavini, "I Conti Aldobrandeschi e la Valdinievole. Una nota sulla situazione politica in Tuscia nei primi anni del secolo XI," in Atti del convegno *Signori e feudatari nella Valdinievole dal X al XII secolo* (Buggiano: Comune di Buggiano, 1992), 101–127, at 123–125; see Simone Collavini, Honorabilis domus

any allusion to the misdeeds of the bishop of Chiusi, but takes all its weight from the context. The drawing up of a contract of this type, like the aforesaid *querimoniae*, was the province of a certain elite, since it presupposed a cultural refinement and economic foundation not within everyone's reach, as well as direct access to the recipient.

(b) When the affair is of general importance, an inventory of possessions might also be drawn in advance of the hearings. This is the rationale behind certain inventories and lists, like those drawn up at Lucca for Bishop Petrus II (896–936) at the beginning of his government, some months before the convocation of a judicial assembly of great importance, of which more will be said later.[20]

(c) If the authority solicited was the prince, he might entrust the affair to his *missi* either orally or with a written mandate (*indiculum, iussio*), which also assured safe conduct while travelling in the designated region. The order could be generic, if the mission covered more than a single dispute. In the few cases that have come down to us, the text of the mandate may be preserved separately or copied at the beginning of the corresponding record.[21]

(d) If the judicial authority decided to treat a complaint and convoked an assembly to rule on it, at least one of the two parties may have had to be summoned if they had not previously reached an agreement to appear together before the judges. This entailed the sending of letter(s) (*epistolae*) which were delivered by the *missi*. This was the case especially in the tenth century, when the procedure of *investitura salva querela* developed, meant to establish the plaintiff's rights for an asset after the absence of the defendant is recorded.[22]

(e) The parties involved had to prepare the hearing as well as possible. When property titles, which usually constitute sufficient argument, were lacking, one had to fall back on witnesses. Either the witnesses were designated by the respective parties, or they were arbitrarily selected by the judges in the context of an *inquisitio*, which proliferated in the ninth century.[23] In either case, it was essential for the success of the plaintiff or the defendant that the testi-

et spetiosissimus comitatus. *Gli Aldobrandeschi da "conti" a "principi territoriali" (secoli IX–XIII)* (Pisa: Edizioni ETS, 1988), 101; Amleto Spicciani, *Protofeudalesimo. Concessioni livellarie, impegni militari non vassallatici e castelli (secoli X–XI)* (Pisa: Edizioni ETS, 2001), 155–157.

20 See n. 56 below.

21 Bougard, *La justice*, 185.

22 See below, "In search of legal certainty," b.

23 Bougard, *La justice*, 194–203.

monies corroborate his case and not contradict each other. The prospective witnesses could thus be solicited by a written engagement, drawn up by a notary, stating what they would say under oath. We have four examples from the county of Piacenza, dating from the years 823 to 915.[24] They can be considered the precursors of the agreements *de placito et bisonnio*, which were common in Tuscany in the eleventh century, in a very different social context, where judicial assistance was reinforced by military support.[25]

(f) Either of the parties might not have an *advocatus*, which prevented the trial from being held. He had then to be appointed, which required the drawing up of a special document, of which there are a few examples in the eleventh century. There even exists a proper formula.[26]

(g) The inquest procedure (*inquisitio*), carried out by the imperial *missi*, was meant to record the testimony in written form. **(h)** And it is not rare that investigators also made an inventory of all or part of the assets of the plaintiff.[27]

(i) The judicial assembly, however, usually produced only one record, which came at the conclusion: a *notitia iudicati*, written in indirect discourse in the kingdom; a *memoratorium* often beginning in direct discourse and in the name of the winning party in Roman territory and, until the end of the tenth century, in the southern Lombard principalities. Court records were written when the proceedings concluded with a judgment, or more rarely with a *convenientia* or a 'friendly' *pactuicio* or *pactum* pronounced before the judges.[28] The content of previous hearings was sometimes recalled, which allows us to follow the geographic and judicial itinerary of the affair: from its opening before a

---

24 François Bougard, "L'église de Varsi et son chartrier: pouvoirs, territoires, communauté, VIIIe–Xe siècle," in *La fabrique des sociétés médiévales méditerranéennes. Les Moyen Âges de François Menant*, ed. Diane Chamboduc de Saint-Pulgent and Marie Dejoux (Paris: Publications de la Sorbonne, 2018), 421–431.

25 Piero Brancoli Busdraghi, "Patti di assistenza giuridica e militare in Toscana fra XI e XII secolo," in *Nobiltà e ceti dirigenti in Toscana nei secoli XI–XIII: strutture e concetti* (Monte Oriolo: F. Papafava, 1982), 29–55; Amleto Spicciani, "Forme giuridiche e condizioni reali nei rapporti tra il vescovo di Lucca e signori laici (secolo XI)" [1996], in *Protofeudalesimo*, 81–139.

26 *Manaresi*, 3: no. 338 (near Tortona, 1035); Volpini, no. 36 (Florence, 1055). Formula: MGH LL 4, 650–651 (Lomello, 1018). Bougard, *La justice*, 268.

27 Bougard, *La justice*, 378–388.

28 Volpini, 447–451 = *ChLA*^{2} LXVIII 20 (county of Piacenza, 832); Manaresi, 1: no. 28 (Spoleto, 814); no. 97 = *ChLA*^{2} LXVI 30 (county of Piacenza, 891 or 890); Manaresi, 2/1: no. 250 (Gaeta, 999); 3/2: 480–481 (Gesino, 1051: *sponsio et perdonatio*). For *amicae pactuiciones* outside the court, or so it seems, see Chris Wickham, "Land disputes and their social framework" [1986], in idem, *Land & Power. Studies in Italian and European Social History, 400–1200* (London: British School at Rome, 1994), 229–256, at 252–253.

first assembly until its conclusion, including a visit to the disputed locations. The whole process could involve three and sometimes four successive hearings.

However, sometimes the account was truncated by the failure of one of the parties to appear, and his absence was recorded in writing, as in a session presided over by the duke of Spoleto in 813, where the abbot of Farfa waited in vain until the "third hearing".[29]

It could also happen that the record was interrupted at an intermediary stage in the procedure, for example: (1) after a commitment, with presentation of *wadia*, to appear again with written titles, witnesses, guarantors or a champion for a duel;[30] (2) after the taking of the witnesses' declarations, especially in the *inquisitio* procedure;[31] (3) after the taking of an oath;[32] (4) to record the stonewalling of one of the parties who remained obstinately silent;[33] (5) to record the powerlessness of the judges, who suspended the hearing after waiting for one of the two parties present at the first hearing to reappear, and whose abstention allowed that party to avoid recognizing its defeat or having to engage in a duel;[34] (6) as an indication of the doubts of the judges themselves, who refused to take a decision, as in the famous *placitum* held in Garfagnolo (Reggio Emilia) in 1098.[35] An exceptional case took place in Rome in 829. The imperial *missi* pronounced in favour of the abbey of Farfa against the Church of Rome con-

29 Manaresi, 1: no. 27: *expectavit ipse abbas secondo et tertio placito.*

30 Witnesses: Manaresi, 1: no. 135 (Parma, 935). Oath for guarantors: Manaresi, 2/2: no. 220 (near Vicenza, 995). Battle: *Placiti*, 2/2: no. 274 (near Arezzo, 1010). On the oath for the guarantors and on the duel, Bougard, *La justice*, 331–339; François Bougard, "Prêter serment en justice dans le royaume d'Italie, VIIIe-XIe siècle," in *Oralité et lien social au Moyen Âge (Occident, Byzance, Islam)*, ed. Marie-France Auzépy and Guillaume Saint-Guillain (Paris: ACHCByz, 2008), 327–339; François Bougard, "Rationalité et irrationalité des procédures autour de l'an mil: le duel judiciaire en Italie," In *La justice en l'an mil* (Paris: La Documentation française, 2003), 93–122.

31 Examples even at the end of the tenth and beginning of the eleventh century: Manaresi, 2:669–675.

32 Manaresi, 2:674–675 (in Tuscany, 1008); 3/2: 447–449 (Flesso, 1046–1047). In Lucca in 1077, the formula *Et hoc modo finita est lis* follows the taking of a sermon, but without allowing to determine the outcome of the decision (Manaresi, 3/2:451–452).

33 Manaresi, 1: no. 133 (Pavia, 927): the defendant categorically refused to respond to the plaintiff and judges, and left the assembly.

34 Manaresi, 1: no. 48 (Milan, 844) = *ChLA*² XCIV 33; Manaresi, 1: no. 135 (Parma, 935); Marta Calleri, ed. *Codice diplomatico del monastero di Santo Stefano di Genova, I*, (Genova: Società ligure di storia patria, 2009), no. 20 (Genova, 1006).

35 Manaresi, 3/2: no. 478 = MGH DD MT, 482–484. See Francesca Santoni, "Fra *lex* e *pugna*: il placito di Garfagnolo (1098)," *Scrineum Rivista* 2 (2004), 5–45, at https://oajournals.fupress.net/index.php/scrineum/article/view/8758/8756 (accessed 10 January 2019).

cerning five *curtes*. But the pope stopped the trial, declaring that he "did not believe" in the judgment so long as the affair had not been treated before the emperor.[36]

Consequently, the same affair treated by the same tribunal is likely to produce several records until it is finally resolved; sometimes it ends with the absence of a ruling, in extreme cases where the losing party refuses to recognize that it has lost. At other times, the ruling in the dispute may be split according to the points treated. A record from 822 in Lucca resolves a land dispute substantively, designating a victor, then puts off until a later date the taking of the oath related to a possible indemnification for the use of land during the time elapsed between the submission of the complaint and the conjoining of justice.[37] The hearing where the oaths were to be taken would have had little chance of being documented because it did not establish rights over the land.

(j) In the case of an *inquisitio*, the decision was theoretically taken by the royal authority, if the entire procedure had not been delegated to its representatives. The testimonies of witnesses were then sent to the sovereign, who pronounced his sentence in a diploma, as was customary north of the Alps.[38]

(k) Lastly, the written record of the rights of the victor did not automatically close the conflict. It only inaugurated a new legal relation between the parties—but that is what made it essential. The execution of the sentence might engender the establishment of a *breve* for the local investiture of the property, and this might happen years later, if the loser was obstructive.[39] Some sought out the additional authority of a diploma in order to confirm what they had obtained and reinforce the authority of the *notitia pro securitate*.[40] Others reignited the controversy through an appeal, at their risk and peril.[41]

---

36 Manaresi, 1: no. 38.

37 Volpini, no. 2 = *ChLA*² LXXV 8.

38 MGH DD L I 176, for Piacenza; MGH DD Lo I 25, for Cremona; 35, for San Salvatore of Brescia; 157, for Como; etc.

39 Manaresi, 1:566–568 (Ostiglia, 827); see Andrea Castagnetti and Antonio Ciaralli, *Falsari a Nonantola. I placiti di Ostiglia (820–827) e le donazioni di Nogara (910–911)* (Spoleto: CISAM, 2011), 22–33. Other examples: Volpini, 458–459 (Ravenna, 1037); Manaresi, 3/2:484–486 (near Ferrara, 1067).

40 MGH DD L I 298: confirmation for S. Vincenzo al Volturno of four *iudicata* in which the monastery was opposed by the *servi* in the valley of *Trita*; MGH DD L II 31: confirmation for Bobbio of several properties gained through judicial cases.

41 Manaresi 1: no. 26 = *ChLA*² LXXIII 50 (Lucca, 813: reopening of a trial against the priest Alpulus, excommunicated in 803, but who then brought the affair before Adalhard of Corbie, *missus* of Charlemagne in Italy). Manaresi, 1: no. 112 (Milan, 901: reopening of an affair adjudged the previous year, which opposed the tax authorities and several men whose liberty was contested). See also Garfagnolo, 1098 (n. 35 above).

Yet others persevered until a compromise settlement was obtained outside the courts, in the form of a property transaction or a waiver of the financial compensation decided upon by the judges against a promise to respect the decision that had barely been pronounced.[42] The historian is fortunate when the corresponding documents state what motivated them. But many common contracts (donations, sales, exchanges, rentals, divisions) were drawn up in response to situations of this kind about which we know nothing. But here we leave the strictly judicial terrain for the more general arena of the 'settlement of conflicts'.

3 Standardization and Diversity of the Records

The foregoing overview illustrates the wide variety of documentation linked with the exercise of justice, especially in the kingdom of Italy, where the *notitia* can be surrounded by many less formal pieces, for the most part *brevia*.[43] However, it must be admitted that often the treatment of a conflict by an assembly probably gave rise to the writing of a single document. It would therefore be abusive to think that an 'ideal-type' can be drawn from that overview, which, moreover, pays little attention to changes in time.

The Italian originality resides above all in the formal transformation of the court record as a documentary genre. Until the second half of the ninth century, court records followed a schema shared with the rest of Carolingian Europe.

42 Examples: CDL II 168 = *ChLA* XXIX 871 (Ceneda, 762: restitution of *omnes res vel pecunia* first attributed to the plaintiff by the ducal court); CDL V 16 and 38 (Rieti, 751 and 764; see Marios Costambeys, "Disputes and courts in Lombard and Carolingian central Italy," *Early Medieval Europe* 15 [2007], 265–289); Manaresi, 3/2:486–488 (Rovereto, 1067), partial payment of the sum duc for the *rupina* of one hundred fifty bulls. See also, in 877, the *amica pactuicio* by virtue of which the son of Sisenandus receives a horse and one hundred *solidi* from S. Clemente a Casauria in exchange for his renunciation of all action concerning the properties that had been confiscated from his father as a result of a trial for adultery: Laurent Feller, *Les Abruzzes médiévales. Territoire, économie et société en Italie centrale du IXe au XIIe siècle* (Rome: École française de Rome, 1998), 671.

43 Attilio Bartoli Langeli, "Sui 'brevi' italiani altomedievali," *Bullettino dell'Istituto storico italiano per il medio evo* 105 (2003), 1–23; Giovanna Nicolaj, *Lezioni di diplomatica generale, I. Istituzioni* (Rome: Bulzoni, 2007), 180; Michele Ansani, "Appunti sui *brevia* di XI e XII secolo," *Scrineum Rivista* 4 (2006–2007), 107–152, at https://oajournals.fupress.net/index.php/scrineum/article/view/8771/8769 (accessed 1 September 2017); Michele Ansani, Caritatis negocia *e fabbriche di falsi. Strategie, imposture, dispure documentarie a Pavia fra XI e XII secolo* (Rome: Istituto storico italiano per il medio evo, 2011), 40–53.

The presentation of the tribunal is followed by the submission of the complaint, then by an exchange in direct discourse between the plaintiff and the defendant (*altercatio*), by the search for and administration of the proof, by the admission of defeat by the losing party, and, finally, by the order given by the president to record in writing the content of the debates and the procedures. Up to this point, the *notitiae iudicati* can be analysed in the same way as elsewhere, not only for matters concerning procedures and proofs, but also for everything that concerns the exchange of responses between parties, directly or through the *advocati*, especially in disputes where large landowners oppose peasants whose status is contested.[44]

In the years 870–890, new ways of recording judicial sessions began to take effect under the impetus of judges and notaries in Pavia, encouraged by the knowledge and experience they had gained in the company of the *missi* during their judicial rounds in the kingdom.[45] The formal palette of the *notitiae iudicati* widened over time, until the closing years of the eleventh century, but it leaves less and less space for an explanation of the origin and unfolding of the conflicts, favouring instead the choice between standardized solutions with immediately recognizable forms, easy to produce serially with minor adaptations (the names of the parties, descriptions of the property) and, consequently, easy to group in a corpus. For the period between the mid-tenth century and 1100, the number of records written according to ancient criteria becomes a minority.

The downside of such a documentary innovation is a considerable impoverishment of the information concerning the nature of conflicts, which notaries were no longer meant to record. To have access to this, the investigation must be widened to include information from other sources.[46] Otherwise, comparison with other corpuses of judicial records can henceforth lead only to an impasse,

44 See n. 12 above; Ross Balzaretti, "Spoken narratives in ninth-century Milanese court records," in *Narrative and History in the early Medieval West*, ed. Elizabeth M. Tyler and Balzaretti (Turnhout: Brepols, 2006), 11–37; Costambeys, "Disputes and courts;" Aneta Pieniądz, "Literacy and the legal culture of the early Middle Ages. Old research—new questions," in *Právní kultura ve středověku*, Colloquia mediaevalia Pragensia 17, ed. Martin Nodl and Piotr Węcowski (Prague: Filosofia, 2016), 13–25 (on Manaresi, 1: no. 71, Lucca 870 = *ChLA*² LXXXII 42).

45 See below, "In search of legal certainty".

46 As noted by Marios Costambeys, *Power and Patronage in Early Medieval Italy. Local Society, Italian Politics and the Abbey of Farfa, c. 700–900* (Cambridge: Cambridge University Press, 2007), 110–131; Marios Costambeys, "Disputes and documents in early medieval Italy," in *Making Early Medieval Societies. Conflict and Belonging in the Latin West*, ed. Kate Cooper and Conrad Leyser (Cambridge: Cambridge University Press, 2016), 125–154.

given the abyss that separates Italy from the rest of Europe. And this black hole is all the more profound in that French scriptoria, for example, develop at the same moment what are called 'narrative' *notitiae*, which distance themselves from the relative sobriety of the Carolingian schema, and wax volubly on all aspects of the disputes. The inflation of the 'monastic trial records', overblown with adjectives, exclamations, psychological and moral considerations, and maledictions, is a feature of writing style, not an institutionalized form, as has often been thought. It is also an excellent indication of the fact that the lands north of the Alps had not adopted the notarial system put into place in the ninth century. The Carolingian reform, which ought to have applied to the entire empire, only took hold in places where the cultural terrain was favourable, and not in those where the mastery of documentary writing remained, for lack of anything better, in the hands of the clergy.[47] Confirmation of this is found in the fact that even in Italy, but outside the kingdom, certain records written by ecclesiastical scribes adopt the same tone and the same vocabulary as those in the north.[48]

The foregoing affirmation should be nuanced, lest it be considered too straightforward. The Po valley and Tuscany are not alone in the movement that comes to favour the documentation of the resolution of a conflict rather than the stages by which one arrives at the ruling. The phenomenon is also seen in Sabina in the eleventh century, with the many *refutationes* in favour of the abbey of Farfa, behind which one can often implicitly imagine the existence of a dispute and an assembly dealing with it, independently of knowledge of whether it was presided over by the count, by the abbot, or by his provost and whether or not in the presence of professional judges.[49] We see it also in France, notably at Cluny, with the *notitiae werpitionis* which appear at the beginning of the tenth century and are related to property, to disputes (*querelae*), and to *malae consuetudines*. Sometimes they look like records of hearings before a public authority and in which it is simply said that the defendant recognizes the rights of the abbot; sometimes they describe a *werpitio*

47 François Bougard, "Notaires d'élite, notaires de l'élite dans le royaume d'Italie," In *La culture au haut Moyen Âge: une question d'élites?*, ed. François Bougard, Régine Le Jan, and Rosamond McKitterick (Turnhout: Brepols, 2009), 438–460; Ronald G. Witt, *The Two Latin Cultures and the Foundation of Renaissance Humanism in Medieval Italy* (Cambridge: Cambridge University Press, 2012), 61–66.

48 E.g. Manaresi, 2/2: no. 285 (a. 1014); François Bougard, "Écrire le procès: le compte rendu judiciaire entre VIIIe et XIe siècle," *Médiévales* 56 (printemps 2009), 23–40, at 37.

49 Toubert, *Les structures du Latium médiéval*, 1274–313; Chris Wickham, "Justice in the kingdom of Italy in the eleventh century," in *La giustizia nell'alto medioevo (secoli IX–XI)*, 179–250, at 222–234.

('déguerpissement', public renunciation of rights or land) before the abbot; in yet others, the *werpitio* is written in direct discourse, in the name of those who renounce property, without any further explanation or simply declaring an end to the dispute. In the last case, it is impossible to know if the settlement comes after one or several judicial hearings have been held, or whether it is a comparable 'private' transaction, as was the case of the *refutatio* made by the count of Sabina in favour of Farfa in 998 in compensation for the abusive occupation of a castle, and in order to avoid a *reclamatio* by the abbot to the emperor.[50]

The *werpitio* certainly spreads further than the small Cluniac world.[51] But the correspondences between the Cluniac sources and those of Farfa make one think that the two abbeys, which were in close contact, shared documentary knowledge. More generally, it is a form of documentation that fits well with the development of monastic seigneurial justice, which is as exceptional in Italy as it is common in the north.

4 Controlling the Legal Implications of the Written Document

North of the Alps, the tendency in Cluny to erase the conflict could also sit alongside the development of narrative records that give an exaggerated account. In the kingdom of Italy, the apparent simplification is accompanied by a very close attention given to documentary writing and its potential. Efforts are made to control the production of charters, and especially their uses in potential litigation.

This control over written documents, which characterizes the ninth century, stems from the concern on the part of large landholders to guarantee free disposition of their properties. In the areas under Lombard law, which inherited the Roman legal tradition, this was already the purpose of the long-term leases, which were limited to 29 years; after 30 years, ownership devolved on the tenant.[52] Moreover, it is not rare that bishops and abbots obtained from the king annulation of the documents by which their predecessors had alien-

50 The abbot, for his part, regularized the situation by drawing up a contract in the name of the count for the castle. The details of the affair are described by Abbot Hugh: Balzani, *Chronicon Farfense*, 1:74.

51 Paul Ourliac, "La tradition romaine dans les actes toulousains des Xe et XIe siècles," *Revue historique de droit français et étranger* 60 (1982), 577–588, at 583–584 (sur la base des actes de l'abbaye de Lézat).

52 Grimoald 4, Liutprand 54, Aistolf 18 (MGH Fontes iuris 2:75, 106, 168–169).

ated property, especially by rental or exchange. The corresponding diplomas, which stretch from the mid-ninth to the mid-eleventh century, are sufficiently numerous to show the universality of the procedure.[53] These reclamations, often justified by criticisms of bad or iniquitous management by the preceding bishop or abbot in charge, was a convenient way for prelates who had just arrived to take control of an often dispersed patrimony; furthermore, the rentals had often been sub-let by the tenants, thus running a risk that the existence of the eminent owner be forgotten.

Cancellation allowed the plaintiff to terminate *de facto* situations, to 'reactivate' his rights, to personalize the contractual relation between contemporaries rather than with generations that had sometimes disappeared. This applied not only to the contracting parties, but also to the witnesses whose presence would be required in case of dispute. If the operation proceeded without incident, the lease was renewed immediately, once the former lease was returned. One has to imagine a procession of tenants at the episcopal palace, at the monastery, or in the rural estates belonging to them. In 874 the bishop of Volterra told Louis II how much he deplored the *invasiones atque demenerationes* to which his church had been subjected *sub occasione libellorum*. The emperor declared null and void all that had been established in the name of the preceding bishop—who, it is carefully noted, had been weakened by sickness—in the form of donation, provisional contract, *libellum* or exchange, with the obligation of the holders of *libelli* to return them to the church.[54]

But the general calling into question of contracts can also unfold in a tenser atmosphere. In 852 Bishop Jeremias of Lucca, who had barely been consecrated, demanded that all *libelli* previous to his installation be nullified. But in the spring of the following year, a court presided over by the *missi* had to be convened in order to force a recalcitrant tenant accused of poor maintenance of his rental property to make restitution. The *missi* required the imperial diploma for the nullification of the contracts be "recited" and reproduced in the record of the court case.[55]

At the end of the century, another bishop of Lucca, Petrus II (896–932), used another strategy. He began his tenure by making an inventory of all the property belonging to his church. He also drew up a list of properties that had been ceded by *libellum* (*cartulae ad censum persolvendum*), and those ceded

53 François Bougard, "Actes privés et transferts patrimoniaux en Italie centro-septentrionale (VIIIe-Xe siècle)," *Mélanges de l'École française de Rome—Moyen Âge* 111 (1999), 539–562, at 553–557.

54 MGH DD L II 69.

55 Manaresi, 1: no. 57 = *ChLA*[2] LXXX 26.

as benefice (*feora*). Then in 897 he began court proceedings against the holders of *libelli* (about 100 people), with a hearing before the imperial *missi*, the marquis of Tuscany and several other bishops. Already convoked several times, the defendants did not appear that time either, which allowed the bishop to obtain an investiture *salva querimonia* for all of the property. Without resolving the case as to the substance, since this type of investiture does not rule on the rights that can be invoked against it, the judges gave Petrus II the legal advantage which allowed him to renegotiate in a stronger position with the tenants.[56]

The examples cited show that among the 'risky' documents, the *libelli* are those that are targeted most often. Italy alone uses these instruments, and their very existence did not fail to surprise, indeed horrify, men coming from other legal worlds. Among them, men like Gerbert of Aurillac spearheaded the battle, and his letter sent to Otto II in 983, shortly after he became abbot of Bobbio, is famous: the *libelli*, according to him, lead to an alienation of property equivalent to a sale and are the road to ruin for the church's patrimony.[57] Simone Collavini has suggested that it is also possible that those who were in charge of fiscal lands, who were furthermore protected by a prescription of 60 years,[58] carefully refrained from using charters in day-to-day management, preferring to retain the northern practice of oral land concessions, thus avoiding the worries faced by bishops, canons and abbots.[59] This was probably one of the rationales behind the success of the *inquisitio* in the ninth century, which can be considered as a measure that complements the cancellation of leases. By placing the property of certain churches and monasteries under the legal

56 Manaresi, 1: no. 102 = *ChLA*² LXXXVI 45; Paolo Tomei, "Un nuovo 'polittico' lucchese del IX secolo: il *breve de multis pensionibus*," *Studi medievali* ser. 3ª, 53 (2012), 567–602.

57 Gerbert d'Aurillac, *Correspondance*, ed. and tr. Pierre Riché and Jean-Pierre-Callu, 2 vols (Paris: Les Belles lettres, 1993), 1:4: *Nescio quibus codicibus, quos libellos dicunt, totum sanctuarium Dei venundatum est.* Cinzio Violante, "Fluidità del feudalesimo nel regno italico (secoli X e XI). Alternanze e compenetrazioni di forme giuridiche nelle concessioni di terre ecclesiastiche a laici," *Annali dell'Istituto storico italo-germanico in Trento* 21 (1995), 11–39.

58 Liutprand 78, Ratchis 6 (MGH Fontes iuris 2:114–115, 156).

59 Simone Collavini and Paolo Tomei, "Beni fiscali e 'scritturazione'. Nuove proposte sui contesti di rilascio e falsificazione di D. OIII. 269 per il monastero di S. Ponziano di Lucca," in *Originale–Fälschungen–Kopien. Kaiser- und Königsurkunden für Empfänger in Deutschland und Italien (9.–11. Jahrhundert) und ihre Nachwirkungen im Hoch- und Spätmittelalter (bis ca. 1500) / Originali—falsi–copie. Documenti imperiali e regi per destinatari tedeschi e italiani (secc. IX–XI) e i loro effetti nel Medioevo e nella prima età moderna (fino al 1500 circa)*, ed. Nicolangelo D'Acunto, Wolfgang Huschner, and Sebastian Roebert (Leipzig-Karlsruhe: Eudora, 2017), 205–216.

regime reserved for fiscal lands, the litigation procedure that applied to them consisted of a hearing of *idonei et credentes homines*,[60] rather than the examination of written titles.

5 In Search of Legal Certainty: New Formulas, New Procedures

The distrust of written forms of concession was coupled with the search for appropriate solutions for avoiding, as much as possible, situations of judicial uncertainty, which led to an inflation of written documents in the judicial context. Care was taken to avoid imprecision in matters of possession by increasing recourse to the notarial act and its presentation before the judges. Even before the written document was considered as a proof in the full sense, its creative power for rights was such that it was simultaneously sought out and feared by all. This was the rationale which affected the *notitiae iudicati* at the end of the ninth and in the tenth century, with the creation of new formulas: (a) *investitura salva querela* (the investiture of contested properties in favour of the plaintiff, in the absence of the defendant); (b) *finis intentionis* (a claim to the possession of a property, rights, or a person, with a demand for confirmation); (c) *ostensio cartae* (the presentation of a charter before judges with a demand for confirmation of its content, the document being summarized or, more often, copied out in full in the *notitia*); and, from the late tenth century, (d) *notitia de banno*, which declares the placement of the property under the protection of the royal or imperial *bannum*, at the initiative of the judges. These innovations have been analysed frequently since the nineteenth century, without completely exhausting the subject, which is why I return to it once again.[61]

60 See MGH DD L II 69, pour l'église de Volterra (874): *Ubicunque* [...] *ecclesiae oeconomis necessarium visum fuerit, ita de rebus seu familiis episcopii ipsius tamquam de dominicatis rebus nostris per idoneos et dredentes homines inquisitionem fieri iubemus.*

61 See, e.g., Guido Mengozzi, *Ricerche sull'attività della scuola di Pavia nell'alto medio evo* (Pavia: Tipografia Cooperativa, 1924); Antonio Padoa-Schioppa, "Aspetti della giustizia milanese dal X al XII secolo" [1989], in idem, *Giustizia medievale italiana*, 137–227; Antonio Padoa-Schioppa, "La scuola di Pavia. Alle fonti della nuova scienza giuridica europea," in *Almum Studium Papiense. Storia dell'Università di Pavia*, vol. 1 *Dalle origini all'età spagnola*, ed. Dario Mantovani, 2 tomes (Pavia: Università di Pavia, 2012), 1:143–164; Bougard, *La justice*, 307–331; Giovanna Nicolaj, "Formulari e nuovo formalismo nei processi del *regnum Italiae*" [1997], in *Storie di documenti, storie di libri: quarant'anni di studi, ricerche e vagabondaggi nell'età antica e medievale* (Dietikon-Zurich: Urs Graf, 2013), 230–246; Michele Ansani, "I giudici palatini, le carte, le leggi. Pratiche documentarie e documentazione di placito sullo scorcio del secolo IX," in *Almum Studium Papiense*, ed. Mantovani, 1:171–186.

(a) As I said earlier, the initiative for these modifications came from the judges and notaries in Pavia. It is thus of more than passing interest that the investiture *salva querela* made one of its first appearances at a trial in 897 very carefully prepared by Petrus II of Lucca, when we know that the new bishop was trained in Pavia, where he had acquired a mastery of chancery writing practices.[62] The investiture *salva querela* brings something truly new, since it resolved the aporia created by the obstinate default of the defendant. With this procedure all rights to a given property could momentarily be attributed to a plaintiff, leaving it up to the absent defendant to produce contradicting evidence at a later date.[63] In the reverse situation the risk was great that the provisional investiture would become definitive. In Roman lands, where it is attested from around the year 1000, the investiture *salva querela* could also give rise to an exegesis and application based on the examination of Justinian law.[64]

(b) As for the *finis intentionis* and the *ostensio cartae*, their elaboration was interrelated to the capitulary promulgated at Pavia by Wido of Spoleto in 891.[65] One of the two articles that the text devotes to the *cartae* is copied word for word from the clause of a diploma of Charles the Fat addressed to several churches in the kingdom (Verona, Arezzo, Cremona, Bergamo) in 882.[66] It provides for the obligation of a court appearance for those who had sold or given away a property without, "notoriously", having the *vestitura legitima*, thus making the recipient of the document of sale or donation run the risk of a lawsuit when he took possession of the property in question (*res invadere*, understood here without the pejorative connotation that the translation 'usurper' gives to it).[67] The formula for private charters already provides that the *auctor cartulae*, unless explicitly stated to the contrary, agrees to "defend" the document if its beneficiary is faced with any dispute. Here the measure is reinforced by soliciting from the *auctor cartulae* that he publicly "claim" the property (*eas* [*res*] *vendicet*), so as not to weigh down the new owner with the possibility of his ownership being called into question.

62 Tomei, "Un nuovo 'polittico' lucchese," 579.

63 An example of reinvestiture after a judgment on the legal foundation: Manaresi, 1: no. 127 (Lucca, 915).

64 Chiodi, "Roma e il diritto romano," 1190–201.

65 MGH Capit. 2, no. 224; Bougard, *La justice*, 312–314; Ansani, "I giudici palatini".

66 MGH DD K III 49–52.

67 MGH Capit. 2, no. 224, cap. 5 (p. 108): *De cartis vero interdicimus nemini alienas res praesumtive invadere occasione cartulae ab eo factae, qui vestituram legitimam non habens dinoscitur invasisse. Sed si quis adquisitor extiterit, non ante invadere alienas res, ecclesiae vel cuiuspiam liberi hominis, praesumat, antequam auctor cartulae legali iudiciali diffinitione eas vendicet, et tunc demum cui vult liberam tradendi habeat facultatem.*

By fixing this procedure within the framework of a *legalis et iudicialis diffinitio*, the property holder is assured of all required publicity. Silence is consent: those who, knowing that a landholding has been occupied illegally (*sine lege*), but do not take this opportunity to oppose its alienation (by sale, donation, or concession), perhaps lacking themselves the necessary titles, would accept ipso facto the transaction. The very occupation of land "without legitimate investiture" has every chance of having been relatively frequent, by virtue of unclaimed legacies, gradual appropriation of public lands, or because of the vagaries of the management of large properties made up of many scattered parcels. Hence the importance, also, of the *brevia* and the *notitiae vestitoriae*, which are limited to recording the actual taking possession of property, its investiture, after a donation or a sale: such *brevia* and *notitiae* document the 'implementation' of the legal transaction. Some of these records imply a visit to the land-site itself; others, written for individuals following Salic law, go so far as to be written on the same piece of parchment after the actual sale, to which they give a legal translation in conformity with the Frankish investiture rites.[68] Either can be considered as useful precautions for avoiding future conflicts.

In other words: the non-opposition to a public declaration of possession entails the 'legitimacy' of the occupation of the land by the declarer. It is certainly doubtful that the judicial claim on land by someone occupying it *sine lege* is a spontaneous action. The occasion was most probably sparked by the existence of a local opposition, overt or latent, confronted by the *auctor cartulae* in a role of plaintiff rather than that of defendant. The potential buyer of property of doubtful origin could also require a judicial guarantee for it before concluding the transaction. Nonetheless, by enacting this new ruling, the capitulary of 891 widened the scope of action of the courts into a form of voluntary jurisdiction because, in the absence of an opponent, the judges had just to confirm with their authority the affirmations of the 'plaintiff'.

(c) While the *finis intentionis* responds exactly to what was prescribed by the capitulary of 891, this is not totally the case of the *ostensio cartae*, which would correspond rather to a later moment in the judicial affirmation of property rights. The law is, however, easily applicable to the *ostensio cartae*. In the

68 Visit to the land-site to invest the beneficiary of a donation: *ChLA*² XCV 9 (Gnignano, near Milan, 856; see Ansani, "I giudici palatini," 181); to invest the beneficiary of a diploma: Ettore Falconi, ed., *Le carte cremonesi dei secoli VIII–XII*, 4 vols (Cremona: Biblioteca Statale di Cremona, 1979), 1: no. 18 (Guastalla, 864). *Notitiae vestitoriae* after a sale: see Cristina Mantegna, "Tra diritto romano e riti germanici: il caso del documento piacentino del IX secolo," *Nuovi annali della Scuola speciale per archivisti e bibliotecari* 19 (2005), 5–19; see also *ChLA*² XCIV 34 (844).

absence of the *auctor cartulae*, he who holds the document can, for example, be obliged to present it before judges, in order to eliminate all uncertainty concerning possession. Especially since once the essential point of law resides in the fact that he who makes the claim is he who concretely holds a property, the way is open to use the judicial assembly as a validation chamber for any document that was liable to be challenged, whether or not the possible adversaries are known. Whence the need to install guarantees that would allow anyone contesting the claim the possibility of appearing during a judicial session.

The motivations behind the *ostensio cartae* can be many and they did evolve with time. As said earlier, it would sometimes remedy the absence of the *auctor*, or a loss of local documentary memory occasioned, for example, by the destruction of an archive. This was probably the reason for the presentation before judges in 892 of five *cartulae* related to the church of Varsi, in the diocese of Piacenza, where the archives were partially destroyed some years earlier.[69] At other times a tense political and social context could provoke the need to affirm rights before an assembly, regardless of the intrinsic authority of the document, such as a royal diploma. Whence the wilfully 'performative' aspect associated with the procedure. Solemnly played out before an audience that supports the presenter of the document, it can be sufficiently intimidating that those who are less well armed will avoid taking the risk of denouncing. This is particularly true for diplomas issued in the wake of a political regime change, marking the link between local powers and the new regime, and for those, more generally, that jeopardize the balance of power within a territory or city. Examples include the *placita* held in 898 at the creation of the county of Modena; or in 964 to seal the strong position accorded the church of Reggio by Otto I; or in 998 to affirm the rights of the bishop of Cremona in the face of the *cives*, reducing to nothing what they had obtained from the emperor two years before.[70]

69 Manaresi, 1: no. 99 = *ChLA*² LXX 36. Ansani, "I giudici palatini," 182–183; Bougard, "L'église de Varsi et son chartrier".

70 Manaresi, 1: no. 106 (Modena); 2: nos. 152 (Reggio) and 207. Tiziana Lazzari, "La creazione di un territorio: il comitato di Modena e i suoi 'confini'," *Reti Medievali Rivista* 7, no. 1 (2006), at http://www.serena.unina.it/index.php/rm/article/view/urn%3Anbn%3Ait%3Aunina-3183 (accessed 1 September 2017); Hagen Keller and Stefan Ast, "*Ostensio cartae*. Italienische Gerichtsurkunden des 10. Jahrhunderts zwischen Schriftlichkeit und Performance," *Deutsches Archiv* 53 (2007), 99–121; François Bougard, "Diplômes et notices de plaid: dialogue et convergence." In *Europäische Herrscher*, ed. Ghignoli, Huschner, and Jaros, 15–22, with other examples; François Bougard and Laurent Morelle, "Prévention, appréciation et sanction du faux documentaire (VIᵉ-XIIᵉ siècle)," In *Juger le faux. Moyen Âge—Temps modernes*, ed. Olivier Poncet (Paris: École nationale des chartes, 2011), 19–58, at 28–30.

These three examples are demonstrations of power, and their staging is meant to mark the collective memory, in an exercise of symbolic communication.[71]

The public presentation of a document can also correspond to the final step in economic affairs like those linked with credit, which were voluntary operations staggered over time and guaranteed by a charter of sale or donation issued by the debtor. The charter would be made definitive or nullified according to whether the sum that had been lent was reimbursed.[72] In the eleventh century other particularly complex affairs related to patrimonial successions, and whose comprehension remains clouded, are also guaranteed by the writing of a chain of charters among which *cartulae promissionis* and several documents of *ostensio cartae*, according to a procedure agreed upon in advance by the "partners".[73] Would these, in the absence of mutual confidence, use a judicial court so that the progress of their transaction, secured with unassailable documents, could not be undercut by the questioning of a previous stage? Perhaps things should not be seen in this light. The preliminary agreement is certainly an act of "collusion", as is noted in the documents themselves. They implicate, moreover, the judges and notaries who are the first to counsel their clients in the meanders of the documentation. But the intent is not to deceive or pretend, but to provide a written document which, when presented in public, is unassailable and incontestable.

No doubt a precise knowledge of the context of each case would enrich that functional logic. But things must also be seen from a strictly documentary point of view, paying attention to the chronological relation between the different pieces. *Notitiae* which were established *pro securitate* sometimes express the opinion of the parties concerning an inserted document that is much earlier in time. It is necessary to delete from the document all wording that could be attacked, not on form but on content. Sometimes the document originates

71 Keller and Ast, "*Ostensio cartae*;" Hagen Keller, "The privilege in the public interaction of the exercise of power: forms of symbolic communication beyond the text," in *Medieval Legal Process: Physical, Spoken and Written Performance in the Middle Ages*, ed. Marco Mostert and Paul S. Barnwell (Turnhout: Brepols, 2011), 75–108, at 77.

72 Bougard, *La justice*, 323–325; Bougard, "*Falsum falsorum judicum consilium*," 301; and, on the mechanisms of credit, François Bougard, "Le crédit dans l'Occident du haut Moyen Âge: documentation et pratique," in *Les élites et la richesse au haut Moyen Âge*, ed. Jean-Pierre Devroey, Laurent Feller, and Régine Le Jan (Turnhout: Brepols, 2010), 439–478.

73 Antonella Ghignoli, ed., *Carte dell'Archivio Arcivescovile di Pisa. Fondo arcivescovile, 1 (720–1100)* (Pisa: Pacini, 2006), no. 102 (Mantova, 1034); Bougard, "*Falsum falsorum judicum consilium*," 301–302; Antonella Ghignoli, "*Repromissionis pagina*. Pratiche di documentazione a Pisa nel secolo XI," *Scrineum Rivista* 4 (2006–2007), 38–107, at https://oajournals.fupress.net/index.php/scrineum/article/view/8770/8768 (accessed 1 September 2017).

from the debate in court: either because a charter (sale or donation) terminates a transaction carried out step by step under the eyes of the judges-notaries who dictated how to proceed to avoid legal uncertainty; or because the charter is the end point of the contradictory debates between the parties. One then integrates into the *ostensio* formula the settlement of a conflict, such a phase of which the adversaries had not perhaps foreseen at the beginning.

As with the *finis intentionis*, the question is not to know if there has been a former conflict when the claimant enquires about a possible opponent or asks a named and present adversary whether he intends to oppose the document whose content is being made public. This is sometimes the case, and sometimes not, but we must keep in mind that the formula will not record the debates, if there were any. The formulas were meant not only to express in different words what the judges had said, by adopting models close to those used for a private charter and its voluntary clauses of obligation, or by allowing the insertion of the full charter in a judicial record. They were also meant to widen the social influence of a legal situation, affirmed unilaterally or as the result of an agreement between two parties, by submitting the validation to a court and requesting from it a written record that would assure future memory of its intervention.

The historiographical debates on whether or not there are 'actual lawsuits' behind the formulas invented in the late ninth century have no foundation. These lawsuits are neither visible nor fictive—no more than the pseudo 'Scheinprozesse' of the Merovingian seventh century[74]—but, depending upon the case, their development does or does not include an adversarial party. Sometimes the affirmation of possession is validated with indifference, sheltered from any conflict right to the end, having failed to find someone with the legal weapons that would have stymied the so blatantly illegitimate *vestitura*, whence such historiographical characterizations as "declaratory judgment" or "undefended case".[75] Other times opponents did exist, who are named. In this case, the *altercatio* recovers its rights, even if it is exceptional that details are given of the arguments exchanged or of the nature of the proof. In 1054 in Zurich, before Emperor Henry III, the bishop of Cremona obtained public recognition of his rights over two properties that, it is said in an interpolation,

74 Alexander C. Murray, "So-called fictitious trial in the Merovingian *Placita*," in *Gallien in Spätantike unf Frühmittelalter: Kulturgeschichte einer Region*, ed. Steffen Diefenbach and Gernot Michael Müller (Berlin: De Gruyter, 2013), 297–327.

75 "Declaratory": Jon N. Sutherland, "Aspects of continuity and change in the Italian *placitum* 962–972," *Journal of Medieval History* 2 (1976), 89–118; "undefended": Costambeys, "Disputes and documents".

had just been the object of a duel; but nothing is said about the proceedings. Again, one must be content that at least an allusion was made, because in 1014, in Pavia, another document says nothing of a judicial duel that decided a dispute, but the fact that it took place is known through a diploma.[76] With the *ostensio cartae*, if there is an element to be judged as apparent or fictive that is not the trial itself, but the charter of sale or donation that is the result of the dispute and which says nothing of the conditions for which, nor under which, it was drawn up.

In any case, it would be wrong to draw an opposition between formulas and procedure. Formulas are certainly a "documentary representation",[77] the most efficient way of validating publicly recognized rights. But, being the result of an abstraction, formulas amount to a real procedure, that of committing to writing, which supplanted all others. There is no reason to doubt that the words exchanged between the judges and the parties were not pronounced, right up to the final declaration of closure of the *causa*. It is a judicial action in its own right, in a trial where one awaits the announcement of the winner. If the way it is recorded is simplified by comparison to the *altercationes*, the court proceedings are often more complicated than before, because the debating time, if it takes place, adds a new ritual.

(d) A final word on the *notitia de banno*, which documents the act of placing a property under the protection of the royal, imperial or ducal (in Tuscany) *bannum*. This threatens with a financial sanction anyone trying to appropriate the property, a sanction which will be split between the royal, imperial or ducal *camera* and the injured person or institution. Here again the court responds to the action of the plaintiff, who makes his request after having made a declaration of ownership. The formula for the imposition of the ban, attested first in the 990s and widely diffused after the mid-eleventh century, looks like an element detached from the text of the *finis intentionis* or the *ostensio cartae*, where it sometimes occurs as an appendix, but which now becomes autonomous. Henceforth, any evidence related to a possible conflict likely to justify the demand is absent. It must be emphasized that the financial sanction, drawn up in *mancosi, bizantei* or pounds, is directly copied from royal diplomas. There is no fundamental difference between what is said in a diploma granting the protection of the king (*mundeburdium*) and a court record documenting the fact that the plaintiff had been placed under the protection of the ban. One can see here a sort of judicial 'democratization' of diplomas, the content of

76 Manaresi, 3/1: no. 391 (Zurich, 1054); 2/2: no. 283 (Pavia, 1014). Bougard, "Rationalité et irrationalité des procédures".

77 Ansani, "I giudici palatini," 185.

which is now accessible to those without easy access to the prince and with little chance of ever obtaining a charter written in chancery script on a good-quality, regularly sized and ruled piece of parchment, and bearing a seal. But diplomas were also a supplementary weapon in the eyes of those who did have access to the prince's written favour. The very gesture of the ban, by which the president of the tribunal poses the *baculus*, the sign of his power, on the head of the appellant, can only reinforce the symbolic importance of the request.[78]

6 Conclusion

By their variety, the Italian judicial records from the ninth through eleventh centuries show the attempt to preserve a written memory of everything that took place before the judges and notaries, whatever its importance for the resolution of the conflict. In this, Italy offers an array of possibilities unequalled elsewhere. From the end of the ninth century, judges and notaries in Pavia lead an autonomous movement, indifferent to the political upheavals, which profoundly renovates the judicial practices and has an immediate spillover effect. Its spectacular success is surely due to its favourable reception by those answerable to the law, for whom the corresponding documents—responding to a wider range of situations—carried as many if not more guarantees than before. It also reveals the documentary and procedural engineering of the practitioners of law, who probably benefitted most from it, materially. Regardless of the situation, or the importance of the actors, or the weight of the context, what is key is the written document and what it certifies, in a time when the written document is always liable to be questioned, and not yet equipped with the probationary force that it will receive in the twelfth century. With these innovations, courts and court records become ever more effective legal tools, reinforcing the written word, because judges are not content simply to supervise the debates, they also guarantee their outcome. Efficiency is the main worry: judicial records follow the proceedings as far as the execution of the court's decision—the 'chose jugée'—something that was unknown before.[79]

78 Keller, "The privilege," 87.

79 The margin of difference with certain Roman *refutationes*, which sometimes enclose the account of a judicial hearing in a private transaction, is not great (Santoni, "*Orta fuit intentio*"). The process of documentation is just inversed.

Bibliography

Abbreviations

CDL: *Codice diplomatico longobardo*. Vols I–II, edited by Luigi Schiaparelli, 1929–1933; Vols III/1 and IV/1, edited by Carlrichard Brühl, 1973–1981; Vols IV/2 and V, edited by Herbert Zielinski, 2003 and 1986. Rome: Istituto storico italiano per il medio evo.

ChLA: Bruckner, Albert, and Robert Marichal, eds. *Chartae Latinae antiquiores: Facsimile-Edition of the Latin Charters prior to the Ninth Century*. Vol. XXIX (Italy 10), edited by Jan-Olaf Tjäder, F. Magistrale, and Guglielmo Cavallo. Dietikon-Zurich: Urs Graf, 1993.

*ChLA*²: Cavallo, Guglielmo, and Giovanna Nicolaj, eds. *Chartae Latinae antiquiores: Facsimile-Edition of the Latin Charters*. 2nd Series, *Ninth Century*. Vol. LXVI (Italy 38), *Piacenza 3*, edited by Cristina Cabonetti Vendittelli, 2005; Vol. LXVIII (Italy 40), *Piacenza 5*, edited by Paola Degni, 2006; Vol. LXX (Italy 42), *Piacenza 7*, edited by Flavia de Rubeis, 2007; Vol. LXXIII (Italy 45), *Lucca 2*, edited by F. Magistrale, 2003; Vol. LXXV (Italy 47), *Lucca 4*, edited by F. Magistrale, Pasquale Cordasco, and Corinna Drago, 2005; Vol. LXXX (Italy 52), *Lucca 9*, edited by F. Magistrale and Clelia Gattagrisi, 2010; Vol. LXXXII (Italy 54), *Lucca 11*, edited by Clelia Gattagrisi, Pasquale Cordasco, and Corinna Drago, 2013; Vol. LXXXVI (Italy 58), *Lucca 15*, edited by Clelia Gattagrisi and Corinna Drago, 2015; Vol. XCIV (Italy 66), *Milano 1*, edited by Maddalena Modesti, 2015; Vol. XCV (Italy 67), *Milano 2*, edited by Annafelicia Zuffrano, 2016. Dietikon-Zurich: Urs Graf.

Manaresi: Manaresi, Cesare, ed. *I Placiti del "Regnum Italiae"*. 3 vols in 5. Roma: Tipografia del Senato, 1955–1960.

MGH Capit. 2: Boretius, Alfred, and Victor Krause, eds. *Capitularia regum Francorum*. Monumenta Germaniae Historica, Legum sectio II. Vol. 2. Hannover: Hahn, 1897.

MGH DD K III: Kehr, Paul, ed. *Die Urkunden Karls III*. Monumenta Germaniae Historica, Diplomata regum Germaniae ex stirpe Karolinorum 2. Berlin: Weidman, 1937.

MGH DD L I: Kölzer, Theo, et al., eds. *Die Urkunden Ludwigs des Frommen*. Monumenta Germaniae Historica, Diplomata Karolinorum 3. 3 vols. Wiesbaden: Harrassowitz, 2016.

MGH DD L II: Wanner, Konrad, ed. *Die Urkunden Ludwigs II*. Monumenta Germaniae Historica, Diplomata Karolinorum 4. Munich: MGH, 1994.

MGH DD Lo. I: Schieffer, Theodor, ed. *Die Urkunden Lothars I. und Lothars II*. Monumenta Germaniae Historica, Diplomata Karolinorum 3. Berlin: Weidman, 1966.

MGH DD MT: Goez, Elke, and Werner Goez, eds. *Die Urkunden und Briefe der Markgräfin Mathilde von Tuszien*. Monumenta Germaniae Historica, Laienfürsten- und Dynastenurkunden der Kaiserzeit 2. Hannover: Hahnsche Buchhandlung, 1998.

MGH Fontes iuris 2: Bluhme, Friedrich, ed. *Edictus ceteraeque Langobardoeum leges cum constitutionibus et pactis principum Beneventanorum*. Monumenta Germaniae Historica, Fontes iuris 2. Hannover: Hahn, 1869.

MGH LL: Bluhme, Friedrich, and Alfred Boretius, eds. *Leges Langobardorum*. Monumenta Germaniae Historica, Leges (in Folio) 4. Hannover: Hahn, 1868.

Volpini: Volpini, Raffaello. "Placiti del *Regnum Italiae* (secc. IX–XI). Primi contributi per un nuovo censimento." In Paolo Zerbi, ed. *Contributi dell'Istituto di storia medioevale [dell'Università cattolica del Sacro Cuore]* III, 245–520. Milan: Vita e pensiero, 1975.

Other Primary Sources

Balzani, Ugo, ed., *Il Chronicon Farfense di Gregorio di Catino*. 2 vols. Rome: Istituto storico italiano per il medio evo, 1903.

Calleri, Marta, ed. *Codice diplomatico del monastero di Santo Stefano di Genova, I (965–1200)*. Genova: Società ligure di storia patria, 2009.

Castagnetti, Andrea, Michele Luzzati, Gianfranco Pasquali, and Augusto Vasina, eds. *Inventari altomedievali di terre, coloni e redditi*. Rome: Istituto storico italiano per il Medio Evo, 1979.

Falconi, Ettore, ed. *Le carte cremonesi dei secoli VIII–XII*. 4 vols. Cremona: Biblioteca Statale di Cremona, 1979–1988.

Gerbert d'Aurillac. *Correspondance*, edited and translated by Pierre Riché and Jean-Pierre-Callu. 2 vols. Paris: Les Belles Lettres, 1993.

Ghignoli, Antonella, ed. *Carte dell'Archivio Arcivescovile di Pisa. Fondo arcivescovile, I (720–1100)*. Pisa: Pacini, 2006.

Kurze, Wilhelm, ed. *Codex diplomaticus Amiatinus*. 2 vols. Tübingen: Max Niemeyer, 1974–1982.

Petrucci, Armando, et al., eds. *Lettere originali del Medioevo latino* (*VII–XI sec.*). Vol. 1 *Italia*. Pisa: Scuola Normale Superiore, 2004.

Secondary Works

Albertoni, Giuseppe. "Law and the peasant: rural society and justice in Carolingian Italy." *Early Medieval Europe* 18 (2010), 417–445.

Ansani, Michele. "Appunti sui brevia di XI e XII secolo." *Scrineum Rivista* 4 (2006–2007), 107–152. Accessed 1 September 2017. https://oajournals.fupress.net/index.php/scrineum/article/view/8771/8769.

Ansani, Michele. Caritatis negocia *e fabbriche di falsi. Strategie, imposture, dispure documentarie a Pavia fra XI e XII secolo*. Rome: Istituto storico italiano per il medio evo, 2011.

Ansani, Michele. "I giudici palatini, le carte, le leggi. Pratiche documentarie e documentazione di placito sullo scorcio del secolo IX." In *Almum Studium Papiense. Storia dell'Università di Pavia*, edited by Dario Mantovani. Vol. 1 *Dalle origini all'età spagnola*, tome 1, 171–186. Pavia: Università di Pavia, 2012.

Balzaretti, Ross. "Spoken narratives in ninth-century Milanese court records." In *Nar-*

rative and History in the early Medieval West, edited by Elizabeth M. Tyler and Ross Balzaretti, 11–37. Turnhout: Brepols, 2006.

Bartoli Langeli, Attilio. "Sui 'brevi' italiani altomedievali." *Bullettino dell'Istituto storico italiano per il medio evo* 105 (2003), 1–23.

Bergmann, Werner. "Untersuchungen zu den Gerichtsurkunden der Merowingerzeit." *Archiv für Diplomatik* 22 (1976), 1–186.

Bougard, François. *La justice dans le royaume d'Italie de la fin du VIIIe siècle au début du XIe siècle*. Rome: École française de Rome, 1995.

Bougard, François. "La justice dans le royaume d'Italie aux IXe-Xe siècles." In *La giustizia nell'alto medioevo (secoli IX–XI)*, Settimane di studio del CISAM 44, 133–176. Spoleto: CISAM, 1997.

Bougard, François. "*Falsum falsorum judicum consilium*: l'écrit et la justice en Italie centro-septentrionale au XIe siècle." *Bibliothèque de l'École des chartes* 155 (1997), 299–314.

Bougard, François. "Actes privés et transferts patrimoniaux en Italie centro-septentrionale (VIIIe-Xe siècle)." *Mélanges de l'École française de Rome—Moyen Âge* 111 (1999), 539–562.

Bougard, François. "Rationalité et irrationalité des procédures autour de l'an mil: le duel judiciaire en Italie." In *La justice en l'an mil*, 93–122. Paris: La Documentation française, 2003.

Bougard, François. "*Tempore barbarici*? La production documentaire publique et privée." In *774. Ipotesi per una transizione*, edited by Stefano Gasparri, 331–351. Turnhout: Brepols, 2008.

Bougard, François. "Prêter serment en justice dans le royaume d'Italie, VIIIe-XIe siècle." In *Oralité et lien social au Moyen Âge (Occident, Byzance, Islam)*, edited by Marie-France Auzépy and Guillaume Saint-Guillain, 327–339. Paris: ACHCByz, 2008.

Bougard, François. "Écrire le procès: le compte rendu judiciaire entre VIIIe et XIe siècle." *Médiévales* 56 (printemps 2009), 23–40.

Bougard, François. "Notaires d'élite, notaires de l'élite dans le royaume d'Italie." In *La culture au haut Moyen Âge: une question d'élites?*, edited by François Bougard, Régine Le Jan, and Rosamond McKitterick, 438–460. Turnhout: Brepols, 2009.

Bougard, François. "Le crédit dans l'Occident du haut Moyen Âge: documentation et pratique." In *Les élites et la richesse au haut Moyen Âge*, edited by Jean-Pierre Devroey, Laurent Feller, and Régine Le Jan, 439–478. Turnhout: Brepols, 2010.

Bougard, François. "Diplômes et notices de plaid: dialogue et convergence." In *Europäische Herrscher und die Toskana im Spiegel der urkundlichen Überlieferung—I sovrani europei e la Toscana nel riflesso della tradizione documentaria (800–1100)*, edited by Antonella Ghignoli, Wolfgang Huschner, and Marie Ulrike Jaros, 15–22. Leipzig: Eudora, 2016.

Bougard, François. "Les plaids pour destinataires toscans." In *Europäische Herrscher*, edited by Ghignoli, Huschner, and Jaros, 165–210.

Bougard, François. "Jugement divin, excommunication, anathème et malédiction: la sanction spirituelle dans les sources diplomatiques." In *Exclure de la communauté chrétienne: Sens et pratiques sociales de l'anathème et de l'excommunication*, edited by Geneviève Büher-Thierry and Stéphane Gioanni, 215–238. Turnhout: Brepols, 2015.

Bougard, François. "L'église de Varsi et son chartrier: pouvoirs, territoires, communauté, VIIIe–Xe siècle." In *La fabrique des sociétés médiévales méditerranéennes. Les Moyen Âges de François Menant*, edited by Diane Chamboduc de Saint-Pulgent, and Marie Dejoux, 421–431. Paris: Publications de la Sorbonne, 2018.

Bougard, François, and Laurent Morelle. "Prévention, appréciation et sanction du faux documentaire (VIe-XIIe siècle)." In *Juger le faux. Moyen Âge—Temps modernes*, edited by Olivier Poncet, 19–58. Paris: École nationale des chartes, 2011.

Brancoli Busdraghi, Piero. "Patti di assistenza giuridica e militare in Toscana fra XI e XII secolo." In *Nobiltà e ceti dirigenti in Toscana nei secoli XI–XIII: strutture e concetti*, 29–55. Monte Oriolo: F. Papafava, 1982.

Cammarosano, Paolo. "Carte di querela nell'Italia dei secoli X–XIII." *Frühmittelalterliche Studien* 36 (2002), 397–402.

Casagrande, Gloria. "Il ritrovamento del testo completo del 'polittico delle malefatte', anno ca. 1040." In *Reggiolo medievale. Atti e memorie del Convegno di studi matildici, Reggiolo, 9 aprile 1978*, edited by Gino Badini, 101–132. Reggio Emilia: G. Bizzocchi, 1979.

Castagnetti, Andrea. *Note e documenti intorno alla caratterizzazione professionale dei giudici (secoli IX-inizio X)*. Verona: Università degli studi di Verona, 2008.

Castagnetti, Andrea, and Antonio Ciaralli. *Falsari a Nonantola. I placiti di Ostiglia (820–827) e le donazioni di Nogara (910–911)*. Spoleto: CISAM, 2011.

Chiodi, Giovanni. "Roma e il diritto romano." In *Roma fra Oriente e Occidente*, Settimane di studio del CISAM 49, 1149–254. Spoleto: CISAM, 2002.

Collavini, Simone. Honorabilis domus et spetiosissimus comitatus. *Gli Aldobrandeschi da "conti" a "principi territoriali" (secoli IX–XIII)*. Pisa: Edizioni ETS, 1988.

Collavini, Simone. "I Conti Aldobrandeschi e la Valdinievole. Una nota sulla situazione politica in Tuscia nei primi anni del secolo XI." In Atti del convegno *Signori e feudatari nella Valdinievole dal X al XII secolo*, 101–127. Buggiano: Comune di Buggiano, 1992.

Collavini, Simone, and Paolo Tomei. "Beni fiscali e 'scritturazione'. Nuove proposte sui contesti di rilascio e falsificazione di D. OIII. 269 per il monastero di S. Ponziano di Lucca." In *Originale–Fälschungen–Kopien. Kaiser- und Königsurkunden für Empfänger in Deutschland und Italien (9.–11. Jahrhundert) und ihre Nachwirkungen im Hoch- und Spätmittelalter (bis ca. 1500) / Originali–falsi–copie. Documenti imperiali e regi per destinatari tedeschi e italiani (secc. IX–XI) e i loro effetti nel Medioevo e nella prima età moderna (fino al 1500 circa)*, edited by Nicolangelo D'Acunto,

Wolfgang Huschner, and Sebastian Roebert, 205–216. Leipzig-Karlsruhe: Eudora, 2017.

Costambeys, Marios. "Disputes and courts in Lombard and Carolingian central Italy." *Early Medieval Europe* 15 (2007), 265–289.

Costambeys, Marios. *Power and Patronage in Early Medieval Italy. Local Society, Italian Politics and the Abbey of Farfa, c. 700–900*. Cambridge: Cambridge University Press, 2007.

Costambeys, Marios. "Disputes and documents in early medieval Italy." In *Making Early Medieval Societies. Conflict and Belonging in the Latin West*, edited by Kate Cooper and Conrad Leyser, 125–154. Cambridge: Cambridge University Press, 2016.

Davies, Wendy. *Windows on Justice in Northern Iberia 800–1000*. Abingdon: Routledge, 2016.

Delogu, Paolo. "La giustizia nell'Italia meridionale longobarda." In *La giustizia nell'alto medioevo (secoli IX–XI)*, Settimane di studio del CISAM 44, 257–308. Spoleto: CISAM, 1997.

Feller, Laurent. *Les Abruzzes médiévales. Territoire, économie et société en Italie centrale du IXe au XIIe siècle*. Rome: École française de Rome, 1998.

Ghignoli, Antonella. "*Repromissionis pagina*. Pratiche di documentazione a Pisa nel secolo XI." *Scrineum Rivista* 4 (2006–2007), 38–107. Accessed 1 September 2017. https://oajournals.fupress.net/index.php/scrineum/article/view/8770/8768.

Ghignoli, Antonella, Wolfgang Huschner, and Marie Ulrike Jaros, eds. *Europäische Herrscher und die Toskana im Spiegel der urkundlichen Überlieferung—I sovrani europei e la Toscana nel riflesso della tradizione documentaria (800–1100)*. Leipzig: Eudora, 2016.

La giustizia nell'alto medioevo (secoli IX–XI), Settimane di studio del CISAM 44. Spoleto: CISAM, 1997.

Heil, Michael W. "Clerics, Courts, and Legal Culture in Early Medieval Italy, c. 650–c. 900." PhD dissertation, Columbia University, 2013.

Hübner, Rudolf. "Gerichtsurkunden der fränkischen Zeit." *Zeitschrift der Savigny-Stiftung für Rechtsgeschichte. Germanistische Abteilung* 12 (1891) [Germany and France up to 1000] and 14 (1893) [Italy up to 1150], with separate pagination. Repr. together: Aalen: Scientia, 1971.

Keller, Hagen. "The privilege in the public interaction of the exercise of power: forms of symbolic communication beyond the text." In *Medieval Legal Process: Physical, Spoken and Written Performance in the Middle Ages*, edited by Marco Mostert and Paul S. Barnwell, 75–108. Turnhout: Brepols, 2011.

Keller, Hagen, and Stefan Ast. "*Ostensio cartae*. Italienische Gerichtsurkunden des 10. Jahrhunderts zwischen Schriftlichkeit und Performance." *Deutsches Archiv* 53 (2007), 99–121.

Lazzari, Tiziana. "La creazione di un territorio: il comitato di Modena e i suoi 'confini'."

Reti Medievali Rivista 7, no. 1 (2006). Accessed 1 September 2017. http://www.serena.unina.it/index.php/rm/article/view/urn%3Anbn%3Ait%3Aunina-3183.

Mantegna, Cristina. "Tra diritto romano e riti germanici: il caso del documento piacentino del IX secolo." *Nuovi annali della Scuola speciale per archivisti e bibliotecari* 19 (2005), 5–19.

Mantovani, Dario, ed. *Almum Studium Papiense. Storia dell'Università di Pavia*. Vol. 1 *Dalle origini all'età spagnola*, 2 tomes. Pavia: Università di Pavia, 2012.

Mengozzi, Guido. *Ricerche sull'attività della scuola di Pavia nell'alto medio evo*. Pavia: Tipografia Cooperativa, 1924.

Murray, Alexander C. "So-called fictitious trial in the Merovingian *Placita*." In *Gallien in Spätantike unf Frühmittelalter: Kulturgeschichte einer Region*, edited by Steffen Diefenbac and Gernot Michael Müller, 297–327. Berlin: De Gruyter, 2013.

Nicolaj, Giovanna. *Lezioni di diplomatica generale, I. Istituzioni*. Rome: Bulzoni, 2007.

Nicolaj, Giovanna. "Formulari e nuovo formalismo nei processi del *regnum Italiae*." In *La giustizia nell'alto medioevo (secoli IX–XI)*, 347–379. Repr. in eadem, *Storie di documenti, storie di libri: quarant'anni di studi, ricerche e vagabondaggi nell'età antica e medievale*, 230–246. Dietikon-Zurich: Urs Graf, 2013.

Ourliac, Paul. "La tradition romaine dans les actes toulousains des Xe et XIe siècles." *Revue historique de droit français et étranger* 60 (1982), 577–588.

Padoa-Schioppa, Antonio. "Aspetti della giustizia milanese dal X al XII secolo." In Atti dell'11° Congresso internazionale di studi sull'alto medioevo (Milano, 26–30 ottobre 1987), 459–549. Spoleto: CISAM, 1989. Repr. in idem, *Giustizia medievale italiana*, 137–227.

Padoa-Schioppa, Antonio. "Processi di libertà nell'Italia altomedievale." *Nuova Rivista storica* 95 (2011), 393–436. Repr. in idem, *Giustizia medievale italiana*, 93–136.

Padoa-Schioppa, Antonio. "La scuola di Pavia. Alle fonti della nuova scienza giuridica europea." In *Almum Studium Papiense. Storia dell'Università di Pavia*. Vol. 1 *Dalle origini all'età spagnola*, ed. Dario Mantovani, 2 tomes (Pavia: Università di Pavia, 2012), 1: 143–164.

Padoa-Schioppa, Antonio. *Giustizia medievale italiana. Dal* regnum *ai comuni*. Spoleto: CISAM, 2015.

Pieniądz, Aneta. "Literacy and the legal culture of the early Middle Ages. Old research—new questions." In *Právní kultura ve středověku*, edited by Martin Nodl and Piotr Węcowski, 13–25. Prague: Filosofia, 2016.

Santoni, Francesca. "*Orta fuit intentio et litis calumpnia*. Processi e documenti nella Roma medievale." In *Roma e il suo territorio nel medioevo. Le fonti scritte fra tradizione e innovazione. Atti del Convegno internazionale di studio dell'Associazione italiana dei Paleografi e Diplomatisti (Roma, 25–29 ottobre 2012)*, edited by Cristina Carbonetti, Santo Lucà, and Maddalena Signorini, 365–394. Spoleto: CISAM, 2015.

Santoni, Francesca. "Fra *lex* e *pugna*: il placito di Garfagnolo (1098)." *Scrineum Rivista* 2

(2004), 5–45. Accessed 1 September 2017. https://oajournals.fupress.net/index.php/scrineum/article/view/8758/8756.

Spicciani, Amleto. "Forme giuridiche e condizioni reali nei rapporti tra il vescovo di Lucca e signori laici (secolo XI)." In *Formazione e strutture dei ceti dominanti nel medioevo: marchesi, conti e visconti nel regno italico (secc. IX–XII)*, edited by Cinzio Violante, 315–375. Rome: Istituto storico italiano per il medio evo: 1996. Repr. in idem, *Protofeudalesimo*, 81–139.

Spicciani, Amleto. *Protofeudalesimo. Concessioni livellarie, impegni militari non vassallatici e castelli (secoli X–XI)*. Pisa: Edizioni ETS, 2001.

Sutherland, Jon N. "Aspects of continuity and change in the Italian *placitum* 962–972." *Journal of Medieval History* 2 (1976), 89–118.

Tomei, Paolo. "Un nuovo 'polittico' lucchese del IX secolo: il *breve de multis pensionibus*." *Studi medievali* ser. 3ª, 53 (2012), 567–602.

Toubert, Pierre. *Les structures du Latium médiéval: le Latium méridional et la Sabine du début du IXe siècle à la fin du XIIe siècle*. 2 vols. Rome: École française de Rome, 1973.

Violante, Cinzio. "Fluidità del feudalesimo nel regno italico (secoli X e XI). Alternanze e compenetrazioni di forme giuridiche nelle concessioni di terre ecclesiastiche a laici." *Annali dell'Istituto storico italo-germanico in Trento* 21 (1995), 11–39.

Wickham, Chris. "Land disputes and their social framework." In *The Settlement of Disputes in Early Medieval Europe*, edited by Wendy Davies and Paul Fouracre, 105–124. Cambridge: Cambridge University Press, 1986. Repr. in idem, *Land & Power. Studies in Italian and European Social History, 400–1200*, 229–256. London: British School at Rome, 1994.

Wickham, Chris. "Justice in the kingdom of Italy in the eleventh century." In *La giustizia nell'alto medioevo (secoli IX–XI)*, Settimane di studio del CISAM 44, 179–250. Spoleto: CISAM, 1997.

Wickham, Chris. *Roma medievale. Crisi e stabilità di una città, 950–1100*. Rome: Viella, 2013.

Witt, Ronald G. *The Two Latin Cultures and the Foundation of Renaissance Humanism in Medieval Italy*. Cambridge: Cambridge University Press, 2012.

CHAPTER 10

Cum suo scripto: Lay *Deperdita* and Ecclesiastical Memory in Dispute Records from Castile-Álava and Tuscany (Ninth-Tenth Centuries)

Igor Santos Salazar

1 Introduction

In recent years, a good deal has been published on the relationship between laypeople, writing, and archives in Western Europe during the medieval period. Beginning with the pioneering studies by Michael Clanchy and, for the early Middle Ages, by Rosamond McKitterick,[1] multiple research groups have addressed the issues of lay literacy and documentary culture going all the way back to the final decades of late antiquity.[2] This research appeared at the same time that other historians were rethinking, with a renewed interest in archival

1 Michael Clanchy, *From Memory to Written Record: England, 1066–1307* (Cambridge, Mass.: Harvard University Press, 1979), and Rosamond McKitterick, *The Carolingians and the Written Word* (Cambridge: Cambridge University Press, 1989). McKitterick's book was a reaction to Clanchy's positions, which were overly pessimistic regarding the role of the laity in early medieval written culture. Clanchy himself has modified this position in later editions of his work. I am grateful to Francesca Tinti for discussing these historiographical points with me. I would like to thank Isabel Alfonso Antón, José Miguel Andrade and André Marques for their comments and criticisms, as well as for those given by Leticia Agúndez, Álvaro Carvajal, Julio Escalona and Francesca Tinti, which have served to improve my text. Any errors are mine alone. This chapter is part of the Marie Skłodowska-Curie Research Project CALOSEMA, grant agreement No. 748161. The abbreviations used in this paper for editions of charters are listed in the bibliography.

2 On literacy, see Rosamond McKitterick, ed., *The Uses of Literacy in Early Mediaeval Europe* (Cambridge: Cambridge University Press, 1990), 1–10. For one approach to the contents of documentary culture—that is, of everything that revolves around written documentation—with particular attention to the laity, see Alice Rio, *Legal Practice and the Written Word in the Early Middle Ages: Frankish formulae, c. 500–c. 1000* (Cambridge: Cambridge University Press, 2009), and Warren Brown et al., eds., *Documentary Culture and the Laity in the Early Middle Ages* (Cambridge: Cambridge University Press, 2013), 1–16. A by no means exhaustive list of other scholarly works includes: Karl Heidecker, ed., *Charters and the Use of the Written Word in Medieval Society* (Turnhout: Brepols, 2000); Marco Mostert, "Communication, Literacy and the Development of Early Medieval Society," in *Comunicare e significare nell'Alto Medioevo*, 2 vols (Spoleto: CISAM, 2005), 1:29–55; Peter Erhart, Karl Heidecker and Bernhard Zeller, eds., *Die Privaturkunden der Karolingerzeit* (Dietikon-Zurich: Urs Graf Verlag, 2009);

 | DOI:10.1163/9789004683006_012

sources, the nature and kinds of document preservation, copying, and transmission undertaken by ecclesiastical institutions—the main if not only institutions that transmitted early medieval documents—and the impact that these archival strategies have had on our notions about medieval society.[3]

Despite this body of research developed over the last thirty years, in what follows I will not consider general issues having to do with the reading and writing competence of different social groups that were active in northern Spain and in Italy. Rather, in these pages I will address one aspect of literacy pertaining to lay documentary practices—that is, the relationship between laypeople and written documents.

To that end I will not focus exclusively on "lay charters", that is, on "documents that record a transaction involving only laymen".[4] That would limit the possibilities that records involving churchmen—such as for example judicial records—offer for the study of lay documentary culture itself. Not for nothing have early medievalists warned about the methodological and conceptual problems that arise as a result of a rigid separation between the labels *laicus* and *clericus*. Even so, the historiography has decided to keep these labels, in order to be able to interpret lay documentary culture with greater clarity and concision, leading to very interesting conclusions that have increased our understanding of the complexities of the phenomenon.[5]

---

and Jonathan Jarrett and Allan S. McKinley, eds., *Problems and Possibilities of Early Medieval Charters* (Turnhout: Brepols, 2013).

3 Patrick J. Geary, *Phantoms of Remembrance: Memory and Oblivion and the End of the First Millenium* (Princeton: Princeton University Press, 1994); Olivier Guyotjeannin, Laurent Morelle, and Michel Parisse, eds., *Les cartulaires* (Paris: École nationale des Chartes, 1993); Adam J. Kosto and Anders Winroth, eds., *Charters, Cartularies and Archives: The Transmission and Preservation of Documents in the Medieval West* (Toronto: Pontifical Institute of Mediaeval Studies, 1999); and Julio Escalona and Hélène Sirantoine, eds., *Charters et cartulaires comme instruments de pouvoir. Espagne et Occident chrétien* (*VIII*^e^–*XII*^e^ *siècles*) (Toulouse: Université de Toulouse-Le Mirail, 2013).

4 Adam J. Kosto, "Laymen, Clerics, and Documentary Practices in the Early Middle Ages: The Example of Catalonia," *Speculum* 80 (2005), 44–74, at 54. In addition, Marios Costambeys, "The Laity, the Clergy, the Scribes and Their Archives: The Documentary Record of Eighth- and Ninth-Century Italy," in *Documentary Culture*, ed. Brown et al., 231–257, has defined "lay charter" as follows: "charters in which neither party carries an explicit clerical designation", at 238.

5 Brown et al., "Introduction," in *Documentary Culture*, 1–16. See also the studies that show some lay families' relationship with documentation: François Bougard, "Pierre de Niviano, dit le Spoletin, sculdassius et le gouvernement du comté de Plaisance à l'époque carolingienne," *Journal des Savants* 2 (1996), 291–337; Stefano Gasparri and Cristina La Rocca, eds., *Carte di famiglia: Strategie, rappresentazione e memoria del gruppo familiare di Totone di campione* (*721–877*) (Rome: Viella, 2005); Laurent Feller, Agnès Gramain, and Florence Weber, *La for-*

In this study, however, I will go beyond this artificial division. For the most part, I will be analyzing the numerous incidental references to documents that are now lost (*deperdita*) in records of sale, gift, and exchange, and especially in judicial documents recording disputes either between men and women, kinship groups, or village communities or between these individuals and groups, on the one hand, and bishops, counts, monasteries, *presbiteri*, deacons, etc., on the other. The reason behind this choice to analyse the *deperdita* (in both lay and ecclesiastical documents) is clear: these incidental references afford the readiest proof of the richness and diversity of written lay culture and of its document typologies. I am thinking of examples such as the "Ghittia list", a parchment dated to the eighth century that enumerates eighty-eight documents that are now lost, among which we find typologies whose first and only mention appears on this list.[6]

Moreover, the choice to focus on these two regions in Western Europe is not accidental. The documents preserved in archives in Tuscany and Emilia belong to some of the largest collections of original parchments preserved in Europe. Among them are records of legal disputes that took place in Piacenza, Parma, Lucca, and Pisa and that provide substantial evidence, as we will later see, about lay documentary culture in the kingdom of Italy during the ninth and tenth centuries. In contrast, in Liébana, Castile, and Álava (Spain) we have a very different situation. Here, written documents were filtered through a system in which old single-sheet originals were copied into cartularies during the eleventh to fourteenth centuries by the largest monastic institutions in the kingdoms of Castile and León, from San Millán de la Cogolla to San Pedro de Arlanza, passing through Santa María de Puerto, Valpuesta, Silos, Cardeña, and Liébana, to cite only some among those of particular importance.[7]

In addition, the kingdom of Italy was an important area of Carolingian Europe, with a strong cultural tradition rooted in its Roman past, where writing continued to play a socially and politically central role from late antiquity right up through the millennium. It is highly interesting to compare this situation with the features of the written legacy from those same centuries in Liébana,

---

tune de Karol: Marché de la terre et liens personnels dans les Abruzzes au haut Moyen Âge (Rome: École française de Rome, 2005). One of the best-known Iberian lay archives outside of Catalonia is that of the Muñoz-Flaínez: Alfonso García Leal, "El archivo de los condes Fruela Muñoz y Pedro Flaínez (854–1048): una visión nueva de viejos documentos," *Signo. Revista de Historia de la Cultura escrita* 13 (2004), 121–147.

6 CDL 265. See also Antonella Ghignoli, "Su due famosi documenti pisani dell'VIII secolo," *Bullettino dell'Istituto Storico Italiano per il Medio Evo* 106/2 (2004), 1–69; and Nicolas Everett, *Literacy in Lombard Italy (c. 568–774)* (Cambridge: Cambridge University Press, 2003).

7 The editions of charters from these monasteries are listed in the bibliography. See also above, Chapter 3.

Castile, and Álava. This is so first of all because only recently has the North of Spain prompted debate about documentary culture among laypeople in the early Middle Ages.[8] Secondly, this region's political tradition exhibits differences that are worth noting. It was, in effect, a peripheral area with respect to the most important political entities in Europe at the time, the Carolingian Empire and the Emirate (then Caliphate, from 929) of Córdoba. On the other hand, it was an area in which various local powers were closely connected to one another, where there were several counties about whose origins, development, and social complexity there is still much debate.[9]

Thus, by comparing these two regions it will be possible to interpret not only the similarities and differences in the documentary culture of the laity in the kingdom of Italy and the county of Castile (together with Liébana and Álava). We will also be able to assess whether the differences between the two systems of transmission of written documents—their structural differences—have influenced the interpretation of the laity's documentary practices in these two southern regions of Western Europe.

2 Originals and Cartularies: Conservation, Transmission, and the Structure of Written Sources in the County of Castile and the Kingdom of Italy

The existence of any group of documents preserved in an archive is not the result of chance. Although archival collections have often been lost as a result of fire or neglect, or human brutality and ignorance, most of those that have survived have not done so through happenstance but rather in spite of the hazards of time and through the careful curating of written memory on the part of an institution (church, monastery, or cathedral) that throughout the *Ancien*

8 Roger Collins, "Literacy and the Laity in Early Medieval Spain," in *The Uses of Literacy*, ed. McKitterick, 109–133; Adam J. Kosto, "*Sicut mos esse solet*: Documentary Practices in Christian Iberia, c. 700–1000," in *Documentary Culture*, ed. Brown et al., 259–282; Julio Escalona, "La documentación de la Castilla Condal: viejos problemas y nuevas perspectivas," in *Mundos Medievales. Espacios, sociedades y poder*, ed. Beatriz Arízaga Bolumburu et al., 2 vols (Santander: Ediciones Universidad de Cantabria, 2012), 1:473–487; Jonathan Jarrett, "Comparing the Earliest Documentary Culture in Carolingian Catalonia," in *Problems and Possibilities*, ed. Jarrett and McKinley, 89–126.

9 Igor Santos Salazar, "Competition in the Frontiers of the Asturian Kingdom: The *Comites* of Castile, Lantarón and Álava (860–940)," in *Rivaliser, coopérer dans les sociétés du haut Moyen Âge (500–1100)*, ed. Regine Le Jan, Geneviève Bührer-Thierry, and Stefano Gasparri (Turnhout: Brepols, 2018), 229–249, with detailed bibliography.

Régime preserved the papers and parchments on which we base our interpretations. Thus, the document collections that are available to us are not only an instrument for analyzing an institution, a society, or a region during a certain period of the Middle Ages; they constitute a *representation* of that institution, that society, or that region, as a consequence of the process of selection and filtering of memory undertaken in its archives.

For all these reasons we cannot approach the study of an archival collection made up of single-sheet parchments as if such a study could re-create a particular historical reality, as has been shown in recent years in various important studies.[10] The selection of records carried out in many ecclesiastical archives determines the methodology of our approach to the history of that time in any part of Christian Western Europe. Indeed, an organized archive tends to divest itself of any records that are no longer needed for the day-to-day administration of the church or monastery to which it belongs. Likewise, when a monastery decided to compile a cartulary, the process almost always entailed the selection of materials amenable to copying as well as the exclusion of those that were not.[11] The examples from central Italy correspond to the first situation. That is, they are early medieval document collections made up mostly of rich groups of *cartulae*, *notitiae*, and *brevia* preserved as single-sheet originals. Prominent among them are the groups at the archiepiscopal archive in Lucca (1800 units from before the year 1000) and at Piacenza (both the cathedral chapter's collection and that of the Basilica of San Antonino; more than 650 units dated before the year 1000).[12] To them we can also add the numerous (though not so bountiful) collections from other institutions such as San Bartolomeo in Pistoia, now kept at the Florence State Archive, as well as the collections of Parma cathedral.[13] Obviously, the documents that will be taken into account here, the

10 Wilhem Kurze, "Lo storico e i fondi diplomatici medievali. Problemi di metodo. Analisi storiche," in *Monasteri e nobiltà nel Senese e nella Toscana medievale. Studi diplomatici, archeologici, genealogici, giuridici e sociali* (Siena: Accademia Senese degli Intronati, 1989), 1–23; Ghignoli, "Su due famosi"; Enrico Faini, "Le fonti diplomatistiche per la storia fiorentina dei secoli XI e XII: una visione d'insieme," *Archivio Storico Italiano* 167 (2009), 3–55.

11 Although there are noteworthy exceptions, such as Saint Gall, which retained its oldest parchments even after they were copied into cartularies; Bernhard Zeller, "Le pergamene di San Gallo tra documentazione e memoria," in *Secoli XI e XII: l'invenzione della memoria*, ed. Simone Allegria and Francesca Cenni (Montepulciano: Le Balze, 2006), 63–71.

12 The figures can be found in François Bougard, "Actes privés et transferts patrimoniaux en Italie centro-septentrionale (VIIIe-Xe siècle)," *Mélanges de l'École française de Rome. Moyen Âge* 111, no. 2 (1999) (*Les transferts patrimoniaux en Europe occidental, VIIIe-Xe siècle*, Actes de la table ronde de Rome, 6–8 May 1999), 539–562, at 540.

13 ChLA² XCII.

placita that shed light on lay documentary culture in these areas of the *regnum*, are only a very small part of the whole corpus, whose size allows for the selection of a large enough group of examples to be significant.

In the north of the Iberian Peninsula, we are confronted with a completely different documentary landscape, especially outside León and Catalonia. In areas such as Liébana, Castile, and Álava large collections of single-sheet originals have failed to survive.[14] Rather, the ecclesiastical archives carried out a much more radical selection of memory, and the judicial documents that we will look at here are preserved in cartularies which do not always copy documents in full. The fact that monastic cartularies such as those of San Millán de la Cogolla and San Pedro de Arlanza open with falsifications is a significant example of this pattern of "memory manipulation."[15]

Moreover, no original documents are extant from the numerous churches and monasteries in Álava and Castile that were gradually annexed to the great monasteries in the kingdom of León-Castile during the eleventh and twelfth centuries.[16] The case in Liébana is different. Some of the records from Santa María de Piasca were preserved in the archive of Sahagún (to which Piasca belonged), together with the rest of its documentation.[17] However, in the cases of Castile and Álava it is difficult to know if the archives of churches and smaller monasteries were gathered at their mother houses or if, on the other hand, they remained *in situ* after the former came under the jurisdiction of the latter. Thus, most of the records related to areas in Álava, for example, have been preserved in the collections of large monasteries (such as San Millán de la Cogolla

14 With one exception, the monastery of Piasca: Julio Escalona, "Antes de los cartularios: gestión de archivos y transmisión de los documentos de la Castilla condal (siglo X-1038)," in *Charters et cartulaires*, ed. Escalona and Sirantoine, 131–151.

15 On San Millán's cartulary, see David Peterson, "Mentiras piadosas: falsificaciones e interpolaciones en la diplomática de San Millán de la Cogolla," in *Las donaciones piadosas en el mundo medieval*, ed. Alfonso García (Oviedo: Universidad de Oviedo, 2012), 295–314. On Arlanza, Julio Escalona, Pilar Azcárate and Miguel Larrañaga, "De la crítica diplomática a la ideología política. Los diplomas fundacionales de San Pedro de Arlanza y la construcción de una identidad para la Castilla Medieval," in *Actas del VI Congreso Internacional de Historia de la Cultura Escrita*, 2 vols (Madrid: Calambur, 2002), 1:159–206.

16 Juan Antonio Quirós Castillo and Igor Santos Salazar, "Founding and Owning Churches in Early Medieval Álava (North Spain): The Creation, Transmission and Monumentalization of Memory," in *Churches and Social Power in Early Medieval Europe. Integrating Archaeological and Historical Approaches*, ed. José C. Sánchez-Pardo and Michael G. Shapland (Turnhout: Brepols, 2015), 35–68.

17 Held today at Madrid, Archivo Histórico Nacional, *Clero, Sahagún, carpeta* (folder) 872.

or Santa María de Valpuesta), which not only filters our knowledge but also breaks up the geography where documents were originally produced and preserved, which is very unlike what happened with the archiepiscopal archives in Lucca and Piacenza.[18]

Even the preservation of original records, which did not go through the filter of a copyist, was never innocent or mechanical, but rather influenced by the interests of the ecclesiastical institutions that kept them. Their archives kept mainly (though not exclusively, as we will see) those records that were of interest to the cathedrals and monasteries, as well as the lay documents that served to preserve the memory of the founding family or the principal benefactors of a given ecclesiastical institution. Many other records are forever lost because the monks and canons often got rid of any written material related to lapsed property rights or contractual relationships.[19]

3 Italian *placita*: Lay Charters as Evidence in Court

In a lawsuit that took place in the early autumn of the year 897 in *villa Pomario*, located in the foothills to the west of Piacenza, Garibertus (the *diaconus* of the city's church) and his lawyer (the scabinus Gaidoaldus) presented to the court, presided over by Elmiric, Viscount of Piacenza, three documents related to a piece of land belonging to the *diaconus* located in Tranquilliano.[20] Their purpose was to defend Garibertus from the accusations of two brothers, Ragimpaldus and Raginaldus, as well as their brother-in-law, Aderaldus, who claimed a

18 The work of reconstructing this geography entails the theoretical reassignment of each document to the institution that might have originally kept it and the attribution of each text to the social context in which it was written. To this end, it is necessary to observe which archives were active in Castile-Álava during the period prior to the annexation of some monasteries by larger ones located in Castile and La Rioja. The picture that emerges is one of a region with a very large number of churches and monasteries that managed estates of variable size, from the widely scattered landed assets belonging to the monastery of San Esteban de Salcedo in Álava, to the more localized estates of a countless number of small ecclesiastical houses of different kinds and varying legal status. For a preliminary reconstruction of this picture focusing on the case of Álava, see Igor Santos Salazar, "Los privilegios de Berbeia y Barrio: elites, memoria y poder en Lantarón durante el siglo x," *Studia Histórica. Historia Medieval* 31 (2013), 51–81.

19 Or they were used for other purposes, such as bindings for notarial books. One of these cases has been recently edited: Paolo Tomei, "Chiese, vassalli, concubine. Su un inedito placito lucchese dell'anno 900," *Mélanges de l'École Française de Rome. Moyen Âge* 126, no. 2 (2014), 1–24.

20 ChLA[2] LXXI 19 = Manaresi 105 ([24–30] September 897).

right to the property. On first examination, this case seems to be related simply to a deacon's estate. However, upon closer examination of the contents of the documents presented by Garibertus, it becomes immediately clear how complex the lay dossiers cited in judicial records were, as well as how difficult it would have been for them to be transmitted were it not for ecclesiastical conservation. Garibertus and his lawyer presented three documents (*ostenserunt moniminas tres*), now lost, to the judges called to rule on the case. The first was a record of sale for the houses and the land located in Tranquilliano made to the deacon by Teutberga, with the approval of her husband, Arimundus. The second document was a record of sale for the above-mentioned properties made by the imperial *vassus* Gotefredus in favour of the aforementioned Teutberga. And the third and final document was a *notitia iudicati* that gave an account of a dispute in February 881 between Teutberga, her husband, and father-in-law, on the one hand, and three men (one of whom was the Ragimpaldus who was contesting the deacon's right to the land) *et suos consortes*. This dispute had been resolved in favour of the woman's claim to the property.

Thus, the *placitum* in which a deacon of the church of Piacenza sought to confirm his property rights (and succeeded in doing so) on the basis of the acceptance of the legitimacy of his title deeds turns out to illustrate the centrality of the written document in the daily lives of the laity and, in particular, the life of a woman, Teutberga. When she sold the land in Tranquilliano to Garibertus, she handed over to him not just the properties that were the object of the transaction but all the documentation demonstrating her legitimate possession of those properties—that is, the second record of sale mentioned above and the *notitia* recording the proceedings in the suit where she and her husband and father-in-law successfully argued their case. These two charters demonstrate the family's awareness of the importance of written documents in defending their economic interests and, thus, the need to retain said documents, which means that we can presume that there was a physical place dedicated to the preservation of these parchments.[21]

This is not an isolated case of judicial documents with indirect references to *deperdita*. There are further examples in documents from Tuscany beginning in the eighth century. Recall the "Ghittia list" mentioned above, which is an enumeration of numerous documents, most of which are of exclusively lay provenance. There are also extant parchments recording legal suits between laymen, such as in a different case in Pisa, dated 762 (preserved in a ninth-century copy

21 I will return to this point in the final section of the chapter.

now at the Pisa State Archive).[22] That year there was a suit between Alpertus and Rottruda over control of a hospital (*xenodochium*) founded by Alpertus's brother, the deceased Auripertus. The entire case hangs on the *cartula convenientiae* that Alpertus presented to the judges, with which he attempted to show the agreement he had reached with his brother to succeed him as administrator of the hospital should the latter die without an heir. Rottruda's lawyer was able to show in court that this *cartula* had formal defects.[23] Thus the clauses in the *cartula ordinationis* that Auripertus prepared at the time of the hospital's founding, which entrusted its administration to Rottruda, prevailed.[24]

The cases from Pisa that have been presented up to now have to do with the agility of officials in the kingdom of Lombardy in navigating the law. However, the greatest number of extant documents from the period of Carolingian rule of the *regnum* (beginning in the year 774)[25] offer new perspectives on the role of the written word in the daily life of people who do not belong to local elites or the cadre of *regnum* officials. For example, in a case dated November 815, we get a glimpse of the documentary culture of individuals and families in rural contexts. A certain Soave attempted to show, in response to an injunction by the diocese of Lucca, that his work in four vineyards located in Bulsiniana (in the Serchio Valley) was legal, according to a *livello* contract (*ad lavorandum*) he entered into with a merchant (*negutiante*) named Gheiprandus, who had bought the vineyards at an earlier, unknown date.[26] The lawyer for Lucca cathedral limited himself to pointing out that the vineyards were not the property of the merchant (as the latter had always believed), so the judges asked Soave to substantiate his claim by calling Gheiprandus as a witness, but unfortunately for Soave, the latter was at that point deceased. Lucca cathedral was victorious in this case, which is of interest to us because it shows, at the local

---

22 ChLA[2] LVIII 15.

23 About this *cartula*, it was stated *stare nullu modo deberit, quia nec per garetihinx nec per launichild factam non erat*—that is, it did not comply with the provisions of the laws of the Lombard kings: Rothari (nos. 172–175) and Liuprand (no. 73) in Claudio Azzara and Stefano Gasparri, eds., *Le leggi dei Longobardi. Storia, memoria e diritto di un popolo germanico* (Rome: Viella, 2005).

24 The case is reminiscent, in part, of the disputes involving the monastery of San Bartolomeo de Pistoia. Its lawyers always presented lay documents to the court in support of their cases before officials of the royal fisc. See Manaresi 19 (August 806) and 25 (March 812), both of which are preserved in eleventh-century copies. See my transcription online, at http://saame.it/fonte/placiti-toscani-toscana-10/ and http://saame.it/fonte/placiti-toscani-toscana-11/, respectively (accessed 17 October 2017).

25 See the contributions in Stefano Gasparri, ed., *774 ipotesi su una transizione* (Turnhout: Brepols, 2008).

26 ChLA[2] LXXIV 12.

level, how ordinary it was for people from the Tuscany countryside to have recourse to writing,[27] whether in contracts or sales, or in legal proceedings that developed into disputes (such as the handing over of *wadie*—that is, guarantees—which sometimes involved drawing up other documents[28]).

It is fitting at this point to recall two parchments preserved at the archiepiscopal archive in Lucca, in which a certain Mintus, the son of the deceased Petrus, and a resident of Pescia (province of Pistoia) appears before the courts.[29] In 865 the lawyer for the Church of Santa Maria a Monte (in what is now the province of Pisa) claimed that Mintus's possession of a field in the *fundus Puciatello* was illegal. The latter was then summoned to a later session of the court and proceeded to present the *cartula* showing his father's purchase of the field. However, the document referred to a different field in another locality, as demonstrated by the *inquisitio* carried out by the court. It was then only necessary for the Church of Santa Maria to present the deed of gift through which it had acquired the property under dispute. Nineteen years later, Mintus appears again in another suit, this time together with one Offus, brought against the diocese of Lucca over houses and other properties located in Pescia Maggiore.[30] During the third hearing of this trial, Mintus and Offus presented the *munimina*: a dossier made up of three charters of sale through which we can trace the successive transfers of title to the houses and other properties from their previous owners to the two men. This time as well, Mintus failed to win the lawsuit. Despite his having presented a rather substantial dossier (most prominently two *cartulae venditionis* between laymen), the lawyer for the diocese in Lucca, in a later session of the case, appealed to statements by three witnesses who swore that the bishop had owned the houses and other properties for more than thirty years. This testimony helped the lawyer to win the case.[31]

His defeat notwithstanding, the evidence mentioned in Mintus's two cases again underlines the proximity between laypeople (both farmers and small/

27 For a similar case, also from the area around Lucca (847), in which the court accepted the validity of a piece of writing, only for the case to hinge on the *auctor* who had previously owned the land, see Chris Wickham, "Land Disputes and their Social Framework in Lombard and Carolingian Italy," now repr. with additions in his *Land and Power: Studies in Italian and European Social History* (London: British School at Rome, 1994), 230–235.

28 See the list of *wadiae* written on parchment in the dossier of Peter of Niviano in ChLA^2 LXVI 42 (a. 890–891). Bougard, "Pierre de Niviano."

29 Manaresi 69 (April 865). See also, for this case, Wickham, "Land Disputes," 241.

30 Manaresi 94 (18 July 884).

31 On proof of thirty years' possession overriding written proof in Italian *placita*, particularly in Lucca, see Wickham "Land Disputes," 234–235.

medium landowners) and written documentation. And it underlines the fact as well that all these people had regular recourse to the courts to argue their cases, and that these cases were backed up by an arsenal of *cartulae* that have largely disappeared without a trace (Mintus's *munimina* have also not survived). This proximity between the laity and parchment documents should not be lost sight of, even though judicial proceedings often privileged oral over written evidence. After all, laypeople did bring their parchments to court, as we have seen clearly and repeatedly.

However, we should also not lose sight of the fact that the greater a family's wealth and social position, the greater its ability to generate written documents (still leaving aside, as we have done to this point, the lay aristocracies of the *regnum*). In this way, the management of a rich patrimony allowed families from the highest rungs among the *possessores*—that is, those with properties scattered throughout an entire diocese, or even in two neighbouring districts—to have in their possession more numerous archives, as has been shown in the well-known cases of Toto of Campione and Peter of Niviano and their respective family groups. Thus, the documents preserved in the ecclesiastical archives in Piacenza present us with another picture of *possessores* who must have had at their disposal some kind of archive for managing and defending their estates, spread out over much of the Piacenza diocese. These estates were ever vulnerable to the pretensions (not all of them legal) of neighbours or members of the same kinship group as their legitimate owners.

This seems to have been the case in a lawsuit involving Maginfredus de Cortenova and his wife, Gernia. In July 874,[32] in a *placitum* presided over by Empress Angilberga herself in person, this couple brought a suit against the *subdiaconus* Ratcausus over properties located in several areas of the *comitatus* of Piacenza. Ratcausus accused the couple of holding *malo ordine* (unlawfully) some *casas et res*. In the second hearing it was Gernia who spoke about the situation. The properties had been ceded by the subdeacon by means of several *cartulae* to both Gernia and her sister, Teutberga. It was also stipulated in a *breve recordationis* that both sisters agreed that she who died first, if she was without heirs, left her properties to the other sister. But when Teutberga died, Ratcausus forcefully took back both the properties and the documents. The court was also reminded how the subdeacon, who was probably a close rela-

32 ChLA² LXV 18 = Manaresi 77. This lawsuit is the continuation of the June 872 suit (records of which are now lost) mentioned in the former and of ChLA² LXV 15 (23 April 873). See Nicola Mancassola, *Uomini senza storia. La piccola proprietà rurale nel territorio di Piacenza dalla conquista carolingia alle invasioni ungariche (774–900)* (Spoleto: CISAM, 2013), 340–341.

tive of the two women, had been sued in absentia around the year 872, which allowed the case to be decided in favour of Gernia even back then.[33] The quantity and quality of the documentary evidence produced in this *placitum*, which ended in a second defeat for Ratcausus, shows once again the large number of *cartulae*, *brevia*, and *notitiae* that must have existed among many lay families throughout north-central Italy.

Local communities—whose various members had intricate social connections with one another—also appear in suits demonstrating their familiarity with written documents (although this is better seen through examples from Álava and Castile). It is enough to recall here the lawsuit between the community of Flexo and the monastery of Nonantola, a well-known case.[34] It was a trial presided over by Wala in the city of Reggio Emilia, and it names a group of ten men, *habitatores in Flexo*, who were demanding that the court protect their fishing and pasture rights in areas located *in finibus Regiensibus et Flexicianis*.[35] The men, among them a notary, presented the judges with a *praeceptum* (diploma) from Liutprand, the king of Lombardy. Despite this document, the lawyer for Nonantola claimed that the monastery had already won the case in an earlier lawsuit, presided over by Adalhard of Corbie. In addition, the lawyer presented other royal *praecepta* and had them read to the court; these had been given to Nonantola by Aistulf and Desiderius, who succeeded

33 Maginfredus also presented the *notitia* from the previous suit to the judges. This is one of the earliest examples of *investitura salva querela*. On the new formalism of Italian judicial documents beginning at the end of the ninth century, see François Bougard, *La justice dans le royaume d'Italie de la fin du* VIII*e siècle au début du* XI*e siècle* (Rome: École française de Rome, 1995), 307–328; and Giovanna Nicolaj, "Formulari e nuovo formalismo nei processi del *regnum Italiae*," in *La giustizia nell'alto medioevo (secoli* IX–XI*)* (Spoleto: CISAM, 1997), 347–379. See also above, Chapter 9.

34 Manaresi 36 (24 December 824, the document has been preserved as an original in the archive of the monastery of Nonantola). Giovanni Tabacco, *I liberi del re nell'Italia carolingia e postcarolingia* (Spoleto: CISAM, 1966) 134–137; Vito Fumagalli, *Terra e società nell'Italia padana. I secoli* IX *e* X (Turin: Einaudi, 1976), 61–63; Massimo Montanari, "Conflitto sociale e protesta contadina nell'Italia altomedievale," *Annali Istituto Alcide Cervi*, 16/1 (1994) (*Protesta e rivolta contadina nell'Italia Medievale*), 17–25; Pierpaolo Bonacini, "Il *territorium* di *Flexum*," in *Terre d'Emilia* (Bologna: Clueb, 2001), 211–233. Recent studies that have returned to this document, taking a novel perspective, include: Chris Wickham, "Space and Society in Early Medieval Peasant Conflicts," in *Uomo e spazio nell'Alto Medioevo*, 2 vols (Spoleto: CISAM, 2003), 1:551–586; and Tiziana Lazzari, "La tutela del patrimonio fiscale: pratiche di salvaguardia del pubblico e autorità regia nel regno longobardo del secolo VIII," *Reti Medievali. Rivista* 18, no. 1 (2017), 99–121.

35 *Flexo* is a rural area that is difficult to identify, situated somewhere on the plains near Reggio and the Po River. The community accused the monastery of unlawfully (*contra legem*) possessing the lands.

Liutprand on the throne of Pavia, and they underlined the legitimacy of the monastery's possession of the rights in question. The ten men protested, but a group of witnesses testified that the royal diplomas presented by the monastery were authentic.[36] The *flexiciani* then went right back and tried to draw the judges' attention to a different *praeceptum* from Liutprand, adding that during the first lawsuit they had been unable to produce it in support of their case because they were not in possession of it at that time (*non habebamus praeceptum*). This explanation has raised some doubts in the minds of scholars more predisposed to interpret this second *praeceptum* from Liutprand as a false document drafted somewhere in the bishopric of Reggio.[37] In other words, they contend that the document was constructed *ad hoc* in order to be presented to the judges to make the case against Nonantola. This hypothesis is likely correct since we know of other examples of documentary forgery perpetrated by learned members of the Reggio episcopal entourage, about which individuals we know nothing.[38]

In any case, the judges did not get into evaluating the veracity of the evidence provided by the men from Flexo. They confined themselves to underlining how the diplomas presented by Nonantola established a change in the beneficiary of the disputed fiscal lands. The rights of the men from the plains had lapsed. However, it is interesting to note how these men clung, almost desperately, to documentary proof in an attempt to win a suit against an imperial monastery like Nonantola.[39] In Italy, local communities also understood the value of writing and the need to manoeuvre through a maze of parchment even though doing so did not always guarantee the desired results.

---

36 *iudices vel ceteri nobiles homines, qui tunc ibi fuerant presentes, eam vera esse testificati sunt*, Manaresi 36, p. 112.

37 Tiziana Lazzari, "Comunità rurali nell'Alto Medioevo: pratiche di descrizione e spie lessicali nella documentazione scritta," *Paesaggi, comunità, villaggi medievali*, ed. Paola Galetti, 2 vols (Spoleto: CISAM, 2012), 1:405–421, at 420. Also, Andrea Castagnetti, *L'organizzazione del territorio rurale nel medioevo. Circoscrizioni ecclesiastiche e civili nella Langobardia e nella Romania* (Bologna: Pàtron, 1982), 84, has suggested that the vocabulary used in the *praeceptum* may belong to the ninth century and not, therefore, to Liutprand's time.

38 ChLA² LXXXVIII 26 (8 June 781). This is a falsified document from the second half of the ninth century, now at the Modena State Archive. In it, Charlemagne confirms the privileges granted by his predecessors and takes the Cathedral of Reggio Emilia under his protection. The parchment is accompanied by a genuine seal, which highlights Reggio's skillfulness in creating forgeries.

39 For other conflicts between monasteries and rural communities over the exploitation rights on properties belonging to the royal fisc, see Chris Wickham, *Studi sulla società degli Appennini nell'Alto Medioevo. Contadini, signori e insediamento nel territoiro di Valva (Sulmona)* (Bologna: Clueb, 1982), 25–50.

There was a negative side as well to the importance that documents had in people's daily lives: for example, when written documents were purposely destroyed or concealed in order to gain an advantage in possible future disputes. This is what a certain Grasevertus, a resident of what is today Grazzano Visconti, in the province of Piacenza, seems to have done. He was forced to promise before the court not to challenge two of his sisters for the properties that their father had left to them *per cartula*. These sisters had taken Grasevertus to court because they believed the document in which their father had stipulated the legacy had not disappeared by accident.[40]

Beginning in the final years of the ninth century, however, we can observe a change in Italian judicial documents that reflects a similar change in the structure of private documents. There is progressively less space for laymen, while eminent personages and especially ecclesiastics or people directly related to them become more numerous among the parties to sales, gifts, and lawsuits.[41] For example, communities hardly figure in *placita* after the second half of the ninth century. As has been recently shown, the church in Piacenza selectively preserved documentation from the mid-tenth century, privileging records associated with its property interests.[42] Thus, other than the cases that have been discussed in the last few pages, there are only a few more examples that show the importance of written documents for laypeople in the tenth century.

The smaller number of examples is also the result of the gradual decrease in the number of lawsuits themselves over the middle of the tenth century.[43] There was a 'crisis' in public justice whose causes are still a matter of debate among specialists.[44] This situation affects our ability to observe the world of the laity even when the original documents have been preserved. However, this situation can still be seen in the few judicial proceedings held to resolve disputes between laymen, who presented their *munimina* and the *notitiae* of

40 ChLA² LXV 40 (23 April 883). On the destruction of documents, see Warren Brown, "When Documents Are Destroyed or Lost: Lay People and Archives in the Early Middle Ages," *Early Medieval Europe* 11, no. 4 (2002), 337–366.

41 Igor Santos Salazar, *Una terra contesa. Spazi, poteri, società nell'Emilia Orientale dei secoli VI–X* (Florence: Le Lettere, 2011), 180–195.

42 Marios Costambeys, "Disputes and Documents in Early Medieval Italy," in *Making Early Medieval Societies. Conflict and Belonging in the Latin West, 300–1200*, ed. Kate Cooper and Conrad Leyser (Cambridge: Cambridge University Press, 2016), 125–154, at 146–148.

43 Costambeys, "Disputes and Documents," 147.

44 Igor Santos Salazar, "Crisis? What Crisis? Political Articulation and Government in the March of Tuscany through Placita and Diplomas from Guy of Spoleto to Berengar II," *Reti Medievali. Rivista* 17, no. 2 (2016), 251–279.

earlier lawsuits,[45] or in the cases where ecclesiastics presented to the court documents mentioning sales involving only laymen.[46]

4 Charters, Communities, and Lay Individuals in Castile, Álava, and Liébana

The documentary evidence available in the case of Iberia is, as was mentioned above, completely different from what we have seen in the case of Italy. The parchments on which trial records were originally written are not extant. We do not even have single-sheet copies from the tenth or eleventh centuries. It is possible, as Isabel Alfonso has recently argued, that trial records never existed at all in Castile, unlike what we have seen in the Italian cases.[47]

So it should be no surprise that all the judicial records that I will study in this section have been transmitted through copies in several monastic cartularies from Castile and Rioja. This affects our perception of the processes by which the disputes we know of were resolved, as well as the information that we can obtain from judicial records about the documentary culture of the laity.[48]

The lack of original procedural records means that there are other important differences with respect to the Italian case: the cartularies contain judicial documents that were copied using very different standards of formalization,[49] unlike what happened in Italy starting at the end of the ninth century, where formulas such as the *ostensio cartae* or the *investiturae salva querela* predominated, as we have seen in the *placita* from the kingdom of Italy starting during the final years of Carolingian rule.[50]

---

45 Raffaello Volpini, "Placiti del *Regnum Italiae* (secc. IX–XI). Primi contributi per un nuovo censimento," in *Contributi dell'Istituto di storia medioevale* [*dell'Università cattolica del Sacro Cuore*], ed. Paolo Zerbi, vol. 3 (Milan: Vita e pensiero, 1975), 245–520, no. 10 (19 October 973).

46 Manaresi 142 (May 944).

47 Isabel Alfonso, "El formato de la información judicial en la Alta Edad Media peninsular," in *Chartes et cartularies*, ed. Escalona and Sirantoine, 191–218, at 193–196.

48 On the justice system in Castile in the tenth century, see Igor Santos Salazar, "Ruling through Court: The Political Meanings of the Settlement of Disputes in Castile and Álava (ca. 900–1038)," *Al-Masaq. Journal of the Medieval Mediterranean* 29, no. 2 (2017), 133–150. For an overview of the legal process in the northwestern part of Christian Spain, see Wendy Davies, *Windows on Justice in Northern Iberia, 800–1000* (Abingdon: Routledge, 2016).

49 On the different types of Iberian legal documents and their lack of formalization, see Isabel Alfonso, "El formato," 199–209.

50 However, there are some formulas that are common to documents produced all over the

Sometimes the copies in the Castilian cartularies follow no apparent order, which might indicate the existence of older document pieces that were already fragmentary by the time they were copied. It has even been suggested that the different ways in which procedural documentation was copied into cartularies might reflect the fact that some scribes 'misunderstood' the original document, a suggestion that has recently been criticized by Isabel Alfonso.[51]

It is important to note another difference with respect to the Italian documents: the cases studied here are concentrated predominantly in the years of Count Fernán González's rule in Castile and Álava (r. ca. 930–970), earlier documents being extremely rare and problematic. In effect, for the ninth century we have only echoes of lay participation in judicial proceedings. There is the case of one Rebelio against the monks of Santa María de Puerto[52] or the case of Lellitus and Lilus, who were obliged to acknowledge before court that they had received a church in Liébana from the abbot of San Martín de Turieno (now Santo Toribio de Liébana).[53]

During the tenth century written evidence becomes more plentiful. Likely, the political consolidation of the county of Castile in the middle of that century encouraged the local elites to go to law more often, as they were also seeking to use the courts to sanction the grounds of their hegemony. In any case, it needs to be remembered that, in these pages, the analysis of this group of documents is not intended to address the format in which the judicial information is transmitted. Here the focus is solely those judicial records with information that can shed light on the intimate relationship between the laity and written documents in a geographical area that is traditionally associated with societies that were politically and socially underdeveloped and, thus, had a rudimentary documentary culture.[54] The importance of writing in early medieval Castilian

Kingdom of Asturias and León, although even these cannot be compared to the rigid formalism of the *placita* in Carolingian Italy. See Davies, *Windows on Justice*, 95–120.

51 Agustín Prieto Morera, "El proceso en el Reino de León a la luz de los diplomas," in *El Reino de León en la Alta Edad Media, II: Ordenamiento jurídico del Reino* (León: Centro de Estudios 'San Isidoro', 1997), 381–518, at 347–348. Criticism of this position in Alfonso, "El formato," 193.

52 This monastery is situated on the sea, in Santoña, modern province of Cantabria. Puerto 1 (13 December 863).

53 Liébana 17, (17 December 885). The church in question had been donated to San Martín by a lay family, but the record cites only the *testamentum* (that is, the donation) granted to the abbot.

54 The study in English by Robert Portass, *The Village World of Early Medieval Northern Spain. Local Community and the Land Market* (London: Boydell & Brewer, 2017), 19–24, recaps these historiographical positions.

lay society can be seen in cases in which the texts refer to the presentation of evidentiary documentation to the court.[55] Let us take a look at some of these cases.

In the spring of 947, Bermudo Gudestioz noted, when he entered the monastery of Cardeña and donated his properties to it, that the *villa* of Lacio (which was included in its entirety in the gift) was acquired in a lawsuit (records for which are not extant) he filed against Menendo and his father, Placio. The charter of gift also mentions how the properties were endowed with certain immunities, confirmed to Bermudo by Fernán González, count of Castile, who had been the judge in the suit in which Bermudo acquired Lacio.[56] Everything in this charter (the reminder about the immunities granted by the count to these properties and the participation in the lawsuit) shows how close Bermudo was to the world of writing that granted rights and awarded properties.

Ten years after this *traditio*, Fernán González again presided over legal proceedings in which a certain García was called to defend his interests against accusations by the lawyers for Cardeña, who maintained that García had usurped properties that his brother, the *presbiter* Oveco, had donated to the monastery in the village of Tobilla, near Torresandino (in the modern province of Burgos). The document has the added attraction of being one of the few cases in which it is possible to follow the judicial proceedings through various sessions. In the third session, García was summoned to appear again before the court with documents (*cum cartas*) to support his case. This he could not do, and he acknowledged that the properties had been donated by his brother to Cardeña via a *cartula tradictione*.[57] The fact that García did not have at his disposal the *cartulae* that might have helped him make whatever case he did have does not preclude taking note of the centrality, in this example as well, of the written word in the attempt to defend an estate.

A short passage in the *fuero* (local code) of Nave de Albura, from a somewhat later period (ca. 1012), might shed better light on documentary culture among

55 However, there are fewer of these cases than those which were resolved with the help of sworn testimony by witnesses. In effect, the *conditiones sacramentorum* abound in the oldest extant judicial documentation: Valpuesta 10 (13 May 911), Valpuesta 11 (25 May 919), and Puerto 2 (26 March 927). Other examples of sworn statements that do not follow the formulae of *conditiones sacramentorum* can be found in SMC 23 (a. 936), SMC 24 (a. 940, two lawsuits concerning property belonging to laypeople in what is now La Rioja), CC 38 (26 February 972). Examples of trials without any documentation presented: Liébana 30 (13 December 922), Cardeña 200 (1 May 932), Piasca 24 (a. 983).

56 CC 22 (27 April 947).

57 Cardeña 210 (14 January 957). The suit continued up to December of the same year.

the laity.[58] When Nuño Álvarez and Justa de Maturana came before the count of Castile in Término to defend their privileges, they did so *cum suo scripto, quod habebant de suo foro*. Such a *scriptum* shows not only the relationship between documents and laypeople but also the custom among the latter of defending their interests using the written word, in this case a single-sheet parchment that would probably date back to the tenth century. Unfortunately, no copy of this piece of writing has survived, and it has excited little exegetical interest in spite of its importance as an incontrovertible example of the existence of legal documentation of a lay nature that must have been preserved and transmitted over generations in archives about which we know almost nothing.

Measures taken by rural communities (commonly referred to as *concilia*[59]) to defend their interests before the courts are one of the main features of judicial documentation from Castile and Álava during the second half of the tenth century. This can be observed in documents as early as the *fuero* of Barrio and Berbeia, which mention three suits (ca. 950–1084) involving negotiations between the comital (and later royal) authorities and rural societies that hinged on the community leaders' defence of their fiscal immunities. These privileges must have been grounded on some type of documentation prior to the date when some of the properties with immunity entered into the patrimony of the monastery of San Millán de la Cogolla, making it very difficult to understand how this information was transmitted.[60]

In other cases it is easier to observe the actions of these groups more directly. In the year 972 the *concilium* of *Agusyn* (Los Ausines), forty members of which are mentioned, confirmed the donation of the pastureland of Lomba to Count García Fernández, executed by the *maiores et minores* of the *concilium* in exchange for an exemption granted by the count for the services that the community was to provide in his castles.[61] There is no extant written record of

58 SMC 144 (ca. 1012).

59 The topic of the *concilia* has interested historians for a long time and has been dealt with from various perspectives. See, among many others, Claudio Sánchez Albornoz, "Repoblación del reino asturleonés. Proceso, dinámica y proyecciones," *Cuadernos de Historia de España* 53–54 (1973), 236–461; Reyna Pastor, *Resistencias y luchas campesinas en la época del crecimiento y consolidación de la formación feudal. Castilla y León, siglos X–XIII* (Madrid: Siglo XXI, 1990); and Wendy Davies, "Lordship and Community: Northern Spain on the Eve of the Year 1000," *Past & Present* Supplement 2 (2007), 18–33, at 31.

60 On the origins of this document and its copying into San Millán's cartulary, see Santos Salazar, "Los privilegios," 55–58. The document was copied on fol. 172 of the *Becerro Galicano* of San Millán de la Cogolla, an online edition of which is now available at http://www.ehu.eus/galicano/id535&l=en&cro=0 (accessed 8 October 2017).

61 Cardeña 3 (28 May 972).

the privilege. However, in light of the statements given by the people called to provide testimony in the *fuero* of Nave de Albura, it is no exaggeration to think that the privilege granted to the members of the *concilium* of *Agusyn* also must have been reflected in some written form (a *scriptum*). There are a few incidental references to these comital diplomas addressed to laypeople and now lost.[62] But there can be no doubt that many of them must have been presented in lawsuits. For example, records of a suit between the "*infanzones* de Espeja" and the count of Castile mention a *mandato* of the count in which his political and military interests were imposed against the will of some elites in rural areas.[63] These comital orders and their rejection by the local people must have left a much more substantial and detailed document trail than the mere echoes that remain in the ecclesiastical archives.

Obviously, the participation of numerous people in these lawsuits should not be interpreted as proof that any and all members of these communities were part of a documentary culture. This culture would very likely have been confined to the community leaders. Ultimately, the assemblies that met with the president of the court and its judges had the purpose of ensuring that the courts' decisions were widely known and that the rulings on disputes remained part of collective memory: as Isabel Alfonso has pointed out, the hearings in a case were also a vehicle for communicating its outcome.[64] This is a clear example of literacy being deployed in social contexts in which the collective reading of a ruling had great political significance, regardless of whether all present knew how to read the text that was made public before the assembly.[65]

Where there is no room for doubt is about the relationship between laypeople and writing from Liébana and the coast of the Cantabrian Sea down to the southernmost reaches of Castile in the tenth century, especially if we

62 As in Cardeña 268 (27 April 947), or Silos 2 (6 April 979).

63 *Et non quisierunt infantiones de Spelia suo mandato facere, proinde presit ille comite tota Spelia, et non eis laxabit nisi suas hereditatelias; et mandabit illa suo maiorino de Clunia.* Antonio Ubieto, *El Cartulario de San Juán de la Peña* (Valencia: Anúbar, 1962–1963), no. 54 (ca. 1030).

64 Isabel Alfonso, "Judicial Rhetoric and Political Legitimation in Medieval León-Castile," in *Building Legitimacy: Political Discourses and Forms of Legitimacy in Medieval Societies*, ed. Isabel Alfonso, Hugh Kennedy, and Julio Escalona (Leiden-Boston: Brill, 2004), 51–87. For the role of assemblies as spaces for the creation of consensus in rural society, see Matthew Innes, "People, Places and Power in Carolingian Society," in *Topographies of Power in the Early Middle Ages*, ed. Mayke de Jong, Frans Theuws, and Carine Van Rhijn (Leiden-Boston: Brill, 2001), 397–437.

65 Warren Brown et al., "Introduction," in *Documentary Culture*, 1–10; Roger Wright, "La difusión inmediata del documento: lenguaje y lectura en el siglo x," in *Charters et cartulaires*, ed. Escalona and Sirantoine, 117–126.

keep in mind that the evidence allowing us to observe this relationship does not come from original documents, as in the case of Italy, but from copies included in cartularies. These copies provide only a filtered reflection of the documentary culture of the laity in northern Spain.

5 Ecclesiastical Archives and Lay Documentary Culture: A Conclusion

In presenting his edition of the document known as the "Ghittia list", Luigi Schiaparelli stressed the large number of *cartulae* that had been forever lost in comparison to the meagre number of documents from the Lombard period that survived down to our day. And he added laconically: "lavoriamo su frammenti."[66] In the case of judicial documentation referring to lay records, these fragments had to pass through two different filters before we ever laid eyes on them: first, the process of being put down in writing, which reflects the degree of formalization of judicial documents by the scribes who wrote them (or copied them, as in the Iberian cases); and second, the process of their archival transmission.

The process of formalizing judicial writing is perhaps the main difference between the two geographical areas studied here. The formalism we observe in Italy between the end of the ninth and the tenth century, when the *ostensio cartae* and *investitura salva querela* became well established, has no counterpart in what can be documented in Castile, where documents of a judicial nature exhibit greater informality. The formulas with which records of cases were prepared in Italy, the "public validation in court" through the *ostensio* or the *investitura* of the documents presented to the court, made it so that the *placitum* itself, which contained the judgment, took the place of much lay documentation, such that it would not have made sense to preserve the documents once the lawsuit was concluded.[67] This change meant that, in Italy, judicial documents in which it was possible to follow the debates argued before judges (as in the *Flexum* case) were replaced by more rigid formularies that provide an account of cases in which, nevertheless, written proof was required of the parties to the dispute.[68]

Moreover, the disparities between the 'judicial systems' of the two areas make for other noteworthy differences. For example, the value of oral testi-

66 CDL 295, p. 440.
67 Costambeys, "The Laity," 249.
68 See above, Chapter 9.

mony seems to have been greater in Castile, where many of the lawsuits that we have either direct or indirect knowledge of, in Liébana, Álava, and La Rioja, were argued on the basis of oaths (sworn testimony: *conditiones sacramentorum*), without any written documents being presented.[69] But even so, the examples that show the force of the written word also in the courts of Castile are significant enough to underline the centrality of writing in the social life of this Iberian county. Laypeople, especially those in rural communities, went to court even in the tenth century (in contrast to Italy) taking their documents with them. Besides, changes over time in the way that disputes were resolved (greater weight given to oral testimony or written proof) and changes in the documents (becoming more or less formal) that recorded these cases argued before the courts seem to be questions about the articulation of power through dispensing justice and, thus, seem to be less useful for calibrating the documentary culture of the laity both in Castile and in Tuscany or Piacenza.[70]

Another important problem is, as we have said, the archival transmission of documentation pertaining to the laity. The customary explanation for why these records ended up in ecclesiastical archives is the following: whenever a monastery, church, or cathedral received a donation or bought or exchanged lands—or any other kind of property that could be transferred or inherited—the written documents related to these properties (*munimina*) might as well be transferred to the ecclesiastical archive. This is true particularly of documents that might be useful as proof of the donor's legitimate possession of the property prior to its definitive transfer: in short, any and all documentation that contained information relating to acquired properties and their legal status in earlier periods, which might prove useful to their new owner as insurance against possible lawsuits.

In recent years, some research has demonstrated that this explanation is more a cliché than a point of fact that can withstand a careful analysis of the extant documentation. The mechanisms of preservation of some lay archives reflect more complex procedures that are at times difficult to reconstruct. Certain churches/monasteries seem to have functioned as archives for the lay families/communities either of their founders (as in the case of Toto and the church of Campione) or of the groups that had donated a large part of their properties to these churches/monasteries (this would be the case of the family of Faquilona, the mother of Abbot Opila of San Martin de Turieno, which

69 See above, n. 55.

70 On the political and social context of these changes, see, for Piacenza, Costambeys, "The Laity," 146–151, and for Castile, Santos Salazar, "Ruling through Court," 142–148.

preserves the family's documents). So, it sometimes happens that there is a juxtaposition of different archives in a single ecclesiastical archive, as is also the case in the "Ghittia list", to the point that Antonella Ghignoli was able to study the collections of the archive by noting the recipients of the documentation mentioned in the list.[71]

This is a situation that we might surmise also existed in Castile when we find rural elites appearing in lawsuits in defense of their political and economic privileges. The *scriptum* presented by Justa de Maturana and Nuño Álvarez may well have been kept in an ecclesiastical building that has been completely lost to memory. Sometimes the relationship between documents, local society, and ecclesiastical archives appears more direct, such as in the case of Villabáscones, in the province of Burgos. There, the community constructed a monastery with which it would end up reaching some informal agreements. Very likely the *testamenta* that sanctioned these pacts on the part of the villagers ended up it the monastery's archive and later were transferred to Cardeña, whose cartulary preserves copies of them.[72] But for the moment, these considerations should be taken as working hypotheses. New research is needed to shed light on these issues.

Looking back again at the documentary culture of the laity, the examples cited here confirm, in the case of Italy, the picture that recent studies have drawn of the presence and dissemination of documents among the laity. Focusing on *deperdita* that are mentioned in judicial proceedings has allowed us, however, to observe the *dynamic* use of these documents—that is, the degree of familiarity with which the records that families preserved in the hope of protecting their rights and making their case were used in public, both in Castile and in Tuscany and Emilia. In addition, we have seen that women played an important role both in the suits and in preserving the documents that were presented in those suits: Rottruda, Gernia, Teutberga, and Justa de Maturana show just how rooted written culture was across the gender divide in local societies throughout much of southern Europe during the ninth and tenth centuries.[73]

71 Ghignoli, "Su due famosi," 53–59, divides the documents cited in the "Ghittia list" into collections, which makes clear that lay and ecclesiastical archives coexisted.

72 Cardeña 54 (23 August 956). The church of San Martín was built on plots of land donated by members of Villabáscones society, as can be seen in Cardeña 42 (a. 944–950?).

73 On the activities of women within early medieval families, see the special issue "Donne in famiglia nell'alto medioevo," *Genesis. Rivista della Società Italiana delle Storiche* IX, no. 1 (2010).

Obviously, Castile does not have the same features and traditions as north-central Italy, but even so, the documentation presented here indicates that the contact between laypeople and writing was both more widespread and more frequent than has been supposed. There is one more thing to note: all the evidence from Liébana, Castile, and Álava comes from rural areas, and although the collections at Monte Amiata in Tuscany also show the importance of writing and its presence among village elites in peripheral, rural areas of the March of Tuscany, in the north of Spain this rural phenomenon is much more pronounced because monasteries absorbed the entirety of our written memory. Moreover, unlike the Italian cases (almost all of which were preserved in diocesan, and thus urban archives: Lucca, Piacenza, Parma), in the Iberian territories that we have considered here, most Roman cities were abandoned, and the new 'urban' centres did not even become episcopal sees until the eleventh century (as in the case of Burgos).[74]

This disparity between the two geographical areas is particularly significant when we reflect on the impact that writing had on the social complexity of early medieval Europe both inside and outside the Carolingian world and its successor states. To cite Luigi Schiaparelli once more, these fragments show the relationship between laypeople and writing not only in north-central Italy but also in the most peripheral areas of rural Spain, where the documentary culture of the laity has left important traces in spite of being filtered by ecclesiastical memory.

Bibliography

Abbreviations

Cardeña: Fernández Flórez, José Antonio, and Sonia Serna Serna, eds. *El Becerro Gótico de Cardeña. El primer gran cartulario hispánico (1086)*. 2 vols. Burgos: Real Academia Española—Instituto Castellano Leonés de la Lengua, 2017.

CC: Zabalza Duque, Manuel, ed. *Colección Diplomática de los Condes de Castilla*. Valladolid: Junta de Castilla y León, 1998.

CDL: Luigi Schiaparelli, ed. *Codice Diplomatico Longobardo*. Vol. II. Rome: Tipografia del Senato, 1929.

74 J.A. Quirós Castillo and I. Santos Salazar, "Territorios sin ciudades y complejidad social. El cantábrico oriental en la Alta Edad Media," in *The Medieval City and Archaeology, La ciutat medieval i arqueologia. VI Curs Internacional d'Arqueologia Medieval*, ed. Flocel Sabaté and Josep Brufal (Lleida: Universitat di Lleida, 2015), 139–174.

ChLA[2]: Cavallo, Guglielmo, and Giovanna Nicolaj, eds. *Chartae Latinae Antiquiores*: Facsimile-edition of the Latin Charters. 2nd Series, *Ninth Century*. Vol. LVIII (Italy 30), *Pisa, Volterra*, edited by Antonino Mastruzzo, 2001; Vol. LXV (Italy 37), *Piacenza 2*, edited by Cristina Mantegna, 2004; Vol. LXVI (Italy 38), *Piacenza 3*, edited by Cristina Carbonetti Vendittelli, 2005; Vol. LXXI (Italy 43), *Piacenza 8*, edited by Cristina Mantegna, 2007; Vol. LXXIV (Italy 46), *Lucca 3*, edited by Francesco Magistrale, Clelia Gattagrissi, and Paola Fioretti, 2004; Vol. LXXXVIII (Italy 60), *Modena, Nonantola 1*, edited by Giovanni Feo, Maddalena Modesti, Matteo Al Kalak, and Melania Mezzetti, 2008; Vol. XCII (Italy 64), *Parma 1*, edited by Francesca Santoni, 2012. Dietikon-Zurich: Urs Graf.

Liébana: Sánchez Belda, Luis, ed. *Cartulario de Santo Toribio de Liébana*. Madrid: Archivo Histórico Nacional, 1948.

Manaresi: Cesare Manaresi, ed. *I placiti del "Regnum Italiae"*. Vol. 1 (*a. 776–945*). Rome: Tipografia del Senato, 1955.

Piasca: Montenegro, Julia, ed. *Colección diplomática de Santa María de Piasca* (*857–1252*). Santander: Gobierno de Cantabria, 1991.

Puerto: Serrano y Sanz, Manuel. "El cartulario de la iglesia de Santa Maria del Puerto (Santoña)." *Boletín de la Real Academia de la Historia* 73 (1918), 420–442 (Digital edition: Biblioteca Virtual Miguel de Cervantes, Alicante, 2009).

SMC: Ubieto Arteta, Antonio, ed. *Cartulario de San Millán de la Cogolla* (*759–1076*). Valencia: Anúbar, 1976.

Valpuesta: Ruiz Asencio, José María, Irene Ruiz Albi, and Mauricio Herrero Jiménez, ed. *Los becerros gótico y galicano de Valpuesta*. Madrid: Real Academia Española—Instituto Castellano y Leonés de la Lengua, 2010.

Other Primary Sources

Álamo, Juan del, ed. *Colección Diplomática de San Salvador de Oña* (*822–1284*). Madrid: CSIC, 1950.

Azzara, Claudio, and Stefano Gasparri, eds. *Le leggi dei Longobardi. Storia, memoria e diritto di un popolo germanico*. Rome: Viella, 2005.

Becerro Galicano Digital. Accessed 30 July 2020. www.ehu.eus/galicano.

Serrano, Luciano, ed. *Cartulario del Infantado de Covarrubias*. Silos: Real Monasterio, 1907.

Serrano, Luciano, ed. *Cartulario de San Pedro de Arlanza*. Madrid: Ibáñez de Aldecoa, 1925.

Ubieto, Antonio, ed. *El Cartulario de San Juán de la Peña*. Valencia: Anúbar, 1962–1963.

Volpini, Raffaello. "Placiti del *Regnum Italiae* (secc. IX–XI). Primi contributi per un nuovo censimento." In *Contributi dell'Istituto di storia medioevale* [*dell'Università cattolica del Sacro Cuore*], edited by Paolo Zerbi, vol. 3, 245–520. Milan: Vita e pensiero, 1975.

Secondary Works

Alfonso, Isabel. "Judicial Rhetoric and Political Legitimation in Medieval León-Castile." In *Building Legitimacy: Political Discourses and Forms of Legitimacy in Medieval Societies*, edited by Isabel Alfonso, Hugh Kennedy, and Julio Escalona, 51–87. Leiden-Boston: Brill, 2004.

Alfonso, Isabel. "El formato de la información judicial en la Alta Edad Media peninsular." In *Charters et cartulaires comme instruments de pouvoir. Espagne et Occident chrétien (VIIIe–XIIe siècles)*, edited by Julio Escalona and Hélène Sirantoine, 191–218. Toulouse: Université de Toulouse-Le Mirail, 2013.

Bonacini, Pierpaolo. "Il *territorium* di *Flexum*." In *Terre d'Emilia*, 211–233. Bologna: Clueb, 2001.

Bougard, François. *La justice dans le royaume d'Italie de la fin du VIIIe siècle au début du XIe siècle*. Rome: École française de Rome, 1995.

Bougard, François. "Pierre de Niviano, dit le Spoletin, sculdassius et le gouvernement du comté de Plaisance à l'époque carolingienne." *Journal des Savants* 2 (1996), 291–337.

Bougard, François. "Actes privés et transferts patrimoniaux en Italie centro-septentrionale (VIIIe-Xe siècle)." *Mélanges de l'École française de Rome. Moyen Âge* 111, no. 2 (1999) (*Les transferts patrimoniaux en Europe occidental, VIIIe-Xe siècle*, Actes de la table ronde de Rome, 6–8 May 1999), 539–562.

Brown, Warren. "When Documents Are Destroyed or Lost: Lay People and Archives in the Early Middle Ages." *Early Medieval Europe* 11, no. 4 (2002), 337–366.

Brown, Warren, Marios Costambeys, Matthew Innes, and Adam J. Kosto, eds. *Documentary Culture and the Laity in the Early Middle Ages*. Cambridge: Cambridge University Press, 2013.

Brown, Warren, Marios Costambeys, Matthew Innes, and Adam J. Kosto, "Introduction." In *Documentary Culture*, edited by Brown et al., 1–16.

Castagnetti, Andrea. *L'organizzazione del territorio rurale nel medioevo. Circoscrizioni ecclesiastiche e civili nella Langobardia e nella Romania*. Bologna: Pàtron, 1982.

Clanchy, Michael. *From Memory to Written Record: England, 1066–1307*. Cambridge, Mass.: Harvard University Press, 1979.

Collins, Roger. "Literacy and the Laity in Early Medieval Spain." In *The Uses of Literacy in Early Mediaeval Europe*, edited by Rosamond McKitterick, 109–133. Cambridge: Cambridge University Press, 1990.

Costambeys, Marios. "The Laity, the Clergy, the Scribes and Their Archives: The Documentary Record of Eighth- and Ninth-Century Italy." In *Documentary Culture and the Laity in the Early Middle Ages*, edited by Warren Brown et al., 231–257. Cambridge: Cambridge University Press, 2013.

Costambeys, Marios. "Disputes and Documents in Early Medieval Italy." In *Making Early Medieval Societies. Conflict and Belonging in the Latin West, 300–1200*, edited by

Kate Cooper and Conrad Leyser, 125–154. Cambridge: Cambridge University Press, 2016.

Davies, Wendy. "Lordship and Community: Northern Spain on the Eve of the Year 1000." *Past & Present* Supplement 2 (2007), 18–33.

Davies, Wendy. *Windows on Justice in Northern Iberia, 800–1000*. Abingdon: Routledge, 2016.

"Donne in famiglia nell'alto medioevo." *Genesis. Rivista della Società Italiana delle Storiche* IX, no. 1 (2010).

Erhart, Peter, Karl Heidecker, and Bernhard Zeller, eds. *Die Privaturkunden der Karolingerzeit*. Dietikon-Zurich: Urs Graf Verlag, 2009.

Escalona, Julio. "La documentación de la Castilla Condal: viejos problemas y nuevas perspectivas." In *Mundos Medievales. Espacios, sociedades y poder*, edited by Beatriz Arízaga Bolumburu et al., 2 vols, vol. 1, 473–487. Santander: Ediciones Universidad de Cantabria, 2012.

Escalona, Julio. "Antes de los cartularios: gestión de archivos y transmisión de los documentos de la Castilla condal (siglo X-1038)." In *Charters et cartulaires*, edited by Escalona and Sirantoine, 131–151.

Escalona, Julio, and Hélène Sirantoine, eds. *Charters et cartulaires comme instruments de pouvoir. Espagne et Occident chrétien (VIIIe-XIIe siècles)*. Toulouse: Université de Toulouse-Le Mirail, 2013.

Escalona, Julio, Pilar Azcárate, and Miguel Larrañaga. "De la crítica diplomática a la ideología política. Los diplomas fundacionales de San Pedro de Arlanza y la construcción de una identidad para la Castilla Medieval." In *Actas del VI Congreso Internacional de Historia de la Cultura Escrita*, 2 vols, vol. 1, 159–206. Madrid: Calambur, 2002.

Everett, Nicolas. *Literacy in Lombard Italy (c. 568–774)*. Cambridge: Cambridge University Press, 2003.

Faini, Enrico. "Le fonti diplomatistiche per la storia fiorentina dei secoli XI e XII: una visione d'inseme." *Archivio Storico Italiano* 167 (2009), 3–55.

Feller, Laurent, Agnès Gramain, and Florence Weber. *La fortune de Karol: Marché de la terre et liens personnels dans les Abruzzes au haut Moyen Âge*. Rome: École française de Rome, 2005.

Fumagalli, Vito. *Terra e società nell'Italia padana. I secoli IX e* X. Turin: Einaudi, 1976.

García Leal, Alfonso. "El archivo de los condes Fruela Muñoz y Pedro Flaínez (854–1048): una visión nueva de viejos documentos." *Signo. Revista de Historia de la Cultura escrita* 13 (2004), 121–147.

Gasparri, Stefano, ed. *774 ipotesi su una transizione*. Turnhout: Brepols, 2008.

Gasparri, Stefano, and Cristina La Rocca, eds. *Carte di famiglia: Strategie, rappresentazione e memoria del gruppo familiare di Totone di Campione (721–877)*. Rome: Viella, 2005.

Geary, Patrick J. *Phantoms of Remembrance: Memory and Oblivion and the End of the First Millenium*. Princeton: Princeton University Press, 1994.

Ghignoli, Antonella. "Su due famosi documenti pisani dell'VIII secolo." *Bullettino dell'Istituto Storico Italiano per il Medio Evo* 106/2 (2004), 1–69.

Guyotjeannin, Olivier, Laurent Morelle, and Michel Parisse, eds. *Les cartulaires*. Paris: École nationale des Chartes, 1993.

Heidecker, Karl, ed. *Charters and the Use of the Written Word in Medieval Society*. Turnhout: Brepols, 2000.

Innes, Matthew. "People, Places and Power in Carolingian Society." In *Topographies of Power in the Early Middle Ages*, edited by Mayke de Jong, Frans Theuws, and Carine Van Rhijn, 397–437. Leiden-Boston: Brill, 2001.

Jarrett, Jonathan. "Comparing the Earliest Documentary Culture in Carolingian Catalonia," in *Problems and Possibilities*, edited by Jarrett and McKinley, 89–126.

Jarrett, Jonathan and Allan S. McKinley, eds. *Problems and Possibilities of Early Medieval Charters*. Turnhout: Brepols, 2013.

Kosto, Adam J. "Laymen, Clerics, and Documentary Practices in the Early Middle Ages: The Example of Catalonia." *Speculum* 80 (2005), 44–74.

Kosto, Adam J. "*Sicut mos esse solet*: Documentary Practices in Christian Iberia, c. 700–1000." In *Documentary Culture and the Laity in the Early Middle Ages*, edited by Warren Brown et al., 259–282. Cambridge: Cambridge University Press, 2013.

Kosto, Adam J., and Anders Winroth, eds. *Charters, Cartularies and Archives: The Transmission and Preservation of Documents in the Medieval West*. Toronto: Pontifical Institute of Mediaeval Studies, 1999.

Kurze, Wilhem. "Lo storico e i fondi diplomatici medievali. Problemi di metodo. Analisi storiche." In *Monasteri e nobiltà nel Senese e nella Toscana medievale. Studi diplomatici, archeologici, genealogici, giuridici e sociali*, 1–23. Siena: Accademia Senese degli Intronati, 1989.

Lazzari, Tiziana. "Comunità rurali nell'Alto Medioevo: pratiche di descrizione e spie lessicali nella documentazione scritta." *Paesaggi, comunità, villaggi medievali*, edited by Paola Galetti, 2 vols, vol. 1, 405–421. Spoleto: CISAM, 2012.

Lazzari, Tiziana. "La tutela del patrimonio fiscale: pratiche di salvaguardia del pubblico e autorità regia nel regno longobardo del secolo VIII." *Reti Medievali. Rivista* 18, no. 1 (2017), 99–121.

Mancassola, Nicola. *Uomini senza storia. La piccola proprietà rurale nel territorio di Piacenza dalla conquista carolingia alle invasioni ungariche (774–900)*. Spoleto: CISAM, 2013.

McKitterick, Rosamond. *The Carolingians and the Written Word*. Cambridge: Cambridge University Press, 1989.

McKitterick, Rosamond, ed. *The Uses of Literacy in Early Mediaeval Europe*. Cambridge: Cambridge University Press, 1990.

Montanari, Massimo. "Conflitto sociale e protesta contadina nell'Italia altomedievale." *Annali Istituto Alcide Cervi*, 16, no. 1 (1994) (*Protesta e rivolta contadina nell'Italia Medievale*), 17–25.

Mostert, Marco. "Communication, Literacy and the Development of Early Medieval Society." In *Comunicare e significare nell'Alto Medioevo*, 2 vols, vol. 1, 29–55. Spoleto: CISAM, 2005.

Nicolaj, Giovanna. "Formulari e nuovo formalismo nei processi del *regnum Italiae*." In *La giustizia nell'alto medioevo (secoli IX–XI)*, 347–379. Spoleto: CISAM, 1997.

Pastor, Reyna. *Resistencias y luchas campesinas en la época del crecimiento y consolidación de la formación feudal. Castilla y León, siglos X–XIII.* Madrid: Siglo XXI, 1990.

Peterson, David. "Mentiras piadosas: falsificaciones e interpolaciones en la diplomática de San Millán de la Cogolla." In *Las donaciones piadosas en el mundo medieval*, edited by Alfonso García, 295–314. Oviedo: Universidad de Oviedo, 2012.

Portass, Robert. *The Village World of Early Medieval Northern Spain. Local Community and the Land Market.* London: Boydell & Brewer, 2017.

Prieto Morera, Agustín. "El proceso en el Reino de León a la luz de los diplomas." In *El Reino de León en la Alta Edad Media, II: Ordenamiento jurídico del Reino*, 381–518. León: Centro de Estudios 'San Isidoro', 1997.

Quirós Castillo, Juan Antonio, and Igor Santos Salazar. "Founding and Owning Churches in Early Medieval Álava (North Spain): The Creation, Transmission and Monumentalization of Memory." In *Churches and Social Power in Early Medieval Europe. Integrating Archaeological and Historical Approaches*, edited by José C. Sánchez-Pardo and Michael G. Shapland, 35–68. Turnhout: Brepols, 2015.

Quirós Castillo, Juan Antonio, and Igor Santos Salazar. "Territorios sin ciudades y complejidad social. El cantábrico oriental en la Alta Edad Media." In *The Medieval City and Archaeology, La ciutat medieval i arqueologia. VI Curs Internacional d'Arqueologia Medieval*, edited by Flocel Sabaté and Josep Brufal, 139–174. Lleida: Universitat di Lleida, 2015.

Rio, Alice. *Legal Practice and the Written Word in the Early Middle Ages: Frankish formulae, c. 500–c. 1000*. Cambridge: Cambridge University Press, 2009.

Sánchez Albornoz, Claudio. "Repoblación del reino asturleonés. Proceso, dinámica y proyecciones." *Cuadernos de Historia de España* 53–54 (1973), 236–461.

Santos Salazar, Igor. *Una terra contesa. Spazi, poteri, società nell'Emilia Orientale dei secoli VI–X.* Florence: Le Lettere, 2011.

Santos Salazar, Igor. "Los privilegios de Berbeia y Barrio: elites, memoria y poder en Lantarón durante el siglo X." *Studia Histórica. Historia Medieval* 31 (2013), 51–81.

Santos Salazar, Igor. "Crisis? What Crisis? Political Articulation and Government in the March of Tuscany through Placita and Diplomas from Guy of Spoleto to Berengar II." *Reti Medievali. Rivista* 17, no. 2 (2016), 251–279.

Santos Salazar, Igor. "Ruling through Court: The Political Meanings of the Settlement of Disputes in Castile and Álava (ca. 900–1038)." *Al-Masaq. Journal of the Medieval Mediterranean* 29, no. 2 (2017), 133–150.

Santos Salazar, Igor. "Competition in the Frontiers of the Asturian Kingdom: The *Comites* of Castile, Lantarón and Álava (860–940)." In *Rivaliser, coopérer dans les sociétés du haut Moyen Âge (500–1100)*, edited by Regine Le Jan, Geneviève Bührer-Thierry, and Stefano Gasparri, 229–249. Turnhout: Brepols, 2018.

Tabacco, Giovanni. *I liberi del re nell'Italia carolingia e postcarolingia.* Spoleto: CISAM, 1966.

Tomei, Paolo. "Chiese, vassalli, concubine. Su un inedito placito lucchese dell'anno 900." *Mélanges de l'École Française de Rome. Moyen Âge* 126, no. 2 (2014), 1–24.

Wickham, Chris. *Studi sulla società degli Appennini nell'Alto Medioevo. Contadini, signori e insediamento nel territoiro di Valva (Sulmona).* Bologna: Clueb, 1982.

Wickham, Chris. "Land Disputes and their Social Framework in Lombard and Carolingian Italy." *Land and Power: Studies in Italian and European Social History*, 230–235. London, British School at Rome, 1994.

Wickham, Chris. "Space and Society in Early Medieval Peasant Conflicts." In *Uomo e spazio nell'Alto Medioevo*, 2 vols, vol. 1, 551–586. Spoleto: CISAM, 2003.

Wright, Roger. "La difusión inmediata del documento: lenguaje y lectura en el siglo x." In *Charters et cartulaires comme instruments de pouvoir. Espagne et Occident chrétien (VIIIe-XIIe siècles)*, edited by Julio Escalona and Hélène Sirantoine, 117–126. Toulouse: Université de Toulouse-Le Mirail, 2013.

Zeller, Bernhard. "Le pergamene di San Gallo tra documentazione e memoria." In *Secoli XI e XII: l'invenzione della memoria*, edited by Simone Allegria and Francesca Cenni, 63–71. Montepulciano: Le Balze, 2006.

PART 3

Framing Disputes: Judicial Authorities and Social Order

CHAPTER 11

Versatile Participants in Medieval Judicial Processes: Catalonia, 900–1100

Adam J. Kosto

1 Introduction

As Jeffrey Bowman observed in his insightful study of law and disputing in medieval Catalonia, "judicial assemblies took place in crowded rooms."[1] We can be more specific. The record of an assembly held in 898 in Girona to decide a case between Count Gausfred and the abbey of Sant Medir and Sant Genís, for example, lists by name: the count and viscount, serving as presidents; six judges, one of whom also served as an advocate for the count; a *saio*, or subordinate judicial official; five clerics and at least twenty laymen in the role of *boni homines*; the advocate for the abbey; twenty-seven witnesses; and a scribe. To them could be added perhaps fourteen subscribers who are not named in the body of the document, although subscriptions do not guarantee presence. Even without those subscribers, the document identifies sixty-three late-ninth-century individuals participating in a fairly routine judicial procedure.[2] Equally striking, for those sceptical of the institutional sophistication of early medieval law, or of reading the specifics of Late Roman procedure as found in the Visigothic Code as a reflection of ninth- and tenth-century practice, is the number of distinct procedural roles that these sixty-three individuals fill, independent of their social roles, such as viscount or priest: president, judge, *saio*, advocate, *bonus homo*, witness, scribe. The assembly was not just crowded; it was complex.

1 Jeffrey A. Bowman, *Shifting Landmarks: Property, Proof, and Dispute in Catalonia around the Year 1000* (Ithaca: Cornell University Press, 2004), 108. The abbreviations used in this paper for editions of charters (cited by document number, unless otherwise indicated) are listed in the bibliography.

2 CC5 91. Subscription, in the absence of some other indication, does not necessarily indicate presence: see, e.g., Benoît-Michel Tock, *Scribes, souscripteurs et témoins dans les actes privés en France (VIIe–début XIIe siècle)* (Turnhout: Brepols, 2005), 12–13, 397–400. For the opposite phenomenon—absence of subscription not necessarily indicating absence—see Nicholas Vincent, "The Court of Henry II," in *Henry II: New Interpretations*, ed. Christopher Harper-Bill and Nicholas Vincent (Woodbridge: Boydell, 2007), 278–334, at 284–299.

 | DOI:10.1163/9789004683006_013

Family or social or even emotional context emerges readily from accounts of later medieval judicial processes, but students of early medieval law often cannot go beyond a study of procedural roles in trying to figure out how judicial procedures worked;[3] even when the evidence is not purely normative, the individuals whose names appear in scattered descriptive sources are difficult to bring to life, especially once one descends below the boldfaced names of the high aristocracy. The famously abundant evidence from Catalonia—1202 records in the PRJ database, out of perhaps 20,000 before the year 1100[4]—provides an opportunity to dig a little deeper, to find the same individuals in multiple records, and thus to create a more detailed picture of judicial assemblies. The present study explores the intersection between the institutional and the social by focusing precisely on individuals who appear in different roles, serving as 'versatile participants.' There are two examples in the case from 898 cited above: one of the judges, Trasuad, also acted as the advocate of the count, Gausfred, who was at once president and litigant. Another sort of versatile actor, one who fulfills different roles in different cases, is represented by the mysterious Abbot Berenguer, who between 1050 and 1061 appeared in a dozen judicial documents involving the count of Barcelona, variously as judge, messenger, ex parte witness, or subscriber.[5] To truly take advantage of the data and attempt to develop a network map of the participants in judicial assemblies requires computational tools that are not yet at hand; even after

3 Paul Ourliac, "Juges et justiciables au XIe siècle: Les *boni homines*," *Recueil de mémoires et travaux publié par la Société d'histoire du droit et des institutions des anciens pays de droit écrit* 16 (1994), 17–33; Karin Nehlsen–von Stryck, *Die* boni homines *des frühen Mittelalters: Unter besonderer Berücksichtigung der fränkischen Quellen* (Berlin: Duncker & Humblot, 1981); and now Wendy Davies, *Windows on Justice in Northern Iberia, 800–1000* (Abingdon: Routledge, 2016), 155–180.

4 This study was prepared using the working database (PRJ) for the project "Procesos judiciales en los reinos del norte peninsular (ss. IX–XI)" [prj.csic.es] as it stood in November 2015, with 1181 dispute records classified as from Catalonia (out of a total of 11,733 Catalonian records surveyed). In its present form, the database includes 1202 records (out of a total 12,105 surveyed). Pierre Bonnassie, *La Catalogne du milieu du Xe à la fin du XIe siècle: Croissance et mutations d'une société*, 2 vols (Toulouse: Association des publications de l'Université de Toulouse-Le Mirail, 1975–1976), 1:22, n. 20, estimated at least 5000 documents for the tenth century and 10,000 for the eleventh. *CC*, when complete, will contain just under 5000 documents for the period before 1000, with very few from earlier than the tenth century. Pierre Bonnassie and Jordi Fernández-Cuadrench, "Les documents catalans des IXe–XIIe siècles: Éditions récentes et publications en cours," *Le Moyen âge* 105 (1999), 149–160, at 153, overestimated 7–8000 documents for *CC*; they estimated over 10,000 *published* documents through the twelfth century. In any case, the PRJ database, assembled from printed collections, is far from complete.

5 Adam J. Kosto, "The Elements of Practical Rulership: Ramon Berenguer I of Barcelona and the Revolt of Mir Geribert," *Viator* 47 (2016), 67–94, at 81–84.

a full-text database is established, there is the challenge, on the one hand, of the sheer volume of named *boni homines* and witnesses, for which automated processing would be useful; and on the other, there is the problem of tying names to unique individuals (is this Ramon the same as that Ramon?), for which probabilistic methods are in order.[6] The present study focuses on the more limited roles, namely judges, advocates, scribes, and *saiones*, and in particular the overlap between judges and the other three categories. A focus on judges makes sense, in that they reliably appear in documentation for judicial processes.

Two sorts of individuals, however, appear in the sources described as *iudices*. The first are professional judges, judicial experts appointed by local authorities such as counts; their status as judge was part of their identity, and they regularly subscribed or were referred to as judges even when they were not acting in a judicial capacity. The second—more common in eleventh-century records—are ad hoc judges, individuals named to adjudicate a specific case.[7] Their status as judges was not part of their identity; they normally do not subscribe or appear elsewhere with the title. The professional judges are more easily traced across documents. Did they fulfill roles other than that of judge, thus serving as versatile participants? To anticipate the conclusion: only rarely—but that result nevertheless enriches our understanding of medieval judicial processes in Catalonia before the year 1100.

2 Scribes

Three judge-scribes active around the year 1000 are already very well known: the father and son Ervig and Ponç Bonfill Marc, and the most famous, Bonhom (Appendix, Table 11.1).[8] As for the latter, Anscari Mundó identified his hand

6 The ChartEx project was an early attempt to develop such methods: diggingintodata.org/awards/2011/project/chartex (accessed 21 July 2023). Much progress has been achieved since then by others.

7 Josep M. Salrach, *Justícia i poder a Catalunya abans de l'any mil* (Vic: Eumo, 2013), 26, n. 10. Cf. Bowman, *Shifting Landmarks*, 82–84. Non-professional *iudices* appear, for example, in *PACBI* 523, 556. It is far from clear that the long lists of judges in late-ninth-century records (e.g., the panel of ten *iudices* in CC6 92 / 17 December 875) were professionals in the same sense as their later counterparts.

8 Anscarí M. Mundó, "El jutge Bonsom de Barcelona, cal·lígraf i copista del 979 al 1024," in idem, *Obres completes*, 1.1, *Catalunya: De la romanitat a la sobirania* (Barcelona: Curial Edicions Catalans / Publicacions de l'Abadia de Montserrat, 1998), 587–610 [orig. *Scribi e colofoni: Le*

not only in manuscripts of a version of the Visigothic Code assembled under his direction, the so-called *Liber iudicum popularis*, and a large-format Bible manuscript, but also on 17 original documents, from among likely 120 that refer to him. At least 33 of the 120 are judicial documents that appear in the PRJ database.[9] Among these 33, those that identify a presiding judge or panel—records of judgment, publication charters of testaments,[10] and executions of forfeited pledges[11]—are evenly split between those where Bonhom presides and acts as scribe, and those where he presides but does not act as scribe. In only four does

---

sottoscrizioni di copisti dalle origini all'avvento della stampa: Atti del seminario di Erice, X colloquio del Comité international de paléographie latine (23–28 ottobre 1993), ed. Emma Condello and Giuseppe De Gregorio (Spoleto: Centro italiano di studi sull'alto medioevo, 1995), 269–288]; Josep Maria Font Rius, "Entorn de la figura de Ponç Bofill Marc, jutge comtal de Barcelona, a les primeries del segle XI," *Boletim da Faculdade de Direito* (Coimbra) 58 (1982), 377–395; José María Font y Rius, "La escuela jurídica de Barcelona," in *Historia de España Menéndez-Pidal*, vol. 7.2, *La España cristiana de los siglos VIII al XI: Los núcleos pirenaicos (718–1035): Navarra, Aragón, Cataluña* (Madrid: Espasa-Calpe, 1999), 729–750. Michel Zimmermann, *Écrire et lire en Catalogne (IXe–XIIe siècle)*, 2 vols (Madrid: Casa de Velázquez, 2003), 1:133, 144–147, addresses the overlap of judges and scribes; see also 2:944–948.

9 *Sant Cugat* 218, 267, 277, 282, 317, 352, 425, 428, 430–431, 438, 452, 468, 491; *DACB1* 265, 268, 328–329, 345; *DACB2* 8, 54, 118, 161, 214, 274, 344; *CC4* 1736, 1849; *Urgellia* 278; *DVic* 720–722; *PACB1* 108. Antoni M. Udina i Abelló, *La successió testada a la Catalunya altomedieval* (Barcelona: Fundació Noguera, 1984), no. 31, not in the database, is a testamentary publication charter of 988 that Mundó thought marks Bonhom's first action as a judge (Mundó, "El jutge," 595).

10 Testamentary procedure might generate three separate types of documents: the testament itself; a testamentary publication, recording the testimony of the witnesses to the bequest; and a testamentary execution, effecting a grant ordered in a testament. Since testamentary publications were normally performed before a judge (and a priest), and testamentary executions noted that they were performed subsequent to a judicial order (*iuditium obligatum*), they have been included in the PRJ database, and in great numbers: 295 publications (25 per cent) and 240 executions (20 per cent). There is a single testament proper: *Urgellia* 300, which includes a restitution of property unjustly seized. On testamentary procedure and its documentation in this corpus, see: Udina i Abelló, *La successió testada*; Jean Bastier, "Le testament en Catalogne du IXe au XIIe siècle: Une survivance wisigothique," *Revue historique de droit français et étranger*, 4th ser., 51 (1973), 373–417; Nathaniel Lane Taylor, "The Will and Society in Medieval Catalonia and Languedoc, 800–1200" (Ph.D. dissertation, Harvard University, 1995); Salrach, *Justícia i poder*, 151–160.

11 The value of a pledge was established with judicial intervention (*insistente iudice*), in keeping with the Visigothic law: *tunc creditor iudici vel preposito civitatis pignus ostendat, ut, quantum iudicio eius et trium honestorum virorum fuerit estimatum, sit licentia distrahendi. Et postmodum de pretio venditi pigneris creditor, quantum ei debetur, sibi evidentius tollat, et relicum ille recipiat, qui pignus seposuerat* ("Lex Visigothorum," in Karl Zeumer, ed., *Leges Visigothorum*, MGH LL nat. Germ. 1 [Hanover: Hahn, 1902], V.6.3, p. 232). See Salrach, *Justícia i poder*, 144–150.

he only act as a scribe or as a subscriber and a scribe, and in one of those it might not even be him.[12] He penned five testamentary executions; these do not normally name the judges involved and appear to have been non-contentious.[13] One 'judgeless' transaction penned by Bonhom is more interesting: a family settlement in which two brothers confirm alienations made by their mother and stepfather during their minority. The document is labelled a *confirmatio et pacificatio*, the latter term likely hinting at the contentious nature of the transaction.[14] One can imagine a respected judge helping arrange the settlement, but without a formal judicial role only appearing as scribe. Thus Bonhom generally acts as a scribe either in contentious cases that he had a formal judicial role in, or in non-contentious cases.

Ervig Marc's profile is slightly different. He appears in at least 23 documents in the PRJ database, half acting as a scribe, half not.[15] But unlike Bonhom, he does not act as a scribe in non-contentious testamentary executions, except in one case, where the executor is his colleague, the judge Oruç.[16] On the other hand, he served as a scribe for four contentious cases that, although 'judgeless,' might have drawn on his expertise: entry into servitude to a church made as expiation for infanticide; an episcopal settlement following an unjust usurpation; a comital sale of land acquired as composition for an unspecified offense; and a grant made in composition to the cathedral of Barcelona for depredations of church property.[17] Ervig's son Ponç Bonfill first appears just as a scribe, in a judgment presided over by his father in 1009,[18] but is then quite active in the 1010s, 20s, and 30s; he is found in at least 40 documents in the PRJ database[19] and was the scribe of 28 of them. Of these, only two are apparently non-

12 *Sant Cugat* 452; *DACB2* 8, 118, 214. *DACB2* 8 reads *Bonushomo, qui hanc evacuationem scripsit die et anno quo supra*; while he sometimes appears simply to subscribe as a *levita*, rather than a *levita* and *iudex*, this is a rare case of just the name (see also *Sant Cugat* 352).

13 *Sant Cugat* 267, 277, 425, 428, 430.

14 *DACB1* 329.

15 As scribe: *CC4* 1526, 1864; *DACB1* 175, 191, 201, 203, 224, 237, 253; *CC5* 512; *PACB2* 14. Not as scribe: *DACB1* 181, 194, 229, 243, 265; *DACB2* 118, 129, 142, 150; *Sant Llorenç* 110; *CC4* 1736; *Sant Cugat* 317.

16 *DACB1* 175.

17 *DACB1* 203, 224, 237, 253. There is an Ervig *levita* among those present in *DACB1* 201, penned by Ervig *presbiter*, but neither is identified as a *iudex*. As this is after Ervig's first appearance as a judge-scribe (*CC4* 1526), this may also be a case of only serving as a scribe. In *DACB1* 243, Ervig is neither scribe nor judge, but is present at an extra-judicial settlement; see Salrach, *Justícia i poder*, 215.

18 *DACB2* 129.

19 As scribe: *DACB2* 129, 257, 353, 356–357, 362, 404, 419, 477, 490; *Carlemany* 77; *Urgellia* 391, 438; *DVic* 809, 937; *PACB1* 142, 154, 214, 221; *Sant Cugat* 494, 497, 506, 509, 512, 523–524, 529;

contentious executory documents.[20] More like Bonhom than his father, when he is mentioned in one of these documents, he is usually presiding; indeed in a few of the cases where he appears as just a scribe or as a subscriber and scribe, judges are referred to but not named, or appear only as subscribers to a document that would normally list judges—these may reflect loosening of formulas more than a change in judicial roles.[21] But as with Ervig, there are 'judgeless' cases where a contentious aspect may indicate that his duties went beyond the secretarial: quitclaims, for example, or a comital sale of land acquired as composition for adultery.[22]

To summarize, these three judges sometimes penned their own judgments, and sometimes left them to others; while their scribal activity occasionally appears in apparently non-judicial documents, a contentious element in these often suggests that the scribes may have had a quasi-judicial role, serving as versatile participants. But what is surprising is how rare this phenomenon of judge-scribes actually is. Aside from these three famous judges, only eleven other judge-scribes appear in the PRJ database—which is weighted toward the sort of judicial business in which one might expect judge-scribes to be found. Only three of these eleven penned more than two of the documents.[23]

Judges obviously might have a role in the composition of the document whether or not they were the scribes: they could act, as Ponç Bonfill identified himself in one judgment, not only as *scriptor*, but also as *auctor*.[24] In an execution of a forfeited pledge settled before him, he subscribed *qui hanc venditionis scripturam scribano dictavi et huius tesits sum*. For a procedure for the reconstitution of lost documents (*reparatio scripturae*), it was *qui haec suprascripta sunt sicut Leges Goticae iubent subscripsit atque ita corroboravit*.[25]

Santa Anna 24. Not as scribe: *DACB2* 233, 241, 370, 465, 504, 517; *DVic* 780; *PACB1* 125, 175, 212; *Sant Cugat* 437, 527. Not in the PRJ database, or included in Appendix, Table 11.1: *Cardona* 98 (scribe, presiding), 106 (scribe, non-contentious sale).

20 *Sant Cugat* 506; *Santa Anna* 24.

21 E.g., *DACB2* 362; *DVic* 809; *Carlemany* 77.

22 *DACB2* 356, 490; *PACB1* 154.

23 *Adalbertus levita et iudex* (*Sant Llorenç* 227); *Arnaldus iudex* (*Urgellia* 1043); *Arnallus Lahos iudex* (*DACB2* 217); *Bernardus sacer atque iudex* (*DOliba* 100); *Ermengaudus lator iuris et legis* (*Urgellia* 926, 951, 1141); *Fedacho iudex* (*Urgellia* 479); *Guisadus iudex* (*DACB2* 573; *PACB1* 223, 280); *Henricus levita monachus et iudex* (*DVic* 1074; *Santa Anna* 54); *Reimundus levita et iudex* (*DACB2* 627–630, 754); *Vivas sacer atque iudex* (CC4 1595); *Wifredus levita et iudex* (*DACB2* 161). Not in the PRJ database: *Sendredus iudex* (*Cardona* 15 / 25 September 982); *Adalbertus levita et iudex* (*Cardona* 95 / 20 August 1033), plausibly the same as the scribe in *Sant Llorenç* 227 (1031).

24 *PACB1* 142: *Poncius, cognomento Bonusfilius, clericus et iudex, huius iudicii auctor et scriptor.*

25 *DVic* 780; *PACB1* 175.

A number of non-judicial scribes also acknowledge judicial authorship—for some reason, all of the evidence comes from the county of Urgell. A judgment in 1027 presided over by the judge Guifré and subscribed by Ponç Bonfill Marc was penned by the *levita* Ermemirus *with* (*cum*) judge Guifré. More clearly, in 1052, the scribe Bonfill wrote the document *precipiente iudice*; in 1065, it was Geravus *sacerdos, dictante Bernardo iudice*.[26] The judge Ermengaudus, *lator iuris*, who acted as a scribe himself in 1079, 1081, and 1096, dictated to a scribe in a judgment he presided over in 1086.[27] But it did not always work this way. Thus in 1100, the *grammaticus* Robert was the one who dictated the document to the scribe, despite the presence of a judge.[28] And in 1091 a scribe composed a memorial of complaint "just as Arnau Guillem (the plaintiff) related and said it to me," again despite the presence of judges in the case.[29] In the context of the thousands of documents and hundreds of scribes, however, and the formulaic nature of many documents, this latter situation—a judge-free composition—was probably the most common. That in turn suggests that scribes possessed a substantial amount of legal knowledge: that they served as versatile participants in both writing the document and shaping the process that it recorded.[30]

3 *Saiones*

The *saio* is usually described as a minor judicial official or court officer or bailiff. The role is linked linguistically and conceptually to the royal retainers of the Ostrogothic kingdom,[31] although in Catalonia, at least through the eleventh century,[32] *saiones* appear to be strictly judicial functionaries. They figure expli-

26 *Urgellia* 416, 656, 772.

27 *Urgellia* 1032; cf. above, n. 23.

28 *Urgellia* 1178.

29 *Urgellia* 1079: *Stefanus levita, qui hec carta comemoracionis vel evacuacionis scripsi sicut Arnallus Guilelmi mihi comemoravit et dixit sub die et anno prefixo.*

30 Salrach, *Justícia i poder*, 181.

31 Gideon Maier, *Amtsträger und Herrscher in der Romania Gothica: Vergleichende Untersuchungen zu den Institutionen der ostgermanischen Völkerwanderungsreiche* (Stuttgart: Franz Steiner Verlag, 2005), 169–196.

32 Most twelfth-century references seem to depict a non-judicial, fiscal officer: Thomas N. Bisson, ed., *Fiscal Accounts of Catalonia under the Early Count-Kings (1151–1213)*, 2 vols (Berkeley: University of California Press, 1984), 1:278. See also *PACB2* 443, 460, 511, 1096, 1103; *Santa Anna* 175 (?); Jordi Bolòs, ed., *Diplomatari del monestir de Santa Maria de Serrateix (segles X–XV)* (Barcelona: Fundació Noguera, 2006), no. 139; José María Font Rius, ed., *Cartas de población y franquicia de Cataluña*, 2 vols in 3 (Madrid: Consejo Superior

citly alongside judges in six chapters of the Visigothic Code, tasked with distraint, imprisonment, confiscation, exacting security for appearance, receiving fines, transferring possession of property, and receiving oaths. The sole chapter in which they are not clearly judicial officials is from the oldest, fifth-century layer of the text.[33]

At least 90 documents from up to the year 1100 refer to *saiones* (Appendix, Table 11.2): 34 from the ninth century, 31 from the tenth, and 25 from the eleventh; adding in references to anonymous *saiones* or simply to the office, it is 31 from the ninth century, 34 from the tenth, and 32 from the eleventh; either way, given the overall survival curve of documents in the region, those figures are even more sharply decreasing than they seem. With respect to the PRJ database, *saiones* are mentioned in 71 of the documents from the region of Catalonia, or about 6 per cent. Fairly systematic searching of databases and indices has uncovered another 18 documents that refer to *saiones* from outside the database, mostly subscriptions to apparently non-contentious, non-testamentary land transfers. There are surely more *saiones* out there to be found, especially for the eleventh century, but this is the most complete set of data on *saiones* from Catalonia yet assembled.[34] On the basis of these data, it is clear that

---

de Investigaciones Científicas, 1969–1983), nos. 149, 209; Federico Udina Martorell, ed., *El "Llibre Blanch" de Santas Creus (Cartulario del siglo XII)* (Barcelona: Consejo Superior de Investigaciones Científicas, 1947), no. 235. The reference to *saiones* in the Usatges de Barcelona (*Et emparamentum quod fecerit princeps per se uel per suum nuncium uel per suum saionem uel per suum sigillum* […]) seems best understood in this twelfth-century, non-judicial context (Joan Bastardas, ed., *Usatges de Barcelona: El codi a mitjan segle XII*, 2nd ed. [Barcelona: Fundació Noguera, 1991], cap. 61 [Us. 66]). *PACB2* 1014 refers to the opening of "Lex Visigothorum," ed. Zeumer, II.2.4.

33 "Lex Visigothorum," ed. Zeumer, II.1.18, 26; II.2.4, 10; VI.1.5; X.2.6; cf. V.3.2 (= Codex Euricianus 311). Other passages (e.g., II.1.19, 21; VII.4.4) may include oblique references to *saiones*. See also "Fragmenta Gaudenziana," in Karl Zeumer, ed., *Leges Visigothorum*, MGH LL nat. Germ. 1 (Hanover: Hahn, 1902), 12, pp. 470–471. For the *saio* as an episcopal subordinate, see "Concilium Emeritense" 8 (Giovanni Domenico Mansi, ed., *Sacrorum conciliorum nova et amplissima collectio*, vol. 11 [Florence: Antonio Zatta, 1765], cols. 80–81).

34 The publication of *CC*7–8 will surely add more. In identifying *saiones*, I am discounting the possibility that in the eleventh century the term may have developed into an anthroponymic element, as some editors seem to indicate. See, e.g., *DACB2* 1079 (1065, Bonifilii Sagoni), 1097 (1066, Archimballus Sagone), 1160 (1068, Bonefilius Sagoni); *Cardona* 151 (1046, Ioan Saio), 289 (1097, Saio); *NH*11 226 (1004, Salone); and below, n. 46 (1013, Arnaldo Sayoni). In what follows (and in Appendix, Table 11.2), names of *saiones* (only) have been lemmatized according to Jordi Bolòs i Masclans and Josep Moran i Ocerinjauregui, *Repertori d'antropònims catalans* (*RAC*), vol. 1 (only) (Barcelona: Institut d'Estudis Catalans, 1994).

when *saiones* do appear, it is almost always in a document recording a judicial process, and even then they are fairly rare. Literature on the subject tends to assume that *saiones* were a normal feature of judicial business in this region;[35] these figures suggest that that was not true.

The counterargument, that *saiones* were common, must be grounded in the fact that although normally the *saiones* are just names, occasionally documents describe what their roles entailed, and these roles conform very closely to the roles described in the Visigothic Code. In 1019, a *saio* received sureties (*fideiussores*) from each side in a property dispute (cf. "Lex Visigothorum," ed. Zeumer, II.2.4).[36] In 817, a *saio* received the oaths of witnesses for the division of property, at the order of the judges and the presiding imperial *missi* (cf. VI.1.5).[37] The *saio* did the same in 843 and 860 (and perhaps 853) for the circumambulation of property boundaries,[38] and in 879 and 930 for *reparatio scripturae* procedures.[39] In 957, a *saio* was one of two individuals who proceeded from a judgment about possession of an allod to take control of the property and hand

35 Bowman, *Shifting Landmarks*, 109 ("a regular, but far from universal, feature of courts in the region") was working from about 25 references from the tenth and eleventh centuries, including the non-Catalan regions of the diocese of Narbonne. Similarly: Salrach, *Justícia i poder*, 21: "una presidència, un o uns jutges [...] un grup d'homes bons i un saig"; Bonnassie, *La Catalogne*, 1:192; Roger Collins, "'Sicut lex Gothorum continet': Law and Charters in Ninth- and Tenth-Century León and Catalonia," *English Historical Review* 100 (1985), 489–512, at 505 ("In virtually all of the [Catalan texts], when at the commencement of the document the judges are listed together with the ecclesiastical and lay *boni homines*, one of the laymen is qualified with the title of *Saio*."). Cf. Zimmermann, *Écrire et lire*, 1:76, 278–279, who claims that *saiones* disappear from *reparatio scripturae* documents from 920 to 930, and that in eleventh-century testamentary publication documents the term is an anachronism. Collins ("'Sicut lex Gothorum continent'," 505) notes the much greater role of *saiones* in León, a point validated now by Davies, *Windows on Justice*, 164–168.

36 *Carlemany* 78: *Deusdedit clerico qui exinde fuit sago et tollit fideiussores ex parte Sancte Marie et suis mandatariis, et de Bernardo de uilla Calabodii.*

37 CC5 7: *Magnetius sagio, qui hunc iuramentum per iussionem de missos dominicos vel iudices recepi.*

38 CC6 26–27: *nos testes accessionem fecimus et pedibus circumdub(i/u)mus (vel / et) manibus nostris (hostensimus / ostensum est) ad Godeschalc(h)o saione.* CC6 49: *nos testes accessionem fecimus et pedibus circumdavimus et manibus insinuavimus ad saionem Goddeforte.* In CC6 56, the *saio* circumambulates the property along with the judges and some of the *boni homines*. In CC5 31/91, *Quiricus saio determinavit*, a reference possibly to the *affrontaciones* referred to earlier.

39 CC5 218: *Eldoardo saione, qui hunc sacramentum fideliter recepi.* CC6 120: *nos iudices ordinamus saionem nomine Nazarius qui fecisset ipsos testes iurare et sicut et fecit* [...] *Nazarius saio +, qui hunc sacramentum recepi*; similarly, CC6 121, 123. Judges, however, could also receive oaths: e.g., CC5 461.

it over publicly to the victors in the dispute (cf. x.2.6).[40] A record of a judgment from 980 describes the judge and *saio* sending a letter and seal to order the appearance of one of the parties (cf. II.1.19).[41] A *reparatio scripturae* describes a quitclaim from 875 in which the *saio* "distrained" the parties (cf. II.1.18).[42] The only departure from these executive procedural functions appears in a well-known trial from the abbey of Sant Cugat in which the abbey's opponent was found to have destroyed evidence. When he failed the ordeal, the *saio*—unusually, not named—"wanted to hand him over into the control of the said advocate of Abbot Odo of the abbey of Sant Cugat, whom he had defrauded, and have him given over into perpetual servitude to the saint, as the law held and ordered"—an essentially correct reference to the Visigothic Code (VII.5.2). The court decided instead to impose a fine (*districtio*) payable to the bishop, the abbey, the judge, and the *saio*—itself a role given to *saiones* by the Code (II.2.10).[43]

The examples just cited are, however, the only ones—thus a little over 10 per cent of the total mentions of *saiones*—in which the document details the *saio*'s involvement in procedure. In the vast majority of cases, *saiones* are simply names. The only information available is who they are and the sort of transactions in which they appear. As for the latter point, as noted, they are rarely found in non-judicial contexts. Within judicial contexts, they are much more common in *contentious* judicial processes. Thus, for example, while close to half of the documents in the PRJ database are testamentary transactions—either publications before judicial assemblies, or grants executing the terms, which did not require a judicial assembly—only six of the 90 documents featuring named *saiones* are routine testamentary transactions.[44] They also appear in

40 CC5 324: *Et perrexerunt Oliba saio et Wisandus ad ipsum alodem et aprehenderunt eum in sua potestate et miserunt eum in postetate Agfredi monachi.*

41 CC5 461: *Unde supradictus iudex vel saione misimus nostrum missum cum epistola vel sigillum.*

42 CC6 91.1: *distringente eos Tractimiro saione.*

43 *Sant Cugat* 218: *Et cum voluit eum tradere ipse saio in potestate de iam dicto assertore de abba Odo s. Cucuphati cenobio cui fraudem fecit, et perpetuo ad servitutem abdicari ipsius s. quemadmodum lex ordinabat et iubebat* [...] *fecissent in aliquantulum concessionem ad supralibato monasterio vel et ad supranominato episcopo pro sua portionis districtio seu et ad saio atque et ad iudice*. Cf. "Lex Visigothorum," ed. Zeumer, VII.5.2, p. 304: *Si vero minor extiterit facultas eorum, quam quod aliis facere conati sunt damnum, ipsi procul dubio cum his, que habere videntur, eius servituti subiciantur, cui fraudem fecisse dinoscitur*. On this dispute, see: Bowman, *Shifting Landmarks*, 109–110, 138–139; Salrach, *Justícia i poder*, 187–189.

44 CC4 890, 951, 1334; *Girona* 262; *DACB2* 1079; *PACB1* 108. For the weight of testamentary transactions, above n. 10.

just a half dozen *reparationes scripturae* and valuations of forfeited pledges,[45] although in these cases their rarity is matched in the overall PRJ corpus. That means that *saiones* figure overwhelmingly in contentious procedures: judgments, quitclaims, and oaths related to them—hardly surprising, given the functions ascribed to them in the Visigothic Code.

In contrast to judges, who often appear in pairs or even large groups, *saiones* almost invariably appear alone; extraordinarily, in one case an assistant *saio* (*subtus saione*) serves alongside the main officer.[46] The names of *saiones* normally appear in two places: in lists of the composition of the judicial assembly, which usually appear at the beginning, and in subscriptions, at the end. In just under half of the judicial cases, the *saio*'s name appears in both locations; he subscribes only in a few; in the rest, he is named without subscribing. In the lists at the beginning, the *saio* normally appears either immediately after the judges or at the end of the list of laymen or *boni homines* named as present. Only two *saiones* are identified as clerics. In 849, a Rodebaldo *diaconus saio* participated in a judicial assembly at Urgell.[47] The second, Deusdedit *clericus*, was the *saio* cited above from 1019 who received sureties, and the wording of that document may hint that something unusual was going on. Instead of naming *Deusdedit clericus, saio*, according to the usual formula, it reads *Deusdedit clerico qui exinde fuit sago*; in only one other case is the function of the *saio* explicitly abstracted from the identification of the *saio*.[48]

This raises the question of whether the *saio* was an office connected to an individual for a period of time, or instead a role assigned ad hoc to someone present at an assembly.[49] One approach to this question is to note that only rarely—five cases—does a *saio* named at the beginning of the document appear in the subscriptions without a title; in three of those, he does subscribe with the title in a related document; in a fourth, he appears in a related document but does not subscribe.[50] A second is to note the few cases where *saiones*

---

45 *Reparatio scripturae*: *CC*4 1840; *CC*6 120–123. Pledges: *DACB*2 1160, 1256.

46 *CC*5 461. SACM3, fol. 9r reproduces (from a thirteenth-century notarial copy) a document of 1013 possibly subscribed by two *saiones*: *Arnaldo Sayoni* and *Oliva saio*. John C. Shideler, *A Medieval Catalan Noble Family: The Montcadas, 1000–1230* (Berkeley: University of California Press, 1983), 46–47, interprets the former mention as a personal name rather than a title.

47 *Urgellia* 15 [= apèndix 4].

48 *Carlemany* 78; cf. *CC*5 461 (*Eldemaris, qui inde fuit sagone*).

49 Jonathan Jarrett, *Rulers and Ruled in Frontier Catalonia, 880–1010: Pathways of Power* (London: Royal Historical Society / Boydell, 2010), 42–43.

50 *CC*4 120 (Anno; cf. no. 119, where he does subscribe with title), 890 (Godemarus); *CC*6 27

subscribe documents or are identified with their titles in non-judicial contexts: donations of land to monasteries and to an individual; an exchange of lands with a cathedral; a reference in a will to land the testator purchased from a *saio*; a sale of land; an exemption granted to a monastery; a comital donation to an individual.[51] Both of these phenomena suggest that *saio* status was inherent in the person: a *saio* played a role in judicial assemblies; a random person did not fill the role of *saio* in judicial assemblies. Of those seven documents, four have a direct connection to counts, which might support an argument for the *saio* as an official attached to comital households, whose presence at judgments was in the role of a comital representative, but who might represent the count in other contexts as well (as would be the case in the twelfth century). While it is true that, from the tenth century, almost all of the contentious judicial assemblies with an identifiable president and a *saio* are in fact comital rather than episcopal or otherwise constituted,[52] the absence of *saiones* from the vast majority of comital judicial assemblies argues against that position. For example, while one of the PRJ documents records a *saio* acting with the countess Ermessenda in 1054, it is the only one of the 188 documents associated with her in which a *saio* is named.[53]

The other way to approach the question is to consider the few occasions when *saiones* might be argued appear on multiple occasions, which offer further support for the idea of *saio* as a long-term office rather than as an ad hoc function. Sixty-six different names of *saiones* appear in the corpus; of those, fifteen appear more than once. Of those, seven only appear in clusters in the same archival fonds and separated by less than thirteen months.[54] That leaves eight that might offer evidence of *saiones* serving for long periods of time.[55] The

(Godescalcus; cf. no. 26, where he does subscribe with title); *DOliba* 87 (Wilielmus; cf. no. 90, where he does subscribe with title); *NH*2 24 (Stephanus; cf. *NH*11 226, where he does not subscribe).

51 *DOliba* 21, 36; *DACB*2 186, 563; *CC*5 394; *DOliba* 96; *Liber feudorum maior* 390.

52 Cf. Bowman, *Shifting Landmarks*, 109, n. 38; Jarrett, *Rulers and Ruled*, 43.

53 Xavier Gil i Román, "Ermesèn, vida y obra de la condesa: Estudio histórico de la documentación, c. 977–+1 marzo de 1058 / Diplomatario de Ermesèn, condesa de Barcelona, Osona y Girona, c. 991–25 octubre 1180" (Ph.D. dissertation, Universitat Autònoma de Barcelona, 2004), no. 74 [= *Liber feudorum maior* 390], cf. no. 72 [= *Carlemany* 77].

54 Anno (*CC*4 119–120 / both 15 June 913); Fortis (*CC*5 19–21 / all 21 August 842); Godescalcus (*CC*6 26–27 / 6–7 February 843); Isselmo (*CC*6 93–94 / 18 and 30 January 876); Leopardus (*CC*5 171–172 / both 25 February 921); Stephanus (*NH*2 24, *NH*11 226 / 4 June 1003, 17 February 1004); Undila (*CC*5 80–82, 84, 86 / 13 November 892–1 December 893). Given orthographic variation, this count of names can only be approximate.

55 *CC*5 31 is a lost document of *c.* 853 implied in *CC*5 91 (898), and thus represents only a single reference to Quiricus *saio*.

saio Eldemares who appeared in 980 before Mir, count of Besalú and bishop of Girona, in a matter concerning the monastery of Ripoll is very probably the same figure who appeared at that same count-bishop's assembly three years later, in another matter concerning that abbey, before at least five of the same laymen.[56] More impressively, the Nazarius *saio* who appears in an assembly of Count Mir II of Conflent in 901 is very likely the same Nazarius who served that role in a series of *reparationes scripturae* in the first two months of 879 at assemblies before many of the same judges under the presidency of the previous count, Mir I, a spread of twenty-two years.[57] Other cases are less secure. A Gauzfredus *saio* subscribed donations in 997 and 1008 to the monastery of Portella, one directly from a count, and one of lands that had been purchased from that same count; there is at least one additional duplicate subscriber.[58] The Bonefilius *saio* who acted alongside the priest and judge Ramon in 1068 and 1074 in documents from the Barcelona cathedral archive are plausibly the same individual, despite no other overlap between the documents; but there is little to connect him to the Bonefilius *saio* who subscribed a testament from that archive in 1065.[59] The Wilielmus *saio* who subscribed an exchange in 1012 and another of the same name who appears as vendor in a testament of 1038 are hard to connect to each other, despite the presence of both of these documents in the Barcelona cathedral archive, even less so to a more or less contemporary Wilielmus *saio* at Vic.[60] An Oliba *saio* served under the same president and in the presence of the same judge and perhaps four other participants at assemblies connected to Besalú in 950 and 957, but in only the earlier one is he given a second name: *Olibane saigone, qui alium nomen vocant Aurugo*.[61]

The evidence is slim, but there nevertheless seems to be sufficient cause to argue that *saio* referred to an office, rather than to an ad hoc function. This stands in contrast to the use of the term *iudex*, which might refer to officially

56 *CC5* 461 (7 May 980), 485 (23 March 983). Oriol, Guilabert, Oliba, Sunifred, and Ennego, in addition to the viscount Wandalgodus, appear on both panels.

57 *CC6* 120–123 (28 January–10 February 879), 164 (2 July 901). Unifortes, Langobardus, Sunifred, and Fulgentius appear in all five documents.

58 *DOliba* 21 (15 July 997), 36 (24 June 1008). Bardina, viscount, subscribes both.

59 *DACB2* 1079 (12 April 1065), 1160 (4 March 1068), 1256 (17 March 1074).

60 *DACB2* 186 (14 September 1012), 563 (14 January 1038); *Doliba* 87, 90 (8 May 1026, 7 January 1027). The dates of the Vic documents argue for the identity of the *saiones* named in them.

61 *CC5* 288 (5 March 950), 324 (14 September 957); Guifré, count of Besalú, the judge Joan, and perhaps Sunifred *sacer*, two Ennegos, and Wandalgodus (*vicarius*) appear in both. There is surely no connection to the Oliba *saio* who appears in a testamentary publication of 1013 (*PACB1* 108), or to the Oliba *saio* in SACM3, fol. 9r, also from 1013—although despite the same date there is nothing to connect these two. Similarly, the Rodebaldo *saio* in *Urgellia* 15 [= apèndix 4] (849) naturally differs from the *saio* of the same name in *PACB1* 136 (1018).

appointed, professional legal experts, who subscribed with that title, but also to designated members of a judicial assembly tasked with the function of judging, who might or might not also be professional judges.[62] On the other hand, the lack of repetition—only a dozen or so *saiones* who might appear more than once; less than half that number who might have acted over several years; and none who appear to have acted in different regions—means that there are no famous regional *saiones*, in the way that there were clearly famous regional judges.

One thing that is striking about the *saiones* is their names, an unusual number of which seem odd on first glance: Ardovaste, Gogino, Aguardo, Chalafo, Isselmo, Magnentius, Godescalcus. The *Repertori d'antropònims catalans* (*RAC*) allows for a test of this impression.[63] It catalogues 39,159 instances of personal names up to the year 1000, which appear in some 13,800 forms, which have in turn been lemmatized into 4176 names. Of the 50 names of *saiones* up to the year 1000, only ten appear in the top 50 names in the *RAC*; 18 occur fewer than ten times in the repertory, 23 fewer than 20 times.[64] For comparison, consider the scribes of the documents up to the year 1000 in which the *saiones* appear, which provide 41 names. Of those, only eight occur fewer than ten times and 16 fewer than 20 times.[65] So the names of *saiones* are objectively rare in relative terms.

62 Above, at n. 7.

63 Bolòs i Masclans and Moran i Ocerinjauregui, *Repertori d'antropònims catalans*.

64 The *subtus saione* in *CC*5 461 (Ermemirus) is included in this calculation; the double name in *CC*4 115 (Bonushomo) is discounted. Lemmatized name (rank if in top 100 / number of appearances): Aguardo (* / 2), Anno (* / 9), Ardovaste (* / *), Argefredus (* / 9), Argemirus (37 / 163), Audesindus (52 / 134), Auritius (* / 14), Aurutius (61 / 120), Bardina (* / 43), Chalafo (* / 2), Durandus (15 / 271), Egica (* / 52), Elaredus (* / 3), Eldemares (70 / 109), Eldoardus (* / 8), Emboladus (* / 27), Enalario (* / 1), Ermemirus (14 /277), Fortis (* / 17), Franco (73 / 105), Gauzfredus (70t / 109), Georgius (* / 48), Godefortes (* / 8), Godescalcus (* / 6), Godemarus (17 / 254), Gogino (* / 1), Isarnus (73t / 105), Isselmo (* / 3), Leopardus (57 / 126), Magnentius (* / 3), Nazarius (* / 8), Nifridius (* / 31), Oliba (5 / 464), Quiricus (* / 16), Rainovardo (* / 18), Ramius (42 / 154), Revellus (* / 48), Rodebaldo (* / 9), Salomon (28 / 188), Sentulfo (* / 2), Sisoaldus (* / 14), Teuderedus (* / 38), Teudericus (30 / 183), Tractemirus (* / 5), Undila (* / 57), Usila (* / 35), Walafonsus (* / 39), Warnerus (* / 7), Wimara (29 / 187), Wintila (* / 16), Wiscafredus (13 / 290).

65 Lemmatized name (rank if in top 100 / number of appearances): Ademirus (* / 28), Adericus (* / 11), Ansefredus (* / 38), Argovadus (* / 27), Armentarius (* / 6), Arnulphus (* / 64), Attila (77t / 102), Auriolus (16 / 263), Baldemares (89 / 91), Baldericus (* / 38), Bonessimo (* / 12), Desiderius (* / 73), Durandus (15 / 271), Egihud (* / 1), Egila (27 / 193), Eizo (* / 42), Elderedus (* / 13), Eldesindus (65 / 117), Exemenus (* / 39), Fredarius (* / 77), Frunimio (* / 5), Garsia (* / 18), Geldefredus (* / 3), Gentiles (* / 37), Honestus (* / 20), Isarnus (73t / 105), Iulio (* / 8), Laurentius (* / 30), Leobesindus (* / 4), Maiorecellus (* / 1), Milo (* / 2),

This rarity of names of *saiones* does allow for more prosopographical certainty, and is in a way relevant to the question about versatility. Is there any evidence that the *saiones* became judges later in their careers, that these were steps on a *cursus honorum*? A search of all of the *saiones* whose names were later held by judges in the *Repertori*, with proximity in time of 20 years and space of the same or an immediately adjacent region, uncovered six plausible conjunctions but nothing particularly convincing.[66] The sole example of a *iudex et saio* appears in the description of a lost document (*deperditum*) embedded in the account of a dispute, where a certain Quiricus is referred to first as a *saio* and then as a *iudex et saio*, but lacunae in the document and the possibly summary nature of the reference render the evidence weak.[67]

So again here, the evidence for versatility—for overlapping functions—is quite limited. That said, even if *saiones* cannot be shown to have served as judges or scribes or representatives or presidents of tribunals, they may be said to have been versatile participants in a more limited sense, in that their placement in the lists of composition of the assembly indicates that they likely served generally as members of the assembly in whose presence the proceedings took place—*boni homines*, and perhaps in some cases also as members of the panel of judges. The opinionated *saio* in the case of the destroyed testament from Sant Cugat may not have been entirely unusual.

Nantulfus (* / 14), Protasius (* / 42), Raimundus (43 / 149), Ramius (42 / 154), Riculfus (45 / 146), Sanciolus (* / 17), Sanctius (86 / 95), Sanctus (* / 20), Suniarius (4 / 469), Sunila (* / 31).

66 Argefredus: *CC*6 56 (*saio*, 865, Conflent), 92 (on panel of judges, 875, Elne). Argemirus: *CC*4 1334 (*saio*, 981, Manresa), 1434 (*iudex*, 983, Vic); cf. *Sant Llorenç* 56 (*iudex*, 979, Terrassa). Teudericus: *CC*4 115 (*saio*, 913, Ripollès), 119–120 (on panel of judges, 913, Ripollès). Oliba: *CC*5 288 (*saio*, 950, Besalú), 295 (on panel of judges, 951, Amer), acting for different counts. Oliba: *CC*5 324 (*saio*, 957, Besalú), 335 (on panel of judges, 959, Empúries), acting for different counts. Walafonsus: *CC*6 92 (*saio*, 875, Elne), 93 (on panel of judges, 876, Elne). Taylor, "'The Will and Society," 142, suggests that *CC*4 890 (961) offers evidence for a *saio* presiding alone at a testamentary publication as well as that the *saio* named there, Godemarus, is the same as the Godemarus *iudex* in *CC*4 951 (964). I do not find either conclusion persuasive. *CC*4 890 is damaged at the top of the parchment, with a lacuna just where the formula might identify a judge; meanwhile, *CC*4 951 was sworn at Castellterçol, some 35 km from Vic, where *CC*4 890 was sworn, and there is no overlap in personnel that might suggest a common context. In *CC*5 171–172 *item / iterum* Leopardus likely refers to two people rather than to a single figure serving as both judge and *saio*, although only one subscribes (as *saio*) the first document and neither the second.

67 *CC*5 31.

4 *Mandatarii*

A third category of potentially versatile participants in judicial proceedings comprises those representatives of the principals called variously *mandatarius* or *assertor*, and very rarely *causidicus* or *causarius*; the designation *advocatus* seems to have been restricted to testamentary executors, otherwise labelled *elimosinarii*, among many other terms.[68] *Mandatarii* appear in the database with roughly the same frequency as *saiones*: again, the assumption that they were a routine part of judicial procedure is not tenable. As in the case of *saiones*, however, their official roles make it possible to explore whether they appear in other roles. In particular, it is possible to explore whether, as one might imagine, judges served as *mandatarii*—whether judicial expertise made one a desirable advocate in a dispute.

The latest example from the PRJ database is an absolutely extraordinary case in which judges interpret the Visigothic Code on the level of the meaning of individual words. In 1049, the brothers Ramon Guillem and Renard de Montcada claimed property that had been granted by their father and uncle to the bishop of Vic. The judges asked the brothers if they wanted to appoint an *assertor* to represent them in the case. They named three individuals. The record continues: "And although the law orders that whoever is not able to speak for himself in his own case or perhaps does not want to do so should appoint an *assertor*—in the singular, *not assertores* in the plural—in writing, confirmed with the signatures or subscriptions of himself and of witnesses, lest however we should seem opposed, by the order of the aforesaid bishop and other advisors, we (i.e., the judges) have received them (i.e., the three *assertores*) according to their (i.e., the brothers') wish to carry out the proceeding."[69] The judges here cited verbatim the Code: *Si quis per se causam dicere non pouterit aut forte noluerit, adsertorem per scripturam, sue manus vel testium signis aut suscriptionibus roboratam, dare debebit.*[70] Immediately preceding this

68 Bastier, "Le testament en Catalogne," 408–409; Taylor, "The Will and Society," 89–90.

69 *DVic* 1075 (21 October 1049): *Et quamvis lex iubeat ut qui causam suam per se dicere non poterit aut forte noluerit assertorem singulari numero, non assertores plurali, per scripturam sue manus vel testium signis aut subscripcionibus roboratam dare debeat, tamen ne contrarii videremur, iubente predicto pontifice et consiliantibus aliis, secundum voluntatem eorum eos ad prosequendum negocium recepimus*. For the context, see Shideler, *A Medieval Catalan Noble Family*, 57. The case is also striking for the fact that the witnesses are interrogated by the court separately: *separati a nobis atque legaliter discussi testimonium dederunt*.

70 "Lex Visigothorum," ed. Zeumer, II.3.3, p. 89.

passage, the judges had ordered, again with a direct quotation from the Code, along with a citation to the book and title (II.3.1), that the bishop was not permitted represent himself in the proceedings but had to provide subordinates to do so; the number was apparently not an issue, as the text of the Code refers to *subditos* in the plural. It is perhaps asking too much to wish that they had engaged in some legal reasoning by connecting the two passages; still the fact that such a technicality arose in this context is a striking illustration of the continued power of the written law.[71]

For present purposes what is noteworthy is that the three *assertores* named by the Montcadas included the judge Guillem Marc, perhaps part of the famous clan;[72] the bishops' representatives, not given a particular designation, included the judge Adalbert. Guillem Marc was seen by the court as the main representative—they refer to "judge Guillem and their other *assertores*,"[73] but expert representation benefitted them little; after the bishop's party presented two witnesses, the Montcada side abandoned the proceedings and lost the case. Perhaps surprisingly, this sort of recourse to 'professional' representation is difficult to find in the sources: there are in the PRJ database only four certain examples, and a handful of other possibilities.

The first is the case with which this study began: at Girona in 898, Trasuad is described as *mandatarius vel iudex* and acts on behalf of the count of Girona in a dispute with the monastery of Sant Medir and Sant Genís. He appears in the initial list of judges of the assembly, although the language of the text suggests that they were not brought together *ad hoc* but instead "for hearing and settling by the laws the cases of many people."[74] The count, as president of the tribunal, participated in the questioning of his own *mandatarius*; the count had the losing position, and his representative subscribed the quitclaim: *Trasovadus iudex, qui sum mandatarius seniori meo, Gauzfredo comite, qui me exvacuavit.* His counterpart in the dispute, the *mandatarius* of the abbey, named Madaxus,

71 For an application of legal reasoning of this sort, see Salrach, *Justícia i poder*, 156.

72 A Guillem Marc *iudex* appears in documentation from Barcelona between 1046 and 1071: *PACB1* 344, 490, 562, 571, 617, 696; *DACB2* 694, 850, 891, 912, 915, 988, 1013–1014, 1027, 1059, 1070, 1079, 1087, 1139, 1206, etc. *HGL5* 194 (1030) may be an earlier instance; see Taylor, "The Will and Society," 142–143. Cf. Zimmerman, *Écrire et lire*, 2:946–947; Bonnassie, *La Catalogne*, 2:711, 722; José Balari Jovany, *Orígenes históricos de Cataluña*, 2nd ed., 2 vols in 3 (Sant Cugat del Vallès: Abadía de San Cugat del Vallés / Instituto Internacional de Cultura Románica, 1964), 2:466–467.

73 *Guilelmum iudicem et alios assertores eorum.*

74 CC5 91: *multorum causas audiendas vel legibus definiendas.* Similarly CC5 53; see Salrach, *Justícia i poder*, 32.

may also be a judge but is not identified as such in the document; a Madaxus appears on the panel of judges, although does not subscribe with the title, in seven documents from 888 to 893, thus within a decade of the dispute with Sant Medir.[75] A case from a century later, in 997, in Urgell, presents a similar structure. The diocese claimed certain tithes on behalf of the monastery of Sant Jaume de Frontanyà against a usurper. The case was heard before a tribunal presided over by the count, with a panel of three judges. One of the three judges is then listed as the representative of the bishop in the case: *predictus Wifredus iudex, qui est assertor vel mandatarius*.[76] The document describes the *suprascripti iudices* as interrogating the usurper, but also Guifré as *mandatarius*; thus he must have been removed from the panel of judges to act as a representative.[77] As in the case of the Montcadas, the bishop's opponents quit the proceedings, although in this instance the judge-*mandatarius* was on the winning side. In 995, in a very similar case of a claim of possession against a cathedral, this time in Barcelona, the judge Marc served as *mandatarius* for the bishop, stating the cathedral's claim and presenting witnesses. As at Girona, Marc is also listed as one of the presiding judges, although this may simply be scribal reflex: when Marc is "diligently questioned by the judges," he is presumably not questioning himself.[78] In this case, too, the cathedral, and the professional *mandatarius*, emerged victorious. Finally, there is one possible case of a *mandatarius* serving as a *saio*: an Anno represented the abbot of the monastery of Ripoll in 900, and an Anno served as *saio* in a famous hearing in 913 involving the nearby abbey of Sant Joan de les Abadesses. An Anno also served as one of the *boni homines* for tribunals in this same region in 904, 913, and 917. If this is in fact the same indi-

75 CC5 63–64, 80–82, 84, 86. The *iudex* and *mandatarius* named Trasovarius at CC5 19–22 (842) are different from the one appearing here.

76 *Urgellia* 252. A Guifré *iudex* appears in documents from Barcelona and Urgell, often in the entourage of Borrell II (d. 993), between 977 and 1000: *Urgellia* 192, 212, 233, 252; *DACB1* 299, 345; *ACondal* 181.

77 *Interrogavimus ergo et Wifredum iudicem adsertorem de supra inserto episcopo*. Although cf. Salrach, *Justícia i poder*, 59.

78 *DACB1* 274: *Et interrogatus pretextus Marchus diligenter a iudices*. This is likely Ervig Marc, active between 975 and 1009; see above, n. 8. The oft-discussed dispute over Aiguatèbia (*Urgellia* 416), which played out as a conflict between judges supporting each of the parties, might be added to this catalogue, but Sendred *iudex* here is not a *mandatarius* or *assertor* proper. After the dispute commenced, one side went and found weighty judicial support for its position, and the other side countered with a different, equally weighty judge; the dynamics of the process, at least as described in the record, are quite different from other cases of judges serving as advocates. Cf. Bowman, *Shifting Landmarks*, 1–9; Bonnassie, *La Catalogne*, 2:561.

vidual, his career would represent less a *cursus honorum* (*mandatarius, bonus homo, saio, bonus homo*, etc.) than simple versatility in fulfilling roles in the judicial process.[79]

5 Conclusion

The evidence adduced here for overlap in the official roles in judicial procedure—judges, *saiones, mandatarii*, and scribes—is quite scanty. This does not exhaust the possible overlap. Judges might serve as litigants or executors,[80] or a clerical co-president at a testamentary execution as both executor and scribe.[81] But versatile actors are more likely to be found among the long lists of names of witnesses, subscribers, and those present at the assembly—names without titles, and thus difficult to match across cases.[82] That is a negative conclusion. On the other hand, this relative lack of overlap in officials' roles may be read in a positive way, as evidence for the remarkable penetration of judicial experience and procedure into Catalan society. Judicial procedures were not the province of a limited number of experts responsible for all of the complexities. Many people knew, and were called upon to know, the rules of the game. This broad social base goes a long way toward explaining the significance of legal procedures to the social and political world of tenth- and eleventh-century Catalonia.

---

79 CC4 45 (900), 57 (904; reg. only, printed at *ACondal* 16), 115 (913), 119–120 (913), 168 (917). An Anno also subscribes CC4 44 (900). See Jarret, *Rulers and Ruled*, 42–43.

80 E.g., *Santa Anna* 54, *DVic* 937.

81 E.g., *Urgellia* 247.

82 Jarrett, *Rulers and Ruled*, is a superb example of what can be accomplished given a sufficient density of documents.

Appendix

TABLE 11.1 Judge-Scribes in Catalonia around the Year 1000

	Judge only	Scribe only	Both	Neither	Total
Bonhom	9	10	12	2	33
Ervig Marc	11	7	4	1	23
Ponç Bonfill Marc	8	7	21	4	40
Nature of case when acting as a scribe					
	Contentious		**Non-contentious**		
Bonhom	9		13		
Ervig Marc	9		2		
Ponç Bonfill Marc	17		11		

TABLE 11.2 Documentary References to *saiones* in Catalonia before 1100

817	*CC*5 7	Magnentius
842	*CC*5 19	Fortis
842	*CC*5 20	Fortis
842	*CC*5 21	Fortis
843	*CC*6 26	Godescalcus
843	*CC*6 27	Godescalcus
849	*Urgellia* 15 [= apèndix 4]	Rodebaldo *diaconus*
853	*CC*5 31	Quiricus
858	*CC*6 49	Godefortes
865	*CC*6 56	Argefredus
868	*CC*6 60	Wintila
872	*Urgellia* 25	Usila
874	*CC*6 81	Enalario
875	*CC*6 91.1	Tractemirus
875	*CC*6 92	Walafonsus
876	*CC*6 93	Isselmo
876	*CC*6 94	Isselmo
879	*CC*5 52	Gogino
879	*CC*6 120	Nazarius
879	*CC*6 121	Nazarius
879	*CC*6 122	Nazarius
879	*CC*6 123	Nazarius

TABLE 11.2 Documentary References to *saiones* in Catalonia before 1100 (*cont.*)

881	*CC*5 53	*Ardovaste*
888	*CC*5 63	Georgius
892	*CC*5 80	Undila
892	*CC*5 81	Undila
892	*CC*5 82	Undila
893	*CC*5 84	Undila
893	*CC*5 86	Undila
898	*CC*4 33	Warnerus
898	*CC*4 34	Egica
898	*CC*5 91 (cf. 31)	Sisoaldus
900	*CC*5 104	Revellus
900	*CC*4 45	Wimara
901	*CC*6 164	Nazarius
903	*CC*5 113	Elaredus
904	*CC*4 57 (*ACondal* 16)	Franco
910	*CC*3 113	Bardina
910	*Urgellia* 67	Wiscafredus
913	*CC*4 115	Teudericus (Bonushomo)
913	*CC*4 119	Anno
913	*CC*4 120	Anno
913	*CC*5 143	Nifridius
917	*CC*4 168	Reinovardo
921	*CC*5 171	Leopardus
921	*CC*5 172	Leopardus
930	*CC*5 218	Eldoardus
938	*CC*4 443	Emboladus
950	*CC*5 288	Oliba (Aurutius)
951	*CC*5 295	Sentulfo
957	*CC*5 324	Oliba
959	*CC*5 335	Chalafo
961	*CC*4 890	Godemarus
961	*Urgellia* 143	Audesindus
964	*CC*4 951	Ramius
969	*CC*5 394	Isarnus
972	*CC*5 413	Auritius
980	*CC*5 461	Eldemares / Ermemirus *subtus saione*
981	*CC*4 1334	Argemirus
983	*CC*5 485	Eldemares

TABLE 11.2 Documentary References to *saiones* in Catalonia before 1100 (*cont.*)

984	CC6 561	Aguardo
987	CC4 1517	Teuderedus
993	CC6 620	Salomon
997	*DOliba* 21	Gauzfredus
1000	CC4 1840	Durandus
1003	*NH2* 24	Stephanus
1004	*NH11* 226	Stephanus
1008	*DOliba* 36	Gauzfredus
1010	*HGL5* 168	Wilielmus Radulfi
1012	*DACB2* 186	Wilielmus
1012	*NH12* 573	*Azemaro*
1013	*PACB1* 108	Oliba
1014	SACM3, fol. 9r	Oliba / Arnaldus
1018	*PACB1* 136	Rodebaldo
1018	*NH11* 256 / *HGL5* 175	*Adals*
1019	*Carlemany* 78	Deusdedit *clericus*
1026	*DOliba* 87	Wilielmus
1027	*DOliba* 90	Wilielmus
1029	*DOliba* 96	Audegarius
1030	*HGL5* 193	Witardus Witardi
1038	*DACB2* 563	Wilielmus
1046	*Cardona* 151	Iohannes
1052	*Girona* 262	Bernardus
1054	*Liber feudorum maior* 390	Suniefredus
1054	*HGL5* 240	Adroarius
1063	*Lavaix* 27	Gelemundus
1065	*DACB2* 1079	Bonefilius
1066	*DACB2* 1097	*Archimballus*
1068	*DACB2* 1160	Bonefilius
1074	*DACB2* 1256	Bonefilius
Anonymous or Generic references		
953	CC4 706	
988	*Sant Cugat* 218	
990	CC4 IX	
1018	*DOliba* 56 / *Carlemany* 77	
1022	*DACB2* 353	
1062	*Àger* 52	

TABLE 11.2 Documentary References to *saiones* in Catalonia before 1100 (*cont.*)

1064	*PACB1* 617	
1092	*PACB2* 240	
1068	*Cartas de población* 32	
1097	*Cardona* 289	
References in Neighbouring Regions		
918	*HGL*5 43 (Narbonne)	*Salvardo*
933	*HGL*5 57 (Narbonne)	*Blastolco*
962	*CC*3 188 (Ribagorça)	Centullus
1008	*HGL*5 166.2 (Narbonne)	Bellutio

Note

Josep Maria Salrach i Marès and Tomàs Montagut i Estragués, eds., *Justícia i resolució de conflictes a la Catalynya medieval: Col·lecció diplomática, segles IX–XI* (Barcelona: Generalitat de Catalunya, 2018), published after this study was initially prepared, contains an index of *saiones* (p. 887), which allows for the following additions to the list above (all new names), several from newly published volumes of *CC*: nos. 4 (*CC*2, pp. 442–444), 14 (*CC*8 45), 30 (*CC*8 72 = *DVic* 1), 33 (*CC*8 82), 71 (*CC*7 240), 79bis, and 339. These are not included in the analysis in this article.

Bibliography

Abbreviations

ACondal: Udina i Martorell, Federico. *El Archivo Condal de Barcelona en los siglos IX–X: Estudio crítico de sus fondos*. Barcelona: Consejo Superior de Investigaciones Científicas, 1951.

Àger: Chesé Lapeña, Ramon, ed. *Col·lecció diplomàtica de Sant Pere d'Àger fins 1198*. 2 vols. Barcelona: Fundació Noguera, 2011.

Cardona: Rodríguez Bernal, Francesc, ed. *Col·lecció diplomàtica de l'Archivo Ducal de Cardona (965–1230)*. Barcelona: Fundació Noguera, 2016.

Carlemany: Marquès, Josep Maria, ed. *Cartoral, dit de Carlemany, del bisbe de Girona (s. IX–XIV)*. 2 vols. Barcelona: Fundació Noguera, 1993.

CC: d'Abadal i de Vinyals, Ramon, et al., eds. *Catalunya carolíngia*. 8 vols. to date. Barcelona: Institut d'Estudis Catalans, 1926– [cited by volume and document number].

DACB1: Fàbrega i Grau, Àngel, ed. *Diplomatari de la Catedral de Barcelona: Documents dels anys 844–1260*. Vol. 1 (only) *Documents dels anys 844–1000*. Barcelona: Arxiu Capitular de la Catedral de Barcelona, 1995.

DACB2: Baucells i Reig, Josep, et al., eds. *Diplomatari de l'Arxiu Capitular de la Catedral de Barcelona: Segle XI*. 5 vols. Barcelona: Fundació Noguera, 2006.

DOliba: Junyent i Subirà, Eduard, ed. *Diplomatari i escrits literaris de l'abat i bisbe Oliba*. Barcelona: Institut d'Estudis Catalans, 1992.

DVic: Junyent i Subirà, Eduard, and Ramon Ordeig i Mata, eds. *Diplomatari de la Catedral de Vic*. Vic: Publicacions del Patronat d'Estudis Osonencs / Publicacions de l'Arxiu i Biblioteca Episcopals de Vic, 1980–.

Girona: Martí, Ramon, ed. *Col·lecció diplomàtica de la Seu de Girona (817–1100)*. Barcelona: Fundació Noguera, 1997.

HGL: de Vic, Claude, and Joseph Vaissete. *Histoire générale de Languedoc avec des notes et les pièces justificatives*. New ed., 16 vols. Toulouse: Privat, 1872–1905 [cited by volume and document number].

Lavaix: Puig i Ferreté, Ignasi, ed. *El cartoral de Santa Maria de Lavaix: El monestir durant els segles XI–XIII*. La Seu d'Urgell: Societat Cultural Urgel·litana, 1984.

Liber feudorum maior: Miquel Rosell, Francisco, ed. *Liber feudorum maior: Cartulario real que se conserva en el Archivo de la Corona de Aragón*. 2 vols. Barcelona: Consejo Superior de Investigaciones Científicas, 1945–1947.

NH: Monsalvatje y Fossas, Francisco. *Noticias históricas*. 26 vols. Olot: Juan Bonet, 1889–1919 [cited by volume and document number].

PACB1: Feliu, Gaspar, and Josep M. Salrach, eds. *Els pergamins de l'Arxiu Comtal de Barcelona, de Ramon Borrell a Ramon Berenguer I*. 3 vols. Barcelona: Fundació Noguera, 1999.

PACB2: Baiges, Ignasi J., Gaspar Feliu, and Josep M. Salrach, eds. *Els pergamins de l'Arxiu Comtal de Barcelona, de Ramon Berenguer II a Ramon Berenguer IV*. 4 vols. Barcelona: Fundació Noguera, 2010.

PRJ: *PRocesos Judiciales en las sociedades medievales del norte peninsular*. Accessed 30 November 2015. http://prj.csic.es/.

SACM: Barcelona, Biblioteca de Catalunya, MS 729 (Jaume Pasqual, "Sacrae antiquitatis Cataloniae Monumenta," 11 vols., s. XVII[ex]–XVIII[in]). Accessed 21 July 2023. mdc.csuc.cat/digital/collection/manuscritBC/id/224125/ [cited by volume and folio number].

Sant Cugat: Rius Serra, José, ed. *Cartulario de "Sant Cugat" del Vallés*. 3 vols. Barcelona: Consejo Superior de Investigaciones Científicas, 1945–1947.

Sant Llorenç: Puig i Ustrell, Pere, ed. *El monestir de Sant Llorenç del Munt sobre Terrassa: Diplomatari dels segles X i XI*. 3 vols. Barcelona: Fundació Noguera, 1995.

Santa Anna: Alturo i Perucho, Jesús. *L'arxiu antic de Santa Anna de Barcelona del 942 al 1200 (Aproximació històrico-lingüística)*. 3 vols. Barcelona: Fundació Noguera, 1985.

Urgellia: Baraut, Cebrià, ed. "Els documents … l'Arxiu Capitular de la Seu d'Urgell," *Urgellia* 2 (1979)–11 (1992–1993).

Other Primary Sources

Bastardas, Joan, ed. *Usatges de Barcelona: El Codi a mitjan segle XII*. 2nd ed. Barcelona: Fundació Noguera, 1991.

Bisson, Thomas N., ed. *Fiscal Accounts of Catalonia under the Early Count-Kings (1151–1213)*. 2 vols. Berkeley: University of California Press, 1984.

Bolòs, Jordi, ed. *Diplomatari del monestir de Santa Maria de Serrateix (segles X–XV)*. Barcelona: Fundació Noguera, 2006.

Font Rius, José María, ed. *Cartas de población y franquicia de Cataluña*. 2 vols in 3. Madrid: Consejo Superior de Investigaciones Científicas, 1969–1983.

Mansi, Giovanni Domenico, ed. "Concilium Emeritense." In *Sacrorum conciliorum nova et amplissima collectio*. Vol. 11, cols. 75–100. Florence: Antonio Zatta, 1765.

Salrach i Marès, Josep Maria, and Tomàs Montagut i Estragués, eds. *Justícia i resolució de conflictes a la Catalynya medieval: Col·lecció diplomàtica, segles IX–XI*. Barcelona: Generalitat de Catalunya, 2018.

Udina Martorell, Federico, ed. *El "Llibre Blanch" de Santas Creus (Cartulario del siglo XII)*. Barcelona: Consejo Superior de Investigaciones Científicas, 1947.

Zeumer, Karl, ed. "Fragmenta Gaudenziana" [Collectionis iuris Romano-Visigothici capita VII–XX (Fragmenta Gaudenziana)]. In *Leges Visigothorum*. Monumenta Germaniae Historica, Leges nationum Germanicarum 1, 469–472. Hanover: Hahn, 1902.

Zeumer, Karl, ed. "Lex Visigothorum" [Liber iudiciorum sive Lex Visigothorum]. In *Leges Visigothorum*. Monumenta Germaniae Historica, Leges nationum Germanicarum 1, 33–456. Hanover: Hahn, 1902.

Secondary Works

Balari Jovany, José. *Orígenes históricos de Cataluña*. 2nd ed., 2 vols in 3. Sant Cugat del Vallès: Abadía de San Cugat del Vallés / Instituto Internacional de Cultura Románica, 1964.

Bastier, Jean. "Le testament en Catalogne du IXe au XIIe siècle: Une survivance wisigothique," *Revue historique de droit français et étranger*, 4th ser., 51 (1973), 373–417.

Bolòs i Masclans, Jordi, and Josep Moran i Ocerinjauregui. *Repertori d'antropònims catalans (RAC)*. Vol. 1 (only). Barcelona: Institut d'Estudis Catalans, 1994.

Bonnassie, Pierre. *La Catalogne du milieu du Xe à la fin du XIe siècle: Croissance et mutations d'une société*. 2 vols. Toulouse: Association des publications de l'Université de Toulouse-Le Mirail, 1975–1976.

Bonnassie, Pierre, and Jordi Fernández-Cuadrench. "Les documents catalans des IXe–XIIe siècles: Éditions récentes et publications en cours," *Le Moyen âge* 105 (1999), 149–160.

Bowman, Jeffrey A. *Shifting Landmarks: Property, Proof, and Dispute in Catalonia around the Year 1000*. Ithaca: Cornell University Press, 2004.

Collins, Roger. "'Sicut lex Gothorum continet': Law and Charters in Ninth- and Tenth-Century León and Catalonia," *English Historical Review* 100 (1985), 489–512.

Davies, Wendy. *Windows on Justice in Northern Iberia, 800–1000*. Abingdon: Routledge, 2016.

Font Rius, Josep Maria. "Entorn de la figura de Ponç Bofill Marc, jutge comtal de Barcelona, a les primeries del segle XI," *Boletim da Faculdade de Direito* (Coimbra) 58 (1982), 377–395.

Font y Rius, José María. "La escuela jurídica de Barcelona." In *Historia de España Menéndez-Pidal*. Vol. 7.2 *La España cristiana de los siglos VIII al XI: Los núcleos pirenaicos (718–1035): Navarra, Aragón, Cataluña*, 729–750. Madrid: Espasa-Calpe, 1999.

Gil i Román, Xavier. "Ermesèn, vida y obra de la condesa: Estudio histórico de la documentación, c. 977–+1 marzo de 1058 / Diplomatario de Ermesèn, condesa de Barcelona, Osona y Girona, c. 991–25 octubre 1180." Ph.D. dissertation, Universitat Autònoma de Barcelona, 2004.

Jarrett, Jonathan. *Rulers and Ruled in Frontier Catalonia, 880–1010: Pathways of Power*. London: Royal Historical Society / Boydell, 2010.

Kosto, Adam J. "The Elements of Practical Rulership: Ramon Berenguer I of Barcelona and the Revolt of Mir Geribert," *Viator* 47 (2016), 67–94.

Maier, Gideon. *Amtsträger und Herrscher in der Romania Gothica: Vergleichende Untersuchungen zu den Institutionen der ostgermanischen Völkerwanderungsreiche*. Stuttgart: Franz Steiner Verlag, 2005.

Mundó, Anscarí M. "El jutge Bonsom de Barcelona, cal·lígraf i copista del 979 al 1024." In idem, *Obres completes*, 1.1, *Catalunya: De la romanitat a la sobirania*, 587–610. Barcelona: Curial Edicions Catalans / Publicacions de l'Abadia de Montserrat, 1998. [Orig. in *Scribi e colofoni: Le sottoscrizioni di copisti dalle origini all'avvento della stampa: Atti del seminario di Erice, X colloquio del Comité international de paléographie latine (23–28 ottobre 1993)*, edited by Emma Condello and Giuseppe De Gregorio, 269–288. Spoleto: Centro italiano di studi sull'alto medioevo, 1995.]

Nehlsen–von Stryck, Karin. *Die* boni homines *des frühen Mittelalters: Unter besonderer Berücksichtigung der fränkischen Quellen*. Berlin: Duncker & Humblot, 1981.

Ourliac, Paul. "Juges et justiciables au XIe siècle: Les *boni homines*," *Recueil de mémoires et travaux publié par la Société d'histoire du droit et des institutions des anciens pays de droit écrit* 16 (1994), 17–33.

Salrach, Josep M. *Justícia i poder a Catalunya abans de l'any mil*. Vic: Eumo, 2013.

Shideler, John C. *A Medieval Catalan Noble Family: The Montcadas, 1000–1230*. Berkeley: University of California Press, 1983.

Taylor, Nathaniel Lane. "The Will and Society in Medieval Catalonia and Languedoc, 800–1200." Ph.D. dissertation, Harvard University, 1995.

Tock, Benoît-Michel. *Scribes, souscripteurs et témoins dans les actes privés en France (VIIe–début XIIe siècle)*. Turnhout: Brepols, 2005.

Udina i Abelló, Antoni M. *La successió testada a la Catalunya altomedieval*. Barcelona: Fundació Noguera, 1984.

Vincent, Nicholas. "The Court of Henry II." In *Henry II: New Interpretations*, edited by Christopher Harper-Bill and Nicholas Vincent, 278–334. Woodbridge: Boydell, 2007.

Zimmermann, Michel. *Écrire et lire en Catalogne (IXe–XIIe siècle)*. 2 vols. Madrid: Casa de Velázquez, 2003.

CHAPTER 12

Lines Traced on Mountains: Delimitations and Territorial Disputes in the Western Pyrenees between the Ninth and Eleventh Centuries

Juan José Larrea

1 Territories, Monasteries, and Memory

In the early Middle Ages, Navarre and Aragon occupied an east-west corridor of pre-Pyrenean basins and a succession of valleys that descend into them from the Pyrenean ridge.[1] The basins were host to a Mediterranean-style agriculture, and the valleys comprise a variety of mountainous terrains, reaching 2000–3000 m in altitude. These territories were organized around two political entities that emerged following the Arab conquest, the kingdom of Pamplona—that is, Navarre—and the county of Aragon (see Map 12.1). Until its establishment as an independent kingdom in 1035, the county of Aragon was in general subordinate to the kingdom of Pamplona, either de facto or de iure, depending on the period.

As was the case in all of the northern part of the Iberian peninsula, the territories of these primitive Christian political entities grew spectacularly in the tenth to twelfth centuries. The first stage of this expansion, in the first quarter of the tenth century, was the conquest by Navarre of part of La Rioja, but the decisive leap was made between the end of the eleventh century and the early decades of the twelfth with the incorporation of vast areas of the Ebro Valley: Huesca in 1096, Zaragoza in 1118, and Tudela in 1119. This inordinate expansion of territory coincided with the Gregorian Reform, such that political and ecclesiastical structures in Navarre and Aragon were radically different from what they had been in the early Middle Ages. We need to keep this in mind if we want to understand the development of the monasteries studied in this article. Over the course of the eleventh century, the older

1 This paper has been developed within the Grupo de Investigación del Sistema Universitario Vasco *Sociedades, Procesos, Culturas* (*siglos VIII–XVIII*) IT 1465-22; research project *Societies on the Edges: A Combinative Approach to Cross-Cultural Connections in Early Medieval Western Europe* (PID 2020-115365GB-100): https://connect-web.eu/. The abbreviations used in this paper for editions of charters are listed in the bibliography.

 | DOI:10.1163/9789004683006_014

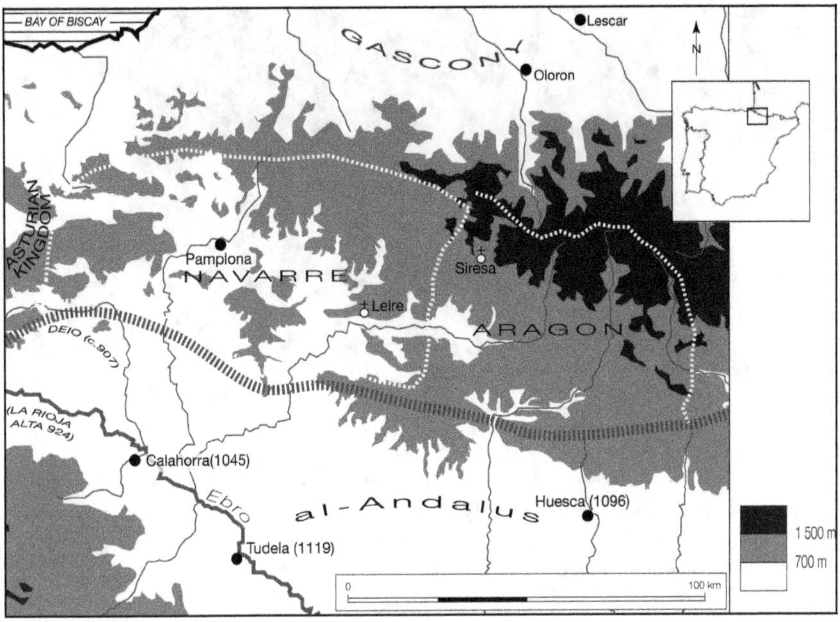

MAP 12.1 The western Pyrenees ca. 900. The dates indicate the years of the Christian conquest of cities and territories
MAP DRAWN BY THE AUTHOR

monasteries in the Pyrenees were in effect relegated to a secondary role in peripheral areas of both kingdoms. But before that time, in the ninth and tenth centuries, they had been important, thriving institutions for Navarre and Aragon.

A very well-known letter addressed to Bishop Wiliesindo of Pamplona by Eulogius of Córdoba attests to the vitality of monastic life in the western Pyrenees in the mid-ninth century. Eulogius says he was favourably impressed by what he had seen during his visit in about 848 to three monasteries in Navarre—San Salvador de Leire, San Vicente de Igal, and San Salvador de Urdaspal—and two in Aragon—San Pedro de Siresa and San Martín de Cillas.[2] In addition to these, three others emerged during the decades following Eulogius's visit: Santa María de Fuenfría, San Julian de Navasal, and the somewhat more distant San Martín de Cercito. This boom in monastic activity was of course inseparable from the development of the kingdom of Navarre and the county of Aragon (see Map 12.2).

2 Eulogius Cordubensis, "Epistula III (ad Wiliesindum)," in Juan Gil, ed., *Corpus Scriptorum Muzarabicorum*, 2 vols (Madrid: CSIC, 1973), 2:498–503; Albarus Cordubensis, "Vita Eulogii," ibid., 1:330–343.

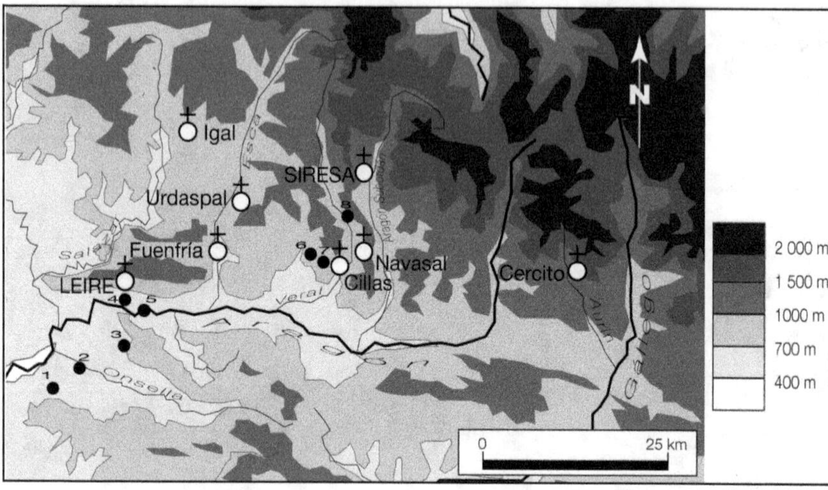

MAP 12.2 The monasteries of the early Middle Ages in the western Pyrenees. Settlements discussed in the paper: 1. Añués, 2. Fillera, 3. Lerda, 4. Benasa, 5. Catamesas, 6. Huértalo, 7. Cabañas, 8. Beralevilla
MAP DRAWN BY THE AUTHOR

The two most important monasteries were San Pedro de Siresa in Aragon and San Salvador de Leire in Navarre. Founded in about 830 on a piece of land belonging to Count Galindo Aznar, Siresa was closely linked to the counts of Aragon during the ninth and tenth centuries. Later, following the birth of the kingdom of Aragon and its expansion to the south, Siresa ended up becoming a priory of the Huesca-Jaca cathedral beginning in 1145. With regard to Leire, the date and the circumstances of its founding are unknown. In any case, it was linked to the Navarrese royal house from the time that this house enters into the historical record around the middle of the ninth century. The monastery even functioned as a royal pantheon during some periods. Unlike Siresa, Leire was able to attract the favour of much of the aristocracy and other notables in Navarre between about 1050 and 1130, thus becoming the most powerful monastery in Navarre.

While the other monasteries also relied on the protection of kings and counts, their influence did not extend much beyond their immediate valleys. In the eleventh century, they were all absorbed by more important institutions: Fuenfría, Cillas, Navasal, and Cercito became dependencies of the Aragonese royal abbey of San Juan de la Peña, while Urdaspal and Igal were subordinated to Leire. Today, the only tangible vestiges of them that remain are some modest ruins.[3]

3 Luis Javier Fortún, *Leire, un señorío monástico en Navarra* (*siglos* IX–XIX) (Pamplona: Go-

The oldest traces of these Pyrenean monasteries have come down to us in the form of a heterogeneous group of single-sheet parchments, *pancartae*, and cartularies that were compiled, edited, and organized mainly in the eleventh century, shortly before or after almost all the monasteries had lost their independence. In Leire, the arrival of a French abbot in 1083 led to the composition of an important cartulary called the *Becerro Antiguo*, but the oldest documents were preserved on single-sheet parchments and in a *pancarta*.[4] Conversely, our knowledge of the early history of Siresa relies on a small cartulary that was compiled in the first half of the twelfth century, only part of which is extant.[5] In addition, the large cartulary from San Juan de la Peña, the *Libro Gótico*, whose composition began in about 1060, contains much of the extant documentation from the monasteries of Fuenfría, Cillas, and Navasal.[6]

As a group, this is a modest documentary dossier, whose interest obviously does not derive from its size, since it contains fewer than 50 records, but rather from the preponderance of narrative texts. The Pyrenean monks knew perfectly well how to compose charters in accordance with the formularies of the Hispano-Visigothic tradition and they sometimes chose to do so,[7] but in these scriptoria the choice was more often made to utilize the narrative account as a source of legitimacy. The preferred document form was the *notitia*, a kind of text that was not subject to the straightjacket of notarial formularies and thus is able to provide rich data about the relationships between these communities of monks and their surroundings. Leire and Siresa, the two largest monasteries, are the only exceptions to this general rule; they built their discourse of legitimacy on their privileged relationship with kings and counts. This explains why the proportion of charters was clearly much larger than that of *notitiae* in the documents from these monasteries.

bierno de Navarra, 1993); Antonio Durán Gudiol, *El monasterio de San Pedro de Siresa* (Zaragoza: Diputación de Aragón, 1989); Ana Isabel Lapeña, *El monasterio de San Juan de la Peña en la Edad Media* (Zaragoza: Caja de Ahorros de la Inmaculada, 1989), 24–44.

4 DML 1, 3–7.

5 CS 1–12.

6 SJP 1, 2, 4–15, 17, 30–32, 34, 156.

7 SJP 5; cf. "Formulae Visigothicae," in Karl Zeumer, ed., *Formulae Merowingici et Karolini Aevi*, MGH LL 5 (Hanover: Hahn, 1886), 579–580 (no. 8 and 9).

2 The Centrality of Territorial Conflicts and Demarcations in the Monasteries' Records

Together with the importance of narrative, another key feature of this documentary dossier is the decisive role played by territorial conflicts and demarcations in the records pertaining to each monastery's origins and development. To a large extent, it is as if these conflicts and demarcations were milestones that gave structure to the relationship between the monasteries and the inhabitants of their surrounding areas.

In the narrative accounts written by the monks, the drawing of boundaries is sometimes presented as the natural, immediate sequel to the construction of a church and the founding of a community of monks. These spaces were vast, extending from one mountain crest to another. The area assigned to Fuenfría, for example, is estimated to have been around 10,000 hectares, and that of Cillas extended some 10 km from north to south.[8] The demarcation of boundaries is also sometimes presented as a mechanism for resolving territorial disputes between the monks and local people, or among peasant communities living in the surrounding area of a monastery. In fact, the drawing of boundaries that took place at the founding of a monastery and the drawing of boundaries as a result of a conflict were sometimes presented as the same event: in Navasal this is explicitly stated, and in Cercito the order of the *notitiae* suggests that the drawing of the monastery's boundaries had brought peace to the valley.[9]

From the point of view of conflict resolution, these narratives tend to emphasize the pacifying role of kings and counts in boundary determinations. To do this, the texts emphasize the violence that preceded such determinations: the men of Lerda, Añués, and Fillera had been ready to kill each other over territorial disputes; the rivers around Cercito ran red from the fighting over boundaries between the inhabitants of two areas in dispute; Navasal was destroyed and along with it, its lands.[10] Royal and comital intervention generally took the form of a solemn *perambulatio* ceremony attended by a crowd, after which peace was established. This is not surprising, as we are dealing here with a topos in monastic narratives throughout western Europe: a community of monks, protected by kings and counts, established itself wherever chaos, violence, and wilderness reigned and in doing so brought order, justice, and peace to the area.

---

8 Juan José Larrea, *La Navarre du IVe au XIIe siècle. Peuplement et société* (Paris-Bruxelles: De Boeck, 1998), 185–190.

9 SJP 7, 9, 11.

10 DML 3; SJP 7, 9.

This is noticeable in the way the drawing of boundaries is described. The sequence of events shows royal perambulation as the mechanism that resolved a dispute. However, the specific procedure does not distinguish it from the setting of boundaries when there was no conflict. In fact, it is the perambulation ritual itself, the physical presence of the rulers and their procession, that was most significant. Thus, in the account of the resolution of a conflict between the monastery of Navasal and its neighbouring communities:

> Et venit illo comite Galindo Asnar et invitavit regem Fortunio Garcianes ut parteret illos terminos illis. Et venerunt ad Labasal et steterunt ibi die sabbato et die dominico, et servivit illis abbas dompnus Bancius. Et die lunis manescente, rege equitante suo caballo rosello, cum totos suos barones, et comite cum suos, sic diviserunt illo termino ut fieret de Labasal de illa zema de Iserui quomodo devaddat ad illa spelunca de Lisue et exit in directo ad illa zema de Iati, ac si quomodo aqua vertit [...].[11]

It should not be forgotten that this document and others like it were not strictly judicial documents. As a revealing contrast, an exceptional document from the cathedral of Jaca shows the endless succession of negotiations, disputes, and agreements behind a territorial conflict in the tenth century.[12] This record is similar to the ones we are examining here, except that in the latter, the monks were silent about important stages and circumstances of the conflict. This silence was a conscious decision and certainly not due to their inability to recount the details. These monastic records are judicial narratives whose logic cannot be considered separately from the overall discourse about the past.

In fact, it is not difficult to perceive the political and symbolic value of the act of setting boundaries. Firstly, the physical presence of the king was highlighted. In the second half of the ninth century, the monarchy of Pamplona was in the process of transforming itself from a fundamentally military form of leadership into a Christian principality.[13] The ceremonies involving the delimitation of boundaries by the king, as a result of the settlement of disputes over collective spaces, sometimes involving churches and monasteries, contributed

11 SJP 7.

12 PRJ database: https://prj.csic.es/consulta_instituciones_en.php?m=2&c=3 (accessed 13 July 2023). See Juan José Larrea, "La condición del campesinado navarro-aragonés entre los siglos IX y XII: una revisión crítica," *En la España Medieval* 29 (2006), 383–409, at 391–392. See also Takashi Adachi, "Documents of Dispute Settlement in Eleventh-Century Aragón and Navarra: King's Tribunal and Compromise," *Imago Temporis. Medium Aevum* 1 (2007), 71–85, which deals primarily with the eleventh century.

13 Juan José Larrea, "Construir un reino en la periferia de al-Andalus: Pamplona entre los

to the creation of mechanisms of territorial government. Furthermore, the relationship between the counts of Aragon and the kings of Pamplona was publicly enacted by such ceremonies. Either the kings confirmed the setting of boundaries made by the counts, or the counts asked them rhetorically to confirm and endorse such boundaries.[14] These ceremonies were also a representation of the seizure of power by the Jimeno family after the change of dynasty in 905: in a text related to the dispute between Benasa and Catamesas, which shall be discussed later, the change of dynasty that had taken place between the two perambulations was expressly recorded.[15]

In sum, what these documents describe is, above all, how the monasteries were invested with power over the territories whose boundaries were defined in such ceremonies. We should recall that the investiture not only made the new right of the beneficiary visible; the *potestas* of the grantor was also made manifest. This twofold potential of the investiture is particularly evident in the ongoing creation of political entities such as Navarre and Aragon in this period.

3 Building Monastic Territories by Drawing Boundary Lines

We have thus identified a discourse about the past that influenced the selection of information to be preserved in monastic documents. However, such a discourse did not prevent actual or potential conflicts over real territories: the monks were thus interested in having specific events, places, and perambulations recorded. This is why the documents can also be used to answer questions about the economic and spatial meaning of the very act of drawing a line in order to construct a monastic territory.

Let us begin with one observation. The documentary dossier being discussed here includes a remarkable variety of terms used to designate arable and pastoral spaces depending on their morphology and their actual or potential use. These terms differentiate between areas being cultivated (*campo*), which may correspond to seasonal fields (*campos cognitos*) and plots within them (*fasca*); between different types of plots according to their greater or lesser exposure to the sun (*solana, opaca*); between pastures and shelters for cattle in the lower

---

siglos VIII y X," in *Symposium Internacional: Poder y simbología en la Europa altomedieval*, ed. Francisco J. Fernández Conde and César García de Castro Valdés (Oviedo: Trea, 2009), 279–308, at 303–305.

14 CS 5, 6, 8; SJP 7.

15 SJP 14.

part of the valleys (*pardina, cubile*) and in the high mountain areas (*estiva*); and mention is also made of places where pastures and crops were alternated (*monte*), forests (*silva*), meadows (*agorral* and perhaps *erbare*), and pastures that were designated in an apparently generic way (*pascuero*); there was even a specific term for the use of water (*acuero*).[16] All of this suggests that there was significant and diversified use being made of the entire valley, from the river-banks to the crests of the mountains.

Looking at the landscape today, marked as it is by rural exodus and extensive reforestation, it is difficult to imagine what it must have been like a thousand years ago, when it teemed with small settlements.[17] These settlements occupied agricultural 'islets' of a few hectares, located on the wide valley floors or on higher terraces (see Fig. 12.1). They were the nuclei of large territories engaged in diverse economic activities that can be recognized from the descriptions in the texts: such 'islets' were suited to intensive agricultural use, given the abundant cattle and therefore the availability of manure; the slopes protected from the north wind made it possible to have seasonal crops with different cultivation cycles;[18] the various pastures fed pigs, cows, and sheep and could be combined with summer pastures higher up in the mountains.

The economic viability of any of these activities and, consequently, of any community depended on access to the full range of spaces, and not only to arable land. This access involved combining different forms of appropriation and circulation—individual, collective, and supra-local—that overlapped, spread or contracted according to the agricultural, pastoral, and forestry cycles. Elisabeth Bille has coined a definition that is apt for any one of these valleys: "un espace modulable dans le temps".[19] It was the specific use that defined the appropriation of spaces: when the monasteries started marking boundaries, no previously traced lines were encountered. The agreements between monks and peasants did not entertain the possibility that the boundary markers and lines might be moved or misplaced; rather, the fear seems to have been that peasants from the surrounding areas might trespass onto the land that the monks wanted to set aside for their own use.

---

16 SJP 1, 2, 4, 5, 7, 11, 15, 31; CS 3, 5, 6.

17 Carlos Laliena and Philippe Sénac, *Musulmans et Chrétiens dans le haut Moyen Age: aux origines de la Reconquête aragonaise* (Paris: Minerve, 1991), 79–82.

18 On the importance of temporary crops in the medieval agrarian economy in general, see Roland Viader and Christine Rendu, eds., *Cultures temporaires et féodalité. Les rotations culturales et l'appropriation du sol dans l'Europe médiévale et moderne. Actes des Journées Internationales d'Histoire de l'abbaye de Flaran* (Toulouse: Presses Universitaires du Midi, 2014).

19 Elisabeth Bille, "Remarques sur les modes de spatialisation des droits et des pratiques sur

FIGURE 12.1 The old peasant settlement of Beralevilla (known today as Santa Lucía). The settlement originated ca. 900 in one of the valley's small areas of arable land.
PHOTOGRAPH BY THE AUTHOR

Under these circumstances, the dominant presence of the monasteries was not due to their being supposedly large agricultural centres with labour resources that could be deployed over an extensive area. Quite the contrary: these monasteries were not much larger than any of the small peasant settlements of the area. As an example, Cillas occupied an area of little more than ten hectares on the bank of the Veral river, and Navasal was perched on a terrace of about five hectares, located some 200 m above the same river (see Fig. 12.2). The case of Siresa may seem at first glance to be different, because it was at the bottom of a valley broad enough to allow for vineyards to be cultivated. But we know that the monastery had to build its estate gradually by buying, exchanging and receiving donations of numerous small plots that even encroached on the property belonging to Count Galindo Aznar where the church had been established.[20] If the viability of the monasteries had depended on their initial economic and human resources, they would have faced very stiff competition

les vacants en Cerdagne aux XIIe-XIVe siècles," in *Les ressources naturelles des Pyrénées du Moyen Âge à l'époque moderne. Exploitation, gestion, appropriation*, ed. Aymat Catafau (Perpignan: Presses Universitaires de Perpignan, 2005), 239–252, at 244.

20 CS 1.

FIGURE 12.2 Location of the monastery of Navasal, on an elevated terrace in the valley of Ansó. The circle marks the ruins of the rural chapel of the Eleven Thousand Maidens, which is the place where the buildings of Navasal originally stood.
PHOTOGRAPH BY THE AUTHOR

from the surrounding communities for access to the different agricultural areas in each valley.

The monasteries were able to thrive because they were recognized (whether willingly or reluctantly is another matter)[21] as having a superior right over the arable, pastures and woodlands, independent of their real use. There is no doubt that the monasteries did exploit some land, but more characteristically they limited the amount of land cleared by the peasants—undoubtedly accustomed to cyclical displacements of the crops—while at the same time they ceded areas to be cleared in exchange for tithes.[22] As far as livestock was concerned, the monasteries assumed or intended to assume the protection of pastures against foreign stockbreeders, and, above all, they obtained donations of *estivas*—that is, alpine pastures—that allowed them to practice transhumance.[23] The combination of winter pastures in the lower valleys and summer pastures on the high mountain slopes has been documented since the

21 The case of the communities living in the surroundings of Navasal epitomizes the opposition to this superior power exercised by the monks: SJP 7.

22 SJP 31, 32, 42; CS 5, 6.

23 SJP 1, 2, SJP 7; CS 3, 6.

Visigothic period,[24] and in the centuries under discussion here, this was apparently dominated by the ruling families and by the pastoral communities located at the north end of the valleys.[25] This activity naturally required the control of the routes used to move cattle.

We should also remember that control of the churches was an instrument for maintaining territorial domination. The monks received some churches and cemeteries by donation, as well as episcopal rights.[26] They naturally claimed control over the appointment of priests, which seemed to be the source of endless litigation with their parishioners.[27] And, of course, they tried to extend their rights to collect tithes, which was clearly a powerful tool of domination.[28] However, it would be a mistake to imagine that the monasteries grew in power through a simple process beginning with the appropriation of churches and only thereafter allowing for the collection of tithes on the lands that depended on those churches in some way. Take the example of Cabañas:[29] a son of one of the village's notable families had been made lame while fleeing Almanzor's armies and had been delivered as an oblate to San Martin de Cillas, along with the donation of a house and a field. At the time of the *oblatio*, or perhaps later, those notable families agreed to give the church of Cabañas (including its tithes) to Cillas. But an additional component of the *convenientia* was that the inhabitants of Cabañas would be entitled to cultivate a plot of land owned by Cillas for which they would also pay a tithe. The criteria for the payment of tithes often pose a problem to researchers; but in terms of what concerns us here, it suffices to say that the prior control of space by Cillas was also an instrument for extending the collection of tithes.

---

24 Céline Martin and Juan José Larrea, eds., *Nouvelles chartes visigothiques du monastère pyrénéen d'Asán* (Bordeaux: Ausonius Éditions, 2021).

25 Juan José Larrea, "Moines et paysans: aux origines de la première croissance agraire dans le Haut Aragon (IXe-Xe s.)," *Cahiers de Civilisation Médiévale* 33 (1990), 219–239; "Notas sobre los orígenes del poblamiento del valle de Salazar (Navarra)," in *Villages pyrénéens. Morphogenèse d'un habitat de montagne*, ed. Maurice Berthe and Benoît Cursente (Toulouse: CNRS-Université de Toulouse-Le Mirail, 2000), 195–207.

26 SJP 8, 13, 17, 30, 31; CS 7, 12; DML 1, 3, 5, 7.

27 SJP 13, 17; José Ángel Lema, ed., *Colección diplomática de Alfonso I de Aragón y Pamplona (1104–1134)* (San Sebastián: Sociedad de Estudios Vascos, 1990), no. 89.

28 Roland Viader, "La dîme dans l'Europe des féodalités. Rapport introductif," in *La dîme dans l'Europe médiévale et moderne. Actes des Journées internationales d'histoire de l'abbaye de Flaran*, ed. Roland Viader (Toulouse: Presses Universitaires du Midi, 2010), 7–36, also for all the following remarks on tithing.

29 SJP 31.

In sum, the way these new monastic players were able to gain access to large swathes of land already in use was by exercising their power through the demarcation of monastic territories. The legitimacy of this act of power derived from the fact that monasteries were considered foci of sacredness.[30] They housed numerous and powerful relics, practised a far more effective liturgy than the modest rural churches, and ensured that the memory of their benefactors was preserved. They acted both as the stage where the power dynamics of the royalty and the counts were played out and as poles of attraction for notable families. As discussed above, they also acted as beacons of peace, justice and compassion for the crippled and the sick (of the important families, it must be said).[31]

In symbolic and visual terms, linear limits seemed particularly effective for projecting monastic spaces.[32] Moreover, this irradiation of the sacred may have to do with the presence of hagio-toponyms in the mountains along some boundary lines.[33] Didier Méhu makes this point about Cluny, noting how a space organized around a spiritual focus needed to be articulated with the physical reality of the territory under the monastery's domination.[34] This is exactly what was done when a precise continuous line was traced along the lines of ridges—*serra serra, dossum dossum, quantum aqua bertit*—connecting several toponyms, landscape features, and different land units being used in sundry activities. The tracing of these lines was always described as being done all at once, rather than over the course of time, and was sometimes recalled in connection to a solemn *perambulatio* (*quomodo partivit rex*), at other times narrated in the first person (*intramus rasos, veniamus*), and still

---

30 See Alain Guerreau, "Quelques caractères spécifiques de l'espace féodal européen," in *L'État ou le Roi. Les fondements de la modernité monarchique en France* (XIVe-XVIIe *siècles*), ed. Neithard Bulst, Robert Descimon, and Alain Guerreau (Paris: Maison des Sciences de l'Homme, 1996), 85–101; Michel Lauwers, "De l'Incastellamento à l'inecclesiamento. Monachisme et logiques spatiales du féodalisme," in *Cluny, les moines et la société au premier âge féodal*, ed. Dominique Iogna-Prat et al. (Rennes: Presses Universitaires de Rennes, 2013), 315–338, at 318.

31 SJP 10, 31.

32 Pierre Toubert, "Frontière et frontières: un objet historique," in *Castrum 4. Frontière et peuplement dans le monde méditerranéen au Moyen Âge* (Rome–Madrid: École française de Rome—Casa de Velázquez, 1992), 9–17, at 12; Michel Lauwers and Laurent Ripart, "Représentation et gestion de l'espace dans l'Occident médiéval," in *Rome et l'État moderne européen*, ed. Jean-Philippe Genêt (Rome: École française de Rome, 2007), 115–171, at 141–142.

33 SJP 1, 5, 7, 14, 32; DML 3.

34 Didier Méhu, *Paix et communautés autour de l'abbaye de Cluny* (x^e^-xve *siècle*) (Lyon: Presses Universitaires de Lyon, 2010), ch. 3.

others, using a verb in the third person, whose subject seems to be the boundary line itself (*et perrexit*).[35]

In any case, it was no accident that the very genesis of these monasteries was closely associated with the demarcation of their territories in the (often later) memory constructed by these institutions.

4 Lines and Conflicts outside Monastic Territories

Let us now undertake an exercise in abstraction. If what has been examined in the previous section is reduced to its basic principles, it can be seen that the drawing of boundary lines introduced a new logic for the appropriation of space. The previous occupants of the territory, as well as the occupants that shared the valleys with the monasteries, delimited space through its actual use, that is, through overlapping cycles of varying intensity and degrees.[36] In contrast, whoever could not claim the use of space, but had enough power to impose their access to it, drew a line. In other words, certain actors appropriated space through specific work (whether their own or performed by subordinates is irrelevant here), and others traced a line that in principle was and would be independent from their actual capacity to exploit the land.

One aspect that blurs the distinction between line and use is precisely the relationship between the drawing of lines and conflict resolution: in fact, linear boundaries often appeared to be a 'natural' solution to a territorial dispute and this is how they are presented in the texts. Fortunately, the documentary dossier under discussion here contains a couple of cases of conflicts between peasant communities that were resolved by drawing boundary lines. This allows us to approach the issue freed from the symbolic weight attached to the monastic territories and to focus the discussion on the contrast between the lines being drawn and the actual use of the land. The aim is to discover to what extent the use of boundary lines under the pretext of restoring peace between peasant communities also projected a spatial logic that was characteristic of the dominant groups.

Both of these conflicts between peasants occurred in the sector of pre-Pyrenean basins located on the border of Navarre and Aragon. This area was much better suited to agriculture than the Pyrenean valleys: the river's lower

35 SJP 2, 4, 7, 11.

36 In some sectors, however, there may have been some kind of temporary or permanent separation mark: in the violent conflict between the two neighbouring communities of Cercito (SJP 9), *ballatos*, i.e., 'fences' are mentioned.

banks had moist and silty soils, good for irrigated crops but also for intensive grain cultivation, as well as for woodlands and pastures for grazing draught animals. However, there were some problems: the susceptibility of many streams to flash flooding caused cyclical damage, so the peasants had to constantly rebuild fragile and non-durable canals. The highest terraces were of mediocre or poor quality, but the climate allowed for more or less extensive cultivation of grains as well as for vineyards.[37] Unfortunately, the settlement reorganization that resulted from setting the border between Navarre and Aragon in the twelfth century, together with the construction of the Yesa reservoir in the 1950s, has radically changed, if not erased, the early medieval settlement pattern.

The first conflict to be discussed is that between the villages of Benasa and Catamesas,[38] located in an area physically dominated and politically controlled by the monastery of Leire, which overlooks the river from a position 300 m above. During the Middle Ages, this area, now flooded by the Yesa reservoir, teemed with small villages. One of them, Benasa, was just below the monastery.[39] Its territory encompassed the lower reaches of the mountain range, the fertile plain on the two banks of the river, and part of the hills bordering this plain to the south. Catamesas was nearby, although it is impossible to know which side of the river it was on; indeed, its territory may also have extended onto both banks.[40]

The *notitia* corresponding to this dispute was composed in 928 at the initiative of Bishop Galindo of Pamplona, an influential figure in this area.[41] The text

---

37 Isidro Escagüés Javierre, "La Valdonsella," *Príncipe de Viana* 6 (1945), 218–344; Salvador Mensúa, *La Navarra Media oriental* (Zaragoza: Diputación Foral de Navarra—CSIC, 1960), 82–86.

38 SJP 14. This conflict has received some attention in recent decades: Roger Collins, "Visigothic Law and Regional Custom in Disputes in Early Medieval Spain," in *The Settlement of Disputes in Early Medieval Europe*, ed. Wendy Davies and Paul Fouracre (Cambridge: Cambridge University Press, 1986), 97–104; Larrea, *Navarre*, 273–274; Chris Wickham, "Espacio y sociedad en los conflictos campesinos en la Alta Edad Media," in *El lugar del campesino. En torno a la obra de Reyna Pastor*, ed. Ana Rodríguez (Valencia: Universitat de València—CSIC, 2007), 33–60, at 35–36.

39 Fortún, *Leire*, 317.

40 Jean Passini, "L'habitat fortifié dans la Canal de Berdún, Aragon. Xe-XIIIe siècles," in *Castrum 3: Guerre, fortification et habitat dans le monde méditerranéen au Moyen Age* (Rome-Madrid: École française de Rome—Casa de Velázquez, 1985), 91–98, at 92, places the inhabited centre to the south, as he also does for Benasa, but there is no conclusive evidence for one location or another.

41 José Goñi Gaztambide, *Historia de los obispos de Pamplona. S. IV–XIII* (Pamplona: EUNSA, 1979), 94–96.

begins by going back to the past to explain that *in temporibus illis* there was a dispute over the boundaries of Benasa and Catamesas, which was resolved by King Fortun Garcés (r. 880–905) through a ceremonial perambulation:

> fecit placitum pro ipso termino, et venit ipse rex cum multitudine virorum et posuerunt terminum. Ipse rex in equo suo pedificando antecedabat, et alii viri post eum. Agmina multitudo confirmaverunt, ipse vero precedebat omnes.

The text then adopts the tone of a chronicle and recalls that King Sancho Garcés I (r. 905–925), the founder of the Jimeno dynasty, had been chosen by God. After recounting his death, the narration returns to the time and place of the document's composition and explains the actions of Bishop Galindo in 928. He gathered the men who were familiar with the disputed boundaries, making more than twenty abbots and priests walk the boundary lines as they had seen Fortun Garcés do long ago. The drawing of the boundaries is then described, and it is recorded that three of the witnesses to the original perambulation swore in the church of San Juan, before the king, that they had closely followed Fortun Garcés's itinerary. The document ends with a long list of the names of the people involved.

The entire ceremony, involving large crowds and arranged into several successive acts, conveyed the idea that the *perambulatio*, linked to the figures and the memory of the kings, was intended to ensure peace. But there are several interesting aspects that reveal a specific logic of territorial domination. Firstly, it is necessary to question Bishop Galindo's motives. While it is true that the document says that the *notitia* was written to ensure that there would be no conflict between an ambiguous *nos et illos*, it had also said previously that the bishop acted *pro confirmatione*. It is telling that, in a text as rich in details as this one, nowhere does it say that the old conflict had re-emerged. Rather it seems that everything was done to affirm the authority of Bishop Galindo over Catamesas. Secondly, the text suggests that the limits were known by those who remembered where King Fortun Garcés rode his horse through between 23 and 48 years earlier: the actual use to which the inhabitants put the land does not seem to have been considered. Thirdly, there is a striking discordance between the Benasa-Catamesas dispute, which gave rise to the *perambulatio*, and the boundaries traced as a result: although it is impossible to locate them with precision, two lines are perfectly identified that descend from the slope to the river bank, more or less perpendicular to it, one to the east and another to the west. If we keep in mind that Benasa and Catamesas were approximately in line with the river and that there were other villages to the east and west of them, it is clear that only one of these lines could have been common to Benasa and Catamesas, and we can grant that it served to ensure peace. However, this was definitely not the case with the other line.

The same questions can be asked about the second dispute, which is recounted in a *notitia* inserted into a charter from Leire.[42] This was a conflict between the villages of Lerda and Añués, on the one hand, and Fillera, on the other, which was resolved through royal intervention. The resolution of the conflict is attributed to King García Íñiguez (r. 850–880), who had given Lerda and Añués to the monastery of Leire. According to the account, the clashes between the men from Lerda and Añués and the men from Fillera had grown murderous. The king was able to restore peace in a formal demarcation, which was attended by crowds and in which he was accompanied by people from his circle with roots in the area, clergymen and at least one judge.

The three villages are now uninhabited, but we know the precise locations of Añués and Fillera, and the approximate location of Lerda. They are situated in a nearly straight line about 12 km long, with Fillera in the middle. These were probably relatively large villages: Lerda was the burial place of Bishop Basilio of Pamplona in 921; Fillera was located in the area occupied by one of the most important settlements in the region, if not the most important, going back to the High Empire and up to at least Visigothic times.[43] The conflict may have erupted around the fertile plains of the final stretch of the Onsella River and the streams that ran parallel to it. Or it might have taken place in the areas used for seasonal crops in the high terraces. In fact, these two possible options are not mutually exclusive. In this region, a village territory was conceived as one in which its inhabitants had the right to make clearings, with the sole exception of some internal areas intended for permanent crops, grassland for draught animals, pastures, and forests for the production of wood.[44]

The *notitia*'s description of the boundaries, drawn according to a linear and circular method (*sicut vertit aqua* [...] *ex inde in suso usque*), allows us to reconstruct the territory of Lerda with confidence, and that of Añués with reasonable precision. The point, precisely, is that these two were the only territories whose boundaries consisted of a circle drawn around them; this was not the case for Fillera, which did not belong to Leire. The king and those who fol-

42 DML 3.

43 Larrea, *Navarre*, 66–68; Javier Andreu et al., "Una ciudad de los *vascones* en el yacimiento de Campo Real/Fillera (Sos del Rey Católico-Sangüesa)," *Archivo Español de Arqueología* 81 (2008), 75–100.

44 One can see this clearly in the document that recounts Leire's failed attempt to create a very modest village at the gates of the monastery in 1173: DML 332.

lowed him drew two circles north and southwest of Fillera. Therefore, for the most part, the lines that were drawn were not even remotely related to the violent dispute that is said to have given rise to the demarcation of boundaries.[45]

Before introducing the list of witnesses, it is noted that the purpose of the document was so that the men of Lerda and Añués would no longer have any conflicts with or bring suit against those from Fillera, or with those from other neighbouring villages. This contains an explicit justification for the circular delimitation that constituted a compromise between dispute resolution and the construction of a territory. What is distinctive here, as in Catamesas, is that this was not a monastic territory, but one whose day-to-day management and defence appears to have been in the hands of a peasant community. This opens up new potential interpretations, since providing the territory of a peasant community with boundaries that were closed and independent of the real use of space, which undoubtedly affirmed the authority of the bishop or the monastery of Leire in both this case and the former, could also benefit the community itself. Somehow, there was a transfer of legitimacy that should put us on guard against two interpretative pitfalls: that of naively imagining that everything can be reduced to an opposition between the way space was organized by the ruling groups versus the way it was organized by peasants; and that of seeing in some judicial inquiries regarding boundaries made among the inhabitants of a certain place equally naive forms of simply ascertaining customary uses of the land.[46]

5 A Brief Comparative Overview

Before moving to some final reflections, it is worth briefly recalling some examples from other regions that suggest the structural character of this play of oppositions between line and use. In general terms, it is clear that the construction of monastic territories in the Navarre-Aragonese Pyrenees was a regional manifestation—at the scale of the small polities in these borderlands of Christendom—of a phenomenon common to other areas of western Europe.[47] More specifically, there is an important historiographical tradition

45 For a rough outline of this demarcation, see Larrea, *Navarre*, 61.

46 See Lauwers and Ripart, "Espace," 129.

47 Yoshiki Morimoto, "Autour du grand domaine carolingien: aperçu critique des recherches récentes sur l'histoire rurale du haut Moyen Âge (1987–1992)," in idem, *Études sur l'économie rurale du haut Moyen Âge* (Bruxelles: De Boeck, 2008), 81–132, at 97–99.

of identifying the different kinds of logic that together determined how territories were constructed. Medieval studies have emphasized the overlapping of different kinds of rights, whether these are enunciated in typically legal terms (*dominium directum* vs. *dominium utilis*) or understood as a variety of situations that it is impossible to reduce to these categories.[48] A very valuable recent contribution to this question is the original interpretation proposed by Nicolas Schroeder for a much-studied topic, the colonization of the Odenwald.[49]

Others have pointed out that linear delimitation becomes a form of *vestitio* in the *perambulationes* of the territories of Fulda and Hammelburg.[50] In the former, the line is represented successively in two different ways. In the original donation dated to ca. 743, the territory of Fulda was described as an ideal space radiating from the newly founded centre (*ab illo loco undique in circuitu, ab oriente scilicet et ab occidente, a septentrione et meridie, marcha per quatuor millia passuum tendatur*).[51] This way of defining a territory is well-documented since the seventh century in Lindisfarne, Bobbio, and Stavelot-Malmedy.[52] Some years later, the description of the boundaries reflected the modification of the territory of Fulda to correspond to the actual terrain; these boundaries were now described as crossing particular streams, passing by certain trees and going over specific hills. Another famous example comes from Michelstadt, whose boundaries were defined as having a radius of two leagues when Einhard received it in 815; this definition became much more specific, and the boundary line itself much more extensive when the territory was ceded to Lorsch in 819.[53]

---

48 Chris Wickham, "European Forests in the Early Middle Ages: Landscape and Land Clearance," in idem, *Land & Power. Studies in Italian and European Social History, 400–1200* (London: British School at Rome, 1994), 155–199, at 167.

49 Nicolas Schroeder, "Der Odenwald im Früh- und Hochmittelalter. Siedlung, Landschaft und Grundherrschaft in einem Mittelgebirge," *Siedlungsforschung: Archäologie, Geschichte, Geographie* 33 (2016), 355–387.

50 See Karl Rübel, *Die Franken. Ihr Eroberungs- und Siedlungssystem im deutschen Volkslande* (Bielefeld: Delhagen und Klajing, 1904; repr. Aalen, 1968), 53–60, and above all, as regards the transmission of the texts, Edmund E. Stengel, "Die Urkundenfälschungen des Rudolf von Fulda (Fuldensia 1)," in idem, *Abhandlungen und Untersuchungen zur Hessischen Geschichte* (Marburg: Elwert: 1960), 40–63.

51 Edmund E. Stengel, ed., *Urkundenbuch des Klosters Fulda. 1. Die Zeit des Abtes Sturmi*, 3 vols (Marburg: Historische Kommission für Hessen und Waldeck, 1956), 1: no. 4, 5 and 83.

52 John Blair, *The Church in Anglo-Saxon Society* (Oxford: Oxford University Press, 2005), 222.

53 Thomas Ludwig, "Vor dem Bau der Basilika," in *Die Einhards-Basilika in Steinbach bei Michelstadt im Odenwald. Tafeln*, ed. Thomas Ludwig, Otto Müller, and Irmgard Widdra-Spiess (Mainz: Philipp von Zabern, 1996), 1–23, at 8–9.

Another case, which resembles the one that concerns us here more closely, comes from the demarcation of the territory immediately surrounding the monastery of Lorsch, since it entailed two successive and different ways of appropriating the same territory. Indeed, for one or two generations, several members of the aristocratic Rupertine family had cobbled together a patchwork of fields, buildings, pastures, and forests in a peripheral sector of the Bürstadt royal *villa*, called Lauresham, using the work of their slaves and appropriation mechanisms such as the *bifang*, which is the equivalent in several German-speaking regions to the southern *aprisio*. During that time, the use to which the lands were put was sufficient to define the boundaries of this compound space, except for the southern part, where a notch in a tree separated the Rupertine lands from the area occupied by another group. Such was the situation on the last day of May 770. As it had been decided that on 1 June this whole sector would be given to the successful monastery that Count Cancor and his mother had founded there six years earlier, on the very morning of the act of donation a continuous boundary was established which, completed by the river, enclosed a circular space: what was now a monastic territory no longer needed to be legitimated by its actual use.[54]

The simultaneity of the establishing of a monastery's territory and the drawing of linear borders is something we also find in the royal donation received in 772 by San Salvatore di Brescia, consisting of a part of the royal forest or *gagium* in Reggio with an estimated area of 4000 *iugera*. Abono, *waldeman* of *gagium*, then drew and put in writing a very detailed boundary line that went through fields, pastures, and clearings.[55]

Another relatively common situation had to do with the resolution of disputes by drawing linear boundaries. In 824, also in Italy, there was a famous legal suit between Flexo's inhabitants and the monastery of Nonantola, concerning access to the old royal forest.[56] The linear boundary statements collec-

---

54 Karl Glöckner, ed., *Codex Laureshamensis. 1. Einleitung, Regesten, Chronik* (Darmstadt: Historischer Verein für Hessen, 1929–1936), no. 10 and 167. Accessible online at https://archivum-laureshamense-digital.de/view/saw_mainz72 (accessed 13 July 2023). See Matthew Innes, "Kings, Monks and Patrons: Political Identity at the Abbey of Lorsch," in *La royauté et les élites dans l'Europe carolingienne*, ed. Régine Le Jan (Lille: Centre d'Histoire de l'Europe du Nord-Ouest, 1998), 301–324; Magdalene Fecher, *Die Namen der Gemarkung Lorsch* (Gießen: Hessische Vereinigung für Volkskunde, 1941).

55 Luciano Lagazzi, *Segni sulla terra: determinazione dei confini e percezione dello spazio nell'alto Medioevo* (Bologna: CLUEB, 1991), 16–22. For the online edition of the diploma, see *Codice diplomatico della Lombardia medievale* at http://www.lombardiabeniculturali.it/cdlm/edizioni/bs/brescia-sgiulia1/carte/sgiulia0772-06-14B (accessed 15 April 2020).

56 Cesare Manaresi, ed., *I Placiti del "Regnum Italiae,"* vol. 1 (*a. 776–945*) (Rome: Tipografia del

ted in previous charters and judicial records were repeatedly invoked by the *advocatus* of the monastery, not by the *consortes* who claimed longstanding fishing and pasture rights. Back in Germany, another well-known case concerns the *captura*, the Latin equivalent of *bifang*, that someone named Walto and his *socii* gave to the monastery of Fulda in 801. The property's linear demarcation does not seem to have been contemporaneous with the *captura* but rather was drawn in the context of a conflict settled around 827 between Fulda and a group of pioneers.[57] As usual, the description of the plot shows that the area had already been in use before the demarcation was made.

Finally, Saint Gall's *formula* for the distribution of access to the forest between the *pagenses*, on the one hand, and royal, episcopal, and monastic representatives, on the other, is also well known.[58] It should be noted that this distribution was made *propter diuturnissimas lites reprimendas et perpetuam pacem conservandam*. Since it is related to the widely studied topic of *Markgenossenschaft* (mark community), Saint Gall's *formula* has been discussed by many different scholars over the past century.[59] I only want to point out here a contrast in the procedure that was established to demarcate each part. There was a clear intention to draw a continuous line for the part belonging to the king and the Church (*a villa ad villam, a vico ad vicum, a monte ad montem, a colle ad collem, a flumine N. ad flumen N.—singula per se—sine ullius communion*), while the description of the boundaries assigned for the collective use of the *pagenses* is much more vague.

6 Conclusion

To the extent that power is inseparable from its spatial expression,[60] an exercise in abstraction that reduces the latter to its basic components can reveal

---

Senato, 1955), no. 36. On the dispute of Flexo, Igor Santos Salazar, *Una terra contesa. Spazi, poteri e società nell'Emilia orientale dei secoli VI–X* (Florence: Le Lettere, 2011), 171–174.

57 Matthew Innes, "Rituals, Rights and Relationships: Some Gifts and their Interpretation in the Fulda Cartulary, c. 827," *Studia Historica. Historia Medieval* 31 (2013), 25–50, at 39.

58 "Collectio Sangallensis Salomonis III. *tempore conscripta*," in Karl Zeumer, ed., *Formulae Merowingici et Karolini Aevi*, MGH LL 5 (Hannover: Hahn, 1886), 403–404 (no. 10).

59 Siegfried Epperlein, *Herrschaft und Volk im karolingischen Imperium*, (Berlin: Akademie-Verlag, 1969), 158–165. More recently, Wickham, "Forests," 188.

60 Anne Mailloux, "Le territoire dans les sources médiévales: perception, culture et expérience de l'espace social. Essai de synthèse," in *Les Territoires du médiéviste*, ed. Benoît Cursente and Mireille Mousnier (Rennes: Presses Universitaires de Rennes, 2005), 223–235, at 225.

tensions and developments concealed beneath apparently innocent procedures. This article suggests that linear forms of demarcation deserve to be studied in themselves, which has rarely been done.[61] Of course, this is already present in the work of medievalists in a more or less intuitive way, but rarely as a problem specifically formulated as such. In addition, studies along these lines have been disconnected from each other: Karl Rübel observed the difference between linear and non-linear demarcation, linking the former to stronger political powers, but provided only a reductive ethnic explanation.[62] Karl Brandi proposed in a brief essay that the diffusion of linear boundaries was a slow and non-universal process that extended from the early Middle Ages to the end of the Ancien Régime. One important take-away from Brandi's study is the idea that this was a top-down process, beginning on royal and noble lands and then extending to local communities; another is its connection with the territorialization of power.[63] More recently, Luciano Lagazzi has applied a semiotic analysis to the delimitation practices documented in the early Middle Ages in Italy, based on the anthropological concept of *liminarità*.[64]

This chapter has analysed some of the implications of linear demarcations. In the first place, judicial procedures and the texts they generated are essential for observing both the demarcation practices and the discourses associated with them. The reason seems obvious: judicial acts are privileged frameworks for the exercise of power and for constructing a political discourse. However, the fact that judicial procedure contributes to deploying a certain spatial logic does not mean that the two things should be confused.

Secondly, churches are presented as a legitimising factor for the control of the surrounding space. The capacity to tithe operated as a key mechanism of domination, although its forms of territorial extension have specific dynamics.

Third, the written document itself forms part of the demarcation practices, insofar as it channels the justifying discourse and ensures the memory of a space defined by a line.

---

61 I am not referring here to the problem of the borders of kingdoms or states, on which there is an abundant bibliography, nor to the specific ways of marking boundaries on the landscape and their legal treatment, which has long been studied by legal historians: Harald Siems, "Flurgrenzen und Grenzmarkierungen in den Stammesrechten," in *Untersuchungen zur eisenzeitlichen und frühmittelalterlichen Flur in Mitteleuropa und ihrer Nutzung*, ed. Heinrich Beck, Dietrich Denecke, and Herbert Jankhun (Göttingen: Vandenhoeck & Ruprecht, 1979), 268–309.

62 Rübel, *Franken*, 89–143.

63 Karl Brandi, "Grundfragen historischer Geographie und der Plan des historischen Atlas," in Karl Brandi, *Ausgewählte Aufsätze* (Oldenburg: Stalling, 1938), 469–490.

64 Lagazzi, *Segni*.

Fourthly, the final Iberian cases examined here warn against naive approaches. The fact that linear demarcation was linked to the territorial logic of the dominant groups does not imply that everything can be reduced to their imposition upon a different logic embraced by the peasantry and based on the actual use of the territory. I have shown how the legitimacy derived from the drawing of a line was transferred to certain peasant communities, with profound implications. If a community no longer needed to justify its control of its territory through use, this changed the way it related to neighbouring communities and also the conditions under which its members' access to their own internal spaces was organized.

Finally, I would like to suggest that for all this to work, there must have been some shared form of legitimacy between dominant groups and peasant communities.[65] Although often treated as marginal issues, appropriation practices—whether they were *presuras*, *aprisiones*, *runcales*, *bifangs*, or the establishing of monastic territories—were a fundamental aspect of the relationship of medieval society with space. In its very initial moment, any appropriation, whether by *potentes* or by peasants, is merely the expression of a will: it is only later that it is legitimized and makes the control of space visible, either through work or through power.

Bibliography

Abbreviations

CS: Ubieto, Antonio, ed. *Cartulario de Siresa*. Zaragoza: Anubar, 1986.

DML: Martín Duque, Ángel J., ed. *Documentación medieval de Leire (siglos IX a XII)*. Pamplona: Príncipe de Viana, 1983.

PRJ: PRocesos JUdiciales en las sociedades medievales del norte peninsular. Accessed 13 July 2023. http://prj.csic.es/index_en.php?c=1#.

SJP: Ubieto, Antonio, ed. *Cartulario de San Juan de la Peña*. Valencia: Anubar, 1962.

65 Juan José Larrea and Roland Viader, "Aprisions et presuras au début du IXe siècle: pour une étude des formes d'appropriation du territoire dans la Tarraconaise du haut Moyen Âge," in *De la Tarraconaise à la Marche supérieure d'Al-Andalus (IVe-XIe siècle). Les habitats ruraux*, ed. Philippe Sénac (Toulouse: Presses Universitaires du Midi, 2005), 167–210; Juan José Larrea, "Défricher la terre et se l'approprier. L'accès aux ressources de l'inculte dans le système agraire du haut Moyen Âge," *Vierteljahrschrift für Sozial- und Wirtschaftsgeschichte* 106/3 (2019), 288–328.

Other Primary Sources

Ansani, Michele, ed. *Codice diplomatico della Lombardia Medievale*. Accessed 15 April 2020. http://www.lombardiabeniculturali.it/cdlm/.

Gil, Juan, ed. *Corpus Scriptorum Muzarabicorum*. 2 vols. Madrid: CSIC, 1973.

Glöckner, Karl, ed. *Codex Laureshamensis. 1. Einleitung, Regesten, Chronik*. Darmstadt: Historischer Verein für Hessen, 1929–1936. Accessed 13 July 2023. https://archivum-laureshamense-digital.de/view/saw_mainz72.

Lema, José Ángel, ed. *Colección diplomática de Alfonso I de Aragón y Pamplona (1104–1134)*. San Sebastián: Sociedad de Estudios Vascos, 1990.

Manaresi, Cesare, ed. *I Placiti del "Regnum Italiae"*. Vol. 1 (*a. 776–945*). Rome: Tipografia del Senato, 1955.

Stengel, Edmund E., ed. *Urkundenbuch des Klosters Fulda. 1. Die Zeit des Abtes Sturmi*. Marburg: Historische Kommission für Hessen und Waldeck, 1956.

Zeumer, Karl, ed. *Formulae Merowingici et Karolini Aevi*. Monumenta Germaniae Historica, Legum Sectio v. Hanover: Hahn, 1886.

Secondary Works

Adachi, Takashi. "Documents of Dispute Settlement in Eleventh-Century Aragón and Navarra: King's Tribunal and Compromise." *Imago Temporis. Medium Aevum* 1 (2007), 71–85.

Andreu, Javier, Javier Armendáriz, Pablo Ozcáriz, María García-Barberena, and Ángel A. Jordán. "Una ciudad de los *vascones* en el yacimiento de Campo Real/Fillera (Sos del Rey Católico-Sangüesa)." *Archivo Español de Arqueología* 81 (2008), 75–100.

Bille, Elisabeth. "Remarques sur les modes de spatialisation des droits et des pratiques sur les vacants en Cerdagne aux XIIe-XIVe siècles." In *Les ressources naturelles des Pyrénées du Moyen Âge à l'époque moderne. Exploitation, gestion, appropriation*, edited by Aymat Catafau, 239–252. Perpignan: Presses Universitaires de Perpignan, 2005.

Blair, John. *The Church in Anglo-Saxon Society*. Oxford: Oxford University Press, 2005.

Brandi, Karl. "Grundfragen historischer Geographie und der Plan des historischen Atlas." In idem, *Ausgewählte Aufsätze*, 469–490. Oldenburg: Stalling, 1938.

Collins, Roger. "Visigothic Law and Regional Custom in Disputes in Early Medieval Spain." In *The Settlement of Disputes in Early Medieval Europe*, edited by Wendy Davies and Paul Fouracre, 85–104. Cambridge: Cambridge University Press, 1986.

Durán Gudiol, Antonio. *El monasterio de San Pedro de Siresa*. Zaragoza: Diputación de Aragón, 1989.

Epperlein, Siegfried. *Herrschaft und Volk im karolingischen Imperium* Berlin: Akademie-Verlag, 1969.

Escagüés Javierre, Isidro. "La Valdonsella." *Príncipe de Viana* 6 (1945), 218–344.

Fecher, Magdalene. *Die Namen der Gemarkung Lorsch*. Gießen: Hessische Vereinigung für Volkskunde, 1941.

Fortún, Luis Javier. *Leire, un señorío monástico en Navarra (siglos IX–XIX)*. Pamplona: Gobierno de Navarra, 1993.

Goñi Gaztambide, José. *Historia de los obispos de Pamplona. S. IV–XIII*. Pamplona: EUNSA, 1979.

Guerreau, Alain. "Quelques caractères spécifiques de l'espace féodal européen." In *L'État ou le Roi. Les fondements de la modernité monarchique en France (XIVe-XVIIe siècles)*, edited by Neithard Bulst, Robert Descimon, and Alain Guerreau, 85–101. Paris: Maison des Sciences de l'Homme, 1996.

Innes, Matthew. "Kings, Monks and Patrons: Political Identity at the Abbey of Lorsch." In *La royauté et les élites dans l'Europe carolingienne*, edited by Régine Le Jan, 301–324. Lille: Centre d'Histoire de l'Europe du Nord-Ouest, 1998.

Innes, Matthew. "Rituals, Rights and Relationships: Some Gifts and their Interpretation in the Fulda Cartulary, c. 827." *Studia Historica. Historia Medieval* 31 (2013), 25–50.

Lagazzi, Luciano. *Segni sulla terra: determinazione dei confini e percezione dello spazio nell'alto Medioevo*. Bologna: CLUEB, 1991.

Laliena, Carlos, and Philippe Sénac. *Musulmans et Chrétiens dans le haut Moyen Age: aux origines de la Reconquête aragonaise*. Paris: Minerve, 1991.

Lapeña, Ana Isabel. *El monasterio de San Juan de la Peña en la Edad Media*. Zaragoza: Caja de Ahorros de la Inmaculada, 1989.

Larrea, Juan José. "Moines et paysans: aux origines de la première croissance agraire dans le Haut Aragon (IXe-Xe s.)." *Cahiers de Civilisation Médiévale* 33 (1990), 219–239.

Larrea, Juan José. *La Navarre du IVe au XIIe siècle. Peuplement et société*. Paris-Brussels: De Boeck, 1998.

Larrea, Juan José. "Notas sobre los orígenes del poblamiento del valle de Salazar (Navarra)." In *Villages pyrénéens. Morphogenèse d'un habitat de montagne*, edited by Maurice Berthe and Benoît Cursente, 195–207. Toulouse: CNRS—Université de Toulouse-Le Mirail, 2000.

Larrea, Juan José. "La condición del campesinado navarro-aragonés entre los siglos IX y XII: una revisión crítica." *En la España Medieval* 29 (2006) 383–409.

Larrea, Juan José. "Construir un reino en la periferia de al-Andalus: Pamplona entre los siglos VIII y X." in *Symposium Internacional: Poder y simbología en la Europa altomedieval*, edited by Francisco J. Fernández Conde and César García de Castro Valdés, 279–308. Oviedo: Trea, 2009.

Larrea, Juan José. "Défricher la terre et se l'approprier. L'accès aux ressources de l'inculte dans le système agraire du haut Moyen Âge." *Vierteljahrschrift für Sozial- und Wirtschaftsgeschichte* 106/3 (2019), 288–328.

Larrea, Juan José, and Roland Viader. "Aprisions et presuras au début du IXe siècle: pour une étude des formes d'appropriation du territoire dans la Tarraconaise du haut Moyen Âge." In *De la Tarraconaise à la Marche supérieure d'Al-Andalus (IVe-XIe siècle). Les habitats ruraux*, edited by Philippe Sénac, 167–210. Toulouse: Presses Universitaires du Midi, 2005.

Larrea, Juan José, and Jesús Lorenzo. "Barbarians of Dâr al-Islâm: The Upper March of al-Andalus and the Western Pyrenees in the Eighth and Ninth Centuries." In *La Transgiordania nei secoli XII–XIII e le 'frontiere' del Mediterraneo medievale*, edited by Guido Vannini and Michele Nucciotti, 277–288. Oxford: *BAR International Series*, 2012.

Lauwers, Michel. "De l'incastellamento à l'inecclesiamento. Monachisme et logiques spatiales du féodalisme." In *Cluny, les moines et la société au premier âge féodal*, edited by Dominique Iogna-Prat, Michel Lauwers, Florian Mazel, and Isabel Rosé, 315–338. Rennes: Presses Universitaires de Rennes, 2013.

Lauwers, Michel, and Laurent Ripart. "Représentation et gestion de l'espace dans l'Occident médiéval." In *Rome et l'État moderne européen*, edited by Jean-Philippe Genêt, 115–171. Rome: École française de Rome, 2007.

Ludwig, Thomas. "Vor dem Bau der Basilika." In *Die Einhards-Basilika in Steinbach bei Michelstadt im Odenwald. Tafeln*, edited by Thomas Ludwig, Otto Müller, and Irmgard Widdra-Spiess, 1–23. Mainz: Philipp von Zabern, 1996.

Mailloux, Anne. "Le territoire dans les sources médiévales: perception, culture et expérience de l'espace social. Essai de synthèse." In *Les Territoires du médiéviste*, edited by Benoît Cursente and Mireille Mousnier, 223–235. Rennes: Presses Universitaires de Rennes, 2005.

Martin, Céline, and Juan José Larrea, eds., *Nouvelles chartes visigothiques du monastère pyrénéen d'Asán*. Bordeaux: Ausonius Éditions, 2021.

Méhu, Didier. *Paix et communautés autour de l'abbaye de Cluny (Xe-XVe siècle)*. Lyon: Presses Universitaires de Lyon, 2010.

Mensúa, Salvador. *La Navarra Media oriental*. Zaragoza: Diputación Foral de Navarra—CSIC, 1960.

Morimoto, Yoshiki. "Autour du grand domaine carolingien: aperçu critique des recherches récentes sur l'histoire rurale du haut Moyen Âge (1987–1992)." In idem, *Études sur l'économie rurale du haut Moyen Âge*, 81–132. Brussels: De Boeck, 2008.

Passini, Jean. "L'habitat fortifié dans la Canal de Berdún, Aragon. Xe-XIIIe siècles." In *Castrum 3: Guerre, fortification et habitat dans le monde méditerranéen au Moyen Age*, 91–98. Rome-Madrid: École française de Rome—Casa de Velázquez, 1985.

Rübel, Karl. *Die Franken. Ihr Eroberungs- und Siedlungssystem im deutschen Volkslande*. Bielefeld: Delhagen und Klajing, 1904; repr. Aalen, 1968.

Santos Salazar, Igor. *Una terra contesa. Spazi, poteri e società nell'Emilia orientale dei secoli VI–X*. Florence: Le Lettere, 2011.

Schroeder, Nicolas. "Der Odenwald im Früh- und Hochmittelalter. Siedlung, Landschaft und Grundherrschaft in einem Mittelgebirge." *Siedlungsforschung: Archäologie, Geschichte, Geographie* 33 (2016), 355–387.

Siems, Harald. "Flurgrenzen und Grenzmarkierungen in den Stammesrechten." In *Untersuchungen zur eisenzeitlichen und frühmittelalterlichen Flur in Mitteleuropa und ihrer Nutzung*, edited by Heinrich Beck, Dietrich Denecke, and Herbert Jankhun, 268–309. Göttingen: Vandenhoeck & Ruprecht, 1979.

Stengel, Edmund E. "Die Urkundenfälschungen des Rudolf von Fulda (Fuldensia I)." In idem, *Abhandlungen und Untersuchungen zur Hessischen Geschichte*, 27–146. Marburg: Elwert, 1960.

Toubert, Pierre. "Frontière et frontières : un objet historique." In *Castrum 4: Frontière et peuplement dans le monde méditerranéen au Moyen Âge*, 9–17. Rome-Madrid: École française de Rome—Casa de Velázquez, 1992.

Viader, Roland. "La dîme dans l'Europe des féodalités. Rapport introductif." In *La dîme dans l'Europe médiévale et moderne. Actes des Journées Internationales d'Histoire de l'abbaye de Flaran*, edited by Roland Viader, 7–36. Toulouse: Presses Universitaires du Midi, 2010.

Viader, Roland, and Christine Rendu, eds. *Cultures temporaires et féodalité. Les rotations culturales et l'appropriation du sol dans l'Europe médiévale et moderne. Actes des Journées Internationales d'Histoire de l'abbaye de Flaran*. Toulouse: Presses Universitaires du Midi, 2014.

Wickham, Chris. "European Forests in the Early Middle Ages: Landscape and Land Clearance." In idem, *Land & Power: Studies in Italian and European Social History, 400–1200*, 155–199. London: British School at Rome, 1994.

Wickham, Chris. "Espacio y sociedad en los conflictos campesinos en la Alta Edad Media." In *El lugar del campesino. En torno a la obra de Reyna Pastor*, edited by Ana Rodríguez, 33–60. Valencia: Universitat de València—CSIC, 2007.

CHAPTER 13

One Monk, One Donkey, One Dead Man: Contexts for a Homicide in a Tenth-Century Sahagún Charter

Julio Escalona

The Archivo Histórico Nacional (Madrid) preserves, among the charters from the monastery of Sahagún, one dated on 11 May 971 by which King Ramiro III of León granted the abbey a village called Grañeras (modern prov. León).[1] This grant (hereafter S1 261) was kept in the monastic archive and copied—not without radical distortions—to the cartulary, composed ca. 1110. The parchment leaf is additionally relevant because it contains a marginal note about a judicial affair that has been largely ignored.[2] This paper is an attempt at exploring and interpreting it.

Formally, S1 261 resembles other contemporary Leonese royal diplomas, but its coarser realization has raised some eyebrows (see Fig. 13.1).[3] The layout is

---

1 This paper was produced with support from the project HAR2016–76094-C4–3-R, funded by the Programa Estatal de Investigación, Desarrollo e Innovación orientada a los Retos de la Sociedad. Preliminary versions were presented in a Seminar at the CCHS-CSIC in 2014 and in the 2015 Santiago de Compostela conference on Judicial Processes in Early Medieval Societies. I am extremely grateful to all those who participated in these events—especially to Juanjo Larrea—for their comments and suggestions. Álvaro Carvajal and Isabel Alfonso read and commented upon drafts of the text, and I am grateful for all the feedback received. I am especially indebted to José Antonio Fernández Flórez and Marta Herrero de la Fuente for their invaluable help with the palaeography of S1 261 and to Luis Miguel de la Cruz for his crucial help at the Archivo Histórico Nacional. Huge thanks are also due to the editors of this volume for their endless patience and encouragement. While all of them contributed a great deal to improving the final text, I am solely responsible for the views here expressed and none of the text's possible shortcomings should be attributed to anyone but the author. The abbreviations used in this paper for editions of charters are listed in the bibliography.

2 S1 261; Madrid, Archivo Histórico Nacional, CLERO-SECULAR_REGULAR, Car. 876, núm. 8. The cartulary version (Becerro Gótico de Sahagún (= BGS); Archivo Histórico Nacional, CODICES, L.989, fol. 10r) omits this marginal note.

3 On these grounds, J. Antonio Fernández Flórez dismissed the charter as a clear forgery executed by an ungifted person, certainly not from among the usual scribes of the Leonese royal charters (José Antonio Fernández Flórez, "El fondo documental del monasterio de Sahagún y sus *scriptores* (siglos IX–X)," in *El monacato en los reinos de León y Castilla (Siglos VII–XIII), X Congreso de Estudios Medievales, León, 26 a 29 de septiembre de 2005*, ed. José Ignacio Ruiz de la Peña Solar (Ávila: Fundación Claudio Sánchez Albornoz, 2007), 125–146, at 140).

 | DOI:10.1163/9789004683006_015

horizontal, with the text in Visigothic cursive script—except for the first line, in Visigothic *elongata*—covering the two upper thirds, and leaving the bottom third to the signatures, which are loosely organized in columns with interspersed blank gaps. Precisely one of these gaps, at the bottom left corner, was used by a different hand to enter, in a more compressed calligraphy, a ten-line note. It is an 83 word-long undated account whose relation to the contents of the royal diploma it invades is not readily apparent.

This brief text has received little attention, maybe in part because its editor, J.M. Mínguez, did not publish it separately, but as a mere footnote to S1 261 that goes easily overlooked.[4] His reading, however, needs correcting at two crucial points.

Minguez's edition	**Suggested alternative reading**
(*Cross*) In presencia frater Verimudo et Iaquinte et Mutarafe iudices et saione Meme. Manifestu sum eo Haione qui peticione Godleo qui tinuit voce de frater Verimudo quia peccatu inpidendu et diabulu inmitendu sic invenit omine de Montesone in ic loqu in Fontes ubi bebebat aqua; et ocisut ipsu ommine qum suo gladio et presumsit ipsu omine uno asinu in Kasigatu de Pice et invenerunt saione con ipsu furtum in suo domu. Eo Haione in hanc manifestu de mea manu signum rovoravi (*signum*). Placenti presbiter noduit (*signum*).	(*Cross*) In presencia frater Verimudo et Iaquinte et Mutarafe iudices et saione Meme. Manifestu sum eo Haione qui peticione Godleo qui tinuit voce de frater Verimudo quia peccatu inpidendu et diabulu inmitendu sic invenit omine de Montesone in ic loqu in Fontes ubi bebiebat aqua; et ocisut ipsu ommine qum suo gladio et presumsit ipsu omine uno asinu **inkarigatu de pice** et invenerunt Haione con ipsu furtum in suo domu. Eo Haione in hanc manifestu de mea manu signum rovoravi (*signum*). Placenti presbiter noduit (*signum*).

His opinion is accepted by Leticia Agúndez San Miguel, *La memoria escrita en el monasterio de Sahagún (años 904–1300)* (Madrid: Consejo Superior de Investigaciones Científicas, 2019), 118 and 124. Wendy Davies considers the charter valid: *Windows on Justice in Northern Iberia, 800–1000* (Abingdon: Routledge, 2016), 47, 85–86.

4 S1, p. 313, n. 1.

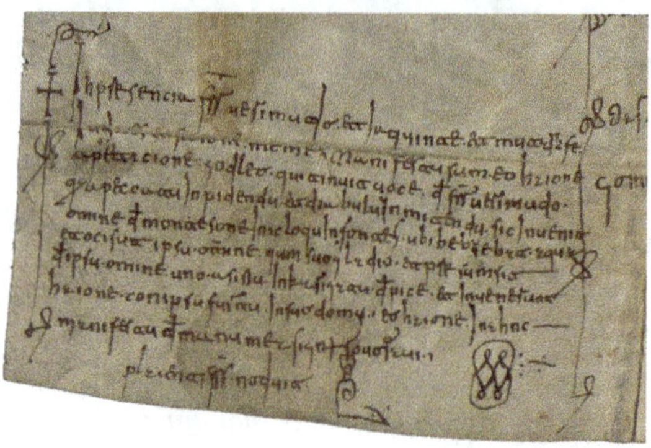

FIGURE 13.1 Sahagún 261. General view of the parchment and detail of the added notice about the dispute
MADRID, ARCHIVO HISTÓRICO NACIONAL, CLERO-SECULAR_REGULAR, CAR. 876, NÚM. 8R. PRINTED WITH PERMISSION

First, the reading *kasigatu de pice* was amended shortly after Mínguez's edition by linguist José Luis Pensado in a largely unnoticed article, where he claimed that this awkward place name (a one-off in the rich Leonese charter collections) actually resulted from misreading an *s* for an *r*, a common error with Visigothic script. The right reading was, thus, *inkarigatu de pice*, that is, 'loaded with fish'.[5] Second, in the sentence *inuenerunt saione con ipsu furtum*, the first letter of the second word is clearly an *H*, not an *s*, and therefore it is Haio, the defendant, and not a *saio*, that is intended.

So, the edited version depicted a man called Haio who, moved by the Devil, found at the place called Fontes a man from Monzón who was drinking water, and killed him with his sword. He then took the dead man's donkey to his home in Kasigatu de Pice, where it was found by the *saio*. The alternative reading, however, is significantly different:

> (*Cross*) In the presence of *frater* Vermudo and the judges Iaquinte and Mutarafe and the *saio* Meme, I, Haio, confess, at the request of Godleo, who speaks for *frater* Vermudo, that, seeking to sin and not fearing the Devil, he found a man from Monzón in the place called Fontes drinking water and killed him with his sword and he seized from that man a donkey that was loaded with fish and said Haio was discovered with that booty at his home. I, Haio, with my own hand signed this confession (*sign*). Placenti, priest, wrote this down (*sign*).

Once 'kasigatu de pice' is ruled out as a place name, the whole story becomes confined to one single location, Fontes. There Haio found and killed a man from Monzón, seized from him a donkey 'loaded with fish' and took it home, where he was found with his booty. The marginal text in S1 261 becomes thus clearer, but a number of obscure points remain. There are at least four important questions that I will try to address one by one: Which is the geographical context of the events described? Who were the actors? What was the dispute about? Why was the story written on a royal diploma?

1 Which Is the Geographical Context of the Events Described?

The setting of the story was a place called Fuentes, some 15 km west from Sahagún. Fuentes was one of a number of small territories in that area where Saha-

5 José Luis Pensado, "Anotaciones marginales latinas, leonesas y gallegas a la *Colección Diplomática del Monasterio de Sahagún* (*siglos* IX *y* X)," *Senara* 3 (1982), 11–54.

gún had interests from the very early tenth century. It is nowadays deserted, only surviving as the name of a small spring east from the modern locality of Las Grañeras. This is in itself relevant, since Las Grañeras is the subject of the 971 donation recorded in the charter on which our judicial account was written.

The extant texts from the tenth and eleventh centuries suggest a highly fragmented settlement pattern in this sector (see Map 13.1).[6] There were several small territories, often called *vallis* (valley), organized along the course of a minor waterway, each of which may have contained one or more settlements called *villae*, although it is not uncommon for the larger 'valley' units to be also called *villa* occasionally.[7] Valdefresno is probably the best documented of them. This was the name of a territory which, albeit comprising several settlements, constituted a community, as suggested by a charter of 943 that was witnessed by people from several localities including some under the heading *De Villa de Fraxeno*.[8] Sahagún acquired land in Valdefresno since the early tenth century,[9] but a series of purchases dated 965 throw the most light on the local geography. In that year, the monastery bought one by one the portions that a number of co-heirs had in a settlement called Villa de Doña Madre that lay within Valdefresno.[10] Judging from the boundaries expressed in the charters, said portions must each have consisted in a number of land plots scattered across a local ter-

6 Despite the many documentary references, the locations of the individual settlements in this area are often elusive. They can be sometimes pinned down with the help of later medieval texts, especially the so-called *Becerro de Presentaciones de la Catedral de León*: José Antonio Fernández Flórez, "El Becerro de Presentaciones. Códice 13 del ACL. Un parroquial leonés de los siglos XIII–XV," in *León y su historia. Miscelánea histórica, V* (León: Centro de Estudios e Investigación 'San Isidoro', 1984), 265–565. Place-name research can also contribute; see Fátima Carrera de la Red, *El valle del Cea a través de la toponimia documental* (Madrid: Liceus, 2010). But many settlements can only be narrowed down to a more or less undefined area, by reference to neighbouring sites. Juan José Sánchez Badiola, *La configuración de un sistema de poblamiento y organización: el territorio de León (siglos IX–XI)* (León: Universidad de León, 2002), 73, 86 and 89, provides valuable clues for locating some of the places.

7 On this issue, see José María Mínguez Fernández, *El dominio del monasterio de Sahagún en el siglo X. Paisajes agrarios, producción y expansión económica* (Salamanca: Universidad de Salamanca, 1980), 85–98; Wendy Davies, *Acts of Giving. Individual, Community and Church in Tenth-Century Christian Spain* (Oxford: Oxford University Press, 2007), 193–199; and especially Álvaro Carvajal Castro, "The Use of the Term *Uilla* in Early Medieval León: A Review of the Economic Base of the Astur-Leonese Monarchy (Ninth–Eleventh Centuries)," in *Polity and Neighbourhood in Early Medieval Europe*, ed. Julio Escalona, Orri Vésteinsson, and Stuart Brookes (Turnhout: Brepols, 2019), 325–350.

8 S1 87.

9 S1 17 (916–919), 50 (932).

10 S1 224–234, 235, 238–241, all dated 965.

ritory that seems to be one and the same in all those documents. Three of these boundaries take consistently as references three neighbouring settlements: on the east the boundaries of Grañera; on the south, those of Villa Nañín; on the west, those of Porvillos. By contrast, the northern side looks undefined: the references are mainly to the boundaries of Villa Asneros, but sometimes landscape features are mentioned, such as the road from Fuentes to Sandoval, the church of San Juan, or the road from León to Villa Mayor, etc. In the mid-tenth century, Villa Asneros lay on the easternmost reaches of the territory controlled from the royal stronghold of Sollanzo.[11] Valdefresno lay right across that major territorial division, a kind of spatial buffer that could explain the hesitations in defining that boundary. Sahagún's pressure to acquire Villa de Doña Madre was not uncontested. In 1005, the heirs of some of the local landowners tried to push the monks out, but where challenged and defeated in court.[12] Thereafter Sahagún seems to have held Villa de Doña Madre firmly under its control, but a conflict of even greater magnitude broke out in 1092, when the place name is last attested.[13]

East from Villa de Doña Madre was Grañeras. This locality, seemingly a polyfocal unit like Valdefresno, was evidenced as a community in the aforementioned 943 charter, featuring eight witnesses under the rubric *De Villa Graniera*.[14] If Sahagún carried out a similar policy of accumulating property in Grañeras, this has gone unrecorded.[15] Instead, the *village* was allegedly transferred to the monastery by King Ramiro III in 971 in S1 261, the charter to which our judicial account was appended. The royal grant included a whole valley comprising more than one settlement: *villas que uocidant Grannarias ad integrum cum suo valle* [...] *ad integrum vobis concedimus ad aula Sancti Iuliani in Fontes per cuntis terminis suis*. The latter mention is somewhat unclear, but it seems to imply that the hamlets that constituted the village of Grañeras were

11 CL2 453 (978).

12 The information comes from a text that, to the best of my knowledge, remains unpublished. It is a short judicial account, not unlike the one added to S1 261, that uses the bottom right corner of a parchment leaf (Madrid, Archivo Histórico Nacional, CLERO-SECULAR_REGULAR, Car. 875, núm. 10) that contains two purchases of land in Villa de Doña Madre, both in 965: S1 226 and 227.

13 S3 900 (1092). By then Villa de Doña Madre concentrated most of Sahagún's property in Valdefresno, while the rest of the valley was controlled by the local elites (*infanzones*).

14 S1 87.

15 A possible exception is S1 123 (ca. 950), the grant of an estate named Villa Mayor, although the heading of the entry in the Sahagún cartulary reads *Testamentum de Albaro Velaz de hereditate sua de Granneras*.

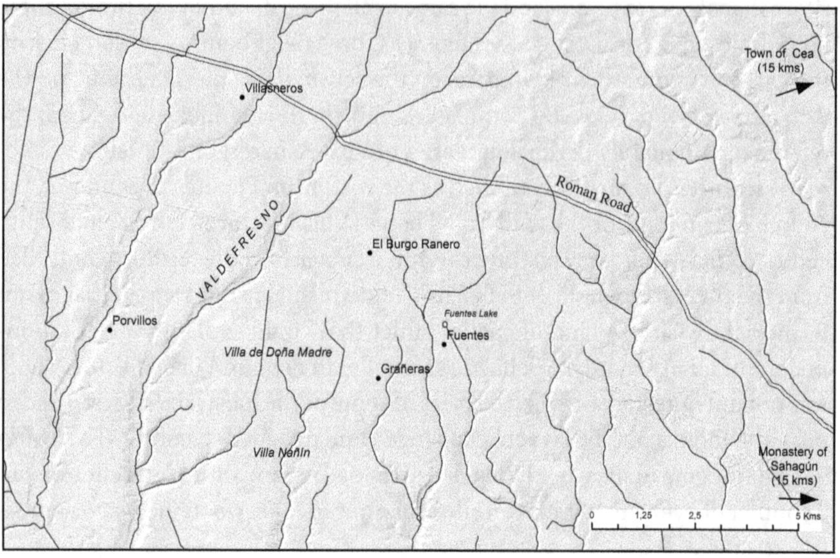

MAP 13.1 Location of the main places cited in the text. Names in italics represent settlements that can only be placed approximately.
MAP DRAWN BY THE AUTHOR

to be subjected to Sahagún's monastery of San Julián de Fuentes. As for the latter, about 1.5 km northeast from modern Las Grañeras there is a place that still today bears the name 'Fuentes', associated to a stream called 'Valle de Fuentes', and a small lagoon called 'Laguna Fuentes'. In the Valley of Fuentes Sahagún bought in 932 a piece of land that was bounded by monastic property on all sides, suggesting that the abbey had been acquiring property there in the same piecemeal fashion as in Villa de Doña Madre, although in this case the records are much more incomplete.[16] The key piece there was the monastery of San Julián de Fuentes, which features from our earliest records as a house and oratory, probably working as the management centre for Sahagún's interests in the area.[17]

Summing up, by 971 Sahagún had developed a strong position in this sector that was based in controlling three elements: (a) the minor monastery of San Julián de Fuentes, as a managerial centre; (b) the small territory of Gra-

16 S1 43 (932).

17 The monastery of Fuentes is first mentioned in 942 in relation to a pasture enclosure located *infra vestros terminos de monasterio de Fontes*, S1 82. In 961 Sahagún bought two fields *infra vestro termino iuxta vestra casa de Fontes et Sancti Iuliani oraculo*, S1 186.

ñeras, which comprised several settlements—at least modern Las Grañeras and whichever settlement derived into what was later called El Burgo Ranero—, arguably with continuous jurisdictional rights in the area;[18] (c) the settlement of Villa de Doña Madre, apparently bought off piecemeal from the locals, although there is no sound indication of jurisdictional control, and the place seems to have remained a part of Valdefresno, as revealed in 1092 by a dispute to which I will refer in detail below. San Julián probably also managed a constellation of small, scattered items of property that Sahagún had in this sector.

The sequence cannot be complete without considering one further document. In 977 Sahagún made an agreement with a number of "men from the *villae* of Fuentes", speaking for themselves and/or acting as sureties for others.[19] They nevertheless operated as a small community, as evidenced by the expression *totos sub uno a maximo usque a minimo roboramus*, which is characteristic of situations of collective action.[20] All of them, once summoned to the monastery, committed to pay Sahagún 100 *solidi* should they accept some other lord (*alia potestate*) in the *villae* that served Fuentes against the interests of Sahagún (*pro adversario de fratres de Sancto Facundo*). This agreement might have a context in the turbulent years of the revolt of Gómez Díaz, count of Cea, against king Ramiro III.[21] It clearly envisages a scenario in which the locals could seek

18 The hypothesis that El Burgo Ranero and Las Grañeras were once two settlements of a single territory is supported not only by the place name (Grannarias> Ranero) and the topography, but also by the fact that they both feature together, albeit with two different churches, in a thirteenth-century jurisdictional dispute between the abbey of Sahagún and the bishop of León: CL6 1849 (1215).

19 S1 29 (977). [...] *Nos homines de villas de Fontes nominati subterius facimus placitum super nos vobis domno Felix abba vel voci Sancti Facundi et damus fideiussores Mirelle et Godeleo qui sunt fidiatores de Veila, Meneize qui est fidiatore de Negrello, Saturnino qui est fidiatore de suo filio Daniel, Iohannes qui es fidiatore de dom Patre monaco, Vela qui est fidiatore de Sarrazino et de Ferro, dom Patre qui est fidiatore de suo germano Iohanne.*

20 Álvaro Carvajal Castro et al., "Collective Action in Local Contexts in the Kingdom of León (9th–11th Centuries): An Exploration of the Charter Evidence," in *Archaeology and History of Peasantries 1: From the Late Prehistory to the Middle Ages*, ed. Juan Antonio Quirós Castillo (Bilbao: Universidad del País Vasco, 2020), 149–161, and Álvaro Carvajal Castro, "Collective Action and Local Leaderships in Early Medieval North-Western Iberia. Ninth-Eleventh Centuries," in *Social Inequality in Early Medieval Europe. Local Societies and Beyond*, ed. Juan Antonio Quirós Castillo (Turnhout: Brepols, 2020), 281–299.

21 A point for which I thank Álvaro Carvajal. See Álvaro Carvajal Castro, *Bajo la máscara del Regnum: la monarquía asturleonesa en León (854–1037)* (Madrid: Consejo Superior de Investigaciones Científicas, 2017), 193–199.

patronage from a lord, as is characteristic of the loose forms of lordship that connected Castilian and Leonese communities to aristocrats who exercised territorial control.[22] Powerful monasteries like Sahagún developed their tighter lordly control of peasants by cutting their way across such basic territorial networks, not without tensions.[23] The 977 agreement seems to reflect such tensions. Moreover, the fact that one of the actors in the agreement is Godleo, who appears in that account as a representative in court for monk Vermudo, helps to pin down the whole sequence: in 971, the royal grant of Grañeras, in 977, the agreement and, slightly before or after the latter, the homicide and trial. In fact, Haio's homicide could very well have triggered the conflict settled by the 977 agreement.

2 Who Were the Actors?

Let us now turn to the actors in the S1 261 judicial account, starting with the judicial assembly that heard the case. As said before, formally the notice is a confession or *agnitio* made by Haio.[24] The usual formula *In presentia de …* introduces the description of an apparently formal court, composed by three officers (two judges and a *saio*), but it also mentions a monk called Vermudo whose role is more ambiguous. This cleric can be easily identified as an agent of the monastery of Sahagún. He is recorded in 949 arranging purchases in the Cofiñal area together with other people related to the monastery, such as the

22 See Julio Escalona, "Supra-Local Territorial Units: On the Origins of *Behetría* Lordship," in *Land, Power and Society in Medieval Castile*, ed. Cristina Jular Pérez-Alfaro and Carlos Estepa Díez (Turnhout: Brepols, 2009), 29–58, and more generally on the Castilian *behetrías*, Carlos Estepa Díez, *Las behetrías castellanas*, 2 vols (Valladolid: Junta de Castilla y León, 2003).

23 See Isabel Alfonso's seminal study "Conflict in the *Behetrías*," in *Land, Power, and Society in Medieval Castile*, ed. Cristina Jular Pérez-Alfaro and Carlos Estepa Díez (Turnhout: Brepols, 2009), 275–316, and, more generally, her "Los nombres de la violencia y el control de su legitimación," *Hispania* 61, no. 208 (2001), 691–706, English translation: Isabel Alfonso "Naming Violence and Controlling its Legitimation," in *Conflict, Language and Social Practice in the Middle Ages. Selected Essays of Isabel Alfonso* (Turnhout: Brepols, forthcoming).

24 On the formal aspects of this kind of text, see the alternative views of Isabel Alfonso, "El formato de la información judicial en la Alta Edad Media peninsular," in *Chartes et cartulaires comme instruments de pouvoir. Espagne et Occident chrétien (VIIIe–XIIe siècles)*, ed. Julio Escalona and Helène Sirantoine (Toulouse: Université de Toulouse le Mirail, 2013), 191–218, and Davies, *Windows on Justice*, 124–130.

monk Maurelo,[25] and he is last seen in 989 representing the abbot of Sahagún in a transaction.[26] S1 261's judicial account, however, is the only instance in which he carries out a judicial role. Which role was that is something I will get back to below.

Thanks to the abundance of mid-tenth-century charters relating to the Fuentes area, Judge Mutarraf is also identified with reasonable certainty as the same individual who participated between 965 and 967 in four of Sahagún's acquisitions in Valdefresno.[27] Conceivably too, the place called 'Villa Motarraf' that is recorded in the vicinity of Fuentes and Valdefresno could derive from this character.[28] The second judge, Iaquinte, is also recorded in several Sahagún charters between 942 and 961. However, the presence of two individuals with the same name in a single text is a warning that this identification may be hampered by homonymy issues.[29] Both judges seem to be members of a non-aristocratic elite of well-to-do local landowners that operated in a small-scale circuit limited to a few neighbouring settlements in the Valdefresno-Grañeras sector. Raúl González González has recently shown that some individuals of a comparable social standing that participated in small-scale transactions in the centre of the Duero basin (Tierra de Campos) were not really members of the local peasant communities, as is often assumed, but of the León urban elites. Some of them are also recorded as judges, and they seem to form a specific learned sub-group within the León elites. Ancestors of those urban elites are known to have expanded the radius of their patrimonies through their cooperation with King Alfonso III in the late ninth-century takeover of the Tierra de Campos.[30] This is a very compelling argument that sheds new light

25 S1 115, 116, 118.

26 S1 315: *Vobis Pascualis abba vel fratri Vermudo et omni collegio Sanctorum Facundi et Primitivi* […].

27 He is witness in S1 224, 230, 247. In S1 236 (965) he sells to the monastery land in Valdefresno jointly with three other co-proprietors.

28 On which see Álvaro Carvajal Castro, "The Use of the Term *Uilla*". The identification is reinforced by Mutarraf's witnessing to a 967 sale that mentions Villa Motarraf as one of its boundaries (S1 247).

29 S1 82 (942), 87 (943, with two Iaquentis), S2 367 (956), S1 227 (965), 186 (961). In the latter, Iaquenti sold Sahagún two land plots adjacent to San Julián de Fuentes, and he got back a lamb skin, one tunic (*saiale*) and a pair of wooden shoes, which strongly suggests non-aristocratic status. S2 367 is an excerpt from a now lost charter in which Iaquinte, his wife Gaudiosa and his children gave to Sahagún their hereditary land in Fuentes.

30 Raúl González González, *Bastiones de tradición. Ciudades y aristocracias urbanas en la Alta Edad Media asturleonesa (siglos IX–XI)* (León: Librería Universitaria de León, 2017), pp. 63–67.

on the composition of the regional landowning elites, but it does not seem to apply to our case.[31] Neither Mutarraf nor Iaquinte appear among the groups of *iudices* of the city of León exhaustively analysed by Raúl González. While they both lack demonstrable links to the city, they seem to be firmly rooted in the Valdefresno-Fuentes area. There is nothing to suggest either that Mutarraf and Iaquinte were professional specialists of the kind that Wendy Davies has defined, and that are more easily detected in the León urban context.[32] Their recorded actions are more in tune with relatively educated individuals of local relevance who may serve as judges of local affairs eventually, without implying a continuous judicial function. The fourth identifiable character is Godleo, spokesman for monk Vermudo in the hearing. There is no mention of Godleo in the abundant preserved transactions from the period before 971. However, he appears as one of the *vicini* of Fuentes that made the 977 agreement with Sahagún. Moreover, he acts, together with someone called Mirelle, as surety for Veila. This seems to qualify him as another member of the non-aristocratic local elites of the Fuentes area.[33] By contrast, there is no documentary trace of the *saio* Meme or the defendant Haio. Neither appear in any of the many documents from this area and period, which invites to consider them as peasants, ordinary members of the local communities. The judicial assembly before which Haio confessed was, therefore, composed by two judges and one executive officer (*saio*) who were all locals, albeit of different social standing, and most likely exercised their functions occasionally, rather than permanently.[34]

The role of *frater* Vermudo in the hearing is the hardest to interpret. The monk was surely a Sahagún agent, but the abbey is not mentioned in the text. Neither is there any explicit indication of a president of the court or any higher authority, nor of the place of the hearing, but the actors' profiles suggest a local assembly, dealing with a local affair. The exception is Vermudo. The opening formula *In presentia frater Verimudo et Iaquinte et Mutarafe iudices et saione Meme* seems to ascribe him a leading role, which can only mean that Sahagún was behind the whole operation. Moreover, the remark that Haio's confession

31 Ibid., table 3, p. 331. However, much earlier than the events studied here, in the early tenth century, two judges from León may have had proprietary links to Valdefresno (ibid., pp. 73–74).

32 Wendy Davies, "Judges and Judging: Truth and Justice in Northern Iberia on the Eve of the Millennium," *Journal of Medieval History* 36, no. 3 (2010), 193–203.

33 S1 289 (977). See Wendy Davies, "On Suretyship in Tenth-Century Northern Iberia," in *Scale and Scale Change in the Early Middle Ages: Exploring Landscape, Local Society and the World Beyond*, ed. Julio Escalona and Andrew Reynolds (Turnhout: Brepols, 2011).

34 Davies, *Windows on Justice*, 168.

was "requested by Godleo who spoke for *frater* Vermudo" means that, while Vermudo presided, Godleo represented him as plaintiff. It seems that it was the monk (hence Sahagún) that took Haio's case to court where he doubled as judger and plaintiff.

3 What Was the Dispute about?

Few details are to be expected from a story that is less than one hundred words long. Nevertheless, the judicial account in S1 261 is as remarkable for what it tells as for what it does not. At least four elements are sorely lacking. Firstly, there is a deafening silence about the victim, vaguely called 'a man from Monzón' (Monzón de Campos, c. 45 kms south-east from Sahagún). Was that provenance established after some sort of inquiry into the deceased's identity? The narrative, careful as it is in identifying by name all actors, is content with just noting that he was from a foreign territory. Neither is there any mention of the victim's relatives and/or friends, nor any suggestion that the case was initiated by an accusation from them. Whoever pressed charges was more interested in the facts than in the victim.

Secondly, the scribe seems to have been eager to silence whichever reasons Haio could have had for his actions. The voices in the text provide a clue to this. The account starts in the first person, as one would expect in an *agnitio*, with Haio admitting his guilt, but then it swiftly turns into an anonymous third-person speech that tells a story of robbery and homicide.[35] Right between both sections, just five words (*peccatu inpidendu et diabulu inmitendu*) portray Haio's actions as diabolic influence. This is the well-known strategy of blaming certain actions on the influence of the Devil, drunkenness, madness, or the like, that strips the other's actions of all rationality and renders them unjustifiable. Haio committed robbery and homicide, and there is no space for alternative views or indeed for the defendant's arguments.

And still, the story does contain traces of Haio's motive. The first clue is that the unnamed victim is marked out as a foreigner. The second is that Haio attacked him when he was "drinking water". This expression, which is frequent in later Castilian-Leonese *fueros* (local codes) and ordinances, designates the

35 See the interesting remarks on changes of voice in dispute-related stories in Gadi Algazi, "Feigned Reciprocities Lords, Peasants, and the Afterlife of Late Medieval Social Strategies," in *Negotiating the Gift: Pre-Modern Figurations of Exchange*, ed. Gadi Algazi, Valentin Groebner, and Bernhard Jussen (Göttingen: Vandenhoeck & Ruprecht, 2003), 99–127, at 112–115.

right to water livestock in waters subject to jurisdictional restrictions, including the villagers' common uses. So, it seems plausible that what the foreigner was doing, rather than drinking water himself, was watering his beast, a donkey that was "loaded with fish". And this is the third clue. The small spring called Arroyo de Fuentes is unlikely to have ever been a fishing spot, but the small lagoon nearby quite probably was.[36] All three facts draw a plausible alternative picture: Haio caught a foreigner fishing in waters subject to shared exploitation by the local community and he conceivably tried to seize the animal with its load, which was a standard response when jurisdictional rights were infringed. If the foreigner put up a fight, this would be the right context for an unintended killing. The sequence of events alone hints at Haio's potential arguments to justify his doings, and the scribe's silences begin to talk aloud. Much as the account tries to conceal it, Haio could actually have had a point, after all. Not everything was about the Devil pushing him to commit robbery and homicide. He might have just done what community members did when someone tried to steal their communal resources: pledge their assets. The way in which the judicial account wiped out this whole side of the story reveals that defining the facts as robbery and homicide was crucial to the interest of the winning party, that is, the monastery of Sahagún. A fine analysis of a similar case by J.J. Larrea shows that community control of commons was linked to *homicidium*, that is, the joint payment of jurisdictional penalties for manslaughter.[37] When someone was killed within a locality and the killer could not be identified, the local community was liable to pay a collective penalty. The obvious rationale was to press on them to give away the killer or pay jointly for his deed. This kind of solidarity was especially likely to operate when the locals' common good was at stake, and anyone interfering with their commons would clearly pose such a threat.[38] Tellingly, the Riojan case studied by Larrea also shows the monastery (in this case San Millán de la Cogolla) strategically invoking diabolic influence

36 I thank Arturo Morales and José Antonio López Sáez for their help with the fascinating issue of fish populations in the endorrheic lagoons of inland Spain.

37 Juan José Larrea Conde, "Obispos efímeros, comunidades y homicidio en La Rioja Alta en los siglos X y XI," *Brocar* 31 (2007), 177–199, esp. 191–192 and 94–196. See also Carvajal Castro et al., "Collective Action in Local Contexts."

38 See, for example, Oña 12 (1011), where a monastic protected enclosure is defined, giving a list of things that the locals are banned from doing, which constitutes a suitable description of what they would normally do on common land. Tellingly, it includes: [...] *si aliquis homo* [...] *intra istos terminos prenominatos pignorauerit aut homine ceperit uel interfecerit aut inde per uim aliquid extraxerit aut aliquam uiolentiam intulerit* (if any man should [...] take pledges, or capture or kill anyone, or forcibly take anything from him, of perform any other violence).

as motivation in order to silence the locals' possible arguments, just like Sahagún did in Haio's case.

This precisely makes the text's fourth silence even more striking: the account ends with Haio's signature and that of the scribe, and we're left with no hint of a sentence, a punishment, or a penalty. The redactors were just as uninterested in the victim or his kin as in Haio's fate. All they wanted was to ensure that the case was treated as plain robbery and homicide, but then why write down such a minor incident, with no obvious higher implications, on a royal charter of donation?

4 Why Was the Note Written on a Royal Diploma?

There is no simple answer to the last question of this enquiry. Besides the documentary context sketched above, the main written traces of this process constitute together a puzzle whose core is S1 261, but involves at least two more documents, each with their own particular history:

(1) S1 261 (971) is the royal donation of Grañeras, with the added judicial account on its left bottom corner (Fig. 13.1). The parchment is preserved at the Archivo Histórico Nacional, but there is also a copy of it in the first Sahagún cartulary, composed ca. 1110 (BGS, fol. 10^r). The scribe responsible for most of BGS, Munio, is known to have frequently altered his sources, a fact that stands out when single parchment versions survive for comparison, but can only be hypothesized otherwise.[39] BGS's copy of S1 261 differs indeed from the parchment.[40]

(2) S1 262 (971) is a royal donation of Fuentes to Sahagún that only survives in a cartulary copy (BGS, fol. 75^v). It seems logical to assume that it might

39 José Antonio Fernández Flórez and Marta Herrero de la Fuente, "Libertades de los copistas en la confección de cartularios: el caso del Becerro Gótico de Sahagún," in *Scribi e colofoni: le sottoscrizioni di copisti dalle origini all'avvento della stampa (Atti del Seminario di Erice: X Colloquio del Comité International de paléographie latine, 23–28 ottobre 1993)*, ed. Emma Condello and Giuseppe De Gregorio (Spoleto: Centro Italiano di Studi sull'alto Medioevo, 1995), 301–324; Sonia Serna Serna, "Munio y el Becerro Gótico de Sahagún: una muestra de su actividad como copista," in *El monacato en los reinos de León y Castilla (Siglos VII–XIII), X Congreso de Estudios Medievales, León, 26 a 29 de septiembre de 2005*, ed. José Ignacio Ruiz de la Peña Solar (Ávila: Fundación Claudio Sánchez Albornoz, 2007), 425–436.

40 To mention only the most relevant differences, it abbreviates quite radically the preamble and the best part of the dispositions, but then it amplifies the sanction clauses by adding to the spiritual curses a pecuniary penalty of two talents of gold. Likewise, it appends a few witness names that are not in the single parchment.

have suffered similar alterations when being copied, but, in the absence of other versions, there is no way to gauge that possibility.

(3) S1 289 (977) is an agreement between Sahagún and the people of Fuentes. The latter commit not to take any other lord that might oppose the interests of the abbey or face a fine of 100 *solidi*. Again, this text is only extant in its cartulary copy (BGS, fol. 230) and there is no way to check the accuracy of its transmission.

In purely geographical terms, the three texts are clearly connected. The two donations refer to the neighbouring villages of Grañeras and Fuentes, and the agreement involves the latter. Still, the most pressing question is, if S1 262 granted Sahagún the village of Fuentes, should it not also be the first choice for recording an account of a trial affecting that same locality? Why was it written on S1 261 instead?

A closer look to S1 261 reveals its enormous complexity. Formally, it keeps to the layout of contemporary Leonese royal diplomas, with a first line in ornamental elongated script. However, the lack of both graphical and linguistic skill of the scribe Iulianus has led J.A. Fernández Flórez to consider it a later forgery.[41] This remains a possibility, but additional issues need to be addressed. Iulianus's hand is certainly idiosyncratic. Maybe its most distinctive trait is the frequent recourse to duplicate strokes on the left side of letters such as *e*, *c*, and *d*. This repeats itself all across the main text, in the signatures, and also in Iulianus's *roboratio*, which is placed on the bottom right margin, rotated anti-clockwise. There is little doubt that the same hand penned all of the royal donation charter. By contrast, the judicial account on the bottom left corner—signed by a different scribe called Placenti—was clearly written by a different hand, one that never employs Iulianus's signature double strokes. There are clearly at least two different stages in the making of S1 261 as we see it now.

There is, however, an element that unifies both parts: prestige charters often show stylized figures of chrismons not only in the opening, but also as frames for the columns of signatures. The ones in S1 261 are distinctive in that they have at the top an ornamental stroke that curls upwards (see the main chrismon on the left margin, and the ones of columns 1, 3, and 4 in Fig. 13.1). They also end with a distinctive lace suggesting an *S* (all except the main one). Most peculiarly, the shaft is sometimes truncated near the upper end, marked by two small horizontal strokes (col. 3) that in two occasions accommodate a cross between them (cols. 1 and 4). A search of tenth- and early eleventh-century Sahagún charters has failed to detect any other comparable instances of chrismons with

41 See above, n. 3.

an inserted cross. This seems to be just another peculiarity of Iulianus's (who, incidentally, never features in any other Sahagún charter, except S1 262). Strikingly, the judicial account on the left bottom corner is framed by very similar figures. On the left, it presents a chrismon with all the traits just described: a curly stroke at the top, a cross inserted in the upper shaft and an S-shaped lace at the bottom. However, this has been executed in small bits (the shaft is fragmented in at least five segments), suggesting that the author was trying to replicate a model, rather than drawing it spontaneously. On the right margin, he clearly extended downwards the chrismon of col. 2, to provide a boundary for his text. In other words, the scribe of the judicial account tried his best to make his addition merge aesthetically with the rest of the charter, but there are still clear traces of his operation.

The judicial notice is undated, but the appearance of Godleo as spokesperson for *frater* Vermudo in Haio's hearing and as surety to one of his neighbours in the 977 agreement strongly connects both. It seems logical to suppose that Haio's trial occurred not too long before or after that. If S1 261 were a later forgery, the account would necessarily have been added even after it was forged, which seems unlikely, given its strongly contextual content. Instead, if the judicial account was inserted in, or slightly after, 977, this leaves a narrow 971×977 range for the writing of the main charter. The diploma could have been made on the spot, maybe on the event of a royal visit, and entrusted to a scribe that was not a regular among the king's notaries (although, for all his shortcomings, he clearly had some idea of how a royal diploma should look). Alternatively, it could be a forgery or a simple copy, but one made already in the 970s, which is not impossible, but much less compelling.

We can reasonably deconstruct how the judicial note ended up on S1 261, but can we explain why not on S1 262, which was more closely related to the matter? With S1 262 we are on a slippery slope, having to work only from a cartulary version. The charter records how King Ramiro III and his wife Elvira granted to Sahagún their *domus* of Fuentes, as well as Villa de Doña Madre. It is dated the very same day as S1 261 (11 May 971), signed by Iulianus too, and the witness lists are very similar, although not identical. Even allowing for significant alterations by the cartulary copyist, this charter is still suspicious. First, the donors offer Sahagún their *domus* of Fuentes, stating its boundaries, which are divided in two sections, marked by the words *a parte orientis* and *de alia pars*. After that, they declare the additional donation of Villa de Doña Matre, without any boundaries expressed. The problem is that what purports to be the eastern limits of Fuentes is actually a huge perimeter—much larger at any rate than Fuentes—comprising several areas over which Sahagún held aspirations in the eleventh century, but did not fully control.

As for *alia pars*, these are actually the boundaries of Villa de Doña Madre, as repeatedly recorded in mid-tenth century charters, despite being presented as surrounding Fuentes on the western side.[42] It seems as if the boundaries of both villages were conflated into a single clause that lacks spatial consistency. Additionally, the boundary clause contains at least two place names—Quintanillas del Páramo and Villamoratiel—that are not recorded until much later.[43]

To complicate things further, there is yet another element connecting S1 261 and S1 262. On the bottom margin of S1 261 there is a line of text, scribbled in a tiny Visigothic cursive hand with a dim sepia-colored ink that is now almost totally faded (Fig. 13.2).[44] It reads: *De Gubara a Quintanellas de Paramo et a Lacuna Maiore et uadit* [...]. The text stops there and resumes further to the right, after the central fold of the leaf: *et inde ad illa Lacuna Maiore qui est inter Ualle Fraxino et Uilla Ambitos*.

This list of place names recalls the one in S1 262. The first half coincides almost literally (*Gubara*, *Quintanellas de Paramo*, and *Lacuna Maiore*). The second half only coincides in the reference to *toto Valle de Fraxino*. Despite its obvious likeness, this line is clearly not a direct rendering of S1 262, since much of the phrasing and place names are missing, including all the boundaries of Villa de Doña Madre. Reaching a safer conclusion about this text would require an entirely different investigation via image processing technology. At this point I can only hypothesize, on the grounds that it appears to be divided in two in order to avoid the parchment fold, that this line—despite being so faded—is an addition to S1 261 made after it was folded for archiving. It might have been written as part of the preparation of S1 262. The Grañeras grant with the judicial note would have been studied in order to forge the Fuentes/Villa

42 *a parte orientis per Guvara et vadit a Quintanellas de Paramo et discurrit ad illa Lacuna Maiore et vadit a monte Sancti Martini et per illo valle que discurrit a Villa Moratelle et inde ad ipsa Villa Moratelle et toto Valle Fraxino; de alia pars de Grannera ad eclesia Sancti Iohannis in Valle Fraxeno et vadit ad Poplellos; de alia vero pars Villa Nannini*, S1 262.

43 Quintanillas del Páramo, a deserted settlement, appears in S1 262 and in a marginal note added to S1 261 (see below). After that, it goes unrecorded until 1136 (S4 1256). Villamoratiel is mentioned in a will dated in 959 (S1 168) that the editor considers to have been redacted in the twelfth century (S1, p. 229). Otherwise, it does not occur until 1089 (S3 848). Its extreme proximity (less than 2 kms) to the location of much cited 'Populellos' marks it as a possible successor to the early medieval settlement.

44 To the best of my knowledge, this line has gone hitherto unnoticed by editors and commentators of S1 261. I must express my immense gratitude to José Antonio Fernández Flórez and Marta Herrero, who most generously offered their reading of the text, and to Luis Miguel de la Cruz (Archivo Histórico Nacional), who helped me checking with the original charter. None of them is accountable for my interpretation.

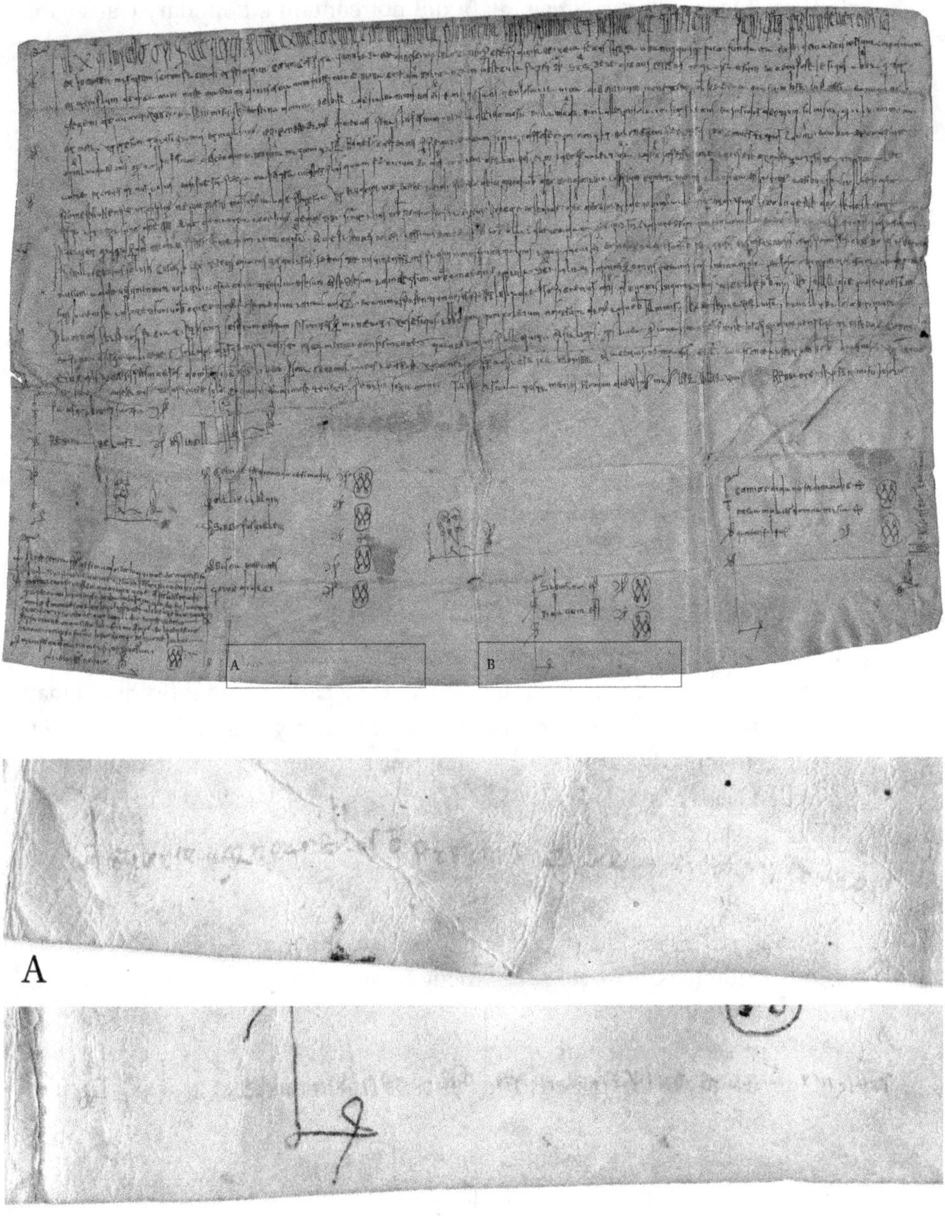

FIGURE 13.2 A much faded line of text at the foot of Sahagún 261 stating a list of place names. Note the hiatus over the fold.

MADRID, ARCHIVO HISTÓRICO NACIONAL, CLERO-SECULAR_REGULAR, CAR. 876, NÚM. 8R. PRINTED WITH PERMISSION de Doña Madre charter. Since S1 261 did not contain a boundary clause, the suitable boundaries were scribbled in very thin ink on the margin, and later incorporated (with changes) into the single parchment version of S1 262, which also took the date, scribe's name and most of the witnesses from S1 261.

There is a credible context for the forging of S1 262 in a dispute that arose in 1092 between Sahagún and the local elites (*infanzones*) of Valdefresno over Villa de Doña Madre, as mentioned above.[45] From that conflict it is clear that, whatever the charter claimed, Sahagún did not hold the undisputed lordship of Villa de Doña Madre. If Fuentes had been granted to Sahagún in 971, the obvious place to write down the Haio trial would have been the charter of donation of Fuentes. The fact that it was written on S1 261 instead strongly suggests that S1 262 did not exist at the time. In that case, the obvious second choice for writing the judicial account should be the 977 agreement, which deals specifically with Sahagún's interests in Fuentes, but this did not happen, either because Haio's trial preceded—maybe triggered?—the agreement, or maybe because the monks simply preferred the symbolic appearance of a royal charter. S1 261 was either the best or the only option for recording this account, especially if—as one would expect—the charter was presented by the monastery as evidence during the hearing.

I must stress that, while I do not think S1 262 can be authentic, S1 261 may very well be a later copy, or even a late eleventh-century forgery, as suggested by Fernández Flórez. In the latter case, however, a convincing explanation should be given for its bearing a judicial note on an obscure, largely prescribed local trial that clearly belongs in the 970s. There is no way to elucidate this until a more sophisticated analysis of S1 261 is carried out with the proper technology.

All that considered, this strenuous deconstruction of the textual evidence yields a credible basic sequence, although it must be considered hypothetical and provisional:

(1) Since the early tenth century, and especially from 965, Sahagún carried out a gradual expansion in Valdefresno (including Villa de Dona Madre), mainly by means of purchases.
(2) In 971 the monastery gained control of Grañeras.
(3) In 977 the people of Fuentes agreed to seek the patronage of no other lord than Sahagún.
(4) Shortly before or after that, the Haio incident took place.

45 See above, n. 13. This charter, which is also preserved only in its cartulary version, was copied on fol. 75^{v}, not far from S1 262 (BGS, fol. 74^{r}), which probably indicates that they were stored in similar locations at the archive.

5 Conclusion

Short as it is, the judicial account added to S1 261 reveals itself as a relevant part of the monastery's strategies to build its seigneurial control over a supralocal rural area. The account of Haio's confession deliberately distorts the events in order to reduce the whole conflict to a qualification of robbery and homicide. Its silences, though, and the nature of the facts, unveil a deeper conflict about local and lordly claims to jurisdiction over common rights. The story is told in a manner that avoids any hint that Haio could be—or feel that he was—entitled to act against the man from Monzón. The underlying message is that only the monastery could legitimately do that. Why, if not, write down such an ordinary crime on a royal grant? With its control of the monastery of San Julián and of Grañeras, Sahagún had a firm grip on the area in which common resources such as pasture and water surely played a major role.[46] The abbey's strategy was to treat the whole area as if it was under its full lordship; hence the 977 agreement that kept the people of Fuentes from seeking another lord's patronage.[47] Hence, too, blocking the locals' claims to jurisdiction over waters, which were crushed in a court composed by two judges closely linked to Sahagún and with an important community member acting as its representative. And yet, over one century later there were still local elites (*infanzones*) in Valdefresno that claimed autonomy from Sahagún, and the monastery had to forge a charter that proved tighter lordly rights over Fuentes than they actually enjoyed. It seems that in some areas of the tenth-century Duero plateau flattening the local communities and building full seigneurial rights was a complicated task that took much more than one monk, one donkey and one dead man.

46 See Iñaki Martín Viso, "Commons and the Construction of Power in the Early Middle Ages: Tenth-Century León and Castile," *Journal of Medieval History* 46, no. 4 (2020), 373–395.

47 The case can be compared to that of *Villa Castellana*, a (now deserted) settlement whose inhabitants committed in 976 to have Bishop Sisnando of León as their only lord, allowing for no interference from any *maior* or *potestas*: CL2 443 (976). I thank Álvaro Carvajal for this reference.

Bibliography

Abbreviations

BGS: *Becerro Gótico de Sahagún*, Madrid, Archivo Histórico Nacional, CODICES, L.989.

CL2, CL6: *Colección Documental del Archivo de la Catedral de León (775–1230)*. Vol. 2 (*953–985*), edited by Emilio Sáez and Carlos Sáez; vol. 6 (*1188–1230*), edited by José María Fernández Catón. León: Centro de Estudios e Investigación 'San Isidoro', 1990.

Oña: Del Álamo, José, ed. *Colección diplomática de San Salvador de Oña (822–1284)*. Vol. I *822–1214*. Madrid: CSIC, 1950.

S1, S2, S3, S4: *Colección Diplomática del Monasterio de Sahagún (857–1230)*. Vol. 1 (*Siglos IX y X*), edited by José María Mínguez Fernández; vol. 2 (*1000–1073*) and vol. 3 (*1073–1109*), edited by Marta Herrero de la Fuente; vol. 4 (*1110–1199*), edited by José Antonio Fernández Flórez. León: Centro de Estudios e Investigación 'San Isidoro', 1976, 1988, 1988, 1991.

Secondary Works

Agúndez San Miguel, Leticia. *La memoria escrita en el monasterio de Sahagún (años 904–1300)*. Madrid: Consejo Superior de Investigaciones Científicas, 2019.

Alfonso, Isabel. "Conflict in the *Behetrías*." In *Land, Power, and Society in Medieval Castile*, edited by Cristina Jular Pérez-Alfaro and Carlos Estepa Díez, 275–316. Turnhout: Brepols, 2009.

Alfonso Antón, Isabel. "Los nombres de la violencia y el control de su legitimación." *Hispania* 61, no. 208 (2001), 691–706. English translation: "Naming Violence and Controlling its Legitimation," in *Conflict, Language and Social Practice in the Middle Ages. Selected Essays of Isabel Alfonso*. Turnhout: Brepols, forthcoming.

Alfonso Antón, Isabel. "El formato de la información judicial en la Alta Edad Media peninsular." In *Chartes et cartulaires comme instruments de pouvoir. Espagne et Occident chrétien (VIIIe–XIIe siècles)*, edited by Julio Escalona and Helène Sirantoine, 191–218. Toulouse: Université de Toulouse le Mirail, 2013.

Algazi, Gadi. "Feigned Reciprocities Lords, Peasants, and the Afterlife of Late Medieval Social Strategies." In *Negotiating the Gift: Pre-Modern Figurations of Exchange*, edited by Gadi Algazi, Valentin Groebner, and Bernhard Jussen, 99–127. Göttingen: Vandenhoeck & Ruprecht, 2003.

Carrera de la Red, Fátima. *El valle del Cea a través de la toponimia documental*. Madrid: Liceus, 2010.

Carvajal Castro, Álvaro. *Bajo la máscara del Regnum: la monarquía asturleonesa en León (854–1037)*. Madrid: Consejo Superior de Investigaciones Científicas, 2017.

Carvajal Castro, Álvaro. "The Use of the Term *Uilla* in Early Medieval León: A Review of the Economic Base of the Astur-Leonese Monarchy (Ninth–Eleventh Centuries)."

In *Polity and Neighbourhood in Early Medieval Europe*, edited by Julio Escalona, Orri Vésteinsson, and Stuart Brookes, 325–350. Turnhout: Brepols, 2019.

Carvajal Castro, Álvaro. "Collective Action and Local Leaderships in Early Medieval North-Western Iberia. Ninth-Eleventh Centuries." In *Social Inequality in Early Medieval Europe. Local Societies and Beyond*, edited by Juan Antonio Quirós Castillo, 281–299. Turnhout: Brepols, 2020.

Carvajal Castro, Álvaro, Julio Escalona, Iñaki Martín Viso, and Igor Santos Salazar. "Collective Action in Local Contexts in the Kingdom of León (9th–11th centuries): An Exploration of the Charter Evidence." In *Archaeology and History of Peasantries 1: From the Late Prehistory to the Middle Ages*, edited by Juan Antonio Quirós Castillo, 149–161. Bilbao: Universidad del País Vasco, 2020.

Davies, Wendy. *Acts of Giving. Individual, Community and Church in Tenth-Century Christian Spain*. Oxford: Oxford University Press, 2007.

Davies, Wendy. "Judges and Judging: Truth and Justice in Northern Iberia on the Eve of the Millennium." *Journal of Medieval History* 36, no. 3 (2010), 193–203.

Davies, Wendy. "On Suretyship in Tenth-Century Northern Iberia." In *Scale and Scale Change in the Early Middle Ages: Exploring Landscape, Local Society and the World Beyond*, edited by Julio Escalona and Andrew Reynolds, 133–152. Turnhout: Brepols, 2011.

Davies, Wendy. *Windows on Justice in Northern Iberia, 800–1000*. Abingdon: Routledge, 2016.

Escalona, Julio. "Supra-Local Territorial Units: On the Origins of *Behetría* Lordship." In *Land, Power and Society in medieval Castile*, edited by Cristina Jular Pérez-Alfaro and Carlos Estepa Díez, 29–58. Turnhout: Brepols, 2009.

Estepa Díez, Carlos. *Las behetrías castellanas*. 2 vols. Valladolid: Junta de Castilla y León, 2003.

Fernández Flórez, José Antonio. "El Becerro de Presentaciones. Códice 13 del ACL. Un parroquial leonés de los siglos XIII–XV." In *León y su historia. Miscelánea histórica, V*, 265–565. León: Centro de Estudios e Investigación 'San Isidoro', 1984.

Fernández Flórez, José Antonio. "El fondo documental del monasterio de Sahagún y sus *scriptores* (siglos IX–X)." In *El monacato en los reinos de León y Castilla (Siglos VII–XIII), X Congreso de Estudios Medievales, León, 26 a 29 de septiembre de 2005*, edited by José Ignacio Ruiz de la Peña Solar, 125–146. Ávila: Fundación Claudio Sánchez Albornoz, 2007.

Fernández Flórez, José Antonio, and Marta Herrero de la Fuente. "Libertades de los copistas en la confección de cartularios: el caso del Becerro Gótico de Sahagún." In *Scribi e colofoni: le sottoscrizioni di copisti dalle origini all'avvento della stampa (Atti del Seminario di Erice: X Colloquio del Comité international de paléographie latine, 23–28 ottobre 1993)*, edited by Emma Condello and Giuseppe De Gregorio, 301–324. Spoleto: Centro Italiano di Studi sull'alto Medioevo, 1995.

González González, Raúl. *Bastiones de tradición. Ciudades y aristocracias urbanas en la Alta Edad Media asturleonesa (siglos IX–XI)*. León: Librería Universitaria de León, 2017.

Larrea Conde, Juan José. "Obispos efímeros, comunidades y homicidio en La Rioja Alta en los siglos X y XI." *Brocar* 31 (2007), 177–200.

Martín Viso, Iñaki. "Commons and the Construction of Power in the Early Middle Ages: Tenth-Century León and Castile." *Journal of Medieval History* 46, no. 4 (2020), 373–395.

Mínguez Fernández, José María. *El dominio del monasterio de Sahagún en el siglo X. Paisajes agrarios, producción y expansión económica*. Salamanca: Universidad de Salamanca, 1980.

Pensado, José Luis. "Anotaciones marginales latinas, leonesas y gallegas a la *Colección Diplomática del Monasterio de Sahagún (siglos IX y X)*." *Senara* 3 (1982), 11–54.

Sánchez Badiola, Juan José. *La configuración de un sistema de poblamiento y organización: el territorio de León (siglos IX–XI)*. León: Universidad de León, 2002.

Serna Serna, Sonia. "Munio y el Becerro Gótico de Sahagún: una muestra de su actividad como copista." In *El monacato en los reinos de León y Castilla (Siglos VII–XIII), X Congreso de Estudios Medievales, León, 26 a 29 de septiembre de 2005*, edited by José Ignacio Ruiz de la Peña Solar, 425–436. Ávila: Fundación Claudio Sánchez Albornoz, 2007.

CHAPTER 14

Double Records: Officializing Dispute Settlement in Twelfth-Century Denmark

Kim Esmark

1 Introduction

At some time around the year 1170, a dispute arose at the Danish metropolitan church of Lund.[1] Florentius, a young canon of the cathedral chapter, claimed to be the rightful inheritor of some land in Villingerød in northern Zealand which his ecclesiastical lord, Archbishop Eskil, had purchased from Florentius's grandfather some 20 odd years before and then donated to his own monastic foundation in Esrum, close to Villingerød. The conflict was soon settled, apparently without recourse to formal legal proceedings or regular judgment. Having considered the issue bilaterally with the archbishop, Florentius agreed to renounce the claim. He and his brother Benedict subsequently granted the disputed estate to Esrum Abbey at a gathering of prominent clerical and lay magnates in Lund.

The case of Villingerød is one of very few extant recorded legal conflicts from Denmark before 1200. As far as the course of the controversy and the measures applied by the involved parties go, it resembles so many other intra-class, out-of-court, settlement-by-compromise property disputes known from the steadily expanding field of medieval 'dispute studies' all around Europe.[2]

1 Lund in Scania, today southern Sweden, until 1658 part of the kingdom of Denmark. On the general history of the archiepiscopal church of Lund, see Lauritz Weibull, *Skånes kyrka från älsta tid till Jacob Erlandsens död 1274* (Copenhagen: Rosenkilde & Bagger, 1946); Erik Buus, ed., *Consuetudines Lundenses: statutter for kannikesamfundet i Lund c. 1123* (Copenhagen: Det danske sprog- og litteraturselskab, 1978); Per-Olov Ahrén and Anders Jarlert, eds., *Lund—medeltida kyrkometropol* (Lund: Stiftshistoriska sällskapet i Lunds stift, 2004); Anna Minara Ciardi, *On the Formation of Cathedral Chapters and Cathedral Culture. Lund, Denmark, and Scandinavia, c. 1060–1225* (Lund: Lund University, 2016). A warm thanks to Anders Leegaard Knudsen (Society for Danish Language and Literature) and Helle Vogt (University of Copenhagen), for invaluable comments and expert help.

2 On this historiography and its reception in Scandinavia, see Kim Esmark and Hans Jacob Orning, "General Introduction," in *Disputing Strategies in Medieval Scandinavia*, ed. Kim Esmark et al. (Leiden: Brill, 2013), 1–28.

 | DOI:10.1163/9789004683006_016

Nothing particularly noteworthy, in other words, except that the Villingerød case happens to be documented in two different, overlapping but not entirely congruent contemporary accounts: a sealed charter issued in the name of the (quit-)claimant Florentius, and an open letter of proclamation by Archbishop Eskil.[3] Two (or more) records of the same dispute is by no means unheard of, neither in a narrow Danish nor in a wider European medieval context. Usually, however, we are dealing with corroborations or ratifications of the same settlement by different authorities or with later confirmations or summaries of one original account.[4] The existence of two parallel records, both addressing the same settlement, but one representing each side of the conflict, is more of a rarity, and allows for interesting glimpses into the ways litigants might seek to frame disputing processes and their public representation.

In the "face-to-face society" of twelfth century Denmark,[5] conflicts like the dispute over Villingerød were handled in a societal context where most of the features associated with modern legal systems were still more or less absent. That implied, among other things, that people engaged in such conflicts did not regard 'law', 'legal procedure' or 'legal facts' as belonging to a separate field isolated from broader socio-cultural norms and practices. Also, what we today would designate as specifically 'judicial authority' was not always (and certainly not easily) distinguishable from other kinds of legitimate social power; it rather seemed to merge into (or indeed rely on) powers derived from being lord, patron, kinsman or friend of specific individuals or groups, and as it was not yet institutionalized the way it later came to be, it had to be continuously claimed and displayed in public manifestations. Finally, in this world of intricate face-to-face relations dispute processes often carried implications beyond the narrowly 'judicial' matter at issue, potentially affecting reputation, rank and local hierarchies, not only among the parties directly involved (litigants, mediators, compurgators, judges, witnesses, etc.), but also within these people's social networks.

---

3 Original documents lost but both preserved as copies in Esrum Abbey's fifteenth-century cartulary, *Codex Esromensis*, Copenhagen, Royal Library, *E. don. var.* 140, 4°, fols. 73^r–74^v. Edited: O. Nielsen, ed., *Codex Esromensis. Esrum Klosters Brevbog* (Copenhagen, 1880–1881; repr. 1973), 89–91, and Herluf Nielsen et al., eds., *Diplomatarium Danicum* (Copenhagen: Munksgaard, 1938–2000) [hereafter DD], 1.2.184 and 1.2.185.

4 See, for example, the resolution of a property dispute in 1174 reported by the king and the local bishop in two separate charters issued on the same day at the same venue, DD 1.3.45 and 1.3.46.

5 Aptly defined in this way by Michael H. Gelting, "Ansigt-til-ansigt-samfundet og de to øvrigheder," in *Gaver, ritualer, konflikter. Et retsantropologisk perspektiv på nordisk middelalderhistorie*, ed. Hans Jacob Orning, Kim Esmark, and Lars Hermanson (Oslo: Unipub, 2010), 301–316.

The interpretation and definition of a conflict and its closure, expressed and enacted in ritual procedure and/or written testimony, was therefore always of concern to disputing parties. Depending on strategy, power, and micropolitical specificities, an objectively lopsided resolution could be publicized as an evenly balanced agreement that all sides would put a good face to, just like a necessary compromise settlement could be presented as a clear-cut vindication of one suitor's claim. In some cases, the function of royal or episcopal judge could be emphasized in order to legitimate the person holding the office (or the office itself), in others it could be downplayed. Specific legal arguments sustaining or undermining particular challenges could be either highlighted or suppressed.[6] To be able in this way to impose a certain perception of a dispute upon others and have it socially consecrated by relevant communities—i.e. made *official* (authoritative, legitimate)—was a real source of symbolic power, hence an object of contention in itself. It therefore animated a wide register of what Pierre Bourdieu has termed 'officializing strategies', that is speech, action, or writing designed to manipulate public opinion and the definition of situations with the aim of "transmuting 'egoistic', private, particular interests [...] into 'disinterested', collective, publicly avowable, legitimate interests".[7]

Production of charters constituted one such strategy. It is beyond the scope of this chapter to explain in comprehensive theoretical terms how officializing effects might potentially be accomplished by way of "sheepskin blackened with ink and weighted with a little lump of lead".[8] Here, attention should be called to but three interrelated aspects. First, when somebody took the effort and invested the necessary means to put their claims or propositions on parchment, scourged in standardized formulas and protective clauses and authenticated by seals, signatures and witness lists, they effectively removed (or purported to remove) these claims or propositions from the world of ordinary, contestable discourse, transferring them instead to a realm of sanctified, inviolable truth.

---

6 For examples derived from Danish source material, see Kim Esmark, "Disputing Property in Zealand: The Records of the Sorø Donation Book," in *Disputing Strategies in Medieval Scandinavia*, ed. Kim Esmark et al., 181–218.

7 Pierre Bourdieu, *The Logic of Practice* (Cambridge: Polity Press, 1990), 108–110. For application of the term 'officializing strategies' in medieval studies, see Stephen D. White, "Inheritances and Legal Arguments in Western France, 1050–1150," *Traditio* 43 (1987), 55–103, at 97, and Kim Esmark, "Just Rituals: Masquerade, Manipulation, and Officializing Strategies in Saxo's *Gesta Danorum*," in *Rituals, Performatives, and Political Order in Northern Europe, c. 650–1350*, ed. Wojtek Jezierski et al. (Turnhout: Brepols, 2015), 237–267.

8 The derogatory term for charter evidence famously put into the mouths of King Henry I's English bishops by the chronicler Eadmer. See Michael Clanchy, *From Memory to Written Record. England 1066–1307*, 2nd ed. (Oxford: Blackwell, 1993), 261.

Second, charters not only communicated certain constatations about rights and privileges, they were also costly textual objectifications of the otherwise fleeting occasions at which they were issued, granted or displayed—occasions which constituted officializing acts in their own right. Thus, as enduring testimonies of such acts, performed publicly by gatherings of prominent people at particular places, charters were also snapshot engravings of authorising social constellations. Thirdly, besides the explicit purposes indicated by their dispositive clauses, charters would often be doing things implicitly by the very (f)act of their confection: displaying power and authority, reconfirming or dismantling networks of friendship and clientage, instituting distance and difference in social space. To issue a charter was essentially a statement that one possessed a socially consecrated power to define, delimit, delegate, and dispose—a power which in a kind of self-confirming circularity rested precisely on acts like issuing charters. These documents, then, were not just attestations of particular rights or judgments. In the words of Isabel Alfonso, "they also served as vehicles for the communication of the means whereby those decisions had been made, and the social networks that had been activated in the process".[9] Charters, in other words, were also *performatives* or *acts of institution*.[10]

Of course, comprehending charter records and the public events they narrate as officializing strategies presupposes, ideally at least, a knowledge of the records' "total local context" which is rarely possible to fully construct on the basis of medieval source material.[11] Bearing this limitation in mind, I shall in the following attempt a sort of contextualized close reading of the two reports of the Villingerød dispute with the aim of exploring and discussing the involved parties' officializing strategies. What constituted the substance of the controversy over Villingerød, according to the canon's charter and the archbishop's proclamation respectively? How and on what basis was the conflict resolved?

9 Isabel Alfonso, "Judicial Rhetoric and Political Legitimation in Medieval Leon-Castile," in *Building Legitimacy. Political Discourses and Forms of Legitimacy in Medieval Societies*, ed. Isabel Alfonso, Hugh Kennedy, and Julio Escalona (Leiden: Brill, 2004), 51–87, at 54.

10 See for much fuller expositions of this line of thoughts, Alfonso, "Judicial Rhetoric;" Geoffrey Koziol, "Making Boso the Clown: Performance and Performativity in a Pseudo-Diploma of the Renegade King (8 December 879)," in *Rituals, Performatives, and Political Order in Northern Europe, c. 650–1350*, ed. Wojtek Jezierski et al. (Turnhout: Brepols, 2015), 43–61; Pierre Bourdieu, *Language and Symbolic Power* (Cambridge: Polity Press, 1991); Michel Foucault, *Power/Knowledge* (New York: Pantheon Books, 1980).

11 "Total local context" referring to the (micro-)political circumstances of the document's issuance, the parties involved, their interrelationships and prehistory, etc.—the knowledge of which one would presumably have had as a member of the society at the time, cf. Koziol, "Making Boso the Clown," 51.

And how can we understand the partly conflicting representations of the process as efforts to bolster micropolitical interests and claims to social power and judicial authority? Before I turn to the Villingerød case itself, however, I shall have a few words to say about the sources for studying property disputes in high medieval Denmark and about these sources' most recent historiography.

2 Medieval Danish Disputes: Sources and Approaches

Scholars inspired by the international current of medieval dispute studies and wishing to explore how things in the Danish realm compared to legal cultures and disputing practices in wider Europe will find themselves left with a somewhat unrewarding undertaking. The source material, quite simply, is discouragingly meagre.

Charters, first of all, which have provided the main bulk of evidence in most of the defining historiography on French, English, Italian, Spanish and other regions' disputes, were introduced comparatively late and have come down in very limited numbers.[12] The earliest known charter issued on Danish soil is a royal donation letter from 1085,[13] and up until 1200 all title deeds, privileges and documents recording grants or affirmations of property rights were issued by kings, clerics or members of the royal kindred. Counting every single reference to disputing activities in this sample, we don't find more than a dozen cases. From the turn of the thirteenth century onwards, the number of records increases, including a growing flow of private charters issued by lay nobles and reports of dispute settlements. Some 75 disputes in total are mentioned in the documents dating from the years between 1200 and 1299.[14] Of all Danish charters from the twelfth and thirteenth century very few have survived the fires, wars, and accidents of the early modern period as originals: the vast

12 *Diplomatarium Danicum*, the all-exhaustive, chronologically ordered, multi-volume edition of Danish medieval charters counts some 420 entries from the twelfth century, but this includes not only all regular charters or diplomas issued in the kingdom, but also brief references to lost records gathered from lists and registers, as well as every single papal letter sent to Denmark, and every single record found in archives across Europe containing mentions of persons or places in the Danish realm.

13 King Knud the Holy's donation charter to the church of Lund, DD 1.2.21. Indirect evidence suggests that a sealed privilege was issued by the bishop of Roskilde in the early 1070s, but the text itself is lost, see DD 1.2.9.

14 Counted by Helle Vogt, "The Power to Judge: Jurisdiction in Property Conflicts in Thirteenth-Century Denmark," in *Disputing Strategies in Medieval Scandinavia*, ed. Kim Esmark et al., 161–180, at 162.

majority, including the Villingerød records, are known from copies, vidimations or summaries in fifteenth-century monastic cartularies and registers. As for the style of the documents the diplomatics vary, but in general the prose is quite terse and formulaic with next to nothing of the kind of extensive narrations sometimes seen in charters from other parts of Europe.

Turning to other types of sources does not add much. Many property disputes in Denmark were dealt with at local and regional assemblies known as the *thing*. But as the *thing* (referred to in Latin as *placitum, ius* or *curia secularis*) had no judges, scribes, legal officials or executive power of its own, and as the legal procedures regulating land transfer and property litigation at these gatherings gave priority to oral testimony (written records alone were not regarded as valid proof of ownership until the fourteenth century), the *thing* has left no court records from the period before 1300.[15] No systematic court records were produced at the ecclesiastical courts either. Litigation in these fora is therefore only known from references in charters. The provincial law-books, written in the vernacular during the late twelfth and early thirteenth century and presumably covering the laws of Jutland, Zealand, and Scania respectively, constitute a rich source for studies of medieval Danish legal, institutional and social history.[16] However, while the law-books provide useful contextual knowledge, especially in regard to legal procedure at the *thing*, they are normative in nature and do not tell much about actual practices of disputing. Chronicles, annals, and legends of royal martyr saints, finally, provide a reasonable corpus of narrative sources. Yet, if many of these texts do indulge in vivid descriptions of conflict in the broad sense—violence, rebellion, feuding, treachery, tension filled *Herschertreffen*, etc.—they are mainly concerned with high politics, and only rarely describe the kind of legal processes primarily under scrutiny here.[17]

By and large, then, investigations of property litigation and dispute processing in high medieval Denmark are bound to rely on a limited dossier of

---

15 Michael H. Gelting, "Circumstantial Evidence: Danish Charters of the Thirteenth Century," in *Medieval Legal Process: Physical, Spoken and Written Performance in the Middle Ages*, ed. Marco Mostert and Paul S. Barnwell (Turnhout: Brepols, 2011), 157–195; Anders Leegaard Knudsen, "Testimonia Placiti—Private Charters as Public Instruments. A Study in Medieval Danish Diplomatics," *Archiv für Diplomatik* 57 (2011), 147–179; Helmuth Schledermann, "Ting (*Danmark*)," *Kulturhistorisk leksikon for nordisk middelalder. Fra vikingetid til reformation*, ed. Bernt Hjejle et al., 22 vols (Copenhagen: Rosenkilde & Bagger, 1957–1978), 18:360–366.

16 Ditlev Tamm and Helle Vogt, eds., *The Danish Medieval Laws—the Laws of Scania, Zealand and Jutland* (London: Routledge, 2017), see especially the editors' introduction, 1–42.

17 In Denmark, writing of hagiographical texts started in the late eleventh century, while chronicles and annals were compiled from around 1140.

cursory accounts found in scattered, not-so-loquacious charters. One way to at least partly overcome this dearth is by applying a combined methodology of contextualized case study and comparative analysis. This approach, well-known and widely practiced among historians of medieval disputes, has also been taken up in recent Danish research on the topic, and the main conclusion to be drawn from the studies conducted so far points to the striking similarities in regard to basic legal culture between Denmark and some much better documented regions around Europe.[18]

Revisiting individual disputes in the dossier and turning even seemingly trivial cases over several times from different analytic angles arguably constitute another necessary element of the research process. The case of Villingerød, for instance, which is analysed here from the particular perspective of officializing strategies, has also been examined by the present author in studies focusing on gift exchange, property conflict as a means of regulating social order, and logics of compromise settlement.[19] Prior to that, other scholars have treated the same case in the contexts of Danish monastic history and of an alleged clash between old Danish inheritance norms and new conceptions of ownership introduced by the incoming Church.[20] While the latter studies do not pay much attention neither to the relation between the two accounts of the dispute, nor to the conflict's 'total local context', these issues are touched upon in varying detail in the former studies, but shall be the specific focus of the following discussion.

---

18 Kim Esmark, "Godsgaver, calumniae og retsantropologi. Esrum kloster og dets naboer, ca. 1150–1250," in *Ett annat 1100-tal. Individ, kollektiv och kulturella mönster i medeltidens Danmark*, ed. Peter Carelli, Lars Hermanson, and Hanne Sanders (Lund: Makadam, 2004), 143–180; Esmark, "Disputing Property in Zealand;" Kim Esmark, "The Settlement of Disputes by Compromise According to Some Early Danish Charters," in *Denmark and Europe in the Middle Ages, c. 1000–1525. Essays in Honour of Professor Michael H. Gelting*, ed. Kerstin Hundahl, Lars Kjær, and Niels Lund (Ashgate, 2015), 11–26; Vogt, "The Power to Judge;" Helle Vogt, "How To Be Remembered: Securing the *Memoria* of a Slain Person in Medieval Denmark," in *Emotion, Violence, Vengeance and Law in the Middle Ages: Essays in Honour of William Ian Miller*, ed. Kate Gilbert and Stephen D. White (Leiden: Brill, 2018), 156–171. On the need for comparative approaches as a way to comprehend the fragmentary sources for Danish medieval history, see Michael H. Gelting, "Det komparative perspektiv i dansk middelalderforskning. Om Familia og familie, Lið, Leding og Landeværn," *Historisk Tidsskrift* 99/1 (1999), 146–188.

19 Esmark, "Godsgaver"; Esmark, "The Settlement of Disputes".

20 Brian P. McGuire, "Property and politics at Esrum Abbey: 1151–1251," *Medieval Scandinavia* 6 (1973), 122–150, at 139–140; Brian P. McGuire, *The Cistercians in Denmark. Their Attitudes, Roles, and Functions in Medieval Society* (Kalamazoo: Cistercian Publications, 1992), 59–60; Helge Paludan, *Familia og familie. To kulturelementers møde i højmiddelalderens Danmark* (Aarhus: Aarhus universitetsforlag, 1995), 85.

3 Archbishop Eskil, Esrum Abbey, and the *Villa* of Villingerød

As mentioned in the opening lines of this chapter, the disputed property of Villingerød first came into the possession of Esrum Abbey through the hands of Archbishop Eskil. To understand the background and possible legal foundation of the claim later raised by the canon Florentius it is necessary to dig into the somewhat complicated prehistory of the estate and the circumstances surrounding its transfer to the monastery.

Historians usually regard Archbishop Eskil (*c.*1100–1181) as one of medieval Denmark's most prominent ecclesiastical princes, and his importance for Danish twelfth-century political and church history is certainly hard to overestimate. A scion of the mighty aristocratic kin group known by historians as the 'Trugond family', Eskil was afforded education abroad in Hildesheim, Germany, and returned to Denmark in the early 1130s to become provost of the cathedral chapter of Lund, where his uncle Asser reigned as archbishop. Quickly promoted to bishop of Roskilde, Eskil finally obtained the archiepiscopal dignity in 1137, following his uncle Asser's death and some intricate political manoeuvrings in the shadow of royal dynastic feuding and attempts from outside to have Denmark's status as an independent church province abolished.[21] Eskil received the pallium in 1138, and remained archbishop of Lund until he was allowed to resign in 1177, whereafter he retired to Clairvaux to spend his last days there as a Cistercian monk.

Archbishop Eskil was probably the most well-connected and widely travelled Danish noble of his time, enjoying the personal friendship of Bernard of Clairvaux, Pope Alexander III, John of Salisbury, and other members of the European clerical elite. As church leader he was a strong proponent of reform, and at times his attitude triggered both conflict with the king and division within the Danish clergy. Eskil also played a major role in the promotion of monasticism and introduction of new religious orders to Denmark. Among his foremost achievements within this field of activity was the foundation in the

21 A separate Danish ecclesiastical province was not established until 1103/4, when Eskil's uncle Asser became the first Danish archbishop. Until then, the dioceses in Denmark had been suffragans of Hamburg-Bremen, whose archbishops continued to threaten the independence of the Danish metropolitan see all up until the 1160s, and even had it abolished between 1133 and 1137. See Carsten Breengaard, *Muren om Israels hus. Regnum og sacerdotium i Danmark 1050–1170* (Copenhagen: G.E.C. Gad, 1982), 211–223, 237–239, 276–286; Michael H. Gelting, "Da Eskil ville være ærkebiskop af Roskilde. Roskildekrøniken, *Liber Daticus Lundensis* og det danske ærkesædes ophævelse 1133–1138," in *Ett annat 1100-tal. Individ, kollektiv och kulturella mönster i medeltidens Danmark*, ed. Peter Carelli, Lars Hermanson, and Hanne Sanders (Lund: Makadam, 2004), 181–229, at 184–197, 214–223.

years around 1150 of the Cistercian Abbey of Esrum, located in northern Zealand within the diocese of Roskilde, where he first served as bishop.

The exact beginnings of the monastery are difficult to establish with certainty, but in the early 1150s Eskil had replaced what seems to have been an early Benedictine community at Esrum with Cistercian monks brought in from the abbey of Clairvaux.[22] At that time, however, the build-up of a solid endowment had already been going on for some years. Thus, the *villa* of Esrum, on whose land the monastery was erected—a place which according to Eskil's own description was "abundant with acres, woods, streams, fishing ponds, meadows and pastures"[23]—had been acquired by the archbishop from King Erik the Lamb (r. 1137–1146) in exchange for land from Eskil's own patrimony and then granted to the monks.[24] Eskil also added other holdings, some of them purchased or acquired by way of *commutatio* from local landowners, and he persuaded both kinsmen and kings to contribute as well.[25]

Villingerød was among the first properties gathered by the archbishop for the new foundation, and seems to have been in place even before the arrival of the first white monks in about 1151/53.[26] In the various documents mentioning the place, Villingerød is designated alternately as *predium, villa, terra, possessio*, and *proprium*. It was located only three km north of the abbey in a fertile and easily accessible area and just like Esrum village it originally belonged to the royal patrimony.[27] In 1145, however, it was granted by King Erik the Lamb to Herman, a German-born canon of the cathedral chapter in Lund, who shared close bonds with Eskil.[28] In the 1130s, Herman had served as Eskil's chaplain at the see of Roskilde and as diplomatic envoy to the papal curia in Rome during the difficult negotiations in 1137/38 over Eskil's access to the bishopric of Lund and the

22 On Esrum Abbey's somewhat obscure beginnings, see Niels Skyum-Nielsen, *Kvinde og slave* (Copenhagen: Munksgaard, 1971), 120; McGuire, *The Cistercians in Denmark*, 49–51; James France, *The Cistercians in Scandinavia* (Kalamazoo: Cistercian Publications, 1992), 46–49; Thomas Hill, *Könige, Fürsten und Klöster. Studien zu den dänischen Klostergründungen des 12. Jahrhunderts* (Frankfurt am Main: Peter Lang, 1992), 193–205; Tore Nyberg, *Monasticism in North-Western Europe, 800–1200* (Aldershot: Ashgate, 2000), 117–118, 136, 145.

23 DD 1.2.126 (Archbishop Eskil's great charter of privileges to Esrum Abbey, 1158): [...] *habundet utilitatibus. in agris. in nemoribus in aquis et piscacionibus. in pratis et pascuis* [...].

24 DD 1.2.107.

25 McGuire, "Property and Politics," 132–134.

26 Villingerød is listed among Esrum Abbey's properties in the papal foundation charter from late 1151, DD 1.2.106.

27 McGuire, "Property and Politics," 123–125 and map.

28 For Herman's career, see Skyum-Nielsen, *Kvinde og slave*, 95; Gelting, "Da Eskil ville være ærkebiskop," 214–219.

status of the Danish metropolitan church. After that, he was ordained bishop of Schleswig in southern Jutland, where he managed to oust a rival candidate until a local rebellion in early 1145 forced him to relinquish the see and return to Lund. For his services to the king Herman was then awarded various estates and revenues in the province of Zealand, including the *predium* of Villingerød which he, according to a royal charter, received "to hold perpetually according to the customs of our law".[29] Herman died not long after and was honourably buried in the crypt of St Lawrence, the recently consecrated cathedral church in Lund.[30] Villingerød was left to his heir, a *decanus* or dean of the cathedral chapter named Johannes. Archbishop Eskil evidently knew this man well and soon persuaded him to sell his newly inherited property, whereafter the archbishop granted it to his own fledgling foundation in Esrum.[31]

No separate written record of Eskil's purchase of Villingerød from Johannes has survived (if there ever was one), and the exact name and identity of Herman's heir is only revealed in the records of the dispute around 1170. But bits of near-contemporary information about the transfer are found in three different charters issued within the following decade to confirm Esrum Abbey's possessions. Thus, in a sealed charter, which can be dated to somewhere between 1151 and 1157, King Svend Grathe (r. 1146–1157) first discusses and corroborates his predecessor, King Erik the Lamb's alienation of the village of Esrum to Archbishop Eskil and the monks of Esrum Abbey, and then goes on to relate how "the aforementioned archbishop has added another village to the aforementioned brothers, namely Villingerød, which he has procured for money from the heir to Herman, bishop of the church of Schleswig".[32]

In the archbishop's own great charter of privileges to the monastery from 1158, in which all lands held by the monks at that time are enumerated, there is no word of the purchase itself from Herman's heir, Johannes; only Eskil's donation is related. Following a short, but not immodest introductory account of his general advancement of monastic life in Denmark and of his foundation of Esrum Abbey, Eskil simply explains that besides the gift to the monks of the village of Esrum "we furthermore gave them the village called Villingerød, with

29 DD 1.2.91: *perpetuo* […] *possessionis iure ut nostre legis mos est.*

30 Lauritz Weibull, ed., *Necrologium Lundense. Lunds domkyrkas nekrologium* (Lund: Berlingska boktryckeriet, 1923), 52–53.

31 The deanery was the second highest office at the cathedral chapter of Lund. The dean was elected by the archbishop after consultation with the provost and the senior canons, cf. Lauritz Weibull, *Skånes kyrka*, 49–50.

32 DD 1.2.107: […] *prenominatus archiepiscopus uillam aliam Widilingeruth uidelicet. quam ab herede Hermanni ecclesie Sleswicensis episcopi pecunia conquisiuit. sumptui fratrum prenominatorum adiecit.*

woods and fishing ponds and other adjoining lands".[33] Among the charter's nine subscribers, however, we do find the vendor of Villingerød, Johannes, dean at the cathedral chapter.

More is to be gained from the royal charter issued around 1160 at the castle of Søborg, less than five km from Esrum and Villingerød, by King Svend Grathe's rival and successor, the young King Valdemar I (r. 1154–1182).[34] This charter specifically concerns the safeguarding of Esrum Abbey's possession of Villingerød and is interesting because it seems to anticipate exactly the kind of claim that was later raised by Florentius. Thus, the charter relates how the village called Villingerød, "which once was subject to the king's right" (*que aliquando iuri subiacebat regio*), had come into the possession of Archbishop Eskil "in a right and lawful way according to Danish custom" (*recte et legittime iuxta morem Danorum*), and subsequently was granted by him to his own foundation in Esrum. But, the text then continues, because Villingerød had formerly belonged to others, the descendants of these former owners—namely "one of the kings, who succeed us, or one of the heirs to Lord Herman" (*aliquo regum nobis succedentium siue* [...] *aliquo heredum domini Hermanni*)—might easily object to the conveyance and raise a *calumnia*, a legal challenge, to Esrum's ownership. To prevent such a situation, says the charter, King Svend Grathe, Valdemar's predecessor, had approved Esrum's acquisition by way of a sealed letter and even granted the property to the monastery himself. Wishing to provide for his own salvation and that of his family, King Valdemar now repeated Svend's pious grant, while also adding the supplementary gift of exempting the peasants on Esrum's lands from services owed to the king.

4 Custom, Consent and Compromise

As it appears, the monks of Esrum, recipients of King Valdemar's charter, evidently harboured fears concerning Villingerød and therefore sought to have their rights officialized by way of a public royal declaration of the legality of their acquisition. The monks' archiepiscopal patron probably worried himself too. Because Villingerød had once been royal property, future kings might claim

33 DD 1.2.126: [...] *superaddentes eis uillam que uocatur Wideligeruth cum silua et piscacione et ceteris appendiciis*. Hereafter follows a detailed review of Esrum Abbey's other acquisitions.

34 DD 1.2.129. Søborg castle was probably raised by Eskil himself and later taken over by the king; see Martin Pavón, "Søborg—Ærkebiskop Eskils borg i Nordsjælland," *Aarbøger for nordisk oldkyndighed og historie* (2011–2012), 263–291.

it back,[35] and even if Eskil's purchase of the property purportedly had been made in a perfectly right way, heirs of the former owner, Bishop Herman, somehow retained a right to reclaim the property or at least to be admitted a say in regard to the alienation. Although not yet codified in written law, customary norms concerning consent by kinsmen to gifts or sales of land were generally recognized in twelfth-century Denmark and seem to have followed the same basic patterns as the *laudatio parentum* known from other parts of Europe.[36] Alienation out of the kindred group was neither unlawful nor impossible, but remained a contentious issue. Complaints by frustrated heirs could be met or refuted, depending on arguments, moral pressure and micropolitical support mobilized by the parties, but at least in intra-class conflicts people often opted for some kind of compromise or compensation. When, for instance, in the early 1120s various *boni uiri* made grants of land to the metropolitan church of Lund, Eskil's uncle and predecessor, Archbishop Asser, paid the donors' close heirs to obtain their consent. Only thus could it be asserted that the transfers were done rightfully according to law (*legittimo ergo iure*), as explained in a charter issued by Asser some ten years later on the express advice and encouragement of his nephew Eskil, at that time still provost at the cathedral chapter.[37] In the church laws of Scania, promulgated later by Eskil as archbishop *c.*1170 after negotiations with local landholders, heirs were admitted the right to object to pious gifts after the death of the donor.[38]

---

35 On Danish royal lands in the twelfth century, see Carsten Porskrog Rasmussen, "Danish Crown Lands AD 1230—and Before?" in *Settlement and Lordship in Early Medieval Scandinavia*, ed. Bjørn Poulsen and Søren Sindbæk (Turnhout: Brepols, 2011), 239–259.

36 Such customary norms should be conceived of as "a fluid set of general principles, characteristically formulated in the shape of proverbs and maxims, neither fixed in quantity nor making up a logically coherent system; applied to individual cases, they might easily support mutually contradictory solutions": Michael H. Gelting, "Odelsrett–lovbydelse–bördsrätt–retrait lignager: Kindred and Land in the Nordic Countries in the Twelfth and Thirteenth Centuries," in *Family, Marriage and Property Devolution in the Middle Ages*, ed. Lars Ivar Hansen (Tromsø: University of Tromsø, 2000), 133–165, at 141–142, drawing on Stephen D. White, *Custom, Kinship, and Gifts to Saints. The Laudatio Parentum in Western France 1050–1150* (Chapel Hill: University of North Carolina Press, 1988), ch. 3, especially 70–74. See also Helle Vogt, *The Function of Kinship in Medieval Nordic Legislation* (Leiden: Brill, 2010), 192–194; Esmark, "Godsgaver."

37 DD 1.2.56: *Acta est hec descripcio* [...] *consilio et ammonicione domini Eskilli eiusdem ecclesie prepositi*. For parallel examples of kinsmen compensated for consenting to gifts, see DD 1.2.99 and the monastic chronicle of Øm Abbey: "Exordium monasterii Carø insula," in Martin Clarentius Gertz, ed., *Scriptores minores historiæ danicæ medii ævi*, 2 vols (Copenhagen, 1918–1920; repr. 1970), 2:168.

38 Tamm and Vogt, *The Danish Medieval Laws*, 53. For complementary examples of consent by kinsmen to gifts of land from around 1200, see DD 1.3.253 and 1.4.82.

And in fact, around the time King Valdemar confirmed Esrum Abbey's right to Villingerød, Eskil had only just been involved in the resolution of a dispute over a *villa* named Veksebo, which a close kinsman of his, Count Niels, had bought from local landowners in the mid-1150s and then donated to Esrum Abbey before entering as a monk. The settlement is attested by a charter issued by Eskil in August 1158.[39] After Count Niels' death, the charter explains, the vendors of Veksebo made a *calumnia*, objecting to the donation, but in the end they opted for peace and reconciliation—presumably after a process of negotiation (and/or pressure). No reference to court or judgement. At the occasion of Eskil's consecration of Esrum's abbey altar, in front of a crowd of witnesses, the suitors surrendered the property to the archbishop himself by way of *scotatio*, the conventional Danish procedure for land conveyance known in the vernacular as *skøte*. The ceremony is not described in the charter (as it was well-known by contemporaries), but its *pars pro toto* symbolism resembles many similar conveyance rites practiced around Europe at this time: the alienator(s) placed a sod from the land that was about to change hand in the corner of the recipient's cloak (the *skøte* in Old Danish, hence literally 'cloak tailing'), while formally declaring the land to be henceforth the rightful possession of the new owner. When the cloak tails had been folded together, the conveyance was complete. In case of an ecclesiastical grantee, the sod would be placed at the altar or in the corner of the altar cloth.[40]

Eskil's charter on the Veksebo controversy was an *officializing act*, aiming to pronounce the unequivocal lawfulness of Count Niels' donation. Yet, a closer look reveals that in practice the former owners' claim was not dismissed as totally unjust: in the archbishop's own charter of privileges to Esrum Abbey (mentioned above), issued before the conclusion of the Veksebo dispute, the contested property was not included in the list of the monastery's properties. The *calumnia*, in other words, was awarded a kind of legal 'suspensive effect' by Eskil and the Esrum monks, who did not claim full possession rights until the dispute had been resolved. Moreover, although the final act of scotation was performed "so that it [Veksebo] could belong rightfully to the aforesaid church [Esrum] in all eternity" (*ut predicte ecclesie iure perpetuo subiaceret*),[41] and showed the archbishop off publicly as peacemaker and protecting patron, the ceremony also admitted the suitors a share in the spiritual benefits of the

39 DD 1.2.127.

40 Gelting, "Circumstantial Evidence," 163–166; Lars Hamre, Gerhard Hafström and Ole Fenger, "Skøyting," in *Kulturhistorisk leksikon for nordisk middelalder*, ed. Hjejle et al., 16:155–167; DD 1.3.238; Tamm and Vogt, *The Danish Medieval Laws*, 29, 69.

41 DD 1.2.127.

gift, as they were now allowed, in public, to confirm the dead count's initial donation themselves.[42] This way of composing and enacting a settlement, that at least could be *said* to leave both parties with something (depending on how it was officialized), prefigures, as we shall see, the way Florentius's *calumnia* concerning Villingerød was dealt with some years later.

5 Florentius *v.* Archbishop Eskil on the Villingerød Dispute

In the summer of 1161, Archbishop Eskil fell out with King Valdemar on account of the papal schism and was forced to leave the realm. A staunch reformer, Eskil naturally sided with the cardinals' pope Alexander III in the expanding conflict, but since the 1130s Danish kings had been vassals of the emperor, and Valdemar—who had only just won the crown after years of dynastic feuding—had to declare his support of the imperial pope Victor IV.[43] As enmities softened, however, the archbishop returned to Denmark and resumed office in Lund in 1167. It was some time after his return from exile and before he travelled abroad again in 1174 that his gift of Villingerød to Esrum Abbey came to be disputed by Florentius.[44]

It is impossible to say which of the two records of the affair was produced first, but we shall follow—somewhat arbitrarily—the order found in the Esrum cartulary and start by looking at Florentius's charter. In its form this is a genuine charter, complete with subscriptions and seals.[45] Most likely it was confected in close cooperation with the recipients, the monks of Esrum, and no doubt reflected a common agreement between Florentius and the Cistercian brothers as to how the resolution of the dispute should be enacted and recorded.

In the opening intitulation, Florentius presents himself as *sancte Marie et sancti Laurentii canonicus*, canon of the cathedral church in Lund.[46] The charter then is addressed "to my kinsmen as well as to strangers, present and

42 Cf. the observations by White, *Custom*, 54–85. More on the Veksebo dispute and the interpretation of the scotation part in Esmark, "Godsgaver," 150–152; Esmark, "The Settlement of Disputes," 15–16.

43 Breengaard, *Muren om Israels hus*, 275–301.

44 On the dating: DD 1.2.184, editors' notes, p. 337.

45 The original, as mentioned earlier, is lost, but an impression of the document's possible layout may be gained by comparing, for instance, Bishop Absalon's privilege to the convent of Our Lady in Roskilde from 1164–1178 (DD 1.2.163), facsimile in Franz Blatt and C.A. Christensen, eds., *Corpus Diplomatum Regni Danici*, 7 vols (Copenhagen, Munksgaard, 1938), 7: pl. 627.

46 DD 1.2.185. Florentius' name and date of death (19 September) was entered in the two cathedral necrologies that were kept at the archiepiscopal see. In the *Liber daticus vetus-*

future" (*propinquis meis quam extraneis presentibus atque futuris*) and continues with Florentius's proclamations about two interrelated acts. First, he announces that before the Lord Archbishop and many others he has renounced, with a full heart and of his own will and devotion, the complaint (*querimonia*) he had against the monastery in Esrum concerning the land of Villingerød, which his grandfather, the dean Johannes, surrendered to the Lord Archbishop for an approved and appropriate price. In order, furthermore, that none of his blood relatives in the course of time should resume the *calumnia* against the monastery, he has supplied the present charter and act with the seal of the church of Lund.

In other words: Florentius had publicly recognized the justness and lawfulness of Eskil's purchase of Villingerød from his grandfather; he had voluntarily given up his claim to the property; and he had refused any rights on the part of his kinsmen to challenge Esrum Abbey's ownership in the future. Those who were present when Florentius made his declaration before the archbishop are then listed. First in an impressive line-up is "the venerable bishop of Roskilde, Lord Absalon", an ecclesiastical prince almost equal in power to the archbishop around this time. Absalon—warleader as much as prelate, according to his own chronicler Saxo[47]—was a leading member of the prominent Hvide-family, old rivals of Eskil's Trugond-clan, and a trusted friend of King Valdemar. He was also the main patron of his own family's *Hauskloster* in Sorø (Western Zealand), which since 1161 had been manned by Cistercian monks from Esrum. In 1178 he would take over from Eskil as both archbishop of Lund and patron of Esrum Abbey.[48] Next among the witnesses are abbots Markus of All Saints and Johannes of Holy Trinity, two monasteries situated in or just outside the city of Lund, both associated through bonds of mutual prayer with the cathedral chapter.[49] Finally, Asser, provost of the cathedral church; magister Walter,

tior, the entry reads *Et de domo sancti Laurencii obiit Florencius, canonicus et sacerdos* (Christian Weeke, ed., *Libri memoriales capituli Lundensis. Lunde domkapitels gavebøger* (Copenhagen, 1884–1889, repr. 1973, 241), while the *Memoriale fratrum* adds that Florentius *dedit fratribus duas marcas argenti* (Weibull, *Necrologium Lundense*, 95). On the complicated relationship between the two necrologies, see Michael H. Gelting, "Forholdet mellem Liber daticus og Memoriale fratrum," in *Mellan evighet och vardag. Lunds domkyrkas martyrologium Liber daticus vetustior*, ed. Eva Nilsson Nylander (Lund: Universitetsbiblioteket Lunds universitet, 2015), 131–150.

47 Saxo Grammaticus, *Gesta Danorum: The History of the Danes*, ed. Karsten Friis-Jensen, transl. Peter Fischer, 2 vols (Oxford: Clarendon Press, 2015), 14.21.3.

48 Frank Birkebæk, Tom Christensen and Inge Skovgård-Petersen, eds., *Absalon—fædrelandets fader* (Roskilde: Roskilde Museums Forlag, 1996); Michael Kræmmer, *Den hvide klan. Absalon, hans slægt og hans tid* (Viborg: Spektrum, 1999).

49 Weibull, *Skånes Kyrka*, 52–53; Tore Nyberg, "Broderlig böngemenskap i 1100- och 1200-talens Lund," in *Mellan evighet och vardag. Lunds domkyrkas martyrologium Liber daticus*

Absalon's chaplain; Niels of Falster, a lay noble associated with Absalon's kin;[50] Knud Karlsen, Eskil's own grandson; "and many others from the Lord Archbishop's *curia* as well as the Lord Bishop Absalon's *curia*" (*et multi alii tam de curia domni archiepiscopi quam de curia domni episcopi Absalonis*). The prominence of the gathering testifies to the importance attached to the affair by Archbishop Eskil, but it also points to the potential pressure exerted upon Florentius to give up his claim.

The second act attested by the canon's charter is a *scotatio* ceremony, which took place one 28 August in Lund, probably shortly after the foregoing renunciation.[51] According to the right of inheritance, the text says, Florentius as well as his brother Benedict really should have possessed the aforesaid estate of Villingerød. Therefore, the two of them performed a scotation of the property to Esrum Abbey, "partly as a gift of alms, partly according to the agreement concluded between us" (*partim pro elemosina. partim pro conuentione inter nos pacta*). The statement almost invalidates the previous renunciation by (re-)invoking the brothers' customary inheritance right and certainly emphasizes the essentially amicable character of the settlement. It also represents the brothers' alienation of Villingerød as a pious gift in its own right, made as part of a mutual agreement with the monks.[52]

Present at the *scotatio* were several local ecclesiastics, all of whom also subscribed the document. The majority—Ebbe, Martin, Svend, Niels, Bjørn, and Anders—were fellow canons of the cathedral chapter, styled familiarly by Florentius as *nostri concanonici* as if to emphasize their corporative bonds.[53]

---

vetustior, ed. Eva Nilsson Nylander (Lund: Universitetsbiblioteket Lunds universitet, 2015), 179–190. Abbot Markus of All Saints monastery seems to have been close to Eskil: Markus subscribed three archiepiscopal charters between 1158 and 1171 and was admitted, along with Eskil, into the prayer fraternity of the church of Rheims in France (DD 1.2.126, 1.2.149, 1.2.151, 1.3.14, 1.3.19). The archbishop himself made donations of both land and revenues to All Saints (DD 1.2.74; Weibull, *Skånes Kyrka*, 101). Florentius' grandfather Johannes may also have had some history with the monastery of All Saints: in the cathedral necrology, his obit, most likely entered before his grandson's *calumnia*, reads *Johannes, sacerdos et conversus Omnium Sanctorum et decanus de domo beati Laurentii* (Weeke, *Libri memoriales capituli Lundensis*, 270; cf. Weibull, *Necrologium Lundense*, 101).

50 Hill, *Könige, Fürsten und Klöster*, 232–233.

51 A *scotatio* of property to Esrum Abbey would sometimes be doubled, performed in the abbey church as well as in the cathedral of Lund; see for example DD 1.3.45.

52 Cf. the interpretation in Gelting, "Odelsrett," 143, and Esmark, "The Settlement of Disputes," 18.

53 All six canons known from the cathedral necrologies and lists of presbyters and deacons (Weibull, *Necrologium Lundense*, 86, 87, 90, 116, 90, 123, 125; Weeke, *Libri memoriales capituli Lundensis*, 200, 220, 303). At the time of the dispute, Archbishop Eskil had just extended the number of prebends attached to the cathedral chapter from sixteen to twenty: DD 1.2.160; Weibull, *Skånes Kyrka*, 75.

Others listed are Esger, prior of St Peter, a Benedictine nunnery in Lund; Othmar, dean at the cathedral church;[54] and, finally, at the bottom of the list despite their rank, abbots Johannes and Markus of Holy Trinity and All Saints, who had already witnessed the foregoing renunciation act—and perhaps took some kind of mediating role in the process? Besides putting their signature on the charter, Esger, Othmar and Abbot Johannes also attached their churches' seals.[55]

Florentius's brother Benedict, who co-performed the *scotatio*, signed the document as well. He may have been the canon of Holy Cross church in Dalby, close to Lund, whose death was recorded in the cathedral necrology around the same time as Florentius's.[56] In that case, he was probably identical with the Benedict credited by the Esrum monks for having supplied them with the aforementioned King Erik's charter of 1145 to Bishop Herman: in the Esrum cartulary the rubric to the copy of this document reads *Privilegium Erici regis de Willingerøth quod habuimus a Benedicto canonico de Dalby*.[57] Apparently the original title deed on Villingerød from the king was passed on within the family, from Bishop Herman through Johannes to Florentius and Benedict, who then granted the document to the monks of Esrum after the two brothers had finally given up their claim to the property.[58]

Moving on to Archbishop Eskil's account we find a somewhat different kind of document. His is not a formal charter, but rather a public declaration in the form of an open letter addressed to "all faithful Christians, present and future".[59] Having introduced himself as archbishop *Dei gracia* of the holy church in Lund, apostolic legate, and primate of Denmark and Sweden, Eskil

54 Cf. Weibull, *Necrologium Lundense*, 55, 116. In 1158, Othmar co-subscribed Archbishop Eskil's charter to Esrum Abbey as *sancti Laurentii thesaurarius* (DD 1.2.126).

55 The monastery of Holy Trinity, along with All Saints Abbey, was one of the first churches in Scandinavia to have its own seal (Weibull, *Skånes Kyrka*, 56).

56 Weeke, *Libri memoriales capituli Lundensis*, 96: *Benedictus, subdiaconus et canonicus Sancte Crucis ecclesie*—day of death 22 April, entered in the necrology in the final third of the twelfth century, cf. DD 1.2.91, editors' notes, p. 173.

57 *Codex Esromensis*, fol. 74^{v}, cf. DD 1.2.91, editors' notes, p. 173.

58 Parallel example of a written title deed donated along with a property: around 1200, a royal chaplain received some lands from King Knud VI along with a charter attesting the gift (DD 1.3.197). When later the chaplain donated the same lands to the Cistercian monastery of Øm, he also granted the royal charter itself to the monks; see "Exordium monasterii Caræ insula," ed. Gertz, 167–168.

59 DD 1.2.184: [...] *omnibus Christi fidelibus tam presentibus. quam futuris*. The text as a whole—length, structure, formulas employed—closely resembles another document issued by Archbishop Eskil not long before the Villingerød dispute to announce that he had exempted the canons of the cathedral chapter from paying tithes of their prebends and benefices: DD 1.2.159.

proclaims that he has bought a property called Villingerød from Johannes, "dean at our church" (*decano ecclesie nostre*), and for the redemption of his soul he has handed it over to the monastery in Esrum to possess in perpetuity. Then, after some time, a young man called Florentius, "son of the aforesaid dean's daughter" (*filius filie predicti decani*), started to "murmur in secret" (*submurmurando*), claiming that the property had been alienated from him in a somewhat unlawful way. However, "summoned before me [Eskil]" (*coram me uocatus*), Florentius accepted the truth and entirely renounced his *calumnia* in the presence of Bishop Absalon, the provost Asser, the abbots of All Saints and Holy Trinity, and many other persons from the churches of Lund and Roskilde. Furthermore, in order that Florentius should not in any way cause future disturbance to the brothers of Esrum, he faithfully repeated his promise, concerning everything, in the presence of the same persons. A short *valedictio* concludes the text.

In his statement Eskil arms himself with the full symbolic weaponry of names, titles and credentials and, by implication, of the institutional capital on which these rest. Speaking, thus, with *official* authority, he first establishes the perfect legality of his purchase of Villingerød, and the no less perfect religious devotion motivating his transfer of the property to Esrum Abbey. Next, he rhetorically undermines Florentius's claim by stripping him of title and affiliation—in Eskil's text Florentius is not a canon of Lund, but simply "a certain young man" (*quidam adolescens*, a term often connoting in medieval charter discourse to unreason and inexperience), who happened to be a grandson of Villingerød's vendor—and by representing his claim not as a valid judicial challenge but as a false rumour, circulated 'in private', hence unofficially, illegitimately. Finally, without speaking explicitly of 'court', 'conviction' or of himself as 'judge', the archbishop invokes the air of legal authority as he describes how Florentius was called (*uocatus*) before him and an assembly of high-ranking ecclesiastics to be lectured about the true facts of the matter and to renounce publicly, under oath, his wrong and unfounded claim. A clear-cut case, in other words. No talk of inheritance right, mutual concord or a symbolically polyvalent conveyance ceremony attended by the canons of the cathedral chapter.[60]

If Eskil's letter implicitly points to his status as an ecclesiastical judicial authority, it also reads as a statement of a patron's efforts to protect his own gift and the holdings of his own monastic foundation. Archbishop Eskil had

60 Unless, of course, the text's last words about Florentius "faithfully repeating his promise" (*testimonio* [...] *fideliter repromisit*) should be interpreted as a somewhat euphemized reference to the second act reported in the canon's charter—in which case the rhetorical suppression of this part of the settlement process only stands out even more.

invested massively (in terms of both economic means and social networking) in the erection of what may have been intended as some sort of *Hauskloster* for the Trugond family, an institution that quickly evolved into one of the wealthiest and most prestigious religious centres in the kingdom.[61] According to the chronicler Saxo, Eskil's own grandson was brought up and educated at Esrum Abbey, and Eskil himself cultivated close ties of friendship with the abbots, who seem to have served him loyally as diplomatic envoys and political go-betweens.[62] Most of the ecclesiastical communities in and around Lund were linked together by formal bonds of intercessory prayer and this network also included the monks of Esrum.[63] In short, Archbishop Eskil had every motive for presenting the settlement of the Villingerød dispute as the outcome of his authoritative intervention, and for trying to establish his version as the *official* story.

6 Conclusion

In-between the double records of the Villingerød settlement the historian may perceive the contours of a fairly trivial legal conflict rooted in overlapping norms of inheritance and property transfer. A process of negotiation and pressure involving circles of clerical and lay nobles leads to a mutual agreement, publicly enacted at ritualized events (renunciation oath, conveyance ceremony) which are, however, open to varying interpretations and officializing strategies, both *in medias res* and in subsequent written accounts.

In regard to factualities, the two records are by no means incompatible, but they cut the picture in different ways. Florentius insists on the basic justness of his challenge, but opts to back down, and claims to do so out of honourable and culturally laudable motives. The conveyance ceremony is presented as the main act of the settlement process and expressly makes him and his brother partakers of the spiritual benefits accruing from the transfer of their grandfather's property. At the ceremony, Florentius is surrounded by his fellow canons and

61 Whether Eskil's foundation of Esrum Abbey was motivated by family strategy or more universal religious considerations is subject to debate; compare, for instance, Hill, *Könige, Fürsten und Klöster*, 197–205, and the views of McGuire, *The Cistercians in Denmark*, and Nyberg, *Monasticism*.

62 DD 1.2.106, with the interpretation by France, *The Cistercians in Scandinavia*, 48–49; Saxo, *Gesta Danorum*, 14.26.7–12.

63 Nyberg, *Monasticism*, 241. Eskil's own relative, Count Niels, who died as a monk at Esrum, was entered in the necrologies of Lund: Weeke, *Libri memoriales capituli Lundensis*, 102; Weibull, *Necrologium Lundense*, 69.

has leading ecclesiastics from Lund lend their attendance, signature and seal—their social and legal authority—to a representation which does not mention Archbishop Eskil's gift of Villingerød to Esrum Abbey with a single word and instead allows Florentius to guarantee the monastery against future claims to Villingerød. Archbishop Eskil, in contrast, bypasses Florentius's conveyance act altogether. For him the decisive moment in the process is the young canon's public, unconditional, oath-sworn surrender of the contested property. Eskil's account invokes the image of a quasi-legal judgement, or the correction of an inferior by his wronged lord. The issuance of an official written statement itself establishes the prelate as someone with the recognized authority to do exactly that: issue an official written statement. As a historian, one can only wonder how it would affect our picture of dispute processes and judicial authority in medieval society if every case of conflict were covered in the sources by more than one voice.

The monks of Esrum did not worry about the differences between Florentius's charter and Archbishop Eskil's letter, but were only too happy to keep both records of a settlement that finally made them undisputed possessors of Villingerød.[64] In fact, they collected every possible piece of parchment relating to Villingerød, including the royal charters cited earlier in this chapter, stored them in their archive and copied them, many years later, into their cartulary. Without having ever heard about 'officializing strategies' they knew as well as any other members of this society that conflict resolutions were designed and orchestrated outcomes of complex social processes. They also knew that any written evidence had to be interpreted in this light and that possession of alternate records of one and the same case might come to good use.

A passage in the fifteenth-century cartulary of Sorø Abbey, Esrum's daughter house in Western Zealand, may in conclusion serve to illustrate the conscious reflexive attitude of practitioners of medieval property disputing. According to a summary of a group of charters, a lay noble around 1300 claimed to be the rightful heir to one of Sorø Abbey's recently acquired estates. The monks possessed a number of sealed documents testifying how the property had been sold by the claimant's late father's widow's new husband and subsequently granted to Sorø Abbey by the buyer. Persuaded by a group of mediators, they nevertheless agreed to a compromise. The claimant was paid a considerable amount of money and he then granted the estate to the monastery as a gift

64 The village or estate was soon transformed into a grange (McGuire, "Property and Politics," 134).

of his own. According to the summary of the case, a charter was set up as official evidence of the nobleman's donation and *scotatio*. In this document the Sorø monks formally gave up all rights to the property before receiving it back as a pious gift. The monk who later summarized the case, however, hesitated to accept this officializing account of the settlement. "It must be understood", he added in a dry commentary, "that this was not consistent with the truth, but a figure of speech, of course, enjoined on both parties by the mediators."[65]

Bibliography

Manuscripts

Copenhagen, Royal Library, *Codex Esromensis, E. don. var.* 140, 4°.

Primary Sources

Blatt, Franz, and C.A. Christensen, eds. *Corpus Diplomatum Regni Danici*. 7 vols. Copenhagen: Munksgaard, 1938.

Buus, Erik, ed. *Consuetudines Lundenses: statutter for kannikesamfundet i Lund c. 1123*. Copenhagen: Det danske sprog- og litteraturselskab, 1978.

Gertz, Martin Clarentius, ed. "Exordium monasterii Carø insula." In *Scriptores minores historiæ danicæ medii ævi*, 2 vols, vol. 2: 153–264. Copenhagen, 1918–1920; repr. 1970.

Nielsen, Herluf, et al., eds. *Diplomatarium Danicum*. Copenhagen: Munksgaard, 1938–2000.

Nielsen, Oluf, ed. *Codex Esromensis. Esrum Klosters Brevbog*. Copenhagen, 1880–1881; repr. 1973.

Saxo Grammaticus. *Gesta Danorum: The History of the Danes*, edited by Karsten Friis-Jensen, translated by Peter Fischer. 2 vols. Oxford: Clarendon Press, 2015.

Tamm, Ditlev, and Helle Vogt, eds. *The Danish Medieval Laws—the Laws of Scania, Zealand and Jutland*. London: Routledge, 2017.

Weeke, Christian, ed. *Libri memoriales capituli Lundensis. Lunde domkapitels gavebøger*. Copenhagen, 1884–1889; repr. 1973.

Weibull, Lauritz, ed. *Necrologium Lundense. Lunds domkyrkas nekrologium*. Lund: Berlingska boktryckeriet, 1923.

65 DD 2.6.306: […] *intelligendum est hoc non fuisse secundum rei veritatem, sed secundum dici, scilicet per modum utrisque partibus a placitatoribus indictum*. For a full analysis of this dispute, see Esmark, "Disputing Property in Zealand," 204–206.

Secondary Works

Ahrén, Per-Olov and Anders Jarlert, eds. *Lund—medeltida kyrkometropol. Symposium i samband med ärkestiftet Lunds 900-årsjubileum, 27–28 april 2003*. Lund: Stiftshistoriska sällskapet i Lunds stift, 2004.

Alfonso, Isabel. "Judicial Rhetoric and Political Legitimation in Medieval Leon-Castile." In *Building Legitimacy. Political Discourses and Forms of Legitimacy in Medieval Societies*, edited by Isabel Alfonso, Hugh Kennedy, and Julio Escalona, 51–87. Leiden: Brill, 2004.

Birkebæk, Frank, Tom Christensen, and Inge Skovgård-Petersen, eds. *Absalon—fædrelandets fader*. Roskilde: Roskilde Museums Forlag, 1996.

Bourdieu, Pierre. *The Logic of Practice*. Cambridge: Polity Press, 1990.

Bourdieu, Pierre. *Language and Symbolic Power*. Cambridge: Polity Press, 1991.

Breengaard, Carsten. *Muren om Israels hus. Regnum og sacerdotium i Danmark 1050–1170*. Copenhagen: G.E.C. Gad, 1982.

Ciardi, Anna Minara. *On the Formation of Cathedral Chapters and Cathedral Culture. Lund, Denmark, and Scandinavia, c. 1060–1225*. Lund: Lund University, 2016.

Clanchy, Michael. *From Memory to Written Record. England 1066–1307*. 2nd ed. Oxford: Blackwell, 1993.

Esmark, Kim. "Godsgaver, calumniae og retsantropologi. Esrum kloster og dets naboer, ca. 1150–1250." In *Ett annat 1100-tal. Individ, kollektiv och kulturella mönster i medeltidens Danmark*, edited by Peter Carelli, Lars Hermanson, and Hanne Sanders, 143–180. Lund: Makadam, 2004.

Esmark, Kim. "Disputing Property in Zealand: The Records of the Sorø Donation Book." In *Disputing Strategies in Medieval Scandinavia*, ed. Kim Esmark, Lars Hermanson, Hans Jacob Orning, and Helle Vogt, 181–218. Leiden: Brill, 2013.

Esmark, Kim. "Just Rituals: Masquerade, Manipulation, and Officializing Strategies in Saxo's *Gesta Danorum*." In *Rituals, Performatives, and Political Order in Northern Europe, c. 650–1350*, edited by Wojtek Jezierski, Lars Hermanson, Hans Jacob Orning, and Thomas Småberg, 237–267. Turnhout: Brepols, 2015.

Esmark, Kim. "The Settlement of Disputes by Compromise According to Some Early Danish Charters." In *Denmark and Europe in the Middle Ages, c. 1000–1525. Essays in Honour of Professor Michael H. Gelting*, edited by Kerstin Hundahl, Lars Kjær, and Niels Lund, 11–26. Farnham: Ashgate, 2015.

Esmark, Kim and Hans Jacob Orning. "General Introduction." In *Disputing Strategies in Medieval Scandinavia*, edited by Kim Esmark, Lars Hermanson, Hans Jacob Orning, and Helle Vogt, 1–28. Leiden: Brill, 2013.

Foucault, Michel. *Power/Knowledge. Selected Interviews and Other Writings, 1972–1977*. New York: Pantheon Books, 1980.

France, James. *The Cistercians in Scandinavia*. Kalamazoo: Cistercian Publications, 1992.

Gelting, Michael H. "Det komparative perspektiv i dansk middelalderforskning. Om Familia og familie, Lið, Leding og Landeværn." *Historisk Tidsskrift* 99/1 (1999), 146–188.

Gelting, Michael H. "Odelsrett–lovbydelse–bördsrätt–retrait lignager: Kindred and Land in the Nordic Countries in the Twelfth and Thirteenth Centuries." In *Family, Marriage and Property Devolution in the Middle Ages*, edited by Lars Ivar Hansen, 133–165. Tromsø: University of Tromsø, 2000.

Gelting, Michael H. "Da Eskil ville være ærkebiskop af Roskilde. Roskildekrøniken, *Liber Daticus Lundensis* og det danske ærkesædes ophævelse 1133–1138." In *Ett annat 1100-tal. Individ, kollektiv och kulturella mönster i medeltidens Danmark*, edited by Peter Carelli, Lars Hermanson, and Hanne Sanders, 181–229. Lund: Makadam, 2004.

Gelting, Michael H. "Ansigt-til-ansigt-samfundet og de to øvrigheder." In *Gaver, ritualer, konflikter. Et retsantropologisk perspektiv på nordisk middelalderhistorie*, edited by Hans Jacob Orning, Kim Esmark, and Lars Hermanson, 301–316. Oslo: Unipub, 2010.

Gelting, Michael H. "Circumstantial Evidence: Danish Charters of the Thirteenth Century." In *Medieval Legal Process: Physical, Spoken and Written Performance in the Middle Ages*, edited by Marco Mostert and Paul S. Barnwell, 157–195. Turnhout: Brepols, 2011.

Gelting, Michael H. "Forholdet mellem Liber daticus og Memoriale fratrum." In *Mellan evighet och vardag. Lunds domkyrkas martyrologium Liber daticus vetustior*, edited by Eva Nilsson Nylander, 131–150. Lund: Universitetsbiblioteket Lunds universitet, 2015.

Hjejle, Bernt, Peter Skautrup, Niels Skyum-Nielsen, Axel Steensberg, Georg Rona, and Allan Karker, eds. *Kulturhistorisk leksikon for nordisk middelalder. Fra vikingetid til reformation* edited by. 22 vols. Copenhagen: Rosenkilde & Bagger, 1957–1978.

Hill, Thomas. *Könige, Fürsten und Klöster. Studien zu den dänischen Klostergründungen des 12. Jahrhunderts*. Frankfurt am Main: Peter Lang, 1992.

Knudsen, Anders Leegaard. "Testimonia Placiti—Private Charters as Public Instruments. A Study in Medieval Danish Diplomatics." *Archiv für Diplomatik* 57 (2011), 147–179.

Koziol, Geoffrey. "Making Boso the Clown: Performance and Performativity in a Pseudo-Diploma of the Renegade King (8 December 879)." In *Rituals, Performatives, and Political Order in Northern Europe, c. 650–1350*, edited by Wojtek Jezierski, Lars Hermanson, Hans Jacob Orning, and Thomas Småberg, 43–61. Turnhout: Brepols, 2015.

Kræmmer, Michael. *Den hvide klan. Absalon, hans slægt og hans tid.* Viborg: Spektrum, 1999.

McGuire, Brian P. "Property and politics at Esrum Abbey: 1151–1251." *Medieval Scandinavia* 6 (1973), 122–150.

McGuire, Brian P. *The Cistercians in Denmark. Their Attitudes, Roles, and Functions in Medieval Society*. Kalamazoo: Cistercian Publications, 1992.

Nyberg, Tore. *Monasticism in North-Western Europe, 800–1200*. Aldershot: Ashgate, 2000.

Nyberg, Tore. "Broderlig böngemenskap i 1100- och 1200-talens Lund." In *Mellan evighet och vardag. Lunds domkyrkas martyrologium Liber daticus vetustior*, edited by Eva Nilsson Nylander, 179–190. Lund: Universitetsbiblioteket Lunds universitet, 2015.

Paludan, Helge. *Familia og familie. To kulturelementers møde i højmiddelalderens Danmark*. Aarhus: Aarhus Universitetsforlag, 1995.

Pavón, Martin. "Søborg—Ærkebiskop Eskils borg i Nordsjælland." *Aarbøger for nordisk oldkyndighed og historie* (2011–2012), 263–291.

Rasmussen, Carsten Porskrog. "Danish Crown Lands AD 1230—and Before?" In *Settlement and Lordship in Early Medieval Scandinavia*, edited by Bjørn Poulsen and Søren Sindbæk, 239–259. Turnhout: Brepols, 2011.

Skyum-Nielsen, Niels. *Kvinde og slave*. Copenhagen: Munksgaard, 1971.

Vogt, Helle. *The Function of Kinship in Medieval Nordic Legislation*. Leiden: Brill, 2010.

Vogt, Helle. "The Power to Judge: Jurisdiction in Property Conflicts in Thirteenth-Century Denmark." In *Disputing Strategies in Medieval Scandinavia*, edited by Kim Esmark, Lars Hermanson, Hans Jacob Orning, and Helle Vogt, 161–180. Leiden: Brill, 2013.

Vogt, Helle. "How To Be Remembered: Securing the *Memoria* of a Slain Person in Medieval Denmark." In *Emotion, Violence, Vengeance and Law in the Middle Ages: Essays in Honour of William Ian Miller*, edited by Kate Gilbert and Stephen D. White, 156–171. Leiden: Brill, 2018.

Weibull, Lauritz. *Skånes kyrka från älsta tid till Jacob Erlandsens död 1274*. Copenhagen: Rosenkilde & Bagger, 1946.

White, Stephen D. "Inheritances and Legal Arguments in Western France, 1050–1150." *Traditio* 43 (1987), 55–103.

White, Stephen D. *Custom, Kinship, and Gifts to Saints. The Laudatio Parentum in Western France 1050–1150*. Chapel Hill: University of North Carolina Press, 1988.

Index

www.ingramcontent.com/pod-product-compliance
Lightning Source LLC
LaVergne TN
LVHW010541300926
849162LV00002B/198